Warman's

Coins &
Paper Money

A Value & Identification Guide

4th Edition

Allen G. Berman

©2008 Krause Publications

Published by

kp **krause publications**
An Imprint of F+W Publications

700 East State Street • Iola, WI 54990-0001
715-445-2214 • 888-457-2873
www.krausebooks.com

Our toll-free number to place an order or obtain
a free catalog is (800) 258-0929.

Library of Congress Control Number: 2008928413

ISBN-13: 978-0-89689-683-3
ISBN-10: 0-89689-683-8

Designed by Wendy Wendt
Edited by Mark Moran

Printed in China

DEDICATION

To Chet Krause and Clifford Mishler,
for a timely favor to us all.
To my parents for a timely favor to me.

CONTENTS

INTRODUCTION

Welcome to a newly revised and updated version of *Warman's Coins and Paper Money*. For 13 years now it has been my privilege to be author of one of the most widely distributed introductory books on coin collecting in the United States. This book was originally conceived to be a basic guide to the hobby, written simply but intelligently for both beginning collectors and curious laymen. It presumes no prior background in numismatics (the study of coins). I have strived to make it a unique book in that it incorporates not only pricing, but also historical backgrounds and many of my own personal observations on various aspects of coin collecting that may fall through the cracks in more conventional coin books. It is also distinctive in that it covers numismatics in its broadest definition, discussing not only United States, world and ancient coins, but also tokens, medals, paper money and checks. This may be quite a bit to fit into one volume, but the point of an introduction is, among other things, to tell the curious reader what collectibles are out there.

New collectors have no way of pursuing the many facets of numismatics if they have not been made aware of them. Moreover, beginning literature simply does not exist for many numismatic specialties. Truly, a full library is necessary to answer every question regarding this 2,700-year-old medium of exchange. More detailed books can be searched out later as needed. But most people go through a stage where one basic book will do just fine. After four editions and lists of endorsements, I must admit, I am gratified to provide a book like this one that fills such a need.

There is much in the way of updates and improvements to this new edition. The addition of color plates two editions ago proved enormously popular. The most exciting change to this edition is the expansion of those color illustrations to the entire book. The reader can now experience the breathtaking beauty of these miniature works of art.

The market has been extremely strong recently, so I have updated market values for all issues worldwide, covering tens of thousands of listings. Indeed, there are relatively few values that I have not increased. Of course I have included complete new-issue and commemorative listings for both the United States and Canada, as well..

Additional improvements include an update of the chapters on ancient and medieval coins. I have long considered early coinage a favorite specialty, having written or edited four other books on medieval coins.

The ownership by F+W Publications (the world's largest numismatic publisher) of the entire series of *Warman's Encyclopedia of Antiques and Collectibles* – this volume included – puts at my disposal vast reference and research facilities, including their world-class photo collection.

Price listings for modern coins in this edition will be based primarily on the hundreds of hours of research conducted by the staff of F+W Publications' numismatic division. This will certainly provide a broader base of reference than any one author is likely to have at his disposal. This pricing foundation has been brought even more up to date by intensive compilation from a variety of sources, reflecting the extreme volatility of this dynamic market.

I have preserved in this edition a hard-boiled approach to the use of coins as investment vehicles. I give some background on the market role of the notorious "slabs" and some methods for attempting to select an honest coin dealer.

(Yes, I'm pleased to say they do exist.) I try to provide the investor with enough information about market practices and safety nets. As a result of reading this book, an investor can comfortably say that he is less likely to be taken advantage of than before reading it. How much less depends on his own willingness to do research and apply a good helping of common sense. I must admit, however, that I do not invest in coins, despite being a full-time dealer in them. I do not believe that the best use for historical artifacts such as these is to lock them away somewhere in the hopes that they may appreciate. I would rather see them in the hands of history buffs and teachers who would be likely to share them either in a classroom, or at a local coin show exhibit or coin club.

Coin collecting can be an extremely social hobby. The many joyful friendships I have made in this field have taught me this firsthand. There are hundreds of local coin clubs throughout the country, where collectors get together at a restaurant or library to swap stories or show off the latest prized additions to their collections. There are also a good number of regional associations that sponsor conventions and coin shows at which dealers display their wares for the collectors' perusal. On a grander scale, there are national-level organizations such as the American Numismatic Association (ANA), which not only sponsor shows but also have libraries and museums. I have included an entire section on clubs and museums and give information on contacting these wonderful organizations.

My beginnings in this field go back to 1970. A Civil War three-cent nickel found in my grandfather's antique desk, and a bag of change from a relative's trip around the world, caught the imagination of an impressionable 10-year old. I was hooked for life. Since then the love of old coins has taken me from travels in Europe to a graduate degree in history. I have had the rare privilege of knowing no other profession, and even on the longest of days, I am still grateful. I know of few hobbies that bring together such a wide array of people from diverse states and countries as intimately and amiably as coin collecting. An interest in coins has even been known to improve a student's grades.

I have never found it difficult to communicate some level of the excitement that I find in coin collecting. In the holding of one small metal disc, the collector is capable of exploring other cultures, philosophies, artistic environments and political systems. Even more exciting, a coin represents a point of contact, where an average person from another age and a modern person come together. It is a meeting point in time and space between two individuals who could only have dreamed of the other's existence.

Any user of this or any other price guide should be warned: Coin prices can be as volatile the stock market, and can go in either direction. Many coins will go up or down with the changes in the precious-metals market. Others will be unaffected. Many coins will skyrocket based on popular fancy, and drop back down again when they become *passé*. Sometimes, the market is stimulated by firms attempting to corner every available fairly priced specimen. But beware; when these firms' orders are filled, those who have accumulated in hopes of "feeding" the market may well dump the same coins at a fraction of what they may have otherwise asked.

This book simply gives an idea of the normal retail value of coins at the time of writing. It is not an offer to buy or sell.

In most cases, neither I nor any other dealer can make a firm offer without personally examining the coin in question.

Besides being a dealer in coins and an appraiser, I am continuously involved in writing new references and guides on coins. I am always eager to hear from readers with suggestions on how I can make this book more useful, or those with coin-related questions or comments. I can be reached at:

Allen G. Berman, M.A.
Professional Numismatist
P.O. Box 605
Fairfield, CT 06824
Send e-mail to agberman@aol.com.

ORGANIZATION

This book is organized for ease of use, but not at the expense of logic or accuracy. As a result of this principle, some changes have been made in this fourth edition. Much of the introductory material provides information that can be of equal use whether the reader is interested in collecting American tokens, African paper money or Roman Imperial coins.

Some arrangements of information are intended to make for quicker and handier to use. As most readers don't wish to continually consult the lists of various in-depth references cited for further reading, they have been gathered into special sections, often with my personal recommendations and background comments. The bibliographical sections on United States and medieval coins should be particularly useful.

Local state coinages have been listed before the series of federally issued United States coins. This is because they were struck earlier, and sequencing them in chronological order makes more sense. Most Biblical coins will be found under the ancient countries that struck them, such as Judea and Rome, rather than in a separate section. This will make them easier to locate. Such coins, however, will be cited in this book as having been specifically mentioned in the Bible.

Foreign coins are generally listed alphabetically within each continent, as this makes it easier for the average person with only a moderate amount of geographic knowledge to locate a country's listings. Keeping the coinages of entire continents together made sense, however, as coinages of neighboring countries will frequently influence each other and reflect similar characteristics. As in the case previously for European coins, now non-European coins of the ancient and medieval periods are grouped together before the modern ones. Each section begins with an historical background as to the origin of the series being discussed. Don't forget that the value we, as a society, assign to these old coins derives primarily from the historical significance they hold for us. Included in each introduction is important background information concerning the coins' characteristics, and collecting practices. It is the intent of the author to incorporate knowledge picked up from decades of experience in numismatics, but not usually found in most books of this nature.

Counterfeits of even inexpensive coins have become increasingly common. Known counterfeits are listed as a separate section for each series. There have been counterfeits made to fool every level of consumer, from the casual and careless tourist on a vacation to explore ancient ruins, to the sophisticated collector seeking to acquire the crowning achievement of his 40-year collecting endeavor. Counterfeits have been made for thousands of years and the reader should be observant.

Prices are given for two different grades of United States and Canadian coins. One is higher for the collector trying to guess what that additional quality acquisition may cost him, one low to give the layman an idea as to the replacement value of the typical "strange old coins" likely to have been handed down by a relative. Prices for ancient and foreign coins are given in the grade in which they are either most commonly collected or encountered on the Western market. In all cases, the exact grade that is being priced is indicated at the top of the first column to which it is being applied.

Coins in this book are chosen to be representative. Most of the coins are common examples of a particular "type," which is what a collector calls a coin design in a particular metal. Sometimes a rare date and a common date of the same type will be given for contrast. It is the intent of the author to list some rare, some average and some common-type coins, and thus give the reader an overview of what the exciting world of numismatics has to offer.

VALUATIONS

The values in this book are intended to represent the average price a professional coin dealer would charge a collector. This is not to say that every dealer will charge the same price for the same coin. Local factors can influence the price of a coin, such as whether or not the dealer has more of a coin than he can use, or conversely, is running low on it. Also a dealer must keep his local clientele in mind. Half a dozen members of a local coin club collecting the exact same field in harmony can easily deplete a dealer's stock. Other factors that can influence the retail price of a coin include a dealer's personal taste and aesthetic sensibilities. Quite simply put, does the dealer like the coin? Nationally and internationally, the prices of some coins can remain stable for years, whereas other coins, particularly those that are bullion-related, or experiencing a sudden rise or fall in popularity, or are being manipulated as investments, can fluctuate weekly. Hence, a book such as this, while it is able to give a general frame of reference, should not be considered an ultimate source of information. The ultimate decision makers on the legitimate retail value of a coin are the dealer selling it and the collector purchasing it.

This book makes no effort to give information on the wholesale value of coins, or what a person disposing of a collection would expect to actually get for his coins. Of course, these prices fluctuate too, both over time and throughout the country. But there are other factors involved, as well. Traditionally, the discount on bullion coins is fairly small. The retail values of particularly inexpensive coins include a handling charge. It costs the dealer just as much labor to sell a $2 coin as a $200 coin, so logically the percentage of the value that is to pay for the dealer's labor is much higher in the case of cheap coins. A dealer may wish to pay 50 to 60 percent of the retail value of an expensive coin that will sell in a medium amount of time. In the case of a coin that sells just a quickly, but for only a couple dollars or so, he may be willing to pay only 20 percent of what he could get. Also, he may be willing to work on a much smaller margin on a coin that sells quickly, than one of the

same value but which might take years to sell. Foreign and ancient coins will also be discounted more as they are much less popular in the U.S. and Canada than the coins of North America. In short, a person attempting to sell a coin may get anywhere from 10 to 90 percent of its retail value, based primarily on the age-old principles of supply and demand.

The grades that have been chosen represent average prices for coins considered either most commonly encountered in the market or ones which are most likely to be sought by the average collector. In very few cases have two consecutive grades on the grading scale been chosen, as a general book such as this can stand to benefit from a greater diversity of grades.

Just because the retail value of a coin is above its face value in mint state does not mean that any dealer would pay over face value to obtain it. The difference represents the dealer's handling charge, which in many cases does not even cover the value of his time or that of his counter help.

Again, it is important to note that the numismatic market at this time is both strong and dynamic. No collector should be shocked to see the next few years bring rapid price inflation in both the popular coin series and bullion-related coins.

NUMISMATIC ABBREVIATIONS

Numismatists often write in their own shorthand. Some commonly used numismatic abbreviations, many of which are used in this book, are listed below. Grades will be discussed later.

AB	Aluminum Bronze
AE	Copper or Bronze
Ag or AR or S	Silver
AL	Aluminum
ANA	American Numismatic Association
ANS	American Numismatic Society
AV or Au or G	Gold
B	Brass
Bil.	Billon (an alloy of copper and silver)
Bullion	when listed instead of a value, means the coin retails for a handling charge above the value of its precious metal.
Ch.	Choice (i.e. nice for the grade)
CN	Copper-Nickel
CNZ	Nickel Silver (an alloy of copper, nickel and zinc)
Cu or C	Copper
IAPN	International Association of Professional Numismatists
l.	left
mm.	mintmark or mintmaster's mark
mm.	diameter in millimeters
ND	Not dated
Obv.	Obverse (Heads)
Or.	Orichalcum (ancient brass rich in zinc)
PNG	Professional Numismatists Guild
r.	right
Rev. or Rx	Reverse (Tails)
Spend	when listed instead of a value, means the coin retails for a handling charge above its face value.
WM	White Metal (a tin alloy)
Z or Zn	Zinc
/	separation of obverse and reverse descriptions
[ ]	not visible on coin

ILLUSTRATIONS

Unless indicated otherwise, all illustrations in this book are of the type of coin described immediately below it. Illustrations of coins enlarged or reduced will be noted. Most illustrations of paper money and primitive money larger than 2 inches (5 cm) are reduced.

ACKNOWLEDGEMENTS

This book, like the four editions that preceded it, could only come to fruition with the help of a vast number of friends, experts and consultants, each of whom brought to this project contributions and advice in their own special fields of expertise. While the prices contained in this book are based on hundreds of sources, I would most like to thank the research staff at Krause Publications for the most substantive contribution. In the field of United States coin prices, I would also like to extend a special thanks to Robert Walter and Bruce Thompson of Sam Sloat Coins Inc. of Westport, Conn., who have taken time out of an extremely busy schedule to provide important advice and critical examination of the manuscript. Walter's vigilant observation of the market has provided him with some very clear insights. I would also like to extend noteworthy thanks to Alex G. Malloy, with whom I collaborated on earlier editions of this book. It was Malloy who gave me my first "basic training" in ancient and medieval coins, as well as my first opportunity to write for publication. Without the education he provided me earlier in life, and his important consultations in the course of writing the previous editions, I would not have felt comfortable pursuing this project. The field of United States paper money is among the most active in all numismatics. I am grateful to David Klein of RaBenco for reviewing the paper-money sections. He is both a nationally successful dealer and a friend, with great expertise in this specialized field. I would like to thank Lucien Birkler, Robert and Phyllis Cohen, Nicholas Economopoulos, Frederick Fleischer, Kyle Mutcher, Camden Percival, Robert Kokotailo, Dr. Gordon A. Singer and Joseph A. Zannella for their own expertise or specialized advice on how to bring a project such as this to a successful conclusion. I would also like to express my gratitude to Paul Kennedy, Acquisitions Editor for Krause Publications, for offering me the opportunity to write this new edition, and to Randy Thern, Krause Publications' Numismatic Cataloging Supervisor, who oversaw my progress through the stages of this project. After many years of association with Randy functioning in various Krause roles, it was a joy to find myself working with him once again. I am also grateful for the talents of my new editor, Mark Moran.

The majority of the illustrations of the coins after 1700 are from the mammoth archives assembled by Krause Publications, Heritage Numismatic Auctions and Stack's, and are the work of hundreds of great numismatic photographers over the years. Most of the illustrations of earlier coins are from the archives of Pegasi Numismatics, Stack's and Heritage Numismatic Auctions. Most of the spectacular color images of paper money are from the Chester L. Krause collection and the Heritage Numismatic Auctions archive.

Lastly, and most importantly, I would like to note my dearest gratitude to my wife, Barbara, whose continuous encouragements kept this project on track and eliminated the worst of my pre-deadline craziness. Her emotional support, material efforts, and good council were essential to the completion of this work.

HOW AND WHERE TO COLLECT

COIN DEALERS

Perhaps the most important thing a beginner can do to get started in coin collecting, besides reading, is to establish a relationship with a good coin dealer. A coin dealer is more than just someone who can sell you coins. If he is a good dealer and well disposed to you, he can be a source of immeasurable knowledge gained from years of experience. Much of the wisdom a dealer can share with his regular customers cannot readily be obtained from books. Either they are fine subtleties, or are personal hints gained through the examination of hundreds of thousands of coins, or are things gleaned just the previous day via the "grapevine." You don't have to be a bid spender to be treated well by a dealer. Just be serious about what you are trying to learn and be consistent. If you are not yet ready to make a purchase, say so, but when you are ready, remember the dealer who helped educate you, or you may find out when you need his advice that his font of wisdom has run dry for you. Realize that the dealer is trying to earn a living and that the time he is able to devote to answering your questions may be limited if it is a busy day, or he trying to get an advertisement ready by a deadline. A good dealer will not begrudge you the opportunity to learn grading by examining his coins, but when he tells you to start by buying a basic grading guide or catalog, do so. Nothing brands a freeloading customer more than the desire to be spoon-fed knowledge without the willingness to contribute to the learning process himself.

Aside from the willingness to share time and knowledge, how can a collector tell a good dealer from one to avoid? There are several elements to judging dealers. First of all there is experience. Most of the knowledge a dealer has comes from many years' experience filtered through curiosity and common sense. A new dealer (including many experienced collectors) may start out with wonderful academic knowledge about coins, but may be lacking in other aspects. Understanding the subtleties of grading and the dynamics of the coin market come almost exclusively from doing, not just reading. A new dealer may be truly honest, but he may not be seasoned to the commercial aspect of numismatics. Also, most small businesses of any kind fail in first few years. If your objective is to establish a long-term relationship, knowing that a dealer has been in business for more than his initial start-up period may indicate that he is here for the long haul.

The size of a firm should not be the sole reason for making it your regular coin firm. While larger firms may offer greater selections, smaller firms may have better prices on certain items. Also, knowledge rests in the mind of the individual numismatist, be he self-employed or one of a dozen in a large firm. Most coin businesses are small operations with one to six full-time employees, so don't be intimidated by the lack of a corporate setting. The smaller firms are the front line of coin collecting.

There are other factors besides longevity that a new collector can use to judge dealers. There are credentials such as membership in professional organizations and service awards. The largest numismatic organization in the world is the American Numismatic Association (ANA). This is open to both dealers and collectors. It has a policy of binding arbitration for any of its members involved in a numismatic business dispute. Any dealer displaying the ANA membership logo must submit himself to such arbitration in order to maintain his membership. Most dealers are members, and while that does not mean that the dealer is automatically to be considered a saint, it is reasonable to presume that he will want to settle his own disputes without letting them fester long enough to force an ANA member

collector to submit it to arbitration. Other organizations with their own arbitration programs are the Professional Numismatists Guild and the International Association of Professional Numismatists. Both these organizations have worldwide membership consisting exclusively of dealers who have met certain criteria. PNG membership is primarily located in the United States and Canada, IAPN members are mostly in Europe and Asia.

Another method of screening dealers, useful particularly when ordering coins by mail, is to make sure that the periodical (or Web site) in which the dealer's advertisement appears has a code of conduct or some other standards for enforcing proper conduct. *World Coin News* and *Numismatic News,* for example, have a set of standard mail-order terms that dealers must adhere to unless specific alternative terms are stated in their ads. Both these, as well as other periodicals such as *The Celator, Coin World* and *The Numismatist*, will generally refuse to accept advertising from problem dealers. One way of identifying those dealers who have long and successful track records is to ask the periodical or Web site how long the dealer in question has been an advertiser.

MEMBER

Symbols of organizations and Krause Customer Service Award.

One distinctive program to promote proper conduct among dealers is *Krause Publication's Customer Service Award*. It sets a particularly high standard for mail-order dealers, permitting a minimal number of customer complaints and no unresolved customer complaints. Those dealers achieving this standard are allowed to display the special logo of this award in their advertising.

Mail-order dealers and local-shop dealers are simply different methods of selling coins, based on the collecting interests and specialties of those they serve. One is not inherently more honest than the other. Local shops are probably better at establishing a personal relationship, and for mainline United States and Canadian coins may be particularly satisfying to do business with. Those collectors interested in world, ancient, medieval and somewhat more esoteric United States material may find that their specialized interests force them to seek the more diverse inventories of mail-order and coin-show dealers.

Lastly, don't ignore the experience of your fellow collectors. Ask which dealers they choose to order from or visit and why. Sometimes a personal introduction or a reference from an established customer or other dealer can get you treated like a VIP the minute you walk in the door. Never forget that coin collecting is a social hobby.

COIN-COLLECTING ON-LINE

Over the last two decades, the Internet has become a pervasive influence in most of our lives. Like in many other fields, the hobby of coin collecting has been greatly affected. Most of the activities a collector would normally pursue via other means can now be effectively pursued over the Internet. Of course, the first activity that comes to mind for most collectors is purchasing coins for their collections.

Most dealers have constructed Web sites of varying size and complexitiy. At this point, it is as strange for a full-time dealer to say, "I don't have a Web site," as it would be to say, "I don't have a business card."

The Internet at large lacks some of the safety mechanisms that exist with periodicals or local shops. There are no customer-service awards or standard policies for advertisers, nor are there local Better Business Bureaus to which one can appeal. This does not mean there are no means by which you can discern legitimate dealers from fly-by-nights. Many of the criteria you would apply to shop, mail-order and show dealers can be applied to Internet dealers. Many of the more serious dealers on the Web will also have active advertising programs in conventional media, permitting you to check with those periodicals. Also, the importance of membership in a professional organization still applies. Ask how long the dealer has been in business, not just collecting coins as a hobbyist. Perhaps the most difficult part of selecting dealers on the Web is telling the difference between who is a legitimate, full-time numismatic expert and who is the skilled home-computer buff with the dream of becoming a real coin dealer.

Many auction sites take no responsibility for the transactions they host, but eBay, for example, does provide one way of screening out some of the worst offenders. Stars are used to indicate the amount of customer feedback the member has. Clicking on the star gives additional information such as whether any customers have left negative comments about their transactions. While even the most honest and knowledgeable dealer may not please everybody, a dealer with more than a few percentage points of his feedback listed as negative should be regarded with caution. A pair of sunglasses instead of a star indicates a new ID. Some unscrupulous dealers booted off eBay have been known to simply take new identities and start over.

Whatever the medium through which a collector seeks out dealers, a collector who is willing to do some research and ask the right questions is bound to end up with a few dealers in whom confidence may be placed and find a certain level of comfort.

In addition to eBay, there are now other specialized auction and sale sites. These consolidate a number of coin dealers' offerings into a series of pages in a common location for ease of searching. One of the best-reviewed in recent years is V-coins (www.vcoins.com), which divides itself into various sections by area of interest. Another, perhaps more dealer-oriented, is Coinnet (www.coinnet.com).

It should be pointed out that these sites are not limited to coins sold at auction. Dealers are able to offer coins at fixed prices through "stores" that function much as print ads would. Also, the collector can use searches within these sites to find coins in just their own area of specialization. They can even search for recently listed items only, so as to avoid viewing the same items day after day.

Many smaller but legitimate dealers are not set up to accept credit cards directly. However, financial service Web sites, such as PayPal (www.paypal.com) have made it possible to send them money just as spontaneously and conveniently. You may even be able to link your own credit card to your account. Other special-purpose vending sites provide a means of paying using a credit card through the site itself.

The Internet can be used for far more than purchases. E-mail is a wonderfully immediate way to correspond. Basic computer caution should be observed in order to avoid viruses. Never open an unexpected enclosure or attachment. Either ask the sender to post an image on a Web site, or verify that it was sent by someone you trust. In the case of the latter, make sure that the attachment is discussed in the accompanying e-mail. Simply recognizing the return e-mail address is not enough, as some viruses steal address books.

Services such as Google and Yahoo are making numismatic research easier. Unfortunately, too many collectors consider the somewhat random scattering of information on the Internet as a substitute for basic books. It does not even come close. All too often I have heard people say, "I tried to look it up on the Internet and couldn't find it." This does not mean that the coin is rare. It more often means that the individual has spent hours using his computer when 10 minutes with a *Standard Catalog of World Coins* would have provided a simple answer, and more likely an accurate one.

Not all numismatic Web sites focus on coins for sale. Many sites are geared towards collector services. By this I mean they endeavor to provide assistance, from attribution (identification) to organizing a collection, as well as news.

Some have searches far more focused than Google and the like, and can be a far greater aid in attributing coins or establishing their values. For Greek, Roman and Byzantine, www.forumancientcoins.com and www.ancients.info have thousands of illustrations and articles. One commercial site, www.exonumia.com, is useful in identifying tokens. Another pair, www.stacks.com and www.ha.com, run by Stacks Rarities and Heritage Auction Galleries, respectively, have excellent auction archives of mostly United States material, including truly wonderful images.

One extensive omnibus site is Krause Publications' Numismaster (www.numismaster.com). This site covers everything from news, coin show listings, grading information and catalog listings (free without values, for a fee with values), to the blogs of numismatic journalists. It even has a database program for organizing your coin collection. Of course, one should reflect on privacy considerations before using a program where the contents of your collection would be stored on someone else's computer, no matter how secure.

Not only do the nation's most important numismatic organizations all have Web sites, listed in the next section, but many local coin clubs do as well. Some can even be found through the A.N.A. website itself. Discussion groups and chat rooms, such as Numis-L and Moneta-L among hundreds of others, can also provide for interesting conversations normally only possible at larger coin shows. But remember to protect your security by not revealing an excess of personal information until you know the trustworthiness of the individual with whom you are communicating. Never give out passwords and home addresses. If you are convinced that a firm should be entrusted with your credit card number, send it to them in parts, contained in separate e-mails.

Many of the world's largest mints have sites, including:
United States Mint: www.usmint.gov
Bureau of Engraving and Printing: www.moneyfactory.com
Royal Canadian Mint: www.rcmint.ca
British Royal Mint: www.royalmint.com

If you are doing a search, remember that most countries do not have mints at all, but contract their minting out

CLUBS AND ASSOCIATIONS

As mentioned earlier, coin collecting can be an extremely social hobby, with national, regional and local clubs. The

largest numismatic organization in the world is the American Numismatic Association. It is an institution chartered by Congress to promote numismatic knowledge, and has attracted hundreds of thousands of collectors and dealers. Not only does it provide the arbitration services mentioned earlier, but holds large conventions twice each year at various locations throughout the country. The summer ANA convention is particularly important, being one of the largest coin shows in the world, and features not only coins dealers, but also representatives of the mints of many foreign countries. Other benefits of ANA membership include a circulating numismatic library, access to its one-week summer seminar in Colorado, and an authentication service. Every member of the ANA also receives a monthly issue of the *Numismatist*, its official journal containing many popular articles and columns, as well as ads by member dealers. Its address is:

American Numismatic Association
818 N. Cascade Ave.
Colorado Springs, CO 80903.
www.money.org.

Another extremely important institution is the American Numismatic Society, which boasts the most important numismatic library in the Western Hemisphere. It has played a significant role in the promotion of original academic numismatic research, and there is little cutting-edge scholarship in which its books or staff are not consulted. It also conducts a summer seminar for graduate students and offers scholarships for students incorporating numismatic research in their theses. Its address is:

American Numismatic Society
75 Varick Street, 11th Floor
New York, NY 10013
www.numismatics.org.

While a many Canadians are active members of the ANA, there is also an important national-level organization founded specifically for Canadian numismatists. It is:

Canadian Numismatic Association
4936 Younge St., Suite 601
North York, Ontario, Canada M2N 6S3
www.canadian-numismatic.org

Coin collectors in Mexico may contact:

Sociedad Numismática de México A.C.
Eugenia 13 - 301
C.P. 03810
México, D.F., Mexico

Many regional associations exist, and most of them sponsor important coins shows. One of the largest such organization is FUN, which stands for Florida United Numismatists, which sponsors a large show of national importance each January in Orlando. Another large regional organization is the Central States Numismatic Association, which sponsors conventions throughout the Midwest. The addresses of some of the more important regional societies are:

Florida United Numismatists
P.O. Box 951988
Lake Mary, FL 32795

Central States Numismatic Society
P.O. Box 841
Logansport, IN 46947

Great Eastern Numismatic Association
1805 Weatherstone Drive
Paoli, PA 19301

New England Numismatic Association
P.O. Box 586
Needham, MA 02192

Pacific Northwest Numismatic Association
P.O. Box 4718
Federal Way, WA 98063-4718

There are, of course, a good many state-level organizations, too numerous to mention here.

There is also a good chance that a local coin club meets regularly in your town or county. There are hundreds of such groups throughout the United States and Canada. Most meetings are low-key and informal. Many of these clubs are members of the ANA. Other good resources include your local library or coin shop.

GRADING

The value of a coin is in part determined by its "grade," or how well preserved it is. The most basic part of grading is determining how much a coin is worn. To describe a coin which is not present, such as in correspondence, numismatists have agreed on a series of terms to describe how much wear there is on a coin. From best (no wear at all) to worst (worn out) they are:

Uncirculated (Mint State)
Almost Uncirculated
Extremely Fine (Extra Fine)
Very Fine
Fine
Very Good
Good
Fair
Poor

For every type of United States and Canadian coin, specific criteria have been agreed on for each degree of wear. For United States coins these criteria were arrived at under the auspices of the American Numismatic Association and have been published in *Official A.N.A. Grading Standards for United States Coins*, usually called *The Gray Book*. It is carried and used by virtually every coin shop. All dealers, however, follow certain general principles. Below are some illustrations of coins in each state of wear, with some of the basic requirements for that grade.

Uncirculated (Unc.) or **Mint State (MS)** coins, those with no wear at all, as though they had just come from the mint, have been divided into 11 basic categories, from 60 to 70, the latter being best. The reason for this is that even with no circulation at all, the coins themselves do hit each other while stored at the mint in large bags, leaving minute scuffs. These scuffs are called "bag marks." While these 11 points are a continuum, the ANA has not traditionally recognized intermediate grades other than the ones listed below. Many coin dealers do. When the legendary numismatic scholar and cataloger Walter Breen was asked if he could tell an MS-61 from and MS-62, he replied "No. Neither, I think can anyone else. It is simply ammunition for those whose motivation is dishonesty and greed."

The description **Brilliant Uncirculated (BU)** does not indicate an exact spot on this 11-point continuum. It simply means that the coin is uncirculated and had all or most of its original mint luster.

Uncirculated or Mint State coins with absolutely no bag marks or any other problems are called **MS-70** but these perfect coins do not really exist for most series. To be MS-70 a coin must be fully struck and have no unpleasant stains or discoloration. Copper must have full luster. Recent made-for-collector coins packaged at the mint have a far better chance of grading MS-70 than a coin made for circulation.

MS67

MS-67 is the nearest thing to a perfect coin that is likely to be practically obtainable. It may have the faintest of bag marks discernable only through a magnifying glass. Copper must have luster.

MS65

MS-65 is a grade describing an exceptional coin. It is the highest grade that can be easily obtained when conservative grading is used. It will have no significant bag marks, particularly in open areas (the "fields") or on the cheek when a face is depicted. Fewer than one coin in hundreds qualify for this grade, and is one of the most popular grade of coins with investors.

MS63

MS-63 coins are pleasant, collectible examples that exhibit enough bag marks to be noticed, but not so many as to be considered marred, with particularly few on open areas such as the field or a cheek.

MS60

MS-60 describes those coins that were quite scuffed up at the mint before their release. They will often have nicks and discoloration. Sometimes called "commercial uncirculated," they may actually be less pleasant to behold than a higher grade circulated coin.

AU

About Uncirculated (AU) describes coins with such slight signs of wear that some people may in fact need a mild magnifying glass to see them. A trace of luster should be visible. One should be careful not to confuse an attractive AU coin for Uncirculated.

EF

Extremely Fine (EF, XF) is the highest grade of coin that exhibits wear significant enough to be seen easily by the unaided eye. It is a coin that still exhibits extremely clear minute detail. In the case of American

coins featuring the word LIBERTY on a headband or shield, all letters must be sharp and clear. Many coins will exhibit luster but it is not necessary.

VF

Very Fine (VF) coins will show obvious signs of wear. Nevertheless, most of the detail of the design will still be clear. It is an overall pleasant coin. On American coins with LIBERTY on a headband or shield, all letters must be clear.

F

Fine (F) is the lowest grade most people would consider collectible. About half the design details will show for most types. On United States coins with LIBERTY described earlier, all letters must be visible if not sharp.

VG

Very Good (VG) coins exhibit heavy wear. All outlines are clear, as is, generally, the rim. Some internal detail will also show, but most will be worn off. At least three letters of LIBERTY described earlier must be legible, all letters on pre-1857 copper and Morgan dollars.

G

Good (G) coins are generally considered uncollectible except for novelty purposes. There will usually be no internal detail to the design at all. Some of the rim may also be worn out. LIBERTY as described earlier will be worn off on most coins, and will show just trace elements on pre-1857 copper and Morgan dollars.

aG or Fair

About Good (aG) and Fair (Fr) are grades in which only truly scarce coins are collected. Many collectors would rather do without a coin than to add it to their collections. The rim will be worn down and some outline to the design may be gone.

Poor (Pr) is the lowest possible grade. Many coins in Poor condition will not even be identifiable. When identifiable, many will still be condemned to the melting pot. Few collectors would consider owning such a coin except in the case of the most extreme rarities.

Proof

Sometimes treated as a grade, but technically not one at all, is **Proof (PF)**. Proof quality is a special way of making coins for presentation. A proof coin is usually double struck with highly polished dies on polished blanks, usually yielding

a mirror-like finish. These days proof coins are mass-marketed by the mint to collectors. Earlier in the century, matte or sandblast proofs were popular, characterized by a non-reflective but highly detailed surface. Cameo proof is a particular kind that has been struck with dies polished only in the fields, but with the details such as the portrait deliberately given a dull finish. For some coins, these cameo proofs have a premium value above regular proofs, which often grade MS-65 or higher.

Other miscellaneous factors can affect the quality of a coin. The presence of all or part of the original luster usually increases a coin's value. Be careful, however, not to be fooled by a coin that has been dipped in a brightener in order to simulate this luster artificially. Toning can be either good or bad. If the toning a coin has acquired is dull, irregular or splotchy, it is likely to be considered unpleasant and many collectors may choose to avoid it even if it is a high-grade coin. On the other hand, if it is mild or displays a "halo effect" around the edge of the coin, or is composed of pleasant iridescent shades, many collectors and dealers would consider paying a premium to obtain it based on its "eye appeal." Standard phrases used to emphasize a coin's eye appeal when grading include Premium Quality (PQ) and Proof Like (PL).

Also, the mint will sometimes strike a coin on a blank that is properly prepared enough not to be considered an error, but is nevertheless in some minor way imperfect. The poor mixing of the metals in the alloy or flaws left by trapped gas from this same process are examples. If trivial they may be ignored on most coins, but on more expensive or high-grade pieces, the level of concern over these flaws may increase.

Even on circulated coins, few collectors wish to have coins with scratches or edge nicks. These will occur even more frequently on larger coins like silver dollars, or on coins with reeded edges. Depending on extent of scratches and nicks, such coins may be discounted by a little or a lot.

Of course, coins with damage are worth far less than coins without. Many coins have been mounted for use in jewelry, and even when the loop or bezel has been removed they still may show slight signs of this unfortunate experience. While discounted heavily, a few collectors consider these opportunities to acquire coins with high-grade detail for a fraction of the cost. It should be remembered that the same heavy discount will apply when that collector goes to sell his coins.

SLABS

The word "slab" is numismatic slang for a tamper-resistant holder used to hold coins graded by third-party grading services. Third-party grading services came into existence to answer a market need in the 1970s and early 1980s. Many investors had become aware of the impressive appreciation of certain coins. Coin values were generally on the rise, and the total population of people suddenly calling themselves coins dealers was on the rise, too. Many of these new dealers actively promoted coins as investments. With so many inexperienced customers and dealers entering the market suddenly, it became apparent that there was a dearth of knowledge. While few in the investment market were concerned about whether the academic numismatic knowledge was being passed along, they were very concerned about properly grading the coins. Thus a neutral arbiter was

needed: the third-party grading service. These firms examine coins and seal them in small transparent rectangular holders containing that firm's opinion of the grade. The holder does not damage the coin as embedding in Lucite would. The coin is fully removable, but any attempt to remove it will cause the holder to exhibit evidence of tampering, thus preventing anyone from placing a low-grade coin in a holder indicating a higher grade.

PCGS "slab"

NGC "slab"

ICG "slab"

ANACS "slab"

There are obvious advantages to having someone without a vested interest in the answer determine the grade of a coin, but there are disadvantages as well. While the criteria applied to coin grading – particularly to United States and Canadian coins – are fairly clear and objective, no two coins wear in exactly the same manner and two individuals will not necessarily evaluate a coin in precisely the same manner. It is quite common to send the same coin to different grading services and get significantly different answers. Sometimes this differs even in resubmitting the same coin to the same grading service. As a result it has become common practice for dealers to review the lots of coins sent into the grading services on their return. Those coins graded too conservatively are usually broken out and resubmitted in hopes of achieving a higher grade. Those receiving grades that the dealer believes to be higher than he would have assigned himself are left in the holders and sold as third-party-graded coins. It is easy to see here that – simply by

means of attrition – the population of third-party-graded coins gradually becomes more and more skewed towards liberally graded examples. This does not mean that third-party coins are miss-graded, because there are always the "middle of the road" grades coming back from the services, which often are left intact. It does mean that no collector (or investor or dealer) should blindly accept the grade printed on a plastic holder as gospel. There is no substitute for study, experience and examining enough coins to the point where you can make your own judgments.

There is, nevertheless, a market for "sight unseen" coins encapsulated in slabs. The values of such coins are determined by what the market perceives as the relative accuracy of the grading service in whose capsule the coin sits. The *Coin Dealer Newsletter* (or *"Greysheet"*) rates the relative merits of these grading services on a weekly basis. While most buyers do not pursue the sight-unseen market, this quantifiable information is useful in determining which grading service to select for coins you are about to either buy or sell.

As reflected in the market, some grading services are statistically more liberal at applying grading standards than others. Both the *Coin Dealer News Letter* and the Professional Numismatists Guild have attempted to survey how accurate the coin-dealing community regards various services. The first rating below is an average of the ratings, based on information available over several months shortly before press time. A value of 100% would be the equivalent of the ideal grading service. The second column reflects the results of the PNG survey most proximate to press time. While that survey also factored in criteria related to customer service, the overwhelming majority of it related to perceived accuracy.

GRADING SERVICE	CDN	PNG
PCGS	83%	Superior
NGC	78%	Superior
ICG	75%	Good
ANACS	56%	Good
PCI	49%	Poor
SEGS	48%	—
NCI	39%	—
INS	28%	—
ACG	—	Unacceptable
ACCGS	—	Unacceptable
HCGS	—	Unacceptable
NTC	—	Unacceptable
SGS	—	Unacceptable

One outgrowth of the certified-grading phenomenon is "population reports." Some services maintain a record of the quantity of specimens in each grade for each coin that passes through their hands. In theory this will indicate to the potential coin buyer how rarely a coin occurs in certain high grades. These reports should be viewed with some caution. While it is officially expected that a dealer submitting a previously graded coin for re-grading will indicate that it is the same coin, most do not. Hence one specimen can easily end up on the population reports as two different coins.

A peculiar reaction to the proliferation of slabs is "slab aversion" by pure collectors who have no interest in investment. This author has seen and heard of numerous instances where collectors have refused to buy needed coins at a grade and price that pleased them simply because the coins were in slabs. While there is no logical support for such conduct (obviously anyone who finds the holder odious can throw it away) this is a rare, but observed, fact.

HANDLING AND TREATMENT OF COINS

How a collector or dealer treats his coins can greatly affect how well they hold their value. Metal is both more reactive and softer than most people would think.

Coin damaged by fingerprints

The human body contains many corrosive chemicals. Simply touching a coin in some cases can contribute to its deterioration. This is especially true of coins exhibiting mint luster or iridescent toning. Touching a bright copper surface with a sweaty thumb can easily result in the appearance of a dark thumbprint several weeks or months later. All this being said, it is easy to understand why the first lesson of coin collecting should be ***"Never touch a coin on its surface."*** If one needs to pick a coin up with bare skin, touch only its edge. In the case of proof coins, even greater precautions must be taken. The highly reflective surfaces are so sensitive that one should avoid even breathing directly on the coin. This will cause what coin collectors call "carbon spots," small black dots. Also, do not leave coins out unprotected where they can be directly exposed to dust, sunlight or changes in temperature.

Coins can be stored in many ways. One of the most convenient is in 2" square plastic "flips." These are transparent holders with two pockets, one to contain the coin, one to contain a cardboard ticket on which information can be recorded. It folds over on itself into a size 2" square. Originally they were made only of a PVC-formula plastic. This was particularly flexible and easy to work with, but eventually it would break down, depositing a green slime on the coins it contained. Today both the PVC formula and a new more inert Mylar formula are available. The Mylar type is prone to cracking, but so far has not been found to damage coins. The PVC type is still popular because it is more flexible, but is now usually used only by dealers and auction houses for temporary storage. Collectors usually repackage coins purchased in such holders before placing a coin into long-term storage.

Another common coin holder is the "two-by-two." This is a pair of cardboard squares with an adhering film of

relatively inert plastic. The coin is sandwiched in between the two layers of plastic, and the two halves are stapled together. While this does not permit the coin to be removed and touched as easily as storage in flips, it does permit the coin to be viewed on both sides without opening the holder. It is important to remember that when you remove coins from these holders, be very careful not to accidentally scratch the coin on the exposed ends of the staples that may poke out if the holder is pulled apart. These careless staple scratches have ruined countless good coins.

Both flips and two-by-twos fit nicely into specially made boxes. They also fit into plastic pages designed to hold 20 of either holder. These are transparent and will fit into most looseleaf binders. It is important to remember not to place coins loose in these pages, as they are often of PVC plastic. Moreover, some of the thumb cuts are large enough for some coins to fall through.

There are many specialized coin albums and folders designed to not only store and exhibit a collection, but to guide the collector through it. Each coin in the series is individually labeled making their use extremely convenient. It is widely believed that one of the main reasons coin collecting was able to catch on with the American middle class in the 1930s is the invention of the "penny board," a one-sheet predecessor of these modern coin folders and albums. Old albums and folders contained elements in the cardboard that would tone the coins, although actual corrosion was rare. Today this has been removed from most albums' composition.

This same phenomenon occurs with the long-term use of the orange-brown 2" coin envelopes, although it is less of a problem with those of other colors. The toning in this case is caused by sulfur in the paper.

Many new collectors ask, "How do I remove the toning?" While it can be done, it is not recommended. Though there are rare exceptions, it should generally be stated that one should *never clean a coin*. It is highly likely that more harm than good will result. Toning is actually part of the coin. It is molecularly bonded to the metal, and the only way to remove the toning is literally to remove part of the coin. This is the way most coin dips work, by means of a mild acid. Physical cleaning is even worse, as microscopic striations almost inevitably are cut into the coin's surface, even with something as mild as a tissue!

A cool, dry environment is best for storing a coin collection. Of course not everyone lives in such a climate. One common answer to this is to store a packet of silica gel in the same container as the coin collection. This is a desiccant and will absorb the moisture in the air. Packets can sometimes be obtained at photo shops, or through your local coin dealer.

SECURITY

For anyone who collects something of value, security is a major issue. Realize that no house is theft proof and take reasonable precautions. Make sure all doors are locked and that access cannot be gained through open windows. Many collectors choose to install alarm systems. If this is what you choose, do not neglect to place a sticker to that effect in the window. Most alarm companies provide them automatically. If your collection warrants it, you may wish to consider a home safe of suitable size.

Perhaps more important than locks and alarms is being discreet. Do not tell everyone you meet that you are a coin collector. Even if your collection is relatively inexpensive, some potential thieves may presume that all coin collections are valuable. They may not realize they have stolen a $100 collection instead of a $10,000 one until it is too late.

The most intelligent choice is to keep all your more valuable coins in a safe-deposit box in a bank. When choosing a safe deposit box, it is important to consider the environment. It is better to have a box on an inside wall of the vault rather than along the outside of the building. This will reduce the exposure to temperature fluctuations. Also, do not forget to place a small packet of silica gel in each box. You may find it more convenient to have multiple boxes of moderate size rather than one large box if your collection is particularly heavy.

Lastly, if you are buying coins through the mail, do not give out your home address. Use a post office box. Not only does this provide you with a security barrier, it also provides a safe place for your coins to sit if they arrive while you are away.

DETECTING COUNTERFEITS

Counterfeiting is on the rise, although most counterfeits have both their origin and circulation overseas. Detailed discussion will be made throughout this edition of a great many of these new and sometimes deceptive counterfeits. Here are the basics:

There are three kinds of counterfeits the collector should be aware of. Some are more deceptive than others. The oldest type of counterfeit is often called a forgery. It is a false coin or piece of paper money made with the intent of passing it in circulation. It is usually of adequate quality not to be obvious at a casual inspection, but is often imperfect. A counterfeiter making such a product can, at most, hope to gain face value of the item he is replicating. Therefore, he is limited as to the expense he is willing to lay out and still make a profit for his risk.

Imitations and evasions are other kinds of counterfeiting. These are made to circulate but are often not faithful to the original because they are made for use in communities that, for various reasons, have come to expect that some of their coinage will be counterfeit. Imitations vary only in style, while evasions deliberately modify some aspect of the inscription or design to provide a meager legal defense against a charge of counterfeiting. (A good example would be halfpennies, which circulated in Colonial America with the inscription BRITAINS ISLES instead of BRITANNIA.) All of these may fool a collector at first glance, but they are usually imperfect enough not to pass close scrutiny. Many of them are historically significant and are frequently collected along with – or instead of – the original series. As such they are called "contemporary counterfeits" because they were struck contemporary to those coins with which they were intended to circulate.

A far greater danger to the collector is the true numismatic counterfeit. These are counterfeits of higher quality created with great care to fool numismatic experts. Many counterfeits are made by casting, even though the original coin may have been made by striking. Look for seams along the edge. They may not be centered and obvious but can be hidden to one side or the other. Also, examine the surface under magnification for a multitude of faint pimples or unnatural porosity. The precise shapes of letters are also something often neglected by counterfeiters. On modern

coins, an inaccurate weight, or incorrect alloy (revealed by specific gravity testing) can be a giveaway. Ancient and medieval coins can vary much more in weight. Be aware that a great many counterfeiters have sought to hide their imperfections by heavy cleaning. The idea is that a collector examining a rare coin will attribute the problems to abuse, rather than forgery.

Souvenir marked COPY

An Altered coin. This 1932 Philadelphia quarter has had D mintmark added.

Some collector counterfeits are actually made from real coins. These are called "altered" because the counterfeiter alters the original coin by adding or removing a mintmark or part of the date, making it appear to be a scarcer variety. You may think the task of adding a mintmark to a coin sounds too minute to be possible, but counterfeiters have demonstrated remarkable skill over the years.

The last type of counterfeit is of virtually no threat to collectors, but pity the poor tourist! These are counterfeits made as souvenirs. This is not to say they are never created to pass off as authentic coins, but the forger is presuming either total credulity on the part of the buyer, or an unwillingness to give a critical inspection. Even the color of the metal is often incorrect. Tens of thousands of these, replicating ancient coins, have been sold at archaeological sites in Turkey and the Middle East. Other similar counterfeits are found in Italy replicating 19th century silver-dollar-sized coins. Often these types of replicas (the more accurate name) are sold clearly marked as such in museum shops, or through legitimate vendors. Often they are even marked "COPY" to prevent confusion with the real thing. Since the passage of the Hobby Protection Act, replicas made in the United States have been required to display this word.

ILLUSTRATION CREDITS

The thousands of illustrations in this book are used by the kind permission of a number of firms and individuals. Without the help of these contributors, this book would not be possible.

In particular I would like to thank Heritage Numismatic Auctions Inc., Dallas, and Stack's, New York and Wolfeboro, N.H., for the vast majority of United States coin images. Chet Krause generously provided the lion's share of U.S. paper money illustrated, along with significant contributions by Heritage and Stack's.

Illustrations of ancient coins were provided primarily by Pegasi Numismatics, of Ann Arbor, Mich., and Holicong, Pa., and by Stack's. Other important contributions were provided by Stephen Album, Santa Rosa, Calif., Heritage, and from examples in my own reference collection.

Chet Krause, worldcoingallery.com (Don Norris), Stack's, Heritage and my own inventory all provided a great number of world and Canadian coin images. Some supplementary images also were supplied by Stephen Album and Pegasi Numismatics.

As in the case of United States paper money, Chet Krause provided the majority of world and Canadian paper money illustrations, along with contributions by myself, Heritage and Stack's.

Copyright for the respective contributions is retained by the contributors. Detailed information as to the source of any particular image is available on request.

UNITED STATES COINS
THE EVOLUTION OF UNITED STATES COINAGE

An average American living in the American Colonies during the 18th century would not have found many English silver or gold coins in his pocket. It was British policy to restrict the export of precious metals to the Colonies. As a result there was nothing but copper struck, and even that was rarely minted. Most of the silver coins circulating in Colonial America were imported from Mexico and South America. Spanish colonial *reales* far outnumbered English shillings. The largest Spanish colonial silver coin was a "piece," valued at eight *reales*, hence the term "pieces of eight," so often associated with pirates.

The English colonists called these big coins "pillar dollars" after the Pillars of Hercules flanking the two globes on them, or "milled dollars" because of the milled design applied to the edge to prevent people from trimming away bits of silver. Because two *reales* were equal to one fourth of a milled dollar, the modern U.S. quarter is still sometimes referred to as "two bits." (Until 2001, the New York Stock Exchange also measured values in eighths of a dollar based on this tradition.) Silver coins were so scarce that Colonial Americans would use any other foreign silver or gold coin that could be pressed into service. Besides Spanish, any French, Portuguese and occasionally German silver and gold would be readily accepted when they would turn up.

British copper coins were much more commonly found in the Colonies than precious-metal coins. Excavations at 18th-century Colonial sites frequently uncover halfpennies of George II (1727-1760) and George III (1760-1820), and even those of William III (1688-1702). Supplies of these too were short, but the colonists were less likely to have foreign sources for their copper than for their precious-metal coins. By the mid-1700s the counterfeiting of copper halfpennies had become a popular industry. People would knowingly accept these as a matter of convenience. Today any counterfeit English halfpenny known to have been made at one of these private colonial "mints" is actually worth more than the real English issue in the same grade.

Counterfeits of the Spanish silver "two bit" pieces mentioned earlier were also common both in the English and Spanish colonies. These were usually just silver-plated brass, so unlike the halfpenny imitations in their correct metal, people would not accept them as emergency money. However they too have value today, as historical artifacts.

Same type coin struck by two different hand-engraved dies. Note top of 1 and bottom of pole.

When neither imported nor counterfeit coins were available, the ingenious and hard-pressed colonists improvised money. They used wampum made from beads of trimmed shell. This form of currency was adopted from the local Indians. As anything of refined metal had value, nails became a standard of exchange. Another medium of exchange was the tobacco twist. Both nails and tobacco currency could also be forced back into practical uses if needed.

Some of the colonial governors also issued paper money valued in terms of discounted British currency, or in Spanish milled dollars. This will be discussed more thoroughly in the chapter on United States paper money.

After the Declaration of Independence, many of the same forms of currency continued. Spanish colonial silver and gold were as popular as ever. All of the new states issued their own paper money. Not only did the counterfeiting of British halfpennies continue, or perhaps even increase, but many private firms issued their own coppers and occasionally their own silver coins, too. Under the Articles of Confederation (the first United States Constitution) each state was essentially a fully sovereign country, and some of them issued official state-sanctioned coinage. Usually they were cents the size of the old British halfpennies. Massachusetts, New Jersey and Vermont all authorized their issue, but by far the most common were those of Connecticut. The Continental Congress placed its own copper in circulation – the Fugio Cent. There were a number of other experimental coinages struck both by and for presentation to the Congress, but few amounted to anything.

When the Constitution took effect in 1789 it put an end to all state-issued coinage. In view of the new stronger federal union, many people began to take the idea of a single national coinage more seriously. Others argued that it was not the place of government go get involved in such

Piece of Eight showing Pillars of Hercules

things. With the personal influence of George Washington himself behind them, the proponents of the new U.S. Mint persevered, and construction began in 1792. For both administrative and technical reasons, things got off to a slow start, but before the end of the year, silver five-cent pieces struck from the first president's tableware were circulating around Philadelphia. The new coinage was based on a decimal system dividing a dollar into 100 cents. The idea of the dollar as the standard unit was inspired by the Spanish pieces of eight. Suffering under a severe shortage of both bullion and labor (and annual epidemics of yellow fever), the early mint never succeeded in placing any substantial coinage in circulation on a national level. Broad circulation was also prevented by the rapid withdrawal and melting of much of the gold and silver coinage by speculators, because American coins had too high a precious-metal content relative to their value. The endeavor became so futile that the striking of many denominations were frequently suspended. It wasn't until the 1830s that the weights of the coins were adjusted to prevent their export.

During the mint's first four decades, every die was engraved by hand so no two looked alike. Also, the coins were struck by hand on a screw press one at a time. Finally in 1836 the industrial revolution came to the U.S. Mint. Steam-powered striking equipment was imported from England. Almost over night American coins became more neat and uniform. The old lettered edges were replaced by modern reeding, those hundreds of parallel lines found on coins today. Also, the quantities that could be produced in the same amount of time increased drastically. This technological improvement roughly coincided with the needed reduction in the coins' bullion content, and with a facelift for all silver denominations. Thus, over the mid-1830s, the nation's coinage was utterly transformed.

The purity of silver coins was increased from 89.24 percent to 90 percent in 1837. Minor adjustments occurred to the weight of the silver coins in 1853 and 1873, signified by the addition of small arrows by the date. The silver three-cent piece and three new gold denominations, $3 (1854) and $1 and $20 (1849) were introduced, partially because of the California Gold Rush. But the big event of the mid-century was the coinage law of 1857. This one act eliminated the half-cent, reduced the size of the one-cent piece from bigger than a quarter to the diameter used today, and most importantly, caused foreign silver and gold to cease to be legal tender in the United States. The mint was finally able to produce enough to provide a true national coinage.

Civil War coin shortages not only resulted in many private tokens but also inspired the two-cent and nickel three-cent pieces, and possibly the five-cent nickel. It also saw the debut of the motto "In God we trust on the coinage." During the late 1860s and 1870s the nation was in the economic doldrums. Mintages were low for many denominations, particularly the silver dollar, and hence many coins of this era are scarce today.

From the late 1870s onwards, coinage was plentiful for half a century, sometimes too plentiful. A dominant political influence was the "Free Silver Movement," which didn't mean people wanted to be given free silver, but that they wanted unlimited quantities to be converted into coin to use up the excess that was being mined. Proponents also intended that this would increase the money supply, thereby causing inflation to erode debts. From 1873 to about 1918,

Walking Liberty Half Dollar

several laws were passed to force the government to buy silver and strike an abundance of silver dollars. Unpopular in the more developed parts of the country, they frequently sat in government or bank vaults for decades. Minor silver ("small change") also became more common during this era.

Early in the last century, Theodore Roosevelt led the nation to a new level of intellectual consciousness, touching upon ideas as diverse as national parks and the artistic merits of the nation's coinage. For the latter he sought the aid of the greatest sculptors of the day, deliberately looking outside the mint staff for talent. Most of the new coin designs reflect neo-classical artistic trends prevalent in Europe, as well. These beautiful designs include the Mercury dime, the Walking Liberty half dollar and the Saint-Gaudens double eagle, as well as the less classically inspired Buffalo nickel.

A commemorative coin program was also getting under way, providing an outlet for artists of various tastes. Most never saw circulation, being sold at a premium to collectors. By 1936, however, this had gotten so far out of hand that in that one year alone 22 different half dollars were struck!

The need for strategic metals for armaments during World War II was the cause for interesting, if not pleasant, aberrations in the cent and nickel. The striking of these in steel and a silver-manganese alloy, respectively, was a response to these shortages.

Idealistic images of Liberty were gradually replaced during the 1930s and 1940s with those of statesmen, while art contests replaced selecting artists.

An increase in the price of silver in 1964 prompted massive hoarding of silver coins as the content approached their face value. As a result, silver was all or partially removed from the coinage in favor of clad coinage that can be readily distinguished by the copper core visible on the edge. Almost 30 years later the cent too was debased, the bronze alloy being replaced by one of zinc simply plated with bronze.

Today the nation's coinage is characterized by a new flood of commemoratives struck for both significant and insignificant reasons, most completely unknown to the American people. Traditionally sold at a high premium by the mint, 1999 was the first time since the Bicentennial that commemoratives circulated at face value, this being the first year of an extensive set of quarters commemorating each state.

MINTS & MINTMARKS

The first U.S. Mint was constructed in Philadelphia in 1792. Over the centuries it has had several different homes in that city, continuously growing. Officially, all other mints are branches, but this does not mean that the largest quantities of each coin are always struck in Philadelphia.

The first branch mints were opened to strike coins from new gold being mined from deposits found in the South. These mints at Charlotte, N.C., and Dahlonega, Ga., were opened in 1838 and closed with the Civil War in 1861. They never struck in any metal but gold, usually in small quantities. Also, opened for the same duration but of far greater importance, was New Orleans. This became the second-largest mint, striking vast numbers of coins in both gold and silver.

The San Francisco mint was opened in 1854 in response to the California Gold Rush. Today it strikes most of the proof issues. In 1870, the boom in Nevada silver mines caused the mint to open a branch in Carson City. It was closed in 1893 and its coins are generally scarce.

Easily rivaling Philadelphia in its current importance is the Denver mint. Opened in 1906, it sometimes strikes more coins than the primary mint itself.

Recently some coins have been struck at West Point, N.Y. These are not circulation strikes, but collector issues and bullion only.

One can usually tell where a coin is struck by a small letter or a mark placed on the coin. In the United States they have usually been on the reverse, but reappeared on the obverse after they were removed from 1965 to 1967. The mintmarks used on United States coins are:

None or

P	Philadelphia
C	Charlotte, N.C.
CC	Carson City, Nev.
D	Dahlonega, Ga.
D	Denver
O	New Orleans
S	San Francisco
W	West Point, N.Y.

VARIETIES

In some instances, small modifications to a certain aspect of a die are made after the production process for the year has already begun. When a new design is put into production, trivial aspects of the design may be modified to improve striking quality. Thus, two different versions of the same type will exist for that year.

One common modification results from the use of different style or size punches to place the date in the die. This will cause some coins to have either a small or large date. In earlier times, the mint sought to economize by reusing the previous year's dies, re-engraved with a new date. On such dies, traces of the old date can sometimes be seen. When these dies wear out, new dies are prepared.

Thus some year's coins bear an "overdate" for part of the production run.

Some variations are caused by accident. Double-die coins are not errors in manufacturing but mistakes in the preparation of the dies themselves, visible on the coins even when they are perfectly manufactured.

BOOKS ABOUT U.S. COINS

One cannot overemphasize the importance of books in fully understanding rare coins. The difference between a person accumulating a few interesting coins and a true numismatist is not how much a person spends, but how much a person learns.

The following books provide a good background to United States coins in general. Other books just dealing with one series are listed below, usually sequenced as the coins they cover are sequenced in this volume. Where it is important, I have made a few comments on these books. Do not be put off by early publication dates, a great many standard works from earlier decades have been reprinted many times and are widely available through coin dealers. This is just a sampling, and many other worthwhile books are available.

Bowers, Q. David, *The History of United States Coinage As Illustrated by the Garrett Collection.*

Breen, Walter, *Walter Breen's Complete Encyclopedia of U.S. and Colonial Coins.* One of the most intelligent, in-depth general catalogs of the series. Excellent!

Breen, Walter, *Walter Breen's Encyclopedia of U.S. and Colonial Proof Coins.*

Fivaz, Bill, and Stanton, J.T., *The Cherry Pickers' Guide to Rare Die Varieties.*

Yeoman, R.S., *A Guide Book of United States Coins.* Popularly called the Red Book, it is the widely acknowledged bible of U.S. coins.

Yeoman, R.S., *Handbook of United States Coins.* Popularly called the Blue Book, a companion to the Redbook above, designed for those with an eye to selling their coins.

Grading

American Numismatic Association, *Official A.N.A. Grading Standards for United States Coins.* No one has any business investing in U.S. coins, or even spending significant money on them as a hobby, if they don't have this book.

Professional Coin Grading Service, *Official Guide to Coin Grading and Counterfeit Detection*

Ruddy, James F., *Photograde*

Detecting Counterfeits

American Numismatic Association, *Counterfeit Detection*, 2 vols.

Fivaz, Bill, *Bill Fivaz's Counterfeit Detection Guide.* Convenient set of blow-up photos of authentic examples by a noted coin photographer.

Harshe, Bert, *How to Detect Altered & Counterfeit Coins and Paper Money.*

John, Lonesome, *Detecting Counterfeit Coins.*

John, Lonesome, *Detecting Counterfeit Gold Coins.*

Kleeberg, John M., ed., *Circulating Counterfeits of the Americas*, American Numismatic Society, N.Y.

Larson, Charles M., *Numismatic Forgery.*

Professional Coin Grading Service, *Official Guide to Coin Grading and Counterfeit Detection.*

Virtually every issue of The Numismatist, the official journal of the American Numismatic Association, has large clear photographs of newly discovered counterfeits. The listings in issues before 1988 are in part summarized in the above A.N.A. references.

Colonials Coins

Breen, Walter, Walter Breen's Complete Encyclopedia of U.S. and Colonial Coins. Despite being a general book, it is also one of the best treatments of Colonials as well.

Crosby, S.S., *The Early Coins of America.*

Kleeberg, John, *Money of Pre-Federal America.*

Maris, Edward, *A Historical Sketch of the Coins of New Jersey*.

Miller, Henry Clay, *State Coinages of Connecticut.*

Newman, Eric P., ed., *Studies on Money in Early America.*

Noe, Sydney, *The New England and Willow Tree Coinage of Massachusetts.*

Noe, Sydney, *The Oak Tree Coinage of Massachusetts.*

Noe, Sydney, *The Pine Tree Coinage of Massachusetts.*

Richardson, A.D., *The Copper Coins of Vermont.* (An extension of the standard numbering system established in Ryder, Hillyer, *The Colonial Coins of Vermont.*)

Vlack, Robert, *Early American Coins.*

Half Cents

Breen, Walter, *Walter Breen's Encyclopedia of United States Half Cents 1793-1857.*

Cohen, Roger, *American Half Cents, The "Little Half Sisters."* Establishes a standard numbering system for die varieties.

Large Cents

Newcomb, H., *United States Copper Cents 1816-1857.* (Covers die varieties.)

Sheldon, William, *Penny Whimsy,* 1958 (Covers die varieties 1793 to 1815, a standard that has survived through many reprints).

Small Cents

Bowers, Q. David, *A Guide Book of Lincoln Cents.*

Snow, *Flying Eagle and Indian Cents.*

Taylor, *The Standard Guide to the Lincoln Cent.*

Wiles, James, *The RPM Book - Lincoln Cents.* Guide to re-punched mintmark varieties.

Two-Cent and Three-Cent Pieces

Kilman, M., *The Two Cent Piece and Varieties, 1977.*

Flynn, Kevin, *Getting Your Two Cents Worth.*

Bowers, Q. David, *U.S. Three-Cent and Five-Cent Pieces.*

Half Dimes and Nickels

Blythe, Al, *The Complete Guide to Liberty Seated Half Dimes.*

Bowers, Q. David, *U.S. Three-Cent and Five-Cent Pieces.*

Lange, David, *The Complete Guide to Buffalo Nickels.*

Valentine, D.W., *The United States Half Dimes, 1931.*

Standard reference on die varieties for the series.

Wescott, Michael, *The United States Nickel Five-Cent Piece.*

Dimes

Bowers, Q. David, *United States Dimes, Quarters and Half Dollars.*

Greer, Brian, *The Complete Guide to Liberty Seated Dimes.*

Lawrence, David, *The Complete Guide to Barber Dimes.*

Lange, David W., *The Complete Guide to Mercury Dimes.*

Rapsus, Ginger, *The United States Clad Coinage.*

Twenty Cent Pieces and Quarters

Bowers, Q. David, *United States Dimes, Quarters and Half Dollars*

Briggs, Larry, *Liberty Seated Quarters.*

Browning, A. W., *The Early Quarter Dollars of the United States.* (The standard reference on die varieties for the series.)

Cline, J.H., *Standing Liberty Quarters.*

Hammer, Ted, "The Twenty Cent Piece," *The Numismatist,* vol. 60, pp. 167-69.

Lawrence, David, *The Complete Guide to Barber Quarters.*

Rapsus, Ginger, *The United States Clad Coinage.*

Half Dollars

Bowers, Q. David, *United States Dimes, Quarters and Half Dollars*

Fox, Bruce, *The Complete Guide to Walking Liberty Half Dollars.*

Lawrence, David, *The Complete Guide to Barber Halves.*

Overton, Al C., *Early Half Dollar Die Varieties 1794-1836.* (Standard reference on die varieties for the series.)

Rapsus, Ginger, *The United States Clad Coinage.*

Silver & Clad Dollars

Bolender, M.H., *The United States Early Silver Dollars from 1794 to 1803.* (Standard reference on die varieties for the series.)

Bowers, Q. David, *Silver Dollars and Trade Dollars of the United States: A Complete Encyclopedia.*

Bowers, Q. David, *A Guide Book of Morgan Silver Dollars.*

Newman, Eric, and Bressett, Kenneth, *The Fantastic 1804 Dollar.*

Rapsus, Ginger, *The United States Clad Coinage.*

Van Allen, Leroy, and Mallis, A. George, *Comprehensive Catalogue and Encyclopedia of U.S. Morgan and Peace Silver **Dollars.***

Willem, John M., *The United States Trade Dollar.*

Gold Coinage

Akers, David, *Handbook of 20th-Century United States Gold Coins.*

Bowers, Q. David, *United States Gold Coins: An Illustrated History.*

Commemoratives

Bowers, Q. David, *Commemorative Coins of the United States: A Complete Encyclopedia.*

Hodder, Michael, and Bowers, Q. David, *A Basic Guide to United States Commemorative Coins.*

Swiatek, Anthony, and Breen, Walter, *Encyclopedia of United States Silver and Gold Commemorative Coins 1892-1989.*

Proofs

Breen, Walter, *Walter Breen's Encyclopedia of United States and Colonial Proof Coins.*

Patterns

Judd, J. Hewett, *United States Pattern, Experimental and Trial Pieces.* The newest edition of this standard has been updated by Q. David Bowers.

Krause, Chester, and Mishler, Clifford, *Standard Catalog of World Coins* and *Standard Catalog of World Coins, 19th Century.*

Errors

Margolis, Arnold, *Error Coin Encyclopedia.*

Spadone, Frank, *Major Variety and Oddity.*

Wiles, James, and Miller, Tom, *The RPM Book* (Guide to re-punched mintmark varieties.)

Tokens

Alpert, Stephen and Smith, Kenneth E., *Video Arcade, Pinball, Slot Machine and other Amusement Tokens of North America.*

Breen, Walter, *Pioneer and Fractional Gold.*

Coffee, John, and Ford, Harold, *Atwood-Coffee Catalogue of United States and Canadian Transportation Tokens,* 5th ed.

Fuld, George and Melvin, *Patriotic Civil War Tokens.*

Fuld, George and Melvin, *U.S. Civil War Store Cards.*

Hibler, Harold, and Kappen, Charles, *So-Called Dollars.* A standard work on dollar-sized tokens or medals, particularly those used temporarily as a medium of exchange or to represent such satirically.

Hodder, Michael J., and Bowers, Q. David, *Standard Catalogue of Encased Postage Stamps.*

Kagin, Donald, *Private Gold Coins and Patterns of the United States.*

Rulau, R., and Fuld, G., *Medallic Portraits of Washington.*

Rulau, Russel, *Standard Catalog of United States Tokens.*

Schenkman, David, *Civil War Suttler Tokens and Cardboard Scrip.*

Sullivan, Edmund B., *American Political Badges and Medalets 1789-1892.*

Token and Medal Society, *TAMS Journal.* The journal of this organization is incredibly useful, with regular listings identifying "mavericks," or private tokens which bear no specific indication of their origin.

Hawaii, Alaska, U.S. Philippines

Basso, Aldo, *Coins, Medals and Tokens of the Philippines.*

Gould, Maurice, *Hawaiian Coins Tokens and Paper Money.*

Krause & Mishler, *Standard Catalog of World Coins.*

Yeoman, R.S., *Guidebook of United States Coins.*

Confederate Coins

Reed III, Fred L., series of articles, *Coin World,* Oct. 4, Oct. 11, Oct. 18, 1989

PERIODICALS

Magazines have a certain immediacy not possible in books. They also put the reader in touch with the thoughts and opinions of their fellow numismatists.

CoinAge (monthly) – A popular newsstand magazine, oriented to the collector and the layman.

Coin Prices (six per year) – Extensive listings of United States coin values in many grades. Articles more oriented towards the market than towards history. Published by Krause Publications, the world's largest numismatic publisher.

Coins (monthly) – Very similar to *CoinAge* but put out by Krause Publications, the world's largest numismatic publisher.

CoinValues (monthly) - Extensive listings of United States coin values in many grades. Articles mostly oriented. Published by Coin World.

Coin World (weekly) – The largest circulation coin newspaper, covering both American and world coins.

Counterfeit Coin Bulletin (three per year) – Detailed reports on newly discovered counterfeits. A joint publication of the American Numismatic Association and the International Association of Professional Numismatists.

Numismatic News (weekly) – A Krause Publications newspaper focusing primarily on United States Coins.

The Numismatist (monthly) – The monthly journal of the American Numismatic Association. All full members automatically receive a subscription.

COLONIAL AND STATE COINAGES

Coinage in Colonial America was a hodge-podge of British coins, British Colonial issues, local tokens and counterfeits, and imported Spanish colonial silver and gold, usually from Mexico, Peru and Bolivia. Sometimes, small silver was made by cutting the large Spanish milled dollars or "pieces of eight" into wedge-shaped eighths. Each eighth was nicknamed a "bit." One quarter of a Spanish dollar was worth two bits. Coinage was always short in Colonial America, so the colonists would readily improvise for small change. The economic principles of the mercantile system prevented Britain from shipping any reasonable quantities of silver or gold to the Colonies.

As to copper, even when regal coppers were brought over by the keg full, there were never enough. Perhaps the single most common coin to circulate in the British Colonies in America was the George II (1727-60) copper halfpenny. The most influential however may have been that of his grandson and America's last king, George III (1760-1820), shown here:

George III Halfpenny

This coin served as a pattern for numerous local Colonial counterfeits. Sometimes the legends would be changed so the issuer could evade charges of out-and-out counterfeiting. Such imitations are today called "evasions." Other counterfeiters sought to make their product as accurate as possible. Legal or not, the average Colonial

subject was probably not too picky as to the authenticity of his coppers. After all, it was better than nothing at all, or bartering for unneeded goods.

Several Colonies were able to supplement their improvised coins with officially struck tokens. These were usually lighter than the true British issues but were sanctioned by the government to a greater or lesser extent. Some were specifically made for shipment to the American Colonies, while others were approved for shipment when they were rejected in Ireland.

After independence, the Colonial issues were replaced by both state copper coinages, and actual and proposed Continental Congress issues. Under the Articles of Confederation, the Continental Congress was the government of the United States before the present constitution. That union permitted the states to keep many more of their sovereign rights, including their own coinages. Several of the state coppers were cents designed to follow closely on the pattern of George II and especially George III halfpennies. To an illiterate public, comfort was influenced by appearance.

Private coinage did not end abruptly when the Constitution took effect in 1789. The coins were gradually transformed into merchant tokens. This section lists those of the 18th century only, as most have more in common with the pre-Federal unofficial coinages than with the later tokens. The latter will be found discussed separately in the section on Merchant Tokens.

Most types of Colonial coppers, and a far larger quantity of 18th-century British halfpennies, are unearthed from old Colonial sites. They exhibit porous surfaces and pitting. The value of such a coin is always discounted, but if not too awful, many collectors of this early material will be willing to own it.

Paper money continued to be issued, and also continued to merit the same bad reputation, perpetually being subject to discount.

AMERICAN PLANTATION TOKENS

In 1688, King James II's secretary suggested that the mint be receptive to the idea of striking tin coins for the American Colonies, which he and others then referred to as the "American Plantations." Having obtained royal sanction, Richard Holt, on behalf of a

consortium of tin miners, requested the mint to prepare such coins depicting James II on a leaping horse, with four shields of arms on the reverse. This was the first official coinage for the British Colonies in North America.

Their denomination was inscribed as 1/24th of a Spanish *real*, which was a silver coin common to the Colonies. Conventionally, they were considered to have the value of about a British halfpenny of the time, perhaps more by some authorities.

The coins met an unsuccessful end however. Their minting was cut short when James II was forced to flee before the advancing forces of his daughter, Mary II, and son-in-law, William of Orange. Beyond that, the coins themselves soon began to crumble. It seems that tin this pure (97.5%) turns to powder in cold New England and New York winters. Most known specimens suffer from "tin pest," pitting or porosity, particularly near their edges.

Known Counterfeits: In 1828, a London coin dealer struck a few hundred restrikes with original but rusted dies. They can be identified by a large die break right of the horse's face.

	G	F
James II 1/24 Real	230.00	500.00
same, 4 of 24 sideways	430.00	1,850.00
same, arms transposed	750.00	2,000.00
same, restrike	100.00	275.00

ROSA AMERICANA TOKENS

The next attempt at a special coinage for the American Colonies was also ill fated. William Wood actively solicited a royal patent to strike such a coin in hopes

of making a profit. It was agreed that he could strike brass pennies, half pennies and two-pence at a standard roughly 40 percent the weight of British regal copper. The coins' weight was to be verified by none other than Sir Isaac Newton. While the document was granted by the king, it was instantly stolen by the king's mistress and held for ransom, making it impossible for Wood to have them struck in the Tower of London mint under controlled conditions. The 75 percent copper, 24.7 percent zinc alloy looked bright when new but soon discolored, in large part due to the cast (instead of cut) blanks. Their arrival in New York and New England was as unwelcome as it was unexpected. Nobody could figure out the denominations!

The common obverse of these coins is the portrait of George I. The crowned Tudor rose on the reverse is derived from a coin of Henry VIII, the uncrowned version from a coin of his son, Edward VI. The reverse inscription, *Rosa Americana Utile Dulci* roughly translates as, "American Rose, Useful [and] Sweet."

These often suffer from dark surfaces and porosity, even when not ground finds.

Known Counterfeits: The 1722 second prototype halfpenny, electrotype copies of 1722 and 1733 pattern two-pence. Some brass halfpennies have been silver plated to pass for the rare 1723 silver strike.

	G	F
No Date 2 Pence	95.00	400.00
1722 ½ Penny	75.00	260.00
1722 Penny	75.00	250.00

	G	F
1722 2 Pence	95.00	285.00
1723 ½ Penny	700.00	1,900.00
same with crown	55.00	180.00
1723 Penny	60.00	175.00

	G	F
1723 2 Pence	95.00	300.00
1724 Penny pattern		*Two Known*
1724 2 Pence pattern		*Extremely Rare*
1733 2 Pence pattern		*Four Known*

HIBERNIA COINAGE

Before William Wood acquired the Rosa Americana patent, he acquired a similar one to strike coins for Ireland. It was agreed that he could strike copper halfpence and farthings at a standard roughly 1/4 lighter than British regal copper. As in the case of the previous patent, the document was granted by the king, but was instantly stolen by his mistress. It cost an additional £10,000 ransom for Wood to retrieve it. Because the Irish Parliament was not consulted before the coins were shipped, and because of the "King's Whore" scandal, these coins were widely rejected. Production ceased by the beginning of 1724. In 1736 they were demonetized. Certain merchants bought up those remaining for their scrap value and shipped them surreptitiously to the Colonies where they entered circulation at face value, since the colonists accepted whatever coins they could get their hands on.

The common obverse of these coins is the portrait of George I. Hibernia, the allegory of Ireland, seated with a harp, graces the reverse. There are a number of varieties for each date.

Porous ground finds are traded at a discount.

Counterfeit Alert: Any silver off-metal strikes should be examined for the possibility of being silver-plated copper business strikes, as well as deceptive struck counterfeits. Counterfeits also exist of the 1723 First Prototype farthing. Few common types have been counterfeited.

	G	F
1722 Farthing	60.00	400.00
1722 ½ Penny, rocks right (pattern)		3,000.00

	G	F
1722 ½ Penny, harp left	25.00	150.00
1722 ½ Penny, harp right	25.00	100.00
1723 Farthing	25.00	100.00
same with D:G:	50.00	165.00
1723 ½ Penny	25.00	75.00
1724 Farthing	40.00	220.00
1724 ½ Penny	30.00	160.00

HIBERNIA/VOCE POPULI COINAGE

These were originally private tokens struck by a Mr. Roche in the 1760s in Dublin. It has been suggested that the idealized head and the legend VOCE POPULI, or "Voice of the People," could refer to Irish support for Stuart pretenders. The meaning of the P in the obverse field of some of these is a mystery. The common reverse is a seated figure of Hibernia with harp. When a large shipment of 1766 regal George III halfpence arrived, the Voce Populi pieces seemed to loose favor, and were bought by entrepreneurs as scrap metal and shipped to the American Colonies where they traded at face value.

Some of these appear quite crude, as many of the blanks were cast, and some of the actual coins as well.

They are often porous, and as such are discounted depending on surface.

Known Counterfeits: Genuine 1760 coins altered to resemble the 1700 error.

	G	F
1760 Farthing	175.00	600.00
1700 ½ Penny	500.00	1,350.00
1760 ½ Penny	60.00	190.00
1760 ½ Penny, P	80.00	240.00

	G	F
1760 ½ Penny, VOOE	80.00	220.00

PITT TOKENS

The Stamp Act of 1765 required tax to be paid on papers, from forms to newspapers. It stirred major protests by the colonists, who were not consulted. They formed protest organizations such as the Friends of Liberty and Trade. Sir William Pitt successfully defended the colonists' position in Parliament, and the organization commissioned this medal in his honor. While commemorative in nature, it is believed to have circulated in the New York area. One tradition holds that it was engraved after a design by Paul Revere. While the larger one is usually called a halfpenny and the smaller a farthing, Breen has suggested that they both traded as halfpennies. All brass farthings were struck on cast blanks and may show natural traces of porosity.

The obverse bears a bust of Pitt, with the legend, "The Restorer of Commerce 1766 - No Stamps." The reverse shows a ship arriving at AMERICA, with "Thanks to the Friends of Liberty and Trade."

Known Counterfeits: Not extensively counterfeited.

	VG	F
1766 Farthing	3,000.00	8,500.00
1766 ½ Penny	350.00	700.00

ELEPHANT TOKENS

Most of what is known of the elephant halfpence is still conjecture. There are three different localities mentioned on their reverses: London, Carolina and New England. Some London pieces have been recovered in the New York/New Jersey area. It has been suggested that the Elephant indicates a connection to the Royal African Co., and they are possibly of West African copper, but this is not known. There are die linkages between them and it is reasonable to consider them related. The date for the undated London types is not known but they have been observed over-struck on halfpennies dated 1672. All known Carolina tokens with the correct spelling have the O re-punched over an E.

Known Counterfeits: Struck counterfeits of the Carolina second (commoner) type and of the New England are known. The lower illustration is a late 1800s copy. While deceptive, it also has some value.

	VG	VF
(1672-84) London	990.00	4,500.00
(1672-84) G-d Preserve London	325.00	1,250.00
1694 Carolina ½ Penny PROPRIETERS		*Five Known*
1694 Carolina ½ Penny PROPRIETORS	4,250.00	13,500.00

	VG	VF
Same, Bolen copy		*XF* 400.00
1694 New England ½ Penny		*Two Known*

CONNECTICUT

Connecticut coppers are probably the single most commonly encountered coins from pre-Federal America. The first Connecticut coppers, however, are extremely rare. Dr. Samuel Higley of Granby, Conn., was a well-educated physician and metallurgist who also operated a copper mine. He struck his own personal copper tokens of extremely pure metal. His first issues of 1737 bore the inscription, "The Value of Three Pence," but were the size of a mere halfpenny. Evidently finding resistance,

he changed the legend to "Value Me As You Please." This was not the only Higley copper that directly addressed the user; others said, "I Am Good Copper." Their obverses show a stag or a wheel, their reverses crowned hammers or an axe, the dates ranging from 1737 to 1739. They are usually found quite worn or porous but are so rare they are still highly desirable even in low grades.

It was not until after independence that another Connecticut copper was issued, this time by the state itself. In 1785 the Legislature authorized the striking of coppers following the rough pattern of the British halfpenny, but with Latin legends translating, "By the Authority of Connecticut," and "Independence and Liberty." The images were quite similar to the halfpenny, with a generic male bust similar to the king's and Liberty seated looking much like Britannia. By the time the official issue of 1.4 million had been struck, these coins were suffering the fate of the British halfpenny itself: counterfeiting. Counterfeit Connecticut coppers were struck in New York, New Jersey and Massachusetts, where there were no laws against counterfeiting "foreign" coin. Some were even struck in Connecticut by the former coining contractor himself! All those dated 1788 were struck at unofficial mints. Both official and unofficial strikes were crude and struck on imperfect blanks. At least 340 varieties, including many misspellings, are known. Only broad categories are listed below.

Known Counterfeit: Many modern and diverse counterfeits of Higley coppers exist, some deceptive. Both contemporary and modern counterfeits of the state coppers are numerous. The contemporary ones from the 1700s are highly regarded by collectors as being simply "unofficial issues." The Higley illustrated here is a counterfeit struck in 1864.

HIGLEY COPPERS

	G	F
1737 The Value of Three Pence / Connecticut (Three crowned hammers)	10,500.00	38,000.00

	G	F
1737 The Value of Three Pence / I Am Good Copper (Three crowned hammers)	—	*Two Known*
1737 Value Me As You Please / I Am Good Copper (Three crowned hammers)	10,500.00	38,000.00
(1737) Value Me As You Please / I Cut My Way Through (Axe)	10,500.00	38,000.00
(1737) The Wheele Goes Round (wheel) / I Cut My Way Through (Axe)	—	*Unique*
1739 Value Me As You Please / I Cut My Way Through (Axe)	—	*Five Known*

STATE COPPERS

	G	F
1785 Bust left	200.00	600.00
1785 Bust right	60.00	200.00
Same, "African Head" variety with fuller features	85.00	500.00
1786 Mailed bust left	60.00	200.00
1786 Draped bust left	95.00	500.00
1786 Hercules bust left	115.00	600.00
1786 Bust right	80.00	350.00
Same, larger head	200.00	850.00
1787 Bust left	50.00	145.00
Same, horn from bust	55.00	175.00
1787 Bust right	95.00	375.00
1788 Mailed bust left	50.00	175.00
1788 Draped bust left	50.00	200.00
1788 Bust right	50.00	220.00

MASSACHUSETTS

Confronted with continuous shortages of any kind of coinage, particularly silver, and combined with British refusal to permit the latter's import, the inhabitants of Massachusetts Bay Colony were forced to barter. When the Puritan Cromwell overthrew the king, fellow Puritans in Massachusetts saw it as an opportunity. They began striking their own formerly forbidden coinage in 1652. At first these were simple silver discs stamped NE, for New England, and XII, VI or III for the values in shilling, six and three pence. Found easily counterfeited and clipped, the designs were made more complex, extending to the edge of the coin. The legend, "Masathvsets in New England An Dom, 1652" was ordered, surrounding a tree on one side and the value on the other. Today we call this first design a willow tree, but in fact is generic. This crude willow design was struck by rough hand-hammering methods until 1660, always carrying the date 1652. This was to avoid the charge of illegally striking coins in the advent of the return of royal government. Thirty years of Massachusetts silver was to be struck with this one date. When new screw press equipment arrived, the design of the tree was modified. It is described as an oak tree. The coins struck from 1667-82 have a modified tree, described as a pine. In 1686 a new harsh royal governor arrived in Boston with orders to restore the colony to barter. Thus ended silver coins from Massachusetts.

Pitted ground finds exist and are discounted, but are still quite valuable. Some specimens were bent in the 1670s through 1690s to use as talismans to keep away witches.

New patterns were made in 1776. Little is known about them, and whatever projects were intended were abandoned. One theory however is that they were proposals engraved by Paul Revere.

After independence, the new Commonwealth of Massachusetts returned to striking coins, but this time copper cents and half cents. Depicted was an Indian standing with bow and arrow. The reverse has an eagle with an American shield on its chest, the shield being inscribed with the value. It was the first time the word "cent" appeared on an American coin. Pitted ground finds are not unusual and are discounted.

Modern copies such as this often fool laymen, but are too even to trick most collectors.

Known Counterfeits Virtually all NE willow, oak and pine tree coins have been counterfeited. Some are deceptive collector counterfeits made during both the 19th and 20th centuries. Others are contemporary counterfeits made to circulate and are quite valuable. Pine tree coins are the most counterfeited of these four series. Many crude, base-metal cast replicas of all series, including 1776 patterns, have been made for sale by museums and as souvenirs. They can be identified by a seam around the edge, or are too even in strike and thickness. Real ones are often a bit wavy.

	G	F
NE 3 Pence	—	*Two Known*
NE 6 Pence	—	*Seven Known*

	G	F
NE Shilling	38,000.00	120,000.00
1652 Willow 3 Pence	—	*Three known*
1652 Willow 6 Pence	19,500.00	66,000.00

	G	F
1652 Willow Shilling	19,000.00	90,000.00
1662 Oak 2 Pence	625.00	2,300.00
1652 Oak 3 Pence	625.00	2,300.00
1652 Oak 6 Pence	700.00	3,300.00

	G	F
1652 Oak Shilling	700.00	3,300.00
1652 Pine 3 Pence	550.00	1,850.00
1652 Pine 6 Pence	600.00	2,000.00

	G	F
1652 Pine Shilling	700.00	2,400.00
1652 Pine Shilling (small diameter)	600.00	2,000.00
1776 Province Halfpenny Pattern	—	Unique
1776 Three Heads Halfpenny Pattern	—	Unique
1776 Penny Pattern	—	Unique

	VG	VF
1787 ½ cent	150.00	635.00

	VG	VF
1787 Cent, arrows in right talon	8,000.00	Rare

	VG	VF
1787 Cent, arrows in left talon	125.00	650.00
1788 ½ Cent	160.00	650.00
1788 Cent	115.00	550.00

MARYLAND

One fascinating bit of Colonial history is the creation of Maryland as a feudal domain in North America. Different from the other colonies, it was a territory under a Lord along medieval lines. As a result of this, Cecil Calvert, Second Lord Baltimore, was able to strike a proper European-style feudal coinage. Previous to this coinage, tobacco, along with musket balls and gunpowder, had been a primary medium of exchange, but the decline in its value caused hardships, prompting the need for coinage. They were struck at the Royal Mint in 1659. Silver shillings, sixpences and "groats" (English silver coins each worth four pennies), and copper pennies were struck. The Cromwell government challenged his right to strike these coins, but when the government fell, Calvert was vindicated. The coins were very European in appearance, with Calvert's bust and lordly titles on the obverse, his crowned arms on the reverse, a crown and flags alone on the penny.

In 1783, a Baltimore silversmith apparently decided to make a pattern for a proposed national coinage to show to the Continental Congress then meeting in Annapolis. While it did not accept his proposal, he decided to continue striking coins of his own design. Thus John Chalmers struck the first silver coins in English America in a hundred years. All his coins show clasped hands on the obverse. The reverses show interlocking rings, birds, a cross or a wreath. Another Baltimore silversmith, Standish Barry, followed him in 1790, striking a private three pence depicting George Washington.

Known Counterfeits: Nineteenth-century struck counterfeits exist of the Lord Baltimore penny, some deceptive, others with incorrect lettering style. Crude casts of other Lord Baltimore coins have been made for sale in museum shops as souvenirs. They may be identified by a seam around the edge. Counterfeits also exist of the "rings"-type of Chalmers shilling.

LORD BALTIMORE

	G	F
Penny (Denarium)		only 5 known
Groat (IV)	2,000.00	6,800.00

	G	F
Sixpence (VI)	1,500.00	5,700.00
Shilling (XII)	2,200.00	6,700.00

JOHN CHALMERS

	VG	VF
1783 3 Pence	1,800.00	6,800.00
1783 6 Pence	2,500.00	13,000.00
1783 Shilling, circle of rings on rev.		Four Known
1783 Shilling, birds on rev.	1,500.00	5,600.00

STANDISH BARRY

	VG	VF
1790 3 Pence	9,000.00	35,000.00

NEW HAMPSHIRE

The New Hampshire Act of June 28, 1776, not only authorized state coinage, but permitted anyone who wanted to conform to state standards to make their own, as well. The state issues were all cast (steel for engraving dies was not available). They all show a tree on the obverse, the reverses are either a large WM, for William Moulton, the contractor, or a harp. The authorized private imitations were sometimes hand engraved.

Known Counterfeits Many cast and struck counterfeits are known, of various qualities. Some authorities question the authenticity of all WM pieces.

	VG
1776 Penny pattern, Tree / WM	Extremely Rare

	VG
1776 Halfpenny pattern, Tree / WM	*Extremely Rare*
1776 ½ Penny, Tree / Harp	— 28,000.00
1776 same, local engraved imitation	*Extremely Rare*

NEW JERSEY

One imported token has a special connection to New Jersey. During the English Civil War, the royalist Long Parliament struck special tokens to pay its forces who were suppressing the 1641-42 Protestant Ulster Rebellion. The Catholics lost and the coins – known as the St. Patrick coppers – were suppressed for years. After the war they reentered circulation and were still current in Ireland in the 1720s. When Mark Newbie, a Quaker, left Ireland for New Jersey in 1681 he took 14,400 of these with him. Having established the first bank in New Jersey, he was able to get the Provincial Assembly to declare his St. Patrick coppers legal tender in 1682. The obverses of these coins show Charles I as King David playing a harp. The large crown above him is struck where a drop of brass has been added to the blank, giving it a golden color on clean specimens. The reverses show St. Patrick either between a crowd and the arms of Dublin (halfpenny), or driving animals away from a church (farthing).

New Jersey coppers are perhaps the second-most common of state coinages. Three million were originally ordered struck by independent contractors. Later unofficial pieces were also made in New York, some with official dies they had bought from the old contractors. The obverse design of a horse head and plow is an adaptation of the crest on the New Jersey arms. The reverse is an American shield. The obverse legend *Nova Caesarea* is Latin for New Jersey. Some of the latest issues are struck over other coins and tokens. Hundreds of varieties are known, some rarer than others. Porous ground finds are common and are discounted.

Known Counterfeits: The silver off-metal St. Patrick's farthing has been counterfeited. Both contemporary and modern counterfeits of the state cents are known but are not abundant. The contemporary ones from the 1700s are highly regarded by collectors.

	G	F
St. Patrick Farthing	110.00	750.00
same but silver	1,800.00	5,500.00
same but gold		*Unique*
St. Patrick Halfpenny	375.00	1,750.00

	VG	VF
1786 Cent, date at bottom	110.00	550.00
1786 Cent, date lower right	19,000.00	95,000.00
1787 Cent	100.00	550.00
1788 Cent	120.00	700.00
1788 Cent, tiny fox	300.00	2,000.00
1788 Cent, horse head left	600.00	4,000.00

NEW YORK

The earliest token to be associated with New York was long considered mysterious and controversial, but recent scholarship seems to have provided it with an origin. A brass (or sometimes pewter) farthing with an eagle surrounded by "New Yorke in America" has been attributed to Gov. William Lovelace (1663/68 - 1673). Its unusual reverse shows a stand of trees dividing Venus and Cupid.

After this no official New York coins were ever struck, neither as a colony nor during the pre-Federal period under the Articles of Confederation (1776-89). Many private tokens and proposals do exist.

One 1786 token struck by James Atlee shows a bust of George Washington with the legend *Non Vi Virtute Vici*, "Not by Force but by Virtue. It's reverse shows Columbia seated and the legend *Neo-Eboracensis*, "Of New York."

Two proposed coins were struck by Ephraim Brasher and John Bailey in 1787. One was a cent or halfpenny showing the arms of New York on the obverse, an American heraldic eagle on the reverse. The other was a bolder suggestion and has become one of the most famous American coins: the Brasher Doubloon. A gold coin worth 16 Spanish pillar dollars, it showed a sun over mountains, the central motif of the New York arms, on the obverse, an American heraldic eagle within a wreath on the reverse. When it became clear that the state Legislature was not going to accept any coinage proposal, Bailey simply took a third pattern, very similar to the Connecticut cent with a generic male head and seated Liberty, but inscribed *Nova Eborac* for New York, and he put it into production himself.

While Brasher and Bailey were making patterns to propose to the Legislature, so were New Jersey engraver James Atlee and New York businessman Thomas Machin. One sample bore a portrait of New York governor George Clinton on the obverse, with the state arms on the reverse. Another showed an Indian standing with tomahawk and bow on obverse paired with the same reverse. A third paired the Indian obverse with an eagle standing on a globe, the crest from the state arms, on the reverse. When they arrived at the same conclusion as their competitors, their answer was to go to Newburgh, N.Y., up the Hudson River, and set up one of the most notorious counterfeiting operations in 18th-century America. Machin's Mills not only produced counterfeit George III halfpennies by the ton, but also produced imitation Connecticut, New Jersey, Vermont and Fugio cents, mixing and matching their dies with those of various tokens.

Two merchant tokens struck during the early Federal period were so important to New York commerce that they are listed here. One is the Mott token of 1789, struck by a gold and silverware dealer and clock importer. The obverse showed a particular brand of grandfather clock, the reverse a heraldic eagle extremely similar to that adopted for U.S. gold coinage from 1807 to 1908. The production of these coins was so heavy that some were produced with incomplete lettering due to worn-out dies.

Another producer of prolific late-18th-century tokes was Talbot, Allum and Lee, importers of goods from India. Their well-made 1794 and 1795 cents were struck in Birmingham, England. The obverse legend, "Liberty and Commerce," is illustrated by a personification of Liberty standing by a bale of goods. The reverse quite naturally depicts a ship under sail. These stayed in circulation well into the next century and formed a source of blanks on which many U.S. large cents were struck.

Known Counterfeits: Many copies of the Brasher doubloon have been made with varying degrees of accuracy, many not deceptive at all. Wrong lettering styles

and seams characterize many. One of several counterfeit George Clinton cents has an "I" substituted for the 1 in the date. Deceptive counterfeits also exist of the Non Vi Virtute Vici, Excelsior and Indian cents.

	VG	F
(1663/8-73) Farthing, Brass	5,800.00	15,000.00
same, pewter		*Four Known*
1786 Cent, Non Vi Virtute Vici (George Washington) / Neo-Eboracensis (seated Columbia)	7,000.00	13,000.00
1787 Brasher Gold Doubloon		*Seven Known*

	VG	F
1787 Cent, Excelsior (New York arms) / E Pluribus Unum (Eagle with shield)	2,700.00	6,800.00

	VG	F
1787 Cent, George Clinton / New York arms (illustration is of a deceptive counterfeit.)	12,500.00	22,000.00
1787 Cent, Standing Indian / as previous	9,000.00	17,000.00
1787 Cent, as previous / Eagle on globe	15,000.00	25,000.00
1787 Cent, as previous / Bust of George III		*Three Known*

	VG	F
1787 Cent, Male bust, Nova Eborac / Liberty seated right, Virt Et Lib	175.00	375.00
same, Liberty left	165.00	360.00

	VG	F
1789 Mott Cent	150.00	250.00
1794 Cent, Liberty standing / Ship, New York above	75.00	175.00
same, New York omitted	550.00	1,100.00
1795 Cent, same	70.00	140.00

VERMONT

When Reuben Harmon Jr. was given the sole contract to supply Vermont with cents, he intended to provide quality coins. He struck the design dictated to him: a rising sun over the Green Mountains, with a plow in the foreground as the obverse, a radiant Eye of Providence within a 13-star constellation on the reverse. The Latin legend on the reverse translates as "Fourteenth star" reflecting the Republic of Vermont's dream of admission to the Union. Harmon struck his coppers even heavier than he was required to make them. This was still true of later coins in a new style, bearing Vermont legends but similar in design to Connecticut coppers. The change was probably so they would blend together in interstate commerce. Harmon could not prepare dies quickly enough so he entered into an arrangement with Machin's Mills in Newburgh, N.Y. The striking of Vermont coppers was subcontracted to the new firm. The poor Vermonter found that his once-proud cents were being struck at ever lighter weights, and being "muled" with odd dies. (Mule in this sense means a coin struck from dies not originally intended to be used together.) But it was out of his hands. Machin's Mills began striking Vermont coppers on their own without legal authorization. Harmon gave up and left for Ohio, abandoning his coining franchise.

The bust-type coppers were usually incompletely struck on irregular blanks. There are many other varieties. Porous ground finds are traded at a discount.

Counterfeit Alert: Both struck and cast contemporary counterfeits exist. Modern ones are also known.

PLOW SERIES

	G	F
1785 Cent VERMONTS	285.00	1,250.00
Same VERMONTIS	300.00	1,500.00
1786 Cent	250.00	900.00

BUST & LIBERTY SERIES

	G	F
1786 Cent, Bust left	165.00	800.00
1786 Cent, Bust right	320.00	1,400.00
1787, BRITANNIA rev.	125.00	320.00
1787 Cent, Bust left	4,000.00	24,000.00
1787 Cent, Bust right	125.00	500.00
1788 Cent	110.00	400.00

VIRGINIA

Virginia boasts one of the scarcest and one of the most common American coins of the 18th century. The Gloucester 1714 Shilling was a private brass token struck by Dawson and Righault, local

landowners in Gloucester County. The legends read "Glovcester Covrt.hovse Virginia / Righavlt Dawson Anno Dom 1714." The obverse shows the building, the reverse a star.

The only Colonial government created with the right to strike coins was Virginia, but it waited more than 150 years to do so. Previously, tobacco had sufficed as small change, but the expansion of its population caused a need for coins. These halfpence were struck at the Royal Mint in 1773, but by the time they could be placed in circulation, the Revolution was brewing and they were hoarded. Ironically many entered circulation in the 1780s. Part of an original keg of these was disbursed in 1929, thus they are not unobtainable in mint state. The silver shilling struck with a larger bust of George III is a pattern.

Known Counterfeits: Replicas for sale at Colonial Williamsburg are marked CWF below bust. More deceptive counterfeits also exist.

	F	VF
1714 Shilling		*only 2 known*
1715 Shilling		*Not confirmed*

	F	EF
1773 ½ Penny	80.00	365.00
1773 Shilling		*Six known*

WASHINGTON PIECES

One of the most common themes of private tokens of the late 1700s was George Washington. One of the earliest was the Georgius Triumpho copper, not only dated 1783, but actually struck then, unlike others of that date. The reverse depicts Liberty at a weaving frame, with the Latin legend for "Voice of the People." They are thought to have circulated in Georgia, Virginia and New Jersey.

Not all Washington pieces are flattering. The second oldest, the Ugly Head, was a satirical political piece. The obverse legend reads "Washington the Great D:G:" in derision of the monarchical pretensions of some Washington supporters. The reverse has the thirteen interlocking circles of the Continental dollar.

One of several engravers who worked on proposals for new federal coinage was Gregory Hancock, an English child prodigy. His Washington cents of 1791 were rejected by the president as being too "monarchical." In revenge for this snub, Hancock engraved a new unflattering obverse with Washington as a Roman emperor.

The most common 1783 Washington pieces were actually struck in the early 1800s in England and shipped to the United States by merchants. The obverse is one of several military busts. Their reverse varies from ONE CENT in a wreath, to a seated Liberty, to a second bust of Washington.

This is simply a cross section of these pieces; others exist.

	VG	VF
1783 Voci Popoli	120.00	700.00
1784 Ugly Head		*Four Known*

	VG	VF
1791 Hancock's Military Bust / ONE CENT over Eagle	275.00	700.00
1791 same / ship	500.00	2,000.00

	VG	VF
1792 same / stars over Eagle		*Rare*
1792 same / Inscription	2,500.00	15,000.00
ND (1792) same	1,750.00	6,000.00
1792 Hancock's Roman Bust / CENT over Eagle		*Very Rare*
1783 (1820s) Roman Bust / Wreath, UNITY STATES	110.00	250.00
1783 (1820s) Roman Bust / Liberty seated left	50.00	200.00
1783 (1820s) Military Bust / Liberty seated left	50.00	200.00

	VG	VF
ND (1815-20) Military Bust / Military Bust	70.00	270.00

PRE-FEDERAL COINAGE

There were several proposals and attempts at a national coinage under the Articles of Confederation.

In 1776, the Continental Congress anticipated a loan of silver from its French ally. It was thought that to strike this silver into dollars would not only show the world a manifestation of its sovereignty but also bolster public confidence in its paper currency. Benjamin Franklin and David Rittenhouse collaborated on the design, which was engraved in secret. The obverse shows a sundial above which is a sun and the Latin word *FUGIO* (I fly). Below it the phrase "Mind your business." The whole ensemble echoes Franklin's saying, "Time flys so mind your business." The reverse has a chain of thirteen links each labeled with the name of a state. At center is "We are one" surrounded by a smaller circle inscribed "American Congress." Most of these prototypes were struck in tin. Unfortunately, only three real silver ones are known, the French loan having fallen through.

In 1783, Governor Morris, the Confederation's Assistant Superintendent for Finance, proposed a decimal system reconciling the various standards of most of the states. Sample coins for 1,000, 500 and 100 in silver, and 5 units in copper, were struck. A radiant eye surrounded by a 13-star "new constellation" and the Latin *Nova Constellatio* adorned the obverse, the value within a wreath on the reverse. This project was soon abandoned due to lack of bullion.

One outgrowth of the project however was the Nova Constellatio copper. Governor Morris made the most of his project's failure. He went to Birmingham, England, where he had quality dies engraved by George Wyon based on his failed decimal designs. Many thousands of these coppers were struck in 1785 and 1786 (not 1783 as they're dated) to Morris' personal order and shipped back to America, becoming popular for a time.

Wyon quickly took the initiative and created his own 1785 patterns for a proposed American cent. The obverse has a seated figure surrounded by the Latin *Immune Columbia*, misspelled by his inept die letterer, Walter Mould. (Columbia

was another name for America at the time.) They were not accepted but the dies were taken by the fleeing Mould, who ended up selling them to none other than the Machin's Mills counterfeiting operation in Newburgh, N.Y.

Besides its paper money, the single most common relic of the Continental Congress is the Fugio cent. In 1787, James Jarvis made a successful bid to strike cents for the Congress. The designs were similar to the old Continental dollars. He acquired tons of copper from the government, bought a controlling interest in the renegade Connecticut mint in New Haven, made a limited amount of Fugios and quickly switched the majority of production (using embezzled government copper) to the more profitable Connecticut cents. Soon he was forced to flee to Europe and his equipment, including both Connecticut and Fugio dies, was sold to, yet again, the Machin's Mills counterfeiters.

Known Counterfeits: Both deceptive and amateurish replicas of Continental dollars have been made in large quantities. A counterfeit exists of Morris' decimal mark of 1,000 Units. Contemporary counterfeits were made of Nova Constellatio coppers. Nineteenth-century counterfeits exist of Immune Columbia coppers. "Restrikes" of the Fugio cent made with false dies were made around 1860.

	VG	VF
1783 Nova Constellatio "100", Silver		*Rare*
1783 Nova Constellatio "500", Silver legend		*Rare*
1783 Nova Constellatio "500", Silver no legend		*Rare*
1783 Nova Constellatio "cent", Copper	100.00	450.00

	VG	VF
1785 same	100.00	475.00
1786 same	*Dubious*	

	VG	VF
1785 Immune Columbia / Nova Constellatio, Copper		*Rare*
1785 Immune Columbia / Eagle, Copper	600.00	3,600.00
1785 Immune Columbia / George III, Copper	7,000.00	12,500.00
1785 Immune Columbia / Vermon Auctori, Copper	8,500.00	30,000.00

	VG	VF
1787 Fugio Cent, Pointed rays	250.00	800.00
1787 Fugio Cent, Club rays	400.00	2,250.00
1787 (1860s) Fugio Cent, New Haven restrike (thin circles)		XF 400.00

	VG	VF
1776 Continental Dollar, Pewter	8,000.00	20,000.00
Same, Brass	25,000.00	60,000.00
Same, Silver		*Rare*
1783 Nova Constellatio "5", Copper		*Unique*

1792 MINT ISSUES

When the United States was created by the Constitution in 1789 (signed 1787) it was not a given that the nation would have a mint, or even a national coinage. Many were opposed to the idea of government involvement in these matters, and some of those who weren't thought that contracting out the manufacture of coinage would be adequate. Even Washington had problems with the original coinage bill, which called for his own name and portrait to appear on each coin. After much protest, the first coinage law of April 2, 1792, replaced Washington with Liberty. It was this law that set up the basic pattern of American coinage still in use today. It seems that the very first coins struck under the federal union that is the United States of America, as opposed to the Continental Congress under the Articles of Confederation, were actually struck in a saw maker's basement rather than the mint. The mint and personnel were not ready but coins were needed! Even Washington had made this point. Small silver was in particularly short supply in general commerce and no one wanted to delay while an old distillery was converted into a mint. According to legend, the first $75 worth of half "dismes" included silver from Washington's own tableware. When the mint moved from the saw maker's basement to its new facilities, coinage continued with a small quantity of dismes. Many have found the early spelling "disme" to be curious. It is a synthetic word that first appeared in French in 1585, later in English in 1608, and refers to the decimal system. It continued to be the prevailing spelling for the tenth part of a dollar until the 1830s, but its pronunciation had long since changed to that used for the modern spelling, dime. The first United States cent was a matter of experimentation. Congress had called for a large copper coin, but Thomas Jefferson thought that it would be more convenient to strike a smaller coin with just a touch of silver added to compensate. Both a central silver plug and a uniform alloy were attempted, but in the end, it was the original congressionally authorized cent that was released. All these coins share the obverse legend, "Liberty, Parent of Science and Industry." One last denomination was considered for the issues of 1792, the quarter, but this was deferred, and only trial strikes are known.

Known Counterfeits: Cent (silver center, small copper, large copper), Half

Disme (copper), Quarter (copper). Be cautious of holed and plugged half dismes.

	G	F
1792 Cent, Copper		*Rare*
1792 same with silver center		*Rare*
1792 Large Cent, Copper		*Rare*
1792 same, White Metal		*Rare*

	G	F
1792 Half Dime, Silver	17,000.00	55,000.00
1792 same, Copper		*Unique?*
1792 Dime, Silver		*only 3 known*
1792 same, Copper		*Rare*
1792 Quarter, Copper		*only 2 known*
1792 Quarter, White Metal		*only 2 known*

REGULAR MINT ISSUES

HALF CENTS

The half cent is far more popular today than it ever was when it actually circulated. While they permitted precise dealings in commerce, they were still considered a nuisance by those who had to spend them. Demand for them was small, mintages were low, and in some years none were struck for circulation at all. They were so low a priority that the mint sometimes allocated no blanks for them, but struck them on secondhand merchant tokens instead. Even the banks didn't want them. From July 1811 until 1825 none were struck because of pressure from the banking industry. The half cent was finally abandoned in 1857.

Though not as popularly collected as the large cent, they are today considered scarce and desirable coins. Like the large cent, half cents are collected by die variety. Rare die combinations can be worth much more than common ones of the same year. Metal-detector finds exhibiting porous surfaces are worth substantially less than the prices listed. Early dates are particularly difficult to find in better than well-worn condition. The Classic Head is much easier to find well preserved.

Known Counterfeits: Cheap cast replicas of the 1793 exist, as do more deceptive counterfeits of that and the

1796 "no pole" variety. Authentic half cents exist with their dates skillfully altered to resemble the rare 1831 date. The 1840s proof restrikes were actually struck by the U.S. Mint in the 1850s and 1860s.

Type Coin Price Range	aG to MS-60
1793-1797	150.00 to 17,500.00
1800-1808	25.00 to 1,200.00
1809-1836	20.00 to 300.00
1840-1857	25.00 to 200.00

LIBERTY CAP TYPE

	VG	VF
1793	4,000.00	10,000.00
1794	800.00	2,200.00
1795	570.00	1,500.00
1796 with pole	20,000.00	35,000.00
1796 no pole	32,000.00	90,000.00
1797	570.00	1,600.00

DRAPED BUST TYPE

	VG	VF
1800	75.00	300.00
1802	1,600.00	8,000.00
1803	70.00	275.00
1804	70.00	150.00
1804 spiked chin	90.00	175.00
1805	75.00	145.00
1806	70.00	145.00
1807	80.00	175.00
1808	70.00	160.00

CLASSIC HEAD TYPE

	VG	VF
1809	65.00	85.00
1810	70.00	220.00
1811	375.00	1,750.00
1825	65.00	110.00

	VG	VF
1826	65.00	90.00
1828	65.00	85.00
1829	65.00	100.00
1831	7,000.00	16,000.00
1831 Restrikes		*Unc.* 6,500.00
1832	65.00	95.00
1833	65.00	95.00
1834	65.00	95.00
1835	65.00	95.00
1836		*Proof only* 6,000.00
1836 Restrike		*Proof only* 20,000.00

BRAIDED HAIR TYPE

	VG	VF
1840 *Proof only*		5,500.00
1840 Restrike *Proof only*		5,500.00
1841 *Proof only*		5,500.00
1841 Restrike *Proof only*		6,000.00
1842	*Proof only*	6,000.00
1842 Restrike	*Proof only*	6,000.00
1843	*Proof only*	6,500.00
1843 Restrike	*Proof only*	6,000.00
1844	*Proof only*	6,000.00
1844 Restrike	*Proof only*	6,000.00
1845	*Proof only*	6,000.00
1845 Restrike	*Proof only*	6,000.00
1846	*Proof only*	6,000.00
1846 Restrike	*Proof only*	6,000.00
1847	*Proof only*	6,000.00
1847 Restrike	*Proof only*	6,000.00
1848	*Proof only*	6,000.00
1848 Restrike	*Proof only*	6,000.00
1849	*Proof only*	6,500.00
1849 Restrike *Proof only*		6,000.00
1849 Large date	70.00	125.00
1850	60.00	125.00
1851	60.00	90.00
1852 *Proof only*		90,000.00
1852 Restrikes *Proof only*		5,000.00
1853	75.00	115.00
1854	75.00	115.00
1855	75.00	125.00
1856	75.00	125.00
1857	90.00	200.00

LARGE CENTS

The United States large cent was a result of dual desires, one for a decimal coin worth one-hundredth of a dollar. The other was the need for a coin to replace British halfpennies and their imitations that had been common in the American Colonies. It was slightly larger than the halfpenny, and the concept of decimal coinage was so innovative that the fraction "1/100" literally had to be written on the coin, along with the edge inscription "ONE HUNDRED FOR A DOLLAR."

The dies for striking early American coins had to be engraved by hand and no two were identical. Because of this it has been popular to collect them – especially the large cents – by die combination.

It is interesting to note that low mintages and mediocre acceptance by the public resulted in the first large cents being little more than local Philadelphia coinage. Metal was in such short supply that junked copper hardware of inconsistent alloy was used for some early cents, giving a poor quality blank on which to strike the coin. People also resented the chain on the first design of 1793 as a symbol contrary to liberty, and laughed at the frightened expression they perceived on the face of Miss Liberty. Later they became so popular that they were considered good luck. In the early 1800s they were nailed to the rafters of new houses to bring good luck to its inhabitants. These old relics, found with characteristic square nail holes through them, have a discounted value but still hold historical interest for collectors, and have been given the nickname "rafter cents." Other large cents were stamped or hand engraved with advertising, personal initials, or risqué comments, then placed back into circulation.

During the 1850s, public irritation with the heaviness of the cent began to grow and, after eight years of research into smaller alternatives, the large cent was abandoned in 1857.

Because the hand-engraved dies with which these coins were struck have been individually identified, large cents are actively collected by die variety. Rare die combinations can be worth much more than common ones of the same year. Metal-detector finds exhibiting porous surfaces are worth substantially less than the prices listed. Early dates are particularly difficult to find in better than well-worn condition.

Known Counterfeits: Large cents were not frequently counterfeited in their day. A few rare dates were later counterfeited by casting (and possibly striking) to fool collectors. They include 1799, 1803, 1805 over 5, and 1851 over inverted 18. The 1799 is also known altered from 1798. Some crude museum souvenirs have been made of Chain Cents as well.

Type Coin Price Range	aG to MS-60
1793-1796	95.00 to 5,000.00
1796-1807	25.00 to 2,200.00
1808-1814	30.00 to 2,800.00
1816-1836	12.00 to 270.00
1837-1857	10.00 to 200.00

FLOWING HAIR TYPE

	VG	VF
1793 Chain Rev.	11,000.00	30,000.00
1793 Wreath Rev.	2,500.00	8,000.00

LIBERTY CAP TYPE

	VG	VF
1793	8,000.00	25,000.00
1794	500.00	1,300.00
1795	500.00	1,200.00
1796	500.00	1,500.00

DRAPED BUST TYPE

	VG	VF
1796	600.00	1,800.00
1797	175.00	450.00
1798	130.00	525.00
1799	5,000.00	17,000.00
1800	95.00	400.00
1801	85.00	360.00
1802	75.00	350.00
1803	80.00	350.00
1804 Original (open wreath)	2,000.00	5,000.00
1804 Restrike (closed wreath)	*Unc.*	1,500.00
1805	90.00	350.00
1806	95.00	400.00
1807	80.00	350.00

CLASSIC HEAD TYPE

	VG	VF
1808	200.00	575.00
1809	350.00	1,300.00
1810	95.00	600.00
1811	175.00	1,000.00
1812	85.00	525.00
1813	175.00	800.00
1814	90.00	530.00

CORONET TYPE

	VG	VF
1816	40.00	110.00
1817 13 stars	35.00	75.00
1817 15 stars	50.00	225.00
1818	30.00	80.00
1819	30.00	70.00
1820	30.00	70.00
1821	75.00	400.00
1822	35.00	110.00
1823	150.00	675.00
1823 Restrike	700.00	990.00
1824	28.00	200.00
1825	35.00	170.00
1826	35.00	120.00
1827	35.00	75.00
1828	35.00	90.00
1829	35.00	100.00
1830	35.00	90.00
1831	35.00	80.00
1832	35.00	80.00
1833	35.00	80.00
1834	35.00	80.00
1835	35.00	80.00
1836	35.00	80.00
1837	30.00	80.00

	VG	VF
1838	30.00	80.00
1839	40.00	90.00

	VG	VF
1840	30.00	50.00
1841	30.00	50.00
1842	30.00	50.00
1843	30.00	50.00
1844	30.00	50.00
1845	30.00	50.00
1846	30.00	50.00
1847	30.00	50.00
1848	30.00	50.00
1849	30.00	50.00
1850	30.00	50.00
1851	30.00	50.00
1852	30.00	50.00
1853	30.00	50.00
1854	30.00	50.00
1855	30.00	50.00
1856	30.00	50.00
1857	125.00	225.00

FLYING EAGLE CENTS

After years of experimenting, the mint introduced its new small cent in 1857. It was less than half the weight of the large cent and was brown to beige in color due to its alloy of 88 percent copper and 12 percent nickel. It depicted an eagle flying left, modeled after "Old Pete," a bird which years earlier had served as a mascot at the mint. Initially these were released in certain quantities at *below face value* to encourage their acceptance, but the old large cents were so bulky that people didn't take long to accept them. It's interesting to observe, in today's health-conscious atmosphere, that the wreath on the reverse contains, among other plants, tobacco.

The 1856 is technically a pattern but was widely distributed at the time, and is generally collected as part of the series.

Known Counterfeits: Most of the 1856 cents encountered are counterfeit. They are usually made from authentic coins with the dates re-engraved.

Type Coin Price Range	G to MS-60
1856-58	25.00 to 325.00

	VG	VF
1856	7,300.00	12,500.00
1857	39.00	50.00
1858 Lg. Letters	40.00	57.00
1858 Small Letters	39.00	50.00

INDIAN HEAD CENTS

The story of the Indian Head Cent is one of the most charming in the field of numismatics. According to legend, James B. Longacre, engraver at the U.S. Mint, was entertaining an Indian chief who happened to be wearing his full war bonnet. As a gesture of whimsy, the chief removed his bonnet and placed it upon the head of Longacre's little girl, Sarah. The engraver instantly perceived that this was the image destined for the next American cent. Admittedly, fewer people believe this story as time goes on, but it does add a quaint bit of sentimentality to the origin of one of America's favorite coin designs.

When the Indian Head Cent was first released, it was struck in the same copper-nickel alloy as the Flying Eagle Cent. The reverse was a simple laurel wreath encircling the words ONE CENT. The following year this was replaced by oak leaves (often considered a symbol of authority) into which was tied a bundle of arrows. Its top was open enough to fit a small American shield.

In 1864, nickel was removed from the alloy, giving the coin the bronze appearance that has since characterized the U.S. cent. It was also made thinner like our modern cent. This new bronze cent was reminiscent in form to the private one-cent "Civil War Tokens," which were circulating at the time, and which cost a fraction of a cent to manufacture. The mint was well aware of this obvious savings.

Known Counterfeits: Struck counterfeits of 1867, 1868, 1873 open 3, and 1877 exist. Counterfeit 1908-S and 1909-S are often made by altering real 1908 and 1909 Indian cents.

Type Coin Price Range	G to MS-60
1859	13.00 to 260.00
1860-64	8.00 to 190.00
1864-1909	2.00 to 30.00

(1864-1909 with original mint red are worth more.)

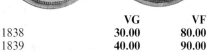

COPPER-NICKEL ALLOY

	F	XF
1859	23.00	120.00
1860	22.00	75.00
1861	45.00	120.00
1862	13.00	32.00
1863	12.00	30.00
1864	36.00	90.00

BRONZE

	F	XF
1864	25.00	75.00
1864 L on ribbon	130.00	280.00
1865	18.00	45.00
1866	75.00	200.00
1867	90.00	200.00
1868	70.00	180.00
1869	235.00	455.00
1870	235.00	415.00
1871	285.00	460.00
1872	380.00	630.00
1873	60.00	175.00
1874	42.00	115.00
1875	55.00	125.00
1876	70.00	240.00
1877	1,600.00	2,850.00
1878	65.00	250.00
1879	16.00	75.00
1880	8.00	29.00
1881	7.00	22.00
1882	7.00	22.00
1883	6.00	18.00
1884	7.00	30.00
1885	12.00	65.00
1886	20.00	140.00
1887	4.00	18.00
1888	5.00	20.00
1889	3.50	12.00
1890	3.00	10.00
1891	3.25	13.00
1892	3.75	18.00
1893	3.25	10.00
1894	12.00	50.00
1895	3.50	13.00
1896	3.00	12.00
1897	3.00	10.00
1898	3.00	10.00
1899	2.60	11.00
1900	2.50	12.50
1901	2.50	10.00
1902	2.50	10.00
1903	2.50	10.00
1904	2.50	10.00
1905	2.50	9.00
1906	2.50	9.00
1907	2.50	8.50
1908	2.50	9.00
1908S	95.00	180.00
1909	8.00	18.00
1909S	575.00	750.00

LINCOLN CENTS

The Lincoln Cent was the first regular-issue United States coin to bear the portrait of a real person. It made its debut in 1909 to celebrate the 100th anniversary of Lincoln's birth. It was designed by a sculptor from outside the mint, Victor David Brenner. His initials are found prominently on the very first examples to be released. Some thought they were featured too prominently, and the outcry forced their removal, resulting in two varieties the first year. Later in 1918, they were added more discretely under the truncation of the shoulder.

Lincoln Cents were a bronze alloy of 95 percent copper until 1943 when they were changed to zinc-coated steel to save copper for the war effort. Because some of them were confused with dimes they were replaced in 1944 and 1945 with cents made from melted shell casings, resulting in a much more conventional appearance. The original alloy was restored from 1946 until 1982 when it was finally abandoned for zinc plated with copper to reduce the expense of manufacturing. If you cut one of the cents struck today in half, it will not be orange or brown inside but white, revealing its true composition.

A new reverse was introduced in 1959 for the 150th anniversary of Lincoln's birth and the 50th anniversary of the Lincoln Cent. Still in use today, it depicts the Lincoln Memorial in Washington, D.C.

The Lincoln Cent is one of the most popularly collected coins on earth. It is collected in most grades, and even the rarities can be found without too long a search.

Known Counterfeits: The 1909S VDB, 1909S, 1914D, 1922-Plain, 1931S, and 1955 double dies have been extensively counterfeited. Most are altered cents of other dates. Counterfeits also exist of the 1972 double die. Virtually all 1943 bronze and 1944 steel cents are counterfeit. A magnet test will reveal the crudest counterfeits made by plating. Other 1943 bronze cents have been made by altering 1948 and by striking with false dies..

In addition to counterfeits, the collector should be aware of "reprocessed" cents. These are circulated 1943 steel cents given a fresh zinc coating to make them appear uncirculated. Many hobbyists are quite willing to have them in their collections, but it is important to know the difference. Don't look for luster, but for traces of flatness at the cheekbone.

Type Coin Price Range	VG to MS-63
1909-1958	.05 to .75
1943	.15 to 2.25
1959-82	spend to .15
1982-date	spend to .15

(Coins with original mint red are worth worth more than toned specimens.)

WHEAT EARS REVERSE

	VF	MS-60
1909 VDB	13.00	14.00
1909S VDB	1,100.00	1.500.00
1909	3.50	15.50
1909S	165.00	310.00
1910	1.00	18.50
1910S	25.00	82.50
1911	2.50	20.00
1911D	15.50	85.00
1911S	38.00	170.00
1912	6.00	30.00
1912D	25.00	150.00
1912S	35.00	140.00
1913	3.50	35.00
1913D	10.50	90.00
1913S	25.00	200.00
1914	6.00	50.00
1914D	450.00	2,000.00
1914S	38.00	300.00
1915	15.00	90.00
1915D	6.50	70.00
1915S	30.00	170.00
1916	2.60	18.00
1916D	6.00	70.00
1916S	7.50	80.00
1917	2.00	17.00
1917D	5.50	65.00
1917S	2.50	60.00
1918	1.30	13.00
1918D	5.50	70.00
1918S	4.00	65.00
1919	.75	9.00
1919D	4.20	55.00
1919S	2.70	45.00
1920	1.50	15.00
1920D	5.50	65.00
1920S	3.00	90.00
1921	3.00	42.00
1921S	6.00	110.00
1922D	25.00	95.00
1922 plain	1,450.00	9,000.00

	VF	MS-60		VF	MS-60		BU
1923	1.50	14.00	1943 steel	.45	1.25	1960 small date	3.00
1923S	8.00	200.00	1943D steel	.50	3.00	1960D large date	.30
1924	1.25	21.00	1943S steel	.65	3.50	1960D small date	.50
1924D	60.00	235.00	1944	.20	.65	1961	.25
1924S	5.00	115.00	1944D	.20	.65	1961D	.25
1925	1.00	10.00	1944 D over S	120.00	400.00	1962	.25
1925D	5.00	60.00	1944S	.20	.65	1962D	.25
1925S	2.75	80.00	1945	.20	.60	1963	.25
1926	.80	8.00	1945D	.20	.70	1963D	.25
1926D	4.50	80.00	1945S	.20	.55	1964	.25
1926S	14.00	120.00	1946	.20	.55	1964D	.25
1927	.80	8.00	1946D	.20	.50	1965	.25
1927D	3.50	60.00	1946S	.20	.60	1966	.25
1927S	5.00	65.00	1947	.15	.90	1967	.25
1928	.80	8.50	1947D	.15	.40	1968	.25
1928D	3.00	34.00	1947S	.20	.65	1968D	.25
1928S	3.50	75.00	1948	.15	.65	1968S	.25
1929	1.00	6.00	1948D	.15	.65	1969	.40
1929D	2.00	22.00	1948S	.20	.75	1969D	.25
1929S	2.50	18.00	1949	.15	.75	1969S	.25
1930	.75	4.00	1949D	.15	.70	1970	.25
1930D	1.25	12.00	1949S	.20	1.00	1970D	.25
1930S	1.00	10.00	1950	.15	.50	1970S small date	40.00
1931	2.00	19.50	1950D	.15	.50	1970S large date	.25
1931D	7.00	55.00	1950S	.15	.80		
1931S	150.00	200.00	1951	.15	.90		
1932	3.50	19.50	1951D	.15	.60		
1932D	3.00	18.00	1951S	.15	.75		
1933	3.00	18.00	1952	.15	.50		
1933D	6.50	25.00	1952D	.15	.50		
1934	.55	8.00	1952S	.15	1.20		
1934D	.95	26.50	1953	.15	.50		
1935	.50	4.50	1953D	.15	.50		
1935D	.50	5.50	1953S	.15	.60		
1935S	1.50	13.00	1954	.15	.75		
1936	.45	2.50	1954D	.15	.50		
1936D	.45	3.75	1954S	.15	.50		
1936S	.45	4.75	1955	.15	.50		
1937	.45	2.00	1955 double die	1,350.00	2,050.00		
1937D	.45	2.50	1955 minor date shift or "poor man's double die"	.20	1.20		
1937S	.45	3.50	1955D	.15	.50		
1938	.45	3.00	1955S	.15	.70		
1938D	.55	3.70	1956	.15	40		
1938S	.70	3.00	1956D	.15	.40		
1939	.45	1.00	1957	.15	.40		
1939D	.60	2.50	1957D	.15	.40		
1939S	.55	2.00	1958	.15	.40		
1940	.35	1.00	1958D	.15	.40		
1940D	.35	1.25					
1940S	.35	1.50					
1941	.35	1.00					
1941D	.35	2.25					
1941S	.50	2.75					
1942	.35	.85					
1942D	.35	.75					
1942S	.70	4.50					

1970S Large Date

1970S Small Date

LINCOLN MEMORIAL REVERSE

	BU
1959	.25
1959D	.30
1960 large date	.25

	BU
1971	.40
1971D	.45
1971S	.45
1972	.25
1972 double die	600.00
1972D	.25
1972S	.25
1973	.25
1973D	.25
1973S	.25

	BU		BU
1974	.25	1992D	.25
1974D	.25	1992S *Proof only*	5.00
1974S	.25	1993	.25
1975	.25	1993D	.25
1975D	.25	1993S *Proof only*	7.00
1975S *Proof only*	4.50	1994	.25
1976	.25	1994D	.25
1976D	.25	1994S *Proof only*	5.00
1976S *Proof only*	4.00	1995	.25
1977	.25	1995 double die	40.00
1977D	.25	1995D	.25
1977S *Proof only*	3.00	1995S *Proof only*	7.50
1978	.25	1996	.25
1978D	.25	1996D	.25
1978S *Proof only*	3.00	1996S *Proof only*	4.50
1979	.25	1997	.25
1979D	.25	1997D	.25
1979S *Proof only*	4.00	1997S *Proof only*	9.50
1980	.25	1998	.25
1980D	.25	1998D	.25
1980S *Proof only*	2.25	1998S *Proof only*	9.00
1981	.25	1999	.25
1981D	.25	1999D	.25
1981S *Proof only*	3.00	1999S *Proof only*	6.00
1982	.25	2000	.25
1982D	.25	2000D	.25
1982S *Proof only*	2.75	2000S *Proof only*	4.00
		2001	.25
COPPER-PLATED ZINC		2001D	.25
1982	.25	2001S *Proof only*	4.00
1982D	.25	2002	.25
1983	.25	2002D	.25
1983 double die rev.	350.00	2002S *Proof only*	4.00
1983D	.50	2003	.25
1983S *Proof only*	4.00	2003D	.25
1984	.25	2003S *Proof only*	4.00
1984 double die	275.00	2004	.25
1984D	.50	2004D	.25
1984S *Proof only*	4.50	2004S *Proof only*	4.00
1985	.25	2005	.25
1985D	.25	2005D	.25
1985S *Proof only*	5.00	2005S *Proof only*	4.00
1986	1.00	2006	.25
1986D	1.00	2006D	.25
1986S *Proof only*	7.50	2006S *Proof only*	4.00
1987	.25	2007	.25
1987D	.25	2007D	.25
1987S *Proof only*	5.00	2007S *Proof only*	4.00
1988	.25	2008	.25
1988D	.25	2008D	.25
1988S *Proof only*	8.00	2008S *Proof only*	4.00
1989	.25		
1989D	.25		
1989S *Proof only*	6.00		
1990	.25		
1990D	.25		
1990S *Proof only*	5.75		
1990S w/o S *Proof only*	2,950.00		
1991	.25		
1991D	.25		
1991S *Proof only*	20.00		
1992	.25		

TWO-CENT PIECES

Throughout the Civil War, people hoarded coins, preferring to spend the less-valuable private tokens and small-denomination paper money then available. If the North fell they thought that, at least, real coins would retain some value. A small-change shortage resulted. The Two-Cent Piece was introduced in an attempt to alleviate this shortage. It was the first coin to carry the inscription "In God We Trust."

These are usually found well worn, with fewer than one in a 100 surviving in fine or better condition.

Known Counterfeits: Counterfeits are not particularly common, though some scarce die-struck ones are known.

Type Coin Price Range	G to MS-60
1864-1873	15.00 to 90.00

	F	XF
1864 Small motto (open D in G-D)	275.00	650.00
1864 Large motto (narrow D in G-D)	25.00	44.00
1865	25.00	44.00
1866	25.00	44.00
1867	40.00	65.00
1868	40.00	65.00
1869	42.00	75.00
1870	50.00	120.00
1871	60.00	130.00
1872	500.00	960.00
1873 Closed 3	*Proof only*	2,200.00
1873 Open 3	*Proof restrike*	2,400.00

SILVER THREE-CENT PIECES

Different times have different priorities, and the reasons for striking coins in one era don't always seem to make sense to the people living in another. This is the case of the silver three-cent piece, often called the "trime." It and the three-dollar gold piece were issued to make it easier to purchase singles and sheets of three-cent, first-class postage stamps. Despite the extreme awkwardness of their small size, they were accepted enough in commerce that they continued to be struck in significant quantities for 12 years.

Its thinness prevented it from striking up well and the mint attempted to modify its design repeatedly. Getting a fully struck coin with no weak spots, even in higher grades, is truly difficult. Another problem resulting from their thinness was frequent bending, denting and crinkling. Prices given are for flat, undamaged examples.

Known Counterfeits: Counterfeits made to pass in circulation were struck in base silver and white metal for early dates, German silver (copper-nickel-zinc) dated 1860 and 1861. A struck counterfeit also exists for 1864.

Type Coin Price Range	G to MS-60
1851-1853	25.00 to 180.00
1854-1858	26.00 to 250.00
1859-1873	30.00 to 200.00

	F	XF
No Border Around Star		
1851	45.00	75.00
1851O	60.00	180.00
1852	45.00	75.00
1853	45.00	75.00
Triple Border Around Star		
1854	50.00	110.00
1855	80.00	215.00
1856	52.00	120.00
1857	52.00	120.00
1858	52.00	110.00
Double Border Around Star		
1859	55.00	90.00
1860	50.00	90.00
1861	50.00	90.00
1862	60.00	100.00
1863	400.00	500.00
1864	400.00	500.00
1865	475.00	565.00
1866	400.00	520.00
1867	475.00	565.00
1868	480.00	575.00
1869	480.00	575.00
1870	500.00	600.00
1871	480.00	575.00
1872	500.00	600.00
1873	*Proof only* 1,700.00	

NICKEL THREE-CENT PIECES

The fact that the tiny silver three-cent piece survived at all indicates that there was some usefulness to that denomination, but its size was impractical. With Civil War silver hoarding occurring, the need for a convenient non-silver coin of this value was even more apparent. The three-cent coin was thus made bigger and changed to an alloy of 75 percent copper and 25 percent nickel, just enough nickel to give it a white color. Despite their active use in commerce for decades, they are not difficult to find well preserved.

Known Counterfeits: Few if any counterfeits of this coin are known.

Type Coin Price Range	G to MS-60
1865 to 1889	15.00 to 100.00

	F	XF
1865	20.00	37.00
1866	20.00	37.00
1867	20.00	37.00
1868	20.00	37.00
1869	20.00	40.00
1870	22.50	42.00
1871	24.00	43.00
1872	25.00	45.00
1873	25.00	45.00
1874	25.00	45.00
1875	30.00	50.00
1876	30.00	55.00
1877 *Proof only*	—	2,550.00
1878 *Proof only*	—	900.00
1879	100.00	120.00
1880	130.00	195.00
1881	20.00	40.00
1882	180.00	275.00
1883	280.00	380.00
1884	575.00	700.00
1885	650.00	800.00
1886 *Proof only*	—	600.00
1887	415.00	585.00
1888	80.00	110.00
1889	150.00	220.00

SHIELD NICKELS

The success of the 25-percent nickel three-cent piece emboldened the mint to strike a larger denomination in the same alloy the following year. Its design was an ornate shield, reminiscent of the then-popular two-cent piece. One unfortunate characteristic of a hard-alloy coin such as this is that its design is not always fully struck. In this case, not all of the horizontal shading lines are always clear, even on mint-state coins. In its second year of issue, the design was simplified, the rays between the stars on the reverse being removed.

Known Counterfeits: Counterfeits intended to pass in circulation were struck bearing the dates 1870 to 1876.

Type Coin Price Range	G to MS-60
1866-1867 Rays	30.00 to 300.00
1867-1883	18.00 to 150.00

	F	XF
1866 Rays	55.00	175.00
1867 Rays	70.00	220.00
1867	29.00	62.00
1868	29.00	62.00
1869	29.00	62.00
1870	53.00	92.00
1871	125.00	265.00
1872	70.00	112.00
1873 Closed 3	65.00	145.00
1873 Open 3	55.00	82.50
1874	75.00	110.00
1875	85.00	150.00
1876	75.00	135.00
1877 *Proof only*	—	3,000.00
1878 *Proof only*	—	1,750.00
1879	620.00	750.00
1880	800.00	1,300.00
1881	450.00	625.00
1882	29.00	62.00
1883	30.00	62.00
1883 3 over 2	400.00	800.00

LIBERTY NICKELS

The Liberty Nickel had one of the most controversial beginnings of all American coins. The original design had the denomination of five cents indicated by the Roman numeral V, with the word cents simply understood. Or so the mint expected. However, some unprincipled people gold-plated these coins and passed them off as the new five-*dollar* coin. These plated frauds became known as "racketeer nickels" and prompted an immediate change in the design of this coin. The word "cents" was added boldly underneath the large V. Today racketeer nickels have some value as collector's novelties, but not as much as a natural, unaltered coin. Interestingly, the original "no cents" nickel is quite common today in medium to high grades, perhaps evidence of it being considered a novelty in its day.

The famous 1913 Liberty Nickel is not an authorized mint issue, but was struck at the U.S. Mint by a scheming employee with an eye to profit. Carefully marketed, the first advertisements to purchase these rare coins were placed by the original seller knowing that no one else had any to sell, but also aware that this would excite interest in the numismatic community. Today it is one of the most valuable coins in the world!

Known Counterfeits: There are counterfeits of the 1913, but they are somewhat less deceptive as all five extant pieces are in known hands. Also, 1912S pieces exist made from altered 1912D nickels.

Type Coin Price Range	G to MS-60
1883 No Cents	5.00 to 30.00
1883-1913	1.75 to 80.00

	F	XF
1883 No Cents	7.00	10.00
1883 With Cents	45.00	90.00
1884	45.00	98.00
1885	900.00	1,400.00
1886	425.00	725.00
1887	35.00	85.00
1888	75.00	200.00
1889	35.00	85.00
1890	30.00	70.00
1891	25.00	65.00
1892	25.00	70.00
1893	25.00	68.00
1894	100.00	250.00
1895	25.00	75.00
1896	45.00	100.00
1897	13.00	47.00
1898	11.50	45.00
1899	8.75	36.00
1900	8.75	36.00
1901	7.50	34.00
1902	4.50	32.50
1903	5.00	32.50
1904	5.00	30.00
1905	4.50	30.00
1906	4.50	30.00
1907	4.50	30.00
1908	4.50	30.00
1909	4.50	30.00
1910	4.50	32.00
1911	4.50	30.00
1912	4.50	30.00
1912D	12.50	85.00
1912S	300.00	950.00
1913 *Proof*	5,000,000.00	

BUFFALO NICKELS

The Buffalo Nickel, also called the Indian Head Nickel, was one of the most artistically progressive American coins when first issued. It was designed by James Earl Fraser, a noted sculptor of the era. Tradition holds that three different Indians posed for the obverse portrait, but this theory has been called into question. The original reverse depicting an American bison standing on a mound was changed for practical reasons the year it was issued, as the words FIVE CENTS were in such high relief that they would quickly wear off. The second reverse has the denomination in a recess below a plane on which the bison stands. The date is also rendered in high relief on these coins, and usually wears off. Such dateless coins are of little value.

One entertaining sidelight is the Hobo Nickel. This relic of American folk art consists of a Buffalo Nickel with the portrait re-engraved by hand into a variety of different portraits. Making these works of art and selling them at a modest profit was some individual's way of fighting poverty during the Great Depression. They have come into their own as collectibles, and attempts to identify individual artists have met with some success.

Known Counterfeits: The most famous counterfeit in the series is the Three-Legged Buffalo of 1937D. It should be noted that a real three-legged buffalo can be distinguished – not simply because of its missing leg – but based on numerous minor missing details where the design meets the field. Other counterfeits are coins altered to appear to be 1913S Type II, 1918/7D, 1921S, 1924S, 1926D, and 1926S.

Type Coin Price Range	VG to MS-63
1913 Mound	11.00 to 55.00
1913-1938	1.50 to 30.00

	F	Unc.
1913 Mound	12.00	35.00
1913D Mound	22.00	65.00
1913S Mound	50.00	130.00
1913 Plain	12.50	35.00
1913D Plain	185.00	300.00
1913S Plain	450.00	900.00
1914	22.00	50.00
1914D	160.00	480.00
1914S	45.00	200.00
1915	8.00	52.00
1915D	45.00	225.00
1915S	105.00	625.00
1916	7.00	45.00
1916D	30.00	150.00
1916S	20.00	175.00
1917	8.00	60.00
1917D	55.00	400.00
1917S	80.00	455.00
1918	8.00	110.00
1918 8 over 7	2,950.00	30,000.00
1918D	65.00	470.00
1918S	55.00	550.00
1919	6.00	60.00
1919D	66.00	575.00
1919S	52.00	550.00

	F	Unc.
1920	3.50	60.00
1920D	37.00	565.00
1920S	30.00	525.00
1921	8.75	125.00
1921S	220.00	1,600.00
1923	4.50	65.00
1923S	27.00	600.00
1924	4.50	75.00
1924D	30.00	400.00
1924S	100.00	2,350.00
1925	3.75	42.00
1925D	40.00	390.00
1925S	17.50	450.00
1926	2.85	35.00
1926D	30.00	325.00
1926S	100.00	5,000.00
1927	2.50	35.00
1927D	8.00	160.00
1927S	6.00	485.00
1928	2.50	35.00
1928D	4.00	59.00
1928S	3.00	220.00
1929	2.50	35.00
1929D	3.00	55.00
1929S	2.25	48.00
1930	2.50	33.00
1930S	3.00	55.00
1931S	20.00	65.00
1934	2.50	50.00
1934D	4.75	83.00
1935	2.25	21.00
1935D	3.00	75.00
1935S	2.50	50.00
1936	2.25	16.00
1936D	2.65	36.00
1936S	2.50	36.00
1937	2.25	15.00
1937D	2.50	30.00

1937D 3-legged Buffalo

	F	Unc.
1937D 3-Legged	950.00	2,750.00
1937S	2.50	28.00
1938D	4.00	20.00
1938D D over S	12.00	50.00

JEFFERSON NICKELS

The Jefferson Nickel was the first circulating United States coin to be designed by public contest. Felix Schlag won $1,000 for his design featuring Jefferson's portrait on one side and Monticello on the other. The initial rendition lacks the designer's initials, which were not added until 1966.

During World War II, nickel was needed for the war effort, so from mid-1942 to the end of 1945, "nickels" were struck in an unusual alloy of 56 percent copper, 35 percent silver and 9 percent manganese. These War Nickels bear a large mintmark over the dome. These coins exhibit great brilliance when new, but quickly turn an ugly dull color with a moderate amount of wear.

Four special nickels were put into circulation in 2004 and 2005, struck to commemorate the bicentennial of the 1804-1806 expedition of "The Corps of Discovery" from St. Louis to the Pacific, led by Meriwether Lewis and William Clark. The first two bear the standard Jefferson obverse, the second pair an impressive profile. One reverse bears clasped hands adapted from a Jefferson-era Indian peace medal, another, an old keelboat used for navigating rivers. The popular buffalo is on the third, and lastly a view of the Pacific coast with the quote, "Ocean in view! O! the joy!" For the second pair, a radical facial profile of Jefferson replaced the original 1938 bust. Beginning in 2006, that was replaced by a facing bust of Jefferson.

Due to the difficulty of getting the metal to flow into every crevice of the die, many coins are struck with the steps of Monticello incompletely struck on the standard reverse. Full-step nickels sometimes command a premium from specialists.

Known Counterfeits: The 1950D. Crude casts were also made to circulate in the 1940s.

Type Coin Price Range	VG to MS-63
1938-date	spend to .35
1942-1945 Silver	1.00 to 8.00

	VF	BU
1938	.80	4.00
1938D	1.25	3.50
1938S	2.50	4.75
1939	.25	1.75
1939D	6.00	110.00
1939S	1.50	30.00
1940	.30	4.00
1940D	.30	3.00
1940S	.30	5.00
1941	.25	3.00
1941D	.30	5.00
1941S	.30	5.00

	VF	BU
1942	.25	6.00
1942D	3.00	50.00

Wartime Silver Alloy

	VF	BU
1942P	1.50	14.00
1942S	2.00	15.00
1943P	1.50	9.00
1943P 3 over 2	75.00	300.00
1943D	1.50	9.00
1943S	1.50	12.00
1944P	1.50	20.00
1944D	1.50	15.00
1944S	1.50	11.00
1945P	1.50	10.00
1945D	1.50	9.50
1945S	1.50	9.00

Regular Alloy

	VF	BU
1946	.25	2.00
1946D	.25	1.85
1946S	.30	1.00
1947	.25	1.00
1947D	.25	1.20
1947S	.25	1.20
1948	.25	1.00
1948D	.25	2.20
1948S	.25	1.50
1949	.25	3.00
1949D	.30	1.75
1949D D over S	40.00	210.00
1949S	.45	2.00
1950	.35	2.50
1950D	13.00	20.00
1951	.40	2.50
1951D	.40	4.00
1951S	.50	2.75
1952	.25	2.00
1952D	.30	3.00
1952S	.25	1.00
1953	.25	1.00
1953D	.25	1.00
1953S	.25	1.00
1954	.25	1.00
1954D	.25	1.00
1954S	.25	1.50
1954S S over D	14.00	50.00
1955	.40	1.00
1955D	—	.50
1955D D over S	12.50	40.00
1956	—	.50
1956D	—	.50
1957	—	.50
1957D	—	.50
1958	—	.50
1958D	—	.50
1959	—	.30
1959D	—	.25
1960	—	.25
1960D	—	.25
1961	—	.25
1961D	—	.25

	VF	BU
1962	—	.25
1962D	—	.25
1963	—	.25
1963D	—	.25
1964	—	.25
1964D	—	.25
1965	—	.25
1966	—	.25
1967	—	.25
1968D	—	.25
1968S	—	.25
1969D	—	.25
1969S	—	.25
1970D	—	.25
1970S	—	.25
1971	—	.75
1971D	—	.25
1971S *Proof only*	—	1.60
1972	—	.25
1972D	—	.25
1972S *Proof only*	—	2.00
1973	—	.25
1973D	—	.25
1973S *Proof only*	—	1.75
1974	—	.25
1974D	—	.25
1974S *Proof only*	—	2.00
1975	—	.25
1975D	—	.25
1975S *Proof only*	—	2.25
1976	—	.25
1976D	—	.25
1976S *Proof only*	—	2.00
1977	—	.25
1977D	—	.25
1977S *Proof only*	—	1.75
1978	—	.25
1978D	—	.25
1978S *Proof only*	—	1.75
1979	—	.25
1979D	—	.25
1979S *Proof only*	—	1.50
1980P	—	.25
1980D	—	.25
1980S *Proof only*	—	1.50
1981P	—	.25
1981D	—	.25
1981S *Proof only*	—	2.00
1982P	—	2.00
1982D	—	1.50
1982 S *Proof only*	—	3.00
1983P	—	1.50
1983D	—	1.00
1983S *Proof only*	—	4.00
1984P	—	1.25
1984D	—	.25
1984S *Proof only*	—	5.00
1985P	—	.30
1985D	—	.30
1985S *Proof only*	—	4.00
1986P	—	.30

	VF	BU
1986D	—	1.00
1986S *Proof only*	—	7.00
1987P	—	.25
1987D	—	.25
1987S *Proof only*	—	3.50
1988P	—	.25
1988D	—	.25
1988S *Proof only*	—	5.50
1989P	—	.25
1989D	—	.25
1989S *Proof only*	—	4.50
1990P	—	.25
1990D	—	.25
1990S *Proof only*	—	5.50
1991P	—	.25
1991D	—	.25
1991S *Proof only*	—	5.00
1992P	—	.75
1992D	—	.25
1992S *Proof only*	—	4.00
1993P	—	.25
1993D	—	.25
1993S *Proof only*	—	4.00
1994P	—	.25
1994P *Matte finish*	—	75.00
1994D	—	.25
1994S *Proof only*	—	4.00
1995P	—	.25
1995D	—	.35
1995S *Proof only*	—	6.50
1996P	—	.25
1996D	—	.25
1996S *Proof only*	—	3.00
1997P	—	.25
1997P *Matte finish*	—	200.00
1997D	—	.25
1997S *Proof only*	—	5.00
1998P	—	.25
1998D	—	.25
1998S *Proof only*	—	4.50
1999P	—	.25
1999D	—	.25
1999S *Proof only*	—	3.50
2000P	—	.25
2000D	—	.25
2000S *Proof only*	—	2.00
2001P	—	.30
2001D	—	.30
2001S *Proof only*	—	2.00
2002P	—	.25
2002D	—	.25
2002S *Proof only*	—	2.00
2003P	—	.30
2003D	—	.30
2003S *Proof only*	—	2.00

	VF	BU
2004P Peace rev.	—	.35
2004D Peace rev.	—	.35
2004S Peace rev. *Proof only*	—	8.00

	VF	BU
2004P Keelboat rev.	—	.35
2004D Keelboat rev.	—	.35
2004S Keelboat rev. *Proof only*	—	8.00

	VF	BU
2005P Bison rev.	—	.35
2005D Bison rev.	—	.35
2005S Bison rev. *Proof only*	—	8.00
2005P Coastline rev.	—	.35
2005D Coastline rev.	—	.35
2005S Coastline rev. *Proof only*	—	7.00

Facing Bust

	VF	BU
2006P	—	.35
2006D	—	.35
2006S *Proof only*	—	6.00
2007P	—	.35
2007D	—	.35
2007S obv. *Proof only*	—	6.00
2008P	—	.35
2008D	—	.35
2008S obv. *Proof only*	—	6.00

BUST HALF DIMES

The United States did not always have nickel fivecent pieces. The original ones were very small silver coins called half dimes. Their designs almost always resembled those used on large whole dimes. Despite it being a priority of George Washington, half dimes were not consistently struck in early America. Between 1805 and 1829 none were struck at all.

The bust half dime's thinness resulted in frequent bending and dents. Prices given are for flat, undamaged examples. Rare die combinations of early specimens command a premium from specialists

Known Counterfeits: 1795.

Type Coin Price Range	G to MS-60
1794-1795	900.00 to 12,500.00
1796-1797	1,000.00 to 14,000.00
1800-1805	700.00 to 11,000.00
1829-1837	30.00 to 350.00

FLOWING HAIR TYPE

	VG	VF
1794	1,400.00	2,800.00
1795	1,100.00	2,400.00

DRAPED BUST / SMALL EAGLE

	VG	VF
1796	1,500.00	3,500.00
1797	1,300.00	3,250.00

DRAPED BUST / HERALDIC EAGLE

	VG	VF
1800	900.00	2,500.00
	VG	VF
1801	950.00	2,800.00
1802	27,000.00	65,000.00
1803	990.00	2,500.00
1805	1,300.00	3,000.00

CAPPED BUST TYPE

	VG	VF
1829	55.00	110.00
1830	45.00	95.00
1831	45.00	95.00
1832	45.00	95.00

	VG	VF
1833	45.00	95.00
1834	45.00	95.00
1835	45.00	95.00
1836	45.00	98.00
1837	50.00	110.00

SEATED LIBERTY HALF DIMES

Following the introduction of the Seated Liberty design by Christian Gobrecht on the silver dollar, the smaller coins were gradually brought into harmony with this design. It is generally accepted that the seated-goddess version of Liberty was directly or indirectly inspired by depictions of the Roman allegory of Britannia on British coins. The half dime and dime, because of their small size, were redesigned to have a laurel wreath encircling the denomination on the reverse, rather than an eagle.

There were several minor changes over the life of this coin. After only a year, the plain obverse was ornamented by 13 stars. Two years later additional drapery was added below Liberty's elbow. The arrows by the date from 1853 to 1855 indicate a 7½ percent reduction in weight. A far more obvious design change was the shift of the words UNITED STATES OF AMERICA from the reverse to the obverse in 1860.

The seated half dime's thinness resulted in frequent bending and dents. Prices given are for flat, undamaged examples.

Known Counterfeits: Counterfeit half dimes are not frequently encountered.

Type Coin Price Range	G to MS-60
1837-1838 No Stars	32.00 to 720.00
1838-1859	16.00 to 190.00
1860-1873	15.00 to 150.00

SEATED LIBERTY—PLAIN OBVERSE FIELD

	VG	VF
1837	42.00	120.00
1838O	150.00	475.00

SEATED LIBERTY—STARS ON OBVERSE

	VG	VF
1838	20.00	30.00
1839	20.00	35.00
1839O	30.00	50.00
1840	20.00	40.00
1840O	30.00	70.00
1841	17.50	30.00
1841O	22.00	55.00
1842	20.00	35.00
1842O	45.00	250.00
1843	20.00	35.00
1844	20.00	35.00
1844O	105.00	450.00
1845	20.00	35.00
1846	550.00	1,250.00
1847	20.00	35.00
1848	20.00	35.00
1848O	25.00	65.00
1849	20.00	60.00
1849 overdates	26.00	62.00
1849O	40.00	225.00
1850	20.00	40.00
1850O	25.00	70.00
1851	20.00	35.00
1851O	20.00	45.00
1852	20.00	35.00
1852O	45.00	145.00
1853 no arrows	50.00	145.00
1853O no arrows	325.00	850.00
1853 arrows	20.00	35.00
1853O arrows	20.00	35.00
1854	20.00	35.00
1854O	20.00	35.00
1855	20.00	35.00
1855O	22.00	55.00
1856	20.00	35.00
1856O	20.00	60.00
1857	20.00	35.00
1857O	20.00	45.00
1858	20.00	35.00
1858O	20.00	45.00
1859	20.00	45.00
1859O	21.00	48.00

SEATED LIBERTY—LEGEND ON OBVERSE

	VG	VF
1860	20.00	35.00
1860O	20.00	35.00
1861	20.00	35.00
1862	30.00	60.00
1863	250.00	400.00
1863S	45.00	95.00
1864	475.00	800.00
1864S	75.00	200.00
1865	475.00	750.00
1865S	40.00	90.00
1866	475.00	700.00

	VG	VF
1866S	40.00	90.00
1867	650.00	900.00
1867S	40.00	90.00
1868	90.00	220.00
1868S	25.00	45.00
1869	25.00	45.00
1869S	22.00	42.00
1870	22.00	42.00
1870S	*Unique*	
1871	20.00	40.00
1871S	30.00	70.00
1872	20.00	40.00
1872S	20.00	40.00
1873	20.00	40.00
1873S	25.00	40.00

BUST DIMES

Due to limited mint capacity, dimes were not struck until 1796, even though other denominations of United States silver began to be struck two years earlier. Dime production was suspended occasionally when enough small Mexican coins were imported to satisfy demand. The initial reverse design, which showed a rather skinny eagle within a wreath, was replaced after two more years with a plumper eagle carrying a heraldic shield. In 1809 a cap was added to Liberty and her bust was turned to the left. In the same year a denomination first appeared, not as a "dime," however, but as "10C." Rare die combinations of early specimens command a premium from specialists

Known Counterfeits: Scarce cast counterfeits are known.

Type Coin Price Range	G to MS-60
1796-1797	1,300.00 to 12,000.00
1798-1807	450.00 to 5,000.00
1809-1837	28.00 to 750.00

DRAPED BUST / SMALL EAGLE

	VG	VF
1796	2,000.00	3,500.00
1797 13 stars	2,000.00	3,500.00
1797 16 stars	2,000.00	3,500.00

DRAPED BUST / HERALDIC EAGLE

	VG	VF
1798 over 97, 13 stars	3,000.00	7,000.00
1798 over 97, 16 stars	850.00	1,700.00
1798	900.00	2,000.00
1800	850.00	1,800.00
1801	900.00	2,500.00
1802	1,400.00	3,200.00
1803	800.00	1,800.00
1804, 13 stars	1,900.00	5,500.00
1804, 14 stars	2,100.00	6,000.00
1805	700.00	1,300.00
1807	700.00	1,300.00

CAPPED BUST TYPE

	VG	VF
1809	250.00	800.00
1811 over 9	200.00	650.00
1814 Small Date	70.00	400.00
1814 Large Date	40.00	200.00
1820	40.00	150.00
1821 Small Date	40.00	175.00
1821 Large Date	40.00	150.00
1822	625.00	1,700.00
1823, 3 over 2	40.00	150.00
1824, 4 over 2	50.00	400.00
1825	40.00	150.00
1827	40.00	140.00
1828 Large Date	110.00	375.00
1828 Small Date	45.00	195.00
1829 (varieties)	40.00	80.00
1830 30 over 29	60.00	250.00
1830	40.00	80.00
1831	40.00	80.00
1832	40.00	80.00
1833	40.00	80.00
1834	40.00	80.00
1835	40.00	80.00
1836	40.00	80.00
1837	40.00	80.00

SEATED LIBERTY DIMES

Following the introduction of the Seated Liberty design by Christian Gobrecht on the silver dollar, the smaller coins were gradually brought into harmony with this design. It is generally accepted that the seated goddess version of Liberty was directly or indirectly inspired by depictions of the Roman allegory of Britannia on British coins. The dime and half dime, because of their small size, were redesigned to have a laurel wreath encircling the denomination on the reverse, rather than an eagle.

There were several minor changes over the life of this coin. After somewhat more than a year, the plain obverse was ornamented by 13 stars. A year later, additional drapery was added below Liberty's elbow. The arrows by the date from 1853 to 1855 indicate a 7 percent reduction in weight, those in 1873 to 1874 a minuscule increase. A far more obvious design change was the shift of the words UNITED STATES OF AMERICA from the reverse to the obverse in 1860.

The seated dime's thinness resulted in frequent bending and dents. Prices given are for flat, undamaged examples.

Known Counterfeits: Collector counterfeits of seated dimes are not frequently encountered, but circulating counterfeits were struck in copper, lead, and white metal (tin and lead alloys), particularly during the 1850s-1860s.

Type Coin Price Range	G to MS-60
1837-1838 No Stars	40.00 to 1,100.00
1838-1860	10.00 to 275.00
1860-1891	10.00 to 175.00

SEATED LIBERTY—OBVERSE FIELD PLAIN

	VG	VF
1837	50.00	300.00
1838O	75.00	400.00

SEATED LIBERTY—STARS ON OBVERSE

	VG	VF
1838 (varieties)	20.00	45.00
1839	20.00	45.00
1839O	22.50	60.00
1840	20.00	45.00
1840O	22.50	70.00
1840 extra drapery from elbow	50.00	200.00
1841	20.00	32.00
1841O	22.00	45.00
1842	20.00	32.00
1842O	23.00	75.00
1843	20.00	32.00
1843O	70.00	325.00
1844	350.00	800.00
1845	20.00	32.00

	VG	VF
1845O	35.00	250.00
1846	300.00	850.00
1847	25.00	85.00
1848	21.50	55.00
1849	20.00	40.00
1849O	30.00	135.00
1850	25.00	35.00
1850O	27.00	90.00
1851	25.00	35.00
1851O	25.00	90.00
1852	20.00	32.00
1852O	30.00	125.00
1853 no arrows	110.00	275.00
1853 arrows	18.00	30.00
1853O arrows	20.00	45.00
1854	20.00	30.00
1854O	20.00	30.00
1855	20.00	30.00
1856	20.00	35.00
1856O	20.00	35.00
1856S	225.00	550.00
1857	20.00	35.00
1857O	20.00	35.00
1858	20.00	35.00
1858O	25.00	90.00
1858S	200.00	475.00
1859	20.00	45.00
1859O	20.00	45.00
1859S	225.00	550.00
1860S	55.00	145.00

SEATED LIBERTY—LEGEND ON OBVERSE

	VG	VF
1860	22.00	36.00
1860O	600.00	1,950.00
1861	20.00	35.00
1861S	90.00	275.00
1862	20.00	35.00
1862S	65.00	185.00
1863	500.00	900.00
1863S	55.00	145.00
1864	500.00	750.00
1864S	45.00	110.00
1865	575.00	875.00
1865S	55.00	135.00
1866	600.00	950.00
1866S	65.00	150.00
1867	700.00	1,100.00
1867S	60.00	150.00
1868	22.00	40.00
1868S	35.00	85.00
1869	35.00	80.00
1869S	30.00	55.00
1870	22.00	40.00
1870S	375.00	650.00

	VG	VF
1871	20.00	33.00
1871CC	3,500.00	8,500.00
1871S	55.00	130.00
1872	20.00	30.00
1872CC	1,100.00	3,000.00
1872S	60.00	150.00
1873 Closed 3	20.00	30.00
1873 Open 3	35.00	75.00
1873CC	Unique	
1873 arrows	20.00	60.00
1873CC arrows	3,000.00	6,000.00
1873S arrows	30.00	70.00
1874 arrows	30.00	50.00
1874CC arrows	6,500.00	12,500.00
1874S arrows	70.00	160.00
1875	20.00	30.00
1875CC	20.00	30.00
1875S	20.00	30.00
1876	20.00	30.00
1876CC	20.00	30.00
1876S	20.00	30.00
1877	20.00	30.00
1877CC	20.00	40.00
1877S	20.00	30.00
1878	20.00	30.00
1878CC	90.00	225.00
1879	310.00	450.00
1880	275.00	375.00
1881	300.00	425.00
1882	20.00	30.00
1883	20.00	30.00
1884	20.00	30.00
1884S	35.00	65.00
1885	20.00	30.00
1885S	650.00	1,750.00
1886	20.00	30.00
1886S	70.00	125.00
1887	20.00	30.00
1887S	20.00	30.00
1888	20.00	30.00
1888S	20.00	30.00
1889	20.00	30.00
1889S	20.00	45.00
1890	20.00	30.00
1890S	20.00	50.00
1891	20.00	30.00
1891O	20.00	30.00
1891S	18.00	30.00

BARBER DIMES

The dime, quarter and half dollar introduced in 1892 bear a portrait head of Liberty instead of an entire figure. They were designed by Chief Engraver Charles E. Barber, after whom they have been named. More practical than artistically adventurous, contemporaries thought the design rather boring if not unpleasant. Because of its small size, the dime differed from the other two denominations in the Barber series in that the reverse simply has the value within a wreath, rather than an eagle, much as occurred with the Seated Liberty coinage.

Known Counterfeits: The rare 1894S has certainly been counterfeited.

Type Coin Price Range	G to MS-60
1892-1916	2.50 to 110.00

	F	XF
1892	16.00	28.00
1892O	32.00	75.00
1892S	200.00	300.00
1893, 3 over 2	175.00	300.00
1893	20.00	46.00
1893O	110.00	200.00
1893S	38.00	85.00
1894	115.00	200.00
1894O	205.00	445.00
1894S	Very Rare Proof	1,300,000.00
1895	300.00	575.00
1895O	880.00	2,500.00
1895S	130.00	240.00
1896	55.00	98.00
1896O	300.00	480.00
1896S	280.00	400.00
1897	8.00	33.00
1897O	280.00	480.00
1897S	96.00	185.00
1898	8.00	32.50
1898O	85.00	205.00
1898S	32.00	80.00
1899	7.50	26.00
1899O	70.00	150.00
1899S	26.00	48.00
1900	7.00	28.00
1900O	110.00	225.00
1900S	12.50	32.00
1901	6.50	27.50
1901O	16.00	67.50
1901S	360.00	520.00
1902	5.50	23.00
1902O	15.00	62.50
1902S	55.00	135.00
1903	4.50	25.00
1903O	13.50	50.00
1903S	340.00	800.00
1904	6.50	25.00
1904S	160.00	350.00
1905	6.00	25.00
1905O	35.00	98.00
1905S	9.00	45.00
1906	4.00	25.00
1906D	8.00	37.00
1906O	48.00	98.00
1906S	12.00	48.00
1907	4.00	25.00
1907D	8.50	46.00
1907O	32.00	63.00

	F	XF
1907S	16.00	67.50
1908	4.00	25.00
1908D	6.00	30.00
1908O	42.50	98.00
1908S	11.50	48.00
1909	4.00	25.00
1909D	60.00	135.00
1909O	12.50	50.00
1909S	85.00	190.00
1910	4.00	25.00
1910D	8.50	48.00
1910S	50.00	110.00
1911	4.00	25.00
1911D	4.00	25.00
1911S	8.50	41.50
1912	4.00	25.00
1912D	4.00	25.00
1912S	6.00	34.00
1913	4.00	25.00
1913S	85.00	240.00
1914	4.00	25.00
1914D	4.00	25.00
1914S	8.00	42.00
1915	4.00	25.00
1915S	32.50	70.00
1916	4.00	25.00
1916S	4.50	25.00

MERCURY DIMES

The name Mercury for this dime is a misnomer. Designed by Adolph Weinman, it actually depicts Liberty wearing a winged cap, representing freedom of thought. It was received with wide acclaim for its artistic merit when it was first released as part of a program for the beautification of United States coinage. The reverse carries the ancient Roman "fasces," a bundle of rods containing an axe with the blade protruding. This symbol of authority is still seen in the United States Senate. The horizontal bands tying the fasces together do not always strike up distinctly from each other, and those coins with "full split bands" often command a premium.

Known Counterfeits: These include 1916D, 1916D, 1921, 1921D, 1931D, 1942/1, 1942/1D, most of which have been made by altering the mintmark on a more common date. The date 1923D is a fantasy, none having been struck.

Type Coin Price Range	G to MS-63
1916-1945	Bullion to 10.00

	VF	MS-60		VF	MS-60		XF	BU
1916	7.00	33.00	1941	3.00	7.00	1952D	2.00	3.50
1916D	4,200.00	14,000.00	1941D	3.00	7.00	1952S	2.00	6.00
1916S	15.00	46.00	1941S	3.00	8.00	1953	2.00	3.50
1917	5.50	30.00	1942, 2 over 1	750.00	2,250.00	1953D	2.00	3.50
1917D	26.00	140.00	1942D, 2 over 1	840.00	2,650.00	1953S	2.00	3.50
1917S	6.50	64.00	1942	3.00	7.00	1954	2.00	3.50
1918	12.00	70.00	1942D	3.00	8.00	1954D	2.00	3.50
1918D	12.00	110.00	1942S	3.00	9.50	1954S	2.00	3.50
1918S	10.00	100.00	1943	3.00	7.00	1955	2.00	3.50
1919	5.50	38.00	1943D	3.00	7.50	1955D	2.00	3.50
1919D	25.00	190.00	1943S	3.00	9.90	1955S	2.00	3.50
1919S	17.00	190.00	1944	3.00	7.00	1956	—	3.00
1920	4.00	27.50	1944D	3.00	7.50	1956D	—	3.00
1920D	8.00	115.00	1944S	3.00	7.50	1957	—	2.50
1920S	8.50	115.00	1945	3.00	7.00	1957D	—	2.50
1921	280.00	1,175.00	1945D	3.00	7.00	1958	—	2.30
1921D	400.00	1,325.00	1945S	3.00	7.00	1958D	—	2.30
1923	4.00	27.50	1945S micro S	9.00	60.00	1959	—	2.30
1923S	18.00	165.00				1959D	—	2.30
1924	4.50	45.00				1960	—	2.30
1924D	22.00	175.00				1960D	—	2.30
1924S	12.00	170.00				1961	—	2.30
1925	4.00	28.00				1961D	—	2.30
1925D	44.00	370.00				1962	—	2.30
1925S	14.00	190.00				1962D	—	2.30
1926	3.00	25.00				1963	—	2.00
1926D	9.90	125.00				1963D	—	2.00
1926S	70.00	900.00				1964	—	2.00
1927	3.50	27.00				1964D	—	2.00

ROOSEVELT DIMES

The fact that the dime was chosen to bear the image of Franklin Roosevelt, a victim of polio, is not a coincidence. It was selected to remind people of the president's involvement in the March of Dimes. The coin was designed on a tight deadline by Chief Engraver John R. Sinnock. There are no true rarities in this series.

Known Counterfeits: Counterfeit Roosevelt dimes are quite rare.

Type Coin Price Range	F to MS-65
1946-1964	Bullion to 2.00
1965-date	.25 to .75

	VF	MS-60
1927D	24.00	200.00
1927S	9.00	290.00
1928	3.50	27.50
1928D	22.00	200.00
1928S	6.50	125.00
1929	3.00	24.00
1929D	8.00	28.00
1929S	5.00	32.50
1930	3.75	26.00
1930S	7.00	82.00
1931	4.50	35.00
1931D	18.00	98.00
1931S	11.00	96.00
1934	3.00	30.00
1934D	7.50	50.00
1935	3.00	11.00
1935D	6.50	38.00
1935S	3.00	25.00
1936	3.00	10.00
1936D	4.20	28.00
1936S	3.00	20.00
1937	2.50	9.00
1937D	3.00	24.00
1937S	3.00	23.00
1938	2.50	14.00
1938D	5.00	18.00
1938S	3.25	21.00
1939	2.50	10.00
1939D	2.50	8.00
1939S	2.50	25.00
1940	3.00	7.00
1940D	3.00	8.00
1940S	3.00	9.00

	XF	BU
1946	2.00	4.50
1946D	2.00	4.50
1946S	2.00	4.50
1947	2.00	7.00
1947D	2.00	8.00
1947S	2.00	6.00
1948	2.00	6.00
1948D	2.00	9.00
1948S	2.00	7.00
1949	3.00	35.00
1949D	2.25	14.00
1949S	7.50	50.00
1950	2.25	16.00
1950D	2.00	7.00
1950S	3.75	50.00
1950S, S over D	70.00	225.00
1951	2.00	4.00
1951D	2.00	3.50
1951S	3.00	18.00
1952	2.00	3.50

CUPRO-NICKEL CLAD COPPER

	XF	BU
1965	—	.60
1966	—	.50
1967	—	.75
1968	—	.50
1968D	—	.50
1968S *Proof only*	—	1.50
1969	—	1.50
1969D	—	.50
1969S *Proof only*	—	1.35
1970	—	.50
1970D	—	.50
1970S *Proof only*	—	1.50
1971	—	1.00
1971D	—	.50
1971S *Proof only*	—	1.50
1972	—	.50
1972D	—	.50
1972S *Proof only*	—	1.50
1973	—	.50
1973D	—	.50
1973S *Proof only*	—	1.50
1974	—	.50
1974D	—	.50
1974S *Proof only*	—	1.50
1975	—	.50
1975D	—	.50
1975S *Proof only*	—	2.25
1976	—	.75
1976D	—	.50
1976S *Proof only*	—	1.50

	XF	BU
1977	—	.50
1977D	—	.50
1977S *Proof only*	—	2.25
1978	—	.50
1978D	—	.50
1978S *Proof only*	—	1.50
1979	—	.50
1979D	—	.50
1979 thick S *Proof only*	—	1.50
1979 thin S *Proof only*	—	2.25
1980P	—	.50
1980D	—	.50
1980S *Proof only*	—	1.50
1981P	—	.50
1981D	—	.50
1981S *Proof only*	—	1.50
1982P	—	3.50
1982 no mintmark error	80.00	200.00
1982D	—	1.50
1982S *Proof only*	—	2.00
1983P	—	3.00
1983D	—	1.25
1983S *Proof only*	—	2.00
1984P	—	.50
1984D	—	1.00
1984S *Proof only*	—	2.00
1985P	—	.50
1985D	—	.50
1985S *Proof only*	—	1.50
1986P	—	1.00
1986D	—	1.00
1986S *Proof only*	—	2.75
1987P	—	.50
1987D	—	.50
1987S *Proof only*	—	1.50
1988P	—	.50
1988D	—	.50
1988S *Proof only*	—	3.00
1989P	—	.50
1989D	—	.50
1989S *Proof only*	—	4.00
1990P	—	.50
1990D	—	.50
1990S *Proof only*	—	2.00
1991P	—	.50
1991D	—	.50
1991S *Proof only*	—	3.00
1992P	—	.50
1992D	—	.50
1992S *Proof only*	—	4.00
1992S Silver *Proof only*	—	5.00
1993P	—	.50
1993D	—	.75
1993S *Proof only*	—	5.00
1993S Silver *Proof only*	—	8.50
1994P	—	.50
1994D	—	.50
1994S *Proof only*	—	5.00
1994S Silver *Proof only*	—	8.50
1995	—	.75
1995D	—	1.00
1995S *Proof only*	—	18.00
1995S Silver *Proof only*	—	25.00

	XF	BU
1996	—	.50
1996D	—	.50
1996W	—	14.00
1996S *Proof only*	—	2.50
1996S Silver *Proof only*	—	8.50
1997P	—	1.00
1997D	—	.50
1997S *Proof only*	—	11.00
1997S Silver *Proof only*	—	25.00
1998P	—	.50
1998D	—	.75
1998S *Proof only*	—	4.00
1998S Silver *Proof only*	—	8.00
1999P	—	.50
1999D	—	.50
1999S *Proof only*	—	4.00
1999S Silver *Proof only*	—	6.50
2000P	—	.50
2000D	—	.50
2000S *Proof only*	—	1.00
2000S Silver *Proof only*	—	4.50
2001P	—	.50
2001D	—	.50
2001S *Proof only*	—	1.50
2001S Silver *Proof only*	—	5.00
2002P	—	.50
2002D	—	.50
2002S *Proof only*	—	1.00
2002S Silver *Proof only*	—	5.50
2003P	—	.50
2003D	—	.50
2003S *Proof only*	—	2.00
2003S Silver *Proof only*	—	4.00
2004P	—	.50
2004D	—	.50
2004S *Proof only*	—	4.75
2004S Silver *Proof only*	—	4.00
2005P	—	.50
2005D	—	.50
2005S *Proof only*	—	2.25
2005S Silver *Proof only*	—	4.00
2006P	—	.50
2006D	—	.50
2006S *Proof only*	—	4.75
2006S Silver *Proof only*	—	4.00
2007P	—	.50
2007D	—	.50
2007S *Proof only*	—	4.75
2007S Silver *Proof only*	—	4.00
2008P	—	.50
2008D	—	.50
2008S *Proof only*	—	5.00
2008S Silver *Proof only*	—	4.25

TWENTY-CENT PIECES

It is evident that, even before its release, the mint was concerned about the public confusing this coin with a quarter. This is indicated by several features distinct from the other silver coins of the day. The reverse design is a mirror image of that on the others, the word LIBERTY on the shield is in relief rather than recessed, and the edge is plain, not reeded. Nevertheless the public was still confused, and the coin was terminated after only two years in circulation, the 1877 and 1878 dates being collectors' issues.

Known Counterfeits: The 1876CC with added mintmark. Some 19th-century charlatans would hand-scrape reeding into the edge of pieces in hopes of passing them off as quarters.

Type Coin Price Range		G to MS-60
1875-78		110.00 to 550.00
	VG	VF
1875	240.00	375.00
1875CC	400.00	600.00
1875S	130.00	200.00
1876	250.00	385.00
1876CC		
Extremely Rare MS-65		175,000.00
1877	—	3,100.00
1878	—	2,500.00

BUST QUARTERS

Due to limited mint capacity, quarters were not struck until 1796, when a small quantity was produced, even though other denominations of United States silver began to be struck two years earlier. These first rare pieces were struck on blanks with crude edges, often exhibiting "adjustment marks" from filing off excess silver before striking. The initial reverse design showing a rather skinny eagle within a wreath had been in use only one year when the striking of quarters was suspended. When striking was resumed a few years later it was replaced with a plumper eagle carrying a heraldic shield. Coinage ceased again until 1815 when a cap was added to Liberty and her bust was turned to the left. In the same year a denomination first appeared, not as "quarter dollar" but "25C."

Rare die combinations of early specimens command a premium from specialists. Cleaning plagues this series, and such pieces are discounted.

Known Counterfeits: Cast counterfeits exist of 1796. Other counterfeits to 1807 are possible.

Type Coin Price Range	G to MS-60
1796	9,000.00 to 90,000.00
1804-1807	240.00 to 6,650.00
1815-1838	68.00 to 1,500.00

DRAPED BUST / SMALL EAGLE

	VG	VF
1796	**16,500.00**	**36,500.00**

DRAPED BUST/HERALDIC EAGLE

	VG	VF
1804	**4,200.00**	**8,600.00**
1805	**360.00**	**1,000.00**
1806, 6 over 5	**400.00**	**1,400.00**
1806	**350.00**	**1,000.00**
1807	**350.00**	**1,000.00**

CAPPED BUST TYPE

	VG	VF
1815	**125.00**	**410.00**
1818 8 over 5	**120.00**	**450.00**
1818	**115.00**	**390.00**
1819	**115.00**	**390.00**
1820	**115.00**	**390.00**
1821	**120.00**	**400.00**
1822 25 over 50c	**3,200.00**	**6,700.00**
1822	**125.00**	**440.00**
1823, 3 over 2	**30,000.00**	**56,000.00**
1824, 4 over 2	**400.00**	**1,500.00**
1825, 5 over 2	**180.00**	**520.00**
1825, 5 over 3	**140.00**	**420.00**
1825, 5 over 4	**125.00**	**400.00**
1827	**70,000.00**	
1827 Proof Restrike	—	**75,000.00**
1828	**110.00**	**375.00**
1828 25 over 50c	**300.00**	**1,200.00**

NO MOTTO, REDUCED SIZE

	VG	VF
1831 Small letters	**95.00**	**140.00**
1831 Large letters	**90.00**	**150.00**
1832	**90.00**	**150.00**
1833	**100.00**	**170.00**
1834	**90.00**	**150.00**
1835	**90.00**	**150.00**
1836	**90.00**	**150.00**
1837	**90.00**	**150.00**
1838	**90.00**	**150.00**

SEATED LIBERTY QUARTERS

Following the introduction of the Seated Liberty design by Christian Gobrecht on the silver dollar, the smaller coins were gradually brought into harmony with this design. It is generally accepted that the seated goddess version of Liberty was directly or indirectly inspired by depictions of the Roman allegory of Britannia on British coins. The eagle on the reverse is not significantly different from that on the last capped-bust coins.

There were several minor changes over the life of this coin. After the first few years, additional drapery was added below Liberty's elbow. The arrows by the date from 1853 to 1855, and the rays on the reverse in 1853, indicate a 7 percent reduction in weight; arrows in 1873 to 1874 indicate a minuscule increase. A ribbon with the motto "In God We Trust" was added over the eagle in 1866.

Known Counterfeits: Genuine 1858 quarters have been re-engraved to pass as 1853 no-arrows pieces. Contemporary counterfeits struck in copper, lead and white metal (tin and lead alloys) exist.

Type Coin Price Range	G to MS-60
1838-1865	35.00 to 1,250.00
1853 arrows and rays	18.00 to 975.00
1854-55 arrows	17.00 to 440.00
1873-1874 arrows	20.00 to 800.00
1866-1891	20.00 to 300.00

NO MOTTO ABOVE EAGLE

	VG	VF
1838	**50.00**	**110.00**
1839	**44.00**	**100.00**
1840O	**55.00**	**135.00**
1840 extra drapery from elbow	**50.00**	**125.00**
1840O extra drapery from elbow	**48.00**	**120.00**
1841	**95.00**	**190.00**
1841O	**35.00**	**100.00**
1842	**125.00**	**285.00**
1842O Small date	**650.00**	**1,950.00**
1842O Large date	**45.00**	**75.00**
1843	**28.00**	**65.00**
1843O	**40.00**	**125.00**
1844	**27.00**	**65.00**
1844O	**35.00**	**85.00**
1845	**27.00**	**65.00**
1846	**27.00**	**70.00**
1847	**27.00**	**68.00**
1847O	**45.00**	**140.00**
1848	**55.00**	**185.00**
1849	**30.00**	**85.00**
1849O	**700.00**	**1,850.00**
1850	**55.00**	**135.00**
1850O	**50.00**	**120.00**
1851	**85.00**	**225.00**
1851O	**275.00**	**875.00**
1852	**80.00**	**195.00**
1852O	**270.00**	**900.00**
1853 no arrows	**550.00**	**1,050.00**

ARROWS AT DATE

	VG	VF
1853	**27.00**	**55.00**
1853, 3 over 4	**75.00**	**250.00**
1853O	**42.00**	**100.00**
1854	**27.00**	**70.00**
1854O	**35.00**	**80.00**
1854O Huge O	**1,400.00**	**4,800.00**
1855	**27.00**	**65.00**
1855O	**75.00**	**300.00**
1855S	**60.00**	**225.00**

ARROWS REMOVED

	VG	VF
1856	**27.00**	**45.00**
1856O	**35.00**	**65.00**
1856S	**70.00**	**350.00**
1856S, S over S	**200.00**	**975.00**
1857	**27.00**	**45.00**
1857O	**30.00**	**50.00**
1857S	**150.00**	**425.00**
1858	**27.00**	**45.00**
1858O	**35.00**	**70.00**
1858S	**110.00**	**300.00**
1859	**27.00**	**45.00**

	VG	VF
1859O	35.00	90.00
1859S	175.00	500.00
1860	27.00	45.00
1860O	40.00	65.00
1860S	350.00	975.00
1861	27.00	45.00
1861S	135.00	450.00
1862	30.00	45.00
1862S	115.00	325.00
1863	47.00	130.00
1864	110.00	225.00
1864S	550.00	1,350.00
1865	110.00	225.00
1865S	150.00	400.00

MOTTO ABOVE EAGLE

	VG	VF
1866	600.00	1,000.00
1866S	365.00	1,050.00
1867	325.00	685.00
1867S	425.00	925.00
1868	225.00	400.00
1868S	125.00	390.00
1869	475.00	800.00
1869S	135.00	385.00
1870	85.00	225.00
1870CC	7,500.00	18,000.00
1871	60.00	135.00
1871CC	4,400.00	14,500.00
1871S	465.00	1,100.00
1872	45.00	120.00
1872CC	1,400.00	4,250.00
1872S	1,250.00	2,600.00
1873 Closed 3	325.00	725.00
1873 Open	345.00	120.00
1873CC	4 known	

ARROWS AT DATE

	VG	VF
1873	27.00	70.00
1873CC	4,000.00	13,000.00
1873S	40.00	180.00
1874	27.00	70.00
1874S	35.00	150.00

ARROWS REMOVED

	VG	VF
1875	27.00	45.00
1875CC	110.00	375.00
1875S	56.00	120.00
1876	27.00	45.00
1876CC	50.00	75.00
1876S	27.00	45.00
1877	27.00	45.00
1877CC	50.00	75.00
1877S	27.00	45.00
1877S over horizontal S	60.00	175.00
1878	27.00	45.00
1878CC	50.00	110.00
1878S	185.00	350.00
1879	235.00	335.00

	VG	VF
1880	235.00	335.00
1881	235.00	375.00
1882	250.00	375.00
1883	265.00	375.00
1884	450.00	700.00
1885	265.00	375.00
1886	600.00	825.00
1887	375.00	575.00
1888	350.00	550.00
1888S	30.00	45.00
1889	300.00	425.00
1890	90.00	150.00
1891	30.00	45.00
1891O	235.00	575.00
1891S	30.00	65.00

BARBER QUARTERS

The quarter, dime and half dollar introduced in 1892 bear a portrait head of Liberty instead of an entire figure. They were designed by Chief Engraver Charles E. Barber, after whom they have been named. More practical than artistically adventurous, contemporaries thought the design rather boring if not unpleasant. The reverse of the quarter and the half have a fully spread heraldic eagle, a ribbon in its beak, with a field of stars above. Barber quarters are common and well-worn examples are often regarded as little better than bullion.

Known Counterfeits: The 1913S is suspected but not confirmed. Contemporary counterfeits in a tin-lead alloy are not rare.

Type Coin Price Range	G to MS-60
1892-1916	Bullion to 215.00

	F	XF
1892	25.00	75.00
1892O	42.00	96.00
1892S	80.00	190.00
1893	28.00	75.00
1893O	30.00	100.00
1893S	63.00	165.00
1894	34.00	95.00
1894O	42.00	125.00
1894S	38.00	120.00
1895	35.00	85.00
1895O	40.00	135.00
1895S	60.00	150.00
1896	25.00	85.00
1896O	115.00	425.00
1896S	1,850.00	4,350.00
1897	25.00	80.00

	F	XF
1897O	115.00	400.00
1897S	275.00	440.00
1898	25.00	80.00
1898O	75.00	300.00
1898S	50.00	100.00
1899	25.00	80.00
1899O	35.00	135.00
1899S	75.00	145.00
1900	25.00	80.00
1900O	65.00	160.00
1900S	40.00	85.00
1901	25.00	85.00
1901O	135.00	470.00
1901S	16,500.00	28,000.00
1902	22.00	70.00
1902O	52.00	160.00
1902S	55.00	175.00
1903	22.00	70.00
1903O	42.00	125.00
1903S	50.00	145.00
1904	22.00	80.00
1904O	63.00	250.00
1905	30.00	80.00
1905O	85.00	260.00
1905S	45.00	125.00
1906	22.00	70.00
1906D	25.00	75.00
1906O	42.00	110.00
1907	22.00	66.00
1907D	30.00	85.00
1907O	22.00	70.00
1907S	50.00	175.00
1908	22.00	75.00
1908D	22.00	75.00
1908O	22.00	80.00
1908S	95.00	320.00
1909	22.00	70.00
1909D	25.00	90.00
1909O	95.00	395.00
1909S	38.00	100.00
1910	30.00	85.00
1910D	50.00	140.00
1911	22.00	80.00
1911D	100.00	350.00
1911S	55.00	175.00
1912	22.00	70.00
1912S	48.00	175.00
1913	75.00	415.00
1913D	40.00	98.00
1913S	3,950.00	6,500.00
1914	22.00	65.00
1914D	22.00	65.00
1914S	205.00	550.00
1915	22.00	66.00
1915D	22.00	66.00
1915S	37.00	120.00
1916	22.00	66.00
1916D	22.00	66.00

STANDING LIBERTY QUARTER

According to many at the time, Hermon MacNeil's Standing Liberty

Quarter was America's first "obscene" coin. Many prominent artists thought it an excellent example of inspired neo-classical art. In either case, it was hotly debated at the time. It's original version, with a bare-breasted Liberty stepping through a gateway while exposing a shield was ultimately replaced by a more modest one on which she is clad in chain mail. The corrective legislation, however, was careful not to criticize the coin's artistic merit or moral standing openly, thus not offending the Commission of Fine Arts, responsible for its approval. Technically, the coin shared with the Buffalo Nickel the problem of a high-relief date that would wear off. This was partially remedied in 1925 by carving out the area of the date and placing it in the recess. Another technical problem with this quarter was the tendency of Liberty's head to be incompletely struck. As a result, high-grade pieces with fully struck heads command a premium. Examples with the date worn off are worth only their bullion value.

Known Counterfeits: 1916 altered from 1917, 1917 Type I, 1918S 8 over 7, 1923S (altered, including all with round-topped 3), 1927S (altered), 1929.

A lead-alloy circulating counterfeit; note the dark-gray color. The extra metal near ED in UNITED is a sign of casting.

Type Coin Price Range	G to MS-60
1916-1917 Type I	22.00 to 250.00
1917-1930 Type II	Bullion to 125.00

	F	XF
1916	9,000.00	14,500.00
1917	52.00	100.00
1917D	60.00	150.00
1917S	65.00	185.00

	F	XF
1917	43.00	80.00
1917D	65.00	125.00
1917S	63.00	125.00
1918	30.00	55.00
1918D	66.00	125.00
1918S	32.00	60.00
1918S, 8 over 7	3,850.00	8,250.00
1919	55.00	85.00
1919D	195.00	600.00
1919S	185.00	540.00
1920	25.00	55.00
1920D	88.00	175.00
1920S	30.00	60.00
1921	450.00	800.00
1923	35.00	60.00
1923S	675.00	1,300.00
1924	25.00	50.00
1924D	108.00	195.00
1924S	43.00	110.00
1925	7.00	45.00
1926	6.50	40.00
1926D	20.00	75.00
1926S	12.00	110.00
1927	6.50	40.00
1927D	32.00	150.00
1927S	110.00	1,200.00
1928	6.50	40.00
1928D	8.00	45.00
1928S	6.50	40.00
1929	6.50	40.00
1929D	7.00	45.00
1929S	6.50	40.00
1930	6.50	40.00
1930S	6.50	40.00

WASHINGTON QUARTER

The Washington quarter was intended to be a one-year commemorative for the 200th anniversary of Washington's birth in 1932, not a regular issue. Its release was delayed because of the Treasury's decision to change designers from Laura Gardin Fraser to John Flanagan. Both designs were based the 1785 bust of Washington by Houdon. Eventually it was decided to replace the unpopular Standing Liberty quarter with the new commemorative, which enjoyed immense initial popularity.

Several dates in the 1930s are characterized by weak rims, making grading difficult. The 1934 and 1935 coins do not have this problem; 1964 pieces were aggressively hoarded in uncirculated rolls, and are excessively common.

A special reverse was used in 1975 and 1976 (both with 1976 obverse) to commemorate the American Bicentennial. It depicts the bust of a Colonial drummer designed by Jack L. Ahr.

Known Counterfeits: 1932D and 1932S exist with false mintmarks.

Counterfeits of high-grade 1932 and 1934 pieces also exist.

Type Coin Price Range	F to MS-65
1932-1964	Bullion to 15.00
1976	Spend to 3.50
1965-date	Spend to 1.00

	VF	BU
1932	7.50	27.00
1932D	250.00	1,100.00
1932S	250.00	525.00
1934	5.20	30.00
1934D	14.00	245.00
1935	5.00	25.00
1935D	14.00	255.00
1935S	7.50	110.00
1936	5.00	25.00
1936D	22.00	625.00
1936S	6.25	150.00
1937	5.00	26.00
1937D	6.25	70.00
1937S	15.00	160.00
1938	7.00	90.00
1938S	10.00	110.00
1939	5.00	16.00
1939D	5.50	45.00
1939S	9.00	110.00
1940	4.50	20.00
1940D	12.50	135.00
1940S	6.50	28.00
1941	—	10.00
1941D	—	35.00
1941S	—	31.00
1942	—	8.00
1942D	—	19.00
1942S	5.00	80.00
1943	—	6.50
1943D	5.00	30.00
1943S	5.00	30.00
1944	—	6.50
1944D	5.00	20.00
1944S	5.00	16.00
1945	—	6.00
1945D	5.00	19.00
1945S	—	10.00
1946	—	6.00
1946D	—	9.50
1946S	—	9.00
1947	—	11.00
1947D	—	9.50
1947S	—	9.50
1948	—	6.00
1948D	—	12.00
1948S	—	8.00
1949	6.50	38.00
1949D	—	18.00

	VF	BU
1950	—	6.50
1950D	—	6.50
1950D, D over S	65.00	295.00
1950S	—	9.50
1950S, S over D	70.00	400.00
1951	—	6.00
1951D	—	7.00
1951S	—	23.00
1952	—	6.50
1952D	—	5.50
1952S	5.00	20.00
1953	—	6.00
1953D	—	5.50
1953S	—	5.50
1954	—	6.00
1954D	—	6.00
1954S	—	5.50
1955	—	5.50
1955D	5.00	6.00
1956	—	6.00
1956D	—	5.50
1957	—	6.00
1957D	—	6.00
1958	—	5.75
1958D	—	5.25
1959	—	5.00
1959D	—	5.00
1960	—	5.00
1960D	—	5.00
1961	—	5.00
1961D	—	5.00
1962	—	5.00
1962D	—	5.00
1963	—	5.00
1963D	—	5.00
1964	—	5.00
1964D	—	5.00

CUPRO-NICKEL CLAD COPPER

	VF	BU
1965	—	1.00
1966	—	1.00
1967	—	1.00
1968	—	1.00
1968D	—	1.25
1968S *Proof only*	—	3.50
1969	—	1.25
1969D	—	1.00
1969S *Proof only*	—	3.50
1970	—	1.00
1970D	—	1.00
1970S *Proof only*	—	3.00
1971	—	1.00
1971D	—	1.00
1971S *Proof only*	—	3.00
1972	—	.75
1972D	—	.75
1972S *Proof only*	—	3.00
1973	—	.75
1973D	—	1.00
1973S *Proof only*	—	3.00
1974	—	.75

	VF	BU
1974D	—	1.00
1974S *Proof only*	—	3.00

	VF	BU
1976 Bicentennial	—	1.00
1976D Bicentennial	—	1.00
1976S Bicentennial *Proof only*	—	2.00
1976S Bicentennial Silver Clad	—	3.00
1977	—	.75
1977D	—	.75
1977S *Proof only*	—	2.00
1978	—	.75
1978D	—	.75
1978S *Proof only*	—	2.00
1979	—	.75
1979D	—	.75
1979 thick S *Proof only*	—	2.00
1979 thin S *Proof only*	—	3.00
1980P	—	.75
1980D	—	.75
1980S *Proof only*	—	2.00
1981P	—	.75
1981D	—	.75
1981S *Proof only*	—	2.00
1982P	—	3.00
1982D	—	1.50
1982S *Proof only*	—	3.00
1983P	—	3.00
1983D	—	2.00
1983S *Proof only*	—	2.75
1984P	—	1.00
1984D	—	1.25
1984S *Proof only*	—	2.75
1985P	—	1.50
1985D	—	2.00
1985S *Proof only*	—	1.75
1986P	—	3.00
1986D	—	2.00
1986S *Proof only*	—	3.00
1987P	—	.75
1987D	—	.75
1987S *Proof only*	—	2.00
1988P	—	1.00
1988D	—	1.00
1988S *Proof only*	—	2.25
1989P	—	.75
1989D	—	.75
1989S *Proof only*	—	2.25
1990P	—	.75
1990D	—	.75
1990S *Proof only*	—	6.00
1991P	—	.75
1991D	—	.75

	VF	BU
1991S *Proof only*	—	3.00
1992P	—	.75
1992D	—	.75
1992S *Proof only*	—	3.25
1992S Silver *Proof only*	—	4.00
1993P	—	.75
1993D	—	.75
1993S *Proof only*	—	3.00
1993S Silver *Proof only*	—	6.50
1994P	—	.75
1994D	—	.75
1994S *Proof only*	—	4.00
1994S Silver *Proof only*	—	12.50
1995P	—	.75
1995D	—	.75
1995S *Proof only*	—	18.00
1995S Silver *Proof only*	—	18.00
1996P	—	.75
1996D	—	.75
1996S *Proof only*	—	4.50
1996S Silver *Proof only*	—	12.50
1997P	—	.75
1997D	—	.75
1997S *Proof only*	—	11.00
1997S Silver *Proof only*	—	22.00
1998P	—	.75
1998D	—	.75
1998S *Proof only*	—	11.00
1998S Silver *Proof only*—		12.50

50 STATE QUARTERS

In 1992, to commemorate its 125th anniversary, Canada released a set of circulating commemorative quarters honoring each province and territory. They were immensely popular with the general public. Partially inspired by this Canadian series, the United States began issuing a similar set of quarters honoring the 50 states. It was the intent of Congress to "promote the diffusion of knowledge among the youth of the United States about the individual states, their history and geography, and the rich diversity of the national heritage."

Five were released from each year 1999 to 2008. Their release dates followed the order in which each state ratified the Constitution, with a new quarter appearing roughly every ten weeks. These are the only quarters issued during this period. None with the eagle reverse were produced at all. The designs meet certain federal criteria, but were designed and submitted at the state level.

In addition to clad circulation strikes, special silver and clad proof coins are being produced for collectors, much as they have been in previous years.

Known Counterfeits: Apparently risqué designs are actually satirical tokens

struck with privately made dies on real quarters.

	BU	PF
1999P Delaware	—	1.50
1999D Delaware	—	1.50
1999S Delaware *Proof only*	—	15.00
1999S Delaware Silver *Proof only*	—	65.00

	BU	PF
1999P Pennsylvania	—	1.50
1999D Pennsylvania	—	1.50
1999S Pennsylvania *Proof only*	—	15.00
1999S Pennsylvania Silver *Proof only*	—	65.00
1999P New Jersey	—	1.50
1999D New Jersey	—	1.50
1999S New Jersey *Proof only*	—	15.00
1999S New Jersey Silver *Proof only*	—	65.00

	BU	PF
1999P Georgia	—	1.50
1999D Georgia	—	1.50
1999S Georgia *Proof only*	—	15.00
1999S Georgia Silver *Proof only*	—	65.00

	BU	PF
1999P Connecticut	—	.75
1999D Connecticut	—	.75
1999S Connecticut *Proof only*	—	15.00
1999S Connecticut Silver *Proof only*	—	65.00

	BU	PF
2000P Massachusetts	—	.75
2000D Massachusetts	—	.75
2000S Massachusetts *Proof only*	—	5.00
2000S Massachusetts Silver *Proof only*	—	10.00
2000P Maryland	—	.75
2000D Maryland	—	.75
2000S Maryland *Proof only*	—	5.00
2000S Maryland Silver *Proof only*	—	10.00

	BU	PF
2000P South Carolina	—	.75
2000D South Carolina	—	.75
2000S South Carolina *Proof only*	—	5.00
2000S South Carolina Silver *Proof only*	—	10.00
2000P New Hampshire	—	.75
2000D New Hampshire	—	.75
2000S New Hampshire *Proof only*	—	5.00
2000S New Hampshire Silver *Proof only*	—	10.00

	BU	PF
2000P Virginia	—	.75
2000D Virginia	—	.75
2000S Virginia *Proof only*	—	5.00
2000S Virginia Silver Proof only	—	10.00
2001P New York	—	.75
2001D New York	—	.75

	BU	PF
2001S New York Proof only	—	9.50
2001S New York Silver Proof only	—	22.50

	BU	PF
2001P North Carolina	—	.75
2001D North Carolina	—	.75
2001S North Carolina *Proof only*	—	9.50
2001S North Carolina Silver *Proof only*	—	22.50
2001P Rhode Island	—	.75
2001D Rhode Island	—	.75
2001S Rhode Island *Proof only*	—	9.50
2001S Rhode Island Silver *Proof only*	—	22.50

	BU	PF
2001P Vermont	—	1.00
2001D Vermont	—	.75
2001S Vermont *Proof only*	—	9.50
2001S Vermont Silver *Proof only*	—	22.50
2001P Kentucky	—	1.00
2001D Kentucky	—	.75
2001S Kentucky *Proof only*	—	9.50
2001S Kentucky Silver *Proof only*	—	22.50

	BU	PF
2002P Tennessee	—	1.75
2002D Tennessee	—	1.75
2002S Tennessee *Proof only*	—	6.00
2002S Tennessee Silver *Proof only*	—	11.00
2002P Ohio	—	.75

	BU	PF
2002D Ohio	—	.75
2002S Ohio *Proof only*	—	6.00
2002S Ohio Silver *Proof only*	—	11.00

	BU	PF
2002P Louisiana	—	.75
2002D Louisiana	—	.75
2002S Louisiana *Proof only*	—	6.00
2002S Louisiana Silver *Proof only*	—	11.00
2002P Indiana	—	.75
2002D Indiana	—	.75
2002S Indiana *Proof only*	—	6.00
2002S Indiana Silver *Proof only*	—	11.00

	BU	PF
2002P Mississippi	—	.75
2002D Mississippi	—	.75
2002S Mississippi *Proof only*	—	6.00
2002S Mississippi Silver *Proof only*	—	11.00
2003P Illinois	—	.75
2003D Illinois	—	.75
2003S Illinois *Proof only*	—	4.00
2003S Illinois Silver Proof only	—	6.00

	BU	PF
2003P Alabama	—	.75
2003D Alabama	—	.75
2003S Alabama *Proof only*	—	4.00
2003S Alabama Silver *Proof only*	—	6.00
2003P Maine	—	.75
2003D Maine	—	.75

	BU	PF
2003S Maine *Proof only*	—	4.00
2003S Maine Silver *Proof only*	—	6.00

	BU	PF
2003P Missouri	—	.75
2003D Missouri	—	.75
2003S Missouri *Proof only*	—	4.00
2003S Missouri Silver *Proof only*	—	6.00
2003P Arkansas	—	.75
2003D Arkansas	—	.75
2003S Arkansas *Proof only*	—	4.00
2003S Arkansas Silver *Proof only*	—	6.00

	BU	PF
2004P Michigan	—	.75
2004D Michigan	—	.75
2004S Michigan *Proof only*	—	5.00
2004S Michigan Silver *Proof only*	—	6.00
2004P Florida	—	.75
2004D Florida	—	.75
2004S Florida *Proof only*	—	5.00
2004S Florida Silver *Proof only*	—	6.00

	BU	PF
2004P Texas	—	.75
2004D Texas	—	.75
2004S Texas *Proof only*	—	5.00
2004S Texas Silver *Proof only*	—	6.00
2004P Iowa	—	.75
2004D Iowa	—	.75
2004S Iowa *Proof only*	—	5.00

	BU	PF
2004S Iowa Silver *Proof only*	—	6.00

	BU	PF
2004P Wisconsin	—	.75
2004D Wisconsin	—	.75
2004D Wisconsin, extra leaf (2 var.)	—	225.00
2004S Wisconsin *Proof only*	—	5.00
2004S Wisconsin Silver *Proof only*	—	6.00
2005P California	—	1.00
2005D California	—	1.00
2005S California *Proof only*	—	3.00
2005S California Silver *Proof only*	—	6.00

	BU	PF
2005P Minnesota	—	1.00
2005D Minnesota	—	1.00
2005S Minnesota *Proof only*	—	3.00
2005S Minnesota Silver Proof only	—	6.00
2005P Oregon	—	1.00
2005D Oregon	—	1.00
2005S Oregon Proof only	—	3.00
2005S Oregon Silver Proof only	—	6.00

	BU	PF
2005P Kansas	—	1.00
2005D Kansas	—	1.00
2005S Kansas *Proof only*	—	3.00
2005S Kansas Silver *Proof only*	—	6.00
2005P West Virginia	—	1.00
2005D West Virginia	—	1.00

	BU	PF
2005S West Virginia *Proof only*	—	3.00
2005S West Virginia Silver Proof only	—	6.00

	BU	PF
2006P Nevada	—	1.00
2006D Nevada	—	1.00
2006S Nevada *Proof only*	—	4.00
2006S Nevada Silver *Proof only*	—	6.00
2006P Nebraska	—	1.00
2006D Nebraska	—	1.00
2006S Nebraska *Proof only*	—	4.00
2006S Nebraska Silver *Proof only*	—	6.00

	BU	PF
2006P Colorado	—	1.00
2006D Colorado	—	1.00
2006S Colorado *Proof only*	—	4.00
2006S Colorado Silver *Proof only*	—	6.00
2006P North Dakota	—	1.00
2006D North Dakota	—	1.00
2006S North Dakota *Proof only*	—	4.00
2006S North Dakota Silver *Proof only*	—	6.00

	BU	PF
2006P South Dakota	—	1.00
2006D South Dakota	—	1.00
2006S South Dakota *Proof only*	—	4.00
2006S South Dakota Silver *Proof only*	—	6.00
2007P Montana	—	1.00
2007D Montana	—	1.00

	BU	PF
2007S Montana *Proof only*	—	4.00
2007S Montana Silver *Proof only*	—	6.00

	BU	PF
2007P Washington	—	1.00
2007D Washington	—	1.00
2007S Washington *Proof only*	—	4.00
2007S Washington Silver *Proof only*	—	6.00
2007P Idaho	—	1.00
2007D Idaho	—	1.00
2007S Idaho *Proof only*	—	4.00
2007S Idaho Silver *Proof only*	—	6.00

	BU	PF
2007P Wyoming	—	1.00
2007D Wyoming	—	1.00
2007S Wyoming *Proof only*	—	4.00
2007S Wyoming Silver *Proof only*	—	6.00
2007P Utah	—	1.00
2007D Utah	—	1.00
2007S Utah *Proof only*	—	4.00
2007S Utah Silver *Proof only*	—	6.00

	BU	PF
2008P Oklahoma	—	1.00
2008D Oklahoma	—	1.00
2008S Oklahoma *Proof only*	—	4.50
2008S Oklahoma Silver *Proof only*	—	6.50
2008P New Mexico	—	1.00
2008D New Mexico	—	1.00
2008S New Mexico *Proof only*	—	4.50

	BU	PF
2008S New Mexico Silver *Proof only*	—	6.50

	BU	PF
2008P Arizona	—	1.00
2008D Arizona	—	1.00
2008S Arizona *Proof only*	—	4.50
2008S Arizona Silver *Proof only*	—	6.50
2008P Alaska	—	1.00
2008D Alaska	—	1.00
2008S Alaska *Proof only*	—	4.50
2008S Alaska Silver *Proof only*	—	6.50

	BU	PF
2008P Hawaii	—	1.00
2008D Hawaii	—	1.00
2008S Hawaii *Proof only*	—	4.50
2008S Hawaii Silver *Proof only*	—	6.50

EARLY HALF DOLLARS

The half dollar, along with the half dime and dollar, was one of the first silver denominations to be released by the new United States Mint. As a result, it first appeared with the briefly used flowing-hair design. These first rare pieces were struck on blanks with crude edges and often exhibit "adjustment marks" from filing off excess silver before striking. The initial reverse design showing a rather skinny eagle within a wreath continued to be used after the flowing-hair obverse was replaced by the rather voluptuous draped bust design. After a brief gap in the issue of halves, the first eagle was replaced with a plumper eagle carrying a heraldic shield. In 1807 a cap was added to Liberty's head and her bust was turned to the left. In the same year a denomination first appeared, not as "half dollar" but "50C." The eagle was also made slightly more

realistic, though it still bore a heraldic shield. With the introduction of this type, production began to increase. By about 1815, halves became so common that banks began to use them as cash reserves to back up their own privately issued paper money. As a result many half dollars made between 1807 and 1839 can be found well preserved. Unfortunately, their high relief caused many of them to be incompletely struck, particularly at the motto over the eagle, and the broach. In 1836 new machinery was introduced and the edges were changed from lettered to reeded.

Rare die combinations of early specimens command a premium from specialists. Cleaning plagues this series, and such pieces are discounted.

Known Counterfeits: Cast counterfeits exist of 1796. Other counterfeits of 1794 to 1802 are possible. Contemporary counterfeits of capped bust halves exist for most dates. They have been struck or cast in brass, copper, tin-lead alloys and German silver. Holed coins are sometimes deceptively plugged.

Type Coin Price Range	G to MS-60
1794-1795	950.00 to 37,000.00
1796-1797	35,000.00 to 265,000.00
1801-1807	175.00 to 8,500.00
1807-1836 lettered	57.50 to 975.00
1836-1839 reeded	60.00 to 1,000.00

FLOWING HAIR TYPE

	VG	VF
1794	6,500.00	19,500.00
1795 two leaves	1,500.00	4,000.00
1795 three leaves	3,000.00	9,900.00

DRAPED BUST / SMALL EAGLE

	VG	VF
1796, 15 stars	39,500.00	87,000.00
1796, 16 stars	48,000.00	90,000.00
1797	39,500.00	87,000.00

DRAPED BUST / HERALDIC EAGLE

	VG	VF
1801	1,200.00	3,950.00
1802	1,100.00	3,900.00
1803 Small 3	270.00	1,100.00
1803 Large 3	240.00	900.00
1805, 5 over 4	325.00	1,200.00
1805	240.00	550.00
1806, 6 over 5	240.00	525.00
1806	240.00	525.00

Note: many varieties of 1806 exist.

	VG	VF
1807	240.00	525.00

CAPPED BUST / LETTERED EDGE

	VG	VF
1807 Small stars	175.00	550.00
1807 Large stars	165.00	475.00
1807, 50 over 20	125.00	350.00
1808, 8 over 7	110.00	250.00
1808	85.00	140.00
1809	85.00	140.00
1810	85.00	140.00
1811, 11 over 10	95.00	155.00
1811	85.00	125.00
1812, 2 over 1, small 8,	90.00	195.00
1812, 2 over 1, large 8,	1,900.00	4,800.00
1812	83.00	130.00
1813	83.00	130.00
1813, 50 C over inverted UNI	95.00	185.00
1814, 4 over 3	135.00	290.00
1814	83.00	130.00
1815, 5 over 2	1,500.00	2,900.00
1817, 7 over 3	185.00	515.00
1817, 7 over 4	80,000.00	200,000.00
1817	83.00	130.00
1818, 8 over 7	100.00	140.00
1818	80.00	115.00
1819, 9 over 8	80.00	120.00
1819	80.00	115.00
1820, 20 over 19	110.00	200.00
1820	80.00	145.00
1821	80.00	115.00
1822, 2 over 1	90.00	190.00
1822	80.00	115.00
1823	80.00	110.00
1824, 4 over 1	80.00	115.00
1824, 4 over 4	80.00	115.00
1824	80.00	115.00
1825	80.00	115.00
1826	80.00	115.00
1827, 7 over 6	100.00	160.00
1827	80.00	115.00

	VG	VF
1828	80.00	115.00

Note: date varieties of 1828 exist.

	VG	VF
1829, 9 over 7	85.00	175.00
1829	75.00	90.00
1830	70.00	90.00
1831	70.00	90.00
1832	70.00	90.00
1833	70.00	90.00
1834	70.00	90.00
1835	70.00	90.00
1836	70.00	90.00
1836, 50 over 00	100.00	195.00

CAPPED BUST / REEDED EDGE

	VG	VF
1836 50 CENTS	1,200.00	2,100.00
1837 50 CENTS	75.00	125.00
1838 HALF DOL	75.00	125.00
	VG	VF
1838O *Proof only*	AU = 300,000.00	
1839 HALF DOL	75.00	150.00
1839O HALF DOL	320.00	675.00

SEATED LIBERTY HALF DOLLARS

Following the introduction of the Seated Liberty design by Christian Gobrecht on the silver dollar, the smaller coins were gradually brought into harmony with this design. The half dollar was the last to make the change. It is generally accepted that the seated goddess version of Liberty was directly or indirectly inspired by depictions of the Roman allegory of Britannia on British coins. The eagle on the reverse is not significantly different from that on the last capped-bust coins.

There were several minor changes over the life of this coin. During its first year, additional drapery was added below Liberty's elbow. The arrows by the date from 1853 to 1855, and the rays on

the reverse in 1853, indicate a 7 percent reduction in weight; arrows in 1873 and 1874 a minuscule increase. Most of the 1861O pieces were struck after Louisiana seceded from the Union. A ribbon with the motto "In God We Trust" was added over the eagle in 1866. Seated halves are often found cleaned. Be careful of re-toned specimens.

Known Counterfeits: Genuine 1858O halves have been re-engraved to pass as 1853O no-arrows pieces. Some "with arrows" pieces have had the arrows removed for the same reason. Contemporary counterfeits struck in tin and lead alloys are often found.

Type Coin Price Range	G to MS-60
1839-1866	28.00 to 500.00
1853 arrows and rays	28.00 to 1,700.00
1854-55 arrows	28.00 to 600.00
1873-1874 arrows	30.00 to 900.00
1866-1891	28.00 to 375.00

NO MOTTO ABOVE EAGLE

	VG	VF
1839 No drapery below elbow	85.00	340.00
1839 With drapery	45.00	88.00
1840 Sm. rev. letters	45.00	85.00
1840 Med. rev. letters (struck at New Orleans with 1838 reverse die)	175.00	325.00
1840O	45.00	90.00
1841	65.00	150.00
1841O	40.00	90.00
1842 Small date	50.00	110.00
1842 Large date	45.00	90.00
1842O Small date	850.00	2,350.00
1842O Large date	40.00	90.00
1843	40.00	70.00
1843O	40.00	70.00
1844	40.00	70.00
1844O	40.00	70.00

	VG	VF
1844O Double date	775.00	1,375.00
1845	40.00	110.00
1845O	40.00	70.00
1845O No Drapery	47.00	115.00
1846	40.00	70.00
1846, 6 over horizontal 6	250.00	435.00
1846O, Med. date	40.00	70.00
1846O, Tall date	285.00	620.00
1847, 7 over 6	2,700.00	5,200.00
1847	45.00	70.00
1847O	40.00	70.00
1848	65.00	190.00
1848O	40.00	70.00
1849	45.00	80.00
1849O	40.00	70.00
1850	320.00	560.00
1850O	40.00	80.00
1851	425.00	800.00
1851O	55.00	120.00
1852	500.00	925.00
1852O	125.00	350.00
1853O no arrows	154,000.00	Rare

ARROWS AT DATE/RAYS ON REVERSE

	VG	VF
1853	35.00	98.00
1853O	35.00	135.00

ARROWS AT DATE / NO RAYS

	VG	VF
1854	38.00	70.00
1854O	38.00	70.00
1855 over 1854	85.00	275.00
1855	40.00	75.00
1855O	38.00	70.00
1855S	500.00	1,500.00

ARROWS REMOVED

	VG	VF
1856	38.00	70.00
1856O	38.00	70.00
1856S	98.00	280.00
1857	38.00	70.00
1857O	38.00	70.00
1857S	115.00	290.00
1858	38.00	70.00
1858O	38.00	70.00
1858S	45.00	115.00
1859	38.00	70.00
1859O	38.00	70.00
1859S	40.00	115.00
1860	40.00	90.00
1860O	38.00	70.00
1860S	38.00	75.00
1861	38.00	70.00
1861O	38.00	70.00
1861S	40.00	70.00
1862	50.00	130.00
1862S	38.00	70.00
1863	45.00	80.00
1863S	40.00	70.00
1864	45.00	110.00
1864S	38.00	70.00
1865	45.00	90.00
1865S	38.00	70.00
1866	Unique	
1866S	325.00	800.00

MOTTO ABOVE EAGLE

	VG	VF
1866	40.00	75.00
1866S	38.00	70.00
1867	48.00	120.00
1867S	40.00	70.00
1868	60.00	195.00
1868S	40.00	70.00
1869	40.00	70.00
1869S	42.00	70.00
1870	40.00	75.00
1870CC	1,600.00	5,500.00
1870S	40.00	75.00
1871	40.00	70.00
1871CC	325.00	1,200.00
1871S	40.00	70.00
1872	40.00	70.00
1872CC	125.00	450.00
1872S	45.00	135.00
1873 Closed 3	45.00	120.00
1873 Open	33,500.00	5,900.00
1873CC	320.00	900.00
1873S	No Known Specimens	

ARROWS AT DATE

	VG	VF
1873	50.00	110.00
1873CC	275.00	925.00
1873S	80.00	265.00
1874	45.00	110.00
1874CC	575.00	1,800.00
1874S	60.00	220.00

ARROWS REMOVED

	VG	VF
1875	38.00	70.00
1875CC	56.00	120.00
1875S	38.00	70.00
1876	38.00	70.00
1876CC	55.00	115.00
1876S	38.00	70.00
1877	38.00	70.00
1877CC	55.00	115.00
1877S	38.00	70.00
1878	45.00	90.00
1878CC	600.00	1,550.00
1878S	35,000.00	44,000.00
1879	325.00	450.00
1880	325.00	450.00
1881	300.00	400.00
1882	400.00	500.00
1883	350.00	460.00
1884	420.00	540.00
1885	425.00	550.00
1886	500.00	725.00
1887	600.00	800.00
1888	325.00	425.00
1889	325.00	425.00
1890	325.00	430.00
1891	65.00	130.00

BARBER HALF DOLLARS

The half dollar, quarter, and dime introduced in 1892 bear a portrait of Liberty's head, instead of an entire figure. They were designed by Chief Engraver Charles E. Barber, after whom they have been named. More practical than artistically adventurous, contemporaries thought the design rather boring if not unpleasant. The reverse of the half and the quarter have a fully spread heraldic eagle, a ribbon in its beak, with a field of stars above. This new design for the half dollar came only a year following its resurrection as an actively minted denomination. Barbers are common and well-worn examples are often regarded as little better than bullion. Strong middle grades on the other hand are surprisingly difficult to obtain.

Known Counterfeits: Contemporary counterfeits in a tin-lead alloy are not rare. Altered 1913, 1914 and 1915 coins exist with mintmarks removed.

Type Coin Price Range	G to MS-60
1892-1916	11.00 to 475.00

	VG	VF
1892	42.00	125.00
1892O	400.00	590.00
1892S	325.00	550.00
1893	30.00	135.00
1893O	60.00	225.00
1893S	225.00	550.00
1894	50.00	200.00
1894O	31.00	175.00
1894S	28.00	125.00
1895	25.00	150.00
1895O	38.00	230.00
1895S	55.00	250.00
1896	28.00	155.00
1896O	55.00	300.00
1896S	135.00	350.00
1897	15.00	100.00
1897O	230.00	850.00
1897S	200.00	550.00
1898	15.00	96.00
1898O	75.00	355.00
1898S	50.00	175.00
1899	15.00	100.00
1899O	36.00	175.00
1899S	33.00	150.00
1900	16.00	96.00
1900O	23.00	175.00
1900S	19.00	100.00
1901	16.00	96.00
1901O	28.00	205.00
1901S	55.00	355.00

	VG	VF
1902	14.00	90.00
1902O	17.00	110.00
1902S	19.00	150.00
1903	16.00	125.00
1903O	17.00	125.00
1903S	18.00	125.00
1904	14.00	90.00
1904O	33.00	225.00
1904S	70.00	550.00
1905	28.00	180.00
1905O	50.00	250.00
1905S	17.00	125.00
1906	15.00	90.00
1906D	14.00	100.00
1906O	14.00	110.00
1906S	16.00	120.00
1907	14.00	90.00
1907D	14.00	85.00
1907O	14.00	100.00
1907S	22.00	175.00
1908	14.00	90.00
1908D	14.00	90.00
1908O	14.00	100.00
1908S	25.00	175.00
1909	16.00	100.00
1909O	23.00	140.00
1909S	14.00	100.00
1910	29.00	175.00
1910S	17.00	100.00
1911	14.00	90.00
1911D	16.00	100.00
1911S	17.00	100.00
1912	14.00	90.00
1912D	14.00	90.00
1912S	20.00	100.00
1913	75.00	420.00
1913D	20.00	100.00
1913S	25.00	120.00
1914	170.00	550.00
1914S	19.00	100.00
1915	165.00	380.00
1915D	14.00	85.00
1915S	20.00	100.00

WALKING LIBERTY HALF DOLLAR

This artistic half dollar was designed by Adolph Weinman, the designer of the Mercury dime released in the same year. It depicts Liberty, the American flag draped about her and flowing in the breeze, progressing towards the dawn of a new day. It was received with wide acclaim for its artistic merit when it was first released as part of a program for the beautification of United States coinage. The reverse carries an eagle perched on a rocky crag. The obverse design proved so popular that it was resurrected in 1986 for use on the new silver one-ounce bullion coins. Originally, the mintmarks on this coin appeared on the obverse, but after a matter of months they were moved to the reverse.

Due to the arrangement of the design, Liberty's head does not always strike up fully. High-grade examples with fully struck heads are worth more.

Known Counterfeits: 1916S, 1938D coins with added mintmark exist; 1928D halves are all counterfeit.

Type Coin Price Range	G to MS-63
1916-1947	Bullion to 45.00

	F	XF
1916	110.00	275.00
1916D	90.00	250.00
1916S	300.00	700.00
1917	11.00	50.00
1917D Obv.	90.00	240.00
1917D Rev.	50.00	300.00
1917S Obv.	150.00	750.00
1917S Rev.	18.00	70.00
1918	18.00	170.00
1918D	38.00	250.00
1918S	17.00	70.00
1919	85.00	575.00
1919D	110.00	850.00
1919S	85.00	990.00
1920	18.00	80.00
1920D	75.00	500.00
1920S	22.00	260.00
1921	375.00	1,750.00
1921D	600.00	2,300.00
1921S	250.00	5,200.00
1923S	30.00	350.00
1927S	15.00	185.00
1928S	16.50	210.00
1929D	19.00	115.00
1929S	13.50	125.00
1933S	13.50	68.00
1934	10.00	14.00
1934D	10.00	35.00
1934S	10.00	30.00
1935	—	10.00

	F	XF
1935D	—	31.00
1935S	—	29.00
1936	—	10.00
1936D	—	20.00
1936S	—	22.00
1937	—	10.00
1937D	—	34.00
1937S	—	25.00
1938	—	11.00
1938D	180.00	240.00
1939	—	10.00
1939D	—	10.00
1939S	—	24.00
1940	—	10.00
1940S	—	11.00
1941	—	10.00
1941D	—	10.00
1941S	—	10.00
1942	—	10.00
1942D	—	10.00
1942D, D over S	45.00	85.00
1942S	—	10.00
1943	—	10.00
1943D	—	10.00
1943S	—	10.00
1944	—	10.00
1944D	—	10.00
1944S	—	10.00
1945	—	10.00
1945D	—	10.00
1945S	—	10.00
1946	—	10.00
1946D	—	23.00
1946S	—	10.00
1947	—	10.00
1947D	—	12.50

FRANKLIN HALF DOLLAR

Like the design for the Washington Quarter, the design for the Franklin Half Dollar was used in opposition to the recommendation of the Commission of Fine Arts. The reverse depicts the Liberty Bell as its prime motif, despite a law requiring all coins larger than a dime to bear an eagle. This is why a small eagle was added at the side of the bell as an afterthought. While the coin was designed by Chief Engraver John R. Sinnock, the minute eagle was actually engraved by a young Frank Gasparro, who went on to become the mint's chief engraver from 1965-1981.

The biggest striking problem of the Franklin Half Dollar is the horizontal lines on the Liberty Bell. Those mint-state examples with fully struck bell lines often sell for significantly more.

Known Counterfeits: None are known.

Type Coin Price Range   **VF to MS-65**
1948-1963   **Bullion to 55.00**

	XF	BU
1948	**10.00**	**17.00**
1948D	**10.00**	**17.00**
1949	**10.00**	**40.00**
1949D	**15.00**	**45.00**
1949S	**20.00**	**65.00**
1950	**10.00**	**27.00**
1950D	**10.00**	**23.00**
1951	—	**12.00**
1951D	**14.00**	**28.00**
1951S	**12.00**	**24.00**
1952	—	**12.00**
1952D	—	**12.00**
1952S	**21.00**	**50.00**
1953	**11.00**	**25.00**
1953D	—	**12.00**
1953S	—	**26.00**
1954	—	**12.00**
1954D	—	**12.00**
1954S	—	**15.00**
1955	**19.00**	**30.00**
1955 Bugs Bunny Teeth	—	**28.00**
1956	**10.00**	**13.00**
1957	—	**12.00**
1957D	—	**12.00**
1958	—	**12.00**
1958D	—	**12.00**
1959	—	**12.00**
1959D	—	**12.00**
1960	—	**12.00**
1960D	—	**12.00**
1961	—	**12.00**
1961D	—	**12.00**
1962	—	**12.00**
1962D	—	**12.00**
1963	—	**12.00**
1963D	—	**12.00**

KENNEDY HALF DOLLAR

Only three days had elapsed between the assassination of President John F. Kennedy on Nov. 22, 1963, and the first notice from the director of the mint to the chief engraver to prepare for the issue of a coin bearing his portrait. Gilroy Roberts fashioned its obverse portrait based on the Kennedy inaugural medal to save time. The reverse is Frank Gasparro's rendition of the presidential seal. Remarkably, working dies were ready by Jan. 2, 1964. Kennedy halves have been struck in three different compositions. The 1964 issue was struck in the traditional 90 percent silver alloy. The following year when dimes and quarters were changed to cupronickel-clad copper, the half dollar was preserved as a silver-alloy coin by striking it in a silver-clad version containing 80 percent silver in its outer layers, and 21 percent silver in its middle layer. The remaining alloy was copper. Finally silver was abandoned in 1971, and only sporadic collector issues have been struck in that metal since. Circulation issues are now struck in the same clad composition as dimes and quarters. Coins dated 1970D, 1987P and 1987D were not issued to circulation, but are widely available from broken-up mint sets.

A special reverse was used in 1975 and 1976 (both with 1976 obverse) to commemorate the American Bicentennial. Designed by Seth G. Huntington, it depicts Independence Hall in Philadelphia.

Known Counterfeits: None are known.

Type Coin Price Range	**XF to MS-65**
1964	**Bullion to 20.00**
1965-70	**Bullion to 14.00**
1971-date	**Spend to 5.00**
1976	**Spend to 8.00**

	BU
1964	**9.00**
1964D	**9.00**

SILVER CLAD

1965	**4.50**
1966	**4.50**
1967	**4.50**
1968D	**4.50**
1968S *Proof only*	**7.00**
1969D	**4.50**
1969S *Proof only*	**7.00**
1970D	**13.00**
1970S *Proof only*	**19.50**

CUPRONICKEL-CLAD COPPER

	BU
1971	**2.00**
1971D	**2.00**
1971S Proof only	**5.00**
1972	**2.00**
1972D	**2.00**
1972S Proof only	**5.50**
1973	**2.00**
1973D	**2.00**
1973S Proof only	**5.50**
1974	**2.00**
1974D	**2.00**
1974S Proof only	**4.00**

BICENTENNIAL REVERSE

	BU
1976 Bicentennial	**2.00**
1976D Bicentennial	**2.00**
1976S Bicentennial *Proof only*	**5.00**
1976S Bicentennial Silver Clad	**4.50**

REGULAR ISSUE CONTINUED

	BU
1977	**2.00**
1977D	**2.00**
1977S *Proof only*	**4.50**
1978	**4.00**
1978D	**4.00**

	BU		BU
1978S Proof only	3.00	1997D	2.00
1979	2.00	1997S Proof only	26.00
1979D	2.00	1997S Silver Proof only	95.00
1979 Filled S Proof only	3.00	1998P	2.00
1979 Clear S Proof only	18.50	1998D	2.00
1980P	2.00	1998S Proof only	15.00
1980D	2.00	1998S Matte Proof only	350.00
1980S Proof only	2.50	1998S Silver Proof only	30.00
1981P	2.00	1999P	2.25
1981D	2.00	1999D	2.25
1981S Proof only	2.50	1999S Proof only	18.00
1982P	3.50	1999S Silver Proof only	35.00
1982D	3.50	2000P	2.50
1982S Proof only	3.00	2000D	2.50
1983P	3.50	2000S Proof only	5.00
1983D	3.50	2000S Silver Proof only	12.50
1983S Proof only	3.00	2001P	2.50
1984P	3.00	2001D	2.50
1984D	3.00	2001S Proof only	10.00
1984S Proof only	3.50	2001S Silver Proof only	18.50
1985P	3.00	2002P	3.00
1985D	3.00	2002D	3.00
1985S Proof only	4.00	2002S Proof only	10.00
1986P	3.50	2002S Silver Proof only	13.50
1986D	3.50	2003P	2.50
1986S Proof only	7.50	2003D	2.50
1987P	4.00	2003S Proof only	7.00
1987D	4.00	2003S Silver Proof only	12.50
1987S Proof only	4.00	2004P	2.00
1988P	3.50	2004D	2.00
1988D	3.50	2004S Proof only	12.00
1988S Proof only	6.50	2004S Silver Proof only	11.00
1989P	2.50	2005P	2.00
1989D	2.50	2005D	2.00
1989S Proof only	7.00	2005S Proof only	9.50
1990P	3.00	2005S Silver Proof only	12.50
1990D	3.00	2006P	2.00
1990S Proof only	5.00	2006D	2.00
1991P	3.50	2006S Proof only	7.00
1991D	3.50	2006S Silver Proof only	12.50
1991S Proof only	11.50	2007P	2.00
1992P	2.50	2007D	2.00
1992D	3.50	2007S Proof only	7.00
1992S Proof only	7.50	2007S Silver Proof only	12.50
1992S Silver Proof only	15.00	2008P	2.50
1993P	3.00	2008D	2.50
1993D	4.00	2008S Proof only	7.50
1993S Proof only	14.00	2008S Silver Proof only	13.50
1993S Silver Proof only	27.00		
1994P	2.00		
1994D	2.00		
1994S Proof only	9.00		
1994S Silver Proof only	35.00		
1995P	2.00		
1995D	2.00		
1995S Proof only	45.00		
1995S Silver Proof only	100.00		
1996P	2.00		
1996D	2.00		
1996S Proof only	10.50		
1996S Silver Proof only	50.00		
1997P	2.00		

EARLY SILVER DOLLARS

The first American silver dollar was intended to fill the same role in commerce as the old Spanish colonial milled dollar. The dollar, along with the half dollar and half dime, was one of the first silver denominations to be released by the new United States Mint. As a result, it first appeared with the briefly used flowing-hair design. These first rare pieces were struck in 1794 and 1795 on crude blanks, often exhibiting "adjustment marks" from the filing off of excess silver before striking. While considered part of the manufacturing process, these marks nevertheless reduce the value of a specimen. The initial reverse design, showing a rather skinny eagle within a wreath, continued to be used after the flowing-hair obverse was replaced by the rather voluptuous draped bust design. After four years of use the first eagle was replaced with a plumper eagle carrying a heraldic shield.

As with the smaller denominations, the government's lack of bullion and skilled labor made it impossible to strike enough pieces to have a significant role in the economy. Another complication soon ended the life of the silver dollar altogether. The average silver content of these coins slightly exceeded that of the Spanish dollar, though it was exchangeable for them at par. Most of them were thus exported and melted, worn Spanish dollars being shipped back in their place. Not willing to change the dollar's specifications, the government simply ceased to strike it for 30 years. During the last year they were struck for circulation, 1804, only old dies, probably dated 1803 were used. In the 1830s, when a few dollars were needed as gifts for foreign heads of state, the mint struck bust dollars appearing as the 1804 dollars *would* have looked like if they had borne that date. These exceedingly rare "1804" dollars have become among the most famous United States coins. A small number were also restruck somewhat later for collectors.

Rare die combinations of early coins can command a premium from specialists.

Known Counterfeits: It is likely that all dates of early dollars have been counterfeited. Some of the cruder counterfeits can be easily distinguished by the plain or reeded edges they have, as opposed to the lettered edges of the authentic pieces. Other counterfeits are more deceptive. A false 1794 is known re-engraved from a real 1795. A great many

counterfeit 1804s exist. Holed coins are sometimes deceptively plugged. Cleaning is a frequent problem, both on real and counterfeit pieces. On the latter it can sometimes make authentication more difficult.

Type Coin Price Range	G to MS-60
1794-95 Flowing Hair	1,550.00 to 46,500.00
1795-98 Small Eagle	1,300.00 to 35,000.00
1798-1804 Heraldic Eagle	875.00 to 19,000.00

FLOWING HAIR TYPE

	VG	VF
1794	90,000.00	160,000.00
1795	19,000.00	5,600.00

DRAPED BUST / SMALL EAGLE

	VG	VF
1795	1,750.00	4,650.00
1796	1,750.00	4,800.00
1797 9 & 7 stars, Small letters	2,750.00	8,000.00
1797 9 & 7 stars, Large letters	1,825.00	5,200.00
1797 10 stars l. & 6 stars r.	1,775.00	4,700.00
1798 15 stars	2,150.00	5,800.00
1798 13 stars	1,650.00	4,900.00

DRAPED BUST /HERALDIC EAGLE

	VG	VF
1798	1,000.00	2,450.00
1799, 9 over 8, 15 stars	1,100.00	2,800.00
1799, 9 over 8, 13 stars	1,100.00	2,850.00
1799	975.00	2,400.00
1799 8 stars l. & 5 stars r.	1,200.00	3,000.00
1800	975.00	2,400.00
1801	1,100.00	2,800.00
1802, 2 over 1	1,100.00	2,800.00
1802	1,050.00	2,700.00
1802 *Proof Restrike*	—	250,000.00
1803	1,050.00	2,500.00
1803 *Proof Restrike*	—	250,000.00
1804 (struck 1834-35) *Proof*	—	4,100,000.00
1804 (struck 1859) *Proof*	—	1,200,000.00

GOBRECHT DOLLARS

It is ironic that the coin for which the Seated Liberty design was first prepared was the last to have it actually appear

on pieces actively struck for circulation. It was the intent, when the striking of silver dollars was resumed, that a design of exceptional artistic merit be used. For this reason, Christian Gobrecht was asked to prepare dies based on a drawing of Liberty seated by artist Thomas Sully. It is generally accepted that his seated goddess concept of Liberty derives from depictions of the Roman allegory of Britannia on British coins. The reverse design was also a radical departure from the staid old heraldic eagle. The new eagle was seen in the realistic attitude of flight. It was prepared by Gobrecht based on a drawing of "Old Pete" by the famous artist, Titian Peale. Old Pete was an eagle who lived at the mint circa 1830-36 and who met an unfortunate end, getting caught in the machinery. While Gobrecht dollars are not all patterns, very few were ever struck for circulation, never more than 1,000 or so of any one variety. Only circulating issues are listed here. Pattern pieces with the engraver's name in the field (as opposed to on the base), as well as 1838 issues, are listed in that section. Later some were restruck for collectors. These can usually be distinguished by the misaligned dies that make the eagle appear to be flying horizontally when the coin is turned around. Originals have the eagle flying slightly upward.

Known Counterfeits: Gobrecht experimental dollars are less counterfeited than other early dollars. Cleaning and polishing are problems, however.

STARS ON REVERSE

	VF	EF
1836 (coin alignment)	8,500.00	12,000.00
1836 (struck 1837, medal alignment)	8,500.00	12,000.00

STARS ON OBVERSE

	VF	EF
1839	15,000.00	20,000.00

SEATED LIBERTY DOLLARS

The active production of silver dollars was finally resumed in 1840. However, the reverse design especially created for it was replaced by a more mundane heraldic eagle, similar to that in use on the minor coinage. While production of these coins continued for most years, those struck from 1853 to about 1867 were primarily intended as bullion pieces for export, each containing more than a dollar's worth of silver. A ribbon with the motto, "In God We Trust," was added over the eagle in 1866. These dollars are often found cleaned. Be careful of retoned specimens as well.

Known Counterfeits: Counterfeits of this type are not common.

Type Coin Price Range	G to MS-60
1840-1865	220.00 to 1,825.00
1866-1873	220.00 to 1,775.00

NO MOTTO ABOVE EAGLE

	F	EF
1840	325.00	600.00
1841	295.00	425.00
1842	295.00	425.00
1843	295.00	400.00
1844	300.00	550.00
1845	385.00	600.00
1846	280.00	550.00
1846O	320.00	750.00
1847	275.00	425.00
1848	480.00	900.00
1849	280.00	480.00

	F	EF
1850	700.00	1,300.00
1850O	475.00	1,500.00
1851 Original	8,000.00	14,500.00
1851 Restrike *Proof*	—	54,000.00
1852 Original	6,500.00	11,500.00
1852 Restrike Proof	—	56,000.00
1853	545.00	850.00
1854	1,900.00	3,800.00
1855	1,400.00	3,600.00
1856	600.00	1,250.00
1857	575.00	1,250.00
1858	4,000.00	5,600.00
1859	400.00	675.00
1859O	300.00	485.00
1859S	490.00	1,750.00
1860	385.00	575.00
1860O	300.00	445.00
1861	950.00	1,350.00
1862	900.00	1,300.00
1863	575.00	750.00
1864	500.00	700.00
1865	400.00	775.00
1866	*2 Known*	

MOTTO ABOVE EAGLE

	F	EF
1866	350.00	600.00
1867	330.00	600.00
1868	325.00	575.00
1869	300.00	475.00
1870	300.00	475.00
1870CC	750.00	1,750.00
1870S	98,000.00	275,000.00
1871	265.00	425.00
1871CC	4,000.00	10,500.00
1872	275.00	450.00
1872CC	2,400.00	5,500.00
1872S	450.00	1,600.00
1873	300.00	475.00

	F	EF
1873CC	6,500.00	17,500.00
1873S	*None known to exist*	

TRADE DOLLARS

Trade dollars were coins struck deliberately for export as bullion, usually to the Far East. They were chiefly intended to compete against the Mexican peso, which had slightly more silver than a standard dollar. They are distinguished by a Liberty and eagle facing the opposite direction from the standard dollars. From the very beginning, their legal-tender status was limited in the United States, but in 1876 when the price of silver dropped, they ceased to be legal tender altogether, not having it restored until 1965. Eight million were redeemed by the government in 1887, however. Any struck between 1879 and 1885 are "Proof Only" collectors' issues. Prices listed for them are for circulated examples, however.

It was typical for Oriental merchants to impress a character into these and other silver coins, to confirm that they accepted them as good quality. These "chop marks" are commonly found on trade dollars, sometimes in quantity. They reduce the value of the coin as a form of mutilation, but have recently been the subject of serious research. Chop-marked dollars may not be as valuable, but are still collectible.

Known Counterfeits: Counterfeits are not abundant and are more likely to be contemporary. Be cautious of cleaned coins.

Type Coin Price Range

	Chopped to MS-60
1873-1885	60.00 to 900.00

	F	EF
1873	145.00	260.00
1873CC	320.00	900.00
1873S	160.00	275.00
1874	160.00	275.00
1874CC	300.00	475.00
1874S	140.00	200.00
1875	375.00	600.00
1875CC	250.00	400.00
1875S	140.00	200.00
1875S, S over CC	400.00	900.00
1876	140.00	200.00
1876CC	285.00	430.00
1876S	138.00	180.00
1877	140.00	180.00
1877CC	300.00	580.00
1877S	138.00	180.00
1878 Proof only	—	3,500.00
1878CC	700.00	2,350.00
1878S	138.00	180.00
1879 Proof only	—	3,500.00
1880 Proof only	—	3,500.00
1881 Proof only	—	3,500.00
1882 Proof only	—	3,500.00
1883 Proof only	—	3,500.00
1884 *Proof only*	—	*10 known*
1885 *Proof only*	—	*5 known*

MORGAN DOLLARS

The Morgan Dollar was introduced as a result of pressure from the silver-mining lobby. For decades, silver dollars had been scarce in circulation. With the boom in silver mining, the price of the metal dropped as more became available. Something needed to be done to remove the excess silver from the market. The new design coincided with the reintroduction of the silver dollar. Because they were inconvenient, however, many (perhaps hundreds of thousands) of these dollars sat for decades in bags, held as private, bank and government reserves. The U.S. Treasury was stuck with such an excess that thousands remained on hand for almost a century, prompting the famous General Services Administration auctions of silver dollars beginning in 1972. Those coins in distinctive GSA cases often command a slight premium.

Artistically, many consider the Morgan Dollar, named after it's designer, George T. Morgan, an aesthetically pleasing but unoriginal design. Morgan's competence (and perhaps his interesting use of Gothic script) may perhaps be attributed to his training at the Royal Mint in London. A long gap exists between 1904 and the last Morgan issue in 1921. During this time the master dies were lost and new ones had to be prepared. As a result, there are subtle differences of relief in the 1921 issue. It is less pleasing, and dealer "bids" are often less for that year than for other bulk Morgan Dollars. Another subtle variation in the appearance of Morgan Dollars is the quality of strike from mint to mint. San Francisco made examples are usually fully struck, Philadelphia's are medium, and New Orleans dollars are usually the most weakly struck. The eagle's breast on high-grade pieces is usually the spot where these differences are most obvious.

Morgans have been among the most popular coins to invest in. This is partially due to their availability in great quantities in uncirculated condition, the typical grade favored by investment promoters and the mass of investors. It is ironic that their sheer commonness has contributed to their desirability.

Known Counterfeits: Genuine coins have been known altered to pass for 1879CC, 1889CC, 1892S, 1893S, 1894, 1895, 1895S, 1896S, 1901, 1903S and 1904S dates. Cast counterfeits are known of 1878, 1878S, 1879S, 1880O, 1881, 1883, 1883S, 1885, 1888O, 1889, 1889O, 1892O, 1899O, 1901, 1902, 1903, 1904S, 1921D and 1921S. Struck counterfeits of certain rare dates are also possible. Cleaned coins are common and are heavily discounted, as are scuffed and heavily edge-knocked pieces. Be careful to avoid coins with false toning.

1891-O lead-tin alloy circulating counterfeit. Note the dark grey color and faintly grainy surface. It also has a slightly "greasy" feel.

Type Coin Price Range	G to MS-65
1878-1904	17.50 to 165.00
1921	16.50 to 170.00

	VF	MS-60
1878, 8 tail feathers	38.00	130.00
1878, 7 over 8 tail feathers	28.00	150.00
1878, 7 feathers	26.00	75.00
1878, 7 feathers, rev. of 1879	24.00	82.00
1878CC	115.00	230.00
1878S	26.00	60.00
1879	24.00	37.00
1879CC	300.00	4,350.00
1879O	24.00	80.00
1879S	24.00	40.00
1880	24.00	37.00
1880CC	220.00	580.00
1880O	24.00	65.00
1880S	24.00	38.00
1881	24.00	38.00
1881CC	450.00	575.00
1881O	24.00	37.00
1881S	24.00	37.00
1882	24.00	37.00
1882CC	120.00	230.00
1882O	24.00	40.50
1882O, O over S	40.00	260.00
1882S	24.00	37.00
1883	24.00	37.00
1883CC	120.00	220.00
1883O	24.00	37.00
1883S	24.00	635.00
1884	24.00	37.00
1884CC	160.00	215.00
1884O	24.00	37.00
1884S	24.00	6,000.00
1885	24.00	37.00
1885CC	600.00	660.00
1885O	24.00	37.00

	VF	MS-60
1885S	40.00	245.00
1886	24.00	37.00
1886O	25.00	700.00
1886S	85.00	330.00
1887, 7 over 6	35.00	450.00
1887	24.00	37.00
1887O, 7 over 6	36.00	350.00
1887O	25.00	55.00
1887S	26.00	115.00
1888	24.00	37.00
1888O	24.00	37.00
1888S	215.00	310.00
1889	24.00	37.00
1889CC	1,750.00	23,000.00
1889O	25.00	140.00
1889S	70.00	215.00
1890	24.00	37.00
1890CC	115.00	460.00
1890O	25.00	58.00
1890S	24.00	58.00
1891	24.00	55.00
1891CC	120.00	375.00
1891O	24.00	140.00
1891S	24.00	60.00
1892	27.00	165.00
1892CC	315.00	1,700.00
1892O	26.00	170.00
1892S	135.00	36,000.00
1893	270.00	800.00
1893CC	335.00	3,800.00
1893O	400.00	2,300.00
1893S	7,500.00	85,000.00
1894	1,900.00	5,000.00
1894O	75.00	600.00
1894S	110.00	700.00
1895 Proof only	—	50,000.00
1895O	620.00	18,000.00
1895S	600.00	4,250.00
1896	24.00	37.00
1896O	24.00	1,450.00
1896S	60.00	1,775.00
1897	24.00	37.00
1897O	25.00	800.00
1897S	24.00	60.00
1898	24.00	37.00
1898O	24.00	37.00
1898S	36.00	270.00
1899	215.00	325.00
1899O	24.00	37.00
1899S	40.00	325.00
1900	24.00	37.00
1900O	24.00	37.00
1900O, O over CC	65.00	370.00
1900S	27.00	350.00
1901	60.00	2,200.00
1901O	24.00	37.00
1901S	32.00	470.00
1902	24.00	45.00
1902O	24.00	37.00
1902S	160.00	450.00
1903	55.00	77.50
1903O	380.00	450.00

	VF	MS-60
1903S	210.00	4,700.00
1904	30.00	80.00
1904O	27.00	38.00
1904S	95.00	1,350.00
1921	19.00	25.50
1921D	19.00	45.00
1921S	19.00	35.00

PEACE DOLLARS

Like the Morgan Dollar before it, the Peace Dollar was the result of Congressional authorization for a new, large coinage of silver dollars. When the famous numismatist Farran Zerbe learned that this new issue of dollars was to bear the old Morgan design, he agitated for a new, artistically more progressive replacement. This was to be a new radiant Liberty head by sculptor Anthony de Francisci. It was not only in harmony with the new designs for the other denominations, especially those by Weinman and Saint-Gaudens, but also commemorated the end of World War I. The word PEACE can be seen upon the rocky perch on which the eagle stands. The first Peace Dollars from 1921 were struck in a much higher relief. Later issues have a lower relief more suitable to mass production. The old silver dollar was last made for circulation in 1935. The Peace Dollar out-lived this death sentence for 30 years in the form of the mysterious issue of 1964. While none have been officially verified there have long been rumors, generally accepted by the numismatic community, that several escaped the mint's melting pot.

Like the Morgan Dollar, this coin is available in mint state in abundant quantities. The broad smooth surfaces, however, permit many mint-state pieces to reveal unsightly bruises and bag marks.

Known Counterfeits: 1928 altered from 1923 or 1928S, as well as other counterfeits of this date.

Type Coin Price Range	G to MS-65
1921	100.00 to 2,400.00
1922-35	16.50 to 180.00

	VF	MS-60
1921	140.00	250.00
1922	18.50	22.00
1922D	18.50	27.00
1922S	18.50	27.00
1923	18.50	21.00
1923D	19.00	53.00
1923S	18.50	30.00
1924	18.50	21.00
1924S	31.00	215.00
1925	18.50	21.00
1925S	25.00	75.00
1926	18.50	40.00
1926D	18.50	66.00
1926S	18.50	40.00
1927	35.00	70.00
1927D	35.00	150.00
1927S	35.00	150.00
1928	455.00	530.00
1928S	40.00	160.00
1934	22.50	120.00
1934D	22.50	135.00
1934S	90.00	1,800.00
1935	22.00	62.00
1935S	21.00	250.00
1964D	*No confirmed examples known*	

EISENHOWER DOLLARS

The "Ike" Dollar was struck as much to commemorate the first manned moon landing in 1969, as to honor President Dwight D. Eisenhower. The reverse of this coin was an adaptation of the Apollo XI insignia, depicting an eagle clutching an olive branch and landing on the moon. The obverse shows a left-facing portrait of Eisenhower. Circulation strikes were of the same cupronickel-clad composition as the dime and quarter. Special collectors' issues were also struck in a silver-clad version similar to the alloy used for the half dollars of 1965-1970. These special silver coins bearing the "S" mintmark were released in blue envelopes for the uncirculated issues, and brown boxes for the proofs. Most dealers and collectors require that they be in the original packaging.

A special reverse was used to commemorate the Bicentennial. It featured the Liberty Bell superimposed on the moon, as arranged by design-contest winner Dennis R. Williams. While all Bicentennial dollars are dated "1776·1976," they were struck in both 1975 and 1976, the reverse of the former year uses heavy block lettering, the latter mostly used slightly finer letters. They are easily identified by the lack of copper on the reeded edge.

Known Counterfeits: Poor-quality counterfeits have come out of China; specifically 1976D is known.

Note absence of copper edge, smaller than normal size, and date running into edge.

Type Coin Price Range		
		MS-60 to PF-65
1971-78		2.75 to 11.00
1976		2.50 to 11.00
1971	—	10.00
1971D	—	5.00
1971S Silver	8.00	11.00
1972	—	6.00

	MS-63	PF
1972D	—	5.50
1972S Silver	8.00	12.00
1973	—	14.00
1973D	—	15.00
1973S *Proof only*	—	12.00
1973S Silver	8.50	32.00
1974	—	5.50
1974D	—	6.00
1974S *Proof only*	—	10.00
1974S Silver	8.00	14.00

BICENTENNIAL REVERSE

	MS-63	PF
1976 Block letters	—	9.50
1976 Finer letters	—	5.00
1976D Block letters	—	6.00
1976D Finer letters	—	5.00
1976S Block letters Proof only	—	13.00
1976S Finer letters Proof only	—	9.00
1976S Silver, Block letters	13.00	20.00

REGULAR ISSUE CONTINUED

	MS-63	PF
1977	—	7.50
1977D	—	7.50
1977S Proof only	—	9.50
1978	—	5.00
1978D	—	5.00
1978S Proof only	—	12.00

SUSAN B. ANTHONY DOLLARS

The Anthony "mini-dollar" was struck to achieve two specific ends. It was intended to save the government money, by replacing the quickly worn-out $1 bill with a coin that would last in circulation for decades. It was also a coin greatly supported and pushed for by the vending-machine lobby. The large Ike Dollars were inconvenient for vending machines but a coin of its value was necessary to facilitate the sale of more expensive items in such machines.

It's obverse depicts Frank Gasparro's portrait of Susan B. Anthony, who was instrumental in gaining women the right to vote. The reverse design is the same Apollo XI motif as on the Eisenhower Dollar.

Certainly one of the least popular coins in the history of the United States, it was far too close in diameter to the quarter, with which it was frequently confused. It was of the same clad composition. The third year of issue was not even placed into circulation, and was just obtainable in mint sets. The final year was only struck in anticipation of its immediate replacement by the Sacagawea dollar.

Known Counterfeits: Not common.

	MS-63	PF
1979P Narrow rim, far date	—	2.50
1979P Wide rim, near date	—	60.00
1979D	—	3.00
1979S	—	3.00
1979S Filled S	—	8.00
1979S Clear S	—	110.00
1980	—	3.00
1980D	—	2.00
1980S	3.50	8.00
1981	—	8.00
1981D	—	8.00
1981S	—	8.00
1981S Filled S	—	8.00
1981S Clear S	—	230.00
1999P	4.00	30.00
1999D	—	4.00

SACAGAWEA DOLLARS

Despite the failure of the Susan B. Anthony Dollar to win popular acceptance, the reasons why it was originally issued remained. The government could save millions by replacing the dollar bill with a more durable coin. Also, a dollar coin of moderate size was still sought by the vending-machine industry.

The confusion caused by the Anthony Dollar was eliminated by changing the color and giving the new coin a broad border. This new, well-designed coin depicts Sacagawea, the Shoshone Indian guide and translator who accompanied the Lewis and Clark Expedition to explore the Northwest (1804-06). She carries her infant son on her back. It is the work of Glenna Goodacre. The reverse, designed by Thomas D. Rogers Jr., depicts a graceful eagle in flight.

While it is the same size as the Anthony dollar, it has a unique composition. It is a brass of 77 percent copper, 12 percent zinc, 7 percent manganese, and 4 percent nickel, bonded to a pure copper core. This coin is prone to spotting. Mint-state examples lacking spots are more desirable.

Known Counterfeits: Quantities are known, primarily made for circulation in Ecuador.

	MS-63	PF
2000P	—	2.00
2000D	—	2.00
2000S	—	10.00
2001P	—	4.00
2001D	—	4.00
2001S	—	95.00
2002P	—	2.00
2002D	—	2.00
2002S	—	28.50
2003P	—	2.50
2003D	—	2.50
2003S	—	12.50
2004P	—	2.50
2004D	—	2.50
2004S	—	22.50
2005P	—	2.50
2005D	—	2.50
2005S	—	22.50
2006P	—	2.50
2006D	—	2.50
2006S	—	22.50
2007P	—	2.50
2007D	—	2.50
2007S	—	22.50

PRESIDENTIAL DOLLARS

Following on the success of the statehood quarter series, the mint has recently introduced a series of circulating dollars depicting the presidents, to be released in chronological order every three months. Their composition is the same as that of the Sacagawea dollar.

A controversial aspect of this series is the edge lettering, which includes not only both mottos but the date and mint mark. "In God We Trust" is expected to be moved to the surface of the coin in 2008.

Known Counterfeits: None reported to date.

	MS-63	PF
2007P Washington	—	2.00
2007D Washington	—	2.00
2007S Washington *proof only*	—	5.00
(2007) Washington, *Plain edge error*	—	75.00

	MS-63	PF
2007P J.Adams	—	2.00
2007P J.Adams, *Doubled edge lettering error*	—	125.00
2007D J.Adams	—	2.00
2007S J.Adams *proof only*	—	5.00
2007P Jefferson	—	2.00
2007D Jefferson	—	2.00
2007S Jefferson *proof only*	—	5.00

	MS-63	PF
2007P Madison	—	2.00
2007D Madison	—	2.00
2007S Madison *proof only*	—	5.00
2008P Monroe	—	2.00
2008D Monroe	—	2.00
2008S Monroe *proof only*	—	5.00

	MS-63	PF
2008P J.Q.Adams	—	2.00
2008D J.Q.Adams	—	2.00
2008S J.Q.Adams proof only	—	5.00
2008P Jackson	—	2.00
2008D Jackson	—	2.00
2008S Jackson proof only	—	5.00

	MS-63	PF
2008P Van Buren	—	2.00
2008D Van Buren	—	2.00
2008S Van Buren proof only	—	5.00

GOLD DOLLARS

Although the gold dollar was originally planned as early as 1791, and patterns were prepared in 1836, it was not until 1849 that they were finally approved. Earlier demand was being filled by privately struck Georgia and Carolina gold of standard United States coinage weight, and the mint director personally opposed their issue. When Congressional intervention was coupled with the new flow of gold from California, the mint had to give in. The first gold dollars, designed as one of James Longacre's early projects, were a mere 12.7mm (half an inch) in diameter and were easily lost. The diameter was increased to 14.3mm and the coin made thinner in 1854 to make them easier to handle, but the new narrow-head design was of too high relief and parts of the date on the reverse did not always strike up. The gold dollar's final modification came in 1856, when the wide "flan" (the blank metal disk before it is stamped to become a coin) was retained but a lower relief portrait of Liberty similar to that on the Three Dollar piece was used.

Many gold dollars were used at the time in jewelry and bear solder marks,

especially the first type. These coins are worth a fraction of the value of untouched coins. Mutilated examples are far more common than worn ones, with few examples grading lower than VF.

Known Counterfeits: 1849C Open Wreath and 1854C exist, made by altering genuine coins of other dates or mints. Cast counterfeits have been made of 1850-54. It is important to note that struck counterfeits exist of virtually every date in this series.

Type Coin Price Range	F to MS-60
1849-1854, Type I	110.00 to 300.00
1854-1856, Type II	220.00 to 2,300.00
1856 to 1889, Type III	125.00 to 320.00

CORONET HEAD—TYPE I

	VF	EF
1849 Open wreath	175.00	220.00
1849 Closed wreath	175.00	200.00
1849C Open wreath	*Extremely Rare*	
1849C Closed wreath	1,200.00	1,950.00
1849D	1,400.00	2,100.00
1849O	180.00	265.00
1850	175.00	200.00
1850C	1,150.00	1,800.00
1850D	1,250.00	2,000.00
1850O	280.00	400.00
1851	175.00	200.00
1851C	995.00	1,300.00
1851D	1,150.00	1,600.00
1851O	175.00	225.00
1852	175.00	200.00
1852C	1,150.00	1,400.00
1852D	1,250.00	1,600.00
1852O	190.00	250.00
1853	175.00	200.00
1853C	1,100.00	1,600.00
1853D	1,250.00	1,750.00
1853O	175.00	235.00
1854	175.00	200.00
1854D	1,400.00	2,400.00
1854S	375.00	550.00

NARROW INDIAN PRINCESS HEAD—TYPE II

	VF	EF
1854	320.00	450.00
1855	320.00	450.00
1855C	1,500.00	4,000.00

	VF	EF
1855D	5,000.00	12,000.00
1855O	440.00	600.00
1856S	925.00	1,325.00

LARGE INDIAN PRINCESS HEAD—TYPE III

	VF	EF
1856 upright 5	185.00	215.00
1856 slanted 5	185.00	210.00
1856D	3,900.00	6,000.00
1857	185.00	210.00
1857C	1,150.00	1,750.00
1857D	1,400.00	2,750.00
1857S	550.00	750.00
1858	185.00	210.00
1858D	1,250.00	1,650.00
1858S	425.00	600.00
1859	185.00	210.00
1859C	1,050.00	1,700.00
1859D	1,400.00	1,800.00
1859S	250.00	600.00
1860	185.00	210.00
1860D	3,000.00	4,000.00
1860S	380.00	500.00
1861	185.00	210.00
1861D (Struck by the Confederacy)	8,000.00	13,500.00
1862	185.00	210.00
1863	500.00	925.00
1864	350.00	440.00
1865	350.00	575.00
1866	360.00	475.00
1867	400.00	525.00
1868	295.00	415.00
1869	335.00	530.00
1870	285.00	400.00
1870S	500.00	800.00
1871	285.00	400.00
1872	275.00	400.00
1873 Closed 3	425.00	820.00
1873 Open 3	185.00	210.00
1874	185.00	210.00
1875	2,350.00	3,850.00
1876	275.00	350.00
1877	185.00	345.00
1878	250.00	350.00
1879	225.00	325.00
1880	185.00	210.00
1881	185.00	210.00
1882	185.00	215.00
1883	185.00	210.00
1884	185.00	210.00
1885	185.00	215.00
1886	185.00	215.00
1887	185.00	210.00
1888	185.00	210.00
1889	185.00	210.00

GOLD 2½ DOLLARS

The first strikes of the quarter eagle (gold 2½ dollar piece) came the year following the first introduction of American gold coinage, the half eagle and eagle preceding it in 1795. However, it preceded the other denominations as being the first coin to depict the heraldic eagle bearing a shield on its chest, later featured on all denominations other than copper. Its first obverse features a bust of Liberty wearing a tall conical cap, traditionally (but inaccurately) referred to by numismatists as a turban. This first bust by Robert Scott was replaced by one designed by John Reich with a smaller cap. A reverse eagle similar, but more realistic, was paired with the new obverse. A large gap in the striking of quarter eagles followed immediately upon the release of this new design, which was finally restored on the same standard – but at a slightly smaller diameter – in 1821.

Through most of its history until the 1830s, the quarter eagle was plagued by mass melting because it was undervalued relative to its gold content, particularly by European standards. In 1834 this was remedied by reducing the coin's gold content. This was indicated to the public by the removal of the motto over the eagle on the reverse, and by a new, capless Liberty head, the "Classic Head" by William Kneass. The final Coronet-type Liberty head design was a rendition by Christian Gobrecht, which continued in use from 1840 to 1907 without change. Those 1848 pieces countermarked CAL were struck with gold that was shipped East by the military governor of California.

In 1908, as part of the same coin design beautification program that later introduced the Walking Liberty half dollar and Saint-Gaudens double eagle, sculptor Bela Lyon Pratt was asked to prepare new designs for the quarter and half eagle in secret under the authority of President Theodore Roosevelt. His work showed the bust of an Indian chief on the obverse and an eagle with closed wings on the reverse. It was both controversial and innovative in that it bore its design in relief, but recessed below the surface of the coin. While some criticized it both for aesthetic reasons, and for fear of it spreading germs in dirt trapped in the recesses, it proved to be a successful method of shielding the design from wear.

Known Counterfeits: Examples of 1848 CAL, 1875 and 1911D exist made by altering genuine coins of other dates or mints. Struck counterfeits exist of virtually every date in this series. All examples of 1905S are counterfeit — no real ones exist. Be cautious of false C mintmarks altered by cutting down an authentic O mintmark. Beware of traces of solder on earlier coins from use as jewelry. Look for interruption in the pattern of edge reeding. Be cautious of cleaned coins. This is harder to detect on gold, which usually does not tone naturally.

Type Coin Price Range	VG to MS-63
1796-1807	2,500.00 to 60,000.00
1808-1834	2,500.00 to 30,000.00
1834-1839	200.00 to 8,600.00
1840-1907	135.00 to 1,300.00
1908-1929	135.00 to 1,100.00

TURBAN BUST RIGHT

	F	XF
1796 No stars on obverse	35,000.00	75,000.00
1796 Stars	30,000.00	65,000.00
1797	17,000.00	30,000.00
1798	6,500.00	13,000.00
1802, 2 over 1	5,000.00	10,000.00
1804, 13 stars	24,500.00	75,000.00
1804, 14 stars	5,000.00	10,000.00
1805	6,000.00	10,000.00
1806, 6 over 4	5,750.00	10,500.00
1806, 6 over 5	9,000.00	18,500.00
1807	5,500.00	10,000.00

CAPPED BUST TYPE

	F	XF
1808	29,500.00	55,000.00
1821	6,000.00	8,000.00
1824, 4 over 1	6,000.00	8,000.00
1825	6,000.00	8,000.00
1826, 6 over 5	6,250.00	10,500.00
1827	6,000.00	9,500.00
1829	5,000.00	7,500.00
1830	5,000.00	7,500.00
1831	5,000.00	7,500.00
1832	5,000.00	7,500.00
1833	5,000.00	7,600.00
1834	9,000.00	16,500.00

CLASSIC HEAD (NO MOTTO)

	F	XF
1834	270.00	800.00
1835	270.00	800.00
1836	270.00	800.00
1837	300.00	950.00
1838	300.00	800.00
1838C	1,400.00	3,000.00
1839	400.00	1,500.00
1839C	1,200.00	3,200.00
1839D	1,350.00	4,000.00
1839O	500.00	1,300.00

CORONET TYPE (NO MOTTO)

	F	EF
1840	160.00	850.00
1840C	1,000.00	1,800.00
1840D	2,100.00	8,800.00
1840O	225.00	800.00
1841	—	87,500.00
1841C	800.00	2,000.00
1841D	1,200.00	4,850.00
1842	450.00	2,900.00
1842C	900.00	3,600.00
1842D	1,000.00	4,350.00
1842O	240.00	1,200.00
1843	165.00	475.00
1843C, Crosslet 4, small date	1,600.00	5,600.00
1843C, Plain 4, large date	850.00	2,200.00
1843D	990.00	2,350.00
1843O, Crosslet 4, small date	165.00	250.00
1843O, Plain 4, large date	200.00	465.00
1844	235.00	850.00
1844C	800.00	2,600.00
1844D	850.00	2,400.00
1845	190.00	350.00
1845D	950.00	2,600.00
1845O	550.00	2,300.00
1846	200.00	500.00
1846C	850.00	3,500.00
1846D	900.00	2,150.00
1846O	190.00	400.00
1847	150.00	370.00
1847C	950.00	2,200.00
1847D	990.00	2,250.00
1847O	160.00	410.00
1848	315.00	850.00

	F	**EF**
1848 CAL.	13,500.00	30,000.00

Quarter eagles with CAL over the eagle were struck with gold shipped to the Dept. of War by the governor of California.

	F	**EF**
1848C	900.00	2,250.00
1848D	2,200.00	2,500.00
1849	200.00	475.00
1849C	900.00	2,250.00
1849D	950.00	2,500.00
1850	160.00	275.00
1850C	900.00	2,250.00
1850D	950.00	2,500.00
1850O	170.00	450.00
1851	150.00	220.00
1851C	990.00	2,300.00
1851D	1,100.00	2,600.00
1851O	150.00	250.00
1852	150.00	210.00
1852C	900.00	2,150.00
1852D	950.00	2,900.00
1852O	160.00	300.00
1853	135.00	225.00
1853D	990.00	3,500.00
1854	150.00	210.00
1854C	700.00	2,000.00
1854D	1,800.00	5,000.00
1854O sss	150.00	240.00
1854S	70,000.00	125,000.00
1855	150.00	230.00
1855C	900.00	3,500.00
1855D	2,000.00	7,500.00
1856	150.00	210.00
1856C	750.00	2,500.00
1856D	4,000.00	12,500.00
1856O	180.00	750.00
1856S	160.00	380.00
1857	150.00	210.00
1857D	900.00	3,000.00
1857O	155.00	350.00
1857S	160.00	340.00
1858	150.00	250.00
1858C	900.00	2,100.00
1859	150.00	265.00
1859D	1,100.00	3,400.00
1859S	200.00	900.00
1860	150.00	265.00
1860C	950.00	2,300.00
1860S	170.00	675.00
1861	150.00	210.00
1861S	200.00	1,000.00
1862, 2 over 1	475.00	2,000.00
1862	160.00	300.00
1862S	500.00	2,100.00
1863 *Proof only*	—	60,000.00
1863S	300.00	1,500.00
1864	2,500.00	10,000.00
1865	2,400.00	8,200.00
1865S	160.00	650.00
1866	650.00	3,500.00
1866S	180.00	650.00
1867	190.00	800.00

	F	**EF**
1867S	170.00	675.00
1868	170.00	400.00
1868S	150.00	350.00
1869	170.00	450.00
1869S	160.00	440.00
1870	165.00	420.00
1870S	155.00	400.00
1871	160.00	325.00
1871S	150.00	300.00
1872	210.00	725.00
1872S	155.00	425.00
1873 Closed 3	150.00	220.00
1873 Open 3	150.00	200.00
1873S	160.00	425.00
1874	170.00	380.00
1875	1,950.00	5,000.00
1875S	150.00	300.00
1876	170.00	650.00
1876S	170.00	525.00
1877	275.00	700.00
1877S	150.00	215.00
1878	150.00	215.00
1878S	150.00	215.00
1879	150.00	215.00
1879S	155.00	275.00
1880	170.00	335.00
1881	850.00	3,200.00
1882	160.00	290.00
1883	175.00	400.00
1884	175.00	400.00
1885	400.00	1,800.00
1886	170.00	270.00
1887	175.00	245.00
1888	160.00	240.00
1889	155.00	230.00
1890	170.00	240.00
1891	165.00	215.00
1892	170.00	250.00
1893	165.00	215.00
1894	170.00	230.00
1895	150.00	225.00
1896	150.00	225.00
1897	150.00	215.00
1898	150.00	215.00
1899	150.00	215.00
1900	150.00	240.00
1901	150.00	215.00
1902	150.00	215.00
1903	150.00	215.00
1904	150.00	215.00
1905	150.00	215.00
1906	150.00	215.00
1907	150.00	215.00

INDIAN HEAD TYPE

	VF	**AU**
1908	175.00	230.00
1909	175.00	230.00
1910	175.00	230.00
1911	175.00	230.00
1911D	2,500.00	5,200.00
1912	175.00	230.00
1913	175.00	230.00
1914	175.00	260.00
1914D	175.00	230.00
1915	175.00	230.00
1925D	175.00	230.00
1926	175.00	230.00
1927	175.00	230.00
1928	175.00	230.00
1929	180.00	250.00

THREE DOLLAR GOLD PIECES

The 1851 law that lowered the rate for first-class mail from 5 cents to 3 cents also authorized a 3-cent coin with which to purchase the new stamps. The prevailing thought at the time continued, and in 1853 another law authorized a $3 gold piece that could be used to conveniently purchase entire sheets of stamps, and could be exchanged for 100 of the small silver "trimes." Popularly called a portrait of an Indian princess, the design is more specifically that of Liberty wearing a feathered headdress, and was also used on the type III gold dollars of 1856. It was never particularly popular, with most years outside the 1850s being struck in insignificant quantities. Mintages became almost ceremonial until striking was finally suspended in 1889.

In its day it was popularly used as jewelry, so collectors must be careful to inspect coins for traces of solder. Look for irregularities in the reeding or discoloration near the edge. Cleaning is both a problem and a hint to other flaws, such as mount marks.

Known Counterfeits: 1877 exists made by altering genuine coins of other dates. Struck counterfeits exist of virtually every date in this series.

Type Coin Price Range		F to MS-60
1854-1889		500.00 to 2,650.00

	VF	**EF**
1854	850.00	1,150.00
1854D	9,000.00	15,000.00
1854O	1,500.00	2,700.00
1855	900.00	1,150.00
1855S	1,200.00	2,500.00
1856	880.00	1,150.00
1856S	900.00	1,600.00
1857	900.00	1,150.00
1857S	950.00	2,800.00

	VF	EF
1858	950.00	2,000.00
1859	900.00	1,800.00
1860	900.00	1,600.00
1860S	950.00	2,350.00
1861	950.00	1,600.00
1862	950.00	1,850.00
1863	900.00	1,500.00
1864	950.00	1,550.00
1865	1,500.00	3,000.00
1866	970.00	1,500.00
1867	950.00	1,500.00
1868	750.00	1,200.00
1869	1,150.00	1,600.00
1870	1,000.00	1,500.00
1870S	Unique	
1871	1,000.00	1,500.00
1872	950.00	1,800.00
1873 Closed 3	4,000.00	6,000.00
1873 Open 3 Proof only	—	65,000.00
1874	800.00	1,300.00
1875 Proof only	—	175,000.00
1876	6,000.00	10,000.00
1877	1,500.00	3,300.00
1878	800.00	1,300.00
1879	850.00	1,300.00
1880	850.00	1,800.00
1881	1,800.00	3,000.00
1882	925.00	1,400.00
1883	1,000.00	1,600.00
1884	1,250.00	1,700.00
1885	1,200.00	1,800.00
1886	1,250.00	1,800.00
1887	900.00	1,300.00
1888	950.00	1,500.00
1889	925.00	1,300.00

FIVE-DOLLAR GOLD PIECES

The first American gold coin to be struck was the half eagle, or $5 gold piece, in 1795. Its first obverse features a bust of Liberty wearing a tall, conical cap, traditionally (but inaccurately) referred to by numismatists as a turban. Originally this was paired with a reverse design featuring a skinny eagle similar to that on the first dollars, but instead of standing within a wreath it is seen holding one above its head. As with the other denominations, this was replaced by a plumper heraldic eagle bearing a shield on its chest, which later was featured on all denominations other than copper. The original bust by Robert Scott was replaced in 1807 by one designed by John Reich, using a smaller cap. A reverse eagle similar, but more realistic, was paired with the new obverse. While the design and net gold content did not change for almost

30 years the coin's diameter was at first increased and then reduced.

Through most of its history until the 1830s, the half eagle was plagued by mass melting, being undervalued relative to its gold content, particularly by European standards. In 1834 this was remedied by reducing the coin's gold content. This was indicated to the public by the removal of the motto over the eagle on the reverse, and by a new capless Liberty head, the "Classic Head" by William Kneass. The final Coronet-type Liberty head design was a rendition by Christian Gobrecht, which continued in use from 1839 to 1908, the motto being replaced over the eagle in 1866.

In 1908, as part of the same coin design beautification program that later introduced the Walking Liberty half dollar and Saint-Gaudens double eagle, sculptor Bela Lyon Pratt was asked to prepare new designs for the quarter and half eagle in secret under the authority of President Theodore Roosevelt. His work showed the bust of an Indian chief on the obverse and an eagle with closed wings on the reverse. It was both controversial and innovative in that it bore its design in relief, but recessed below the surface of the coin. While some criticized it both for aesthetic reasons, and for fear of it spreading germs in dirt trapped in the recesses, it proved to be a successful method of shielding the design from wear.

Known Counterfeits: 1811, 1815 (altered), 1841O (probable), 1852C, 1854S (altered), 1858, 1870CC (altered), 1875, 1877 (altered), 1885, 1885S, 1887 Proof (altered), 1892, 1892O (altered), 1906S, 1907D, 1908 (Liberty), 1908D, 1909 Matte Proof, 1909D, 1909O, 1910D, 1914D, 1914S, and 1915D (all counterfeit), among others. Be cautious of false C mintmarks altered by cutting down an authentic O mintmark. Beware of traces of solder on earlier coins from use as jewelry. Look for interruption in the pattern of edge reeding. Be cautious of cleaned coins. This is harder to detect on gold, which usually does not tone naturally.

Type Coin Price Range	VG to MS-63
1795-1798	6,000.00 to 160,000.00
1795-1807	1,200.00 to 30,000.00
1807-1834	1,000.00 to 23,000.00
1834-1838	290.00 to 10,500.00
1839-1866	250.00 to 7,800.00
1866-1908	250.00 to 990.00
1908-1929	250.00 to 3,600.00

TURBAN BUST/SMALL EAGLE

	F	VF
1795	14,500.00	20,000.00
1796, 6 over 5	16,000.00	21,500.00
1797, 15 stars	23,500.00	30,000.00
1797, 16 stars	18,000.00	22,500.00
1798	100,00.00	190,000.00

TURBAN BUST/HERALDIC EAGLE

	F	VF
1795	10,000.00	17,500.00
1797, 7 over 5	14,000.00	21,500.00
1797, 16 star obv.	—	Unique
1798 Small 8	4,000.00	7,000.00
1798 Large 8, 13 star rev.	3,300.00	4,000.00
1798 Large 8, 14 star rev.	3,500.00	5,000.00
1799	3,500.00	5,000.00
1800	3,500.00	5,000.00
1802, 2 over 1	3,500.00	5,500.00
1803, 3 over 2	3,500.00	5,000.00
1804, Small 8	3,500.00	5,000.00
1804, Small 8 over Large 8	3,500.00	5,000.00
1805	3,500.00	5,000.00
1806, Pointed 6	3,600.00	5,000.00
1806, Round 6	3,500.00	5,000.00
1807	3,500.00	5,100.00

CAPPED BUST TYPE

	F	VF
1807	2,500.00	3,500.00
1808, 8 over 7	3,200.00	4,300.00
1808	2,500.00	3,500.00
1809, 9 over 8	2,500.00	3,500.00
1810 Small date, small 5	12,000.00	23,000.00
1810 Small date, tall 5	2,500.00	3,800.00

	F	VF
1810 Large date, small 5	**15,000.00**	**30,000.00**
1810 Large date, large 5	**2,800.00**	**3,500.00**
1811 Small 5	**2,800.00**	**3,500.00**
1811 Tall 5	**2,700.00**	**3,500.00**
1812	**2,500.00**	**3,500.00**
1813	**2,700.00**	**3,600.00**
1814, 4 over 3	**2,700.00**	**3,600.00**
1815	*EF*	**85,000.00**
1818	**3,000.00**	**4,000.00**
1818 STATESOF	**3,000.00**	**3,800.00**
1818, 5D over 50	**3,000.00**	**4,000.00**
1819	**13,500.00**	**26,500.00**
1819, 5D over 50	—	**25,000.00**
1820, Curved-base 2	**3,500.00**	**4,800.00**
1820, Square-base 2	**3,500.00**	**4,800.00**
1821	**14,000.00**	**24,000.00**
1822	**1,500,000.00**	
1823	**3,000.00**	**4,000.00**
1824	**6,000.00**	**12,000.00**
1825, 5 over 1	**6,100.00**	**14,000.00**
1825, 5 over 4		*Only 2 known*
1826	**5,000.00**	**8,500.00**
1827	**6,000.00**	**10,000.00**
1828, 8 over 7	**20,000.00**	**32,000.00**
1828	**8,000.00**	**17,500.00**
1829	—	*Extremely Rare*

CAPPED BUST/REDUCED DIAMETER

1829	**40,000.00**	**65,000.00**
1830	**16,500.00**	**20,000.00**
1831	**16,500.00**	**20,000.00**
1832, 12 stars		*Only 6 known*
1832, 13 stars	**16,500.00**	**20,000.00**
1833	**16,500.00**	**20,000.00**
1834 Plain 4	**16,500.00**	**20,000.00**
1834 Crosslet 4	**16,500.00**	**20,000.00**

CLASSIC HEAD (NO MOTTO)

	VF	EF
1834 Plain 4	**500.00**	**840.00**
1834 Crosslet 4	**2,000.00**	**3,600.00**
1835	**500.00**	**850.00**
1836	**500.00**	**840.00**
1837	**500.00**	**870.00**
1838	**500.00**	**840.00**
1838C	**2,850.00**	**5,850.00**
1838D	**2,450.00**	**4,500.00**

CORONET TYPE (NO MOTTO)

	VF	EF
1839	**275.00**	**480.00**
1839C	**2,300.00**	**3,000.00**
1839D	**2,200.00**	**3,200.00**
1840	**275.00**	**360.00**
1840C	**2,300.00**	**3,100.00**
1840D	**2,300.00**	**3,200.00**
1840O	**375.00**	**900.00**
1841	**400.00**	**950.00**
1841C	**1,800.00**	**2,400.00**
1841D	**1,800.00**	**2,400.00**
1841O	—	*2 Known*
1842 Small letters	**345.00**	**1,100.00**
1842 Large letters	**750.00**	**2,000.00**
1842C Small date	**9,950.00**	**23,000.00**
1842C Large date	**1,800.00**	**2,300.00**
1842D Small letters	**2,000.00**	**2,350.00**
1842D Large letters	**2,500.00**	**6,700.00**
1842O	**1,000.00**	**3,400.00**
1843	**275.00**	**330.00**
1843C	**1,850.00**	**2,500.00**
1843D	**1,950.00**	**2,600.00**
1843O Small letters	**660.00**	**1,800.00**
1843O Large letters	**265.00**	**1,175.00**
1844	**275.00**	**330.00**
1844C	**1,900.00**	**3,000.00**
1844D	**1,950.00**	**2,400.00**
1844O	**275.00**	**375.00**
1845	**275.00**	**280.00**
1845D	**1,900.00**	**2,400.00**
1845O	**415.00**	**800.00**
1846 Small date	**275.00**	**330.00**
1846	**275.00**	**330.00**
1846C	**1,900.00**	**3,000.00**
1846D	**1,800.00**	**2,400.00**
1846O	**375.00**	**1,000.00**
1847	**275.00**	**280.00**
1847C	**1,850.00**	**2,500.00**
1847D	**2,000.00**	**2,500.00**
1847O	**2,400.00**	**6,700.00**
1848	**275.00**	**285.00**
1848C	**1,900.00**	**2,250.00**
1848D	**2,000.00**	**2,350.00**

	VF	EF
1849	**275.00**	**280.00**
1849C	**1,900.00**	**2,400.00**
1849D	**2,000.00**	**2,575.00**
1850	**300.00**	**625.00**
1850C	**1,850.00**	**2,300.00**
1850D	**1,950.00**	**2,500.00**
1851	**275.00**	**280.00**
1851C	**1,900.00**	**2,350.00**
1851D	**1,950.00**	**2,400.00**
1851O	**590.00**	**1,450.00**
1852	**275.00**	**280.00**
1852C	**1,900.00**	**2,450.00**
1852D	**2,000.00**	**2,450.00**
1853	**275.00**	**280.00**
1853C	**1,950.00**	**2,350.00**
1853D	**2,000.00**	**2,500.00**
1854	**275.00**	**280.00**
1854C	**1,900.00**	**2,300.00**
1854D	**1,875.00**	**2,200.00**
1854O	**300.00**	**525.00**
1854S	—	*Extremely Rare*
1855	**275.00**	**280.00**
1855C	**1,950.00**	**2,300.00**
1855D	**1,950.00**	**2,400.00**
1855O	**675.00**	**2,100.00**
1855S	**390.00**	**1,000.00**
1856	**275.00**	**280.00**
1856C	**1,875.00**	**2,400.00**
1856D	**1,950.00**	**26900.00**
1856O	**650.00**	**1,600.00**
1856S	**300.00**	**700.00**
1857	**275.00**	**280.00**
1857C	**1,900.00**	**2,500.00**
1857D	**2,000.00**	**2,600.00**
1857O	**640.00**	**1,400.00**
1857S	**300.00**	**700.00**
1858	**275.00**	**550.00**
1858C	**1,900.00**	**2,350.00**
1858D	**2,000.00**	**2,450.00**
1858S	**825.00**	**2,400.00**
1859	**325.00**	**625.00**
1859C	**1,900.00**	**2,450.00**
1859D	**2,150.00**	**2,600.00**
1859S	**1,800.00**	**4,100.00**
1860	**280.00**	**575.00**
1860C	**2,100.00**	**2,950.00**
1860D	**1,900.00**	**2,600.00**
1860S	**1,100.00**	**2,100.00**
1861	**275.00**	**280.00**
1861C	**2,400.00**	**4,000.00**
1861D	**4,800.00**	**7,000.00**
1861S	**1,000.00**	**4,500.00**
1862	**800.00**	**1,850.00**
1862S	**3,000.00**	**6,000.00**
1863	**1,200.00**	**3,700.00**
1863S	**1,450.00**	**4,100.00**
1864	**650.00**	**1,850.00**
1864S	**6,000.00**	**16,000.00**
1865	**1,400.00**	**4,000.00**
1865S	**1,400.00**	**2,400.00**
1866S	**1,700.00**	**4,000.00**

CORONET TYPE (WITH MOTTO)

	VF	EF
1866	800.00	1,600.00
1866S	900.00	2,600.00
1867	500.00	1,500.00
1867S	1,400.00	2,900.00
1868	650.00	1,000.00
1868S	400.00	1,550.00
1869	925.00	1,900.00
1869S	500.00	1,750.00
1870	800.00	1,950.00
1870CC	5,250.00	15,000.00
1870S	950.00	2,600.00
1871	875.00	1,700.00
1871CC	1,200.00	3,000.00
1871S	500.00	1,000.00
1872	675.00	1,700.00
1872CC	1,200.00	5,000.00
1872S	460.00	800.00
1873 Closed 3	265.00	280.00
1873 Open 3	265.00	280.00
1873CC	2,600.00	12,500.00
1873S	525.00	1,400.00
1874	660.00	1,450.00
1874CC	850.00	1,750.00
1874S	650.00	2,100.00
1875	34,000.00	45,000.00
1875CC	1,400.00	4,500.00
1875S	715.00	2,250.00
1876	1,100.00	2,500.00
1876CC	1,500.00	5,000.00
1876S	2,000.00	3,600.00
1877	900.00	2,700.00
1877CC	1,000.00	3,300.00
1877S	400.00	650.00
1878	265.00	280.00
1878CC	3,100.00	9,500.00
1878S	265.00	280.00
1879	265.00	280.00
1879CC	575.00	1,500.00
1879S	265.00	280.00
1880	265.00	280.00
1880CC	425.00	800.00
1880S	265.00	280.00
1881, 1 over 0	330.00	600.00
1881	265.00	280.00
1881CC	550.00	1,500.00
1881S	265.00	280.00
1882	265.00	280.00
1882CC	420.00	625.00
1882S	265.00	280.00
1883	265.00	280.00
1883CC	460.00	1,100.00
1883S	265.00	280.00
1884	265.00	280.00
1884CC	575.00	985.00

	VF	EF
1884S	265.00	280.00
1885	265.00	280.00
1885S	265.00	280.00
1886	265.00	280.00
1886S	265.00	280.00
1887 Proof only	—	60,000.00
1887S	265.00	280.00
1888	265.00	280.00
1888S	265.00	280.00
1889	350.00	440.00
1890	390.00	475.00
1890CC	350.00	460.00
1891	265.00	280.00
1891CC	350.00	450.00
1892	265.00	280.00
1892CC	350.00	450.00
1892O	520.00	990.00
1892S	265.00	280.00
1893	265.00	280.00
1893CC	350.00	465.00
1893O	265.00	315.00
1893S	265.00	280.00
1894	265.00	280.00
1894O	265.00	360.00
1894S	265.00	375.00
1895	265.00	280.00
1895S	265.00	295.00
1896	265.00	280.00
1896S	265.00	285.00
1897	265.00	280.00
1897S	265.00	280.00
1898	265.00	280.00
1898S	265.00	280.00
1899	265.00	280.00
1899S	265.00	280.00
1900	265.00	280.00
1900S	265.00	280.00
1901	265.00	280.00
1901S, 1 over 0	265.00	280.00
1901S	265.00	280.00
1902	265.00	280.00
1902S	265.00	280.00
1903	265.00	280.00
1903S	265.00	280.00
1904	265.00	280.00
1904S	270.00	295.00
1905	265.00	280.00
1905S	265.00	280.00
1906	265.00	280.00
1906D	265.00	280.00
1906S	265.00	280.00
1907	265.00	280.00
1907D	265.00	280.00
1908	265.00	280.00

INDIAN HEAD TYPE

	VF	EF
1908	330.00	360.00
1908D	330.00	360.00
1908S	380.00	425.00
1909	330.00	360.00
1909D	330.00	360.00
1909O	2,100.00	3,500.00
1909S	330.00	360.00
1910	330.00	360.00
1910D	330.00	360.00
1910S	330.00	360.00
1911	330.00	360.00
1911D	475.00	540.00
1911S	330.00	360.00
1912	330.00	360.00
1912S	330.00	360.00
1913	330.00	360.00
1913S	340.00	370.00
1914	330.00	360.00
1914D	335.00	365.00
1914S	340.00	375.00
1915	330.00	360.00
1915S	340.00	400.00
1916S	330.00	360.00
1929	5,000.00	10,000.00

TEN-DOLLAR GOLD PIECES

Among the first two American gold coins to be struck was the eagle, or $10 gold piece, in 1795, and it was George Washington himself who received the first example. Its first obverse features a bust of Liberty by Robert Scot, wearing a tall conical cap, traditionally (but inaccurately) referred to by numismatists as a turban. Originally this was paired with a reverse design featuring a skinny eagle similar to that on the first silver dollars, but instead of standing within a wreath, it is seen holding one above its head. As with the other denominations, this was replaced by a plumper heraldic eagle bearing a shield on its chest, which later was featured on all denominations other than copper. All these early eagles were struck on a primitive screw press with hand-engraved dies, no two of which were identical. Many will show evidence of adjustment marks, a scraping of metal from the blank before striking to prevent the coin from being overweight. While not desirable, they are not considered damage, as they are part of the manufacturing process.

The initial issue of 1795-1804 was plagued by mass melting and wholesale export, being undervalued relative to its gold content, particularly by European standards. As a result, its coinage was completely suspended for more than 30 years. It was reintroduced in 1838 on the reduced gold standard adopted in 1834 to prevent these abuses. The new gold

eagle featured a Liberty head wearing a coronet, being Christian Gobrecht's interpretation of a painting of Venus by Benjamin West. A new, more realistic reverse eagle still wore a heraldic shield. This design continued in use until 1907, the motto being replaced over the eagle in 1866.

In 1908, as part of the same coin design beautification trend that later introduced the Walking Liberty half dollar and Mercury dime, noted sculptor Augustus Saint-Gaudens was asked to prepare new designs for the eagle and double eagle by President Theodore Roosevelt. His work showed the head of Liberty wearing an Indian war bonnet, the headdress being added to Saint-Gaudens' head originally designed as Victory at the President's instruction. The reverse featured a proud eagle with closed wings.

As Roosevelt believed the use of the motto "In God We Trust" on coinage to be a debased use of the divine name, it was omitted from the initial issues. This upset Congress so much that a law was enacted that restored it during 1908.

Known Counterfeits: 1799, 1858 (altered), 1889 (altered from Ps), 1901S, 1906D, 1906S, 1907, 1908 with Motto Proof, 1908S, 1909 Matte Proof, 1909S, 1910 Proof, 1910S, 1911 Proof, 1911D, 1911S, 1912S, 1913, 1913S, 1914S, 1915S, 1916S, 1926, 1932, 1933, among others especially 1870 to 1933. Be cautious of false C mintmarks altered by cutting down an authentic O mintmark. Beware of traces of solder on earlier coins from use as jewelry. Look for interruption in the pattern of edge reeding. Be cautious of cleaned coins. This is harder to detect on gold, which usually does not tone naturally.

Type Coin Price Range	VG to MS-63
1795-1797	12,000.00 to 300,000.00
1797-1804	3,000.00 to 55,000.00
1838-1866	550.00 to 14,500.00
1866-1907	500.00 to 1,200.00
1907-1908	500.00 to 4,000.00
1908-1933	500.00 to 1,600.00

TURBAN BUST/SMALL EAGLE

	F	VF
1795, 9 leaves below eagle	35,000.00	50,000.00
1795, 13 leaves	24,000.00	32,000.00
1796	26,000.00	37,000.00
1797	30,000.00	45,000.00

TURBAN BUST / HERALDIC EAGLE

	F	VF
1797	11,500.00	15,500.00
1798/97, 9 stars l., 4 r.	18,000.00	28,000.00
1798/97, 7 stars l., 6 r.	35,000.00	55,000.00
1799	9,500.00	11,000.00
1800	9,500.00	11,000.00
1801	9,500.00	11,000.00
1803	9,500.00	11,000.00
1804	13,500.00	19,500.00

CORONET TYPE (NO MOTTO)

	VF	EF
1838	1,200.00	2,900.00
1839 Large letters	1,150.00	1,950.00
1839 Small letters	1,600.00	3,500.00
1840	515.00	650.00
1841	515.00	550.00
1841O	3,200.00	6,000.00

	VF	EF
1842 Small date	515.00	600.00
1842 Large date	515.00	535.00
1842O	515.00	530.00
1843	515.00	535.00
1843O	515.00	535.00
1844	1,350.00	2,900.00
1844O	515.00	535.00
1845	600.00	775.00
1845O	515.00	750.00
1846	625.00	950.00
1846O	515.00	800.00
1847	515.00	535.00
1847O	515.00	535.00
1848	515.00	535.00
1848O	575.00	1,100.00
1849	515.00	535.00
1849O	710.00	2,100.00
1850 Large date	515.00	535.00
1850 Small date	515.00	535.00
1850O	515.00	875.00
1851	515.00	535.00
1851O	515.00	535.00
1852	515.00	535.00
1852O	650.00	1,100.00
1853, 3 over 2	600.00	800.00
1853	515.00	535.00
1853O	515.00	535.00
1854	515.00	535.00
1854O Small date	515.00	675.00
1854O Large date	515.00	865.00
1854S	515.00	535.00
1855	515.00	535.00
1855O	600.00	1,200.00
1855S	1,500.00	2,500.00
1856	515.00	535.00
1856O	725.00	1,250.00
1856S	515.00	535.00
1857	520.00	850.00
1857O	995.00	1,850.00
1857S	515.00	995.00
1858	5,200.00	8,200.00
1858O	515.00	750.00
1858S	1,600.00	3,100.00
1859	515.00	750.00
1859O	4,000.00	8,500.00
1859S	2,000.00	5,000.00
1860	515.00	775.00
1860O	575.00	1,250.00
1860S	3,250.00	6,100.00
1861	515.00	535.00
1861S	1,600.00	2,950.00
1862	550.00	1,200.00
1862S	2,000.00	3,000.00
1863	3,850.00	9,950.00
1863S	1,700.00	3,500.00
1864	1,700.00	4,500.00
1864S	5,100.00	13,000.00
1865	1,950.00	3,600.00
1865S	5,800.00	12,000.00
1865S, 865 over inverted 186	3,100.00	6,500.00
1866S	2,800.00	3,800.00

CORONET TYPE (WITH MOTTO)

	VF	EF
1866	850.00	1,800.00
1866S	1,550.00	4,000.00
1867	1,500.00	2,600.00
1867S	2,100.00	6,000.00
1868	550.00	800.00
1868S	1,300.00	2,600.00
1869	1,600.00	2,950.00
1869S	1,600.00	2,700.00
1870	850.00	1,475.00
1870CC	9,990.00	30,000.00
1870S	1,300.00	2,950.00
1871	1,600.00	3,000.00
1871CC	2,600.00	5,950.00
1871S	1,300.00	1,750.00
1872	2,400.00	3,600.00
1872CC	3,100.00	11,000.00
1872S	550.00	950.00
1873	4,500.00	9,500.00
1873CC	5,000.00	10,000.00
1873S	950.00	2,400.00
1874	515.00	530.00
1874CC	950.00	3,100.00
1874S	1,150.00	3,250.00
1875	40,000.00	59,000.00
1875CC	4,200.00	11,000.00
1876	3,500.00	6,300.00
1876CC	2,500.00	8,000.00
1876S	1,450.00	1,900.00
1877	2,600.00	5,700.00
1877CC	2,600.00	6,750.00
1877S	530.00	850.00
1878	515.00	530.00
1878CC	4,000.00	10,000.00
1878S	515.00	615.00
1879	515.00	530.00
1879CC	9,500.00	15,000.00
1879O	2,300.00	3,800.00
1879S	515.00	530.00
1880	515.00	530.00
1880CC	590.00	900.00
1880O	505.00	780.00
1880S	515.00	530.00
1881	515.00	530.00
1881CC	525.00	800.00
1881O	525.00	800.00
1881S	515.00	530.00
1882	515.00	530.00
1882CC	950.00	1,300.00
1882O	515.00	575.00
1882S	515.00	530.00
1883	515.00	530.00
1883CC	575.00	915.00

	VF	EF
1883O	3,300.00	7,200.00
1883S	515.00	530.00
1884	515.00	530.00
1884CC	600.00	1,100.00
1884S	515.00	530.00
1885	515.00	530.00
1885S	515.00	530.00
1886	515.00	530.00
1886S	515.00	530.00
1887	515.00	530.00
1887S	515.00	530.00
1888	515.00	530.00
1888O	515.00	530.00
1888S	515.00	530.00
1889	575.00	675.00
1889S	515.00	530.00
1890	515.00	530.00
1890CC	535.00	575.00
1891	515.00	530.00
1891CC	535.00	600.00
1892	515.00	530.00
1892CC	535.00	600.00
1892O	515.00	530.00
1892S	515.00	530.00
1893	515.00	530.00
1893CC	565.00	900.00
1893O	515.00	530.00
1893S	515.00	530.00
1894	515.00	530.00
1894O	515.00	530.00
1894S	515.00	540.00
1895	515.00	530.00
1895O	515.00	530.00
1895S	515.00	530.00
1896	515.00	530.00
1896S	515.00	530.00
1897	515.00	530.00
1897O	515.00	530.00
1897S	515.00	530.00
1898	515.00	530.00
1898S	515.00	530.00
1899	515.00	530.00
1899O	515.00	530.00
1899S	515.00	530.00
1900	515.00	530.00
1900S	515.00	530.00
1901	515.00	530.00
1901O	515.00	530.00
1901S	515.00	530.00
1902	515.00	530.00
1902S	515.00	530.00
1903	515.00	530.00
1903O	515.00	530.00
1903S	515.00	530.00
1904	515.00	530.00
1904O	515.00	530.00
1905	515.00	530.00
1905S	515.00	530.00
1906	515.00	530.00
1906D	515.00	530.00
1906O	515.00	530.00
1906S	515.00	530.00
1907	515.00	530.00

	VF	EF
1907D	515.00	530.00
1907S	515.00	530.00

INDIAN HEAD / NO MOTTO

	VF	EF
1907 Wire rim, periods	—	15,00.00
1907 Rounded rim, periods	39,000.00	
1907 No periods	580.00	620.00
1908	580.00	630.00
1908D	580.00	620.00

INDIAN HEAD / WITH MOTTO

	VF	EF
1908	580.00	620.00
1908D	580.00	620.00
1908S	580.00	620.00
1909	580.00	620.00
1909D	580.00	620.00
1909S	580.00	620.00
1910	580.00	620.00
1910D	580.00	620.00
1910S	580.00	620.00
1911	580.00	620.00
1911D	625.00	725.00
1911S	600.00	650.00
1912	580.00	620.00
1912S	580.00	620.00
1913	580.00	625.00
1913S	600.00	660.00
1914	580.00	620.00
1914D	580.00	620.00
1914S	580.00	620.00
1915	580.00	620.00
1915S	625.00	750.00
1916S	580.00	620.00
1920S	7,800.00	11,000.00
1926	580.00	620.00
1930S	5,500.00	8,000.00
1932	580.00	620.00
1933	*MS-60*	200,000.00

FIRST SPOUSE TEN-DOLLAR GOLD PIECES

Issued in conjunction with the circulating Presidential Dollars, this

series of $10 gold pieces depicts the First Lady of each presidency. The Jefferson administration's coin depicts Liberty, as there was no First Lady during this period.

Known Counterfeits: None reported to date.

	MS-63	PF
2007W Washington	600.00	600.00

	MS-63	PF
2007W Adams	600.00	600.00

	MS-63	PF
2007W Jefferson	600.00	600.00

	MS-63	PF
2007W D.Madison	600.00	600.00

	MS-63	PF
2008W Monroe	600.00	600.00

	MS-63	PF
2008W J.Q.Adams	600.00	600.00

	MS-63	PF
2008W Jackson	600.00	600.00

	MS-63	PF
2008W Van Buren	600.00	600.00

TWENTY-DOLLAR GOLD PIECES

The California Gold Rush of the 1840s resulted in large quantities of bullion being received at the mint for coinage. Partially to make this massive coinage more expedient (and partially because of the obvious convenience of using fewer coins for large international payments), the bill proposing the introduction of gold dollars was amended to include a large $20 gold piece called a "double eagle." James B. Longacre engraved a bust of Liberty wearing a coronet similar to, but of much more refined style than, the one in use on smaller gold since 1838. A facing heraldic eagle with a circlet of stars and a radiant arc above graced the reverse, the two motto ribbons at its sides suggesting the denomination of two eagles. This design continued in use until 1907, the

motto being placed within the circlet over the eagle in 1866. Two other minor modifications were attempted. The first (1861), called the Paquet reverse, is a subtle rearrangement of details, and for technical reasons was abandoned almost immediately. The other was the replacement in 1877 of the abbreviation D with the word "dollars."

In 1908, as part of the same coin design beautification trend that later introduced the Walking Liberty half dollar and Mercury dime, noted sculptor Augustus Saint-Gaudens was asked by President Theodore Roosevelt to prepare new designs for the double eagle and eagle. His work showed a full figure of Liberty, holding a torch and olive branch, striding towards the viewer. It was much inspired by Hellenistic sculpture, as correspondence between the two men clearly confirms. The reverse featured an eagle in mid-flight with a rising sun and rays in the background.

Roosevelt believed the use of the motto "In God We Trust" on coinage to be a debased use of the divine name, and it was omitted from the initial issues. This upset Congress so much that a law was enacted replacing it during 1908. To avoid public confusion, the date was changed from Roman numerals to Arabic ones, and because the initial design was of such high relief that it took three strikes by the dies, it's relief was lowered, as well.

Both the Liberty type and the Saint-Gaudens type are often found with heavy bag marks due to their soft metal and heavy weight. Examples virtually free from bagging command a substantial premium.

Known Counterfeits: 1879, 1879O, 1881 (altered), 1882 (altered), 1887 (altered), 1891, 1894, 1897S, 1898S, 1899S, 1900, 1900S, 1901S, 1903, 1903S, 1904, 1904S, 1906, 1906S, MCMVII, 1907 (Saint-Gaudens), 1908, 1909, 1910D, 1910S, 1911D, 1914D, 1914S, 1915, 1916S, 1919, 1920, 1921, 1922, 1923, 1924, 1925, 1926, 1927, 1927D (altered), 1928, 1929, among others especially 1870 to 1932. This series generally has been extensively counterfeited, be cautious. Beware of traces of solder on earlier coins from use as jewelry. Look for interruption in the pattern of edge reeding. Be cautious of cleaned coins. This is harder to detect on gold, which usually does not tone naturally.

Type Coin Price Range	F to MS-63
1849-1866	1,035.00 to 8,000.00
1866-1876	1,035.00 to 11,500.00
1877-1907	1,035.00 to 1,600.00

Type Coin Price Range	F to MS-63
1907-1908	1,035.00 to 1,300.00
1908-1933	1,035.00 to 1,300.00

LIBERTY HEAD - TYPE I

	VF	EF
1849	Unique	
1850	1,045.00	1,325.00
1850O	1,100.00	2,400.00
1851	1,045.00	1,090.00
1851O	1,050.00	1,400.00
1852	1,045.00	1,090.00
1852O	1,200.00	1,400.00
1853, 3 over 2	1,050.00	1,300.00
1853	1,045.00	1,090.00
1853O	1,045.00	2,200.00
1854	1,045.00	1,090.00
1854O	90,000.00	180,000.00
1854S	1,045.00	1,090.00
1855	1,045.00	1,090.00
1855O	3,200.00	9,500.00
1855S	1,045.00	1,090.00
1856	1,045.00	1,090.00
1856O	90,000.00	150,000.00
1856S	1,045.00	1,090.00
1857	1,045.00	1,090.00
1857O	1,300.00	2,600.00
1857S	1,045.00	1,090.00
1858	1,045.00	1,090.00
1858O	1,800.00	2,750.00
1858S	1,045.00	1,090.00
1859	1,150.00	2,450.00
1859O	4,700.00	9,000.00
1859S	1,045.00	1,090.00
1860	1,045.00	1,090.00
1860O	4,550.00	9,000.00
1860S	1,045.00	1,090.00
1861	1,045.00	1,090.00
1861O	3,300.00	6,700.00

Most of these were struck by Louisiana and the Confederacy after withdrawal from the Union.

	VF	EF
1861S	1,050.00	1,100.00
1861 Paquet rev.	Proof-67	660,000.00

	VF	EF
1861S Paquet rev.	20,000.00	38,000.00
1862	1,050.00	2,000.00
1862S	1,045.00	1,500.00
1863	1,045.00	1,500.00
1863S	1,045.00	1,400.00
1864	1,050.00	1,100.00
1864S	1,045.00	1,090.00
1865	1,045.00	1,090.00
1865S	1,045.00	1,090.00
1866S	3,000.00	11,000.00

LIBERTY HEAD (WITH MOTTO) - TYPE II

	VF	EF
1866	1,045.00	1,100.00
1866S	1,045.00	1,085.00
1867	1,045.00	1,085.00
1867S	1,045.00	1,085.00
1868	1,050.00	1,200.00
1868S	1,045.00	1,085.00
1869	1,045.00	1,085.00
1869S	1,045.00	1,085.00
1870	1,045.00	1,200.00
1870CC	150,000.00	200,000.00
1870S	1,045.00	1,085.00
1871	1,045.00	1,085.00
1871CC	8,000.00	15,000.00
1871S	1,045.00	1,085.00
1872	1,045.00	1,085.00
1872CC	2,400.00	3,300.00
1872S	1,045.00	1,085.00
1873 Closed 3	1,045.00	1,085.00
1873 Open 3	1,045.00	1,085.00
1873CC	2,500.00	4,500.00
1873S	1,045.00	1,085.00
1874	1,045.00	1,085.00
1874CC	1,500.00	1,900.00
1874S	1,045.00	1,085.00
1875	1,045.00	1,085.00
1875CC	1,300.00	1,500.00
1875S	1,045.00	1,085.00
1876	1,045.00	1,085.00
1876CC	1,300.00	1,500.00
1876S	1,045.00	1,085.00

LIBERTY HEAD - TYPE III

	VF	EF
1877	1,040.00	1,080.00
1877CC	1,500.00	1,900.00
1877S	1,040.00	1,080.00
1878	1,040.00	1,080.00
1878CC	2,200.00	3,300.00
1878S	1,040.00	1,080.00
1879	1,040.00	1,080.00
1879CC	2,500.00	4,000.00
1879O	9,500.00	15,000.00
1879S	1,040.00	1,080.00
1880	1,040.00	1,080.00
1880S	1,040.00	1,080.00
1881	5,000.00	8,000.00
1881S	1,040.00	1,080.00
1882	8,000.00	23,500.00
1882CC	1,200.00	1,500.00
1882S	1,040.00	1,080.00
1883	Proof only	100,000.00
1883CC	1,350.00	1,600.00
1883S	1,040.00	1,080.00
1884	Proof only	100,000.00
1884CC	1,250.00	1,550.00
1884S	1,040.00	1,080.00
1885	7,000.00	9,800.00
1885CC	2,900.00	4,000.00
1885S	1,040.00	1,080.00
1886	12,000.00	18,500.00
1887	Proof only	60,000.00
1887S	1,040.00	1,080.00
1888	1,040.00	1,080.00
1888S	1,040.00	1,080.00
1889	1,040.00	1,080.00
1889CC	1,500.00	1,600.00
1889S	1,040.00	1,080.00
1890	1,040.00	1,080.00
1890CC	1,250.00	1,600.00
1890S	1,040.00	1,080.00
1891	4,000.00	6,500.00
1891CC	3,800.00	8,000.00
1891S	1,040.00	1,080.00
1892	1,300.00	2,100.00
1892CC	1,350.00	1,650.00
1892S	1,040.00	1,080.00
1893	1,040.00	1,080.00
1893CC	1,600.00	1,950.00
1893S	1,040.00	1,080.00

	VF	EF
1894	1,040.00	1,080.00
1894S	1,040.00	1,080.00
1895	1,040.00	1,080.00
1895S	1,040.00	1,080.00
1896	1,040.00	1,080.00
1896S	1,040.00	1,080.00
1897	1,040.00	1,080.00
1897S	1,040.00	1,080.00
1898	1,040.00	1,080.00
1898S	1,040.00	1,080.00
1899	1,040.00	1,080.00
1899S	1,040.00	1,080.00
1900	1,040.00	1,080.00
1900S	1,040.00	1,080.00
1901	1,040.00	1,080.00
1901S	1,040.00	1,080.00
1902	1,040.00	1,080.00
1902S	1,040.00	1,080.00
1903	1,040.00	1,080.00
1903S	1,040.00	1,080.00
1904	1,040.00	1,080.00
1904S	1,040.00	1,080.00
1905	1,040.00	1,080.00
1905S	1,040.00	1,080.00
1906	1,040.00	1,080.00
1906D	1,040.00	1,080.00
1906S	1,040.00	1,080.00
1907	1,040.00	1,080.00
1907D	1,040.00	1,080.00
1907S	1,040.00	1,080.00

SAINT-GAUDENS / NO MOTTO

	VF	EF
1907 High relief, wire rim	7,250.00	9,750.00
1907 High relief, flat rim	7,500.00	10,250.00
1907 Arabic numerals	1,040.00	1,090.00
1908	1,040.00	1,080.00
1908D	1,040.00	1,080.00

SAINT-GAUDENS / WITH MOTTO

	VF	EF
1908	1,040.00	1,080.00
1908D	1,040.00	1,080.00
1908S	1,450.00	2,200.00
1909/8	1,040.00	1,080.00
1909	1,040.00	1,080.00
1909D	1,040.00	1,080.00
1909S	1,040.00	1,080.00
1910	1,040.00	1,080.00
1910D	1,040.00	1,080.00
1910S	1,040.00	1,080.00
1911	1,040.00	1,080.00
1911D	1,040.00	1,080.00
1911S	1,040.00	1,080.00
1912	1,040.00	1,080.00
1913	1,040.00	1,080.00
1913D	1,040.00	1,080.00
1913S	1,060.00	1,150.00
1914	1,040.00	1,080.00
1914D	1,040.00	1,080.00
1914S	1,040.00	1,080.00
1915	1,040.00	1,080.00
1915S	1,040.00	1,080.00
1916S	1,040.00	1,080.00
1920	1,040.00	1,080.00
1920S	12,500.00	18,000.00
1921	20,000.00	30,000.00
1922	1,040.00	1,080.00
1922S	1,040.00	1,080.00
1923	1,040.00	1,080.00
1923D	1,040.00	1,080.00
1924	1,040.00	1,080.00
1924D	1,200.00	1,550.00
1924S	1,200.00	1,600.00
1925	1,040.00	1,080.00
1925D	1,600.00	2,200.00
1925S	1,400.00	2,000.00
1926	1,040.00	1,080.00
1926D	7,500.00	11,000.00
1926S	1,100.00	1,550.00
1927	1,000.00	1,080.00
1927D	—	350,000.00
1927S	5,000.00	8,500.00
1928	1,040.00	1,080.00
1929	5,750.00	9,000.00
1930S	15,000.00	27,500.00
1931	9,900.00	14,500.00
1931D	9,000.00	12,500.00
1932	8,200.00	15,000.00
1933 MS-65		9,000,000.00

COMMEMORATIVE COINAGE

From the beginning of Federal coinage in 1792 until a century later in 1892, there was no such thing as commemorative coinage. Then came a celebration of world-class proportions. The World's Columbian Exposition of 1892-93 was America's first chance to show the entire world that it could put on a world's fair equal to those of Europe. It was a matter of national pride and for the first time a specific event was noted on United States coinage. The exposition's success was considered so important in the eyes of the government that two special coins were struck and sold at *over* their face value in order to subsidize the construction and running of the exposition site. A new and innovative turn had been made in America's otherwise mundane coinage, providing a proud manifestation for the nation's medal artists. It also served collectors, the numbers of whom had been growing steadily with the development of America's middle class. (It is no coincidence that these were the days of the American Numismatic Association's birth as well.) Over the next 40 years commemorative silver half dollars — usually sold at a premium as fundraisers for civic causes — became a normal part of the nation's coinage. Commemoratives were struck in gold as well, and between the two metals the mint produced commemorative coins at a rate of slightly less than one per year. By 1934 these issues had become little more than pork for congressmen and special interests. In the short span of five years, 1934-1938, 43 different commemorative half dollars were issued. Many collectors considered it a national scandal, and a debasement of the dignity of the coinage. Clearly they were not alone, as the flow of commemoratives trickled off to one or two per year, and after 1954 this series ended. It took the Bicentennial of American independence to embolden anyone to approve commemoratives again.

Commemorative coins of this early period are often more available in uncirculated than circulated grades. This is primarily due to the surcharges that their original purchasers were required to pay. Sometimes they are even available in their original packaging. These boxes or envelopes can add anywhere from $1 to $100 to the value of the coin.

Because many of these coins were held by laymen who prized them, but had little numismatic knowledge, many have been cleaned. One telltale sign is fine striations. Cleaned specimens are worth less than the prices quoted. The lowest grade in which these are usually collected is XF. Lower grades are often considered undesirable.

The silver commemorative coins here are all half dollars, except for the Isabella Quarter and the Lafayette Dollar. It has long been traditional to sequence the earlier series of U.S. commemorative coins alphabetically. This provides for quick reference, and is how they are listed here:

ISABELLA QUARTER

	AU	MS-60
1893	600.00	690.00

Struck to raise funds for the Board of Lady Managers of the World's Columbian Exposition. It depicts Queen Isabella and a kneeling woman holding distaff and spindle, emblematic of woman's industry. It's issue was instigated by Susan B. Anthony.

ALABAMA CENTENNIAL

	AU	MS-60
1921, with 2x2	325.00	335.00
1921, no 2x2	200.00	220.00

This was the first U.S. coin to bear the portrait of a living person. Depicted are Alabama's first governor, William W. Bibb, and then-governor, Thomas E. Kilby. Struck to raise money for the Alabama centennial commission two years after the centennial.

ALBANY, N.Y.

	AU	MS-60
1936	330.00	345.00

Struck to celebrate the 250th anniversary of Albany's city charter. The obverse depicts a beaver, basis for the city's 17th-century economy. The reverse shows the colonial governor of New York and the city's two founders.

Known Counterfeits: Some counterfeits have been sold as proofs.

ANTIETAM

	AU	MS-60
1937	730.00	765.00

Struck for sale at the battle site commemorations of the 75th anniversary of the Civil War Battle of Antietam. They depict Union General George McClellan and Confederate General Robert E. Lee. Offered at $1.65 each, most went unsold and were melted.

Known Counterfeits: Some are known in high grade.

ARKANSAS CENTENNIAL

	AU	MS-60
1935	105.00	110.00
1935D	110.00	130.00
1935S	110.00	130.00
1936	105.00	115.00
1936D	110.00	115.00
1936S	110.00	115.00
1937	115.00	120.00
1937D	115.00	120.00
1937S	115.00	120.00
1938	165.00	195.00
1938D	165.00	195.00
1938S	165.00	195.00
1939	340.00	400.00
1939D	340.00	400.00
1939S	340.00	400.00

These were struck for the Arkansas Centennial Commission, which originally sold the 1935 Philadelphia for $1 each. Other issues were sold in their entirety to dealers at such high prices that the public outcry stimulated Congress to end the entire commemorative program. Another coin for the same purpose was the Robinson-Arkansas half.

BAY BRIDGE

	AU	MS-60
1936S	170.00	180.00

Not only were these coins struck to commemorate the opening of a world-class bridge from San Francisco to Oakland, they could actually be purchased by motorists at that bridge without even getting out of their cars. The grizzly bear on the obverse was actually a San Francisco resident. The reverse view of the bridge is from the San Francisco side.

DANIEL BOONE

	AU	MS-60
1934	135.00	140.00
1935	135.00	140.00
1935D	135.00	140.00
1935S	135.00	140.00
1935 w/"1934"	310.00	335.00
1935D w/"1934"	310.00	335.00
1935S w/"1934"	310.00	335.00
1936	135.00	140.00
1936D	135.00	140.00
1936S	135.00	140.00
1937	290.00	315.00
1937D	290.00	315.00
1937S	290.00	315.00
1938	375.00	410.00
1938D	375.00	410.00
1938S	375.00	410.00

Originally made to raise money to restore historic sites, this issue was characterized by high-handed marketing tactics. The distribution price increased consistently and the commissioner responsible for their issue falsely announced the 1937 issue as the final year to promote sales.

BRIDGEPORT, CONNECTICUT

	AU	MS-60
1936	120.00	130.00

The world's most famous circus promoter and former Bridgeport, Conn., mayor, P.T. Barnum, was featured on a half dollar commemorating the 100th anniversary of Bridgeport's incorporation as a city. Sold at $2 each, they were distributed rather equitably, and were available locally through official channels for 40 years! Many have said that the eagle on the reverse, when inverted, resembles a shark. Original boxes are common.

CALIFORNIA DIAMOND JUBILEE

	AU	MS-60
1925S	220.00	240.00

This attractive half depicts a "Forty-Niner" panning for gold, with a ferocious grizzly bear on the reverse. It celebrates the 75th anniversary of California statehood.

CARVER - WASHINGTON

	AU	MS-60
1951	30.00	42.00
1951D	40.00	55.00
1951S	40.00	55.00
1952	20.00	22.00
1952D	55.00	60.00

	AU	MS-60
1952S>	55.00	60.00
1953	40.00	55.00
1953D	40.00	55.00
1953S	30.00	35.00
1954	40.00	52.00
1954D	40.00	52.00
1954S	28.00	35.00

The original legislation pushed this coin "to oppose the spread of communism among Negroes in the interest of National Defense," but this was just to hook the McCarthy-ites into passing the bill. In reality it was to help pay off the debts of S.J. Phillips, marketer of the Booker T. Washington half. The reverse design is a replacement for one rejected by the State Department. Many actually saw circulation.

CINCINNATI MUSIC CENTER

	AU	MS-60
1936	320.00	330.00
1936D	320.00	330.00
1936S	320.00	330.00

This coin was made for the 50th anniversary of nothing! It was struck almost exclusively for coin dealer Thomas Melish, who worked with promoters to drive the price per set up from $7.75 to $75 within months. The 1886 date noted on the coin has not been found to have any historical relevance. Stephen Foster, composer of *Oh! Susannah*, whose bust appears here, did, however, live in Cincinnati.

Known Counterfeits: Deceptive casts exist.

CLEVELAND - GREAT LAKES

	AU	MS-60
1936	130.00	135.00

While this coin was legitimately struck for the Great Lakes Exposition at which some were sold, most of them, like the Cincinnati half, fell to the control of coin dealer Thomas Melish, who contrived their issue. The Exposition coincided with Cleveland's 100th anniversary, and it's founder, Gen. Moses Cleaveland is portrayed. (The name changed to its current spelling in 1831 when the first "a" was dropped in order to fit the city's name on a newspaper masthead.)

COLUMBIA, S.C.

	AU	MS-60
1936	275.00	290.00
1936D	275.00	290.00
1936S	275.00	290.00

These were struck for the March 1936 festivities in celebration of Columbia's 150th anniversary as capitol of South Carolina. Unfortunately, they arrived in October. The figure depicted is that of Justice. The tree on the reverse is a palmetto.

COLUMBIAN EXPOSITION

	AU	MS-60
1892	19.50	30.00
1893	16.00	30.00

This is the first United States commemorative coin. It was struck to help raise funds for the 1892-93 World's Columbian Exposition held in celebration of the 400th anniversary of Columbus' voyage of discovery. The obverse portrait is a conjectural one of Christopher Columbus, the reverse shows his ship, the Santa Maria. While initially sold to fairgoers at a premium, too many were ordered and a great many of them later entered circulation at face value.

CONNECTICUT TERCENTENARY

	AU	MS-60
1935	260.00	300.00

Struck to subsidize the statewide celebrations of Connecticut's 300th anniversary. It depicts the Charter Oak, where the colonists hid their royal charter from a governor who sought to revoke it. The distribution of this coin was notably fair, and many went to non-collectors.

Known Counterfeits: Multiple examples reported.

DELAWARE TERCENTENARY

	AU	MS-60
1936	225.00	245.00

Struck to commemorate the landing of Swedish settlers in Delaware in 1638.

Old Swedes Church (1699) is shown, as well as the ship that brought the first settlers.

ELGIN, ILL.

	AU	MS-60
1936	240.00	255.00

This coin was struck to help pay for construction of the statue *Pioneer Memorial* by Trygve Rovelstad, the same sculptor who designed the coin. The statue itself, not completed and dedicated until 2001, is seen on the reverse. The obverse is the head of a typical pioneer of the 1830s, the date 1673 being incorrect.

BATTLE OF GETTYSBURG

	AU	MS-60
1936	430.00	465.00

Struck to commemorate the 75th anniversary of the Battle of Gettysburg, as well as the coinciding Blue and Gray Reunion, a gathering of Civil War veterans on the field of battle.

GRANT MEMORIAL

	AU	MS-60
1922 star in r. field	1,010.00	1,335.00
1922 no star	120.00	135.00

This coin was struck for the 100th anniversary of Grant's birth. A Mathew Brady photograph formed the basis for Laura Gardin Fraser's bust of Grant on both the half dollar and the gold dollar. The proceeds from this coin were supposed to fund the construction of four museum buildings and a highway. None were ever built. A few of these have a recessed star in the obverse field.

Known Counterfeits: Some plain-field Grant halves have been altered by punching a false star in the field. On these, a corresponding flat spot may show on the reverse.

HAWAII SESQUICENTENNIAL

	AU	MS-60
1928	1,900.00	2,800.00

Struck for the 150th anniversary of Capt. Cook's discovery of Hawaii, his bust is on the obverse. While the warrior chief on the reverse is not technically King Kamehameha I, it is based on a statue of him. This is one of the scarcest commemorative-type coins. It was distributed almost exclusively in Hawaii at $2 each.

Known Counterfeits: Counterfeits are a serious problem for this issue.

HUDSON, N.Y.

	AU	MS-60
1935	750.00	940.00

The 150th anniversary of Hudson, N.Y., was not an event of national importance, but in 1935 that was hardly a criterion for a commemorative half dollar. Even worse, after one coin dealer was given permission to purchase 75 percent of them before they were released, only 2,500 remained for the general public to buy at $1 each. The designs are Hudson's ship and the city's seal.

Known Counterfeits: Both regular strikes and matte proofs have been counterfeited.

HUGUENOT-WALLOON TERCENTENARY

	AU	MS-60
1924	140.00	160.00

Struck to commemorate the 300th anniversary of Protestant settlement in America and the founding of New Netherland territory, today New York. The ship *Nieuw Nederlandt* is on the

reverse, while the obverse shows Adm. Coligny and William the Silent, 16th-century Protestant martyrs. More than one third are reported to have entered general circulation.

ILLINOIS STATEHOOD

	AU	MS-60
1918	140.00	160.00

Struck to finance the celebration of Illinois' 100th anniversary of statehood. The statue of a beardless Lincoln depicted was unveiled at the celebrations. Many were spent.

IOWA STATEHOOD

	AU	MS-60
1946	115.00	125.00

Struck to celebrate Iowa's 100th anniversary as a state. Iowa residents were allowed to purchase them at $2.50, others at $3. The design is the state seal and the Old Stone Capitol in Iowa City. Specimens are often plagued with bag marks.

LEXINGTON-CONCORD

	AU	MS-60
1925	105.00	120.00

This coin commemorates the beginning of the Revolutionary War in 1775. The obverse depicts an 1875 statue of a Minute Man, the reverse the Old Belfry that called them to arms. The original wooden box of this coin is among the most common original holders.

LONG ISLAND TERCENTENARY

	AU	MS-60
1936	90.00	100.00

Struck to commemorate the 300th anniversary of Dutch settlement on Long Island. Depicted are a Dutch settler and Algonquin Indian, a 17th-century ship on the reverse. Unlike some 1930s commemoratives, this coin was fairly distributed to the public through Long Island's local banks. Bag marks are a particular problem.

LYNCHBURG, VA.

	AU	MS-60
1936	240.00	275.00

Struck for the "150th Birthday" of Lynchburg, Va. Sen. Carter Glass, then still living, is depicted. Liberty is on the reverse. Glass was the founder of the FDIC.

MAINE CENTENNIAL

	AU	MS-60
1920	140.00	175.00

This half showing the Maine arms honored the centennial of its admission as a state. It was, unlike most halves, distributed by the state treasurer, and was popular with the public.

Known Counterfeits: Those of proof strikes have been seen.

MARYLAND TERCENTENARY

	AU	MS-60
1934	160.00	195.00

Subsidizing the 300th anniversary celebration of Maryland's settlement, this half portrays Cecil Calvert, Lord Baltimore, showing his full arms on the reverse. It was well distributed and fairly popular at the time.

Known Counterfeits: False matte proofs are known, modified from authentic regular issues.

MISSOURI CENTENNIAL

	AU	MS-60
1921, 2★4 in field	675.00	850.00
1921, no 2★4	430.00	700.00

Struck a year late to finance the Missouri Centennial Exposition, also after the statehood centennial. The portrait is that of Daniel Boone, who helped settle Missouri. The 2★4 in the field of some of them indicates that it is the 24th state. On early strikes it is recessed, not in relief.

Known Counterfeits: Type with plain field.

MONROE DOCTRINE

	AU	MS-60
1923S	60.00	80.00

This coin, allegedly to commemorate the Monroe Doctrine, was instigated by promoters of a film industry exposition, hence "Los Angeles" on the reverse. The continents shown are formed of two allegorical figures. John Quincy Adams is shown with Monroe because Adams actually wrote this policy against European intervention in the Americas. Most of these ended up in circulation.

Known Counterfeits: Actual counterfeits are not common, but cleaned or AU coins passing for MS-60 are.

NEW ROCHELLE, N.Y.

	AU	MS-60
1938	425.00	450.00

This coin was made for the 250th anniversary of the settlement of New Rochelle, N.Y., by Huguenots from La Rochelle, France. They owed John Pell, from whom they obtained their land, "one fatt calfe" every June 24. Pell receiving it is depicted.

Known Counterfeits: Matte proofs.

NORFOLK, VA.

	AU	MS-60
1936	540.00	560.00

Despite the 1936 date of the celebration of Norfolk's anniversary, the legislation approving this coin was not even passed by Congress until 1937. The Royal Mace depicted was presented to the city in 1753.

OREGON TRAIL MEMORIAL

	AU	MS-60
1926	145.00	180.00
1926S	145.00	180.00
1928	230.00	260.00
1933D	390.00	420.00
1934D	210.00	225.00
1936	175.00	200.00
1936S	190.00	200.00
1937D	190.00	210.00
1938	165.00	185.00
1938D	165.00	185.00
1938S	165.00	185.00
1939	535.00	610.00
1939D	535.00	610.00
1939S	535.00	610.00

Struck to finance the Oregon Trail Memorial Association's placement of landmarks along the historic route west. This issue was divided between various mints and dates, instead of one large production run. The association's organizers realized that this would force collectors to buy many coins to have a complete set.

PANAMA PACIFIC EXPOSITION

	AU	MS-60
1915S	480.00	555.00

Struck for San Francisco's celebration of the opening of the Panama Canal. It was sold individually at $1 each, and as part of five-piece sets with four gold commemoratives (or in 10-piece double sets.). The original copper frames are valuable.

Known Counterfeits: Some exist with less sharp details.

PILGRIM TERCENTENARY

	AU	MS-60
1920	85.00	115.00
1921	180.00	210.00

Struck to honor the 300th anniversary of the Pilgrims' landing at Plymouth Rock. The bust is a hypothetical one of Gov. William Bradford. The reverse ship represents the Mayflower. Many were melted, making the 1921 issue scarcer.

Known Counterfeits: Reported, not verified.

RHODE ISLAND TERCENTENARY

	AU	MS-60
1936	110.00	115.00
1936D	65.00	115.00
1936S	65.00	115.00

Struck for the 300th anniversary of the founding of Rhode Island by Roger Williams. The obverse and reverse are adaptations of the Providence and Rhode Island arms, respectively. Most went to Rhode Island Hospital National Bank and to Grant's Hobby Shop, with far fewer distributed nationally.

ROANOKE ISLAND, N.C.

	AU	MS-60
1937	260.00	285.00

Struck to honor the 1587 settlement founded by Sir Walter Raleigh, and the birth of the first European child in the New World.

ROBINSON - ARKANSAS

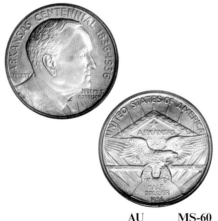

	AU	MS-60
1936	150.00	155.00

The Arkansas Centennial Commission decided that if there were more varieties of its coins it would sell more, so it got approval to replace the allegorical portraits on its half with one of the still-living Sen. Joseph Robinson of Arkansas, then Senate Majority Leader. The entire publicly available mintage was handled by the numismatic firm of Stack's, which offered them at $1.85 each.

SAN DIEGO - CALIFORNIA PACIFIC

	AU	MS-60
1935S	110.00	130.00
1936D	110.00	135.00

Struck to promote the World's Fair in San Diego, the original 1935 quantities did not sell well to attendees, so they were shipped back to the mint to be melted and restruck with a 1936 date, prompting collectors to buy them to maintain a complete set

SESQUICENTENNIAL OF INDEPENDENCE

	AU	MS-60
1926	90.00	120.00

Intended for distribution at the exposition celebrating the 150th anniversary of American independence, most did not sell. This may have been due their low relief, and many were melted. President Calvin Coolidge, then still in office, is depicted with George Washington. A $2½ gold piece was also struck for this celebration.

Known Counterfeits: Beware of false proofs made by treating regular issues.

OLD SPANISH TRAIL

	AU	MS-60
1935	1,300.00	1,400.00

Designed by, struck for and entirely purchased by L.W. Hoffecker, later ANA president. Some proceeds went to the El Paso Museum. Shown is Álvar Núñez Cabeza de Vaca's route west.

Known Counterfeits: Those of matte proofs are possible. Those of regular strikes sometimes lack normal die polish marks.

STONE MOUNTAIN MEMORIAL

	AU	MS-60
1925	75.00	80.00

Struck to raise funds for the construction of the mammoth sculpture (completed 1970) honoring Confederate heroes at Stone Mountain, near Atlanta. Depicted is a section showing generals Thomas Jonathan "Stonewall" Jackson and Robert E. Lee. About half were placed in circulation.

TEXAS CENTENNIAL

	AU	MS-60
1934	145.00	150.00
1935	145.00	150.00
1935D	145.00	150.00
1935S	145.00	150.00
1936	145.00	150.00
1936D	145.00	150.00
1936S	145.00	150.00
1937	145.00	150.00
1937D	145.00	150.00
1937S	145.00	150.00
1938	250.00	310.00
1938D	250.00	310.00
1938S	250.00	310.00

Struck to commemorate the centennial of Texas' independence from Mexico. The obverse shows an eagle against a Lone Star background. The complex reverse shows Victory holding the Alamo, busts of Sam Houston and Stephen Austin at her sides. The reason this issue was divided between various mints and dates, instead of one large production run, was the realization that it would prompt collectors to buy many coins to have a complete set.

FORT VANCOUVER

	AU	MS-60
1925	340.00	415.00

Struck to pay for the celebration of the centennial of the founding of Fort Vancouver, Wash. The bust is that of Dr. John McLoughlin, chief Hudson's Bay Company representative in the area.

Known Counterfeits: Exist both for proofs and regular strikes. They lack sharpness.

VERMONT SESQUICENTENNIAL

	AU	MS-60
1927	245.00	300.00

Struck to commemorate the 150th anniversary of the battle of Bennington and to raise money for local museums. Depicted is Ira Allen, a leader of the Green Mountain Boys, and an inaccurately rendered Vermont catamount. The relief on this coin is notably high.

BOOKER T. WASHINGTON

	AU	MS-60
1946	15.00	19.00
1946D	15.00	19.00
1946S	15.00	19.00
1947	35.00	45.00

	AU	MS-60
1947D	35.00	45.00
1947S	35.00	45.00
1948	55.00	70.00
1948D	55.00	70.00
1948S	55.00	70.00
1949	75.00	95.00
1949D	75.00	95.00
1949S	75.00	95.00
1950	50.00	75.00
1950D	50.00	75.00
1950S	15.00	19.00
1951	15.00	19.00
1951D	50.00	50.00
1951S	50.00	50.00

Ostensibly struck to construct memorials to the great educator, and "to perpetuate [his] ideals and teachings." Many, however, considered them a profit-making scheme of S.J. Phillips, their promoter. Some dates are scarce, and other more common ones ended up in circulation.

WISCONSIN CENTENNIAL

	AU	MS-60
1936	235.00	265.00

Struck not for the centennial of Wisconsin's statehood, but as a territory. One side displays a badger, the other side derived from the territorial flag, showing an arm with pickaxe.

YORK COUNTY, MAINE

	AU	MS-60
1936	230.00	250.00

Struck for the 300th anniversary of the founding of Brown's Garrison, York County, Maine. One third of the production was reserved for Maine residents, who were able to buy them for 20 years.

LAFAYETTE DOLLAR

	AU	MS-60
1900	670.00	1,000.00

The only silver dollar in the original commemorative series. Profits were to pay for an equestrian statue (depicted on reverse) of Lafayette at the 1900 Paris Exposition. The portraits are those of Washington and Lafayette.

Known Counterfeits: Several counterfeits have been reported.

GRANT MEMORIAL GOLD DOLLARS

	AU	MS-60
1922 with star	1,750.00	1,850.00
1922 no star	1,900.00	1,950.00

Struck for the 100th anniversary of Grant's birth. A Mathew Brady photograph formed the basis for Laura Gardin Fraser's bust of Grant on both the half dollar and the gold dollar. It was intended that four museum buildings and a highway be constructed with the proceeds from this coin, none of which were constructed. Some of these have a star above the word GRANT on the obverse.

Known Counterfeits: Casts are known.

LEWIS AND CLARK EXPOSITION GOLD DOLLARS

	AU	MS-60
1904	1,050.00	1,350.00
1905	1,300.00	1,650.00

These were struck to commemorate Lewis and Clark's 1804-06 expedition to the newly acquired Louisiana Territory. They were sold to finance an exposition honoring their explorations in Portland, Ore., and to construct a memorial to Sacagawea. A bust of one explorer is on each side.

Known Counterfeits: Both pieces have been counterfeited.

LOUISIANA PURCHASE EXPOSITION GOLD DOLLARS

	AU	MS-60
1903 Jefferson	700.00	750.00
1903 McKinley	700.00	750.00

Struck to raise money for the 1904 Louisiana Purchase Exposition in St. Louis, and ultimately to commemorate Jefferson's 1803 Louisiana Purchase from France. The McKinley obverse also serves as a memorial, as he was assassinated in 1901.

Known Counterfeits: Both have been counterfeited.

WILLIAM McKINLEY MEMORIAL GOLD DOLLARS

	AU	MS-60
1916	625.00	700.00
1917	790.00	820.00

Struck to pay for the construction of a memorial to the assassinated president in Niles, Ohio. They sold poorly, and 10,000 were bought by coin dealer B. Max Mehl.

Known Counterfeits: Those of the 1917 date are known.

PANAMA-PACIFIC EXPOSITION GOLD SERIES

	AU	MS-60
1915S $1	675.00	750.00

	AU	MS-60
1915S $2½	1,700.00	2,150.00

	AU	MS-60
1915S $50 round	55,500.00	61,200.00

	AU	MS-60
1915S $50 octagonal	54,300.00	55,700.00

Struck for San Francisco's celebration of the opening of the Panama Canal. At the Exposition, the gold dollar – depicting a canal worker – was available for $2, the $2½ showing Columbia astride a seahorse for $4. The giant $50 depicting Minerva and an owl was often bought as part of five-piece sets, with one silver and four gold commemoratives (or in 10-piece double sets.). This was the first time the United States issued a $50 coin, and the last until 1986. The original copper frames are valuable.

Known Counterfeits: Certainly the $1 and $2½, possibly the $50 as well.

INDEPENDENCE SESQUICENTENNIAL $2½ GOLD

	AU	MS-60
1926	525.00	550.00

Intended for distribution at the exposition celebrating the 150th anniversary of American independence. Most did not sell, perhaps due to their low relief or expense, and were melted. The design is Liberty standing with torch and Declaration of Independence, Independence Hall in Philadelphia is on the reverse. A half dollar was also struck for this celebration.

Known Counterfeits: Beware of false proofs made by treating regular issues. Regular issues have also been counterfeited.

RECENT COMMEMORATIVE COINAGE

After the Bicentennial, with the War of Independence still in the popular consciousness, it seemed only right and fitting to strike a commemorative half dollar to honor the 250th anniversary of the birth of the father of our country. Unlike the Bicentennial coins however, no circulation strikes were ever made. Washington halves were sold at a high premium and most Americans never knew of their existence. Congress and the mint had entered the world of modern mass marketing and there was no turning back. Within a few years the mint was selling so many different specialized numismatic products that former ANA president David Ganz, then on the mint's commemorative coin committee, announced in a speech that the full annual coin budget of the average American collector could not even afford to purchase one of each item, let alone do so and have money left over for older coins.

Conversely, the fact that certain coins have been oversold via mass marketing to soon-disinterested non-collectors has placed a great many on the secondary market. Some of these can now be bought at *below* what the government originally charged for them.

Unlike the earlier commemoratives, which are considered special if in the original holders, these are considered undesirable without them. Original holders are the norm. Also, unlike the previous series, these are listed in chronological order, rather than alphabetically, as many of them are collected in sets of issue.

Known Counterfeits: None are known.

WASHINGTON HALF DOLLAR

	MS-65	PF
1982D	7.50	
1982S		7.50

Issued to honor the 250th anniversary of George Washington's birth in 1732.

LOS ANGELES OLYMPICS

	MS-65	PF
1983P $1 Silver	19.00	—
1983D $1 Silver	19.00	—
1983S $1 Silver	19.00	19.00

	MS-65	PF
1984P $1 Silver	19.00	—
1984D $1 Silver	19.00	—
1984S $1 Silver	19.00	19.00

	MS-65	PF
1984P $10 Gold	—	575.00
1984D $10 Gold	575.00	—
1984S $10 Gold	—	575.00
1984W $10 Gold	575.00	575.00

Struck to raise funds for the U.S. Olympic Committee. The 1983 dollar shows three stylized discus throwers, and was disliked by most collectors. The 1984 depiction of the headless statues before the Los Angeles Coliseum was rejected by the national Fine Arts Commission. The first gold eagle since 1933 depicts runners carrying the Olympic Torch.

STATUE OF LIBERTY

	MS-65	PF
1986D $½ Clad	6.50	—
1986S $½ Clad	—	6.50

	MS-65	PF
1986P $1 Silver	19.00	—
1986S $1 Silver	—	19.50

	MS-65	PF
1988W $5 Gold	275.00	275.00

These two coins were struck to benefit the U.S. Olympic Committee, and to finance the U.S. participation in the Olympics held in Seoul, South Korea, that year.

CONGRESS BICENTENNIAL

	MS-65	PF
1989D $½ Clad	9.50	—
1989S $½ Clad	—	9.50

	MS-65	PF
1986W $5 Gold	275.00	275.00

The 100th anniversary of the Statue of Liberty was occasion for thee coins to benefit it and Ellis Island reconstruction. The half dollar depicts an immigrant family of the turn of the century. The dollar bears the Statue of Liberty with Ellis Island in the background, and the $5 gold the head of the Statue of Liberty as seen from slightly below.

	MS-65	PF
1987W $5 Gold	275.00	275.00

These two coins, celebrating the drafting of the Constitution, were deigned by invitational competition. It is interesting to observe the quill pen in the eagle's talons rather than arrows, alluding to the power of words.

SEOUL OLYMPICS

	MS-65	PF
1989D $1 Silver	19.00	—
1989S $1 Silver	—	20.00

CONSTITUTION BICENTENNIAL

	MS-65	PF
1987P $1 Silver	19.00	—
1987S $1 Silver	—	19.05

	MS-65	PF
1988D $1 Silver	19.00	—
1988S $1 Silver	—	19.00

	MS-65	PF
1989W $5 Gold	**275.00**	**275.00**

Because the Constitution did not go into effect in 1789, the Congress celebrated its bicentennial two years after the Constitution itself, hence another series of coins. Part of the profits from this issue went to repair the Capitol Building and to pay down the national debt.

EISENHOWER CENTENNIAL

	MS-65	PF
1990W $1 Silver	**20.00**	—
1990P $1 Silver	—	**20.00**

Despite the prior issue of the "Ike" dollar of 1971-78, it was decided that a coin was needed to honor the 100th anniversary of the Eisenhower's birth. He is depicted both as general and as president.

MOUNT RUSHMORE

	MS-65	PF
1991D ½ Clad	**22.00**	—
1991S ½ Clad	—	**21.50**

	MS-65	PF
1991P $1 Silver	**34.00**	—
1991S $1 Silver	—	**30.00**

	MS-65	PF
1991W $5 Gold	**365.00**	**275.00**

Despite the depiction of his sculpture on the 1925 Stone Mountain half, Gutzon Borglum's most famous work, Mt. Rushmore was not honored on a coin until its 50th anniversary. The eagle on the $5 is shown wielding the sculptor's tools, a hammer and chisel.

KOREAN WAR MEMORIAL

	MS-65	PF
1991D $1 Silver	**19.00**	—
1991P $1 Silver	—	**22.00**

Struck to honor veterans of the Korean War and to finance construction of the Korean War Memorial.

USO ANNIVERSARY

	MS-65	PF
1991D $1 Silver	**19.00**	—
1991S $1 Silver	—	**22.00**

Issued to commemorate the 50th anniversary of the USO, the United Service Organization, famous for providing entertainment to American troops worldwide.

BARCELONA OLYMPICS

to finance the U.S. participation in the Olympics held in Barcelona, Spain, that year.

WHITE HOUSE BICENTENNIAL

	MS-65	PF
1992D $1 Silver	34.00	—
1992W $1 Silver	—	34.00

Issued to mark the bicentennial of the laying of the cornerstone of the White House. The building was designed by architect James Hoban, who is depicted on this dollar's reverse.

COLUMBUS QUINCENTENARY

Among the better-executed designs in recent years, this set of three coins commemorates the 500th anniversary of Columbus' voyage of discovery. It was this historical event that prompted the very first U.S. commemorative coin in 1892.

BILL OF RIGHTS

	MS-65	PF
1993W $½ Silver	22.50	—
1993S $½ Silver	—	18.50

	MS-65	PF
1993D $1 Silver	30.00	—
1993S $1 Silver	—	22.00

	MS-65	PF
1992P $½ Clad	10.00	—
1992S $½ Clad	—	10.00

	MS-65	PF
1992D $1 Silver	25.00	—
1992S $1 Silver	—	27.00

	MS-65	PF
1992D $½ Clad	13.00	—
1992S $½ Clad	—	12.50
1992D $1 Silver	32.50	—
1992P $1 Silver	—	40.00

	MS-65	PF
1992W $5 Gold	365.00	280.00

These three coins were struck to benefit the U.S. Olympic Committee, and

	MS-60	PF
1992W $5 Gold	385.00	330.00

	MS-65	PF
1993W $5 Gold	375.00	350.00

These three coins honor the 1789 approval of the first 10 amendments to the Constitution, which guaranteed

American liberties, and are collectively called the Bill of Rights.

WORLD WAR II

	MS-65	PF
1993P $½ Clad	35.00	30.00

	MS-65	PF
1993D $1 Silver	35.00	—
1993W $1 Silver	—	45.00

	MS-65	PF
1993W $5 Gold	400.00	390.00

This three-piece set was struck to commemorate the 50th anniversary of World War II. The dollar also commemorates D-Day, the decisive allied landing in Normandy that led to the end of the war.

WORLD CUP

	MS-65	PF
1994D $½ Clad	11.00	—
1994P $½ Silver	—	10.00

	MS-65	PF
1994D $1 Silver	29.00	—
1994S $1 Silver	—	32.00

	MS-65	PF
1994W $5 Gold	365.00	295.00

Struck to note the World Cup, the highest international competition of soccer, which was held in the United Stares that year for the first time.

JEFFERSON MEMORIAL

	MS-65	PF
1993P (1994)	29.00	—
1993S (1994)	31.50	—

This coin was struck to commemorate the 250th anniversary of the birth of Thomas Jefferson, third president and author of the Declaration of Independence.

VIETNAM WAR MEMORIAL

	MS-65	PF
1994W $1 Silver	95.00	—
1994P $1 Silver	—	75.00

Issued to mark the 10th anniversary of the Vietnam Veteran's War Memorial in Washington, D.C. The obverse depicts the memorial's primary element, its famous wall of names.

PRISONERS OF WAR

	MS-65	PF
1994W $1 Silver	100.00	—
1994P $1 Silver	—	50.00

Struck to remember American prisoners of war. Proceeds were used to support the National Prisoner of War Museum.

WOMEN VETERANS

	MS-65	PF
1994W $1 Silver	42.50	—
1994P $1 Silver	—	38.50

Struck to honor women who have served in the nation's five branches of the military.

U.S. CAPITOL

	MS-65	PF
1994D $1 Silver	22.50	—
1994S $1 Silver	—	33.00

Struck to commemorate the beginning of construction of the Capitol Building in 1793. It was finally completed in 1830.

SPECIAL OLYMPICS

	MS-65	PF
1995W $1 Silver	31.00	—
1995P $1 Silver	28.00	—

This coin honors the Special Olympic World Games held in the United States, and the movement's founder, Eunice Kennedy Shriver. Considered scandalous by many, this is one of the rare instances where a living person is depicted on a United States coin.

CIVIL WAR BATTLEFIELDS

	MS-65	PF
1995S $½ Clad	45.00	42.00

	MS-65	PF
1995P $1 Silver	80.00	—
1995S $1 Silver	—	85.00

	MS-65	PF
1995W $5 Gold	900.00	600.00

These mark the 100th anniversary of the establishment of Gettysburg as a national park. Like two commemoratives of the 1930s, these coins were struck, in part, to raise money to help preserve Civil War sites.

ATLANTA OLYMPICS

	MS-65	PF
1995S $½ Clad Basketball	23.00	19.00
1995S $½ Clad Baseball	24.00	20.00
1996S $½ Clad Swimming	165.00	40.00
1996S $½ Clad Soccer	140.00	110.00

	MS-65	PF
1995D $1 Silver Gymnast	80.00	—
1995P $1 Silver same	—	60.00
1995D $1 Silver Paralympics	100.00	—
1995P $1 Silver same	—	65.00
1995D $1 Silver Track & Field	105.00	—
1995P $1 Silver same	—	60.00
1995D $1 Silver Cycling	155.00	—

	MS-65	PF
1995P $1 Silver same	—	50.00
1996D $1 Silver Tennis	340.00	—
1996P $1 Silver same	—	95.00
1996D $1 Silver Wheelchair Athlete	—	400.00
1996P $1 Silver same	98.00	—
1996D $1 Silver Rowing	365.00	—
1996P $1 Silver same	—	75.00
1996D $1 Silver High Jump	405.00	—
1996P $1 Silver same	—	62.50

	MS-65	PF
1995W $5 Gold Torch Runner	800.00	355.00
1995W $5 Gold Stadium	1,200.00	550.00
1995W $5 Gold Flag Bearer	1,050.00	675.00
1996W $5 Gold Cauldron	1,060.00	675.00

In 1996 the Olympics were held in Atlanta. This extensive set of commemoratives honors the many facets of these games.

COMMUNITY SERVICE

	MS-65	PF
1996P $1	250.00	—
1996S $1	90.00	—

Struck to commemorate those who volunteer for community service. Part of the money raised from their sale was donated to an organization dedicated to help encourage such activities.

SMITHSONIAN

	MS-65	PF
1996D $1 Silver	160.00	—
1996P $1 Silver	—	68.00

	MS-65	PF
1996W $5 Gold	1,500.00	700.00

This two-piece set was struck to commemorate the 150th anniversary of the founding of the Smithsonian Institution.

BOTANIC GARDEN

	MS-65	PF
1997P $1	50.00	48.00

Struck two years after the fact to honor the 175th anniversary of the founding of the United States Botanic Garden in Washington, D.C.

ROOSEVELT

	MS-65	PF
1997W $5 Gold	1,100.00	600.00

Struck to honor Franklin Delano Roosevelt, the only president to be elected to four terms (1933-1945).

JACKIE ROBINSON

	MS-65	PF
1997S $1 Silver	105.00	125.00

	MS-65	PF
1997W $5 Gold	5,750.00	990.00

This two-piece set was struck to honor the nation's first black Major League Baseball player, on the 50th anniversary of that important event.

LAW ENFORCEMENT

	MS-65	PF
1997P $1	200.00	165.00

Struck to honor those who serve in law enforcement. Proceeds from the sale of this coin contributed $1.4 million towards the National Law Enforcement Officers Memorial.

ROBERT F. KENNEDY

	MS-65	PF
1998S $1 Silver	35.00	50.00

Struck to memorialize Robert F. Kennedy, former Senator and Attorney General, assassinated in 1968.

BLACK PATRIOTS

	MS-65	PF
1998S $1	175.00	120.00

Struck to honor black patriots, and in particular, to recall Crispus Attucks, who was the first American killed in the Boston Massacre of 1770.

GEORGE WASHINGTON

	MS-65	PF
1999W $5 Gold	535.00	510.00

Struck for the bicentennial of Washington's death, its design was based on Laura Gardin Fraser's original design for the 1932 Washington quarter; $35 from the sale of each coin went to preserve Mount Vernon, Washington's home.

DOLLEY MADISON

	MS-65	PF
1999P $1	50.00	50.00

Struck to honor the wife of James Madison. Dolly Madison (1768-1849) saved important historical treasures before the British burnt the White House. Part of the coin's proceeds went to preserve her home, Montpelier, shown on the reverse.

YELLOWSTONE

	MS-65	PF
1999P $1	58.00	60.00

Struck to commemorate the 125th anniversary of the America's first national park, it depicts a geyser on the obverse, a buffalo against a mountainous background on the reverse. A portion of the proceeds from sales went to support the National Park Foundation.

LIBRARY OF CONGRESS

	MS-65	PF
2000P $1	44.00	45.00

	MS-65	PF
2000 $10		
Platinum/Gold	4,000.00	1,500.00

This pair celebrated the bicentennial of the Library of Congress. The $10 piece was the first bimetallic commemorative of the United States, combining a center of platinum within a ring of gold. It depicts the hand of Minerva raising the torch of learning over the library's dome. The reverse contains the library's logo. The dollar shows an open book superimposed over a torch. Its reverse is a rendering of the dome. A portion of the proceeds went to help support outreach programs to make the library's collection accessible to all Americans.

LIEF ERICKSON

	MS-65	PF
2000P $1	95.00	75.00

Struck to celebrate the millennium of Leif Erickson's landing in North America; $10 from the sale of each coin went to fund United States-Icelandic student exchanges. It was available in two-piece sets with a corresponding Icelandic commemorative.

U.S. CAPITOL VISITOR CENTER

	MS-65	PF
2001 $½ Clad	14.50	19.00

	MS-65	PF
2001 $1 Silver	40.00	47.00
2001 $5 Gold	2,000.00	500.00

These coins commemorate the first convening of Congress in the present Capitol Building in 1800. A portion

of the revenue from sale of these coins was used for the Capitol Visitor Center, intended to provide a high-security, educational experience for the five million people who visit the Capitol each year.

BUFFALO DOLLAR

	MS-65	PF
2001P $1	220.00	230.00

Struck to honor the Buffalo Nickel of 1913-38, considered by many to be the quintessential American coin. Part of the proceeds from the coin's sales went to support the Smithsonian Institution's Museum of the American Indian.

WEST POINT

	MS-65	PF
2002W $1	32.00	32.00

Struck to commemorate the bicentennial of the United States Military Academy at West Point, N.Y.

SALT LAKE OLYMPICS

	MS-65	PF
2002P $1 Silver	35.00	45.00
2002W $5 Gold	600.00	575.00

These coins were struck to promote the Winter Olympic Games held in 2002 in Salt Lake City.

FIRST FLIGHT CENTENNIAL

	MS-65	PF
2003P $½ Clad	17.00	18.00

	MS-65	PF
2003P $1 Silver	38.00	35.00

	MS-65	PF
2003W $10 Gold	675.00	550.00

This set commemorates the centennial off the Wright brothers' first heavier-than-air flight. The dollar and $10 obverses portray the brothers, the half shows the Wright Monument. The reverses of all three depict the Wright brothers' 1903 airplane flying. In the case of the gold piece, a bald eagle is flying above.

THOMAS A. EDISON

	MS-65	PF
2004P $1	40.00	40.00

Struck to honor the famous inventor Thomas Alva Edison, developer of the phonograph, light bulb and movies.

LEWIS AND CLARK

	MS-65	PF
2004P $1	40.00	35.00

Struck to commemorate the bicentennial of the "Corps of Discovery," from St. Louis to the Pacific, led by Meriwether Lewis and William Clark.

MARINE CORPS

	MS-65	PF
2005P $1	50.00	55.00

Struck to commemorate the 230th anniversary of the founding of the Marines. The obverse depicts the raising of the flag at Iwo Jima during World War II.

JOHN MARSHALL

	MS-65	PF
2005P $1	40.00	50.00

Struck to honor John Marshall, Chief Justice of the Supreme Court from 1801 to 1835.

BENJAMIN FRANKLIN

	MS-65	PF
2006P $1 "Scientist"	55.00	60.00
2006P $1 "Founding Father"	55.00	55.00

Struck to commemorate the 300th anniversary of the birth of Benjamin Franklin, whose interests were so diverse that two different dollars were deemed necessary, one for his role as a scientist, another for his efforts in helping to found the United States.

OLD MINT, SAN FRANCISCO

	MS-65	PF
2006S $1	65.00	65.00

	MS-65	PF
2006S $5	325.00	315.00

Struck on the centennial of the great San Francisco earthquake and fire, this pair of coins cites the mint's role as an anchor of hope around which the city was able to rebuild.

JAMESTOWN ANNIVERSARY

	MS-65	PF
2007P $1	45.00	45.00

	MS-65	PF
2007W $5	325.00	315.00

Struck to commemorate the 400th anniversary of the founding of the first successful English settlement in North America.

SCHOOL DESEGREGATION

	MS-65	PF
2007P $1	55.00	60.00

Struck to commemorate the 50th anniversary of the desegregation of Little Rock Arkansas' Central High School.

U.S. PROOF SETS

Proof coins have their origins centuries ago when special, carefully produced strikings were prepared as examples of the "ideal" coin, often for reference or for royal approval. American proof coins are known at least from the early 1800s, but those proofs were not widely available. They were struck for VIPs and for those special collectors and coin dealers with personal connections at the mint.

As the proof coin developed through the late 19th and early 20th centuries, certain criteria began to characterize their manufacture. Generally these days, they are struck twice with highly polished dies on carefully prepared polished blanks. Early in the 20th century the dies were given a matte or sandblasted finish, but this soon fell out of favor. Recently some proofs have been struck with a combination of finishes: a dull matte finish on the motifs, such as portraits, with a highly reflective, mirror-like surface in the fields. These are called cameo proofs and are more desirable than conventional proofs with a mirror-like finish over the entire surface.

Beginning 1936, the mint began the active sale of proof sets to the general public. Each set usually contains one coin of each circulating denomination. They have been released every year since with the exceptions of 1943-1949 and 1965-1967. Proof sets of the 1950s were originally sold in cardboard boxes, later in flat cellophane sheets inside special envelopes. Today they come in hard-plastic cases. Proof sets not in their original holders are usually traded at a discount. Such removal can damage their fragile surfaces by exposure to humidity, which can cause what collectors call "carbon spots" to form.

Since the mint has begun active marketing of recent commemoratives, they have also offered special proof sets containing a commemorative dollar as well as the minor coins. These are called "Prestige sets." Another option the government has offered proof-set buyers since 1992 is the traditional alloy of 90% silver, despite the fact that no coins for circulation are struck in that composition. Special sets are also sold containing just the statehood quarters of that year.

Known Counterfeits: Proof sets are not generally counterfeited, but regular coins can be treated to look like matte proofs. This is called "pickling."

	PF
1936	7,850.00
1937	4,200.00
1938	1,950.00
1939	1,850.00

	PF
1940	1,550.00
1941	1,550.00
1942 5 coins	1,375.00
1942 6 coins	1,550.00
1950	700.00
1951	550.00
1952	300.00
1953	265.00
1954	120.00
1955 box	120.00
1955 flat pack	170.00
1956	65.00
1957	30.00
1958	55.00
1959	29.00
1960	22.00
1960 small date cent	35.00
1961	16.00
1962	15.00
1963	15.00
1964	16.00
1968S	8.00
1968S no mint mark dime	17,500.00
1969S	7.50
1970S large date cent	11.00
1970S small date cent	110.00
1970S no mint mark dime	1,450.00
1971S	5.00
1971S no mint mark nickel	2,000.00
1972S	5.00
1973S	10.00
1974S	11.50
1975S	12.75
1975S no mint mark dime	50,000.00
1976S	11.00
1976S 3-pc. silver	18.50
1977S	9.00
1978S	10.00
1979S Filled S	9.00
1979S Clear S	120.00
1980S	10.00
1981S	9.00
1982S	5.00
1983S	7.50
1983S no mint mark dime	1,150.00

	PF
1983S Prestige	100.00
1984S	9.00
1984S Prestige	28.00
1985S	6.00
1986S	11.50
1986S Prestige	32.50
1987S	7.00
1987S Prestige	26.00
1988S	7.50
1988S Prestige	34.00
1989S	8.00
1989S Prestige	42.00
1990S	9.00
1990S no mint mark cent	6,800.00
1990S Prestige	27.00
1990S Prestige, no mint mark cent	7,000.00
1991S	13.50
1991S Prestige	65.00
1992S	7.50
1992S Prestige	80.00
1992S Silver	17.50
1992S Silver Premier	17.50
1993S	14.00
1993S Prestige	38.00
1993S Silver	36.00
1993S Silver Premier	36.00
1994S	13.00
1994S Prestige	45.00
1994S Silver	44.00
1994S Silver Premier	44.00
1995S	40.00
1995S Prestige	135.00
1995S Silver	100.00
1995S Silver Premier	100.00
1996S	16.00
1996S Prestige	500.00
1996S Silver	45.00
1996S Silver Premier	45.00
1997S	30.00
1997S Prestige	175.00
1997S Silver	70.00
1997S Silver Premier	70.00
1998S	32150
1998S Silver	30.00
1998 Silver Premier	30.50
1999S	70.50
1999S Silver	355.00
1999 Quarters	55.00
2000S	20.00
2000S Silver	33.00
2000S Quarters	11.00
2001S	105.00
2001S Silver	165.00
2001S Quarters	55.50
2002S	35.00
2002S Silver	63.50
2002S Quarters	21.00
2003S	23.50
2003S Silver	33.00
2003S Quarters	15.50
2004S	38.00

	PF
2004S Silver	35.00
2004S Quarters	21.00
2004S Silver Quarters	24.00
2005S	20.00
2005S Silver	35.00
2005S Quarters	16.00
2005S Silver Quarters	20.00
2005S American Legacy	150.00
2006S	25.00
2006S Silver	35.00
2006S Quarters	16.00
2006S Silver Quarters	21.00
2006S American Legacy	120.00
2007S	25.00
2006S Silver	40.00
2007S Quarters	15.00
2007S Silver Quarters	21.00

U.S. MINT SETS

Mint sets do not necessarily contain coins superior to those placed in circulation. They are sold as a convenience to collectors who wish to obtain one example of each coins struck for circulation from each mint used to strike that denomination.

Mint sets from 1947 to 1958 contain two of each coin. No conventional mint sets were packaged from 1965 to 1967. The Special Mint Sets of these years were of a superior quality (despite initial government claims to the contrary) perhaps to compensate the public for the lack of proof sets available in those years. While Philadelphia, Denver and San Francisco were all striking coins for circulation, no mintmarks were used so their products cannot be told apart. The 1966 and 1967 sets came in rigid cases within a tight-fitting cardboard box. When the use of mintmarks was resumed in 1968, the coins of the different mints were separated by placing them in blue or red plastic sleeves. Some recent mint sets also contain commemoratives. In 1982 and 1983, souvenir sets sold at the mint replaced mint sets.

Even more than with proof sets, mint sets must be in their original packaging to command a premium above loose, uncirculated coins. Removing them from their protective packaging can damage mint-state coins by exposure to moisture. Such maltreatment can cause "carbon spots" to form, much as they do on proof coins.

Known Counterfeits: When mint sets are presented in unofficial holders, be careful that a slightly circulated coin is not inserted in hopes of passing it off among the others. Coins that originally

constituted a mint set and have been simply placed in another holder will usually have matching toning typical of early sets. The plastic holders of 1966 and 1967 can easily be opened and other coins substituted.

	PF
1947	1,500.00
1948	770.00
1949	960.00
1950	None released
1951	950.00
1952	850.00
1953	600.00
1954	270.00
1955	165.00
1956	165.00
1957	260.00
1958	160.00
1959	60.00
1960	32.00
1961	50.00
1962	25.00
1963	25.00
1964	24.50
1965 Special Mint Set	9.50
1966 Special Mint Set	9.00
1967 Special Mint Set	18.00
1968	6.50
1969	7.50
1970	18.50
1970 small date cent	72.50
1971	6.50
1972	7.00
1973	18.00

	PF
1974	7.00
1975	10.00
1976	10.00
1976S 3-pc. silver	15.00
1977	8.50
1978	7.50
1979	7.50

Above set was incomplete in that it lacks the Susan B. Anthony dollar.

	PF
1980	7.50
1981	15.00
1982	*Souvenir Sets Only*
1983	*Souvenir Sets Only*
1984	7.50
1985	7.25
1986	14.50

	PF
1987	7.25
1988	7.00
1989	7.00
1990	7.50
1991	9.00
1992	8.00
1993	8.00
1994	7.50
1995	16.50
1996	24.00
1997	20.00
1998	7.00
1999	26.00
2000	10.50
2001	19.00
2002	16.00
2003	24.00
2004	65.00
2005	16.00
2006	18.00
2007	27.00

BULLION ISSUES

A bullion coin is a coin with a value in precious metal intended to be higher than its face value. They are sold by the issuing authority at or near the value of the metal. People buy these as a means of investing in precious metal, much as they might otherwise buy ingots. The difference is that a bullion coin is not only guaranteed by the government that issued it but can also be spent in the unlikely event that the value of its metal should evaporate. Beginning on Jan. 1 1975, for the first time since the Depression, it became legal for Americans to own gold bullion. From then until 1980, the United States market in bullion was dominated by imported coins.

An attempt was made to capitalize on this domestic market with a product the U.S. government could easily produce. The first endeavor was the American Arts Medallion series of gold pieces. Struck in one and half-ounce sizes, they depicted important Americans in the arts on the obverse, and a reverse emblematic of their works. Despite some limited success with direct distribution and sales through post offices, this series was not deemed successful, perhaps due to the lack of a denomination and legal-tender status.

In an effort to capture a greater share of that market, and specifically to compete with the South African Krugerrand, which had fallen out of favor because of the anti-Apartheid movement, the United States started issuing its own gold bullion coin. The new gold Eagle, with a face value of $50 rather than $10 like the eagle of 1795-1933, has specifications virtually identical to the Krugerrand's. It contains one ounce

of pure gold, but weighs a bit more because of the addition of an alloy added to harden it. Its purity is 97.67 percent. Although they bear denominations, it is customary in the bullion market to refer to these pieces by their net gold content instead.

The obverses of both the gold and the silver coins hark back to the Hellenistic designs of the early 20th century. The gold ounce and its fractions have Liberty striding towards the viewer as on Saint-Gaudens' $20 gold piece of 1907-1933. The silver revives Weinman's Walking Liberty used on half dollars of 1916-1947. The new reverses depict a family of eagles on the gold, a dignified heraldic eagle on the silver.

In 1997 this series was rounded out by the addition of a $100 one-ounce platinum eagle and its fractions. The proof versions of this coin, depicting a bust of the Statue of Liberty and a soaring eagle, is unusual in its rendering. Rather than having its fields brilliant and its details matte, it is reversed. The major part of the surface has a matte texture, with only selected details reflective. Not only does this make for a striking appearance, it is one more tool to help discern a genuine coin from a counterfeit.

In an effort to maintain a low premium over the bullion content, U.S. bullion coins are only available in bulk quantities. This is not true of proof strikes, which are available individually by mail order. When buying these coins retail, remember that the larger the size, the smaller the percentage premium. Smaller fractions are usually better as gifts than investments.

Known Counterfeits: Despite the fact that the U.S. bullion coins are less counterfeited than many others, it is important to be cautious. Check for detail and for any trace of an edge seam. When the coin is placed upon the tip of a finger and the edge is struck with a pencil, an extended ring should be heard. Many privately made silver bullion pieces resemble the U.S. silver Eagle but differ in their inscriptions. All those larger than one ounce are privately made.

NOTICE: The values of most of these issues, including many proofs, vary at least daily with the value of their metal content. **The prices listed here are based on a platinum value of $2,000, gold $1,000, and silver $20.** Updated prices on commodities such as precious metals, though not on single coins, can be found both in most newspapers and on the Internet. However, for any firm quote on bullion it is best to call your local coin or bullion dealer.

AMERICAN ARTS GOLD MEDALLIONS

1/2 oz.	BU
1980 Marian Anderson	550.00
1981 Willa Cather	550.00
1982 Frank Lloyd Wright	550.00
1983 Alexander Calder	550.00
1984 John Steinbeck	550.00

1 oz.	BU
1980 Grant Wood	1,060.00
1981 Mark Twain	1,060.00
1982 Louis Armstrong	1,060.00
1983 Robert Frost	1,060.00
1984 Helen Hayes	1,060.00

AMERICAN EAGLE SILVER COINS

1 oz. / $1	Unc.	PF
1986	29.00	—
1986S	—	35.00
1987	24.50	—
1987S	—	35.00
1988	26.50	—
1988S	—	55.00
1989	24.50	—
1989S	—	38.00
1990	26.50	—
1990S	—	35.00
1991	24.50	—
1991S	—	50.00
1992	25.50	—
1992S	—	45.00
1993	24.50	—
1993P	—	190.00
1994	26.50	—
1994P	—	240.00
1995	25.50	—
1995P	—	220.00
1995W	—	5,250.00
1996	70.00	—
1996P	—	70.00
1997	30.00	—
1997P	—	130.00
1998	24.50	—
1998P	—	60.00
1999	24.50	—
1999P	—	60.00
2000	24.50	—
2000P	—	38.00
2001	24.50	—
2001W	—	37.00
2002	24.50	—
2002W	—	37.00
2003	24.50	—
2003W	—	37.00
2004	24.50	—
2004W	—	37.00
2005	24.50	—
2005W	—	36.00
2006W	24.50	50.00
2006P *Reverse Proof*	275.00	—
2007	26.00	—
2007W	—	36.00

AMERICAN EAGLE GOLD COINS

1/10 oz. / $5	Unc.	PF
1986	110.00	—
1987	110.00	—
1988	220.00	—
1988P	—	115.00
1989	110.00	—
1989P	—	115.00
1990	110.00	—

1/10 oz. / $5	Unc.	PF
1990P	—	115.00
1991	125.00	—
1991P	—	115.00
1992	110.00	—
1992P	—	115.00
1993	110.00	—
1993P	—	115.00
1994	110.00	—
1994W	—	115.00
1995	110.00	—
1995W	—	115.00
1996	110.00	—
1996W	—	115.00
1997	110.00	—
1997	115.00	—
1998	110.00	—
1998W	—	115.00
1999	110.00	—
1999W	—	165.00
2000	110.00	—
2000W	—	115.00
2001	110.00	—
2001W	—	115.00
2002	110.00	—
2002W	—	115.00
2003	110.00	—
2003W	—	115.00
2004	110.00	—
2004W	—	115.00
2005	110.00	—
2005W	—	115.00
2006	110.00	—
2006W	—	115.00
2007	110.00	—
2007W	—	115.00

1/4 oz. / $10	Unc.	PF
1986	270.00	—
1987	270.00	—
1988	270.00	—
1988P	—	275.00
1989	270.00	—
1989P	—	275.00
1990	270.00	—
1990P	—	275.00
1991	400.00	—
1991P	—	275.00
1992	270.00	—
1992P	—	275.00
1993	270.00	—
1993P	—	275.00
1994	270.00	—
1994W	—	275.00
1995	270.00	—
1995W	—	275.00
1996	270.00	—

1/4 oz. / $10	Unc.	PF
1996W	—	275.00
1997	270.00	—
1997	275.00	—
1998	270.00	—
1998W	—	275.00
1999	270.00	—
1999W	—	275.00
2000	270.00	—
2000W	—	275.00
2001	270.00	—
2001W	—	275.00
2002	270.00	—
2002W	—	275.00
2003	270.00	—
2003W	—	275.00
2004	270.00	—
2004W	—	275.00
2005	270.00	—
2005W	—	275.00
2006	270.00	—
2006W	—	275.00
2007	270.00	—
2007W	—	275.00

1/2 oz. / $25	Unc.	PF
1986	585.00	—
1987	535.00	—
1987P	—	575.00
1988	575.00	—
1988P	—	575.00
1989	625.00	—
1989P	—	575.00
1990	700.00	—
1990P	—	575.00
1991	1,300.00	—
1991P	—	575.00
1992	535.00	—
1992P	—	575.00
1993	535.00	—
1993P	—	575.00
1994	535.00	—
1994W	—	575.00
1995	535.00	—
1995W	—	575.00
1996	535.00	—
1996W	—	575.00
1997	535.00	—
1997W	—	575.00
1998	535.00	—
1998W	—	575.00
1999	535.00	—
1999W	—	575.00
2000	535.00	—
2000W	—	575.00
2001	535.00	—

1/2 oz. / $25	Unc.	PF
2001W	—	575.00
2002	535.00	—
2002W	—	575.00
2003	535.00	—
2003W	—	575.00
2004	535.00	—
2004W	—	575.00
2005	535.00	—
2005W	—	575.00
2006	535.00	—
2006W	—	575.00
2007	535.00	—
2007W	—	575.00

1 oz. / $50	Unc.	PF
1986	1,070.00	—
1986W	—	1,100.00
1987	1,070.00	—
1987W	—	1,100.00
1988	1,070.00	—
1988W	—	1,100.00
1989	1,070.00	—
1989W	—	1,100.00
1990	1,070.00	—
1990W	—	1,100.00
1991	1,070.00	—
1991W	—	1,100.00
1992	1,070.00	—
1992W	—	1,100.00
1993	1,070.00	—
1993W	—	1,100.00
1994	1,070.00	—
1994W	—	1,100.00
1995	1,070.00	—
1995W	—	1,100.00
1996	1,070.00	—
1996W	—	1,100.00
1997	1,070.00	—
1997W	—	1,100.00
1998	1,070.00	—
1998W	—	1,100.00
1999	1,070.00	—

1 oz. / $50	Unc.	PF
1999W	—	1,100.00
2000	1,070.00	—
2000W	—	1,100.00
2001	1,070.00	—
2001W	—	1,100.00
2002	1,070.00	—
2002W	—	1,100.00
2003	1,070.00	—
2003W	—	1,100.00
2004	1,070.00	—
2004W	—	1,100.00
2005	1,070.00	—
2005W	—	1,100.00
2006	1,070.00	—
2006W	—	1,100.00
2007	1,070.00	—
2007W	—	1,100.00

AMERICAN EAGLE PLATINUM COINS

1/10 oz. / $10	BU	PF
1997	220.00	—
1997W	—	225.00
1998	220.00	—
1998W	—	225.00
1999	220.00	—
1999W	—	225.00
2000	220.00	—
2000W	—	225.00
2001	220.00	—
2001W	—	225.00
2002	220.00	—
2002W	—	225.00
2003	220.00	—
2003W	—	250.00
2004	220.00	—
2004W	—	700.00
2005	220.00	—
2005W	—	400.00
2006	220.00	—
2006W	—	250.00
2007	220.00	—
2007W	—	250.00

1/4 oz. / $25	BU	PF
1997	535.00	—
1997W	—	540.00
1998	535.00	—
1998W	—	540.00
1999	535.00	—
1999W	—	540.00
2000	535.00	—
2000W	—	540.00
2001	535.00	—
2001W	—	540.00
2002	535.00	—
2002W	—	540.00
2003	535.00	—
2003W	—	600.00
2004	535.00	—
2004W	—	1,700.00
2005	535.00	—

1/4 oz. / $25	BU	PF
2005W	—	850.00
2006	535.00	—
2006W	—	575.00
2007	535.00	—
2007W	—	575.00

1/2 oz. / $50	BU	PF
1997	1,070.00	—
1997W	—	1,075.00
1998	1,070.00	—
1998W	—	1,075.00
1999	1,070.00	—
1999W	—	1,075.00
2000	1,070.00	—
2000W	—	1,075.00
2001	1,070.00	—
2001W	—	1,075.00
2002	1,070.00	—
2002W	—	1,075.00
2003	1,070.00	—
2003W	—	900.00
2004	1,070.00	—
2004W	—	2,600.00
2005	1,070.00	—
2005W	—	1,600.00
2006	1,070.00	—
2006W	—	1,080.00
2007	1,070.00	—
2007W	—	1,080.00

1 oz. / $100	BU	PF
1997	2,130.00	—
1997W	—	2,140.00
1998	2,130.00	—
1998W	—	2,140.00
1999	2,130.00	—
1999W	—	2,140.00
2000	2,130.00	—
2000W	—	2,140.00
2001	2,130.00	—
2001W	—	2,140.00
2002	2,130.00	—

1 oz. / $100	BU	PF
2002W	—	2,140.00
2003	2,130.00	—
2003W	—	2,140.00
2004	2,130.00	—
2004W	—	3,200.00
2005	2,130.00	—
2005W	—	2,600.00
2006	2,130.00	—
2006W	—	2,140.00
2007	2,130.00	—
2007W	—	2,140.00

PATTERNS

Patterns are trial or experimental coins. They are projects that have gone one step beyond the stages of sketches and plaster sculpture, to the point of engraving dies and striking examples, to see what the coin might look like if it went into production. Such patterns are useful to government officials trying to determine if a particular design is suitable, or if a size or shape or denomination is practical. Also they are useful to mint employees in determining how to adjust the dies or mix the alloy for the best strike. Patterns of successful designs sometimes exist dated *before* the year they were first put into circulation, from the period when they were being developed.

During the 19th and very early 20th centuries, those patterns the mint was no longer using were given or sold to employees, politicians or simply well-connected coin collectors or dealers. At some point, mint employees even struck extra patterns or used pattern dies to strike examples in off metals specifically for sale. Since 1916, it has been forbidden to release them.

Distinguishing fine differences between composition varieties may require specific gravity testing.

All patterns are scarce and all pricing is conjectural, as the arrival or departure of as few as 30 serious collectors in the pattern market can alter the pricing structure.

Known Counterfeits: Restrikes are known of the 1836 2 cent. They are of incorrect weight and show signs of die failure. Electrotype copies have been made of some patterns. One should also not confuse private proposals or fantasies for actual U.S. Mint pattern coins. Overt counterfeiting is not extensive, however. Serious research is recommended.

AU-Unc.

1794 Half Dollar, as regular issue but no stars on obv., struck in copper   *Unique*

AU-Unc.

1808 $5, obv. as regular issue, reverse heraldic eagle as type of 1795-1807, struck in silver, Restrikes only   *Scarce*

1814 Half Dollar, as regular issue but struck in platinum, obv. counter-stamped with 33 P's, reverse engraved Platina over eagle.   *Three Known*

AU-Unc.

1836 2¢, Eagle standing wings open on cloud, rev. TWO CENTS in wreath, 90% copper, 10% silver. 60 grs.   **3,000.00**

1836 Dollar, Seated Liberty, rev. flying eagle, copper, reeded edge   *Rare*

Same, plain edge, Restrike   **25,000.00**

AU-Unc.

1853 Small Cent, Liberty Head rev. Value in wreath, Nickel-silver   **2,200.00**

1855 Large Cent, Flying eagle, rev. Value in wreath, copper   **2,200.00**

1858 Small Cent, Indian head and wreath as regular 1859 issue, Copper Nickel, plain edge   **1,600.00**

1866 5 Cent, Washington, rev. Value in wreath, Nickel   **2,200.00**

AU-Unc.

1869 25 Cent, Liberty Head rev. Value in wreath, Copper   **2,200.00**

AU-Unc.

1870 Dollar, Liberty Seated on Globe, rev. Value in wreath, Silver   **8,000.00**

1873 Trade Dollar, Liberty Seated on Globe, rev. Eagle r. on shield, silver, reeded edge   **4,500.00**

AU-Unc.

1879 $4 "Stella," Liberty Head with coiled hair, rev. Star, gold   **200,000**

1891 Dime, as Barber type of 1892-1916, Silver   *Rare*

1896 1 Cent Shield, rev. Value within circular branch, Aluminum   **3,000.00**

1916 Half Dollar, Walking Liberty with LIBERTY to right, Walking Eagle, Value above, silver   **36,000.00**

AU-Unc.

1942 1 Cent, Liberty head from Colombia 2 centavos, rev. United States Mint in wreath, Zinc coated Steel   **3,500.00**

1942 1 Cent, same but Plastic   **7,000.00**

1974 1 Cent, Lincoln Memorial type, Aluminum   *Rare*

ERRORS

An error is a coin that is manufactured incorrectly, or one manufactured correctly with dies on which a mistake has been made or have been damaged. There are a great many types of error, ranging from the wrong

metal being used to the coin being struck off center. The mint usually tries to prevent such coins from getting out. They are usually caught and melted. Because the modern automated manufacturing process creates far fewer errors and greater uniformity than in ancient times, collectors of modern coins actually prize such mistakes. (Similar errors may actually reduce the value of ancient coins.) Errors in larger coins, proofs and commemoratives tend to be scarcer because more attention is paid to the inspection process. Over the last 50 years more have been getting out than in the past, and as a result, recent errors are not as valuable as early ones.

How each basic type of error occurs is explained below, along with what a typical example of such an error would retail for. Prices are for coins struck within the last 30 years. Coins may be worth more or less depending on the extent of the error. Values for most popular double-die cents appear in the regular listings.

Known Counterfeits: Most major double-die cents have been counterfeited. Virtually all examples of 1943 copper and 1944 steel cents are counterfeit. A magnet test will reveal deceptive plating, but not cleverly altered dates. Also, it is easy to cause apparent errors by striking a coin with a coin or hammering foreign matter into it. Apparent off-metal strikes can simply be a coin plated after it was released from the mint. Some thin coins have been bathed in acid. (Is the surface abraded?) Clipped coins are easily confused for clip errors. Almost all two-headed American coins are concoctions. Do not presume a coin is a mint error until you determine how it was made. There are thousands of such "hoax coins" out there.

Some illustrations here are of foreign coins in order to best show the effects of these errors.

EF-MS-60

BIE Cent - A special kind of die chip in which a small chip out of the die between B and E in liberty looks like an extra letter I. Fairly common in the 1950s .... .50

Blank - A blank, or planchet, is the piece of metal on which a coin is struck. Sometimes they escape the mint with no processing whatsoever. Other times they escape unstruck, but do make it through the machine that upsets the edge slightly. These are called type I and type II blanks, respectively.

	EF-MS-60
Cent	.50
Nickel	2.50
Dime	2.00
Quarter	4.00
Half	12.00
Dollar	30.00

Broadstruck - Coin struck without the collar which keeps it round, thus the metal spreads out.

	EF-MS-60
Cent	4.00
Nickel	12.00
Dime	9.00
Quarter	18.00
Half	60.00
Dollar	60.00

Brockage - Coin struck with a coin and a die instead of two dies. Caused by the previous coin adhering to one die. If it covers the whole die it causes a "full brockage." Partial brockage may be worth less.

	EF-MS-60
Cent	15.00
Nickel	38.00
Dime	50.00
Quarter	50.00
Half	275.00
Dollar	275.00

Clashed Dies - Coin struck with a die that has been previously struck by another die leaving some of its impression behind. On the coin, the image of the primary die will be bold, the image of the residual impression will be faint.

	EF-MS-60
Cent	1.00
Nickel	1.25
Dime	2.00
Quarter	7.50
Half	20.00
Dollar	20.00

Clip (2 types) - Coin struck on a blank that has part of its edge missing. There are two causes: A regular clip is caused by the punching device attempting to cutout the form of another coin before a previously punched blank is out of the way. A straight clip is caused when a blank is punched out from too near to the end of the sheet of metal.

	EF-MS-60
Cent	.50
Nickel	2.50
Dime	2.00
Quarter	2.50
Half	11.00
Dollar	24.00

Cud - A cud is a raised area of the coin near its edge. It is caused by a piece of the die chipping away. There is no striking surface in that spot to force the coin's metal down.

	EF-MS-60
Cent	1.00
Nickel	3.00
Dime	3.50
Quarter	7.00
Half	22.50
Dollar	36.00

Die chip - A die chip is similar to a cud, but it can be quite small and occur anywhere in the die, not just the edge.

	EF-MS-60
Cent	.25 to 1.00
Nickel	.25 to 3.50
Dime	.50 to 3.50
Quarter	2.00 to 7.00
Half	5.00 to 25.00
Dollar	5.00 to 35.00

Die crack - A crack in the die will cause a fine raised line across the surface of the coin it strikes. Larger cracks are worth more than values listed.

	EF-MS-60
Cent	.50
Nickel	.75
Dime	.75
Quarter	1.50
Half	2.50
Dollar	6.00

Double die - Caused by several factors, all in the die-manufacturing process. They will appear blurred at first glance, but upon inspection, the details will be doubled.

Prices vary widely, $10 to $500 or more

Double struck - When the coin that has been struck fails to eject from between the pair of dies it will receive a second impression, usually not centered.

	EF-MS-60
Cent	10.00
Nickel	12.00
Dime	12.00
Quarter	40.00
Half	135.00
Dollar	400.00

Lamination - Occasionally called an "Occluded Gas Lamination," it is caused by improper mixture of the metal when the alloy is being made. It will appear as flaking on the surface.

	EF-MS-60
Cent	.50
Nickel	3.00
Dime	4.00
Quarter	7.00
Half	12.00
Dollar	25.00

Mismatched dies - This occurs when one of the two dies is that intended for another coin. To date, all but one has been struck on a blank intended for the larger coin.

	EF-MS-60
Cent and Dime	*Two known*
Dollar and Quarter	47,500.00

Off center - When the blank is not lined up with the dies, only part of the impression is made. The other part of the blank remains just that – blank!

	EF-MS-60
Cent	1.00
Nickel	2.50
Dime	3.00
Quarter	8.00
Half	30.00
Dollar	40.00

Struck through - A coin that had foreign matter on the blank. This matter was impressed into the surface by the force of the die.

	EF-MS-60
Cent	1.50
Nickel	1.50
Dime	1.50
Quarter	3.50
Half	9.00
Dollar	11.00

Wrong metal - When a blank intended for one coin is accidentally mixed into blanks destined for another and gets struck with those dies.

	EF-MS-60
Cent	100.00
Nickel	40.00
Dime	40.00
Quarter	45.00
Half	125.00
Dollar	375.00

UNITED STATES PAPER MONEY

INTRODUCTION

Before the Civil War there was no such thing as United States government paper money. During the Revolutionary War the states and the Continental Congress printed so much paper money to finance their expenses that its value evaporated. As a result, when the Constitution was written, it contained the words, "No state shall ... make anything but gold and silver coin a tender in payment of debts. (1§10)." Because of this the government avoided issuing paper money until the Civil War, and even then it was issued under limited circumstances. The first type of paper money, Demand Notes, even bore interest.

Most of the paper money issued by the United States over the next century was, in fact, redeemable for gold or silver. There are many different kinds of American paper money, as the following sections will show. Their names, usually found at the top of the note as a heading, and often the colors of their seals indicate the law that authorized their issue and the nature of their backing.

Almost all U.S. paper currency bears a date, but this is not necessarily the year it was actually printed. It was the year of the act authorizing the series or the year the series went into production. The signature combinations on banknotes can often be used to date them.

Originally, paper money was larger than today. Until 1928 the bills were about 7 1/2" by 3 1/8". Beginning with the series of 1928 (released 1929) they have been 6 1/8" by 2 5/8". The fractional notes of the Civil War were smaller than current notes, but varied in size.

GRADING PAPER MONEY

State of preservation is as important for paper money as it is for coins. Paper money is primarily graded to describe the amount of wear, but other factors can influence value. Many of the terms used to describe the grades of paper money are the same as for coins. Of course the physical nature of paper requires a whole different set of definitions. They are briefly described here.

Crisp Uncirculated (CU) - This is a note that is pristine as issued. It is literally crisp, with sharply pointed corners. It must have absolutely no folds, tears, or edge rounding. It can have no stains or staple holes.

Extremely Fine (XF) -This is a particularly nice note with only the slightest sign of wear. It will still be crisp to the touch. Slight rounding of the corner points is possible but no significant folds or creases. No tears, stains or staple holes at all.

(A convenient method of detecting creases in a note is to hold the note pointed at a narrow light source and look at it from an acute angle, though not directly in the direction of the light.)

Very Fine (VF) - This is a nice clean note with obvious but moderate signs of wear. Creases that break the ink will be visible, but generally only one in each direction, and neither crease too deep. Its corner points will be dull. While not limp, it will have only some of the crispness of better-grade notes. No significant stains are visible.

Fine (F) - This is a worn but not worn out note. It has no crispness left. It will have heavy creases, but none that threaten the structural integrity of the note. Its edges may not be perfectly smooth, but are not irregularly worn. Trivial ink marks and smudges are acceptable.

Very Good (VG) - This note is worn and limp. It has serious, deep creases. The edges are worn and not even. Some ink marks or smudges are visible. Tiny tears may be present but no parts missing. Small staple or pinholes are acceptable.

Good (G) - This condition is not considered collectible for most purposes. Only the rarest of notes in this grade could find a home with most collectors. It is usually limp, heavily creased, stained, ripped and pinned or stapled. Some of the creases will permit spots of light to shine through the note at their intersections.

HANDLING AND TREATMENT OF PAPER CURRENCY

The most important thing to know about handling currency is to NEVER FOLD PAPER MONEY. This instantly reduces its value. When in doubt as to whether a note has value or not, place it flat in a book until you can consult a numismatist or coin dealer. Do not carry an interesting note around in your wallet. When handling a note remember that its most fragile parts are its corners. Never touch them. Also, never repair a tear in a note with tape. The tape usually is a greater detriment to the note's value than the tear.

Attempts to clean a note are also likely to cause damage.

DETECTING COUNTERFEITS

Detecting counterfeit notes is not as difficult or as mysterious a business as many presume. Also, many of the methods used by merchants are so inefficient as to be of no value.

First it must be realized that, almost since the beginning, U.S. paper money has been printed not on paper but on cloth. It is part cotton and part linen with some silk. The silk is in the form of minute red and blue threads which dive in and out of the surface of the note. A color copier may be able to reproduce the colors of these tiny threads, but it cannot reproduce the texture of them entering and leaving the surface of the note. Another key to detecting counterfeits is crispness of the ink in the design. Images and lines should be sharp and distinct.

Most counterfeit bills passed in circulation are accepted not because the counterfeits are deceptive, but because little or no effort is put into determining if they are real at all. In recent years, Federal Reserve Notes have incorporated many new counterfeit-detection devices. These are fully described in that section.

Real notes have been used occasionally to create counterfeits. A counterfeiter will take the value numbers from the corners of a note and glue them to a note of a lower face value. Such notes will often feel too thick or irregular at the corners. More importantly, such a criminal is presuming the recipients will pay virtually no attention to the notes they are accepting. Such counterfeits can be detected by even a brief comparison with a real note.

Certain practices are designed to take an authentic note and make it appear to be in a better grade of preservation than it is. These include ironing a note to make it look less worn, and expertly gluing tears. Light will pass through a glued repair differently than through undamaged currency.

When choosing a dealer in rare currency, make sure they have the skills to know if a note is real, and the ethics to accept it back if it is not. There are specialized organizations that enforce codes of ethics. Two of the largest are the International Banknote Society (IBNS) and the Professional Currency Dealers Association (PCDA). These insignia in advertising indicate that the dealer is a member.

BOOKS ABOUT UNITED STATES PAPER MONEY

Bressett, Kenneth, *Guide Book of United States Currency*.
Donlon, William, et al., *United States Large Size Paper Money 1861 to 1923*.
Friedberg, Robert, *Paper Money of the United States*. An important basic reference.
Gengerke, Martin, *United States Paper Money Records*. A compilation of price history for rare notes.
Lloyd, H. Robert, *National Bank Notes, Federal Reserve Bank Notes, Federal Reserve Notes 1928-50*.
Schwan, C.F., and Boling, J.E., *World War II Military Currency*.
Schwartz and Oakes, *U.S. Small Size Currency*.
Continental and State Issues
Newman, Eric, *The Early Paper Money of America*.
Obsoletes
Haxby, James, *Obsolete Bank Notes*.
Fractionals
Rothert, Matt, *A Guide Book of United States Fractional Currency*.
Nationals
Hickman and Oakes, *National Bank Notes*.
Confederate
Slabaugh, Arlie, *Confederate States Paper Money*.
Scrip
Mitchell, Ralph, and Schafer, Neil, *Standard Catalog of Depression Scrip*.
Schingoethe, H. and M., *College Currency*.
Personal Checks
Scott Publishing Co., *Specialized Catalogue of United States Stamps*.
Periodicals
Bank Note Reporter
Paper Money, Society of Paper Money Collectors.

ILLUSTRATIONS

Unless indicated otherwise, all illustrations in this section are that of the type of currency described immediately below it. Most illustrations of paper money larger than 3" wide (7.6 cm) are reduced.

CONTINENTAL AND STATE CURRENCY

The first paper money to circulate in the United States was issued in the Colonial era. The assemblies of all original 13 Colonies issued small square-ish notes valued in either English Pounds or in Spanish milled dollars. Due to British mercantile policies, there was always a shortage of precious-metal coinage in the colonies and these notes helped fill the void.

During the Revolutionary War, the governors and legislatures of the newly independent states continued to print paper money, as did the Continental Congress. Unfortunately, printing un-backed paper currency is inflationary. This situation worsened when the public realized that redeeming the money for real silver or gold varied from difficult to impossible. Rapid inflation soon caused these notes to be devalued, and they traded at a sharp discount. Continental currency issued by the Congress had such a poor reputation that the saying "Not worth a Continental" sprang up. The slang term "shinplasters" for these notes also implies their worthlessness, recalling how 1700s Americans would stick them in their boots to keep warm.

Designs on state notes varied, but the majority featured inscriptions in elaborate borders. Coats of arms and, initially, crowns were also common. During the mid-1770s, designs got more elaborate as farm panoramas and buildings came into vogue. This coincided with the appearance of Continental currency, almost all of which bore intricate circular seals of an allegorical nature.

There are many interesting aspects to American paper currency of the 18th century. The most fascinating was a unique form of printing whereby an actual leaf was used in the printing process, producing fine detail difficult to artificially duplicate. This was intended to deter counterfeiting, as was the saying, "To counterfeit is death" featured on so many notes. Each note bore a hand signature. This is of particular interest to the historian, as many of these signers were either then or soon to be important people. Some became signers of the Declaration of Independence or the Constitution. Signatures of historical figures add to the value of a note. There is also the quaint 18th-century habit of sewing together, instead of gluing, torn notes.

Those notes that were ultimately redeemed were not always destroyed. Sometimes they were cancelled by either cutting an X into them or by cutting out a round hold. These notes, particularly the latter, are today sold at a discount.

Known Counterfeits: The most common counterfeits are those made during the mid-20th century as souvenirs and novelty items. They can be identified by their crackly, brownish-yellow paper. Real notes are printed on thick, soft white paper with a coarse grain. Contemporary counterfeits made to spend at the time are known and are collectible. Serious counterfeits meant to fool collectors are less common.

Note: There are a great many types and varieties. The prices given here are for representative common types.

	VG	VF
Connecticut		
Colony 1709-64	975.00	Rare
Colony 1770-76	85.00	125.00
State 1777-80	85.00	125.00
Delaware		
Colony 1723-60	130.00	350.00
Colony 1776	95.00	135.00
State 1777	95.00	135.00
Georgia		
Colony 1735-75	775.00	Scarce
State 1775-86	400.00	800.00
Maryland		
Colony 1733	95.00	2,500.00
Colony 1740-56	Rare	
Colony 1767-74	75.00	120.00
State 1775-81	75.00	120.00
Massachusetts		
Colony 1690-1744	Rare	
Colony 1750-76	750.00	Rare
State 1776-80	130.00	175.00
New Hampshire		
Colony 1709-63	Rare	
Colony 1775-76 (hole cancelled)	300.00	600.00
State 1777-80	75.00	350.00
New Jersey		
Colony 1709-Jan. 1756	Rare	
Colony June 1756-76	90.00	125.00
State 1780-86	90.00	125.00
New York		
Colony 1709	3,000.00	Rare
Colony 1711-55	Rare	
Colony 1756-76	95.00	200.00
State 1776-88	95.00	200.00
North Carolina		
Colony 1712-35	Rare	
Colony 1748-61	120.00	450.00
Colony & Province 1768-76	100.00	300.00
State 1778-85	100.00	220.00
Pennsylvania		
Colony 1723-49	Rare	

	VG	VF
Colony 1755-56	105.00	200.00
Colony 1757-76	90.00	110.00
Commonwealth 1777-85	90.00	110.00
Rhode Island		
Colony 1710-67	700.00	Rare
Colony 1775-76	95.00	275.00
State 1776-86	85.00	120.00
South Carolina		
Colony 1703-70	Rare	

	VG	VF
Colony 1774-75	Scarce	
State 1776-87	135.00	350.00
Vermont		
State 1781	8,500.00	Rare
Virginia		
Colony 1755-70	Rare	
Colony 1771-76	135.00	250.00
State 1776-81	135.00	250.00

	VG	VF
Continental Currency		
1775	80.00	150.00
1776	80.00	150.00
1777	90.00	225.00
1778	80.00	150.00
1779	85.00	175.00

OBSOLETES

Before the Civil War, the United States government did not issue paper money. It was generally held that it would violate the Constitution. Instead, paper money was issued privately by banks and other firms throughout the country. No one had to accept it. People were at liberty to refuse any note if they thought the issuing bank unsound or unfamiliar, or simply too far away. Usually these notes would simply pass from one consumer to another as modern government-issue notes do. Sound banks keep coin reserves on hand to back the notes and this is why bust half dollars are commonly available in high grades today. Some fraudulent banks released notes without any backing at all. "Obsoletes" were produced in especially large numbers in the 1830s and 1850s. These notes ceased to be issued in the 1860s when many of the banks went bankrupt and others simply redeemed the notes and stopped issuing them. This is why today they are called obsolete notes, or more informally, broken bank notes. They are a wonderful way to trace local history. Many of the vignettes are artistic and represent local industries such as shipping or cotton. Others have generic patriotic vignettes provided by the printer. Some even show their value in coins: a $1.25 note would show pictures of two half dollars and a quarter. Most notes are one-sided.

Known Counterfeits: Many notes were counterfeited at the time. These counterfeits are of some value but usually less than the real ones. Also, some authentic notes were stamped "counterfeit" by rival banks so they would not have to honor them.

Another scam of the day was the passing of "raised" notes. A counterfeiter would take the value numbers from a high-value note and glue them to a note of a lower face value.

Such notes will often feel too thick or where the values were attached. They are collectible, but of less value than unaltered notes.

Most "Bank of the United States" notes of this period are modern replicas, particularly those of high denomination. They may be identified by their crackly, brownish-yellow paper. Real notes are printed on thin, limp paper.

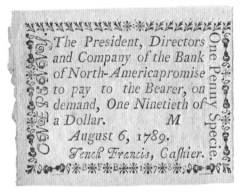

	VG	VF
Bank of North America, 1 Penny, 1789	200.00	450.00
Connecticut: Bridgeport, The Connecticut Bank, $3, 1856 (Locomotive)	200.00	300.00
Same, spurious	30.00	50.00

	VG	VF
__: Fairfield, Fairfield Loan & Trust Company, $1¾, 1839 (Coins, cows and pigs)	135.00	275.00
Delaware: Wilmington, Bank of Wilmington and Brandywine, $5, 1839	150.00	300.00
District of Columbia: Washington, Columbia Bank, Washington, 1852, $1	10.00	25.00
Florida: State of Florida, $50, 1861	27.50	115.00

	VG	VF
Georgia: Savannah, Farmers and Mechanics Bank, $5, 1860 (Statue of Columbia)	15.00	90.00
Illinois: Lockport, State Bank, $10, 1839	10.00	20.00

	VG	VF
Indiana: Bloomfield, Indiana State Bank, $2, 1856	50.00	150.00
Maine: Calais, Washington County Bank, $5, 1835 (Blacksmith, Mercury, Agriculture)	20.00	50.00
Massachusetts: Boston, Cochituate Bank, $5, 1853 (Early steam ship and sailor)	18.00	50.00
Mississippi: State of Mississippi, $1, 1864	10.00	38.00
Nebraska: Omaha, Western Exchange Fire & Marine Insurance, $2, 1856 (Indian, horse & train)	16.00	45.00
New York: Roundout, Bank of Roundout, $10	25.00	98.00
__: Ithaca, Village of Ithaca, 3¢, 1863	25.00	100.00

	VG	VF
North Carolina: Lexington, Bank of Lexington, $5, 1860 (Cotton picker at left)	15.00	40.00
Ohio: Wilmington, Goshen, Wilmington & Columbus Turnpike Co., $10, 1840	35.00	135.00
Virginia: Fincastle, Farmers Bank of Fincastle, $10, 1857	100.00	250.00

FRACTIONAL AND POSTAL CURRENCY

As a result of the Civil War, people began to hoard coins, not only precious metal but copper, too. Much of the silver coinage was also being shipped to Canada. One improvised answer to the shortage created was to spend postage stamps as small change. The U.S. Treasury even sanctioned this practice, much to the chagrin of the Post Office, which was running out of stamps. It was a useful concept, but impractical. Small envelopes printed with a value were devised to convey the stamps as they were spent, but the stamps soon became a

sticky mess, and the envelopes quickly deteriorated. Merchants found an alternative: give customers their own miniature paper currency for small change, requiring the customers to return with more business in order to spend them. These were made illegal. The problem was solved in 1862 by a hybrid between postage stamps and paper money. Small rectangles of paper depicting stamps and labeled "Postage Currency" were issued. They could be redeemed for postage at any post office, but generally they circulated at the value of the stamps depicted. These sheets initially had stamp-like perforations around the edges, but they were soon removed. The miniature notes were a more convenient size and lacked the adhesive which had made stamps a mess. These special stamps were replaced in March 1863 by small notes of a similar size, but which were designed more in the form of paper money, with no reference to stamps. They were now labeled "Fractional Currency." These continued through several issues, surviving the Civil War well into the period of Reconstruction. More than 99 percent of these notes were redeemed and destroyed. Despite this, fractionals are today quite common. They are a popular and easy series to collect, available in virtually every state of preservation from crisp to pulverized. The latter have slightly more than novelty value.

Fractional currency can be divided into four different series. The first is the postage currency already mentioned. It contains several varieties of ink and paper color, as well as notes with and without "ABNCo." These are the initials of the American Bank Note Co., the printing contractor.

When these were replaced by the fractional currency notes of the second series, an interesting counterfeit-prevention device was incorporated. A metallic bronze ink was used to frame Washington's bust and to overprint the value on the reverse. Like bronze coins, they can both tone down and corrode green. Collectors prefer those notes with the bright, original color. These notes were printed by the government itself, instead of by a private contractor.

Attempts to prevent counterfeiting continued with hard-to-imitate details incorporated into a set of all-new designs. (The notes of the second series were all identical.) Actual hand signatures were also tried. This third series has the interesting distinction of having two government officials place their portraits on different notes. Both United States Treasurer Frances Spinner, and Superintendent of the National Currency Bureau, Spencer M. Clark, deemed themselves worthy of depiction. Evidently Congress did not agree. It quickly passed a law to prevent the likeness of a living person from being depicted on these notes again. It has been suggested that Clark accidentally placed himself on the 5-cent note in a case of mistaken identity with the explorer of the Northwest, William Clark! A document allegedly called for a portrait of "Clark." Nevertheless these notes continued to be printed for two years.

A new anti-counterfeiting measure was also introduced for the fourth series. Perhaps even more important, these notes incorporated new, almost inimitable paper containing silk threads. It was an oversized treasury seal, superimposed over the entire height of the face of the note. Some also have a bright pink background over the entire face, and are worth more than prices listed.

The final series of notes lasted only two years. It was decided that the country had recovered from the Civil War enough to redeem its fractional paper. New silver coins were struck and virtually all fractional paper was turned in.

Known Counterfeits: Contemporary counterfeits of fractional currency were a problem from the very first series

of postal currency. It continued to an extent for years into the following series. Nevertheless, these counterfeits were mostly destroyed in the 1860s and 1870s, and they are not abundant today. The bronze metallic ink overprints can be removed in order to create what appears to be a rare variety.

FIRST ISSUE - POSTAGE CURRENCY

	VG	VF
5¢ Jefferson, perforated edges	30.00	85.00
5¢ Jefferson, straight edges	25.00	60.00
10¢ Washington, perforated edges	30.00	95.00
10¢ Washington, straight edges	25.00	60.00
25¢ Five Stamps, perforated edges	30.00	85.00
25¢ Five Stamps, straight edges	25.00	70.00
50¢ Five Stamps, perforated edges	40.00	125.00
50¢ Five Stamps, straight edges	30.00	80.00

SECOND ISSUE - 1863-64

	VG	VF
5¢ Washington in bronze oval	20.00	50.00
10¢ same	20.00	55.00
25¢ same	22.00	70.00
50¢ same	22.00	70.00

THIRD ISSUE - 1864-69

Note: All read "Act of March 3, 1863"

	VG	VF
3¢ Washington	40.00	70.00
5¢ Clark	25.00	65.50
10¢ Washington	20.00	50.00
15¢ Specimen only		CU 120.00
25¢ Fessenden	20.00	55.00
50¢ Justice seated	60.00	150.00

	VG	VF
50¢ Spinner	40.00	85.00

FOURTH ISSUE - 1869-75

Note: All read "Act of March 3, 1863" and have large treasury seal on face.

	VG	VF
10¢ Liberty bust	20.00	55.00
15¢ Columbia bust	55.00	90.00
25¢ Washington	20.00	60.00
50¢ Lincoln	70.00	180.00
50¢ Stanton	30.00	100.00
50¢ Samuel Dexter	25.00	90.00

FIFTH ISSUE - 1874-76

	VG	VF
10¢ Wm. Meredith	20.00	35.00
25¢ Robert. Walker	20.00	35.00
50¢ Wm. Crawford	22.00	40.00

DEMAND NOTES

The demand notes of 1861 were the first regular paper money issued by the United States. They were put into circulation under the emergency circumstances of the Civil War. The bad experiences of the overproduction of paper money during the Revolutionary War were still remembered, so limits were set on the uses of these notes. They differed from modern currency mostly in that they were not properly legal tender, but rather were "receivable in payment for all public dues." That is to say they were not good for "all debts public and private," and not by initial obligation for any private debts at all. One could use them to pay taxes, but did not have to accept them otherwise. Later a law was passed requiring their acceptance. The name "demand note" derives from another phrase on their face, "The United States promises to pay to the bearer on *demand*."

On the other hand, there were limits as to how they could be redeemed. These notes were issued at five cities and could only be redeemed by the assistant treasurers in the individual note's city of issue. Designs were uniform from city to city. The $5 note shows at left the statue of Columbia from the Capitol building, a portrait of Alexander Hamilton right. The $10 shows Lincoln, then in office, left, an eagle centered, and an allegorical figure of Art right. The $20 depicts Liberty holding a sword and shield.

The nickname "greenback" for paper money began with these notes because of their back color. The privately issued paper money circulating until then had blank backs.

There are two major varieties of these, resulting from the government being ill prepared for the practical reality of hand-signing millions of notes. The original intent was that clerks would be able to sign them "N. for the" Register of the Treasury and "N. for the" Treasurer of the United States. The time it took to sign the words "for the" millions of times quickly became excessive, so the words were printed instead. The earlier varieties are worth more than the prices listed here.

High-grade notes in this series are rare.

Known Counterfeits: Examine detail, check to make sure notes are hand signed, and use reasonable caution.

	G	VG
$5 Boston	450.00	3,500.00
$5 Cincinnati	Rare	
$5 New York	450.00	3,500.00
$5 Philadelphia	450.00	3,500.00
$5 St. Louis	1,000.00	Rare

	G	VG
$10 Boston	950.00	3,700.00
$10 Cincinnati	Rare	
$10 New York	950.00	3,400.00
$10 Philadelphia	950.00	3,400.00
$10 St. Louis	3,000.00	8,000.00

	G	VG
$20 Boston	12,500.00	22,000.00
$20 Cincinnati		Rare
$20 New York	8,500.00	22,000.00
$20 Philadelphia	8,500.00	22,000.00

TREASURY NOTES

These notes, designated "Treasury Notes" by the titles on their face inscriptions, are also called "Coin Notes." This was because, according to law, the Secretary of the Treasury was instructed to redeem these notes in coin, either gold or silver, at his or her choosing. Interestingly, they were not actually backed by coin at all, but rather by silver bullion.

This series was of short duration, being issued only in 1890 and 1891. Both years have the same face designs, generally of military heroes. The original reverse designs featured the values spelled out in large letters. For 1891, they were redesigned to allow more blank space. The ornamentation of the two 0s in 100 on the reverse of the $100 notes is reminiscent of the pattern on the skin of a watermelon, hence they are known by the collecting community as "watermelon notes."

Known Counterfeits: Examine detail, silk threads in paper and use reasonable caution.

	F	XF
$1 1890 Edwin M. Stanton	650.00	2,500.00
$1 1891 same	350.00	650.00

	F	XF
$2 1890 Gen. James D. McPherson	1,000.00	6,500.00
$2 1891 same	500.00	2,000.00
$5 1890 Gen. George H Thomas	600.00	3,000.00
$5 1891 same	350.00	750.00

	F	XF
$10 1890 Gen. Philip H. Sheridan	1,500.00	3,500.00
$10 1891 same	950.00	1,900.00
$20 1890 John Marshall	3,400.00	7,500.00
$20 1891 same	3,000.00	7,400.00
$50 1891 William H. Seward	40,000.00	120,000.00

	F	XF
$100 1890 Adm. David G. Farragut	70,000.00	150,000.00
$100 1891 same	70,000.00	150,000.00
$1000 1890 Gen. George Meade	Rare	
$1000 1891 same	Rare	

NATIONAL BANK NOTES

National banknotes are a hybrid of government-issued and private paper money. The notes, titled "National Currency" on their face, were issued by individual private banks, but printed by the U.S. government. Not every bank could issue them, only "national banks." To qualify, each bank had to meet certain criteria, which included keeping a predetermined value of U.S. government bonds on deposit with the United States Treasurer. In exchange for this commitment, the notes issued by the bank were considered legal tender of the United States and were good anywhere United States currency was good. The treasury would stand behind them.

Designs did not vary from bank to bank, but they used those types designated by the Treasury. The face of each note would indicate the issuing bank's name (usually including the word "national") and its charter number. Many earlier notes would also show the coat of arms of its native state.

Each of more than 1,300 issuing banks was assigned a charter number. There were three periods under which banks could apply for a 20-year charter. The first period was 1863-1882. Those banks securing their charters during this period could issue notes of the first charter reverse design as late as 1902. Those banks receiving their charters from 1882 to 1902, the second period, issued notes of a new type back designed for

second-charter banks. These were actually printed 1882 to 1922. Those banks receiving their charters during the third period of authorization, 1902 to 1922, issued different designs from 1902 to 1929. It is seen that this system determines the design (and often apparent "date") on a note not by when it was issued, but by when the issuing bank first received its charter. Hence, different designs of national banknotes could be issued at the same time with different dates! A very confusing situation.

Just as with all other currency, nationals were reduced in size in 1929. Type 1 notes (1929-33) have the charter number on the face twice. Type 2 notes (1933-35) have it four times. When, in May 1935, the treasury recalled many of the bonds that the national banks were using as security, national banknotes ceased to be issued

Nationals have been among the most sought after notes in a generally active U.S. paper money market. Not all nationals of a given type are worth the same, as certain states and cities are more popularly collected than others. Also, some banks ordered small quantities of notes. The values below are for the most common and least expensive notes. Large-size nationals from Alaska, Arizona, Hawaii, Idaho, Indian Territory, Mississippi, Nevada, New Mexico, Puerto Rico and South Dakota are automatically worth more. The same is true for small-size nationals from Alaska, Arizona, Hawaii, Idaho, Montana, Nevada and Wyoming.

Known Counterfeits: Examine detail, silk threads in paper and use reasonable caution.

FIRST CHARTER (1863-1875)

	VG	VF
$1 Allegory of Concord / Pilgrims Landing, ND (Original series)	950.00	2,000.00
same, 1875	950.00	2,000.00

	VG	VF
$2 Lazy 2 / Sir Walter Raleigh, ND (Original series)	3,000.00	5,000.00
same, 1875	3,000.00	5,000.00

	VG	VF
$5 Columbus Sighting Land / Landing of Columbus, ND (Original series)	1,300.00	2,600.00
same, 1875	1,300.00	2,600.00

	VG	VF
$10 Franklin experimenting with lightning / DeSoto, ND (original series)	1,900.00	3,600.00
same, 1875	1,900.00	3,600.00
$20 Battle of Lexington / Baptism of Pocahontas, ND (original series)	2,700.00	4,500.00
same, 1875	2,700.00	4,250.00
$50 Washington Crossing Delaware and at prayer / Pilgrims, ND (original series)	15,000.00	20,000.00
same, 1875	15,000.00	20,000.00
$100 Battle of Lake Erie / Signing of the Declaration of Independence, ND (original series)	17,000.00	23,000.00
same, 1875	17,000.00	23,000.00
$500		*Unique*
$1000		*Unique*

SECOND CHARTER / Series of 1882

"Brown Backs" with charter number

	VG	VF
$5 James Garfield	700.00	1,100.00
$10 as 1st charter	1,000.00	1,700.00
$20 as 1st charter	1,200.00	2,000.00
$50 as 1st charter	5,500.00	7,000.00
$100 as 1st charter	6,700.00	8,000.00

SECOND CHARTER / Series of 1882

"Date Backs" with large "1882*1908"

	VG	VF
$5 James Garfield	650.00	850.00
$10 as 1st charter	870.00	1,250.00
$20 as 1st charter	1,200.00	1,700.00
$50 as 1st charter	5,500.00	6,500.00
$100 as 1st charter	7,500.00	8,200.00

SECOND CHARTER / Series of 1882

"Value Backs" large spelled-out value

	VG	VF
$5 James Garfield	750.00	1,150.00
$10 as 1st charter	900.00	1,200.00
$20 as 1st charter	1,200.00	1,750.00
$50 as 1st charter	45,000.00	70,000.00
$100 as 2nd series	90,000.00	Extremely Rare

THIRD CHARTER / Series of 1902

Red Treasury Seal on face

	VG	VF
$5 Benjamin Harrison / Pilgrims Landing	700.00	1,100.00
$10 William McKinley / Columbia between ships	1,000.00	1,250.00
$20 Hugh McCulloch / Columbia and Capitol	1,200.00	4,800.00
$50 John Sherman / Train	5,700.00	6,500.00
$100 John Knox / Eagle on Shield	7,500.00	11,000.00

THIRD CHARTER / Series of 1902

Blue Treasury Seal, "1902-1908" on back

	VG	VF
$5 as Red Seals	200.00	350.00
$10 as Red Seals	200.00	400.00
$20 as Red Seals	200.00	400.00

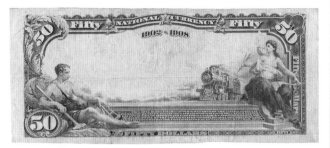

	VG	VF
$50 as Red Seals	1,300.00	2,000.00
$100 as Red Seals	1,200.00	2,700.00

THIRD CHARTER / Series of 1902

Blue Treasury Seal, "Plain Backs" without dates

	VG	VF
$5 as Red Seals	160.00	300.00
$10 as Red Seals	160.00	300.00
$20 as Red Seals	160.00	350.00

	VG	VF
$50 as Red Seals	1,200.00	1,800.00
$100 as Red Seals	1,100.00	2,700.00

THIRD CHARTER / Series of 1929

Brown Treasury Seal, Small Size Notes,

Charter Nmber on Face Twice (1929-33)

	VG	VF
$5 Type 1	60.00	100.00
$10 Type 1	75.00	120.00
$20 Type 1	75.00	120.00
$50 Type 1	300.00	450.00
$100 Type 1	375.00	600.00

THIRD CHARTER / Series of 1929

Brown Treasury Seal, Small Size Notes,

Charter Number on Face Four Times (1933-35)

	VG	VF
$5 Type 2	70.00	120.00
$10 Type 2	90.00	175.00
$20 Type 2	80.00	150.00

	VG	VF
$50 Type 2	350.00	650.00
$100 Type 2	375.00	650.00

NATIONAL GOLD BANK NOTES

These notes were like national banknotes, but they were specifically redeemable in gold coin. They were a co-operative issue of the individual National Gold Banks, which held the obligation, and the U.S. Treasury. Every bank had to be a regular national bank as well, and meet all the reserve requirements. But these national banks were authorized by the treasury to issue notes redeemable in gold.

The reason for their issue from 1870-75 was to relieve the banks in California of the daily handling of massive quantities of gold coins. All but one of the banks authorized to issue these was located in California. The very design of these notes reflects their backing by gold. The paper is a golden yellow, and the reverse bears an array of United States gold coins of every denomination. Their remarkably fine engraving gives the coins a realistic appearance. Because other types of notes were not as popular in California, these notes got some hard use and today are rare in all but worn-out condition.

Known Counterfeits: Examine detail, and look for correct yellow paper, which occasionally may tone down. Use reasonable caution.

	G	F
$5 Columbus Sighting Land	1,700.00	6,000.00
$10 Franklin experimenting with lightning	2,500.00	15,000.00
$20 Battle of Lexington	8,000.00	15,000.00
$50 Washington crossing Delaware and at prayer	15,000.00	Rare
$100 Battle of Lake Erie	38,000.00	Rare

UNITED STATES / LEGAL TENDER NOTES

While most of these notes will carry the title "United States Note" at the top or bottom of their face, some earlier ones actually say "Treasury Note" instead. The very first notes omit both. They are, however, the same according to the legislation that authorized them. They are the longest-lasting kind of American paper money, being issued for more than a century, from 1862 until 1966. There are a great many different designs, of which the "Bison Ten" is the most famous and most popular. Just like all other currency, United States Notes were reduced in size with the "series of 1928" in 1929. Small-size notes are occasionally found in circulation today and are characterized by a red Treasury seal. The latter, when worn, are not generally considered collectible.

This series includes popular "star" notes. These are notes with part of the serial number replaced by a star. They were printed to replace notes accidentally destroyed in manufacturing. These were introduced first on $20 notes in 1880 and eventually descended to $1 notes by 1917. They usually are worth more.

Known Counterfeits: Examine detail, silk threads in paper and use reasonable caution. In addition to counterfeits made to fool collectors, early circulation counterfeits of the 1863 $50, 1869 $50 and 1863 $100 exist.

	F	XF
$1 1862 Salmon P. Chase, red seal	600.00	1,250.00
$1 1869 Washington, Columbus scene / US intertwined	600.00	1,500.00

	F	XF
$1 1874-1917 same / Large X	95.00	140.00
$1 1923 Washington bust	185.00	450.00
$2 1862 Alexander Hamilton / Double circle	775.00	2,200.00
$2 1869 Jefferson and Capitol / II•2•TWO	950.00	3,500.00

	F	XF
$2 1874-1917 same / II•*TWO* omitted	140.00	225.00
$5 1862 Statue of Columbia l., Alexander Hamilton r.	465.00	1,250.00

	F	XF
$5 1863 same, different obligation on back	500.00	875.00

	F	XF
$5 1869 Jackson l., Pioneer family center / Circle with 5	600.00	1,750.00
$5 1875-1907 same, red seal / Circle with concentric pattern	190.00	350.00
$5 1880 same, brown seal	435.00	850.00
$10 1862 Lincoln and allegory of Art, obligation in octalobe on back	1,375.00	3,000.00

	F	XF
$10 1862-63 same, obligation in circle on back	1,375.00	3,000.00
$10 1869 Daniel Webster and Pocahontas / Inscription centered	750.00	3,500.00
$10 1875-80 same / Inscription at right	500.00	1,400.00
$10 1880 same, brown seal	535.00	1,100.00

	F	XF
$10 1901 Bison / Columbia standing between pillars	750.00	2,200.00
$10 1923 Andrew Jackson / Value	1,300.00	5,000.00
$20 1862 Liberty with sword and shield, obligation in octalobe on back	2,000.00	16,000.00
$20 1862-63 same, different obligation in circle on back	2,000.00	6,800.00

	F	XF
$20 1869 Alexander Hamilton l., Victory standing r.	2,900.00	9,900.00
$20 1875-80 same / No inscription at center	400.00	1,200.00
$20 1880 same, brown seal	1,000.00	2,500.00
$50 1862 Alexander Hamilton	30,000.00	43,000.00
$50 1863 same	12,500.00	300,000.00
$50 1869 Peace and Henry Clay	32,000.00	50,000.00
$50 1874-80 Franklin and Columbia	3,000.00	9,500.00
$50 same, brown seal	4,500.00	30,000.00

	F	XF
$100 1862 Eagle	30,000.00	50,000.00
$100 1862-63 same, different obligation on back	30,000.00	65,000.00
$100 1869 Lincoln and allegory of Architecture / Inscription centered	17,500.00	50,000.00

	F	XF
$100 1875-80 same, Inscription at left	9,000.00	17,500.00
$100 1880, same, brown seal	9,000.00	30,000.00
$500 1862 Albert Gallatin	Rare	
$500 1862-63 same, different obligation on back	Rare	
$500 1869 John Quincy Adams	Rare	
$500 1874-80 Gen. Joseph Mansfield	Rare	
$500 1880 same, brown seal	Rare	
$1000 1862 Robert Morris	Rare	
$1000 1862-63 same, different obligation on back	Rare	
$1000 1869 Columbus and DeWitt Clinton / Inscription centered	Rare	
$1000 1878-80 same, Inscription at left	Rare	
$1000 1880 same, brown seal	Rare	

SMALL SIZE NOTES - RED SEAL

$1 1928 Washington / ONE
$2 1928-63A Jefferson / Monticello
$5 1928-63 Lincoln / Lincoln Memorial
$100 1966-66A Franklin / Indep.Hall

	F	XF
$1 1928	75.00	250.00
$2 1928	18.00	50.00
$2 1928A	40.00	100.00
$2 1928B	90.00	450.00
$2 1928C	15.00	27.00
$2 1928D	15.00	25.00
$2 1928E	15.00	30.00
$2 1928F	15.00	25.00
$2 1928G	13.50	24.00

	CU
$2 1953	18.00
$2 1953A	11.00
$2 1953B	10.00
$2 1953C	9.00
$2 1963	8.00
$2 1963A	9.00

	F	XF
$5 1928	15.00	28.00
$5 1928A	15.00	45.00
$5 1928B	14.00	28.00
$5 1928C	13.00	25.00
$5 1928D	35.00	75.00
$5 1928E	13.00	25.00
$5 1928F	10.00	25.00
$5 1953	9.00	15.00
$5 1953A	7.00	18.00
$5 1953B	7.00	15.00
$5 1953C	7.50	25.00
$5 1963	7.00	15.00

	XF	CU
$100 1966	220.00	350.00
$100 1966A	365.00	900.00

GOLD CERTIFICATES

As the title on these notes implies, these were both backed by reserves in gold coin and payable to the bearer in that coin. The first gold certificates were issued in 1865-75 but were used for transactions between banks. Notes of this period not listed below are not known to have survived. The issue of 1882 was the first for general circulation. Again, the issues of 1888-89 were only of $5,000 and $10,000, and not widely circulated. Regular issues were again placed in circulation in 1905-07. This series includes a $20 note so beautifully colored with black, red and gold ink on white gold-tinted paper that it has come to have the nickname of "Technicolor." Those of the series of 1913-28 are the most common.

Like all other notes of the 1928 series, these gold certificates were printed on the reduced-size paper still used today. These are distinguished from other kinds of small-size notes by a gold treasury seal. The final issues, those of 1934, were again just for bank transactions. The government recalled these notes from general circulation in 1933 when it withdrew gold coinage. Today they are perfectly legal to own, but far scarcer due to the recall in 1933.

Known Counterfeits: Examine detail, on 1882 and later silk threads in paper, and use reasonable caution.

FIRST ISSUE - 1863

	F	XF
$20 Eagle on Shield		500,000.00
$100 Eagle on Shield		Extremely Rare

SECOND ISSUE - 1870-71

No notes known to have survived.

THIRD ISSUE - 1870s

	F	XF
$100 Thomas H. Benton		Extremely Rare

FOURTH ISSUE - Series of 1882

	F	XF
$20 James Garfield	950.00	5,000.00
$50 Silas Wright	1,750.00	5,000.00

	F	XF
$20 Washington	300.00	700.00
$50 Ulysses S. Grant	850.00	2,500.00
$100 Thomas Benton	950.00	3,500.00
$500 Abraham Lincoln	Rare	
$1000 Alexander Hamilton	Rare	

	F	XF
$100 Thomas Benton	1,150.00	2,800.00
$500 Abraham Lincoln	10,500.00	25,000.00
$1000 Alexander Hamilton	Rare	
$5000 James Madison	Rare	
$10,000 Andrew Jackson	Rare	

SMALL SIZE - Series of 1928

FIFTH ISSUE - Series of 1888

$5000 James Madison		Rare
$10,000 Andrew Jackson		Rare

SIXTH ISSUE - Series of 1900

$10,000 Jackson	Cut Cancelled	3,000.00

SEVENTH ISSUE - Series of 1905-07

	F	XF
$10 Michael Hillegas	250.00	675.00
$20 Washington 1905 "technicolor note"	2,300.00	8,000.00
$20 Washington 1906	300.00	800.00

EIGHTH ISSUE - Series of 1907

	F	XF
$1000 Alexander Hamilton	12,000.00	38,000.00

	F	XF
$10 Alex. Hamilton	125.00	350.00

NINTH ISSUE - Series of 1913

	F	XF
$20 Andrew Jackson	125.00	300.00
$50 Ulysses S. Grant	400.00	1,200.00
$100 Ben.Franklin	650.00	2,000.00
$500 W. McKinley	5,000.00	15,000.00
$1000 G. Cleveland	8,500.00	22,000.00
$5000 James Madison	Rare	

	F	XF
$50 Ulysses S. Grant	900.00	3,000.00

TENTH ISSUE - Series of 1922

	F	XF
$10 Michael Hillegas	250.00	650.00

SILVER CERTIFICATES

On the same day, Feb. 28, 1878, as the authorization by Congress for the striking of millions of silver dollars, it also passed legislation authorizing silver certificates. This was no coincidence. Silver certificates were not simply backed up by silver bullion, but represented actual silver dollars held by the treasury.

Some of the most famous or beautiful banknotes issued by the U.S. are silver certificates. These include the "Educational" $1, $2 and $5 of 1896, the "Onepapa Five," and the "Porthole Five." The name "Onepapa Five" is a misnomer. It depicts

Chief Running Antelope of the Uncpapa Sioux, but because the name sounded so unfamiliar to early collectors, it was quickly mispronounced "Chief One Papa."

Just like all other currency, silver certificates were reduced in size with the "series of 1928" in 1929.

During World War II there was fear that supplies of U.S. currency would fall into enemy hands if certain territories were overrun. The response to this was to make sure that notes distributed in these territories had distinguishing features that would permit their identification and repudiation if captured. Those silver certificates issued to troops in North Africa were printed with a yellow treasury seal instead of a blue one. Notes distributed in Hawaii feature the word HAWAII overprinted large on the back.

The motto "In God We Trust." was added to the $1 note for the 1935G and H, and all 1957 series. They continued to be issued until the 1957B series in 1963. Small-size silver certificates are occasionally found in circulation today and are easily recognized by a blue treasury seal. These notes when worn are not generally considered collectible, but do have some novelty value. They have not been redeemable for silver dollars since 1968.

This series includes popular "star" notes, with part of the serial number replaced by a star. They were printed to replace notes accidentally destroyed in the manufacturing process. These were introduced first in 1899 and are often worth somewhat more.

Known Counterfeits: Examine detail, silk threads in paper and use reasonable caution. Circulating counterfeits exist for this series and are slightly less deceptive.

	F	XF
$1 1886 Martha Washington / Inscription in oval	400.00	850.00
$1 1891 same / Inscription in rosette	500.00	950.00

	F	XF
$1 1896 History Instructing Youth / George and Martha Washington	450.00	1,100.00

	F	XF
$1 1899 Eagle	150.00	275.00
$1 1923 Washington	45.00	75.00
$2 1886 Gen. Winfield Scott Hancock	700.00	1,750.00
$2 1891 Sen. William Windom	650.00	2,500.00

	F	XF
$2 1896 Science Presenting Steam and Electricity to Commerce and Industry / Fulton and Morse	1,000.00	4,500.00
$2 1899 Washington, Mechanics and Agriculture	265.00	900.00
$5 1886 Ulysses S. Grant / Morgan Silver Dollars	1,250.00	4,600.00
$5 1891 same / Inscription	800.00	2,000.00
$5 1896 Winged Electricity lighting the World	2,500.00	6,300.00

	F	XF
$50 1891 same / Inscription in center	2,500.00	4,500.00
$100 1878-80 James Monroe /		
S I L V E R	16,000.00	45,000.00
$100 1891 same / Inscription in center	8,000.00	44,000.00
$500 1878-80 Sen. Charles Sumner /		
S I L V E R	Rare	
$1000 1878-80 William Marcy	Rare	
$1000 1891 Columbia and Marcy	Rare	

SMALL SIZE NOTES - BLUE SEAL

$1 1928-28E Washington / ONE
$1 1934-57B Washington / Great Seal
$5 1934-53C Lincoln / Lincoln Memorial
$10 1933-53B Hamilton / Treasury

	F	XF
$5 1899 Chief "Onepapa"	650.00	1,900.00
$5 1923 Lincoln in porthole-like frame /		
Great Seal	1,700.00	2,750.00
$10 1878-80 Robert Morris /		
S I L V E R	1,700.00	8,500.00
$10 1886 Thomas Hendricks in		
tombstone-like frame	1,250.00	4,000.00

	F	XF
$1 1928	26.00	45.00
$1 1928A	26.00	45.00
$1 1928B	26.00	45.00
$1 1928C	120.00	400.00
$1 1928D	45.00	200.00
$1 1928E	600.00	1,150.00
$1 1934	40.00	55.00
$1 1935	6.00	10.00
$1 1935A	4.00	5.00
$1 1935A HAWAII	40.00	70.00
$1 1935A Yellow seal	45.00	75.00
$1 1935A Red R	75.00	130.00
$1 1935A Red S	75.00	150.00
$1 1935B	4.00	5.00
$1 1935C	3.00	4.00
$1 1935D	3.00	4.00

	F	XF
$10 1891-1908 same / UNITED STATES		
in oval	750.00	1,850.00
$20 1878-80 Capt. Stephen Decatur /		
S I L V E R	3,700.00	12,500.00
$20 1886 Daniel Manning /		
Double Diamond	4,000.00	13,000.00
$20 1891 same / Double Circle	1,500.00	3,750.00
$50 1878-80 Edward Everett /		
S I L V E R	9,900.00	35,000.00

	XF	CU
$1 1935E		9.00
$1 1935F	9.00	
$1 1935G	9.50	
same with motto	6.00	30.00
$1 1935H	10.00	
$1 1957	9.00	
$1 1957A	9.00	
$1 1957B	9.00	

	XF	CU
$5 1934	18.00	35.00
$5 1934A	15.00	25.00
$5 1934A Yellow seal	95.00	220.00
$5 1934B	12.00	30.00
$5 1934C	10.00	23.00
$5 1934D	10.00	23.00
$5 1953	21.00	
$5 1953A	20.00	
$5 1953B	20.00	

	XF	CU
$10 1934A Yellow seal	100.00	250.00
$10 1934B	400.00	1,400.00
$10 1934C	50.00	125.00
$10 1934D	40.00	115.00
$10 1953	65.00	125.00
$10 1953A	125.00	200.00
$10 1953B	75.00	150.00

FEDERAL RESERVE NOTES

The Federal Reserve System was created in 1913. Under this system there are twelve Federal Reserve Banks. They are governed in part through the Federal Reserve Board, appointed by the president and confirmed by the Senate. Each of the Federal Reserve Banks is composed of various member banks. Today in the United States, the paper currency is not directly issued by the treasury but by the Federal Reserve Banks. Originally, Federal Reserve notes bore an obligation of the government to redeem them in gold. This was changed in 1934. Today, Federal Reserve notes are the only type of paper money issued in the United States.

Just like all other currency, Federal Reserve notes were reduced in size with the "series of 1928" in 1929.

Since 1993, major innovations have been gradually incorporated into these notes to prevent counterfeiting. At first, micro printing was incorporated into the design and around the frame of the portrait. Also, a transparent strip bearing the value and USA was imbedded in the paper. It can only be seen when the note is held up to the light and cannot be photocopied.

	XF	CU
$10 1933	8,000.00	15,500.00
$10 1933A	*Unique*	
$10 1934	75.00	100.00
$10 1934A	80.00	125.00
$10 1934 Yellow seal	9,000.00	15,000.00

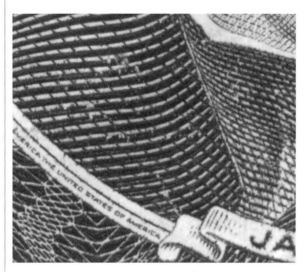

Micro Printing (Enlargement)

Color Shifting Ink

These improvements were only a precursor to the first major overhaul of the currency designs since the 1920s. Beginning in 1996 with the $100 note, the portraits were enlarged to show more detail. The reverse was modified to incorporate more white space, making it possible to successfully have a watermark incorporated into the paper. This is an image neither printed on nor imbedded inside the paper, but one created by the pressure of a pattern pressed against the paper during its drying stage. Like the transparent printed strip, it can only be seen when the note is held up to the light. Among the most ingenious high-tech safeguards on the new notes is the use of color shifting ink, which alters its color depending on the angle of the light hitting it. The green U.S. Treasury seal has been retained but the old letter seal indicating the Federal Reserve Bank of distribution is now replaced by the seal of the Federal Reserve system. These innovations were also incorporated into the 1996 series $50 and $20 notes, with the $10 and $5 notes following during the 1999 series. The $1 note is intended to remain basically the same.

Additional steps were taken to prevent counterfeiting in 2004. Both the $20 and $50 note received multicolor background designs. The $10 was changed in 2005.

A recent experiment with the use of a web press in the manufacture of $1 notes has resulted in less than total success. Interestingly enough for collectors, however, is the fact that this has resulted in some paper money being printed outside the Bureau of Engraving and Printing for the first time since the 19th century, and the appearance of an actual mintmark, FW being used to designate Fort Worth, Texas.

Most Federal Reserve notes since the 1930s are only collected in high grade. Dealers may be unwilling to buy even scarce pieces if not crisp uncirculated. Star replacement notes are popularly collected in this series, but again, must usually be crisp to be desirable. Recent ones command no premium at all, and are sold at face value plus a handling fee.

Known Counterfeits: Examine detail, silk threads in paper and use reasonable caution. Circulating counterfeits exist, particularly $20, and to a lesser extent the $10. Most are imperfect, and can be easily detected on close examination. The $100 is the most counterfeited outside the United States.

F   XF

RED SEAL - SERIES OF 1914

	F	XF
$5 Abraham Lincoln / Columbus and Pilgrims	550.00	1,500.00

Transparent Strip

	F	XF
$10 Andrew Jackson / Reaper and Factory	675.00	1,500.00
$20 Grover Cleveland / Train and Ship	725.00	2,100.00
$50 Ulysses S. Grant / Allegory of Panama	2,700.00	4,500.00
$100 Franklin / Five allegories including commerce and agriculture	1,850.00	4,000.00

	F	XF
$10 Andrew Jackson / Reaper and Factory	110.00	240.00
$20 Grover Cleveland / Train and Ship	200.00	400.00
$50 Ulysses S. Grant / Allegory of Panama	300.00	750.00
$100 Franklin / Five allegories including commerce and agriculture	625.00	1,000.00

BLUE SEAL - SERIES OF 1914

BLUE SEAL - SERIES OF 1918

	F	XF
$500 John Marshall / DeSoto discovering Mississippi	8,000.00	22,000.00

	F	XF
$5 Abraham Lincoln / Columbus and Pilgrims	100.00	200.00

	F	XF
$1,000 Alexander Hamilton / Eagle	9,200.00	24,000.00
$5,000 Madison	*Extremely Rare*	
$10,000 Chase	*Extremely Rare*	

SMALL SIZE NOTES - GREEN SEAL

$1 1963 Washington / Great Seal
$2 1976 Jefferson / Signing Declaration
$5 1928 Lincoln / Lincoln Memorial
$10 1928 Hamilton / Treasury Building
$20 1928 Jackson / White House
$50 1928 Grant / Capitol
$100 1928 Franklin / Independence Hall
$500 1928-34A McKinley / 500
$1000 1928-34A Cleveland / Inscription
$5000 1928-34B Madison / 5000
$10,000 1928-34B Chase / 10,000

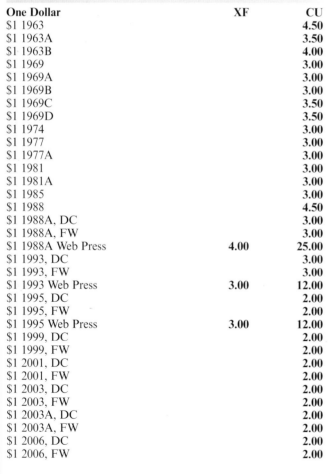

One Dollar	XF	CU
$1 1963		4.50
$1 1963A		3.50
$1 1963B		4.00
$1 1969		3.00
$1 1969A		3.00
$1 1969B		3.00
$1 1969C		3.50
$1 1969D		3.50
$1 1974		3.00
$1 1977		3.00
$1 1977A		3.00
$1 1981		3.00
$1 1981A		3.00
$1 1985		3.00
$1 1988		4.50
$1 1988A, DC		3.00
$1 1988A, FW		3.00
$1 1988A Web Press	4.00	25.00
$1 1993, DC		3.00
$1 1993, FW		3.00
$1 1993 Web Press	3.00	12.00
$1 1995, DC		2.00
$1 1995, FW		2.00
$1 1995 Web Press	3.00	12.00
$1 1999, DC		2.00
$1 1999, FW		2.00
$1 2001, DC		2.00
$1 2001, FW		2.00
$1 2003, DC		2.00
$1 2003, FW		2.00
$1 2003A, DC		2.00
$1 2003A, FW		2.00
$1 2006, DC		2.00
$1 2006, FW		2.00

Two Dollars		CU
$2 1976		5.00
$2 1995		15.00
$2 2003		4.00
$2 2003A		4.00

Five Dollars	XF	CU
$5 1928	50.00	175.00
$5 1928A	60.00	150.00
$5 1928B	40.00	75.00
$5 1928C	220.00	600.00
$5 1928D	1,500.00	2,500.00
$5 1934	25.00	55.00
$5 1934A	18.00	40.00
$5 1934 HAWAII	200.00	950.00
$5 1934A HAWAII	200.00	650.00
$5 1934B	25.00	50.00
$5 1934C	20.00	55.00
$5 1934D	25.00	60.00
$5 1950		35.00

Five Dollars	XF	CU
$5 1950A		20.00
$5 1950B		20.00
$5 1950C		17.00
$5 1950D		25.00
$5 1950E		55.00
$5 1963		18.00
$5 1963A		15.00
$5 1969		12.00
$5 1969A		13.00
$5 1969B		45.00
$5 1969C		12.00
$5 1974		10.00
$5 1977		10.00
$5 1977A		15.00
$5 1981		12.00
$5 1981A		15.00
$5 1985		10.00
$5 1988		10.00
$5 1988A		10.00
$5 1993		10.00
$5 1995		9.00

Large Portrait

	XF	CU
$5 1999 DC		9.00
$5 1999 FW		9.00
$5 2001		10.00
$5 2003 DC		10.00
$5 2003 FW		10.00
$5 2006 Purple in Background		9.00

Ten Dollars	XF	CU
$10 1928	100.00	180.00
$10 1928A	80.00	200.00
$10 1928B	40.00	75.00
$10 1928C	150.00	450.00
$10 1934	38.00	65.00
$10 1934A	20.00	35.00
$10 1934A HAWAII	200.00	500.00
$10 1934B	30.00	70.00
$10 1934C	20.00	35.00
$10 1934D	25.00	55.00
$10 1950	20.00	60.00
$10 1950A	20.00	55.00
$10 1950B		35.00

Ten Dollars	XF	CU
$10 1950C		40.00
$10 1950D		30.00
$10 1950E		95.00
$10 1963		30.00
$10 1963A		30.00

Ten Dollars	XF	CU
$10 1969		25.00
$10 1969A		20.00
$10 1969B		95.00
$10 1969C		35.00
$10 1974		25.00
$10 1977		25.00
$10 1977A		30.00
$10 1981		30.00
$10 1981A		20.00
$10 1985		20.00
$10 1988A		20.00
$10 1990		15.00
$10 1993		15.00
$10 1995		15.00

Large Portrait

	XF	CU
$10 1999 DC		15.00
$10 1999 FW		15.00
$10 2001 DC		15.00
$10 2001 FW		15.00

	XF	CU
$10 2003 DC		15.00
$10 2003 FW		15.00
$10 2004A FW		15.00
$10 2006		15.00

Twenty Dollars

	XF	CU
$20 1928	85.00	200.00
$20 1928A	150.00	400.00
$20 1928B	60.00	125.00
$20 1928C	850.00	2,500.00
$20 1934	40.00	75.00
$20 1934A	30.00	65.00
$20 1934 HAWAII	250.00	1,100.00
$20 1934A HAWAII	150.00	600.00
$20 1934B	40.00	90.00
$20 1934C	40.00	65.00
$20 1934D	30.00	85.00
$20 1950		50.00
$20 1950A		50.00
$20 1950B		45.00
$20 1950C		50.00

	XF	CU
$20 1950D		55.00
$20 1950E		95.00
$20 1963		60.00
$20 1963A		40.00
$20 1969		45.00
$20 1969A		55.00
$20 1969B		150.00
$20 1969C		45.00
$20 1974		45.00
$20 1977		45.00
$20 1981		60.00
$20 1981A		45.00
$20 1985		40.00
$20 1988A		45.00
$20 1990		35.00
$20 1993		30.00
$20 1995		30.00

Large Portrait

	CU
$20 1996	30.00
$20 1999 DC	25.00
$20 1999 FW	25.00
$20 2001 DC	25.00
$20 2001 FW	25.00

Large Portrait & Colorized Background

	XF	CU
$20 2004 DC		25.00
$20 2004 FW		25.00
$20 2004A DC		25.00
$20 2004A FW		25.00
$20 2006 DC		25.00
$20 2006 FW		25.00

Fifty Dollars

	XF	CU
$50 1928	375.00	550.00
$50 1928A	110.00	375.00
$50 1934	75.00	225.00
$50 1934A	125.00	290.00
$50 1934B	175.00	400.00
$50 1934C	110.00	200.00
$50 1934D	150.00	250.00

	XF	CU
$50 1950	95.00	175.00
$50 1950A	90.00	180.00
$50 1950B	70.00	125.00
$50 1950C	65.00	150.00
$50 1950D	65.00	150.00
$50 1950E	300.00	450.00
$50 1963A		100.00
$50 1969		125.00
$50 1969A		110.00
$50 1969B		900.00
$50 1969C		80.00
$50 1974		80.00
$50 1977		90.00
$50 1981		100.00
$50 1981A		120.00
$50 1985		80.00
$50 1988		95.00
$50 1990		65.00
$50 1993		65.00

Large Portrait

		CU
$50 1996		60.00
$50 2001		60.00

Large Portrait & Colorized Background

	XF	CU
$50 2004		60.00
$50 2004A		60.00
$50 2006		60.00

One Hundred Dollars

	XF	CU
$100 1928	250.00	600.00
$100 1928A	250.00	300.00
$100 1934	200.00	300.00
$100 1934A	125.00	200.00
$100 1934B	225.00	325.00
$100 1934C	175.00	300.00
$100 1934D	350.00	450.00
$100 1950		350.00
$100 1950A		200.00
$100 1950B		200.00
$100 1950C		175.00
$100 1950D		200.00
$100 1950E		400.00

	XF	CU
$100 1963A		175.00
$100 1969		160.00
$100 1969A		150.00
$100 1969C		150.00
$100 1974		140.00
$100 1977		140.00
$100 1981		175.00
$100 1981A		175.00
$100 1985		140.00
$100 1988		140.00
$100 1990		135.00
$100 1993		135.00
Large Portrait		
$100 1996		120.00
$100 1999 DC		120.00
$100 1999 FW		120.00
$100 2001		120.00
$100 2003		120.00
$100 2003A		120.00
$100 2006 DC		120.00
$100 2006 FW		120.00
Five Hundred Dollars		
$500 1928	1,600.00	2,800.00
$500 1934	1,200.00	1,750.00
$500 1934A	1,000.00	1,600.00
$500 1934B	—	—
$500 1934C	—	—
One Thousand Dollars		
$1000 1928	2,250.00	3,800.00
$1000 1934	2,250.00	3,400.00
$1000 1934A	2,000.00	3,200.00
$1000 1934C	—	—
Five Thousand Dollars		
$5000 1928	65,000.00	75,000.00
$5000 1934	65,000.00	75,000.00
$5000 1934A	—	—
$5000 1934B	—	—
Ten Thousand Dollars		
$10,000 1928	75,000.00	150,000.00
$10,000 1934	60,000.00	80,000.00
$10,000 1934A	—	—
$10,000 1934B	—	—

FEDERAL RESERVE BANK NOTES

Federal Reserve Banknotes are a type of national currency issued not by individual National Banks but directly by the 12 Federal Reserve Banks. These are regional banks under the partial control of the Board of Governors of the Federal Reserve, appointed by the president. Unlike Federal Reserve notes, these were legal tender but not a government obligation. The obligation to redeem Federal Reserve Banknotes fell to the individual Federal Reserve Banks and not directly with the U.S. Treasury. They were issued for a fairly short duration.

Small-size Federal Reserve Banknotes are actually emergency currency printed on notes originally intended to become regular 1929 series national currency. The identity of the Federal Reserve Bank is printed where the name of the National Bank would have been and small details of text are either blocked out or added. They were issued in 1933 and have a brown treasury seal, unlike the large-size notes, which feature a blue one.

Star replacement notes are scarce and command a significant premium.

Known Counterfeits: Examine detail, silk threads in paper and use reasonable caution.

	F	XF
$1 1918 George Washington / Eagle on Flag	110.00	250.00
$2 1918 Thomas Jefferson / Battle Ship	500.00	1,300.00
$5 1915 Abraham Lincoln / Columbus, Pilgrims landing	400.00	700.00
$5 1918 same	375.00	650.00
$10 1915 Andrew Jackson / Horse-drawn Reaper and Factory	1,300.00	2,750.00
$10 1918 same	1,250.00	2,750.00
$20 1915 Grover Cleveland / Train and Ship	2,500.00	5,000.00
$20 1918 same	2,650.00	5,250.00
$50 1918 Ulysses S. Grant / Allegory of Panama	9,500.00	17,000.00

SMALL SIZE NOTES - BROWN SEAL

	F	XF
$5 Boston	25.00	60.00
$5 New York	20.00	50.00
$5 Philadelphia	20.00	75.00
$5 Cleveland	20.00	50.00
$5 Atlanta	35.00	50.00
$5 Chicago	20.00	50.00
$5 St. Louis	300.00	1,500.00
$5 Minneapolis	75.00	225.00
$5 Kansas City	75.00	225.00
$5 Dallas	55.00	75.00
$5 San Francisco	950.00	4,500.00

	F	XF
$10 Boston	30.00	75.00
$10 New York	90.00	300.00
$10 Philadelphia	22.00	65.00
$10 Cleveland	20.00	90.00
$10 Richmond	30.00	95.00
$10 Atlanta	25.00	75.00
$10 Chicago	30.00	70.00
$10 St. Louis	25.00	60.00
$10 Minneapolis	30.00	75.00
$10 Kansas City	25.00	50.00
$10 Dallas	300.00	800.00
$10 San Francisco	200.00	500.00

	F	XF
$20 Boston	30.00	75.00
$20 New York	35.00	50.00
$20 Philadelphia	35.00	90.00
$20 Cleveland	30.00	70.00
$20 Richmond	30.00	175.00
$20 Atlanta	35.00	150.00
$20 Chicago	30.00	60.00
$20 St. Louis	30.00	95.00
$20 Minneapolis	30.00	90.00
$20 Kansas City	35.00	150.00
$20 Dallas	300.00	900.00
$20 San Francisco	100.00	200.00
$50 New York	75.00	150.00
$50 Cleveland	70.00	115.00
$50 Chicago	85.00	150.00
$50 Minneapolis	70.00	150.00
$50 Kansas City	75.00	160.00
$50 Dallas	375.00	1,700.00
$50 San Francisco	90.00	300.00

	F	XF
$100 New York	130.00	175.00
$100 Cleveland	135.00	175.00
$100 Richmond	150.00	300.00
$100 Chicago	150.00	225.00
$100 Minneapolis	150.00	250.00
$100 Kansas City	125.00	210.00
$100 Dallas	400.00	1,500.00

INTEREST-BEARING NOTES

In an effort to raise money during the Civil War, Congress authorized a form of paper money that was a cross between a banknote and a bond. This was called an Interest Bearing Note. Authorized by legislation of 1861 and 1863, they were legal tender for their face value but they also bore interest. Those issued with one- and two-year maturity could be redeemed at that time for more than their face value. Those that matured in three years actually had coupons attached that could be redeemed at six-month intervals for interest payments. They were issued in $10, $20, $50, $100, $1,000, and $5,000 denominations.

These notes are incredibly rare because most were redeemed. They are far too specialized to include a complete listing here, but an example of an 1864 $20 one-year note is illustrated below.

Known Counterfeits: All such notes should be examined by an expert for authenticity and value.

	VF
$10+5% 1864 Salmon Chase, eagle and Peace	**15,000.00**

	VF
$20 +5% 1864 Lincoln, mortar, and Victory	*RARE*

COMPOUND INTEREST TREASURY NOTES

Continuing the precedent of the Interest Bearing Notes of 1861-63, as the Civil War had vastly depleted the U.S. Treasury, Congress authorized another form of paper money that incorporated the features of a zero-coupon bond.

This was called a Compound Interest Treasury Note, a name displayed conspicuously in gold letters. On some notes, this overprint has been known to dissolve through the note or to turn green. Issued in 1863 and 1864, they were legal tender for their face value but they also bore compounded interest payable at maturity in three years. An interest-calculation table was displayed on the back. They were issued in $10, $20, $50, $100, $500, and $1,000 denominations.

Most of these notes were turned in at maturity, hence they too are incredibly rare and are too specialized to include

a complete listing here. The face design of a $10 note is similar to the Interest Bearing Note depicted earlier, but with its gold overprint.

Known Counterfeits: All such notes should be examined by an expert for authenticity and value.

	VF
$10 1864	**10,000.00**
All others	*Rare*

REFUNDING CERTIFICATE

This last type of circulating government security was authorized by Congress in 1879. The small denomination of $10 was intended to make such notes more widely available, however, they could only be redeemed in groups of five or more. They accrued interest at 4 percent per year until 1907. In that year, Congress voted to suspend interest accrual, freezing them at their 1907 value of $10 plus an additional $11.30 interest.

Known Counterfeits: All such notes should be examined by an expert for authenticity and value.

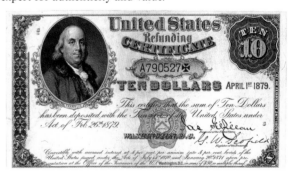

	XF
10 1879, Benjamin Franklin / Assignment form	**Two** known
10 1879, similar / Large TEN and interest table	**8,000.00**

CONFEDERATE STATES ISSUES

The story of Confederate paper money is, in some ways, reminiscent of Continental currency. Under desperate wartime circumstances and with the best intentions, the government attempted to finance the war effort by printing unbacked paper currency. The initial series, backed by cotton, held its value at first and restraint was used in the quantities issued, but as the war continued, more and more were printed, causing inflation. According to the legends on the later notes, they could not be redeemed until "two years after the ratification of a treaty of peace between the Confederate States and United States." Ultimately the seventh and final issue was authorized in unlimited quantity. After two billion dollars were issued, the currency's value eroded almost completely. Measured in gold dollars its decline can be seen as follows, along with rough quantities issued or authorized:

	VG	VF
1861 March	$150,000,000	95¢
1862	$265,000,000	
1863	$515,000,000	33¢
1864	$1,000,000,000	
1865 April	none	1 ¢
1865 May	none	1/12¢

For many years Confederate currency was synonymous with worthlessness, and some people even burned it. From the 1960s onward, however, it has become collectible. Since the late 1990s, there has been a particularly strong market for this series. Prices have increased drastically.

The first Confederate currency of March 1861 was initially issued in Montgomery, Ala., but the wording was changed to Richmond, Va. This is because the capitol of the Confederacy was moved to Richmond in May after Virginia withdrew from the Union. Throughout the war, the production of Confederate notes was plagued with difficulties. The Northern printers, who had originally been hired to print notes before hostilities erupted, were no longer available. Paper was in short supply. It was not always practical to import notes, paper or even plates due to the Union blockade of Southern ports. Some paper was brought in from the North by smugglers and from Great Britain by blockade runners. As a result some of the designs use improvised images not initially prepared for Confederate currency. More suitable images used include portraits of President Jefferson Davis and members of his cabinet, as well as of Southern agriculture.

Known Counterfeits: It has been suggested that contemporary counterfeits were made of virtually every type of Confederate currency. True or false, a vast array of contemporary counterfeits of Confederate notes have survived. Most are printed from very crudely engraved plates. Like real examples, they are often printed on thin, limp paper. Not all the counterfeits made during the Civil War were actually meant to circulate. Samuel Upham of Philadelphia made 1.5 million Confederate and Southern state notes as a spoof, all with the notice, "Facsimile Confederate Note - Sold wholesale and retail, by S.C. Upham, 403 Chestnut Street, Philadelphia" in the margin. Many had this notice cut off and intact examples are worth at least a few dollars each. In 1954, reproductions were distributed in Cheerios cereal as a promotion. Other similar notes printed on brittle brownish-yellow paper were printed in the 1960s. Many (but not all) have the word FACSIMILE near the margin.

Some "fantasy" notes were also made to circulate during the Civil War period. These were notes claiming to be Confederate, but with designs which the Confederate government never used. The most famous of these notes is the "female riding a deer" note, which actually depicted Artemis riding a stag. It is illustrated here. Most of the counterfeits, both contemporary and modern, have printed signatures, while all authentic notes are hand signed except for the 50-cent denomination.

	VG	VF

FIRST ISSUE, MONTGOMERY 1861

$50 Three slaves hoeing cotton	2,250.00	5,200.00

	VG	VF
$100 Train	850.00	4,400.00
$500 Train on bridge, Cattle below	1,400.00	8,800.00
$1000 John Calhoun and Andrew Jackson	1,700.00	8,000.00

FIRST ISSUE, RICHMOND 1861

$50 Industry and Agriculture seated on cotton	110.00	700.00
$100 Train	140.00	750.00

SECOND ISSUE, July 25, 1861

$5 Inscription	250.00	2,100.00
$5 Liberty and Eagle, Sailor left	220.00	1,600.00
$10 Liberty and Eagle, Commerce left	38.00	450.00
$20 Sailing Ship	20.00	110.00
$20 Artemis riding Stag, Indian seated left *Contemporary Fantasy*	18.00	70.00
$50 Washington	22.00	125.00
$100 Ceres and Proserpina	110.00	700.00

THIRD ISSUE, September 2, 1861

	VG	VF
$2 Confederacy striking down Union, Judah Benjamin l.	90.00	400.00
$5 Cotton being loaded onto Steamboat left, Indian Princess right	1,300.00	7,750.00

	VG	VF
$5 Commerce seated on bale of cotton	17.00	45.00
$5 Allegories of Commerce, Agriculture, Liberty, Industry and Justice, Minerva left	80.00	500.00
$5 Sailor with cotton bales, C.G. Memminger left	32.00	75.00
$5 Boy's bust left, Blacksmith seated right	130.00	700.00
$5 C.G. Memminger, V at lower right	27.00	85.00
$5 same, but FIVE at lower right	27.00	85.00
$10 Liberty with Eagle left	650.00	4,250.00
$10 Ceres and Commerce left	17.00	75.00
$10 Indian Family	80.00	425.00
$10 Cotton Picker	35.00	200.00
$10 Revolutionary War Generals with sweet potatoes, Minerva standing r.	17.00	75.00
$10 Wagon with cotton, John Ward left	200.00	950.00
$10 Robert Hunter left, Child right	30.00	200.00
$10 Hope with Anchor, Robert Hunter left, C.G. Memminger rt.	22.00	150.00
$10 same, with X X overprint	27.00	125.00

	VG	VF
$20 Ceres between Commerce and Navigation	80.00	450.00
$20 Sailing Ship	17.00	65.00
$20 Navigation seated with globe	350.00	1,800.00

	VG	VF
$20 Industry seated behind large 20	12.00	50.00
$20 Alexander Stephens	40.00	200.00
$50 Moneta & chest	20.00	100.00
$50 Train	450.00	3,600.00
$50 Jefferson Davis	27.00	175.00
$100 Loading cotton onto wagon, Sailor left	27.00	120.00

FOURTH ISSUE, April 17, 1862

$1 Steamship	22.00	100.00
$1 same with ONE overprint	26.00	140.00
$2 Confederacy striking down Union, Judah Benjamin l.	22.00	75.00
$2 same with "2 TWO" overprint	30.00	125.00
$10 Commerce reclining	Rare	
$10 Ceres seated	Rare	
$20 Liberty with shield	650.00	3,600.00
$100 Train	27.00	75.00
$100 Hoeing Cotton	27.00	75.00

FIFTH ISSUE, December 2, 1862

$1 Clement Clay	26.00	85.00
$2 Judah Benjamin	24.00	75.00
$5 Confederate Capitol at Richmond, Memminger right	12.00	42.00
$10 South Carolina Capitol, Robert Hunter right	12.00	42.00
$20 Tennessee Capitol, Alexander Stephens right	22.00	110.00
$50 Jefferson Davis	27.00	150.00
$100 Lucy Pickens	35.00	150.00

SIXTH ISSUE, April 6, 1863

50¢ Jefferson Davis	12.00	38.00
$1 Clement Clay	25.00	85.00
$2 Judah Benjamin	25.00	175.00
$5 Confederate Capitol at Richmond, Memminger right	20.00	8.00
$10 South Carolina Capitol, Robert Hunter right	18.00	45.00
$20 Tennessee Capitol, Alexander Stephens right	16.00	50.00
$50 Jefferson Davis	22.00	85.00
$100 Lucy Pickens center, Soldiers left, George Randolph right	27.00	85.00

SEVENTH ISSUE, February 17, 1864

	VG	VF
50¢ Jefferson Davis	10.00	35.00
$1 Clement Clay	32.00	110.00
$2 Judah Benjamin	27.00	90.00
$5 Confederate Capitol at Richmond, Memminger right	10.00	35.00

	VG	VF
$10 Field Artillery, Robert Hunter right	10.00	30.00
$20 Tennessee Capitol, Alexander Stephens right	10.00	30.00

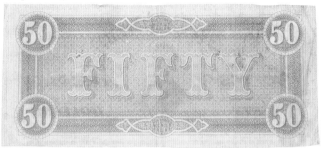

	VG	VF
$50 Jefferson Davis	22.00	65.00
$100 Lucy Pickens, Soldiers left, George Randolph right	27.00	70.00

	VG	VF
$500 Flag and seal left, Stonewall Jackson right	130.00	450.00

ADVERTISING AND OTHER SCRIP

During the Great Depression there was very little money in circulation. In order to facilitate local business, many chambers of commerce, city governments and various firms printed their own paper money. Through various methods, which varied by issuer, it could be placed into circulation at a more rapid rate than normal money could. To force it into the stream of currency rather than being sidetracked into savings, it usually carried an expiration date.

Even in times when there is no shortage of coin or currency, it is often useful for businesses to print their own paper money-like certificates, which can be redeemed for products or services. Sometimes this is issued as a reward for patronage. Other times it facilitates purchases of goods in a closed economic environment, such as a camp or convention. These notes often serve no practical purpose at all, but merely serve to remind the customer of the merchant's business in an entertaining way. One less common, and to an extent, outmoded form of scrip, is college currency. This is essentially "play money" used by business schools for practicing commercial situations. "Real" play money of course has a very long history too, and some early issues can actually have numismatic value.

There is no thorough reference for this type of material, so it is a wide-open area for those interested in doing original research in local history. Prices for these types of notes are often minimal.

Known Counterfeits: Negligible risk.

	XF-CU
1860-85 National School Bank, 2 left, girl right $2	80.00
1860-85 Salt Lake City, Utah, Latter Day Saints College Currency $1000	400.00

	XF-CU
1862 National College Bank, NY, blacksmith, couple with horse and dog, $1	90.00

	XF-CU
1876 Imperial Government of Norton I, woman standing with flag, bust of Emperor Norton, 50¢	20,000.00
1912 (actually 1998) United States of DiCaprio, Bust of Leonardo DiCaprio, $20,000,000	.35
1920s Astor and Colonial Theatre, Los Angeles, Calif., Auction Scrip, overprinted by Greenblatt... Delicatessen and Fine Kosher Meats, Lincoln Silhouette	20.00

	XF-CU
1930 R-K-O Proctor's 58th St. Theatre, R.C.A. Victor Radio Auction, 100 Shekels	6.00
1933 San Diego (Calif.) Clearing House Certificate, Inscription $20	45.00
1933 St. Petersburg (Florida) Citizens Emergency Committee, 10¢	35.00
1935 State of Washington Tax Token Scrip, 10¢	1.00
1935 Parker Brothers, Monopoly $5, house l., locomotive r. (salmon paper)	1.00

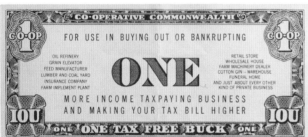

	XF-CU
(c.1940) Anti-co-op note, Cartoon of Big Business, $1	4.00
(1940) "Buck Benny Rides Again," Portrait of Jack Benny, 1 Benny Buck	10.00
1970s (Parker Brothers, Monopoly) $5, house l., locomotive r. (pink paper)	.10
1970s Fairfield County (Conn.) Council, Boy Scouts of America, Eagle, Cub Bucks $1	.50

	XF-CU
1988 American Numismatic Association, ANA logo right, ANA Collector Currency $1	1.50
1988 International Association of Millionaire, Statue of Liberty, $1,000,000 (engraved printing)	2.50

A Canadian fantasy note similar to this has also been printed.

	XF-CU
1988 Attorney Lester E. Blank (Bridgeport, Conn.), Bust of Blank, $1,000,000	.25

	XF-CU
1990 Krause Publications Currency Collector Series, Five Cherubs with oversized Seated Liberty Dollars / Krause building $5	5.00
1994 Chicago International Coin Fair, Three women and Cupid frolicking in Water, Revolutionary War Soldier left, $1	.50

	XF-CU
1997 Stack's, New York, Stack's logo (inscription and borders as colonial note of the 1700s) £5	.25
2000 $200 spoof note, after the style of a Federal Reserve Note but depicting George W. Bush	2.00

(Some of these spoof notes have actually been accepted as real — yet more proof that most people rarely pay attention to the notes they get in circulation!)

MILITARY PAYMENT CERTIFICATES

U.S. military payment certificates are special currency paid to personnel overseas. It is good only at military installations. The reason for its issue is to prevent the speculation in currency by merchants in surrounding communities. To prevent local entrepreneurs from speculating in the certificates themselves, they are frequently recalled and demonetized with little notice, at which time the military base is sealed off. Even the soldiers off base run the risk of being stuck with worthless paper if they ignore the notice. The use of MPC also affords some of the advantages of the old World War II North Africa and Hawaii notes, in that if captured by the enemy, they can be easily identified and easily repudiated without reflecting poorly on the integrity of the U.S. dollar.

Most MPC is smaller than regular currency. While humble in appearance, earlier examples can be quite valuable in high grade. Dates do not appear on MPC, but they can be dated by the series number.

Known Counterfeits: Few known.

	VF	CU
Series 461 (1946) $110.00		110.00
Series 471 (1947) $5	1,000.00	8,000.00
Series 472 (1948) 5¢ Great Seal / Great Seal	2.00	8.00
Series 481 (1951) 5¢ Seated female with compass and sphere	3.00	25.00

	VF	CU
Series 521 (1954) $10 Female wearing wreath	160.00	1,300.00
Series 541 (1958) 25¢ Female wearing wreath	9.00	38.00
Series 591 (1961) 50¢ Bust of statue of Liberty	36.00	210.00
Series 641 (1968) 50¢ Female head l.	3.00	20.00

	VF	CU
Series 641 (1968) $10 Female portrait	20.00	155.00
Series 661 (1968) $5 Female in antique clothes, holding flowers	3.75	24.00
Series 681 (1969) 25¢ Submarine	2.00	15.00

	VF	CU
Series 692 (1970) $20 Indian Chief Ouray	130.00	650.00

BANK & PERSONAL CHECKS

The use of personal checks has its origins in the letters of credit written during the Renaissance. They represent the transfer of a certain sum of money stored in a bank from one specific individual to a second individual's account at another bank. It permits a great amount of convenience and security in not having to transfer actual precious metal or currency from one distant location to another. Because it is usually not a document issued to a bearer but rather to a specific individual, if it is lost or stolen the funds are usually recoverable.

Checks have been used in the United States for most of its existence. From 1862 to 1882, all checks written were required to have a revenue stamp either affixed to its face or pre-printed on its paper. For a brief time during the Spanish-American War (1898), these tax stamps were again required. Most checks have traditionally been boring and utilitarian in appearance. Early in the 20th century, certain firms began to display their logos on them. New styles of artistic checks have become more popular in recent years, depicting background images ranging from *Star Trek* to prairie scenes.

Checks are usually collected as an adjunct to other collections. Traditionally, depictions of actual local buildings are of interest to local-history collectors. They will also peruse checks written by important community founders. National Bank Note collectors find interest in checks drawn on banks that also issued paper money. Autograph collectors also can find checks of interest, as even famous historical figures are known to have signed checks. Finally, stamp collectors have long been interested in the varieties of revenue stamps found on checks, some of which can be valuable.

While economists have long considered personal checks a form of money, it is only recently that collectors have begun to give them reasonable attention in their own right.

Known Counterfeits: The alterations and other frauds that are occasionally a concern when checks are used in commerce are irrelevant to the collector of cancelled checks.

XF Cancelled

1849 P.T.Barnum, Bridgeport Bank, Conn., View
of Barnum's mansion Iranistan, unissued — **125.00**
1864 Deposit Bank, Deposit, NY, View of Bank,
2¢ revenue stamp affixed — **2.50**
1870 Connecticut National Bank of Bridgeport
(Connecticut), pre-printed 2¢ stamp depicting eagle — **2.00**

XF Cancelled

1874 The Bank of California, San Francisco,
Calif., $135.46, printed on orange 2¢ stamp — **10.00**
1874 First National Bank of Rushville, Ill., $112.30,
Semi-nude woman and eagle — **3.00**
1879 Shawmut National Bank, Boston, Mass.,
$600.00, Steam Locomotive — **25.00**
1883 Asylum for the Chronic Insane, on City
National Bank of Worcester, shield of
Massachusetts, $46.54 — **25.00**

XF Cancelled

1895 Centennial National Bank of Philadelphia,
$15.00, Bank Building — **30.00**
1899 Dime Savings Bank / Western Savings and
Deposit Bank, $21.20, three revenue stamps affixed. — **5.00**
*Part of the difference in value between the above two checks
is that more people collect "national" banks than other banks
because many national banks also issued paper money.*
1899 Bank of Clinch Valley, Tazewell, Va.,
$100.00, 2¢ stamp depicting battle ship affixed — **1.00**
1906 Central National Bank, Philadelphia, Penn.,
$27.00 — **1.00**
1912 All Night and Day Bank, Los Angeles, CA,
$420.00 — **2.25**
1916 The First-Bridgeport National Bank, Conn.,
$7.50 — **.50**
1918 The First State Bank, Clarita, Okla., $ 292.60
Cashier's Check, issued to Postmaster Coalgate. *Of
interest to postal history collectors* — **2.00**
1925 The Farmers and Mechanics National Bank,
Washington, DC, $75.00, Portrait of founder
William Marbury — **.75**

XF Cancelled

1939 Fort Worth National Bank, Ft. Worth,
Texas, issued on account of famous coin
dealer B. Max Mehl, $3.40, Mehl Building
and Fugio Cent — **3.00**
1947 Denmark State Bank, Denmark, Wis.,
issued on account of Beneckes General
Merchandise, $277.93, Assortment of groceries — **1.00**
1998 First National Bank of Chicago,
$69.00, View of Chicago shore — **.10**

CANADIAN COINS

EVOLUTION OF CANADIAN COINAGE

Like the situation south of the border in the United States, and formerly in the 13 Colonies, Canadian coinage before the 1870s was a hodgepodge of various coins and tokens struck by a number of authorities, firms, countries and individuals. Throughout the 1700s and early 1800s, the British policies of Mercantilism prevented the royal government from shipping reasonable quantities of sterling to British North America. By the time the idea was seriously considered, there was already chaos. When official coinage was finally struck by the various pre-Confederation colonial provinces, they had already recognized slightly different standards, sometimes as much as 20 percent different from each other in value. The first coins to be struck in the name of "Canada" were not struck by the Canadian Confederation, but rather by the Province of Canada. This was the collective name for Upper Canada (Ontario) and Lower Canada (Quebec). Bronze cents and silver five, 10 and 20 cents were struck in 1858-59. During the intervening years before these two provinces combined with New Brunswick and Nova Scotia to form the independent Canadian Confederation in 1867, all of them had already struck their own unique coins. Despite all this complexity of coinage, there still persisted a shortage of small change in circulation. Neither bank tokens nor poorly made "blacksmith" counterfeits could be suppressed. During the American Civil War, when U.S. silver coins were being discounted in terms of gold, some firms bought it up in quantity and imported it. Unfortunately, it soon became the tool of scams, whereby it was paid out at par but only taken for deposit at a discount. Finally, in 1869-70, a three-step program was used to cure this dilemma. The United States silver was bought up and $4 million worth re-exported south. An order was placed with the Royal Mint for an issue of millions of new sterling silver Canadian five-cent, 10-cent, 25-cent and 50-cent pieces. Lastly, a temporary issue of fractional paper money redeemable in gold was released immediately to make due until the new coins arrived. (This small paper money proved so popular that it continued to be issued until the 1930s.).

The new Canadian silver coins, nominally valued at one United States dollar's worth of gold per Canada dollar, were struck in quantity, except for the depression of the late 1870s, supplemented by a large initial issue of cents in 1876. These were slightly heavier than the Province's old cents, and continued from 1881 onward. The standards for cents and silver remained unchanged until World War I. During the 1800s Canadian coins were struck at the Royal Mint in London, and sometimes by contract at the Heaton Mint, Birmingham, England. In 1908, after years of agitation, a branch of the Royal Mint was opened in Ottawa. With it came the ability to mint the gold then being mined in Canada into internationally recognized British-design sovereigns, and soon after that a domestic gold coinage was initiated.

While the basic designs for most Canadian coins remained fairly stable from the beginning until 1937, many smaller changes occurred as needed. Of course, with the passing of each monarch, a new royal portrait was designed, one for Edward VII in 1902, another for George V in 1911. The gold sovereigns only, instead of using the crowned busts, used bareheaded ones to match British gold sovereigns. There was a bit of a ruckus in 1911 when the new obverse of George V was found to be lacking the Latin *Dei Gratia* for "by the grace of God." The mint responded to the public outcry and beginning in 1912 these titles were added. World War I and its aftermath resulted in more modifications. The large cent was replaced in 1920 by a small cent

and the five-cent silver in 1922 was replaced by one of pure nickel, both similar in size to their American counterparts. Also, as a result of a wartime increase in the price of silver, the alloy of coins in that metal was reduced from 92.5 percent pure (sterling) to 80 percent beginning with 1920.

The entire visual style of Canadian coins began to change in 1935, when a new, artistic commemorative silver dollar for the jubilee of George V was released. It depicted the now-famous design of a fur trapper and an Indian paddling a canoe. When the obverses were changed to portray the new King George VI in 1937, the opportunity was taken to revise all the reverses of the smaller denominations with creative and distinctly Canadian designs. The cent was given a more naturalistic sprig of maple leaves, the five cents a beaver on its dam, a schooner graced the 10-cent pieces and the bust of a caribou the 25 cent. The 50-cent coins displayed a more conservative coat of arms. Because of the time taken to design the new coinage, some 1936-dated coins were struck in 1937 bearing a minute dot to distinguish them. These are quite rare. The reverses introduced in 1937 have continued in use today with some alteration.

Like World War I, the Second World War had its effects on the coinage. Shortages of nickel caused the five-cent piece to be struck in a copper-zinc alloy called "tombac," and later in chromium-plated steel. It was not finally restored to its old nickel composition until 1955. A special reverse design was used to boost wartime morale, that of a torch superimposed on a "V" for victory. Because of the time taken to modify the royal titles to reflect the independence of India, some 1947 coins were struck in 1948 with a tiny maple leaf after the date. While not at all rare, these are quite popular.

No monarch has had as many different portraits on Canadian coins as Elizabeth II. The first portrait, designed by Mary Gillick, had some minor difficulties in striking and as a result was subtly modified after being placed in production. In 1965, a new bust wearing a tiara was introduced, years before Britain itself began using it. When a mature head of the Queen was desired, the Canadian choice for the first time differed from that of Britain. A design with an open crown, by Canadian artist Dora de Pédery-Hunt, was used beginning in 1990. It was replaced in mid-2003 by a bareheaded, grandmotherly portrait designed by Susanna Blunt.

The centennial of Canadian independence resulted in some of Canada's most beautiful and dignified wildlife coins. Animals emblematic of Canada shown against stark open backgrounds were portrayed on the reverses of the 1967 issues, along with a $20 gold piece with the national arms. Unfortunately, the rising price of silver forced these animal coins out of circulation. In mid-year the 10-cent and 25-cent pieces were reduced to 50 percent pure, and beginning in 1968, pure nickel replaced all circulating silver.

From the 1970s through 1990s, various modifications were made to reduce the expenses of producing coins, which no longer had any tie to their intrinsic value. The cent went through several modifications in weight and shape before it was switched to copper-plated zinc in 1997, later supplemented by issues in copper-plated steel. In 1982, the five-cent piece was changed from nickel to cupronickel, then to nickel-plated steel in 2000, along with the 10-cent, 25-cent and 50-cent pieces. Radical new dollar and two-dollar coins were introduced to save the expense of producing perishable paper money. A small golden-

bronze-plated nickel dollar was introduced in 1987 depicting a swimming loon. In 1996, a two-dollar coin depicting a polar bear and composed of a nickel ring surrounding an aluminum bronze center followed. Today these two coins are popularly known as the "loonie" and "twonie," respectively.

Since the 1970s, Canada has had an aggressive collector-coin program, with several different designs in various precious metals being offered in quality strikings each year. Some of these are quite scarce and are made in limited quantities. Others, particularly those of the 1970s, are so common as to be frequently melted for scrap. Some of the more unusual pieces are the silver Canadian Aviation series, which actually boast a small portrait inlay of gold. This decade also saw the old cellophane-packaged, proof-like sets supplemented with the more market-oriented cased-proof sets.

Circulating commemoratives were struck for the 125th anniversary of the Canadian Confederation in 1992. While most coins just bore the 1867-1992 legend, an extremely popular series of 25-cent coins bore reverses emblematic of each province and territory. A dollar depicting children before Parliament was issued as well.

As one of the world's richest nations in terms of precious metals, it is not surprising to note that Canada has for years produced some of the world's most popular bullion coins. Silver one-ounce, gold 1/20- to one-ounce, and platinum 1/20- to one-ounce pieces are struck bearing an intricate and difficult-to-counterfeit maple leaf reverse.

CANADIAN MINT MARKS

C	Ottawa, Ontario
H	Heaton, Birmingham, England
None (1858-1907)	Royal Mint, London
None (1908-	Ottawa, Ontario
None (1968)	Philadelphia
None (1973)	Hull, Quebec,
None (1975-)	Winnipeg, Manitoba
B (1999-)	Plated on steel blank
W (1998-)	Winnipeg, Manitoba

GRADING CANADIAN COINS

There are certain convenient key reference points that greatly facilitate the grading of Canadian coins. In the case of the portraits of Queen Victoria, it is the hair over or braid below the ear. In the case of both Edward VII and George V, it is the band of the crown.

Two special bits of wisdom should be imparted to those who would grade Canadian coins. First, even though the typical reverse of a pre-1937 Canadian coin is usually in better grade than the obverse, the value of a coin in the real marketplace is primarily determined by the grade of its obverse. Second, pure nickel George V five-cent pieces are quite difficult to grade. Because of nickel's hardness, the dies did not always leave a sharp impression. Thus the understanding of the texture and surface of the metal is always useful in grading this series.

Uncirculated coins with particularly unpleasant bagging, color or toning may trade at a heavy discount.

MS-65 or Gem Uncirculated – This is the highest grade one is likely to encounter. It has utterly no wear. It has no significant bag marks, particularly in open areas such as the field or cheek of a portrait. Copper must have luster.

MS-63 or Choice Uncirculated – This is a pleasant coin with absolutely no wear but enough bag marks to be noticed. Still, there are few enough bag marks not to be considered marred, particularly few in open areas such as the field or cheek.

MS-60 or Uncirculated – While there is technically no wear at all on an MS-60 coin, it is not necessarily attractive. It will bear scuffs and bag marks acquired from handling at the mint before release. Copper will usually be toned and some coins of either metal may be discolored.

AU or Almost Uncirculated – This describes a coin with such slight signs of wear that some people may need a mild magnifying glass to see them. One should be careful not to confuse an attractive AU coin for uncirculated. Look for the texture of the metal.

XF or Extremely Fine – This is the highest grade of coin that exhibits wear significant enough to be seen easily by the unaided eye. It still exhibits extremely clear, minute detail. In the case of Victorian coins, the hair over ear and jewels of diadem, or segments of braid, are sharp. In the case of Edward VII and George V, the jewels in the band of the crown are sharp. George VI coins will have only the slightest wear in the hair over the ear.

VF or Very Fine – These coins will show obvious signs of wear. Nevertheless, most of the detail of the design will still be clear. In the case of Victorian coins, the hair over ear, or segments of braid, are visible but not sharp. The same is true of the jewels in the diadem. In the case of Edward VII and George V, the jewels in the band of the crown are visible but not sharp. George VI coins will have about 80 percent of hair detail visible.

F or Fine – This is the lowest grade most people would consider collectible. About half the design detail will show for most types. In the case of Victorian coins, the strands of the hair over ear or segments of braid begin to run into each other. Some of the details in the diadem will be obscured. In the case of Edward VII and George V, the jewels in the band of the crown will be unclear, but the band will be distinct from the head. George VI coins will have only about half the hair detail visible.

VG or Very Good – These coins exhibit heavy wear. All outlines are clear, as is generally the rim. Some internal detail will also show, but most will be worn off. In the case of Victorian coins, the details in the strands of the hair over ear or segments of braid will be obscured. Most of the details in the diadem will be obscured. In the case of Edward VII and George V, the band of the crown will be worn through at its center. George VI coins will have only about one-third the hair detail visible.

G or Good – These coins are generally considered uncollectible except for novelty purposes. There will usually be little or no internal detail to the design. Some of the rim may also be barely visible on silver. In the case of Victorian coins, the hair over ear or the braid will be much obscured, as will the majority of the diadem. In the case of Edward VII and George V, the band of the crown will be worn through along most of its width. George VI coins will have no hair detail at all.

BOOKS ON CANADIAN COINS

Charlton, J.E., *Canadian Colonial Tokens*
Cross, W.K., *Charlton Standard Catalogue: Canadian Coins*
Harper, David C., ed., *North American Coins & Prices*
Haxby, James, *The Royal Canadian Mint and Canadian Coinage: Striking Impressions*
Haxby, James, and Willey, R.C., *Coins of Canada*

Periodical
Canadian Coin News

CENTS

One-inch-wide large cents were among the first coins to be struck by the Province of Canada in 1858-59 before the formation of the Confederation. These coins with the head of a young Queen Victoria were struck in such quantities that they were still in bank coffers until 1875. The following year another large order for cents was placed, this time with a heavier weight and a mature head of the queen. This order lasted for five years. Since 1881 Canadian cents have been struck almost continuously.

With the passing of Queen Victoria, a new portrait was designed for Edward VII in 1902, another for George V in 1911. There was a bit of a ruckus in 1911 when the new obverse of George V was found to be lacking the Latin *Dei Gratia* – "by the grace of God." The mint responded to the public outcry and beginning in 1912 these titles were added. More public complaint was heard about the traditional size of the cent. The large cent was replaced in 1920 by a small cent much like America's.

When the obverse was changed to portray the new King George VI in 1937, the opportunity was taken to revise the reverse of the cent. It was given a more naturalistic sprig of maple leaves, designed by G.E. Kruger-Gray. Because of the time taken to design the new cents, some 1936-dated coins were struck in 1937 bearing a minute dot to distinguish them. These are quite rare. The reverse introduced in 1937 has (with some alteration) continued in use today.

Because of the time taken to modify the royal titles to reflect the independence of India, some 1947 cents were struck in 1948 with a tiny maple leaf after the date. While not at all rare, these are quite popular.

No monarch has had as many different portraits on Canadian coins as Elizabeth II. The first portrait, designed by Mary Gillick, had some minor difficulties in striking and as a result was subtly modified after being placed in production. In 1965 a new bust wearing a tiara was introduced, years before Britain itself began using it. When a mature head of the queen was desired, the Canadian choice differed from that of Britain. A design with an open crown, by Canadian artist Dora de Pédery-Hunt, was used beginning 1990. It was replaced in mid-2003 by a bareheaded, grandmotherly portrait designed by Susanna Blunt.

As part of a set of wildlife coins struck for the centennial of Canadian independence, the 1967 cent depicted a rock dove. For its 125th anniversary, the double date 1867-1992 was displayed.

In an economizing measure, the weight of the cent was reduced in 1979, 1980 and 1982. Its copper alloy was switched to copper-plated zinc in 1997. Most years since 1999, these cents were supplemented by some struck on copper-plated steel. The latter are marked with a P on the obverse. From 1982 to 1996, Canadian cents were twelve-sided.

Known Counterfeits: The 1936 dot variety is a prime target.

VICTORIA

	VG	VF
1858	60.00	95.00
1859, 9 over 8	30.00	70.00
1859, Narrow 9	2.50	5.50
1859, Double punched		
9 (2 vars.)	60.00	120.00
1876H	2.00	4.00
1881H	3.00	9.50
1882H	2.00	4.50
1884	3.00	6.00
1886	4.00	12.00
1887	3.00	8.00
1888	2.00	4.50
1890H	8.00	18.00
1891 Large date	6.50	17.00
1891 Small date, Large		
Leaves	70.00	130.00
1891 Small date, Small		
Leaves	50.00	90.00
1892	5.00	12.00
1893	2.50	5.00
1894	8.50	21.00
1895	4.00	12.00
1896	2.75	4.75
1897	2.75	6.00
1898H	6.00	15.00
1899	2.25	4.00
1900	7.00	17.00
1900H	2.50	5.00
1901	2.50	5.00

EDWARD VII

	VG	VF
1902	2.00	3.50
1903	2.00	3.50
1904	2.00	5.00
1905	3.50	7.50
1906	2.00	3.50
1907	2.00	3.50
1907H	9.00	25.00
1908	2.25	5.00
1909	1.50	2.50
1910	1.50	2.50

GEORGE V - LARGE

	F	XF
1911	1.50	3.50
1912	1.50	3.50
1913	1.50	4.00
1914	1.50	4.00
1915	1.50	4.00
1916	.75	3.00
1917	.75	2.25
1918	.75	2.25
1919	.75	2.25
1920	.75	2.25

GEORGE V - SMALL

	F	XF
1920	.50	2.00
1921	.75	5.00
1922	17.00	40.00
1923	30.00	55.00
1924	7.00	15.00
1925	25.00	42.00
1926	5.00	12.00
1927	1.25	6.00
1928	.30	1.50
1929	.30	1.50
1930	2.00	8.50
1931	1.00	5.50

	F	XF
1932	.30	1.50
1933	.30	1.50
1934	.30	1.50
1935	.30	1.50
1936	.30	1.50
1936 Dot below date	*Rare*	

GEORGE VI

	XF	MS-63
1937	1.50	9.50
1938	.85	9.00
1939	.85	6.00
1940	.65	6.00
1941	.65	50.00
1942	.50	40.00
1943	.50	30.00
1944	.65	90.00
1945	.50	18.00
1946	.50	6.00
1947	.50	6.00
1947 Maple Leaf	.50	5.00
1948	.80	25.00
1949	.35	7.00
1950	.35	7.00
1951	.25	8.00
1952	.25	5.00

ELIZABETH II

Gillick bust   *none*

Machin bust

	MS-63
1953 without fold	2.00
1953 with fold	35.00
1954 without fold	*Prooflike only* 300.00
1954 with fold	4.00
1955 without fold	975.00
1955 with fold	1.50
1956	.90
1957	.70
1958	.70
1959	.50
1960	.50

	MS-63
1961	.25
1962	.20
1963	.20
1964	.20
1965	.40
1966	.20
1967 Centennial	.20
1968	.20
1969	.20
1970	.20
1971	.20
1972	.20
1973	.20
1974	.20
1975	.20
1976	.20
1977	.20
1978	.20
1979	.20
1980	.15
1981	.15
1982	.15
1983	.15
1984	.15
1985	.15
1986	.15
1987	.15
1988	.15
1989	.15

Centennial

Crowned bust   *125th Anniv. rev.*

Crowned bust

	MS-63
1990	.15
1991	.15
1992 "1867-1992"	.15
1993	.15
1994	.15
1995	.15
1996	.15

Copper-plated Zinc

1997	.15
1998	.15

	MS-63
1998 Bronze *in sets only*	.75
1998W	1.75

	MS-63
1998 Large Cent as 1908	16.50

Copper-plated Zinc & Copper-plated Steel

	MS-63
1999	.15
1999P *steel*	6.00
2000	.15
2000P *steel*	*Rare*
2000W	PL 1.75
2001	.15
2001 Bronze	*Proof only* 2.75
2001P *steel*	PL 5.00
2002 "1952-2002"	.15
2002P "1952-2002" *steel*	.15
2003 Crowned bust	.15
2003P Crowned bust *steel*	.15
2003 Gillick bust, copper	*Proof only* 2.50

Bare head

	MS-63
2003	.25
2003P steel	.25
2003WP bare head	1.50
2004	.25
2004P *steel*	2.50
2005	.25
2005P *steel*	15.00
2006	.25
2006P *steel*	2.00
2007	.25

THREE CENTS

This most unusual denomination for the Canadian series commemorates the 150th anniversary of the first Canadian postage stamp. It is a collector issue struck in gold-plated silver. Depicted is a beaver from that stamp.

	PF
2001	20.00

FIVE CENTS

Tiny sterling silver five-cent pieces were among the first coins to be struck by the Province of Canada in 1858 before the formation of the Confederation. These coins bore the head of a young Queen Victoria. Twelve years later the new Confederation started issuing five-cent silver coins, making no significant changes form the earlier provincial piece.

With the passing of Queen Victoria, a new portrait was designed for Edward VII in 1902, followed the next year by a change of the reverse crown from St. Edward's to the Imperial crown. There was a bit of a ruckus in 1911 when the new obverse with George V's portrait was found to be lacking the Latin *Dei Gratia* – "by the grace of God." The mint responded to the public outcry, and beginning in 1912, these titles were added.

As a result of a World War I increase in the price of silver, the alloy was reduced from 92.5 percent pure (sterling) to 80 percent beginning with 1920. Public complaint persisted about the small size of this coin. Not only were they prone to loss and fumbling, their thinness resulted in the dents, edge dings and bends that collectors object to today. It was replaced in 1922 by a larger coin much like America's, but of pure nickel.

When the obverse was changed to portray the new King George VI in 1937, the opportunity was taken to revise the reverse of the five-cent piece. A naturalistic beaver on its dam was portrayed, designed by G.E. Kruger-Gray. This new reverse, with some alteration, is still used today.

Like World War I, the Second World War had its effects on the coinage. Shortages of nickel caused the five-cent piece to be struck in a copper-zinc alloy called "tombac" from 1942-44, and later in 1944-45 and 1951-54, in chromium-plated steel. A special reverse design was used to boost wartime morale, that of a torch superimposed on a "V" for victory

Because of the time taken to modify the royal titles to reflect the independence of India, some 1947 coins were struck in 1948 with a tiny dot or maple leaf after the date. The dot is scarce, the leaf common, but both are quite popular.

No monarch has had as many different portraits on Canadian coins as Elizabeth II. The first portrait, designed by Mary Gillick, had some minor difficulties in striking and as a result was subtly modified after being placed in production. In 1965 a new bust wearing a tiara was introduced, years before Britain itself began using it. When a mature head of the Queen was desired, the Canadian choice differed from that of Britain. A design with an open crown, by Canadian artist Dora de Pédery-Hunt, was used beginning 1990. It was replaced in mid-2003 by a bareheaded, grandmotherly portrait designed by Susanna Blunt.

As part of a set of wildlife coins struck for the centennial of Canadian independence, the 1967 five-cent piece depicted a rabbit running. For its 125th anniversary, the double date 1867-1992 was displayed. Recently, a series of commemorative reverse five-cent pieces has been struck in silver.

In an economizing measure, the alloy of the five-cent coin was changed to 75 percent copper, 25 percent nickel in 1982. It was switched to nickel-plated steel gradually from 1999 to 2001, with proofs being struck in sterling.

Modern counting machines occasionally leave an X-shaped scratch on these coins, and such damaged coins are virtually worthless unless bearing scarcer dates.

Known Counterfeits: For the small-size pieces, only the 1921, most of which were melted. For the large-size, crude contemporary counterfeits are occasionally encountered.

VICTORIA

	VG	VF
1858	19.00	45.00
1858, Large date over small date	130.00	320.00
1870 Flat rim	15.00	50.00
1870 Wire rim	16.00	45.00
1871	18.00	50.00
1872H	13.00	38.00
1874H Plain 4	22.50	85.00
1874H Crosslet 4	15.00	70.00
1875H Large date	250.00	725.00

	VG	VF
1875H Small date	120.00	350.00
1880H	6.00	27.00
1881H	9.00	30.00
1882H	12.00	30.00
1883H	22.50	80.00
1884	120.00	350.00
1885	13.00	45.00
1886	8.50	25.00
1887	19.50	60.00
1888	5.50	22.00
1889	24.00	80.00
1890H	6.50	27.00
1891	6.00	18.00
1892	6.00	25.00
1893	6.00	17.00
1894	19.00	60.00
1896	5.50	16.00
1897	4.50	20.00
1898	9.00	37.00
1899	4.50	13.00
1900 Oval 0's	4.50	13.00
1900 Round 0's	17.00	60.00
1901	4.50	13.00

EDWARD VII

	VG	VF
1902	2.25	5.00
1902H Broad H	2.25	4.50
1902H Narrow H	7.50	24.00
1903	4.00	17.00
1903H	1.75	7.00
1904	2.75	7.00
1905	1.75	6.00
1906	2.25	6.00
1907	2.25	4.00
1908	6.00	23.00
1909	3.00	9.50
1910	2.25	5.00

GEORGE V - SILVER

	VG	XF
1911	2.00	10.00
1912	2.00	9.00
1913	2.00	7.00
1914	2.00	9.00
1915	11.00	50.00
1916	2.75	22.00
1917	1.75	7.00
1918	1.75	6.00
1919	1.75	6.00
1920	1.75	6.00
1921	2,600.00	6,700.00

GEORGE V – NICKEL

	VG	VF
1922	.25	7.00
1923	.40	16.00
1924	.30	9.50
1925	55.00	200.00
1926 near 6	2.50	60.00
1926 far 6	95.00	600.00
1927	.25	9.50
1928	.25	9.50
1929	.25	9.50
1930	.25	11.00
1931	.25	18.00
1932	.25	16.00
1933	.40	18.00
1934	.25	16.00
1935	.25	11.00
1936	.25	9.00

GEORGE VI

	XF	Unc.
1937	2.50	9.00
1938	7.00	75.00
1939	3.50	30.00
1940	2.25	18.00
1941	2.25	23.00
1942 Nickel	1.75	18.00
1942 Brass	1.75	3.00

Nickel Reverse

	XF	Unc.
1943 Brass	.85	3.00
1944 Brass	*Rare*	

	XF	Unc.
1944 Steel	1.00	2.00
1945 Steel	1.00	2.00
1946	2.00	14.00
1947	1.25	9.50
1947 Dot	60.00	180.00
1947 Maple Leaf	1.25	9.50
1948	3.00	18.00
1949	.75	6.00
1950	.75	6.00
1951 Steel	.85	2.50
1951 Nickel	.50	1.75
1952 Steel	.85	3.00

ELIZABETH II

	BU
1953 Steel, without strap	3.00
1953 Steel, with strap	3.50
1954 Steel	4.00
1955	2.50
1956	1.50
1957	1.25
1958	1.25
1959	.55
1960	.35
1961	.20
1962	.20
1963	.20
1964	.20

Tiara bust   *Centennial Rev.*

	BU
1965	.20
1966	.20
1967 Centennial	.20
1968	.20
1969	.20
1970	.35
1971	.20
1972	.20
1973	.20
1974	.20
1975	.20
1976	.20
1977	.20
1978	.20
1979	.20

	BU
1980	.20
1981	.20

Cupro-Nickel

	BU
1982	.20
1983	.20
1984	.20
1985	.20
1986	.20
1987	.20
1988	.20
1989	.20

Crowned bust   *"V" reverse*

		BU
1990		.20
1991		.20
1992 "1867-1992"		.20
1993		.20
1994		.20
1995		.20
1996		.20
1996 Silver	*Proof only*	5.50
1997		.20
1997 Silver	*Proof only*	5.50
1998		.20
1998 Silver	*Proof only*	4.50
1998W		2.75
1998 "1908-1998" Silver		2.75
1999		.20
1999 Silver	*Proof only*	4.50
1999P		9.75
2000		.20
2000 Silver	*Proof only*	4.50
2000P		5.50
2000W		PL 3.75
2000 Voltigeurs, Silver	*Proof only*	10.00
2001		.20
2001 Silver	*Proof only*	4.50

Military

		BU
2001 Military Colleges, Silver	*Proof only*	12.00
2001P		.20
2002P "1952-2002"		.20
2002 "1952-2002" Silver	*Proof only*	9.50

	BU
2002 Vimy Ridge, Silver	*Proof only* 11.50
2003P	.20
2003, Silver	4.50
Uncrowned Portrait	
2003	.20
2003P	.20
2003, Silver	3.00
2003WP	1.50
2004	.20
2004P	.20
2004 D-Day, Silver	40.00
2005	.20
2005P	.20
2006	.20
2006P	.20
2007	.20

TEN CENTS

Sterling silver 10-cent pieces were among the first coins to be struck by the Province of Canada in 1858 before the formation of the Confederation. These coins bore the head of a young Queen Victoria. Twelve years later the new Confederation started issuing 10-cent silver coins, making no significant changes form the earlier provincial piece.

With the passing of Queen Victoria, a new portrait was designed for Edward VII in 1902. There was a bit of a ruckus in 1911 when the new obverse with George V's portrait was found to be lacking the Latin *Dei Gratia* – "by the grace of God." The mint responded to the public outcry, and beginning in 1912, these titles were added.

As a result of a World War I increase in the price of silver, the alloy was reduced from 92.5 percent pure (sterling) to 80 percent beginning with 1920.

When the obverse was changed to portray the new King George VI in 1937, the opportunity was taken to revise the reverse of the 10-cent piece. A fishing schooner under sail is depicted, designed by Emmanuel Hahn. Because of the time taken to design the new reverse, some 1936-dated coins were struck in 1937 bearing a minute dot to distinguish them. These are quite rare. This new reverse is, with some alteration, still in use today.

Because of the time taken to modify the royal titles on the dies to reflect the independence of India, some 1947 coins were struck in 1948 with a maple leaf after the date. These are common, but are quite popular.

No monarch has had as many different portraits on Canadian coins as Elizabeth II. The first portrait, designed by Mary Gillick, had some minor

difficulties in striking and as a result was subtly modified after being placed in production. In 1965 a new bust wearing a tiara was introduced, years before Britain itself began using it. When a mature head of the Queen was desired, the Canadian choice differed from that of Britain. A design with an open crown, by Canadian artist Dora de Pédery-Hunt, was used beginning 1990. It was replaced in mid-2003 by a bareheaded, grandmotherly portrait designed by Susanna Blunt.

As part of a set of wildlife coins struck for the centennial of Canadian independence the 1967, 10-cent piece depicted a mackerel. Unfortunately, the rising price of silver forced the centennial coins out of circulation. In mid-year, the 10-cent piece was reduced to 50 percent pure, and beginning in 1968, to pure nickel. It was switched to nickel-plated steel in 2001, with proofs being struck in sterling.

For the Confederation's 125th anniversary, the double date 1867-1992 was displayed on the regular type. The 1997 issue commemorating the voyages of John Cabot began a series of commemorative 10-cent pieces.

Modern counting machines occasionally leave a circular scratch on these coins, and such damaged coins are virtually worthless unless bearing scarcer dates.

Known Counterfeits: The 1936 dot should be examined by an expert; 1930 circulation counterfeits are known.

VICTORIA

	VG	VF
1858, 8 over 5	800.00	2,200.00
1858	20.00	65.00
1870 Narrow 0	18.00	75.00
1870 Wide 0	25.00	95.00
1871	22.00	90.00
1871H	30.00	95.00
1872H	125.00	300.00
1874H	12.00	45.00
1875H	300.00	975.00
1880H	12.00	65.00
1881H	17.00	60.00
1882H	17.00	60.00
1883H	65.00	200.00
1884	250.00	950.00
1885	62.00	200.00

	VG	VF
1886 Small 6	30.00	125.00
1886 Large 6	30.00	150.00
1887	63.00	175.00
1888	16.00	45.00
1889	500.00	1,500.00
1890H	20.00	80.00
1891, 21 leaves	20.00	85.00
1891, 22 leaves	20.00	85.00
1892/1	175.00	600.00
1892	19.50	75.00
1893 Flat top 3	44.00	125.00
1893 Round 3	550.00	2,700.00
1894	45.00	150.00
1896	12.00	45.00
1898	12.00	45.00
1899 Small 9's	8.50	35.00
1899 Large 9's	16.00	60.00
1900	8.50	40.00
1901	8.50	40.00

EDWARD VII

	VG	VF
1902	7.50	30.00
1902H	3.75	18.00
1903	14.00	75.00
1903H	7.00	30.00
1904	11.00	45.00
1905	6.50	55.00
1906	6.50	30.00
1907	4.00	23.00
1908	8.00	55.00
1909 Victorian Leaves	5.50	40.00
1909 Broad Leaves	9.50	55.00
1910	3.75	18.00

GEORGE V

	VG	XF
1911	4.50	40.00
1912	2.25	30.00
1913 Large Leaves	95.00	900.00
1913 Small Leaves	2.25	23.00
1914	2.25	25.00
1915	6.00	95.00
1916	2.25	17.00
1917	2.25	9.75
1918	2.25	8.75
1919	2.25	8.75
1920	2.00	12.00
1921	2.00	20.00

	VG	XF
1928	2.00	12.00
1929	2.00	12.00
1930	2.00	14.00
1931	2.00	12.00
1932	2.00	23.00
1933	2.25	35.00
1934	3.00	60.00
1935	3.50	60.00
1936	2.00	9.00
1936 Dot		*4 Known*

	XF	BU
1961	—	2.00
1962	—	2.00
1963	—	2.00
1964	—	2.00

Tiara Portrait   *Centennial*

	XF	BU
1965	—	2.00
1966	—	2.00
1967 Centennial	—	1.50
1968	—	1.50

Nickel

	XF	BU
1968	—	.25
1969	—	.25
1970	—	.65
1971	—	.25
1972	—	.25
1973	—	.25
1974	—	.25
1975	—	.25
1976	—	.25
1977	—	.25
1978	—	.25
1979	—	.25
1980	—	.25
1981	—	.25
1982	—	.25
1983	—	.25
1984	—	.25
1985	—	.25
1986	—	.25
1987	—	.25
1988	—	.25
1989	—	.25

	XF	BU
1996		.25
1996 Silver	*Proof only*	5.50
1997		.25
1997 Silver	*Proof only*	5.50
1997 John Cabot, Silver	*Proof only*	17.50
1998	—	.25
1998 Silver	*Proof only*	4.00
1998O Silver	*Proof only*	4.00
1998W	—	1.00
1998 "1908-1998" Silver		9.50
1999	—	.35
1999 Silver	*Proof only*	5.00
2000	—	.35
2000 Silver	*Proof only*	5.00
2000W	**PL 1.75**	
2000 Credit Unions, Silver	*Proof only*	10.00

Nickel-plated Steel

	XF	BU
1999P	—	10.00
2000P	*14 known*	
2001P	—	.35
2001 Silver	*Proof only*	5.00
2001P Volunteer	—	.50
2001 Volunteer, Silver	*Proof only*	10.00
2002P "1952-2002"	—	.35
2002 "1952-2002" Silver	*Proof only*	9.50
2003P	—	.35
2003, Silver	*Proof only*	5.00

Uncrowned Portrait

	XF	BU
2003P	—	.35
2003, Silver	*Proof only*	4.00
2004P	—	.35
2004, Silver	*Proof only*	5.00
2004 Golf	—	25.00
2005P	—	.35
2006P	—	.35

GEORGE VI

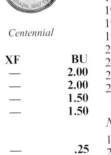

	XF	Unc.
1937	3.75	12.00
1938	6.50	40.00
1939	5.00	45.00
1940	3.00	15.00
1941	6.00	35.00
1942	4.00	30.00
1943	4.00	18.00
1944	4.50	25.00
1945	4.00	18.00
1946	4.50	30.00
1947	6.00	30.00
1947 Maple Leaf	3.00	9.50
1948	13.00	45.00
1949	2.00	9.00
1950	2.00	8.00
1951	2.00	6.00
1952	2.00	5.00

ELIZABETH II

	XF	BU
1953 without straps	—	3.00
1953 with fold	—	5.00
1954	2.25	10.00
1955	—	3.00
1956	—	3.00
1956 Dot below date	5.00	13.00
1957	—	2.25
1958	—	2.25
1959	—	2.25
1960	—	2.00

Crowned bust   *Volunteers*

Crowned Portrait

	XF	BU
1990	—	.25
1991	—	.25
1992 "1867-1992"	—	.25
1993	—	.25
1994	—	.25
1995	—	.25

TWENTY CENTS

Sterling silver 20-cent pieces were the largest of the first coins to be struck by the Province of Canada in 1858 before the formation of the Confederation. These coins bore the head of a young Queen Victoria. During the American Civil War, when U.S. silver coins were being discounted in terms of gold, some firms bought them up in quantity and imported them into Canada. With so many U.S. quarters circulating at the same time, it became easy to confuse the 20-cent piece with them. Because of this it was decided to withdraw the denomination in 1870.

It has since become one of the most desirable and salable Canadian coins

Known Counterfeits: Few.

	VG	VF
1858	**45.00**	**100.00**

TWENTY-FIVE CENTS

Sterling silver 25-cent pieces were first struck in 1870 the decision to abandon the old 20-cent denomination. The new coin was more in harmony with the flood of United States quarters that had been imported into Canada during the American Civil War. These coins bore an older head of Queen Victoria. They saw hard service, not being actively replaced by the government as they wore out, hence they are more difficult to find than one would expect in middle to upper grades.

With the passing of Queen Victoria, a new portrait was designed for Edward VII in 1902. There was a bit of a ruckus in 1911 when the new obverse with George V's portrait was found to be lacking the Latin *Dei Gratia* – "by the grace of God." The mint responded to the public outcry and beginning in 1912 these titles were added.

As a result of a World War I increase in the price of silver, the alloy was reduced from 92.5 percent pure (sterling) to 80 percent beginning with 1920.

When the obverse was changed to portray the new King George VI in 1937, the opportunity was taken to revise the reverse of the 25-cent piece. A Caribou's head is depicted, designed by Emanuel Hahn. Because of the time taken to design the new reverse, some 1936-dated coins were struck in 1937 bearing a minute dot to distinguish them. These are quite rare. This new reverse is, with some alteration, still in use today.

Because of the time taken to modify the royal titles on the dies to reflect the independence of India, some 1947 coins were struck in 1948 with a tiny dot or maple leaf after the date. The dot is scarce, the leaf is not, but both are quite popular.

No monarch has had as many different portraits on Canadian coins as Elizabeth II. The first portrait, designed by Mary Gillick, had some minor difficulties in striking and as a result was subtly modified after being placed in production. In 1965 a new bust wearing a tiara was introduced, years before Britain itself began using it. When a mature head of the Queen was desired, the Canadian choice differed from that of Britain. A design with an open crown, by Canadian artist Dora de Pédery-Hunt, was used beginning 1990. It was replaced in mid-2003 by a bareheaded, grandmotherly portrait designed by Susanna Blunt.

As part of a set of wildlife coins struck for the centennial of Canadian independence, the 1967 25-cent piece depicted a bobcat. Unfortunately, the rising price of silver forced the centennial coins out of circulation. In mid-year this coin was reduced to 50 percent pure, and beginning in 1968, to pure nickel. It was switched to nickel-plated steel in 2000, with proofs being struck in sterling.

A special reverse was used in 1973 to commemorate the centenary of the Royal Canadian Mounted Police. A whole set of circulating commemorative 25-cent pieces was struck for the 125th anniversary of the Canadian Confederation in 1992. While one of the coins simply bore a "1867-1992" legend, a dozen others of the extremely popular series bore reverses emblematic of each province and territory. A series of monthly "Millennium" 25-cent pieces was initiated in 1999 and 2000, and were struck in the old nickel composition.

Most common 1912-1968 pieces in Very Good or lower are worth only their scrap value. Modern counting machines occasionally leave a circular scratch on these coins, and such damaged coins are virtually worthless unless bearing scarcer dates.

Known Counterfeits: The 1936 dot should be examined by an expert.

VICTORIA

	VG	VF
1870	**22.00**	**75.00**
1871	**22.00**	**125.00**
1871H	**25.00**	**115.00**
1872H	**10.00**	**45.00**
1874H	**10.00**	**45.00**
1875H	**275.00**	**1,350.00**

	VG	VF
1880H Narrow 0	60.00	300.00
1880H Wide 0	125.00	600.00
1880H Wide over narrow 0	95.00	400.00
1881H	30.00	125.00
1882H	30.00	110.00
1883H	16.00	75.00
1885	150.00	450.00
1886, 6 over 3	55.00	250.00
1886	30.00	110.00
1887	125.00	450.00
1888	20.00	80.00
1889	145.00	500.00
1890H	25.00	125.00
1891	75.00	350.00
1892	15.00	75.00
1893	125.00	385.00
1894	28.00	125.00
1899	9.50	55.00
1900	9.50	45.00
1901	12.00	50.00

EDWARD VII

	VG	VF
1902	9.50	65.00
1902H	6.50	45.00
1903	15.00	75.00
1904	20.00	150.00
1905	15.00	95.00
1906 Small crown	2,500.00	6,000.00
1906 Large crown	8.00	55.00
1907	6.50	55.00
1908	15.00	95.00
1909	13.00	70.00
1910	5.50	40.00

GEORGE V

	F	XF
1911	18.00	85.00
1912	9.00	55.00
1913	8.50	50.00
1914	9.00	60.00
1915	45.00	425.00
1916	5.25	40.00
1917	4.50	30.00
1918	4.50	25.00

	F	XF
1919	4.50	25.00
1920	4.50	30.00
1921	24.00	225.00
1927	50.00	225.00
1928	4.50	35.00
1929	4.00	35.00
1930	5.00	40.00
1931	5.50	50.00
1932	6.00	50.00
1933	6.50	65.00
1934	9.00	70.00
1935	7.50	50.00
1936	4.00	20.00
1936 Dot	65.00	300.00

GEORGE VI

	XF	Unc.
1937	6.00	16.00
1938	9.50	65.00
1939	7.00	50.00
1940	4.00	15.00
1941	4.00	16.00
1942	4.00	17.00
1943	4.00	16.00
1944	4.00	26.00
1945	4.00	16.00
1946	8.00	45.00
1947	8.00	50.00
1947 Dot after date	150.00	250.00
1947 Maple Leaf	4.00	16.00
1948	12.00	55.00
1949	4.00	10.00
1950	4.00	8.00
1951	4.00	7.00
1952	4.00	6.00

ELIZABETH II

	XF	BU
1953 without strap		5.00
1953 with strap		6.50
1954	6.00	25.00
1955	—	6.00
1956	—	4.25
1957	—	4.00
1958	—	4.00

	XF	BU
1959		4.00
1960		4.00
1961		4.00
1962		4.00
1963		4.00
1964		4.00
1965		4.00
1966		4.00

Centennial   *R.C.M.P.*

	MS-60
1967 Centennial	2.75
1968	2.50

Nickel

1968	.50
1969	.50
1970	1.00
1971	.50
1972	.50
1973 R.C.M.P.	.50
1974	.50
1975	.50
1976	.50
1977	.50
1978	.50
1979	.50
1980	.50
1981	.50
1982	.50
1983	.75
1984	.50
1985	.50
1986	.50
1987	.65
1988	.65
1989	.50

Crowned Portrait

1990	.60
1991	8.00
1992 "1867-1992"	12.50
1992 Alberta	.50
1992 Alberta *Silver proof*	7.50
1992 British Columbia	.50
1992 Br. Columbia *Silver proof*	7.50

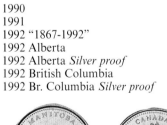

	MS-60
1992 Manitoba	.50
1992 Manitoba *Silver*	*proof* 7.50
1992 New Brunswick	.50
1992 New Brunswick *Silver*	*proof* 7.50

	MS-60
1992 Newfoundland	.50
1992 Newfoundland *Silver*	*proof* 7.50
1992 North West Terr.	.50
1992 North West Terr. *Silver*	*proof* 7.50

	MS-60
1992 Nova Scotia	.50
1992 Nova Scotia *Silver*	*proof* 7.50
1992 Ontario	.50
1992 Ontario *Silver*	*proof* 7.50
1992 Prince Edward Island	.50
1992 Prince Edward Island *Silver*	*proof* 7.50
1992 Quebec	.50
1992 Quebec *Silver*	*proof* 7.50
1992 Saskatchewan	.50
1992 Saskatchewan *Silver*	*proof* 7.50
1992 Yukon	.50
1992 Yukon *Silver*	*proof* 7.50
1993	.65
1994	.65
1995	.65
1996	.65
1996 Silver	*Proof only* 6.50
1997	*In sets only* 4.00
1997 Silver	*Proof only* 5.00
1998	*In sets only* 6.00
1998 Silver	*Proof only* 5.50
1998O Silver	*Proof only* 5.50
1998W	5.00
1998 "1908-1998" Silver	15.00
1999	*In sets only* 3.50
1999 Silver	*Proof only* 6.00
1999P	16.00
1999 January	.50
1999 January Silver	*Proof only* 8.50
1999 February	.50
1999 February Silver	*Proof only* 8.50
1999 March	.50
1999 March Silver	*Proof only* 8.50
1999 April	.50

	MS-60
1999 April Silver	*Proof only* **8.50**
1999 May	**.50**
1999 May Silver	*Proof only* **8.50**
1999 June	**.50**
1999 June Silver	*Proof only* **8.50**
1999 July	**.50**
1999 July, Silver	*Proof only* **8.50**
1999 August	**.50**
1999 August, Silver	*Proof only* **8.50**

	MS-60
1999 September	**.50**
1999 September, Silver	*Proof only* **8.50**
1999 October	**.50**
1999 October, Silver	*Proof only* **8.50**
1999 November	**.50**
1999 November, Silver	*Proof only* **8.50**
1999 December	**.50**
1999 December, Silver	*Proof only* **8.50**
2000	**4.00**
2000 Silver	*Proof only* **8.00**
2000W	*PL Only* **5.00**
2000 Health	**.50**
2000 Health, Silver	*Proof only* **8.50**
2000 Freedom	**.50**
2000 Freedom, Silver	*Proof only* **8.50**

	MS-60
2000 Family	**.50**
2000 Family, Silver	*Proof only* **8.50**
2000 Community	**.50**
2000 Community, Silver	*Proof only* **8.50**

	MS-60
2000 Harmony	**.50**
2000 Harmony, Silver	*Proof only* **8.50**
2000 Wisdom	**.50**
2000 Wisdom, Silver	*Proof only* **8.50**
2000 Creativity	**.50**
2000 Creativity, Silver	*Proof only* **8.50**

	MS-60
2000 Ingenuity	**.50**
2000 Ingenuity, Silver	*Proof only* **8.50**
2000 Achievement	**.50**
2000 Achievement, Silver	*Proof only* **8.50**

	MS-60
2000 Natural Legacy	**.50**
2000 Natural Legacy, Silver	*Proof only* **8.50**
2000 Celebration	**.50**
2000 Celebration, Colorized	**50.00**
2000 Celebration, Silver	*Proof only* **8.50**
2000 Pride	**.50**
2000 Pride, Colorized	**15.00**
2000 Pride, Silver	*Proof only* **8.50**
2001	**1.00**
2001 Silver	*Proof only* **6.50**

Nickel-plated Steel

1999P	**1.00**
2000P	*3-5 known*
2001P	**1.00**

	MS-60
2001 Canada Day, reverse colorized	**12.00**
2002 "1952-2002" Silver	*Proof only* **6.50**
2002P "1952-2002"	**1.00**
2002P Canada Day Reverse	**1.00**
2002P Canada Day Reverse, Colorized	**8.00**
2003, Silver	*Proof only* **4.00**
2003P	**.65**
2003P Canada Day Reverse, Colorized	**8.00**

Uncrowned Portrait

2003, Silver	*Proof only* **4.00**
2003P	**1.00**
2003WP	**2.75**
2004	**2.75**
2004 Silver	*Proof only* **4.00**
2004P	**1.00**
2004P Canada Day Reverse Colorized	**12.00**
2004 Citizenship	**12.00**
2004 Colorized Poppy	**3.00**
2004 Silver, Gilt Poppy	**20.00**

	MS-60
2004 Santa Claus	**18.00**
2004 Colorized Maple Leaf	**4.00**
2005P	**1.00**
2005 Canada Day	**12.00**
2005 Three Soldiers	**10.00**
2005 Alberta	**2.00**
2005 Beaver	**4.00**
2005 Saskatchewan	**2.00**
2005 Bear in Stocking	**5.00**
2005 Netherlands Liberation	**25.00**
2005 Veterans	**2.00**
2006P	**1.00**
2006 Canada Day	**12.00**
2006P Toronto Maple Leafs	**9.00**
2006P Montreal Canadiens	**9.00**
2006P Ottawa Senators	**9.00**
2006 Snowman	**5.00**
2006 Bravery Medal	**2.00**
2006 Queen's Birthday	**8.00**
2006 Breast Cancer, colorized	**7.00**

	MS-60
2007P	**2.00**
2007 Canada Day	**12.00**
2007 Hockey	**2.00**
2007 Wheelchair Curling	**2.00**
2007 Biathlon	**2.00**
2007 Skiing	**2.00**
2007 Hummingbird	**12.00**

FIFTY CENTS

Sterling silver 50-cent pieces were the largest coin struck for domestic circulation from the beginning of Confederation coinage in 1870 until 1912. These coins bore an older head of Queen Victoria. Initial mintages were moderate and for some time it was not the government's policy to replace worn-out coins, so these coins saw hard service. They are more difficult to find than one would expect in middle to upper grades.

With the passing of Queen Victoria, a new portrait was designed for Edward VII in 1902. The first coin struck at the new Canadian Mint in 1908 was one of these pieces. There was a bit of a ruckus in 1911 when the new obverse with George V's portrait was found to be lacking the Latin *Dei Gratia* – "by the grace of God." The mint responded to the public outcry and beginning in 1912 these titles were added.

As a result of a World War I increase in the price of silver, the alloy was reduced from 92.5 percent pure (sterling) to 80 percent beginning with 1920. Most 1921 pieces were melted before they could be released, and no more 50-cent pieces were struck until 1929. The 1921 coin is today one of the greatest of Canadian rarities.

When the obverse was changed to portray the new King George VI in 1937, the opportunity was taken to revise the reverse of the 50-cent piece. The crowned coat of arms of Canada was selected, as designed by George Kruger-Gray. This new reverse motif has, with significant alterations, continued in use today.

Because of the time taken to modify the royal titles on the dies to reflect the independence of India, some 1947 coins were struck in 1948 with a tiny maple leaf after the date. This is not common and quite popular.

No monarch has had as many different portraits on Canadian coins as Elizabeth II. The first portrait, designed by Mary Gillick, had some minor difficulties in striking and as a result was subtly modified after being placed in production. In 1965 a new bust wearing a tiara was introduced, years before Britain itself began using it. When a mature head of the Queen was desired, the Canadian choice differed from that of Britain. A design with an open crown, by Canadian artist Dora de Pédery-Hunt, was used beginning 1990. It was replaced in mid-2003 by a bareheaded, grandmotherly portrait designed by Susanna Blunt.

During this reign the coat of arms on the reverse went through its own evolutions. A version with a motto and more elaborate crest was introduced in 1959, only to be modified the next year. The 1959 version was heraldically inaccurate, using the symbol for blue instead of white in the lowest section. In 1997, an additional collar was added around the shield.

As part of a set of wildlife coins struck for the centennial of Canadian independence the 1967, 50-cent piece depicted a howling wolf. Unfortunately, the rising price of silver forced the centennial coins out of circulation. Production of the silver 50-cent piece was suspended, and beginning in 1968 it was reduced in size and produced in pure nickel. It was switched to nickel-plated steel in 2000, with proofs being struck in sterling.

For the Confederation's 125th anniversary, the double date "1867-1992" was displayed on the regular type. Since then commemoratives have become more common, with most placed on sale at a premium.

Most common 1937-1968 pieces in Fine or lower are worth only their scrap value.

Known Counterfeits: Any 1921 should be examined by an expert.

VICTORIA

	VG	VF
1870	800.00	2,000.00
1870 LCW	45.00	180.00
1871	55.00	275.00
1871H	90.00	400.00
1872H	40.00	175.00
1872H inverted A over V	250.00	1,300.00
1881H	45.00	200.00
1888	170.00	600.00
1890H	950.00	3,200.00
1892	50.00	320.00
1894	350.00	1,100.00
1898	75.00	350.00
1899	150.00	700.00
1900	38.00	175.00
1901	55.00	225.00

EDWARD VII

	VG	VF
1902	15.00	98.00
1903H	22.00	175.00
1904	150.00	600.00
1905	150.00	600.00
1906	12.00	95.00
1907	12.00	95.00
1908	20.00	175.00

	VG	VF
1909	17.00	175.00
1910 Victorian Leaves	22.00	175.00
1910 Edwardian Leaves	8.00	85.00

GEORGE V

	F	XF
1911	70.00	550.00
1912	24.00	225.00
1913	24.00	300.00
1914	55.00	550.00
1916	14.00	175.00
1917	11.00	100.00
1918	10.00	90.00
1919	10.00	90.00
1920	13.00	125.00
1921	22,000.00	32,000.00
1929	13.00	100.00
1931	30.00	225.00
1932	185.00	800.00
1934	30.00	225.00
1936	30.00	175.00

GEORGE VI

	XF	Unc.
1937	9.50	30.00
1938	25.00	95.00

	XF	Unc.
1939	17.00	60.00
1940	7.00	27.00
1941	7.00	27.00
1942	7.00	27.00
1943	7.00	27.00
1944	7.00	27.00
1945	7.00	30.00
1946	8.00	60.00
1946 Hoof in 6	150.00	1,100.00
1947 Straight 7	12.00	65.00
1947 Curved 7	15.00	98.00
1947 Straight 7, Maple Leaf	70.00	160.00
1947 Curved 7, Maple Leaf	2,200.00	3,900.00
1948	98.00	250.00
1949	7.00	35.00
1949 Hoof over 9	60.00	325.00
1950	35.00	125.00
1950 Lines in 0	7.00	9.00
1951		9.00
1952		7.50

ELIZABETH II

	XF	BU
1953 Small date, without strap		7.00
1953 Large date, without strap	14.00	75.00
1953 Large date, with strap		15.00
1954	7.00	20.00
1955		15.00
1956		7.50
1957		7.50
1958		7.00
1959		7.00

	MS-60
1960	7.00
1961	7.00
1962	7.00
1963	7.00
1964	7.00
1965	7.00
1966	7.00
1967 Centennial (Wolf)	7.00

Nickel

1968	.75
1969	.75
1970	.75
1971	.75
1972	.75

	MS-60
1973	.75
1974	.75
1975	.75
1976	.75
1977	1.35
1978	.75
1979	.75
1980	.75
1981	.75
1982	.75
1983	.75
1984	.75
1985	.75
1986	1.00
1987	1.00
1988	1.00
1989	1.00

Crowned Portrait

1990	1.00
1991	.85
1992 "1867-1992"	1.00
1993	.85

	MS-60
1994	.75
1995	.75
1995 Puffin, Silver	*Proof only* 22.00
1995 Whooping Crane, Silver	*Proof only* 22.00
1995 Gray Jays, Silver	*Proof only* 22.00
1995 Ptarmigans, Silver	*Proof only* 22.00
1996	.75
1996 Silver	*Proof only* 9.00
1996 Moose calf, Silver	*Proof only* 22.00
1996 Wood Ducklings, Silver	*Proof only* 22.00

	MS-60
1996 Cougar Kittens, Silver	*Proof only* 22.00
1996 Black Bear Cubs, Silver	*Proof only* 22.00
1997	.75
1997 Silver	*Proof only* 9.50
1997 Duck Tolling Retriever, Silver	*Proof only* 17.00
1997 Labrador Retriever, Silver	*Proof only* 17.00
1997 Newfoundland, Silver	*Proof only* 17.00
1997 Eskimo Dog, Silver	*Proof only* 17.00
1998	.75
1998 Silver	*Proof only* 9.50
1998W	*In sets only* 3.00
1998 "1908-1998" Silver	15.00
1998 Skaters, Silver	*Proof only* 10.00
1998 Ski Jumper, Silver	*Proof only* 10.00
1998 Soccer Players, Silver	*Proof only* 10.00
1998 Race Car, Silver	*Proof only* 10.00
1998 Killer Whales, Silver	*Proof only* 15.00
1998 Humpback Whale, Silver	*Proof only* 15.00
1998 Beluga Whales, Silver	*Proof only* 15.00
1998 Blue Whale, Silver	*Proof only* 15.00
1999	.75
1999 Silver	*Proof only* 9.00
1999P	8.00
1999 Golfers, Silver	*Proof only* 13.50
1999 Yacht Race, Silver	*Proof only* 10.00
1999 Football, Silver	*Proof only* 10.00
1999 Basketball, Silver	*Proof only* 10.00
1999 Cymric Cat, Silver	*Proof only* 17.50
1999 Tonkinese Cat, Silver	*Proof only* 17.50
1999 Cougar, Silver	*Proof only* 17.50
1999 Lynx, Silver	*Proof only* 17.50

	MS-60
2000	1.00
2000 Silver	*Proof only* 9.00
2000P	*approximately 200 struck*
2000W	*In sets only* 2.00
2000 Hockey, Silver	*Proof only* 12.00

	MS-60
2000 Curling, Silver	Proof only 12.00
2000 Steeplechase, Silver	Proof only 12.00
2000 Bowling, Silver	Proof only 12.00

	MS-60
2000 Great Horned Owl, Silver	Proof only 13.50
2000 Red Tailed Hawk, Silver	Proof only 13.50
2000 Osprey, Silver	Proof only 13.50
2000 Bald Eagle, Silver	Proof only 13.50
2001 Silver	Proof only 7.50
2001P	1.00
2001 Quebec Winter Carnival, Silver	Proof only 15.00
2001 Nunavut Toonik Tyme, Silver	Proof only 15.00
2001 Newfoundland Folk Festival, Silver	Proof only 15.00
2001 P.E.I. Festival, Silver	Proof only 15.00
2001 The Sled, Silver	Proof only 17.00
2001 The Maiden's Cave, Silver	Proof only 17.00
2001 Les Petits Sauteux, Silver	Proof only 17.00
2002 Silver	Proof only 8.00
2002P "1952-2002"	1.75
2002 "1952-2002", Silver	17.50
2002 "1952-2002", Gilt Silver	25.00
2002 Nova Scotia Festival, Silver	Proof only 15.00
2002 Ontario Stratford Festival, Silver	Proof only 15.00
2002 Manitoba Folklorama, Silver	Proof only 15.00
2002 Alberta Calgary Stampede, Silver	Proof only 15.00
2002 British Columbia Squamish Days, Silver	Proof only 15.00
2002 The Pig ... over the Stile, Silver	Proof only 15.00
2002 Shoemaker in Heaven, Silver	Proof only 15.00
2002 Le Vaisseau Fantome, Silver	Proof only 15.00
2002 Tulip Festival, Gilt Silver	Proof only 25.00
2003 crowned portrait	1.00
2003 crowned portrait, Silver	Proof only 5.00

	MS-60
2003 bare portrait, Silver	Proof only 5.00
2003W bare portrait	3.00
2003WP bare portrait	2.00
2003 Yukon Festival, Silver	Proof only 15.00
2003 Manitoba Back to Batoche, Silver	Proof only 15.00
2003 Saskatchewan Arts Festival, Silver	Proof only 15.00
2003 New Brunswick Festival, Silver	Proof only 15.00
2003 N.W.Terr. Festival, Silver	Proof only 15.00
2003 Daffodil, Gilt Silver	Proof only 25.00
2004	4.00
2004, Silver	7.00
2004 Easter Lily, Gilt Silver	Proof only 25.00
2004 Swallowtail Butterfly, hologram	Proof only 22.00
2004 Sulphur Butterfly, hologram	Proof only 22.00
2005 Golden Rose, Gilt Silver	Proof only 20.00
2005 Spangled Fritillary Butterfly, hologram	Proof only 22.00
2005 Monarch Butterfly	Proof only 22.00
2005 Toronto Maple Leafs (4 types)	17.50
2005 Montreal Canadiens (4 types)	17.50
2005 Battle of Britain	20.00
2005 Battle of Scheldt	20.00
2005 Battle of the Atlantic	20.00
2005 Conquest of Sicily	20.00
2005 Liberation of Netherlands	20.00
2005 Raid of Dieppe	20.00
2006 Golden Daisy	22.00
2006 Swallowtail Butterfly	22.00
2006 Silvery Blue Butterfly	22.00
2007 Forget-me-Not	22.00
2007 Christmas ornaments	—

DOLLARS

Despite patterns having been produced as early as 1911, Canada did not issue a silver dollar until 1935. The entire visual style of Canadian coins began to change then, when a new, artistic commemorative dollar for the jubilee of George V was released. It depicted the now-famous Voyageur design of a fur company agent and an Indian paddling a canoe past an islet. This design was retained when the reverses of all the other denominations were modernized with appearance of the new George VI portrait in 1937.

Because of the time taken to modify the royal titles to reflect the independence of India, some 1947 dollars were struck in 1948 with a tiny maple leaf after the date. This variety is both scarce and popular. The 1950-52 Arnprior varieties have only 1 1/2 water lines to the right of the canoe, due to over-polishing of the die.

No monarch has had as many different portraits on Canadian coins as Elizabeth II. The first portrait, designed by Mary Gillick, had some minor difficulties in striking and as a result was subtly modified after being placed in production. In 1965 a new bust wearing a tiara was introduced, years before Britain itself began using it. When a mature head of the Queen was desired, the Canadian choice differed from that of Britain. A design with an open crown, by Canadian artist Dora de Pédery-Hunt, was used beginning 1990. It was replaced in mid-2003 by a bareheaded, grandmotherly portrait designed by Susanna Blunt.

The 1967 centennial of Canadian independence resulted in some of Canada's most beautiful and dignified wildlife coins. On the dollar, a majestic Canada goose is shown against a stark, open background. Unfortunately, the rising price of silver forced this coins out of circulation. Beginning in 1968, the 80 percent silver dollar was replaced by a smaller one of pure nickel.

In 1987, a radical new dollar coin was introduced to save the expense of producing perishable paper money. A small golden-bronze plated nickel dollar was introduced depicting a swimming loon. It was originally intended to use the standard Voyageur reverse, but the master dies were temporarily lost in transit. Today this coin is popularly know as the "loonie."

With a long history of being used as a commemorative (one or more being struck every decade since its creation), it is natural that one-dollar commemoratives would spearhead the modern, aggressive collector coin program initiated during the 1970s. Most years, a special cased silver-alloy dollar is produced for the numismatic market. In some years a base-metal commemorative is also issued, available in both circulation and collector's versions. If cased versions in either silver or base metal are not kept in their cases of issue, they are considered less salable.

Known Counterfeits: Any 1948 dollar should be examined by an expert.

GEORGE V

	XF	Unc.
1935 Jubilee	30.00	45.00
1936	25.00	47.50

GEORGE VI

	XF	Unc.
1937	20.00	35.00
1938	60.00	110.00

Royal Visit

	XF	Unc.
1939 Royal Visit	15.00	18.50
1945	200.00	350.00
1946	40.00	100.00
1947 Pointed 7	110.00	300.00
1947 Blunt 7	100.00	150.00
1947 Maple Leaf	175.00	300.00
1948	950.00	1,350.00

Newfoundland

	XF	Unc.
1949 Newfoundland	20.00	30.00
1950, 4 water lines	16.00	25.00
1950, Arnprior	17.50	35.00
1951, 4 water lines	14.00	16.00
1951, Arnprior	70.00	200.00
1952, 4 water lines	15.00	35.00
1952, Arnprior	20.00	50.00
1952, No water lines	15.00	36.50

ELIZABETH II

	XF	BU
1953 Wire rim, without shoulder strap	—	17.00
1953 Flat rim, with shoulder strap	—	17.00
1954	10.00	20.00
1955, four water lines	9.00	18.00
1955, Arnprior	50.00	135.00
1956	12.50	25.00
1957, four water lines	—	18.00
1957, Arnprior	—	25.00

Charlottetown

	XF	BU
1958 British Columbia	—	16.00
1959	—	15.00
1960	15.00	

	XF	BU
1961	—	15.00
1962	—	15.00
1963	—	15.00
1964 Charlottetown	—	15.00
1965	—	14.50
1966	—	14.50

	BU
1967 Centennial	15.00

Nickel, Voyageur reverse to 1987 unless noted

	BU
1968	2.00
1969	2.00
1970 Manitoba	2.00
1971 British Columbia	2.00
1971 British Columbia, *silver*	PL 10.00
1972	2.00
1973 Pr. Edward Is.	2.00
1973 R.C.M.P., *silver*	PL 10.00

Winnipeg

	BU
1974 Winnipeg	2.00
1974 Winnipeg, *silver*	PL 10.00
1975	2.00
1975 Calgary, *silver*	PL 10.00
1976	2.00
1976 Library of Parliament, *silver*	PL 10.00
1977	2.50

Queen's Jubilee

	BU	PF
1987 Loon	2.25	8.00
1988 Loon	2.25	6.75

	BU	
1977 Queen's Jubilee, *silver*	PL 10.00	
1978	2.00	
1978 Edmonton Games, *silver*	PL 10.00	
1979	2.00	
1979 Sailing Ship, *silver*	PL 10.00	
1980	2.00	
1980 Arctic Territories, *silver*	20.00	

	BU	PF
1981	2.00	5.50
1981 Railroad, *silver*	10.00	15.50
1982	2.00	5.25
1982 Constitution	2.50	6.00
1982 Regina, *silver*	10.00	12.00
1983	2.00	6.50
1983 Edmonton Games, *silver*	10.00	10.00
1984	2.00	6.00
1984 Cartier	2.25	6.00
1984 Toronto, *silver*	14.75	11.00
1985	2.00	6.25

	BU	PF
1985 National Parks, *silver*	11.00	11.00
1986	2.25	8.00
1986 Vancouver, *silver*	10.00	10.00
1987	In sets only 3.50	8.50
1987 Davis Strait, *silver*	10.00	10.00

	BU	PF
1988 Ironworks	16.00	17.00
1989 Loon	2.25	6.75
1989 MacKenzie River	22.50	24.00
1990 Loon	2.00	7.00
1990 Kelsey	22.50	24.00
1991 Loon	2.00	13.00
1991 S.S. Frontenac, Silver,	10.00	23.50
1992 "1867-1992" Loon	2.00	8.00

	BU	PF
1992 "1867-1992" Parliament, *Aureate-bronze plated nickel*	2.25	9.00
1992 Stagecoach	10.75	12.50
1993 Loon	2.00	6.00
1993 Stanley Cup	8.50	12.50
1994 Loon	2.00	7.00

	BU	PF
1994 War Memorial, *Aureate-bronze plated nickel*	2.25	10.00
1994 R.C.M.P. Dog Sled	16.00	24.50
1995 Loon	2.00	7.00
1995 Peacekeeping Monument, *Aureate-bronze plated nickel*	2.25	10.00
1995 Hudson's Bay Co.	16.00	22.00
1996 Loon	2.00	7.50
1996 McIntosh Apple	16.00	26.00
1997 Loon In sets only	5.00	8.00
1997 Loon Flying PL 18.00		
1997 Loon Flying, *silver*	75.00	
1997 Hockey	10.75	24.00
1998 Loon In sets only	2.50	10.00
1998W Loon PL 5.00		
1998 R.C.M.P.	16.00	22.00
1999 Loon In sets only	2.00	8.00
1999 Year of Old Persons		40.00
1999 Ship	16.00	24.00
2000 Loon In sets only	2.00	8.00
2000W Loon PL 5.00		
2000 Human and Space Shuttle	16.00	24.00
2001 Loon In sets only	2.00	8.00
2001P	2.50	8.00

	BU	PF
2001 Ballet	16.00	24.00
2001 "1911-2001" Wreath	55.00	
2002 "1952-2002" Loon	3.00	9.00
2002P Loon	5.00	
2002 Loon family	15.00	
2002 Loon with privy mark	35.00	
2002 Queen in Coach	12.00	40.00
2002 as above but gilt	40.00	
2002 Queen Mother	200.00	
2003 Loon, de Pédery-Hunt portrait	5.00	12.00

	BU	PF
2003 Cobalt	**20.00**	**28.00**
2003 Loon, bare portrait	—	**12.00**
2003P Loon	—	**5.00**
2003W Loon	—	**6.00**
2003 Voyageurs, young portrait	—	**35.00**
2003 Voyageurs, bare portrait	—	**38.00**
Same, Gold	*Unique*	
(2003) Queen in Coach, bare portrait, Gold	*Unique*	
2004 Loon	**3.00**	**12.00**
2004WP Loon	—	**5.00**
2004 Loons flying	—	**5.00**
2004 Elusive Loon	—	**15.00**
2004 Ship	**20.00**	**40.00**
2004 Loon & olympics, silver		**50.00**
2005 Loon	**3.00**	**7.50**

	BU	PF
2005 Terry Fox	—	**8.00**
2005 Flag	**23.00**	**33.00**
2005 similar, gilt	—	**65.00**
2005 Puffin	—	**30.00**
2006 Loon	**3.00**	**7.50**
2006 Loon, Teddy bear	—	**3.50**
2006 Owl	—	**30.00**
2006 Victoria Cross	**27.00**	**35.00**
2006 Same, gilt	—	**60.00**

	BU	PF
2006 Olympic	—	—
2007 The Arts	—	**45.00**
2008 NHL Hockey (6 different)	—	—

Note: Since 1988 uncirculated silver commemorative dollars have had a proof-like finish.

BI-METALLIC TWO DOLLARS

In 1996, a radical new two-dollar coin was introduced to save the expense of producing perishable paper money. It is composed of a central disc composed of aluminum-bronze, surrounded by a washer-like ring of nickel. The reverse design is that of a polar bear.

This is not unique, and such bi-metallic coins have been appearing in more countries since 1982.

Known Counterfeits: Beware of false "errors" created outside the mint by separating the inner and outer sections of the coin. These are of no numismatic value.

	BU	PF
1996 Bear	**3.25**	**10.00**
1996 *gold, silver ring*	—	**190.00**
1996 *gold plated silver, silver ring*	—	**12.00**
1997 Bear	—	**3.25**
1997 *gold plated silver, silver ring*	—	**11.00**
1998 Bear	—	**3.25**
1998 *gold plated silver, silver ring*	—	**12.00**
1998W	**PL 4.00**	
1999 Bear		...

	BU	PF
1999 Nunavut	—	**3.25**
1999 *gold plated silver, silver ring*	—	**15.00**
1999 *gold, base gold ring*	—	**180.00**

	BU	PF
2000 Bear	—	**15.00**
2000W Bear	—	**4.00**
2000 Bear and Cubs	—	**3.25**
2000 *gold plated silver, silver ring*	—	**15.00**
2000 *gold, base gold ring*	—	**180.00**
2001 Bear	**5.00**	**15.00**
2001P Bear	—	**5.00**
2001 *gold plated silver, silver ring*	—	**15.00**
2002 "1952-2002" Bear	**5.00**	**15.00**
2002P "1952-2002" Bear	—	**5.00**
2003 Bear, crowned portrait	**5.00**	**15.00**
2003P Bear, crowned portrait	—	**5.00**
2003 Bear, bare portrait	**3.25**	**15.00**
2003WP Bear, bare portrait	—	**5.00**
2004 Bear	**5.00**	**15.00**
2004 Bear, Silver	—	**15.00**
2005 Bear	**5.00**	**15.00**
2006 Bear	**5.00**	**15.00**
2006 *gold plated silver, silver ring*	—	**15.00**
2006 *gold*	—	**400.00**

SILVER TWO DOLLARS

Despite being struck in the same year, different standards were used for these two coins. The latter is part of a four-coin set based on the designs of the 1993 platinum set.

Known Counterfeits: None.

	BU	PF
2004 Bear, Silver	—	**25.00**
2004 Arctic Fox Bust	—	**25.00**

SILVER THREE DOLLARS

This unusual denomination is part of a four-coin set based on the designs of the 1993 platinum set. It set a precedent for similar later wildlife issues

Known Counterfeits: None.

	BU	PF
2004 Arctic Foxes	—	**35.00**
2006 Beaver	—	**35.00**

SILVER FOUR DOLLARS

This unusual denomination is part of a four-coin set based on the designs of the 1993 platinum set.

Known Counterfeits: None.

	BU	PF
2004 Arctic Fox	—	—

GOLD FIVE DOLLARS

Part of the motivation for establishing a Canadian Mint in 1908 was the ability to convert domestically mined gold into coin. Four years after the mint's opening, this dream was realized. The crowned portrait of George V is the same as on the minor coins. The coat of arms on the reverse is the original one granted in 1868, reflecting the four original provinces: Ontario, Quebec, New Brunswick and Nova Scotia. Bag marks and edge knocks can be a problem on these, also cleaning, although to a lesser extent.

Known Counterfeits: It is believed counterfeits exist for this type.

	VF	XF
1912	260.00	300.00
1913	260.00	300.00
1914	300.00	500.00

SILVER FIVE DOLLARS

Among the most over-sold coins marketed to the general public were the silver commemoratives struck to raise money for the 1976 Olympics in Montreal. Produced over four years, most were sold to laymen, leaving no secondary market for those who no longer wanted to own them. Literally tons were melted during the great silver boom of 1979-80. Ambiguous redemption procedures and limits to the legal-tender status also contributed to the collapse of the market for this series.

This denomination was revived for commemorative use in 1998. The first three of this new series of $5 coins were sold jointly with a related Chinese, Norwegian and British commemorative respectively. The Norwegian piece is base metal and is listed in the following section.

The Arctic Fox coin is part of a four-coin set based on the designs of the 1993 platinum set.

Known Counterfeits: None.

	MS-63	PF
1973 Sailboats	15.00	16.00
1973 Map	15.00	16.00

	MS-63	PF
1974 Olympic Symbol	15.00	16.00

reduced

	MS-63	PF
1974 Ancient Athlete	15.00	16.00
1974 Rowing	15.00	16.00
1974 Canoeing	15.00	16.00
1975 Running	15.00	16.00
1975 Javelin Thrower	15.00	16.00
1975 Swimmer	15.00	16.00
1975 Diver	15.00	16.00
1976 Fencing	15.00	16.00
1976 Boxing	15.00	16.00
1976 Olympic Village	15.00	16.00
1976 Olympic Flame	15.00	16.00
1998 Norman Bethune	—	30.00
2001 Guglieilmo Marconi	—	28.00
2002 Arms	—	225.00
2003 Soccer	—	30.00
2004 Moose	—	125.00
2004 Arctic Fox Family	—	—
2004 Golf	—	28.00
2005 W.W.II	—	35.00
2005 Alberta	—	38.00
2005 Saskatchewan	—	38.00
2005 Deer	—	38.00
2005 Walrus	—	38.00
2006 Falcon	—	40.00
2006 Horse & foal	—	40.00

SILVER EIGHT DOLLARS

A new denomination struck in sterling silver (92.5 percent). All are proof-only collector issues.

2004 Grizzly Bear		60.00
2004 Railroad Bridge		60.00
2005 Chinese Memorial		60.00

BRASS FIVE DOLLARS

This coin was struck to honor the early Viking voyages to Vinland (probably Newfoundland and Labrador). It was sold in sets jointly with the 1999 Norway 20 kroner.

1999 Viking Ship **Proof only 20.00**
Known Counterfeits: None.

GOLD TEN DOLLARS

Part of the motivation for establishing a Canadian mint in 1908 was the ability to convert domestically mined gold into coin. Four years after the mint's opening, this dream was realized. The crowned portrait of George V is the same as on the minor coins. The coat of arms on the reverse is the original one granted in 1868, reflecting the four original provinces: Ontario, Quebec, New Brunswick and Nova Scotia. Bag marks and edge knocks can be a problem on these, also cleaning, to a lesser extent.

Later commemorative revivals of the 10-dollar gold piece are expected to be free from edge knocks.

Known Counterfeits: It is believed counterfeits exist for this type.

	VF	XF
1912	525.00	575.00
1913	525.00	575.00
1914	525.00	590.00
2002 Arms	*Proof only* **550.00**

SILVER TEN DOLLARS

Among the most over-sold coins marketed to the general public were the silver commemoratives struck to raise money for the 1976 Olympics in Montreal. Produced over four years, most were sold to laymen, leaving no secondary market for those who no longer wanted to own them. Literally tons were melted during the great silver boom of 1979-80. Ambiguous redemption procedures and limits to the legal-tender status also contributed to the collapse of the market for this series.

Known Counterfeits: None.

	MS-63	PF
1973 Montreal Skyline	30.00	32.50
1973 World Map	30.00	32.50

	MS-63	PF
1974 World Map	300.00	—
1974 Head of Zeus	30.00	32.50
1974 Temple of Zeus	30.00	32.50
1974 Bicycling	30.00	32.50
1974 Lacrosse	30.00	32.50
1975 Men's Hurdles	30.00	32.50
1975 Ladies' Shot Put	30.00	32.50
1975 Sailing	30.00	32.50
1975 Canoeing	30.00	32.50
1976 Soccer	30.00	32.50
1976 Field Hockey	30.00	32.50
1976 Round Stadium	30.00	32.50
1976 Velodrome	30.00	32.50
2005 Veteran	*Proof only*	40.00
2005 Pope John Paul II		
	Proof only	45.00
2006 Louisbourg	*Proof only*	40.00

SILVER FIFTEEN DOLLARS

This pair of odd-denomination coins was struck as part of a series ordered by the International Olympic Commission. It commemorates the centennial of the founding of the modern Olympic Games. The gold $175 piece is also part of this series.

Known Counterfeits: None.

	PF
1992 Track	35.00
1992 Gymnast, Skater, Jumper	35.00
2008	—

GOLD ON SILVER FIFTEEN DOLLARS

This series of odd-denomination coins marks each Chinese year. Each year in a 12-year cycle is represented by a specific animal. That animal is shown on a distinctive, octagonal gold-inlay in the coin.

Known Counterfeits: None.

	PF
1998 Year of the Tiger	350.00
1999 Year of the Rabbit	40.00
2000 Year of the Dragon	130.00
2001 Year of the Snake	40.00
2002 Year of the Horse	60.00
2003 Year of the Sheep	60.00
2004 Year of the Monkey	85.00
2005 Year of the Rooster	80.00
2006 Year of the Dog	80.00
2007 Year of the Pig	70.00
2008 Year of the Rat	—

GOLD TWENTY DOLLARS

In addition to the wildlife cent through dollar, the 1967 Confederation Centennial was commemorated by Canada's first gold coin since 1919. The reverse of this coins, all of which were originally released in proof-like sets, bear a coat of arms similar to the half dollar of 1960-96. Its proof-like surface makes it particularly susceptible to fingerprinting and other mishandling.

Known Counterfeits: Deceptive counterfeits of this coin are known but not common.

	PL
1967	575.00

SILVER TWENTY DOLLARS

To help raise money for the 1988 Winter Olympic Games in Calgary, a set of coins was sold. Its issue extended over four years and all pieces were Proof $20 pieces. The normal edge is lettered, all plain-edge coins being struck in error.

Known Counterfeits: None.

	PF
1985 Downhill Skier	21.50
1985 Same, plain edge	160.00
1985 Speed Skater	21.50
1985 Same, plain edge	160.00
1986 Biathlon	21.50
1986 Same, plain edge	160.00
1986 Hockey	21.50
1986 Same, plain edge	160.00
1986 Cross-country Skier	21.50
1986 Free-style Skier	21.50
1986 Same, plain edge	160.00

	PF
1987 Figure Skaters	21.50
1987 Curler	21.50
1987 Ski Jumper	21.50

	PF
1987 Bobsledders	21.50

GOLD ON SILVER TWENTY DOLLARS

This series honored Canadian pioneers in the field of powered aviation. It is distinctive in having the portrait of each hero set on a small oval gold inlay.
Known Counterfeits: None.

	PF
1990 Lancaster Bomber	120.00
1990 Two 1940s Airplanes	35.00
1991 1909 Biplane	35.00
1991 1947 Pontoon Airplane	35.00
1992 Curtis Canuck left	35.00
1992 de Haviland Gypsy Moth r.	35.00
1993 Pontoon Airplane	35.00
1993 Lockheed 14 Super Electra	35.00
1994 Curtiss HS-2L and Trees	35.00
1994 Canadian Vickers Vedette	35.00
1995 Fleet Canuck flying l.	35.00
1995 "Chipmunk" flying upward	35.00
1996 "Arrow" two Jets right	75.00
1996 "Canuck" two Jets left	35.00
1997 Sabre Jet left	35.00
1997 Tutor Jet right	40.00
1998 Anti-submarine Bomber l	40.00
1998 Waterbomber Aircraft r.	40.00
1999 Twin Otter	45.00
1999 Dash 8	45.00

MULTICOLOR SILVER TWENTY DOLLARS

The first series celebrates Canadian achievements in the field of transportation. It is unusual in having a small, multicolor hologram applied to the reverse of each coin. It was followed by a "natural wonders" series having an even larger proportion of the coin's surface devoted to the hologram. Some later issues have a selective gold plating instead.

Known Counterfeits: None.

	PF
2000 Schooner Bluenose	150.00
2000 Locomotive of 1853	40.00
2000 Steam Buggy of 1867	40.00
2001 Ship Marco Polo	40.00
2001 Locomotive Scotia	40.00
2001 Russell Touring Car	40.00
2002 Gray-Dort Auto	40.00
2002 Ship William Lawrence	40.00
2002 10-D Locomotive	40.00
2003 Hydrofoil HMCS Bras d'Or	45.00
2003 FA-1 Diesel Locomotive	45.00
2003 Bricklin SV-1 Auto of 1974	45.00
2003 Niagara Falls	70.00
2003 Rocky Mountains	50.00
2003 Northern Lights	60.00
2004 Icebergs	65.00
2004 Hopewell Rocks	60.00
2004 Sambro Lighthouse	60.00
2005 Three-masted ship	55.00
2005 N.W.Terr. Diamonds	50.00
2005 Mingan Archipelago Nat'l. Pk.	60.00
2005 Rainforests	60.00
2005 Toronto Is. Lighthouse	62.50
2006 Georgian Bay Nat'l. Park	60.00
2006 Nahanni Nat'l. Park	60.00
2006 Jasper Nat'l. Park	60.00
2006 Notre Dame Basilica	60.00
2006 CN Tower	60.00
2006 Saddledome	60.00
2006 Ketch (ship)	60.00
2007 Brigantine (ship)	60.00

PLATINUM THIRTY DOLLARS

Another ongoing group of collector coins is the platinum wildlife proof sets of four. These coins are not sold individually. Despite reports to the contrary, these are not bullion coins and are all scarce due to the small quantities struck.

Known Counterfeits: None.

	PF
1990 Polar Bear Bust	225.00
1991 Snowy Owl Bust	225.00
1992 Cougar Bust	225.00
1993 Arctic Fox Bust	230.00
1994 Sea Otter Bust	230.00
1995 Canadian Lynx Bust	225.00
1996 Falcon Bust	225.00
1997 Bison Bust	225.00
1998 Gray Wolf Bust	225.00
1999 Musk Ox Bust	225.00
2000 Pronghorn Antelope Head	225.00
2001 Harlequin Duck Bust	225.00
2002 Great Blue Heron Pair	225.00
2003 Atlantic Walrus Bust	225.00
2004 Grizzly Bear	225.00
2005	—

Known Counterfeits: None.

SILVER FIFTY DOLLARS

2006 Wood Carvings	*Proof only* 65.00

GOLD FIFTY DOLLARS

2005 W.W.II Portraits	450.00

SILVER FIFTY DOLLARS

2005 W.W.II - Battle of Britain	30.00

PLATINUM SEVENTY-FIVE DOLLARS

See remarks on the Platinum 30 dollar earlier.
Known Counterfeits: None.
Part of:

	PF
1990 Polar Bear	550.00
1991 Snowy Owls	550.00
1992 Cougar	550.00
1993 Arctic Foxes	550.00
1994 Sea Otter	550.00
1995 Canadian Lynx kittens	550.00
1996 Falcons	550.00
1997 Bisons	550.00
1998 Gray Wolf	550.00
1999 Musk Ox	550.00
2000 Pronghorn Antelope	550.00
2001 Harlequin Duck Flying	550.00
2002 Great Blue Heron Flying	550.00
2003 Atlantic Walrus Swimming	550.00
2004 Grizzly Bear Eating	550.00

GOLD SEVENTY-FIVE DOLLARS

	PF
2005 Pope John Paul II	*Proof only* 450.00
2007 R.C.M.P.	425.00
2007 Athletes	425.00
2007 Canada Geese	425.00

GOLD HUNDRED DOLLARS

Similar to the collector-issue silver dollars, each year a different topic of Canadian history or culture is honored. Except for the first year, only proof versions are struck. They are all released in special mint packaging and are priced here for examples in that packaging. Those without may occasionally be discounted. From 1976-86, all proofs

contained one-half ounce pure gold, one-quarter ounce from 1987 onward.

Known Counterfeits: None likely.

	MS-63	PF
1976 Olympics	275.00	550.00

	MS-63	PF
1977 Queen's Jubilee		550.00
1978 Geese flying		550.00

	MS-63	PF
1979 Year of the Child	—	550.00
1980 Arctic Territories	—	550.00
1981 National Anthem	—	550.00

	MS-63	PF
1982 New Constitution	—	550.00
1983 St. John's, Newfoundland	—	550.00
1984 Jacques Cartier	—	550.00

	MS-63	PF
1985 National Parks	—	550.00
1986 Peace - Paix	—	550.00
1987 Calgary Olympics	—	275.00
1988 Whales	—	275.00
1989 Sainte-Marie, Ontario	—	275.00
1990 Literacy Year	—	275.00
1991 Ship *Empress of India*	—	275.00

	MS-63	PF
1992 Montreal founding	—	275.00
1993 Antique 1893 Car	—	275.00
1994 WWII: Home Front	—	270.00
1995 Louisbourg	—	270.00
1996 Klondike Gold Rush	—	270.00
1997 Alexander Graham Bell	—	275.00
1998 Discovery of Insulin	—	275.00
1999 Newfoundland	—	285.00
2000 Arctic Expedition	—	285.00
2001 Library of Parliament	—	285.00
2002 Oil Industry	—	450.00
2003 Marquis Wheat	—	285.00
2004 St. Lawrence Seaway	—	300.00
2005 Supreme Court	—	300.00
2006 Hockey	—	300.00
2007 140th Anniv.	—	375.00

PLATINUM 150 DOLLARS

See remarks on the platinum 30-dollar above.

Known Counterfeits: None.

Part of:

	PF
1990 Polar Bear	1,100.00
1991 Snowy Owl Flying	1,100.00
1992 Cougars	1,100.00
1993 Arctic Fox	1,100.00
1994 Two Sea Otters	1,150.00
1995 Canadian Lynx	1,100.00
1996 Falcon on Branch	1,100.00
1997 Bisons	1,100.00
1998 Two Gray Wolf cubs	1,100.00
1999 Musk Ox and calf	1,150.00
2000 Pronghorn Antelopes	1,150.00
2001 Harlequin Duck Pair	1,150.00
2002 Great Blue Heron Bust	1,150.00
2003 Atlantic Walrus Pair	1,175.00
2004 Grizzly Bears	1,175.00

GOLD HOLOGRAPHIC 150 DOLLARS

This series marks each Chinese year. According to tradition, each year of a 12-year cycle is represented by a specific animal. That animal is shown on a distinctive hologram covering the entire reverse of the coin.

Known Counterfeits: None.

	PF
2000 Year of the Dragon	1,200.00
2001 Year of the Snake	365.00
2002 Year of the Horse	390.00
2003 Year of the Sheep	365.00
2004 Year of the Monkey	475.00
2005 Year of the Rooster	450.00
2006 Year of the Dog	450.00
2007 Year of the Pig	450.00
2008 Year of the Rat	—

GOLD OLYMPIC 175 DOLLARS

See remarks on the silver 15-dollar above. Each coin contains one-half ounce of gold.

Known Counterfeits: None.

	PF
1992	550.00

GOLD 200 DOLLARS

Similar to the collector-issue silver dollars and $100 coins, each year a different topic of Canadian history or culture is honored. Only proof versions are struck. They are released in special mint packaging and are priced here for examples in that packaging. Those without may occasionally be discounted. Each contains slightly over half an ounce pure gold.

Known Counterfeits: None likely.

	PF
1990 Canadian Flag Jubilee	550.00
1991 Hockey	550.00
1992 Niagara Falls	550.00
1993 Mounted Police	550.00
1994 Anne of Green Gables	550.00
1995 Maple Syrup Harvesting	
	550.00
1996 Transcontinental Railway	550.00
1997 Haida Mask	650.00
1998 White Buffalo	560.00
1999 Mikmaq Butterfly	560.00
2000 Inuit Mother with infant	550.00
2001 *Habitant Farm* by Krieghoff	550.00
2002 *The Jack Pine* by Thompson	550.00
2003 *Houses* by Fitzgerald	550.00
2004 *Fragments* by Pellan	550.00

	PF
2005 Fur Traders	575.00
2006 Supreme Court	575.00
2006 Lumberjacks	585.00
2007 Fishing Trade	590.00

GOLD 250 DOLLARS

2006 Dog Sled	900.00

PLATINUM 300 DOLLARS

See remarks on the platinum 30-dollar earlier.

Known Counterfeits: None.

	PF
1990 Polar Bears	2,200.00
1991 Snowy Owl with chicks	
	2,200.00
1992 Cougar in Tree	2,200.00
1993 Arctic Fox with kits	2,200.00
1994 Sea Otters	2,200.00
1995 Lynx with kittens	2,200.00
1996 Falcon with chicks	2,200.00
1997 Bisons	2,200.00
1998 Gray Wolf and two cubs	
	2,200.00
1999 Musk Oxen	2,200.00
2000 Pronghorn Antelopes	2,200.00
2001 Harlequin Duck Pair	2,200.00
2002 Great Blue Heron	2,200.00
2003 Atlantic Walrus Family	2,200.00
2004 Grizzly Bear Family	2,200.00

GOLD 300 DOLLARS

This series commemorates the 50th anniversary of Elizabeth II's accession and coronation. The first is actually bi-metallic gold and silver.

Known Counterfeits: None.

	PF
2002 Triple Portraits	1,500.00
2003 Great Seal of Canada	1,400.00
2004 Four Portraits	1,400.00
2005 Standard Time	1,400.00
2005 Shinplaster	1,400.00
2005 Totem Pole	1,400.00
2006 Shinplaster of 1900	1,400.00
2006 colorized	1,400.00
2006 Queen's 80th Birthday	1,650.00
2006 Snowflake	1,500.00
2007 Shinplaster of 1923	1,400.00
2007 Olympics	1,500.00

GOLD 350 DOLLARS

This largest denomination of all Canadian coins depicts the country's flora. In the case of the first year's issue, Canada's heraldic flowers are featured: the English rose, Scottish thistle, Irish shamrock and French fleur-de-lis.

Known Counterfeits: None.

	PF
1998 Heraldic flowers	1,400.00
1999 Lady's slipper	1,400.00
2000 Pacific Dogwood	1,400.00
2001 Mayflower	1,400.00
2002 Wild Rose	1,400.00
2003 White Trillium	1,400.00
2004 Fireweed	1,400.00
2005 Western Red Lilly	1,400.00
2006 Iris Vericolor	1,450.00
2007 Purple Violet	1,475.00

BULLION COINS

GOLD SOVEREIGNS

It was the production of gold sovereigns that was part of the motivation for the opening of the Canadian Mint in 1908. It is also why, until 1931, it had the status of "British Royal Mint, Ottawa Branch." These coins are identical in every aspect to those made for Great Britain. The reverse design of St. George slaying the dragon was originally designed in 1816 by Benedetto Pistrucci. The mintmark "C" for Canada is found on the ground below the horse's hoof. Their production permitted the convenient coinage of locally mined gold into an internationally standard coin (.2354 Troy ounce net). During World War I, they also permitted the transfer of gold from Britain to the United States without the risk of being sunk during a trans-Atlantic crossing.

Known Counterfeits: A great many sovereign counterfeits are known. Some are more deceptive than others. Look for even border patterns and crispness where the field meets the design. Avoid any with a pebbly texture in field.

EDWARD VII

	VF	XF
1908C	1,750.00	2,000.00
1909C	170.00	200.00
1910C	150.00	180.00

GEORGE V

	VF	XF
1911C	130.00	135.00
1913C	450.00	550.00
1914C	200.00	275.00
1916C	12,500.00	14,000.00
1917C	130.00	135.00
1918C	130.00	135.00
1919C	130.00	135.00

MAPLE LEAF BULLION COINS

A bullion coin is a coin intended as a store of precious metal, not necessarily for circulation. While they have face values on them, their values in precious metal are usually much higher; therefore, no one would reasonably spend them. Bullion coins are not collector coins, but are sold by the mint at a modest premium above the value of the metal they contain.

The Maple Leaf series is one of the most popular and difficult to counterfeit bullion series in the world. It began in 1979 with the .999 pure one Troy ounce gold piece. At the time, it was considered unusual to manufacture a bullion gold piece with no alloy at all. Most other countries' pieces weighed more than an ounce to compensate for the addition of an alloy. The metal was further refined to .9999 pure in 1982 and the first fractional gold pieces – the tenth ounce and quarter ounce – were released, followed by a half ounce four years later. Having established a high degree of recognition in the bullion market, it was decided to expand into silver and platinum in 1988, releasing a one-ounce coin in the former metal, three different sizes in the latter. Small gold and platinum pieces, mostly suitable for gift giving, were added to the array in 1993 and 1994.

Beginning in 1999, a number of privy mark and colorization varieties were produced. Such details on bullion issues are outside the scope of a basic book such as this. For more details on these issues, see the references listed at beginning of the Canada section.

Known Counterfeits: None, but the one-ounce gold is always a potential target due to its liquidity.

Notice: The values of most of these issues vary at least daily with the value of their metal content. The prices listed here are based on a platinum value of $2,000, gold $1,000 and silver $20. Updated prices on commodities such as precious metals, though not on single coins, can be found both in most newspapers and on the Internet. For any firm quote on bullion, however, it is best to call your local coin or bullion dealer. Values given here for gold and platinum are in terms of percent premium typically charged above the actual bullion content. Some dealers will add a handling charge to very small orders.

SILVER MAPLE LEAF

1 ounce / $5	MS-63	PF
1988 to date	24.50	
1989	30.00	
10 ounce / $50		
1998	225.00	

GOLD MAPLE LEAF

	MS-63	PF
1/20 oz. ($1) 1993	—	30%
1/15 oz. ($2) 1994	—	90.00
1/10 oz. ($5) 1982	—	15%
1/10 oz. ($5) 1989	—	120.00
1/4 oz. ($10) 1982	—	11%
1/4 oz. ($10) 1989	—	285.00
1/2 oz. ($20) 1986	—	7%
1/2 oz. ($20) 1989	—	550.00

	MS-63	PF
1 oz. ($50) 1979	—	5%
1 oz. ($50) 1989		1,100.00

GOLD MOUNTIE

	MS-63	PF
1 oz. ($50) 1997	685.00	

PLATINUM MAPLE LEAF

	MS-63	PF
1/20 oz. ($1) 1993	—	30%
1/15 oz. ($2) 1994		250.00
1/10 oz. ($5) 1988	—	17%
1/10 oz. ($5) 1989		240.00

	MS-63	PF
1/4 oz. ($10) 1988	—	12%
1/4 oz. ($10) 1989		570.00
1/2 oz. ($20) 1988	—	8%
1/2 oz. ($20) 1989		1,100.00
1 oz. ($50) 1988	—	6%
1 oz. ($50) 1989		2,200.00

PROVINCIAL COINS & TOKENS

Like the situation in the United States and formerly in the 13 Colonies, Canadian coinage before the 1870s was a hodgepodge of various coins and tokens struck by a number of authorities, firms, countries and individuals. Throughout the 1700s and early 1800s, the British policies of Mercantilism prevented the royal government from shipping reasonable quantities of sterling to British North America. Chaos ensued. Numerous merchants throughout the country struck or imported hundreds of different types of local copper tokens. Some were well made, like most bank issues. Others were wretched.

When official coinage was finally struck by the various pre-Confederation provinces, they had already recognized slightly different standards, sometimes as much as 20 percent different from each other in value. Generally, provincial coins started out on the British sterling system, but changed over to a decimal system in the 1860s.

The union of Upper Canada (Ontario), Lower Canada (Quebec), New Brunswick and Nova Scotia, which formed the independent Canadian Confederation in 1867, was not enough to bring order from discord, at least not immediately. There still persisted a shortage of small change in circulation. Neither bank tokens nor poorly made "blacksmith" counterfeits could be suppressed. In 1870 the government announced that certain specified bank tokens would be officially recognized as one-cent and two-cent pieces.

The provincial coinage of Newfoundland continued for decades and is far more extensive than the others. This is because Newfoundland did not join Canada until 1949. Mintages of these coins is often remarkably low, but the

prices have remained moderate despite that fact. Contrary to this, Newfoundland 50-cent pieces are often more common than contemporary Canadian ones.

Known Counterfeits: Contemporary counterfeits of George III Irish halfpennies circulated in Canada and are worth more than real ones. Those of George IV Nova Scotia halfpennies are common and worth about the same as real ones.

LOWER CANADA BANK TOKENS

UN SOU - HALF PENNY (after 1870 1¢)

Boquet / Wreath	VG	VF
Montreal	2.50	10.00
Bank of Montreal	3.00	12.50
Banque du Peuple	2.00	9.00
Standing figure / Oval shield		
1837 City Bank	2.00	9.00
1837 Quebec Bank	2.00	9.00
1837 Bank of Montreal	3.00	12.00
1837 Banque du Peuple	3.50	15.00
Side View Building / Oval shield		
1838 Bank of Montreal	300.00	800.00
1839 Bank of Montreal	300.00	750.00

Front View Building / Oval Shield	VG	VF
1842 Bank of Montreal	5.00	15.00
1844 Bank of Montreal	2.50	7.50
1845 Bank of Montreal		Rare
Standing figure / Allegorical scene		
1852 Quebec Bank	2.50	10.00

DEUX SOU - ONE PENNY (after 1870 2¢)

	VG	VF
Standing figure / Oval shield		
1837 City Bank	3.50	15.00
1837 Bank of Montreal	5.00	22.00
1837 Banque du Peuple	7.00	35.00
1837 Quebec Bank	3.00	13.00
Side View Building / Oval shield		
1838 Bank of Montreal	300.00	750.00
1839 Bank of Montreal	300.00	750.00
Front View Building / Oval Shield		
1839 Banque du Peuple		Rare
1842 Bank of Montreal	4.00	17.50

Standing figure / Allegorical scene	VG	VF
1852 Quebec Bank	4.50	20.00

NEW BRUNSWICK

HALF PENNY	VG	VF
1843	3.50	11.50
1854	3.50	11.50

PENNY	VG	VF
1843	3.75	15.00
1854	3.75	15.00

HALF CENT	VG	VF
1861	95.00	225.00

ONE CENT

	VG	VF
1861	3.00	9.00
1864	3.00	9.00

FIVE CENTS

	VG	VF
1862	60.00	175.00
1864	60.00	175.00

TEN CENTS

	VG	VF
1862	60.00	175.00
1864	60.00	175.00

TWENTY CENTS

	VG	VF
1862	30.00	80.00
1864	30.00	80.00

NEWFOUNDLAND

LARGE CENT Victoria	VG	VF
1865	3.00	12.00
1872H	2.50	7.00
1873	4.00	20.00
1876H	3.00	7.00
1880 Round 0	3.00	7.00
1880 Oval 0	120.00	320.00

	VG	VF
1885	27.00	75.00
1888	30.00	80.00
1890	3.00	15.00
1894	3.00	10.00
1896	3.00	7.00

Edward VII

	VG	VF
1904H	7.00	22.00
1907	2.00	8.00
1909	2.00	7.00

George V

	VG	VF
1913	1.00	3.00
1917C	1.00	3.00
1919C	1.00	3.00
1920C	1.00	3.50
1929	1.00	3.00
1936	1.00	2.50

SMALL CENT

George VI

	VF	XF
1938	1.50	2.75
1940	3.00	9.50
1941C	.75	2.00
1942	.75	2.00
1943C	.75	2.00
1944C	9.00	25.00
1947C	4.00	11.00

SILVER FIVE CENTS

Victoria	VG	VF
1865	35.00	150.00
1870	65.00	220.00
1872H	40.00	125.00

	VG	VF
1873	125.00	450.00
1873H	750.00	2,000.00
1876H	125.00	350.00
1880	45.00	150.00
1881	45.00	150.00
1882H	23.00	90.00
1885	130.00	330.00
1888	40.00	225.00
1890	11.00	45.00
1894	10.00	30.00
1896	4.00	20.00

Edward VII

	VG	VF
1903	4.00	20.00
1904H	3.00	15.00
1908	3.00	12.00

George V

	VG	VF
1912	2.00	6.00
1917C	2.00	7.00
1919C	4.00	20.00
1929	2.00	4.00

George VI	VF	XF
1938	2.00	7.00
1940C	2.00	7.00
1941C	2.00	4.00
1942C	2.00	4.00
1943C	2.00	4.00
1944C	3.00	7.00
1945C	2.00	4.00
1946C	350.00	420.00
1947C	5.00	17.00

SILVER TEN CENTS

Victoria	VG	VF
1865	27.00	75.00
1870	120.00	190.00
1871 (produced in error) *Rare*		
1872H	22.00	80.00
1873	55.00	250.00

	VG	VF
1876H	55.00	225.00
1880, 8 over 7	55.00	255.00
1882H	30.00	150.00
1885	70.00	300.00
1888	35.00	200.00
1890	9.00	35.00
1894	8.00	30.00
1896	5.00	25.00

Edward VII

	VG	VF
1903	8.00	70.00
1904H	4.00	30.00

George V

	VG	VF
1912	2.00	10.00
1917C	2.00	10.00
1919C	2.00	18.00

George VI	VF	XF
1938	3.00	11.00
1940	3.00	10.00
1941C	2.50	5.00
1942C	2.50	5.00
1943C	2.50	6.00
1944C	9.00	25.00
1945C	2.25	4.50
1946C	9.00	25.00
1947C	4.50	14.00

SILVER TWENTY CENTS

Victoria	VG	VF
1865	16.00	65.00
1870	20.00	98.00
1872H	12.00	60.00
1873	20.00	175.00
1876H	25.00	80.00
1880, 80 over 70	27.00	95.00
1881	12.00	80.00
1882H	9.00	50.00

	VG	VF		VG	VF
1885	14.00	80.00	1872H	18.00	90.00
1888	12.00	70.00	1873	40.00	200.00
1890	9.00	45.00	1874	25.00	125.00
1894	15.00	95.00	1876H	35.00	150.00
1896	6.00	35.00	1880	45.00	250.00
1899	5.00	30.00	1881	20.00	135.00
1900	5.00	25.00	1882H	12.00	95.00
			1885	30.00	175.00
			1888	50.00	250.00
			1894	12.00	75.00
			1896	9.00	65.00
			1898	9.00	60.00
			1899	9.00	45.00
			1900	9.00	45.00

GOLD TWO DOLLARS

Victoria	F	XF
1865	150.00	300.00
1870	175.00	325.00
1872	190.00	385.00
1880	900.00	1,100.00
1881	145.00	225.00
1882H	145.00	210.00
1885	145.00	235.00
1888	135.00	200.00

Edward VII

Edward VII

NOVA SCOTIA

HALF PENNY

Bust / Thistle	VG	VF
1823	3.00	13.00
1824	6.00	27.00
1832	3.00	7.50
1382 *error*	450.00	1,650.00
1840	3.50	14.00
1843	3.00	16.00
Bust / Mayflowers		
1856	2.00	7.50

	VG	VF
1904H	10.00	60.00

George V	VG	VF
1912	3.50	14.00

ONE PENNY

SILVER TWENTY-FIVE CENTS

George V	VG	VF
1917C	3.50	7.00
1919C	3.50	14.00

	VG	VF
1904H	9.00	20.00
1907	9.00	25.00
1908	9.00	20.00
1909	9.00	22.00

George V

SILVER FIFTY CENTS

Victoria

	VG	VF
1870	25.00	150.00

	VG	VF
1911	9.00	14.00
1917C	8.50	12.00
1918C	8.50	12.00
1919C	8.50	14.00

Bust / Thistle	VG	VF
1824	4.00	26.00
1832	4.00	15.00
1840	3.50	14.00
1843, 3 over 0	42.00	175.00
1843	4.00	23.00

Bust / Mayflowers

	VG	VF
1856 No LCW	4.00	13.00
1856 with LCW	2.50	12.00

HALF CENT

	VG	VF
1861	5.00	8.00
1864	5.00	8.00

ONE CENT

	VG	VF
1861	3.00	5.00
1862	45.00	150.00
1864	3.00	5.00

PRINCE EDWARD ISLAND

MERCHANTS' TOKENS

	VG	VF
Ships, Colonies & Commerce / Sailing Ship	2.50	12.50
1855 Self Government and Free Trade	2.50	12.50

ONE CENT

	VG	VF
1871	2.50	6.50

UPPER CANADA

HALF PENNY BANK TOKENS
St. George slaying dragon / Bank emblem

	VG	VF
1850	2.50	6.50
1852	2.50	6.50
1854	2.50	6.50
1854 Crosslet 4	8.00	35.00
1857	2.50	6.50

ONE PENNY BANK TOKEN

St. George slaying dragon / Bank emblem

	VG	VF
1850	3.00	10.00
1850 Dot between cornucopias	5.00	20.00
1852	2.00	8.00
1854	2.00	7.00
1854 Crosslet 4	6.00	22.00
1857	2.00	7.00

ANCIENT COINS

Ancient coins are among the most universally popular coins to collect. While most Americans consider them strange and exotic, perhaps even museum pieces, few can grow up in countries like England, Italy or Israel without commonly seeing a Roman or Greek coin that some friend or relative found while on a hike or plowing a field. While most dealers in North America have boxes filled with coins left over from tourist trips across the globe, dealers in most European capitals have boxes filled with coins left over from mankind's trip across the centuries. Much to the surprise of visiting Americans, these Roman coins, while not very well preserved, sell for as little as a dollar or two each. Many other ancient coins, the great rarities of art or grade, can sell at European auctions for tens of thousands of dollars. Clearly, collectors around the world have created an active market in these small relics.

Not only hobbyists find them interesting. Many teachers and professors have found that providing genuine ancient coins for their students to examine has stirred a vital and unexpected interest in the cultures that created them. Coins are among the earliest things which humanity has mass-produced. Because Greek and Roman coins have survived in the millions, they are today among the few genuine ancient artifacts that the average person can own.

THE EVOLUTION OF COINAGE

The ancient Egyptians in the days of the pharaohs, or the Babylonians in the days of Hammurabi, had no coins. They traded precious metal – often in convenient shapes such as rings – but the purity and weight of these items varied and at each transaction they had to be weighed and sometimes even tested. In Asia Minor in present-day Turkey, irregular clumps of electrum, a natural alloy of gold and silver, were popularly traded for their bullion value. As time went by it became apparent that having these clumps be of a known alloy and a regular weight would make commercial transactions much easier. By the seventh century B.C., the kings of Lydia, in western Asia Minor, started impressing their symbols on one side of these clumps to guarantee to their subjects their weight and purity. At first these symbols were engraved at the end of an iron punch. Soon after, the symbols were engraved on the surface of an anvil and a chisel was used to force the metal down into the design. It wasn't long until people realized that if the end of the chisel point could leave its impression on the reverse of the coin, so could a second design engraved into the end of the chisel point. At first this secondary design was little more than a simple geometric pattern, but it quickly took on the complexity of the primary design. In this way, the modern concept of a two-sided struck coin was invented.

GRADE VS. QUALITY

When collecting, it is important to remember that ancient coins were not made by the same methods as modern coins. You should not expect to find perfectly round ancient coins – although there were many exceptions. This is because they were not struck within collars like modern coins, so when the dies pressed down on the metal, it would spread out in unpredictable directions. Also, because the blanks were placed between the dies by hand, they may not have been perfectly centered. Modern automation has caused off-center coins to be scarce collectors' items, but slightly off-center coins were far more common in ancient times. Except for the most radically off-center specimens, modern collectors of Greek and Roman coins consider off-center specimens less desirable, and they often command lower prices. This is especially true if the portrait is affected. Would you want a portrait of a Greek god or Roman emperor with the nose missing?

Another thing that many collectors consider more important than whether or not an ancient coin is worn is the strength of the strike. A coin's design is made by metal being forced into the recessed parts of a die engraved with a negative image of the design. Today, this metal is forced to flow by powerful machines striking the dies against the blank with thousands of pounds of pressure. In ancient day it was only the strength of the minter's arm that determined how much pressure the dies would exert – and maybe whether or not he was paying attention while he was striking. If the craftsman struck the dies with too little pressure, the metal would not flow into every crevice of the die, and even when brand-new, the resulting coin would not have a fully detailed image.

Ancient coins survive today because they were often buried in the ground. Most ancient civilizations did not have banks in the modern sense. To protect their wealth from thieves or invading armies, many ancient peoples would place their wealth in a pottery jar, or a cloth or leather bag, and bury it in a secret place until they could safely retrieve it. Unfortunately for them, many did not live long enough to regain their fortunes, and their secrets died with them. Coins buried in sealed pottery usually survive to modern times well preserved. Those buried in cloth are usually covered with porous or pitted surfaces. Such porous coins, even if high-grade pieces with little circulation wear and much detail, are considered by many collectors undesirable, and are usually sold at a discount.

All these factors together – centering, strike and surface texture – probably affect the value of an ancient coin far more than its technical grade in wear. It is not unusual for a dealer to pay more for a coin in Very Fine than for the same type of coin in Extremely Fine if the strike and centering are superior on the lower-grade coin.

COUNTERFEITS

Modern people have been counterfeiting ancient coins as long as they have had a fascination with them. But not all these creations have been intended to deceive. Many were made either to educate or to inspire. Because they were never intended to deceive an expert, certain characteristics that give a modern creation away were neither hidden nor avoided. Hundreds of thousands have been sold, or given away as promotions, by museums or civic organizations. Others have been sold as souvenirs by vendors at historic sites around the world. Sometimes they are packaged as replicas, sometimes they come with a fistful of dirt and the line, "Mister, Mister, I just dug these up!" Tens of thousands of counterfeit coins have also been sold via the Internet. Choose your dealer carefully (see the "Coin Dealers" section earlier.) But most of these classes are not at all deceptive once certain basic principles of authentication are learned. Here are some of the earmarks of a counterfeit to look for:

1) The word COPY on the surface or the edge. Sometimes COPIA, C, R, hallmarks or a modern date or manufacturer's name may serve the same purpose.

2) A seam on the edge. Most ancients are made by striking

between dies. A seam indicates it was cast in a mold.

3) File marks on the edge. These are sometimes used to remove a seam.

4) The coin being manufactured in the wrong metal, such as a silver coin being brass colored, or vice versa.

5) A grainy surface, with many tiny pimples, another sign of casting.

6) Signs of plating that has worn through at the highest points.

7) Crispness of design may be lacking. It may appear as though you are viewing the design through a veil.

This little checklist will eliminate 90 percent of all the counterfeits you are likely to encounter. Then there are the other 10 percent, and they are more challenging. The counterfeiter in these cases has put in the extra effort to deceive, and presumed that the potential purchaser has some knowledge. Recently, these more serious counterfeiters have been aided by improved technology. Now collectors must put in the extra effort to fight back. Here are some further steps.

1) Look for signs of COPY or other marks having been removed.

2) Look for a seam where the edge meets the surface of the coin. It is easier to miss there.

3) Look for file marks under magnification. They may be very fine.

4) Silver, tin and white metal can look alike at a glance, but usually not if you have ever compared them. Learn the difference in the shades of these light-colored metals. It is not that hard. Similarly, do not confuse the light color of brass with the browner color of bronze or copper.

5) A quality cast may have the same grainy surface as a rough one, but it will be a much finer grain. Use a magnifying glass. Be careful, however, not to confuse the corrosion and crystallization of a coin that has been buried in the ground with this casting porosity.

6) A thick plating may not wear through, and may even be protected by another layer of false patina. While not always convenient, weighing a coin and doing a specific gravity test can reveal an incorrect composition without damaging the surface.

7) On a fine cast, the lack of crispness of design may be less obvious, but it will be there if you know where to look. Check where the design meets the field under magnification. It should be sharply delineated. If the design gradually curves into the field, check for other signs of counterfeiting. Again, it may appear as though you are viewing the design through a veil.

8) Style can often be incorrect when a counterfeit is struck with engraved dies. Often the craftsman will leave a trace of his own style of art, or will engrave the portraiture in an ancient stule, and neglect to perfectly replicate the lettering.

Of course, ancient coins were counterfeited in their own time, too. Most ancient counterfeits are distinctive in either style or metal. More problematic are "fourrées," counterfeits thought to have been made by a government or mint workers using real dies. A fourrée is similar to a modern clad coin in that it has a thick layer of silver over a copper core. Both ancient (called "contemporary") counterfeits and fourrées are considered collectible, and worth most of what a real coin would be valued.

A.C.C.G.

The Ancient Coin Collectors Guild (ACCG) was formed in 2004 to promote and nurture the free and independent collecting of coins from antiquity through education, political action and consumer protection. Its stated goal is "to foster an environment in which the general public can confidently and legally acquire and hold ... any numismatic item of historical interest regardless of date or place of origin." Its Web site is www.accg.us.

GREEK COINS

As the concept of uniform, predictable coinage took root, electrum was generally replaced by separate coinages of gold and silver. During this early stage of development there were no copper coins. If small values were needed, extremely small coins of gold or silver were struck. Some of these minute coins were less than 1/10th the size of a United States dime. In the early 6th century B.C. coinage was still too new a concept for people to accept copper coins of a convenient size just because the government would promise to redeem them for silver. During this early first stage of coinage, it was confined to Asia Minor and Greece. Gradually, coinage spread westward to Italy and Gaul (France) as Greeks established colonies of settlers on their coasts. Coinage expanded eastward to Phoenicia (Lebanon), Syria and Judea (Israel) as people of these lands came into contact with Greek coinage and found it convenient. The Phoenicians spread the use of coinage to North Africa and Spain through their settlement of Carthage.

Ancient Greek coinage has long been divided by numismatists into specific stages based on artistic and political developments. The first stage, beginning with the invention of coinage, is called "archaic." The style of archaic art is stiff, formal and unrealistic. Like ancient Egyptian art, from which it derives, eyes are usually shown in full facing view, even when the head looks towards the side. Faces also have what is called an "archaic smile," and body movements are seen with unnatural exaggeration. Some coin designs continued to use archaic design forms, particularly the simple geometric reverse designs, long after Greek painting and sculpture moved beyond this stage. This was to convince people of the coin's stable weight and value. The idea was that if there was no change in the coin's appearance, there was, theoretically, no change in its content. (Similar logic was brought to the United States $1 bill, the basic design of which has not changed since 1923.)

Much of the authority for issuing archaic coinage came from the many Greek city-states. The designs of these coins usually consisted of the patron deities of these cities, symbols of those gods, or sometimes plants or animals important to the local economy. One example is Athens, named after the goddess Athena. Most ancient Athenian coins bear her portrait on one side, and an owl on the other. The owl was considered a symbol of Athena, who was goddess of wisdom. Coins of ancient Sicily sometimes bore an octopus or a crab, important food animals in Sicily both then and now. Some designs even had puns! Coins of the island of Rhodes in the Aegean Sea usually bore a rose because the Greek word *rhodos* meant both Rhodes and rose.

The next stage in the evolution of Greek coinage is called the Classical period. Roughly mid-5th to mid-4th century B.C., it was the period of finest artistic achievement. The same imagery persisted, but rendered in a more realistic and elaborate style. As designs became more complex, the quality of die engraving became so important that some of the dies were actually signed by the engraver as though they were works of art. Many to this day believe that this

was the high point of numismatic art. By this time virtually all coins were struck with two fully engraved dies. Also, the acceptance of the role of coinage was such that token copper coins replaced minute silver pieces for local use. Copper coins were usually not accepted outside their region of origin, but larger silver and gold coins were available for international commerce. In order to enforce some responsibility for metal purity, at this time some of the magistrates responsible for the coinage were required to sign their name clearly on the dies.

Alexander the Great (reign 336-323 B.C.) changed the political structure of the world forever. Before Alexander, the typical government was the city-state. Alexander's world conquests introduced the concept of a large poly-ethnic state. Even after he died and his empire was divided among his generals, the known world continued to be divided mostly into large kingdoms and federations rather than city-states. This third period of Greek history and coinage is called "Hellenistic." The most notable innovation to be found at this stage is the introduction of real human portraits. Many accept the idea that Alexander, depicted as though he were Hercules wearing a lion's skin, was the first living human being to appear on a coin. Even if this were not true, the generation of the coins that followed his death certainly saw dozens of Hellenistic kings placing their somewhat idealized portraits on their coins. During this period, coins were extremely common and many actually bear the year of issue indicated in many different local calendars, often based on the founding date of a city or dynasty, or a king's accession.

The eclipse of the Hellenistic kingdoms and the Greek federations by the Roman Empire did not completely eliminate Greek coinage. Some of the most important internationally accepted Greek silver coins, such as the shekel of Tyre and the tetradrachm of Philip Philadelphos, continued to be struck under Roman domination. Often, especially in Asia Minor and the Middle East, the new Roman overlords would permit large municipalities to continue striking Greek-style coinage for local use, with no apparent change. Also, many lands, rather than being conquered by the Romans, would submit to them as client states, preserving much of their autonomy and usually keeping their traditional coinage.

Greek gold coins were usually called *staters*. Most staters weighed eight to ten grams and were the size of a cent or nickel.

Greek silver coins were usually called *drachms, obols* and staters. While the size of a drachm could vary from city to city, many shared standards. An average drachm weighed about 4½ grams and resembled a thick dime. One sixth of a *drachm* was called an obol. The term stater, as used at Corinth, referred to its principal coin, worth three drachms.

For both gold and silver, the prefix *hemi-* always meant half. *Deka-, octa-, tetra-*, and *di-* meant ten times, eight times, four times, and double, respectively.

In most cases we do not know the names of ancient Greek bronze coins. Generally, numismatists call them by diameter in millimeters. A coin 15mm in diameter is called an AE15, one 20mm an AE20.

The images on most Greek coins are either of ancient deities or their symbols. Local flora and fauna, such as a horse or a plant, are also common.

Some of the most common ancient gods and goddesses depicted on coins may be recognized by their attire or their symbols. The list here will also prove useful for identifying

the reverses of Roman and Greek Imperial coins. The Roman versions are named in parentheses:

Ammon - Bearded older male, ram's horns on sides of head. Mostly Egyptian.

Aphrodite (Venus) - Female, usually nude or semi-nude. Symbols: Apple, poppy, dove, swan.

Apollo - Beardless male with slightly feminine face, often seen seated on a thimble-shaped object called an omphalos. Symbol: lyre, arrow, tripod (three-legged altar).

Artemis (Diana) - Female with bow and arrow. Symbol: stag.

Ares (Mars) - Helmeted male.

Athena (Minerva) - Woman wearing crested helmet. Symbol: owl.

Baal - Semitic equivalent of Zeus.

Dionysus (Bacchus) - Young man, bearded or not, wearing ivy wreath. Symbols: panther, ivy, grapes.

Dioscuri - The twins Castor and Pollux, usually riding horses together. Symbol: two conical caps. two stars.

Eros (Cupid) - Winged boy. Symbol: bow and arrow.

Heracles (Hercules) - Male, usually bearded, wearing lion's skin. Symbol: club.

Hermes (Mercury) - Beardless male wearing winged broad hat. Symbol: caduceus.

Janus - Bearded male with two faces.

Poseidon (Neptune) - Bearded older male, often naked, wearing wreath or diadem. Symbol: trident, dolphin.

Serapis - Bearded older male, wearing "modius" on head. (A modius is an ancient conical grain measure, with extended feet.)

Nike (Victory) - Winged female. Symbol: trophy of arms.

Tyche (Fortuna) of the city - Female wearing turreted city wall as crown.

Zeus (Jupiter, Jove) - Bearded older male, usually with wreath, often enthroned. Symbols: Thunderbolt, eagle.

BOOKS ABOUT GREEK COINS

Books about ancient Greek coins listed here are confined to only the most basic or the most important references.

British Museum, *Catalogue of Greek Coins in the*, 29 volumes (various authors).

Danish National Museum. *Sylloge Numorum Graecorum* (SNG).

Head, Barclay. *Historia Numorum.*

Klawans, Zander. *Handbook of Ancient Greek and Roman Coins.* Certainly the easiest introduction.

Kraay, Colin. *Archaic and Classical Greek Coins.*

Melville Jones, John, *A Dictionary of Ancient Greek Coins.*

Sayles, Wayne. *Ancient Coin Collecting: Numismatic Art of the Greek World.*

Sear, David. *Greek Coins and their Values,* Vol. 1 & 2. The most commonly used catalogue of representative coins.

Bulletin on Counterfeits, 1995-2000. This journal published by the IAPN and the International Bureau for the Suppression of Counterfeit Coins, focuses on ancients and contains many clear, enlarged images of the most deceptive counterfeits.

The Celator. Popular monthly magazine devoted to ancient coins.

Certain specialized works not mentioned here will be noted in each sub-section.

Values for Greek coins are for **Very Fine** examples for gold (**AV**) and silver (**AR**), **Fine** for bronze and copper (**AE**).

SPAIN & GAUL

The chief cities in ancient Spain were Phoenician colonies of Carthage. By the 1st century B.C., most had fallen under Roman control. The coins of ancient Spain show a blend of Carthaginian, Roman, Greek and local Iberian influences. The alphabet used is unique to the area.

Greek influence in Gaul was primarily focused at the colony of Massalia on the southern coast. The interior was inhabited by Celts.

Additional Specialized Books:

Heiss, *Description Generales Des Monnaies Antiques de L'Espagne.*

Osca. 150-100 B.C. AR Denarius. Bearded head r. / Horseman r. **200.00**
Rhoda. before 250 B.C. AR Drachm. Head of Persephone l. / Rose viewed from beneath (leaves appear as four spokes) **550.00**
Gaul: Massalia (Marseilles). 375-200 B.C. AR Drachm. Head of Artemis r. / Lion r. **150.00**

THE CELTS

The Celts were an ancient people inhabiting an area stretching from Bulgaria and the Danube to Spain and Ireland. As the eastern areas became inhabited by other peoples, the Celts remained more dominant in the British Isles and Gaul through the Roman era. Most Celtic coins, beginning in the 3rd century B.C. and ending in the 1st A.D., derive their form from Hellenistic and Roman Republican types. These usually show a distinctive artistic interpretation, often showing the person or animal as disjointed and conveying more of a sense of motion than a realistic depiction.

Distinctive features also include the use of tin and the casting rather than striking of some base-metal issues in the West.

Additional Specialized Books:

Allen, Derek. *Catalogue of the Celtic Coins in the British Museum*, 3 vols.

Nash, Daphne. *Coinage in the Celtic World.*

VanArsdell, R.D., *Celtic Coinage of Britain.*

England. 45-20 B.C. AV Stater. Abstract design devolved from head of Apollo / Horse leaping r. **500.00**
__. Cunobeline, 10-20 A.D. AV Stater. CA M, Ear of grain / Horse, CVN below. **950.00**

__. Similar AV 1/4 Stater **450.00**
__: Thames and South, 1st century B.C. Tin 18mm. Linear abstract head / Linear abstract bull **90.00**
__: **The Iceni.** 10 B.C - A.D. 60. AR Unit (14mm.). Geometric pattern / Horse r., ECEN below **150.00**

Channel Islands. Armorican. 75-50 B.C. Billon Stater. Stylized head r. / Abstract horse r. **175.00**
Gaul: Aedui or Lingones. 1st century B.C. AR Quinarius. Helmeted head l. / Horse l., wheel below............................... **95.00**
__: **Allobroges.** 1st century B.C. AR Quinarius. Helmeted head of Roma r. / Horseman r., BR COMA below. *Crude imitation of coin of Roman Republic.* **125.00**

__: **Veneti.** 2nd cent. B.C. AV Stater. Stylized male head r./ Horseman galloping r. **1,200.00**
__: **Volcae Tectosages.** 3-2nd cent. B.C. AR Drachm. Degenerate head of Persephone l. / Cross dividing field, crescent in each angle. *Crude imitation of the coin of Rhoda above*.............. **85.00**

Eastern Celts. 200s B.C. AR Tetradrachm. Stylized head of Zeus /

Stylized horseman l. This coin is based on one of Philip II of Macedon. **275.00**
__: 3-2nd century B.C. AR Drachm. Crude head of Alexander the Great in extremely high relief / Disjointed figure of Zeus std. l. **95.00**

GREEK ITALY

Before the expansion of Rome, the majority of settlements in southern Italy and eastern Sicily were Greek, not Italian. They were usually settlements of larger Greek cities, such as Corinth, and their coinage was much in keeping with Greek traditions. Greek Syracuse in particular was notable for the quality of its numismatic art, to the point where some engravers actually signed their works.

Known Counterfeits: High-quality Greek silver has been the target of counterfeiters for more than a century. Many counterfeits are quite deceptive.

Agrigentum, Sicily. 500-450 B.C. AE Trias (tooth-shaped). Eagles' heads / crab / Three pellets................................. **150.00**
Brettian League, Bruttium. 215-205 B.C. AE22. Head of Zeus r. / Naked warrior r. with spear and shield **38.00**
Caulonia, Bruttium. c.525 B.C. AR Stater. Apollo, stg. naked, stag stg. r. looking back, KAVΛ / same incuse and reversed **4,500.00**
Gela, Sicily. 450-430 B.C. AR Tetradrachm. Chariot r. / Forepart of man-headed bull....................... **1,200.00**

Gela Tetradrachm (modern copy)

Same, base metal copy with depression on reverse. This is often marked COPY, but not always. It is a crude cast, with a clear seam. It is perhaps the most commonly encountered copy of any ancient Greek coin.

Neapolis (Naples), Campania. 300-276 B.C. AR Didrachm. Head of Nymph r. / Man-headed bull r., Victory above **500.00**

__: 270-240 B.C. AE20. Head of Apollo l. / Man-headed bull r., Victory above **38.00**

Posedonia, Lucania. c.400 B.C. AE14. Poseidon walking r. / Bull r. **35.00**

Rhegium, Bruttium. 415-387 B.C. AR Tetradrachm. Lion's face / Hd. of Apollo r. **5,000.00**

__: Bruttium. 270-218 B.C. AE21. Laureate head of Apollo l. / Tripod-alter **38.00**

Syracuse, Sicily. 405-344 B.C. AE18 Hd. of Arethusa l. / Dolphin r. over shell **40.00**

__:__, 400-370 B.C. AR Dekadrachm. Fast chariot, driver crowned by Nike (Victory) flying above / Head of Arethusa, signature of Euainetos below ....**VF 12,000.00**

One of the few ancient coins whose dies were signed by the engraver, it is prized for its artistic merit.

__: Agathokles, 317-289 B.C. AV Tetraobol. Head of Apollo l. / Chariot r. **1,500.00**

__. Hieron II, 274-216 B.C. AE22. Head of Poseidon l. / Trident **45.00**

Tarentum, Calabria. 4-3rd century B.C. AR Didrachm. Naked young horseman / Taras riding dolphin..................... **350.00**

Velia, Lucania. 350-300 B.C. AE16. Zeus / Owl with wings spread **40.00**

GREECE & ASIA MINOR

As mentioned earlier, coinage was invented in Lydia, Asia Minor (Turkey). It soon spread throughout the Greek cities of western Asia Minor, the Aegean and the Greek mainland.

Because Alexander the Great of the Kingdom of Macedon, in northern Greece, conquered most of the Greek world and vast regions to its east, he made Greek standards for coinage almost ubiquitous in the ancient world. His coins continued to be struck by dozens of mints throughout his vast former empire for more than a century after his death.

Known Counterfeits: High-quality Greek silver has been the target of counterfeiters for more than a century. Many are quite deceptive. Counterfeits of most denominations of Alexander the Great are abundant.

The works of famous 19th century counterfeiters, including Carl Wilhelm Becker (1772-1830), command values as collectibles themselves. Counterfeit diobols of Apollonia Pontica and Mesembria were widely distributed in 1988.

Achaean League. 200-146 B.C. AR Hemidrachm. Head of Zeus r. / AX monogram in wreath **100.00**

Aegina. 400-340 B.C. AR Stater. Tortoise / Five-part incuse square **950.00**

Apollonia Pontica, Thrace. 400-350 B.C. AR Diobol. Facing head of Apollo / Anchor **100.00**

Amisus, Pontus. 121-63 B.C. AE21. Shield with Medusa head / Victory walking r. **30.00**

Aspendos, Pamphylia. 370-333B.C. AR Stater. Two wrestlers / Slinger r. ... **300.00**

Athens, 449-404 B.C. AR Tetradrachm. Helmeted head of Athena with archaic eye r. / Owl, leaves and crescent moon l., AΘE r., all in incuse square.......... **600.00**

__. Similar, clumpy and irregular... **275.00**

Corinth, 370-320 B.C AR Stater, Pegasus, Q below / Helmeted head. of Athena. **300.00**

Cyzicus, Mysia. 480-450 B.C. AR Obol. Forepart of running boar / Forepart of lion.. **90.00**

Ephesus, Ionia. 280-258 B.C. AE18. Bee, E Φ at sides / Stag stg. r., quiver above **40.00**

__: __. 1st cent. B.C. AR Tetradrachm. Serpent emerging from container, all in wreath / Bow case between two coiled serpents **225.00**

These coins were struck by more than a dozen cities in Asia Minor.

Istros, Black Sea Area, 6th - 5th Century B.C. Arrowhead shaped bronze, 32mm **35.00**

Lydia, Kingdom, Croesus, 561-546 B.C. AR ½ Stater. Busts of lion and bull facing each other / Two incuse squares **600.00**

__:__.__. AR 1/6 Stater. Similar..... **450.00**

See Persia for Lydia under that empire.

Macedon, Kingdom. Amyntas III, 389-383 B.C. AE15. Head of Hercules r. / Eagle r., wings closed, AMYNTA.. **45.00**

__: Philip II, 359-336 B.C. AR Tetradrachm. Head of Zeus r. / King riding l. **450.00**

__:__,__. Head of Zeus r. / Naked horseman r. **350.00**

__: Alexander III the Great, 336-323 B.C. AV Stater. Helmeted head of Athena r. / Victory stg., AΛEΞANΔPoY r. **2,500.00**

__:__. AR Tetradrachm. Head of Alexander as Hercules r. / Zeus std. l., legs parallel. *Usually struck before his death, unlike the following*............. **300.00**

__:__. same, legs crossed. *Almost always struck after his death.* **275.00**
__:__. Similar, but AR Drachm **125.00**
__:__. AE20. Head of Alexander as Hercules / club and bow in case **40.00**
__: Philip III, 323-317 B.C. AV Stater. as that of Alexander above, but ΦΙΛΙΠΠοΥ r. **2,000.00**

Maroneia, Thrace. 400-350 B.C. AE15. Horse galloping r. / Vine in square **30.00**

Mesembria, Thrace. 450-350 B.C. AR Diobol. Crested helmet facing / Four-spoked wheel, META **110.00**

Mytilene, Lesbos. 450-330 B.C. Electrum 1/6 Stater. Head of Apollo r. / Female head in square. **450.00**

Olbia, Black Sea area, 5th Century B.C. Dolphin shaped bronze, 32mm, *value of examples with broken tail.* **30.00**

__: 320-300 B.C. AE21. Head of Borysthenes / Axe and bow case..... **30.00**

Olynthos, Macedon. 6th Century B.C gold Stater. Horse / Mill-sale pattern. *A deceptive modern, die-struck counterfeit.*
Panticapaeum, Northern Black coast, 350-200 B.C. AE17. Head of Pan l. / Head of bull l................................ **30.00**

__. 3rd century B.C. AE10. Rose / Rose, P O at sides.. **30.00**

Sinope, Paphlagonia. 330-300 B.C. AR Drachm. Nymph Sinope / Eagle on dolphin.. **300.00**
Tenedus, Troas, 160-140 B.C. AR Tetradrachm. Janiform head with male and female faces / Double axe in wreath **4,000.00**

Tarsus, Cilicia. 300s B.C. AR Stater. Baal std. l. / Lion attacking bull **450.00**
__,__. 2nd-1st century B.C. AE17. Zeus std. l. / Club in wreath.................... **35.00**
Thasos, Thrace. 411-350 B.C. AR Trihemiobol. Satyr kneeling l. / Amphora..................................... **400.00**

ANCIENT NEAR EAST

At first dominated by the municipal issues of the Phoenician cities in the 500s B.C., as well as of the Persian Empire, this region was incorporated by Alexander the Great into his vast empire. From his death until the Roman conquest of the area, the municipal issues combined with those of the larger Hellenistic kingdoms, particularly the Seleucids, descended from one of Alexander's generals.
Additional Specialized Books:
Houghton, Arthur. *Coins of the Seleucid Empire from the Collection of Arthur Houghton.*
Known Counterfeits: High-quality Greek silver has been the target of counterfeiters for more than a century. Many counterfeits are quite deceptive. Counterfeit shekels of Tyre in every quality are abundant.

Seleucid Empire

Seleucus I, 312-280. AR Tetradrachm. Head of Alexander as Hercules / Zeus std. l., ΣΕΛΕΥΚοΥ r.................... **350.00**
Antiochus I, 280-261 B.C. AE18. Head of Apollo / Tripod **40.00**
Antiochus II, 261-246. AE17. Head r. / Apollo stg. l. **40.00**
Seleucus II, 246-226 B.C. AE17. Head of Hercules / Apollo std. l.................... **40.00**
Antiochus III, 223-187 B.C. AR Tetradrachm. Diad head r. / Apollo std. l.. **325.00**
Molon, 222-220 B.C. AE18. Head of Apollo / Victory stg. l.................... **250.00**
Seleucus IV, 187-175 B.C. AE17. Bust of Artemis, quiver at shoulder / Artemis stg. with deer.................................. **30.00**
Antiochus IV, 175-164B.C. AE16. His radiate head r., AX l. / Tyche std. l. holding small Victory.................... **25.00**
Alexander I, 150-145B.C. AR Tetradrachm. Alexander's bust r. / Eagle l. on prow, club l. **300.00**

Antiochus VII, 138-129 B.C. AR Tetradrachm. Diademed bust r. / Athena stg. l. **240.00**
__. AE18. Bust of Eros r. / Headdress of Isis... **30.00**
Alexander II, 128-123 B.C. AE21. Radiate bust r. / Cornucopia **30.00**
Tigranes II of Armenia, 95-56 B.C. AR Tetradrachm. Bust in Armenian tiara / Tyche std. r............................... **1,200.00**
__. AE22. Similar **80.00**
Philip Philadelphos, 93-83 B.C. AR Tetradrachm. Philip's bust r. / Zeus std. l holding victory and scepter, four line inscription, all in wreath **175.00**

Syria

Antioch. 1st century B.C. AE20 Head of Zeus r. / Zeus std. l......................... **30.00**

Phoenicia

Arados. 2nd century B.C. AE17. Head of Zeus r. / Ram of galley................. **25.00**

Sidon. 4th cent. B.C. AR 1/8 Stater. Galley / King confronting Lion.... **100.00**
__. A.D. 44. AE15. Turreted head of Tyche r. / War galley l., ΣΙΔΩΝΟΣ... above... **30.00**
Tripolis. 2nd century B.C. Veiled bust of Tyche / Prow of galley, two caps above. **30.00**

Tyre. 2nd-1st century B.C. AR Shekel (tetradrachm). Head of Melkarth r. / Eagle l., club l. *There is great demand for this coin for its Biblical connection. It is believed the most likely coin to have been*

used to pay Judas the thirty pieces of silver.............................. **550.00**

__: __. Similar but modern tourist counterfeit. Note the dark grey metal, and flat surface on the obverse. Even more telling is the heavy casting seam on the edge.

__. Half shekel, Similar. *Thought to be the amount of standard donation at the Temple in Jerusalem*..................... **300.00**

Arabia

Himyarites. 1st Century B.C. - 1st Century A.D. AR Denarius. Diademed head / Head of Bull...................... **125.00**

JUDEA

There were no coins in the time of the Patriarchs. The first ones to be made in Judea were tiny silver pieces struck during the Persian occupation and marked "Yehud." Independent Jewish coinage began under John Hyrcanus I, nephew of Judah Maccabee, who led the fight against the Seleucid King Antiochus IV. Ancient Jewish coins are virtually all crudely made small bronzes. Except for two periods of revolt against the Romans, there are no proven silver coins of the Judean kingdom. During the end period when Judean kings were clients of the Romans some of their coins actually depict the Roman emperor on one side, while referring to the king on the other.

The revolt coins are often struck over Roman coins, which sometimes had their designs partially filed off first. Occasionally a fragment of the old coin actually shows through the new design.

Despite their crudeness, Judean coins are extremely popular because of their Biblical connection.

Additional Specialized Books:
Hendin, David. *Guide to Biblical Coins.*

Known Counterfeits: Many poor replicas have been made over the last century, often recognizable by their extreme uniformity or blatant edge seams. High-quality counterfeits exist of many of the revolt silver pieces.

Persian Period, before 333 B.C. AR Hemiobol. Head of Persian king / Falcon, *Yhd* r............................... **650.00**

__,__. AR Drachm. Helmeted , bearded head r. / Male deity std. on winged wheel. ....*Unique*

John Hyrcanus I, 134-104 B.C. AE Prutah. *Yehohanan the High Priest and the Council of the Jews*, in wreath / Two cornucopiae, pomegranate between **30.00**

Anonymous. 1st century B.C. AR Shekel (tetradrachm). Head of Melkarth r. / Eagle l., club l., KP r. *Some scholars believe that Tyre shekels with KP were struck in Jerusalem to use as donations at the Temple.* **475.00**

Alexander Jannaeus, 103-76 B.C. AE Prutah. Anchor / Star within diadem. *This is the coin most often considered the widow's mite mentioned in the New Testament. Because of this it is always popular despite its usual crudeness and poor grade.* Fine **25.00**
same, Low grade **9.50**

Herod I the Great, 40 B.C - A.D. 4. AE27. Cap on couch between branches / Tripod **250.00**

__. AE Prutah. Anchor, HPωΔ BACI / Two cornucopia, caduceus between. **40.00**

Herod Archelaus, 4 B.C - A.D. 6. AE Prutah. Bunch of Grape / Helmet with plumes.. **38.00**

Herod Antipas, 4 B.C - 40 A.D. AE19. HPωΔ TETPAP, Reed / TIBEPIAC in wreath **350.00**

Agrippa I, 37-44. AE Prutah. Umbrella / Three ears of barley **25.00**

Pontius Pilate, 26-36, for Tiberius. AE Lepton. Astrologer's staff / LIZ in wreath **95.00**

Nero, 54-68. AE Lepton. Palm branch / NEPωNOC in wreath..................... **30.00**

Agripa II, 56-95. AE 18. Bust of Roman Emperor Domitian / Victory writing on shield, ETO KΔ BA AΓPIΠΙ around **165.00**

First Revolt, 66-70. AR Shekel. Chalice / Three pomegranates. **2,400.00**

__. AE Prutah. Amphora / Vine leaf **35.00**

Second Revolt, 132-135. AR Tetradrachm. Facade of Temple / Lulav and etrog, "For the freedom of Jerusalem" around **2,500.00**

__. AR Denarius. Bunch of grapes / Lyre **400.00**

ANCIENT PERSIA

Ancient Persian coins are among the most common of the 6th century B.C. Gold *darics* and silver *sigloi* were struck in quantity, both in the homeland of their large empire, and in their possessions in Asia Minor. Many of these coins have a test punched applied by ancient bankers. They reduce the value, but if only on the reverse, not significantly.

After a century of being part of Greek empires, Persia again asserted its independence (238 B.C.) as Parthia. It is interesting to see the evolution of the artistic style of the Parthian drachm, from Hellenistic Greek realism to a stylized and linear oriental rendering.

Three vassal kingdoms of Parthia also struck coins: Characene, Elymais and Persis.

The Sassanian dynasty of Persis overthrew the Parthians, their former overlords (A.D. 224), but continued their empire, calling it Ayran. They also continued the oriental trend in portraiture. Their drachms are notable for their broad, thin fabric and the elaborate crowns worn by their emperors.

Additional Specialized Books:
Gobl, Robert, *Sassanian Numismatics.*
Sellwood, David, *An Introduction to the Coinage of Parthia.*
Sellwood, Whitting, and Williams, *An Introduction to Sassanian Coins.*
Shore, F., *Parthian Coins and History.*

Known Counterfeits: While not as aggressively counterfeited as Greek coins, collector counterfeits of varying quality have been made of these series for almost a century.

Note: All Parthian and Sassanian coins here are silver drachms unless noted.

PERSIAN EMPIRE

500-330 B.C. AV Daric. King kneeling r. holding spear and bow / Crude incuse square....................................... **1,200.00**

500-330 B.C. AR Siglos. Similar **90.00**
Also struck by Persians in Lydia.

PARTHIA

Arsaces I, 238-211 B.C. Beardless bust l.
  wearing leather cap / Archer std. l.
  .... **2,250.00**

Arsaces II, 211-191 B.C. AR Drachm.
  Beardless bust l. wearing leather cap /
  Archer std. r. **375.00**
Mithradates I, 171-138 B.C. Similar, but
  archer seated on omphalos........... **140.00**
Phraates II, 138-127 B.C. Bearded bust l.
  wearing diadem / Similar.............. **200.00**
Artabanos I, 127-124 B.C. Similar to
  above... **250.00**

Mithradates II, 123-88 B.C. Similar but
  archer on chair **90.00**
__. AE17. Similar / Horse head **35.00**
Gotarzes I, 95-87 B.C. Bearded bust in
  tiara l. / Archer std. r. on chair....... **70.00**
Orodes I, 90-77 B.C. Similar. **70.00**
Sinatruces, 77-70 B.C. Similar but anchor
  behind head................................. **250.00**

Phraates III, 70-57 B.C. Bust l. wearing
  short beard and diadem / Similar to
  above... **200.00**
Mithradates III, 57-54 B.C. Similar.
  .... **90.00**
Orodes II, 57-38 B.C. Similar........... **60.00**
Pakoros I, 50 B.C. Beardless bust l. / as
  above.. *Rare*
Phraates IV, 38-2 B.C. Bust l. with short
  beard and diadem / as above **60.00**
Phraataces, 2B.C - A.D.4. Similar but
  Nike behind head **60.00**
Vonones I, 8-12 A.D. Bearded bust l. /
  Victory flying r. **150.00**

Artabanos II, 10-38. Bearded bust l. /
  Archer std. r. **55.00**
Vardanes I, 40-45. Similar................ **90.00**
Gotarzes II, 40-51. Similar **75.00**
Vonones II, 51. Facing bust / Archer std.
  r... **125.00**
Vologases I, 51-78. Bust l. with beard and
  diadem / as above.......................... **80.00**
Vardanes II, 55-58. Similar **90.00**
Vologases II, 77-80. Bust l. with beard
  and tiara / as above **300.00**
Pakoros II, 78-105. Beardless bust l. / as
  above **175.00**
Artabanos III, 80-90. Bust l. with beard
  and diadem. / as above **90.00**
Vologases III, 105-147. Similar. **55.00**
Osroes I, 109-129. Similar but hair is
  gathered in puffy balls.................. **750.00**
__. AR Tetradrachm. Beaded bust l. in
  diadem. **1,250.00**
Parthamaspates, 116. Bearded bust l. in
  tiara / Similar **200.00**
Mithradatess IV, 140. Bust l. with beard
  and diadem / Similar **70.00**
Vologases IV, 147-191. Bust l. with beard
  and tiara / Similar **55.00**
__. Similar / Tyche giving diadem to
  seated king **150.00**
Osroes II, 190. Similar **55.00**
Vologases V, 191-208. Facing bearded
  bust with hair gathered in puffy balls /
  Crude archer std. r **750.00**
Vologases VI, 208-228. Bust l. with beard
  and tiara, Ie r. / as above................ **55.00**
Artabanos IV, 216-224. Similar, >_ to r.
  .... **350.00**

Characene. Attambelos III, 53-72.
  AE Tetradrachm. Beardless head r. /
  Hercules std. l. **60.00**
Elymais. Kamnaskires Ores III, mid-100s.
  Billon tetradrachm. Facing bust and
  anchor / dashes **75.00**
__: Orodes II, c.150-200. AE Drachm.
  Facing bust with tiara, anchor r. / dashes
  .... **12.00**
Persis. 1-2nd cent. AR Hemidrachm.
  Bust in tiara l. / double diadem **75.00**

Sassanian. Ardashir I, 224-241. Bust in
  high crown / Fire altar aflame **150.00**
Shapur I, 241-272. Crowned bust / Fire
  altar between attendants **85.00**
Hormazd I, 272-273. Similar **2,000.00**
Varhran I, 273-276. Bust in spiked crown
  / as above.................................... **300.00**
Varhran II, 276-293. Bust in winged
  crown / as above. **225.00**

Narseh, 293-303. Bust in floral crown / as
  above... **175.00**
Hormazd II, 303-309. Bust in eagle crown
  / as above.................................... **140.00**
Shapur II, 309-379. Crowned bust / as
  above... **65.00**
Ardashir II, 379-383. Bust in cap-crown /
  as above **225.00**
Shapur III, 383-388. Bust in low crown /
  as above....................................... **100.00**
Varhran IV, 388-399. Bust in winged
  crown / as above **55.00**
Yazdgard I, 399-420. Bust in cap-crown /
  as above **65.00**

Varhran V, 420-438. Crowned bust / as
  above, face within flames................ **55.00**
Yazdgard II, 438-457. Crowned bust /
  Fire altar between attendants **45.00**
Firuz, 457-484. Similar **38.00**
Valkash, 484-488. Similar **135.00**
Zamasp, 497-499. Crowned bust, small
  bust before / as above **120.00**
Kavad I, 484-531. Crowned bust / as
  above... **30.00**
Khusru I, 531-579. Similar **30.00**
Hormazd IV, 579-590. Similar **30.00**
Varhran VI, 590-591. Similar......... **300.00**
Vistahm, 591-597. Similar.............. **210.00**
Khusru II, 590-628. Bust in winged
  crown / as above (crude style)......... **22.00**
same (but bold style)........................ **38.00**
Kavad II, 628. Crowned bust / as above
  .... **300.00**

Ardashir III, 628-630. Similar........ **115.00**
Buran, 630-631. Beardless bust / as above
  .... **700.00**
Azarmidukht, 631-632. Bust in winged
  crown / as above...................... **5,000.00**
Hormazd V, 631-632. Similar......... **225.00**

Khusru V, 631-33. Beardless bust / as above **300.00**
Yazdgard III, 632-651. Similar **135.00**

Sassanian Kushanshahs.

Peroz II, 325-c.328. AE14. Peroz in tiara / Bust of deity emerging from altar **15.00**

FURTHER ASIA

Despite the brevity of Alexander the Great's occupation of "further Asia" – areas as far as modern Afghanistan, Pakistan and even India – his cultural and monetary influence was lasting. The Hellenistic kingdom of Bactria continued for hundreds of years until wiped out by invaders from the North. On many of their coins, a Greek obverse inscription is combined with a reverse legend in local Karoshti characters. The later reverse types also show a synthesis of Greek and Indian cultures. Other unusual feature of their coinage was the use of a natural nickel alloy, thousands of years before the isolation of the element nickel, and the use of square coins, again centuries before they were widely used.

Additional Specialized Books:
Mitchiner, Michael, *Oriental Coins and their Values: Ancient and Classical World.*

Known Counterfeits: Many tetradrachms, especially heroic bust types, are magnets for counterfeiters. All must be examined by an expert. Even the small drachms have been subject to frequent counterfeiting. The quality of these counterfeits varies from "tourist" to "expert."

Bactria. Euthydemus I, 230-190 B.C. AE22. Bearded head r. / Horse running r. **90.00**
__. Demetrius I, 190-171 B.C. AE Trichalkon. Head of Elephant / Caduceus **150.00**
__. Antimachus I, 185-170 B.C. AR Tetradrachm. Bust in broad hat / Poseidon stg. **2,500.00**
__. Diomedes, 110-80 B.C. AE17x22 rectangular. Dioscuri stg. / Humped bull **75.00**
Indo-Greeks. Menander I, 155-130 B.C. AR Tetradrachm. Heroic bust l. throwing spear / Athena stg. l. **500.00**
__.__. AR Drachm. Similar **100.00**
__. Strato I, 130-110 B.C. AE20 square. Bust of Hercules r. / Victory walking r. **35.00**
Indo-Scythians. Azes I, 57-35 B.C. AR Tetradrachm. Zeus stg. l. / Victory walking r. **300.00**

__:__. AE 1/2 Unit. King on Camel / Yak **40.00**

EGYPT & AFRICA

The Egyptians found little use for coinage before Alexander the Great. With the founding of the Greek Ptolemaic dynasty (305 B.C.) and the increase in Greek influence, its coinage became prolific. Silver was similar to that of the other Hellenistic kingdoms, but its copper coins were unique for the immense size of their larger denominations. Their "centration holes," actually dimples, are a distinct feature of their manufacturing process.

Carthage was a Phoenician city in North Africa, near modern Tunis. A bitter rival of the Roman Republic during the Punic Wars, it colonized Spain, western Sicily and Sardinia.

Egypt. Nektanebo II, 361-350B.C. AV Stater. Horse galloping r. / Ornamented collar over heart and wind-pipe (hieroglyphic for fine gold) **6,000.00**
Ptolemy II, 285-246B.C. AE16. Head of Zeus-Ammon / Eagle stg. l. on thunderbolt, wings open, Δ between legs **25.00**

Ptolemy IV, 221-204 B.C. AE41. Head of Zeus-Ammon r. / Eagle l. on thunderbolt. cornucopia l. **125.00**
Ptolemy VIII, 145-116B.C. AR Tetradrachm. Idealized head of Ptolemy I / Eagle l. on thunderbolt l., ΠΑ r **175.00**

Cleopatra VII, 51-30B.C. AE26. Her bust r. / Eagle stg. on thunderbolt **600.00**
Carthage. 320-280 B.C Electrum Stater. Head of Tanit l. / Horse stg. r. **985.00**

__. 250-200 B.C. AE18. Head of Tanit / Horse head r. **30.00**

ROMAN COINS

Roman coins are among the most universally collected. In fact, the origin of coin collecting in the West and the rediscovery of realistic portraiture, evolves form the finding of Roman coins by Italians at the dawn of the Renaissance. Roman coins are divided into three different stages, although the middle one actually overlaps the first. They are the Roman Republic, Imperatorial and Roman Empire. The evolution of coinage from the first to the last is a development from primitive to almost modern.

ROMAN REPUBLIC

The Roman word for money, *pecunia*, derives from their earliest measure of wealth: sheep (*pecus*). Less sophisticated than the Greeks at the time, the Romans' next step was to trade in large cast bars of copper (*aes*). Alas, the Greek invention of coinage was still more convenient, and as the Romans expanded their territories and traded over greater distances, their cast-bronze ingots gradually became round and took on the form of coins. When Rome began producing its first silver coins, they were not cast in the Roman tradition, but struck in the Greek manner. Their weights and values were Greek as well. The coasts of southern Italy and Sicily were covered with Greek colonies. In the late 3rd century B.C., the Romans were powerful enough to decide to strike a silver coin on their own standard, and replaced the *drachm* with the new dime-sized *denarius*. In the meantime, the old cast-copper aes had evolved into a struck copper coin of large size, the *As*. It originally weighed one pound or *libra*. The new *denarius* was valued at 10 of these, and later at 16. Most Romans were illiterate, so a system was devised for reading the value of coins by counting dots or simple symbols. It survived for many years as follows:

Roman Republic Bronze

```
(none) .................... = Semuncia 1/2 Uncia
• .................................. = Uncia (ounce)
•• ................................. = Sextans 1/6 As
••• .............................. = Quadrans 1/4 As
•••• ................................ = Triens 1/3 As
S ...................................... = Semis 1/2 As
I ......................................... = As 12 Unciae
```

Roman Republic Silver

```
IIS ......................... = Sestertius 2½ Asses
V .............................. = Quinarius 5 Asses
X .............................= Denarius 10 Asses
✕ ..................... = Denarius, late 16 Asses
```

Most bronzes of the republic depicted a god or goddess on the obverse, the prow of a ship on the reverse. Silver, particularly the denarius, usually had a portrait of the personification of Roma on the obverse, and a chariot on the reverse. Living people were not depicted, but late in the Republic the magistrates responsible for managing the mint would sometimes depict their famous ancestors or deities from which they claimed descent.

BOOKS ABOUT ROMAN REPUBLIC & IMPERATORIAL COINS

Because the imperatorial period is technically the end of the Republic, many of the same books can be useful for both series. Hundreds of pages can be written on books about ancient Roman coins. The list here will be confined to only the most basic or the most important references.

Klawans, Zander, *Handbook of Ancient Greek and Roman Coins*. The simplest introduction.

Sayles, Wayne, *Ancient Coin Collecting: The Roman World - Politics and Propaganda.*

Melville Jones, John, *A Dictionary of Ancient Roman Coins.*

Sear, David, *Roman Coins and their Values.* The most-used catalogue of representative coins.

Sear, David, *Roman Silver Coins*, v. I.

Known Counterfeits: Modern counterfeits of the Republican series proper are few. There are, however, a great many counterfeits of imperatorial coins due to the notoriety of the historical figures involved. Included are both high-quality and poor counterfeits of Julius Caesar (portrait and elephant denarii) and Marc Antony (portrait and legionary denarii).

Fourrées of Roman Republican coins are quite common.

AV 60 Asses, after 211 B.C. Head of Mars / Eagle stg. r. **2,500.00**

Values for Greek coins are for **Very Fine** examples for gold (**AV**) and silver (**AR**), **Fine** for bronze and copper (**AE**).

AR Quadrigatus, 225-213 B.C. Beardless janiform head / Jupiter and Victory in chariot r., ROMA below **950.00**
Same but baser, 213-211 B.C **300.00**

AR Denarius, c.136 B.C. Helmeted head of Roma r., X behind / Dioscuri galloping, ROMA below **120.00**
AR Denarius, 90 B.C. Head of Apollo / Horseman r., L.PISO.FRVGI. **90.00**
AR Denarius, 90 B.C. Bearded head r. / Pegasus r. **120.00**

AR Denarius, 82 B.C. Head of Mercury / Ulysses greeted by dog **175.00**
AR Denarius, 79 B.C. Head of Juno / Griffin leaping r., L.PAPI. This coin has a *serrate* edge, which looks like a series of cuts **120.00**

AR Denarius, 64 B.C. Head of Juno in goatskin r. / Girl feeding erect serpent. **125.00**
AR Victoriatus, 206-195 B.C. Head of Jupiter / Victory crowning trophy **75.00**
AR Quinarius, 98 B.C. Similar but Q at bottom of reverse **80.00**
AR Sestertius, 211-207 B.C. Head of Roma, IIS behind / Dioscuri galloping r. **220.00**
AE Aes Grave As, Liberal Standard (288 grams), 240-225 B.C. Head of Janus / Prow, I above .... **VF 1,000.00**

Early Roman bronzes were made by casting instead of striking, unlike most Roman coins.

AE Semuncia, c.215 B.C. Head of Mercury / Prow r., no mark of value **65.00**
AE Uncia, 217-215 B.C. Helmeted head of Roma l., • r. / Prow r., ROMA above, • below... **125.00**
AE Uncia, 211-207 B.C. same but smaller **90.00**

AE Sextans, 289-245 B.C. Scallop shell, •• / Caduceus, •• **350.00**
AE Sextans, 211-207 B.C. Head of Mercury, •• above / Prow r., •• below **100.00**
AE Quadrans, 2nd cent. B.C. Head of Hercules, ••• behind / Prow r. **60.00**

AE Semis, 211-209 B.C. Head of Saturn r., S behind / Prow, S above **135.00**
AE As, 206-195 B.C. Head of Janus, I above / Prow r., bird and rudder above, I r., ROMA below.......................... **150.00**
AE As, c.190-150 B.C. Head of Janus, I above / Prow r., monogram above **125.00**

ROMAN IMPERATORIAL

Towards the end of the Roman Republic, many important generals took control from each other, eclipsing the power of the senate. During this time their power and audacity caused them to do the previously unthinkable: place their own names and even images on the coinage. These generals include the famous Julius Caesar, who died before his nephew, Octavian, became the first Roman Emperor under the name of Augustus. Numismatists call the coinage in the name of these rulers, who's civil wars caused the demise of the Republic, "Imperatorial" after the Latin name for general, *Imperator*.

Pompey the Great, d. 48 B.C. AE As, 45 B.C. Janiform head of Pompey / Prow **300.00**

Pompey Junior, d. 45 B.C. AR Denarius. Head of Roma / Pompey the Great on prow, receiving palm from Hispania **400.00**

Sextus Pompey, d. 35 B.C. AR Denarius, 44-43 B.C. Head of Pompey the Great / Galley...................................... **2,500.00**

Julius Caesar, d. 44 B.C. AR Denarius, 44 B.C. Bust of Julius Caesar / Venus stg. holding Victory.................. **2,200.00**

___. AR Denarius. Elephant r. trampling serpent, CAESAR below / Priestly implements.................................... **425.00**

Marc Antony, d. 30 B.C. AR Legionary Denarius, 32-31B.C. Galley / Legionary eagle between two standards **225.00**

Marc Antony and Octavian. AR Denarius. 41 B.C. Head of Marc Antony / Head of Octavian...................................... **400.00**

Lepidus and Octavian. AR Denarius. c. 42 B.C. Head of Lepidus / Head of Octavian.................................... **1,800.00**

ROMAN EMPIRE

As Rome grew from a city to a Republic and then to an Empire, larger denominations were needed to facilitate even greater financial transactions. The monetary system as it looked during most of the Empire (27 B.C. to A.D. 286) follows, but not all coins were struck during all periods.

Roman Copper and Brass to 295

Coin	Value	Size
Quadrans	1/4 As	16 to 15
Semis	1/2 As	21 to 18
As	1/16 Denarius	28 to 23
Dupondius	2 Asses	28 to 23
Sestertius	4 Asses	34 to 30

Roman Silver to 286

Quinarius	8 Asses	15 to 14
Denarius	16 Asses	18 to 15
Antoninianus	2 Denarii	24 to 18

(Late silver alloy coins appear copper)

Roman Gold to 286

Quinarius	12½ Denarii	16 to 15
Aureus	25 Denarii	20 to 19

At the end of this 300-year span there was great inflation. The amount of silver in the *antoninianus* (double denarius) was not a whole lot more than that in the original denarius. The denarius itself declined from a dime-size coin of good silver to one of less than half silver by the 250s, and by the 270s it was a small copper containing only a trace of silver. When silver is less than 50 percent pure it is called *billon*.

Diocletian (reign 284-305) attempted to put the degenerate Roman coinage in order. He based his reforms on a heavier gold *aureus* weighing 1/60th instead of 1/70th Roman pound, a small coin of good silver, the *argenteus*, and a large bronze coin, the *follis*, almost the size of an American half dollar. The *argenteus* was particularly innovative, as it had been decades since a good quality silver coin had been minted.

Unfortunately, with Diocletian's passing, his currency began to erode. Constantine the Great (reign 307-337) replaced the *aureus* with the slightly lighter *solidus* (1/72 Roman pound), but from then on the purity and weight of the gold coinage were maintained for centuries into the Byzantine period. He renamed the *argenteus* the *siliqua* and added a 1 1/3 *siliqua* called a *miliarense*, and maintained the purity of both. However, he let the *follis* continue to deteriorate. By His death in 337, it had declined to a size smaller than a dime.

During the late Roman period the sizes of bronze coins declined so rapidly – and surviving records are so scarce – that numismatists have taken to categorizing them by diameter instead of name.

Name	Size	Similar to U.S.:
AE1	**over 24** mm.	mini-dollar
AE2	**21-24 mm.**	quarter
AE3	**17-20 mm.**	cent
AE4	**below 17** mm.	half dime

IMPERIAL COIN DESIGNS

The obverses of most coins of the Roman Empire show the portrait of the emperor or a member of his family, generally the empress or a son. AVG for *augustus* or *augusta* on the obverse meant the person was emperor or empress. *Caesar* after the first dynasty meant junior emperor. The portrait could also tell the average Roman the face value of the coin. If the emperor wore a radiate (spiked) crown, the value was doubled. Dupondii and Antoniniani (the double denarius) both had radiate crowns. For an empress, a crescent below the shoulder substituted for a crown.

First and 2nd century Roman coins have realistic portraits. This realism begins to fade somewhat by the 250s. The Tetrarchy period replaces realistic portraiture altogether with well-executed, angular images of an emperor, still conveying a strong sense of authority. The addition or deletion of a beard aside, these stereotyped images persist through the end of the Empire, although usually lacking the original inspiration.

Most base-metal coins until well into the 3rd century have the letters SC in the reverse field. This indicates that they were issued with the consent of the Senate.

The reverses often depicted gods and goddesses just as the Greeks had. The descriptions of deities given in the Greek section earlier will help for Roman coins, too. The Romans depicted virtues in allegorical form, perhaps more than they showed deities. Often their names were clearly written. Their Latin names and English translations are given here, with an attribute or two given afterward. The V was used both for V and U on Roman coins. Allegories are female unless noted.

ABVNDANTIA - Abundance. Cornucopia and ears of grain.

AEQVITAS - Equity. Balance scales.

AETERNITAS - Eternity. Globe, torch, scepter, phoenix..

ANNONA - Harvest. Ears of grain, grain measure (*modius*), cornucopia.

CLEMENTIA - Clemency. Branch, scepter.

CONCORDIA - Concord. Dish (*patera*), cornucopia.

CONCORDIA MILITVM - Military Concord. Two military standards.

CONSTANTIA - Firmness. Right hand to face, spear.

FECVNDITAS - Fertility. Child or children, scepter.

FELICITAS - Felicity. Caduceus, cornucopia, scepter.

FIDES - Faith. *Patera*, cornucopia, grain-ears, fruit basket.

FORTVNA - Fortune. Rudder, cornucopia, wheel.

GENIVS - Spirit. Male holding *patera* and cornucopia.

HILARITAS - Cheerfulness. Palm branch, cornucopia, scepter, patera.

INDVLGENTIA - Mercy. *Patera*, scepter.

IVSTITIA - Justice. Olive branch, *patera*, scepter.

LAETITIA - Joy. Wreath, scepter.

LIBERALITAS - Liberality. Tablet, cornucopia.

LIBERTAS - Liberty. Pointed cap in hand, scepter.

MONETA - Money. Scale, cornucopia.

PAX - Peace. Olive branch, scepter, cornucopia, caduceus.

PIETAS - Piety. Veil, *patera*, scepter, altar by feet.

PROVIDENTIA - Providence. Baton, globe, scepter.

PVDICITIA - Modesty. Veil, scepter.

SALVS - Health. Scepter, serpent.

SECVRITAS - Security. *Patera*, scepter, column.

SPES - Hope. Raises dress slightly.

VBERITAS - Fertility. Cornucopia, purse, bunch of grapes.

VICTORIA - Victory. Depicted as a winged female. Wreath, palm branch.

VIRTVS - Military Virtue, Courage. Armored male, holding Victory, sword, spear, shield.

ROMAN MINTS

There were many mints throughout the Roman Empire, some as distant from each other as England and Egypt. Most of those operating during the 280s and later placed mintmarks clearly on the reverse.

A Roman mintmark often consisted of three parts. One was an indication of money generally. P, M and SM were used to mean *Pecunia, Moneta* or *Sacra Moneta*. Next, the city was abbreviated. Also, a letter indicating the workshop within the mint, called an *officina*, often followed or preceded the city abbreviation. Some of the more common city abbreviations used in mintmarks are:

AL ....Alexandria, Egypt
AN or ANT.......................Antioch, Syria
AQ ....Aquileia, Italy
AR ....Arles, France
CON or CONS....Constantinople, Turkey
CON or CONST ....Arles, France
H or HERAC ....Heraclea, Turkey
K or CVZ ....Cyzicus, Turkey
K or KART ....Carthage, Tunisia
L or LON ....London
LG or LVG .... Lyons, France
N, NIC or NIK.......... Nicomedia, Turkey
R or ROM ....Rome
S or SIR...................Sirmium, Yugoslavia
SIS or SISC ....Siscia, Croatia
TS or TES............... Thessalonica, Greece
T ....Ticinum, Italy
TR ....Trier, Germany

Coins from more-popularly collected and smaller mints, such as London, command a premium above others.

BOOKS ABOUT ROMAN IMPERIAL COINS

Hundreds of pages can be written on books about Roman Imperial coins. The list here will be confined to only the most basic or the most important references.

Carson, Hill, & Kent, *Late Roman Bronze Coinage.*

Cohen, Henri, Description *Historique des Monneis Frappees sous L'Empire Romain.*

Klawans, Zander, *Handbook of Ancient Greek and Roman Coins.*

Mattingly, H. and Sydenham, E.A., *The Roman Imperial Coinage*, 10 vols.

Melville Jones, John, *A Dictionary of Ancient Roman Coins.*

Sear, David, *Roman Coins and their Values.*

Sear, David, *Roman Silver Coins*, vols. II-V.

Vagi, David, *Coinage and History of the Roman Empire*, 2 vols.

Known Counterfeits: Counterfeits of Roman Imperial coins are extremely common. The sestertii were first counterfeited by Renaissance artists intending to create medals closely resembling the originals. These are called "Paduans" after the Italian city where many early ones were made. They are too bold and uniform, and the fields are too flat. Early Paduans are somewhat valuable, but later casts are worth much less.

"Silver" Denarius of Marc Antony and Julius Caesar, 43 B.C. One of many poor quality, base metal counterfeits.

Caligula and Augustus, Brass Dupondius, 37-41 A.D. *A deceptive counterfeit with nice style and well-done "aging." It has evidence of an artificial edge, is a bit too thick, and has too even a surface.*

Modern counterfeits vary from deceptive and expert reproductions of sestertii and denari to extremely crude copies made for sale to tourists. Many uncirculated Roman silver counterfeits have appeared on the market in the last decade, having been struck by expert engravers in Bulgaria.

Julio-Claudian Dynasty

Augustus, 27 B.C. - A.D. 14. AR Denarius. Caius and Lucius Caesars stg. with shields and spears................ **275.00**
__. AE As. Altar of Lugdunum **60.00**
Livia, wife of Augustus, d. A.D. 29. AE Dupondius. PIETAS below bust / Large SC **275.00**
Agrippa, d. 12 B.C. AE As. Busts of Augustus and Agrippa / Crocodile chained to palm tree.................... **165.00**
Tiberius, 14-37. AV Aureus. Livia as Peace std. r. **2,500.00**

__. AR Denarius. Livia as Peace std. r. This coins is mentioned in the Bible and is often called the "Tribute Penny"...... **350.00**

Counterfeit Tribute Pennies:

Modern cast, plated with silver. Note lack of detail and base metal showing at high points..

Struck with modern dies. Note different style and flat fields.

Drusus, son of Tiberius, d. A.D. 23. AE As. Large SC **200.00**

Germanicus, father of Caligula, d. A.D. 19. Germanicus in chariot / Germanicus standing **200.00**

Caligula, 37-41. AE As. Vesta veiled, std. l. **225.00**
Caligula was a nickname. His real name Caius, or C., appears on his coins.

Claudius, 41-54. AE Quadrans. Modius / SC **35.00**

__. AE As. Constantia stg. **100.00**

Nero, 54-68. AE As. Victory flying l. with shield inscribed SPQR **100.00**

__. AE Sestertius. Nero riding prancing horse, soldier riding in background **1,200.00**

Galba, 68-69. AE As. Liberty stg. holding pileus and scepter. **350.00**

Otho, 69. AR Denarius. Security stg. l. **975.00**

Vitellius, 69. AR Denarius. Tripod altar, dolphin above, raven on base **500.00**

Flavian Dynasty 69-96

Vespasian, 69-79. AR Denarius. Female Jew std. r., trophy of arms behind, IVDAEA below **500.00**

__: AR Denarius. Peace std. l. **125.00**

Titus, 79-81. AR Denarius. Chair .. **250.00**

Julia Titi, daughter of Titus, d. A.D. 83. AR Denarius. Venus leaning on column **1,000.00**

Domitian, 81-96. AR Denarius. Minerva stg. l. with spear **110.00**

The Good Emperors 96-180
Nerva, 96-98. AE As. Clasped hands. **75.00**

Trajan, 98-117. AE Sestertius. Roma stg. l., Dacia kneeling at feet. *This example shows an emerald green patina, highly valued by collecors of ancient coins* **110.00**

Hadrian, 117-138. AV Aureus. Hadrian riding horse r. **1,800.00**

__. AR Denarius. Fortune stg. **100.00**

Sabina, wife of Hadrian, d. 137. AR denarius. Concord std. **200.00**

Aelius, Caesar 136-138. AR Denarius. Concord std.. .... **350.00**

Antoninus Pius, 138-161. AV Aureus. Emperor stg. **2,500.00**

__. AR Denarius. Emperor sacrificing at tripod altar **90.00**

Faustina, Sr., wife of Antoninus Pius, d. 141. AR Denarius. Eternity stg. **80.00**

Marcus Aurelius, 161-180. AV Aureus. Emperor crowned by victory. **2,200.00**

__. AR Denarius. Fortune std. **120.00**

__. AE Sestertius. Minerva stg. with spear and shield. **90.00**

Faustina, Jr., wife of Marcus Aurelius, d. 175. AR Denarius. Fecundity. **75.00**

Lucius Verus, 161-169. AR Denarius. Roma walking l. holdingtrophy.... **150.00**

Lucilla, wife of Lucius Verus, d. 182. AE As. Concord std. **75.00**

Commodus, 177-192. AR Denarius. Bust of Commodus wearing lion-skin headdress of Hercules / Club in wreath **180.00**

AE Dupondius. Minerva **45.00**

Crispina, wife of Commodus, d. 183. AE As. Juno and peacock **75.00**

Pertinax, 193. AR Denarius. Equity stg. with scales and cornucopia........... **850.00**

Didius Julianus, 193. AE Sestertius. Fortune stg. **900.00**

Pescennius Niger, 193-194. AR Denarius. Basket of fruit **1,600.00**

Clodius Albinus, as Caesar 193-195. AE As. Felicity stg. **200.00**

The Severan Era 193-235

Septimius Severus, 193-211. AR Denarius. Victory walking with shield. **60.00**

Julia Domna, wife of Septimius Severus, d. 217. AR Denarius. Venus std. **60.00**

__. AE Sestertius. Venus stg. A modern cast, it has an "applied" patina of the wrong color, and is much too flat and too thin.

Caracalla, 198-217. AE Sestertius. Providence stg. holding rod over globe and long scepter **90.00**

__. Sestertius. Circus Maximus. *This authentic example shows "tooling," scraping with a knife intended to make it look like it has less wear than it really does.* **2,000.00**
Caracalla was a nickname. His real name, Antoninus, appears on his coins.
Plautilla, wife of Caracalla, d. 212. AR Denarius. Piety stg. with child...... **125.00**
Geta, as Caesar, 198-209. AR Denarius. Genius stg. l. holding dish and grain ears... **65.00**
__, as Emperor, 209-212. AR Denarius. Genius stg. l. holding dish and grain ears.. **110.00**

Macrinus, 217-218. AR Denarius. Jupiter stg. holding thunderbolt and scepter **150.00**
Diadumenian, 218. AE As as augustus, 217-218. Diadumenian stg............ **250.00**

Elagabalus, 218-222. AR Denarius. Chariot pulling sacred stone of Emesa **100.00**
__. AR Denarius. Health feeding serpent. **60.00**
Elagabalus was a nickname. His real name, Antoninus, appears on his coins.
Julia Paula, wife of Elagabalus, div.220. AR Denarius. Concord std........... **250.00**
Aquilia Severa, wife of Elagabalus, div. 221. AR Denarius. Concord std. **275.00**

Julia Somaeias, mother of Elagabalus, d. 222. AR Denarius. Venus std. **100.00**
Julia Maesa, grandmother of Elagabalus and Severus Alexander, d. 225. AR Denarius. Juno stg......................... **65.00**

Severus Alexander, 222-235. AR Denarius. Virtus std. l. **40.00**
Julia Mamaea, mother of Severus Alexander, d. 235. AR Denarius. Venus stg. **60.00**
Maximinus, 235-238. AR Denarius. Emperor stg. between two military standards.. **90.00**

__. AE Sestertius. Faith holding standards... **55.00**
Gordian I, 238. AR Denarius. Roma std. l.. **1,350.00**
Gordian II, 238. AE Sestertius. Victory walking l..................................... **725.00**

Balbinus, 238. AE Antoninianus. Clasped hands... **450.00**
Pupienus, 238. AR Antoninianus. Clasped hands... **500.00**
Gordian III, 238-244. AR Antoninianus. Virtus or Mars with spear and shield stg. **55.00**

__. AE Sestertius. Sol stg.. .... **45.00**

Philip I, 244-49. AR Antoninianus. Rome stg.. .... **45.00**
Otacilia Severa, wife of Philip I. AE As. Concord std. **50.00**
Philip II, 247-249. AR Antoninianus. Sol walking l. holding whip................. **45.00**
Pacatian, 248. AR Antoninianus. Fortune std. holding rudder and cornucopia .... *Rare*
Jotapian, 248. AR Antoninianus. Victory walking l....................................... *Rare*
Trajan Decius, 249-251. AR Antoninianus. Allegory of the province of Pannonia stg............................. **45.00**
__. AE Double Sestertius. Felicity stg. holding caduceus and cornucopia. **475.00**

Herennia Etruscilla, wife of Trajan Decius. AR Antoninianus. Modesty stg **50.00**
The second example is one of many recent, deceptive, die struck Eastern European counterfeits.
Herennius Etruscus, as Caesar 250-251. AR Antoninianus. Priestly implements. **85.00**
Hostillian, as Caesar 251. base AR Antoninianus. Apollo std. with lyre **190.00**
Trebonianus Gallus, 251-253. AR Antoninianus. Liberty.................... **40.00**
Volusian, 251-253. AR Antoninianus. Virtue. **50.00**

Aemilian, 253. AR Antoninianus. Virtus. **275.00**
Valerian, 253-260. AR Antoninianus. Faith stg. with two military standards **38.00**

Gallienus, 253-268. Billon Antoninianus. Hippocamp. **60.00**
__. Billon Antoninianus. Security leaning on column. **15.00**

Salonina, wife of Gallienus. Billon Antoninianus. Venus stg. **18.00**

Valerian II, as Caesar 253-55. Billon Antoninianus. Priestly implements **50.00**

Saloninus, as Caesar 255-59. Billon Antoninianus. Priestly implements **50.00**

Macrianus, 260-261. Billon Antoninianus. Jupiter std. l. **150.00**

Quietus, 260-261. Billon Antoninianus. Equity stg. l. **150.00**

Postumus, 259-268 in Gaul. AE Antoninianus. Sol advancing.......... **13.00**

Laelianus, 268 in Gaul. AE Antoninianus. Victory walking r. **875.00**

Marius, 268 in Gaul. AE Antoninianus. Felicity stg. l. **150.00**

Victorinus, 268-270 in Gaul. AE Antoninianus. Piety stg. l., altar at feet **12.00**

Tetricus I, 270-273 in Gaul. AE Antoninianus. Joy stg. with wreath and anchor **12.00**

Tetricus II, caesar 270-273 in Gaul. AE Antoninianus. Hope advancing **12.00**

Claudius II Gothicus, 268-270. AE Antoninianus. Felicity stg. l. **10.00**

Quintillus, 270. AE Antoninius. Faith stg. **70.00**

Aurelian, 270-275. AE Antoninianus. Sol and captive **13.00**

__. AE Denarius. Victory walking l. **35.00**

Severina, wife of Aurelian. AE Antoninianus. Concord stg. **40.00**

Vabalathus, with Aurelian, 270-271. AE Antoninianus **40.00**

Tacitus, 275-276. AE Antoninianus. Tacitus receiving globe from Jupiter **30.00**

Florianus, 276. AE Antoninianus. Felicity stg. **85.00**

Probus, 276-282. AE Antoninianus. Jupiter giving globe to Probus........ **13.00**

__.__. Bust with spear and shield / Rome in temple **20.00**

Carus, 282-283. AE Antoninianus. Female giving wreath to Carus....... **30.00**

Numerian, 283-284. AE Antoninianus. Roma std. l. **25.00**

Carinus, 283-285. AE Antoninianus. Virtue holding spear and sword. **25.00**

Julian I, 284-285. AE Antoninianus. Felicity **2,000.00**

The Tetrarchy 284-324

Diocletian, 284-305. AE Follis. Genius (spirit) of the Romans stg. l. **22.00**

Carausius, 287-293 in Britain. AE Antoninianus. Peace stg. **65.00**

Allectus, 293-296 in Britain. AE Quinarius. Galley........................... **90.00**

Domitius Domitianus, 296-297 in Egypt. AE Follis. Genius of the Romans stg. l. **550.00**

Maximianus, 286-305. AR Argenteus. Tetrarchs before fort with six towers. **265.00**

__. AE Antoninianus. Jupiter stg., eagle at feet **12.00**

Constantius I, 305-306. AE Follis. Genius of the Romans stg. **35.00**

Galerius, as Caesar 293-305. AR Argentius. Four emperors, city gate in background. **325.00**

__. AE Follis. Genius of the Romans stg. **22.00**

On his coins as Caesar, Galerius is often called *Maximianvs Nob Caes*, not Galerius.

__, as Emperor 305-311. AE Follis. Genius of Imperator stg................ **30.00**

Galeria Valeria, wife of Galerius. AE Follis. Venus holding apple............. **40.00**

Severus II, 306-307. AE Antoninianus. Severus and Jupiter stg.................. **45.00**

Maximinus II, 309-313. AE Follis. Jupiter stg., eagle at feet............................ **18.00**

Maxentius, 306-312. AE Follis. Faith with two standards................................. **35.00**

__.__. Wolf suckling twins. **90.00**

Alexander, 308-311 in Carthage. AE Follis. Carthage stg................... **1,700.00**

Licinius I, 308-324. AE3. Jupiter stg. **12.00**

Licinius II, caesar 317-324. AE3. Jupiter stg. **10.00**

Martinian, 324. AE3. Jupiter with eagle and captive at feet. **1,600.00**

House of Constantine 307-363

Constantine I the Great, 307-337. AE3. Victory running r. over captive, *Sarmatia Devicta* around............................. **22.00**

__. AE3. VOT XX in wreath........... **12.00**

AE3/4. Helmeted bust of Roma / Wolf suckling twins................................. **9.00**

AE3/4. Helmeted bust of Constantinople / Winged Victory on prow **9.00**

Above two struck from 330 to 346.

Fausta, wife of Constantine I. AE3. Salus holding two children in arms, *Salus Reipublicae* around **20.00**

Helena, mother of Constantine I. AE3. Helena depicted as Security stg. **20.00**

Crispus, caesar 317-326. AE3. Wreath **12.00**

__. Silver AE3. Jupiter stg. A counterfeit, but one which could not fool a collector. It is a silver cast of a bronze coin.

Delmatius, caesar 335-337. AE3/4. Two soldiers with standard. **30.00**

Hanniballianus, rex 335-337. AE4. River Euphrates reclining. **125.00**

Constantine II, as Caesar 317-337. AE3 Two soldiers standing with standards between **10.00**

AE3. Camp gate **12.00**

Constans, 337-350. AE Centennionalis. Emperor in galley steered by Victory. **16.00**

Constantius II, 337-361. AE Centenionalis. Soldier spearing fallen horseman **15.00**

__.__. Roman soldier dragging barbarian child from hut **18.00**

Magnentius, 350-353. AE Double Centenionalis. Christogram **75.00**

Decentius, Caesar 351-353. AE Centenionalis. Two victories holding shield... **25.00**

Vetranio, 350. AE Centenionalis. Vetranio stg. **150.00**

Nepotian, 350. AE Centenionalis. Roma std. l **1,300.00**

Constantius Gallus, Caesar 351-354. AE Centenionalis. Bareheaded bust / Soldier spearing fallen horseman **20.00**

Julian II the Apostate, 360-363. AE1. Bull. **80.00**

__. AE 3. Wreath. **35.00**

Jovian, 363-364. AE3. Wreath.......... **50.00**

Valentinian I, 364-375. AV Solidus. Emperor stg. **550.00**

__. AE3. Emperor dragging captive **18.00**

Valens, 364-378. AE3. Victory **18.00**

Procopius, 365-366. AE3. Emperor stg. **150.00**

Gratian, 367-383. AE3. Victory walking l. **18.00**

Valentinian II, 375-392. AR Siliqua. Roma std. l. **125.00**

__. AE4. VOT XX MVLT XXX in wreath. Not all die engravers were literate. The illustrated example shows the the emperor's name misspelled. **20.00**

Theodosius I, 379-395. AR Siliqua. Roma std. **200.00**

__. AE 2. Theodosius stg. raising kneeling female **30.00**

Aelia Flaccilla, wife of Theodosius I. AE4. Victory std. **25.00**

Magnus Maximus, 383-388. AE4. Camp gate **55.00**

Flavius Victor, 387-388. AR Siliqua. Roma std. **500.00**

Eugenius, 392-394. AR Siliqua. Roma std. **600.00**

Arcadius, 383-408. AE4. Victory with trophy and captive.......................... **15.00**

Eudoxia, wife of Arcadius. AE3. Eudoxia enthroned...................................... **25.00**

Honorius, 393-423. AV Solidus. Emperor, foot on captive............................. **550.00**

__. AE3. Honorius crowned by Victory. **18.00**

Theodosius II, 402-450. AV Solidus. Victory stg. holding large cross **550.00**

__. AE4. Cross in wreath. **20.00**

Eudocia, wife of Theodosius II. AE4. Eudocia enthroned. **75.00**

Pulcheria, sister of Theodosius II. AE4. Victory std. **90.00**

Constantine III, 407-411. AR Siliqua. Roma std...................................... **600.00**

Constans (II), 408-411. AR Siliqua. Roma std. **4,000.00**

Maximus, 409-411. AR Siliqua. Roma std. **4,000.00**

Priscus Attalus, 409-415. AE3. Victory .... *Rare*

Jovinus, 411-413. AR Siliqua. Roma std. **950.00**

Sebastianus, 412-413. AR Siliqua. Roma std. **6,000.00**

Constantius III, 421. AV Tremissis. Victory with wreath and globe. **5,000.00**

Galla Placidia, mother of Valentinian III. AV Tremissis. Cross in wreath. .. **2,200.00**

Johannes, 423-425. AE4. Victory with trophy and captive........................ **225.00**

Valentinian III, 425-455. AV Solidus. Emperor stg. holding cross and Victory **550.00**

__. AE4. Camp gate......................... **60.00**

Marcian, 450-457. AE4. Monogram **50.00**

Petronius Maximus, 455. AV Solidus. Emperor stg. holding cross and Victory .... *Rare*

Avitus, 455-456. AV Tremissis. Cross in wreath. **4,000.00**

Leo I, 457-474. AV Tremissis. Victory. **600.00**
__. AE4. Monogram. **50.00**
Verina, wife of Leo I. AE2. Victory std. **350.00**
Leo II, 473-474. AV Tremissis. Victory. **850.00**
Majorian, 457-461. AV Solidus. Emperor stg. with cross and Victory **3,600.00**
__. AE4. Victory **310.00**
Severus III, 461-465. AE4. Victory **285.00**
Anthemius, 467-472. AE4. Monogram **335.00**
Olybrius, 472. AV Tremissis. Cross in wreath. **7,500.00**
Glycerius, 473-434. AR Siliqua. Victory walking l. **4,200.00**
Julius Nepos, 474-480. AE4. Monogram **425.00**
Romulus Augustus, 475-476. AV Tremissis. Cross in wreath **4,200.00**

Zeno, 474-491. AV Tremissis. Winged Victory. **300.00**
__. AE4. Monogram **60.00**

GREEK IMPERIALS

In most of the Mediterranean, Greek coinage was replaced with a unique type of coinage, blending Greek, local non-Greek and Roman traditions. Numismatists usually call these coins "Greek Imperial." Greek was the international language of business in the eastern Mediterranean, even in Roman times. These Greek Imperial coins usually bore the portrait of the Roman Emperor or a member of his family, but instead of Latin their titles were usually translated into Greek. Also, the denominations of these coins didn't match the values of regular Roman coins, but were intended to match the values of old Greek-style coins that had been in use for centuries. Lastly, the images on the reverses were not always the favorite Roman deities, but

often local ones, such as river gods. Local industries were also reflected on the coins, such as grapes in wine-producing areas like Thrace and Moesia (Bulgaria), or horses in Asia Minor. Some of the most desirable Greek Imperials depict local temples and shrines, thus preserving a tangible record of numerous buildings that have since fallen into ruin.

Greek Imperial coins provide an exciting avenue for collectors who wish to follow uncharted paths. While the literature on them is extensive, new types of coins may still be discovered by the average hobbyist. On the other hand, those who are particularly concerned about surface quality may find the series disappointing. The majority of Greek Imperial coins are found with slightly to very porous surfaces.

BOOKS ABOUT GREEK IMPERIAL COINS

Burnett, Amandry, and Ripoles, *Roman Provincial Coinage, vol. I, 44 B.C. - A.D. 69; vol.II, 69-96 - A.D.; VII, Asia 238-244 A.D.*

Butcher, Kevin, *Roman Provincial Coins: An Introduction to the Greek Imperials.* A coherent introduction.

Curtis, James, *The Tetradrachms of Roman Egypt.*

Sayles, Wayne, *Ancient Coin Collecting: Roman Provincial Coins.*

Sear, *Greek Imperial Coins and their Values.*

Note: All coins have bust of emperor on obverse unless noted otherwise. For issues of the Roman Procurators of Judea, see Judea in the Greek section.

Province of Syria, 61-35B.C. AR Tetradrachm. Bust of Philip Philadelphos r. / Zeus std. l holding victory and scepter, four line inscription, Greek numbers 3 to 29 below throne, all in wreath **200.00**
Augustus, 27 B.C - A.D. 14. Antioch, Syria. AR Tetradrachm. Tyche std. r., river-god swimming at feet **250.00**
Caligula, 37-41. Caesaraugusta, Spain. AE As. Priest plowing r. with yoke of oxen.. **175.00**
Nero, 54-68. Caesarea, Cappadocia. AR Didrachm. Bust of Agrippina, Jr. r. **500.00**
Domitian, 81-96. Ascalon, Judaea. AE19. War-god Phenebal **65.00**
Trajan, 98-117. Caesarea, Cappadocia. AE17. Winged caduceus. **25.00**
Hadrian, 117-138. Side, Pamphylia. AE20. CIΔHTωN, Athena l. **35.00**

__. Gaza, Palestine. AE26. Io and Tyche. **85.00**
__. Alexandria, Egypt. Billon Tetradrachm. Serapis std. with Cerberus before. **75.00**
Marcus Aurelius, 161-180. Alexandria, Egypt. Billon Tetradrachm. Tyche std. **40.00**
Septimius Severus, 193-211. Heliopolis, Syria. AE27. Temple of Jupiter Heliopolitanus. This coin shows anearly attempt at perspective **125.00**
Elagabalus, 218-222. Nicaea, Bithynia, Asia Minor. AE20. Three military standards. **20.00**
Severus Alexander, 222-235. Alexandria Troas, Asia Minor. AE22. Horse feeding r. **25.00**

Gordian III, 238-44. Marcianopolis, Moesia Inferior. AE28. Confronted heads of Gordian and Sarapis / Sarapis stg. with *modius* on head **75.00**
Philip I, 244-49. Viminacium, Moesia Inferior. Female between bull and lion. **25.00**

__. Antioch, Syria. AR Tetradrachm. Eagle **120.00**
Gallienus, 253-268. Side, Pamphylia. AE30. Bust over eagle / Apollo stg. **60.00**

Maximianus, 286-305. Alexandria, Egypt. Victory **25.00**

EUROPEAN COINS

Modern coinage as we know it began in Europe during the 1500s and spread throughout the world with the establishment of European colonies, or with the opening of European trade relations. Since that time, the manufacture of coinage has progressed from hand hammering, to screw press and roller dies, to steam-powered presses. Today's high-tech, electronic minting machines, capable of striking thousands of coins per minute, are basically an improved version of the steam-powered ones first used in the late 1700s.

Many people collect European and other world coins by "type." This means one of each design, or of each design in each different alloy in which it is struck. Others collect one of each date and mintmark, much as United States coins are collected. There is no right or wrong way to collect coins. The most important thing to remember is to enjoy the experience, and perhaps to learn by the process. There is no series more extensively documented in catalogs than the coinage of modern Europe, so whatever path the collector chooses, one need not do it in the dark. With the introduction of the euro in 2002, people are becoming more aware of the changes in European coinage, past, present and future.

Because many colonial coins feature the name and symbolism of the colonizing power more prominently than any reference to the colony itself, such coins are included in this chapter. This should make it easier for the layman to find the type of coin in question.

BOOKS ABOUT EUROPEAN COINS

While there are thousands of specialized books, a few basic titles will go a long way. Many collectors never feel the need to progress much further than the following volumes:

Bruce II, Colin R., Unusual World Coins. Special listings of fantasies and non-circulating coins.

Krause, Chester, and Mishler, Clifford, Standard Catalog of World Coins, 1601-1700.

Krause, Chester, and Mishler, Clifford, Standard Catalog of World Coins, 1701-1800.

Krause, Chester, and Mishler, Clifford, Standard Catalog of World Coins, 1801-1900.

Krause, Chester, and Mishler, Clifford, Standard Catalog of World Coins, 1901-2000.

Bruce II, Colin R., ed., Standard Catalog of World Coins, 2001-Date.

The above books are virtually an entire library in compact form. Coverage is extensive from the 1600s through the mid-1700s, and is near complete with individual date and mint listings from that time to the present.

Yeoman, R.S., Current Coins of the World.

Yeoman, R.S., *Modern World Coins, 1850-1964.*

ILLUSTRATIONS in this section represent types of coins, not specific dates, and are actual size unless noted.

COUNTERFEIT EUROPEAN COINS

While many individual counterfeits will be listed under each specific country, it is always important to remember that new counterfeits of the more expensive European coins appear every year. This also applies to many more common gold-bullion issues.

As a general rule, Crown- and Thaler-size coins are more prone to be counterfeited for the collector market. During the 19th and 20th centuries, tin or lead-alloy circulation counterfeits of silver coins were likely to be of those coins 20 to 28mm diameter. Recently, more circulation counterfeits of high-denomination, base-metal coins have been reported.

AUSTRIA

The modern coinage of Austria, until 1918, was used in a much larger area than present-day Austria. It circulated in the many lands of the Hapsburg Dynasty, and of their dependent nobles. While modern coin production with the use of roller dies began before his reign, the later coinage of Leopold I the Hogmouth (1657-1705), took it to a new height of uniformity. The excellent portraits are a perfect example of the Baroque style. Collectors should remember that coins struck with roller dies usually appear slightly curved and that this is not a flaw.

The standard design formula is an obverse portrait and a double-headed eagle reverse. It continued through the 1890s, when a crown and values became the commonest designs. A few commemoratives were also struck during this time. Austria is one of three modern countries to have used the double-headed eagle. They are easily distinguished. A Hapsburg shield is on its breast (see illustration). Russia's eagle has St. George slaying a dragon on its breast. Serbia's (later Yugoslavia's) eagle has a shield depicting a cross with C's in the angles. The later Yugoslav shield may be more complex but still contains this element.

After World War I, Austria became a republic and was reduced to its present size. It's circulating coins and commemoratives both depict aspects of local history and culture, such as a Royal Lipizzaner stallion or fauna such as the edelweiss. During World War II, Austria was part of Germany, and Nazi coins with the mintmark "B" were struck in Vienna.

In January 2002, Austria replaced the schilling with coins denominated in euros, the currency of the European Union. On the circulating denominations – one cent through two euros – there is one side that carries an Austrian design, the other a common European design. On higher-denomination commemoratives, both sides are distinctively Austrian.

During most of Austria's history, powerful nobles and bishops were allowed to strike their own coins. The Counts of Tyrol were the most prolific issuers of coins. Their three kreuzers are particularly common. The Archbishops of Salzburg also struck vast numbers of coins at several mints from 996 through 1806.

Additional Specialized Books:

Aicholz, Miller Zu, *Oesterreichische Munzpragungen, 1519-1938.*

Probszt, G., *Die Münzen Salzburgs.*

Known Counterfeits: All 1780 Maria Theresa thalers with mintmarks SF are modern re-strikes. The same is true for most 1915 gold four ducat, one ducat, 20 corona and 100 corona, and 1892 eight florin and four florin.

VF

Leopold I the Hogmouth, 1657-1705. 2 pfennig (S). Three shields / blank
.... **16.00**

VF

__. 3 Kreuzer. Bust r. / Austria and Tyrol shields **35.00**
__. 15 Kreuzer. Bust / Two headed eagle
.... **55.00**
__. Thaler. Similar **275.00**
__. Double Thaler. Bust r. / One headed eagle (for Tyrol)........................... **500.00**

Eighteenth Century

F

1746 1/4 Kreuzer. Crowned Eagle / Blank
.... **22.00**
1761 Kreuzer. Bust of Maria Theresa r. / Cartouche (C) **9.00**
1800 Kreuzer Bust of Francis II r. / Eagle (C)...**3.50**
1714 3 Kreuzer. Bust of Charles VI r. / Eagle (S).. **24.00**
1765 3 Kreuzer. Bust of Maria Theresa (Billon)... **25.00**
1754 10 Kreuzer. Bust of Francis I in wreath / Eagle, 10 on altar (S)........ **27.50**
1795 12 Kreuzer. Eagle / Inscription (Billon)..**9.00**

F

1778 20 Kreuzer. Bust of Joseph II in Wreath / Eagle (S) **8.00**
1800 24 Kreuzer. Eagle / Inscription (Billon).. **25.00**
1746 30 Kreuzer. Bust in diamond / Eagle in diamond (S) **45.00**
1751 ½ Thaler. Bust of Francis I r. / Eagle (S)... **70.00**

F

1780 SF Thaler *restrike*. Bust of Maria Theresa / Eagle. *Unc.* **20.00**
1798 Thaler. Bust of Francis II r. / Arms. (S) **85.00**
1773 Ducat. Bust of Maria Theresa r. / Eagle (G)..................................... **275.00**
1773 3 Ducat. Bust of Joseph II r. / Eagle (G) **1,500.00**

Nineteenth Century to 1920

VF

1851 1/4 Kreuzer Crowned Eagle / Value (C)...**1.50**
1816 Kreuzer. Crowned shield / Inscription (C)................................**2.25**
1885 Kreuzer. Crowned Eagle / Wreath (C)..**.50**
1860 4 Kreuzer. Eagle / Wreath (C)
.... **6.50**
1812 20 Kreuzer. Bust of Francis I in wreath / Eagle (S) **13.00**
1870 20 Kreuzer. Bust of Franz Josef / Eagle (Billon) **2.00**
1841 ½ Thaler. Bust of Ferdinand I / Eagle (S)..................................... **100.00**

VF

1886 Florin. Bust of Franz Josef / Eagle (S) **12.00**

F

1857 2 Thaler. Bust of Franz Josef / Tower between train and ship.... **1,200.00**
1893 1 Heller. Eagle (C) **35**
1908 2 Heller. Eagle (C) ....**.25**

VF

1893 10 Heller. Eagle (N).....................**.50**
1893 1 Corona. Head of Franz Josef / Crown (S)..**3.50**
1900 5 Corona. Head of Franz Josef / Double-headed eagle (S) **20.00**

VF

1868 Ducat. Head of Franz Josef / Eagle (G) **150.00**
1915 (restrike) Ducat. Same.......... **120.00**

Republic Coinage 1923 to 1938

XF

1924 100 Kronen. Eagle head / Oak sprig (C)... **1.50**

XF

1925 Schilling. Neo-classical building / Shield (S)....................................... **4.00**
1928 2 Schilling. Schubert / Ten shields (S) **12.00**
1935 5 Schilling. Madonna and Child / Eagle (S)..................................... **33.00**
1926 25 Schilling. Eagle (G).......... **225.00**

Republic Coinage 1946 to date

BU

1972 2 Groschen. Eagle (AL)...............**.20**

BU

1947 Schilling. Sower (AL) **7.00**
1957 10 Schilling. Shield / Girl's head (S)
.... **8.00**
1974 10 Schilling. Eagle / Girl's head (CN)... **2.00**
1996 20 Schilling. Anton Bruckner (ALB)
.... **4.50**
1956 25 Schilling. Mozart (S)............. **9.50**
2001 100 Schilling. Airplane, Train, Car, Truck / Engine (S around Titanium)
.... **PF 45.00**
1982 500 Schilling. Printing press (S)
.... **55.00**

Euro Coinage 2002 to date

BU

2002 1 Cent. Flower / Globe. (C plated Steel) ....**.35**
2002 5 Euro. Building and animals / Circle of shield, in card (S) **15.00**

BALKANS

The Ottoman conquest of the Balkan Peninsula ended European-style coinage for most of the region, and it was not restored until the 1800s. The only surviving coinages were those of Transylvania, and the small Venetian and Ragusan settlements along the Adriatic coast. The former were all copper, the latter a variety of metals.

The first country to regain its independence from the Ottoman Turks was Greece. Its first coinage was quite distinctive, and portrayed the mythological Phoenix reborn from its ashes, alluding to the rebirth of the Greek nation. Soon its coinage took on the less-creative forms popular elsewhere in Europe: shields, royal portraits and a denomination within a wreath. The coinages of the two Greek republics, 1925-1935 and 1974 to date, are also distinctive in harking back to ancient times for their inspiration.

Soon, Serbia (1868), Romania (1867), Bulgaria (1881), and Montenegro (1906) struck their first modern coins, on much the same European pattern as mentioned earlier. Albania lagged behind until 1926. After the First World War, Montenegro and the former Austrian territories of Slovenia, Croatia and Bosnia-Herzegovina were joined under the king of Serbia to form Yugoslavia. Following World War II, these kingdoms were overthrown by Communists. Most communist coins follow the typical pattern of a state seal on the obverse and a value or a symbol of agricultural or industrial labor on the reverse. As a result of the Yugoslav civil war, Slovenia, Croatia, Macedonia and Bosnia-Herzegovina were established as independent states. With the later withdrawal of Montenegro and Kosovo, the remaining region reverted to the name Serbia. Moldova came into being as a result of the breakup of the Soviet Union.

Bermanian coins (created by this writer) are typical fantasies. Fantasy coins are different from medals in that they bear denominations even though there is no ability to actually spend them. They are struck by those who claim (but do not have) political authority over real or fictional countries. In this case the entire country is fictional, being the focus of a series of stories created for the enjoyment of the author's friends.

Post-Communist Balkan coinage varies form monotonous bank monograms to exquisite depictions of flora and fauna. Some of these new governments have even chosen to use the same heraldic motifs that were found on their coins during the 1930s. All these countries have struck collector coins. Some, such as Bosnia's, have been actively marketed in North America. Others, such as Romania's, have been scantily distributed.

Because the alphabets and languages used may seem unusual to North American readers, it is useful here to give some Balkan country names in their native forms:

Albania .... **SHQIPNI or SHQIPERI**
Bulgaria ....**БЪЛГАРИЯ**
Croatia ....**HRVATSKA**
Greece.................................... **ΕΛΛΑΣ**
Macedonia.....................**МАКΕΔΟΗЗΙΑ**
Montenegro ....**цРНА г ОРА**
Serbia.................**СРБИЈА or СРПИЈА**
Yugoslavia ....**ЈУГОСΛΑΒИЈΑ**

Additional Specialized Books: See general European listings.

Known Counterfeits: Albanian gold and dollar-sized silver coins of the 1920s and 1930s, particularly the 1938 gold. Modern-style counterfeits exist of the 1600s Venetian coppers for Dalmatia and Albania.

ALBANIA

XF

1935 Qindar Ar. Eagle (C) **12.00**
1926 ½ Lek. Two headed eagle / Man fighting lion (N) **18.00**
1935 Frang Ar. Head of King Zog / Arms **25.00**
1926 100 Franga Ar. Head of Amet Zogu / Chariot (G) **1,200.00**
1941 0.20 Lek. King of Italy in helmet / Eagle between fasces (Steel) **4.00**
1939 10 Lek. King of Italy / Similar (S) **135.00**
1947 ½ Lek. Eagle (Z) **1.50**

XF

1964 1 Lek. Eagle (AL)...................... **2.00**

BU

1988 5 Lek. Train / Train. (CN) **12.00**
1996 50 Lek. Ancient horseman (CN) **2.00**

BERMANIA

BU

1998 5 Denari Plumbi. Arms / Bear and Wolf dancing. (CNZ)..................... **15.00**

BOSNIA-HERZEGOVINA

BU

1994 500 Dinara. Arms over bridge / Wolf (CN)....................................... **9.00**
1998 10 fennig. Triangle / Map (C plated Steel) .... **.1.00**

BU

2000 2 Convertible Marks. Dove (CN in NB, bimetallic)................................ **13.50**

BULGARIA

VF

1912 2 Stotinki. Arms / Wreath. (C) **1.00**
1881 5 Stotinki. Similar. (C) **5.00**
1883 50 Stotinki. Similar. (S) **4.00**
1925 1 Lev. Similar (CN) .... **.60**
1882 2 Leva. Similar (S).................. **12.00**
1943 5 Leva. Medieval horseman r. / Wreath **1.00**

VF

1930 10 Leva. Similar. (CN).............. **1.50**
1894 20 Leva. Head of Ferdinand I l. / Arms (G)..................................... **225.00**
1934 100 Leva. Head of Boris III / Art Deco wreath (S) **7.00**

Postwar Issues   **BU**
1951 1 Stotinka. Arms / Grain (ALB) ..**.25**
1977 50 Stotinki. Runner / Arms (CN)
.... **2.00**
1976 1 Lev. Gun and knife / Lion (C)
.... **3.00**

         BU
1979 10 Leva. Children (S)......... **PF 22.50**
1992 10 Leva. Madara horseman (CN)
.... **2.50**
1996 1000 Leva. Sailing ship / Weath (S)
....*Proof only* **40.00**

CROATIA

         VF
Ragusa, 1626-1761. Grosetto. Christ
  standing amid stars / St. Blasius stg.
  (AR)... **30.00**
         UNC
1941 2 Kune. Shield. (Z) **40.00**
1993 1 Lipa. Corn. (AL)......................**.25**
1995 2 Kune. Tuna. (CN)................... **1.75**
1994 5 Kune. Bear. (CN)................... **3.00**
1998 25 Kune. Sailboat. (Brass in CN
  bimetallic) **10.00**

         UNC
1994 100 Kune. St.Blaza Church (S)
.... **PF 75.00**

GREECE

         F
Venetian Morea. 1688-90s Gazetta. Bust
  of winged lion, II below / ARMATA ET
  MOREA (C)................................... **45.00**
1828 1 Lepton. Phoenix / Wreath (C)
.... **150.00**
1851 2 Lepta. Crowned shield / Wreath
  (C)... **35.00**

         F
1828 5 Lepta. Phoenix / Wreath (C)
.... **150.00**
1869 5 Lepta. Head of George / Wreath
  (C)...**5.00**
1895 10 Lepta. Crown / Wreath (CN)
....**2.00**
1831 20 Lepta. Phoenix / Wreath (C)
.... **100.00**
1833 Drachma. Head of Otto / Arms (S)
.... **150.00**
1875 5 Drachmai. Head of George /
  Arms (S)...................................... **30.00**
         VF
1884 20 Drachmai. Similar. (G)..... **225.00**
1922 10 Lepta. Crown / Branch (AL)
....**2.00**
1926 50 Lepta. Head. of Athena (CN)
....**1.00**

         VF
1911 2 Drachmai. Head of George /
  Thetis std. on hippocamp (S) **30.00**
         BU
1954 5 Lepta. Crowned wreath / Wheat
  (AL, holed) **2.00**
1971 50 Lepta. Head. of Constantine II /
  Phoenix and soldier.......................... **2.00**
1988 1 Drachma. Bouboulina / Ship. (C)
....**.50**
1973 20 Drachmai. Phoenix / Bust of
  Athena. (CN) **2.00**
1964 30 Drachmai. Busts of King and
  Queen / Double headed eagle (S)
.... **13.00**

         BU
1994 50 Drachmes. Kallergis / Parliament
  (ALB).. **4.00**
1998 100 Drachmes. Basketball players
  (ALB).. **4.00**
1991 500 Drachmes. Cartoon fish / Flags
  (S) ....*Proof only* **60.00**
2000 500 Drachmes. Woman handing
  torch to athlete / Olympic symbols (CN)
....**5.00**
2002 10 Euro Cent. Bust of Feriaou /
  Map (B)... **1.25**

         BU
2002 1 Euro. Owl on Athenian coin /
  Map. (CN clad N in NB, bimetallic)
....**4.00**

         BU
2004 2 Euro. Discus thrower / Map. (CN
  clad N around NB, bimetallic).........**8.00**

MACEDONIA

         BU
1993 50 Deni. Sea gull (Brass) ....**.65**

         BU
1993 1 Denar. Dog. (Brass)..................**.85**
2000 1 Denar. Elaborate cross / Byzantine
  coin (Brass) **8.75**
1995 2 Denari. Fish / FAO symbol.
  (Brass)... **1.00**

MOLDOVA

         BU
1993 25 Bani. Arms / Wreath (AL).......**.50**
1993 5 Lei. Arms. (CN) **3.50**

MONTENEGRO

         VF
1906 2 Pare. Eagle. (C).......................**8.00**
1908 20 Pare. Eagle. (N)....................**7.50**
1912 1 Perper. Head of Nicholas / Arms
  (S) **15.00**
1910 2 Perpera. Similar (S) **35.00**
1910 10 Perpera. Similar (G) **250.00**

ROMANIA

         VF
1900 1 Ban. Head of Carol I / Arms (C)
....**3.00**

VF

1867 5 Bani. Arms / Wreath (C).........**7.00**
1900 10 Bani. Crown in wreath (CN)
....**2.50**
1921 25 Bani. Eagle (AL)..................**1.00**
1939 1 Leu. Crown / Corn (Brass) ....**.50**
1924 2 Lei. Arms (CN) **1.75**
1880 5 Lei. Head of Carol I / Arms (S)
.... **36.00**
1930 10 Lei. Head of Carol II / Eagle
(Brass)......................................**3.00**
1942 20 Lei. Crown / Wreath (Z) **1.50**
1935 250 Lei. Head of Carol II / Arms on
eagle (S)......................................**16.00**
1946 2000 Lei. Head of Michael / Arms
(Brass)......................................**1.50**
1946 100,00 Lei. Head of Michael /
Woman releasing dove (S) **20.00**

Unc.

1952 1 Ban. Arms (Brass) **3.00**
1963 5 Bani. Arms (N clad Steel).......**2.00**

Unc.

1966 3 Lei. Arms / Factory (N clad Steel)
....**3.50**
1994 1 Leu. Arms (C clad Steel) **1.00**
1996 10 Lei. Arms / Sailboat (N clad
Steel)......................................**9.50**
1993 20 Lei. Bust of King Stefan (Brass
clad Steel)......................................**2.75**
1999 500 Lei. Solar Eclipse (AL) **4.00**
2003 5,000 Lei. Arms (AL) ....**.60**

SERBIA

VF

1868 1 Para. Head of Obrenovich III /
Wreath (C) **13.00**
1884 10 Pare. Eagle (CN).................**2.00**
1915 50 Para. Head of Petar I / Wreath
(S) **3.00**
1897 2 Dinara. Head of Alexander I /
Wreath (S)....................................**18.00**
1879 5 Dinara. Head of Milan I l. /
Wreath (S)....................................**70.00**
1882 10 Dinara. Head of Milan I r. /
Wreath (G)..................................**165.00**
1943 10 Dinara. Eagle / Wreath (Z) ...**2.50**

VF

2006 1 Dinar. Royal arms / Bank building
(CNZ) .... *Unc.* **1.00**

SLOVENIA

BU

1992 10 Stotinov. Salamander (AL)......**.25**
1996 50 Stotinov. Bee. (AL) ....**.35**
1996 5 Tolarjev Locomotive (Brass)... **1.75**

BU

2000 10 Tolarjev Horse (CN) **3.75**
1994 500 Tolarjev. Quill pen. (S)
.... *Proof only* **30.00**
1993 5000 Tolarjev. Bees around hive. (G)
.... *Proof only* **300.00**

YUGOSLAVIA

VF

1925 50 Para. Head of Alexander I /
Wreath (CN) **1.00**
1925 1 Dinar. Head of Alexander I /
Wreath (CN) **2.00**
1938 2 Dinara. Crown (ALB) **1.00**
1932 50 Dinara. Head of Alexander I /
Eagle. (S)......................................**25.00**
1945 Dinar. Arms. (Z).......................**1.00**

BU

1953 50 Para. Arms (AL).....................**.25**
1981 10 Dinar . Arms (B) ....**.25**
1983 500 Dinara. Olympic symbols /
Skier (S) .... *Proof only* **20.00**
1990 1 Dinara. Arms. (CNZ)...............**.25**

BU

1992 1 Dinar. Bank monogram (Brass)
....**.60**

BU

1980 1,000 Dinar. Tito / Map (S)..... **25.00**
1996 1 New Dinar. Eagle shield (Brass)
....**1.25**
1996 20 New Dinar. Eagle shield / Bust
of Nikola Tesla (CNZ)
.... *Proof only* **16.00**

BALTIC STATES

The regions that are today Estonia, Latvia, Lithuania and Finland were, until 1918, submerged under the domination of Russia, Poland, Germany and Sweden in various combinations. Usually, these greater powers would permit certain cities such as Riga, or certain nobles, to strike their own coins. These were somewhat common in the 1600s, but by the 1700s they ceased to be significant. During the 1800s virtually none of these states were permitted their own coinage besides Finland, which was a semi-autonomous Grand Duchy under Russia.

The collapse of the great European Empires during World War I liberated these countries from Russia, the most recent power to dominate the area. The coats of arms of these newly independent states were used on one side or the other of virtually every coin struck between the World Wars. While in most cases the other side was a monotonous indication of value, certain other pieces were exceptionally attractive. Most notable are beautiful renditions of the personification of Latvia. Lithuania also struck interesting commemoratives.

With the exception of Finland, all these countries were conquered by the Soviet Union in 1940. They reemerged with the breakup of the Soviet empire in 1989. It is almost shocking how closely some of the new post-Soviet Baltic coins resemble the coins struck by these countries in the 1930s. The exception is Finland, whose coinage had the opportunity to evolve naturally during its longer independence. Since 1951, its modernistic commemoratives have been released in quantity to the world collector market.

In January 2002, Finland replaced the Markka with coins denominated in euros, the currency of the European Union. Some coins were struck years in advance, and held until 2002. On the circulating denominations, one cent through two euros, there is one side that carries a Finnish design, the other a common European design. On higher-denomination commemoratives, both sides are distinctively Finnish.

Additional Specialized Books: See general European listings.

Known Counterfeits:

Known Finnish counterfeits include the 1951 500 Markka and possibly the 1918 Red Government five pennia.

ESTONIA

	F
Reval, 1663-67. 1 Rundstück. Crowned shield / MON NOV CIVITA REVAL (AR)	45.00
	VF
1922 3 Marka. Three lions (CN)	5.00
1926 5 Marka. Shield in wreath (CN)	160.00
1929 1 Sent. Three lions / Oak leaves (C)	1.50
1935 20 Senti. Shield (CN)	2.25
1934 1 Kroon. Shield in wreath / Viking ship (ALB)	7.50
1930 2 Krooni. Shield in wreath / Castle (S)	9.00
1932 2 Krooni. Shield in wreath / University building (S)	25.00
	BU
1991 5 Senti. Three lions (Brass)	.25
1993 5 Krooni. Doe (Brass)	3.50
1992 100 Krooni. Three lions / Three swallows (S)	*Proof only* 40.00

	BU
1998 100 Krooni. Man on eagle head (S)	*Proof only* 38.00

FINLAND

	VF
Under Russia	
1873 1 Penni. Crowned AII (C)	9.50
1913 1 Penni. Crowned NII (C)	.75
1889 5 Penniä. Crowned AIII (C)	7.00
1900 10 Penniä. Crowned NII (C)	9.00
1917 25 Penniä. Russian eagle (S)	1.00

	VF
1874 50 Penniä. Russian eagle (S)	15.00
1890 1 Markka. Similar (S)	12.00
1882 10 Markka. Similar. (G)	175.00

Republics	XF
1917 25 Penniä. Eagle without crown. *Civil War issue* (S)	1.00
1918 5 Pennia. Trumpets. (C)	50.00
1919 1 Penni. Lion. (C)	1.75

	BU
1943 10 Penniä. Branches / Roses (C)	3.00
1986 50 Penniä. Lion / Tree (ALB)	.50
1993 10 Markka. Capercaille bird / Branches (Brass in CN, *bimetallic*)	3.50
1956 100 Markka. Shield / Trees (S)	3.00
1990 100 Markka. Lyre / Owl (S)	40.00
1952 500 Markka. Olympic rings / Wreath (S)	40.00
1999 2 Cent. Lion / Globe. (C plated Steel)	2.00
2002 1 Euro. Two swans flying / Map. (CN clad N in NB, bimetallic)	4.00

	BU
2002 10 Euro. Globe / Coin (S)	38.00

LATVIA

	F
Riga, 1660-65. Schilling. CR monogram / SOLIDVS CIVI RIG, crossed keys (Billon)	30.00
Republic	**VF**
1935 1 Santims. Shield. (C)	1.50
1939 2 Santimi. Shield (C)	3.00
1922 5 Santimi. Shield (C)	1.50
1922 10 Santimu. Shield (N)	1.50
1922 50 Santimu. Shield / Latvia gazing from rudder of ship (N)	4.00
1924 1 Lats. Shield / Wreath (S)	5.50
1925 2 Lati. Similar. (S)	7.00
1931 5 Lati. Head of Latvia r. / Arms (S)	20.00
Restored Republic	**BU**
1992 2 Santimi. Shield (C plated Steel)	.50
1992 1 Lats. Arms / Fish (CN)	3.75

	BU
2001 1 Lats. Arms / Hockey Player (S)	*Proof only* 50.00
1992 2 Lati. Arms / Cow (CN)	7.00
1995 10 Latu. Arms / Schooner (S)	*Proof only* 50.00
1998 100 Latu. Arms / Logo (G)	*Proof only* 600.00

LITHUANIA

	F
John III Sobieski, 1674-1696. 1679, 6 Groszy. Bust r. / Knight riding. (S)	*Rare*
Augustus II, 1697-1704. 1706 6 Groszy. Crowned bust r. / Three shields (S)	165.00
Republic	**VF**
1936 1 Centas. Knight riding l. (C)	3.50
1936 2 Centai. Similar. (C)	6.00
1925 10 Centu. Knight riding l. / Ear of grain. (Brass)	5.00
1925 50 Centu. Similar. (Brass)	8.00
1925 1 Litas. Similar / Oak branch (S)	3.00
1925 2 Litu. Similar / Wreath (S)	6.00
1925 5 Litai. Similar. (S)	10.00
1936 5 Litai. Similar / Bust l. (S)	7.00

	VF
1936 10 Litai. Knight riding l. / Crowned bust (S)	18.00
1938 10 Litai. Stylized castle / Bust l. (S)	30.00
Restored Republic	**BU**
1991 5 Centai. Knight riding l. (AL)	.40
1997 50 Centai. Similar. (Brass)	.85
1997 1 Litas. Bust / Knight riding l. (CN)	2.00

BU

2002 5 Litai. Knight riding l. / Owl (S)
...................................*Proof only* **45.00**
1994 10 Litu. Two harps / Similar (CN)
...................................*Proof only* **12.00**
1996 50 Litu. Basketball players / Shield
(S) ....*Proof only* **35.00**

LIVONIA & ESTONIA

F

1757 2 Kopeks. Two Shields / Double
headed eagle (base S) **125.00**
1757 4 Kopeks. LIVO ESTHONICA,
Two Shields / Double headed eagle (S)
.... **50.00**

BRITISH ISLES

Despite successful experiments with milled (screw press) coinage during the reign of Elizabeth I (1558-1603), this means of striking uniform, well-made coins was not finally adopted in England until 1663, after the restoration of the monarchy. By this time there were a great many different denominations in silver, from the tiny silver penny, to the crown (60 pence), which had finally become common.

By the end of the 17th century, most of the silver denominations below six pence were being struck only for ceremonial distribution on Maundy Thursday, the week before Easter. These silver coins were given to the poor but usually passed into circulation. After the mid-1700s, their value as collectibles was so established that almost all were immediately sold by their recipients to collectors, and today survive in high grade.

Another change was the replacement of puny, privately made royal-contract farthings with officially struck regal farthings and halfpennies of good weight. For a while, the government replaced these coppers with ones of tin, but this was soon abandoned due to their tendency to corrode.

The designs on British coins have usually been conservative. The shield on a cross, used before the English Civil War, was continued after it. New designs were often heraldic as well, sometimes showing one shield, other times showing arrangements of the shields of England, Scotland, Ireland and France. (England claimed France until the early 1800s.) The new copper coins show a seated female, Britannia, an allegory for Britain dating back to Roman days.

During the 1700s, the government failed to provide enough coins to satisfy Britain's growing industrial economy.

The Industrial Revolution also provided the answer to this dilemma. Merchants and miners took matters into their own hands and contracted with modern factories to strike their own money. These tokens, common from the late 1780s and 1790s, as well as from 1811-15, depict a delightful array of scenes from Gothic cathedrals to the very machines of the Industrial Revolution.

Gradually the government responded. New steam-power-struck coppers were introduced in 1797-99, including the first penny to be struck in copper instead of silver. A massive issue of machine-struck silver and gold was released in 1816. Notable is the powerful Baroque-style depiction of St. George slaying the dragon by Benedetto Pistrucci, used on the crown and gold pieces.

During the reign of Queen Victoria (1837-1901), old designs were sometimes given a beautiful neo-Gothic interpretation. Another innovation on the practical side was the replacement of the copper coins with slightly smaller ones of bronze. These wore much better than pure copper.

The two World Wars took their toll on British coinage. The purity of the silver was lowered from 92.5 percent to 50 percent in 1920 after the First World War. It was replaced completely by cupronickel in 1947. From the Great Depression onward, gold ceased to circulate. The gold sovereigns struck from then until today were solely for bullion or collector purposes.

After 1,100 years of using a coinage derived from the penny of Charlemagne, and based on multiples of 12, Britain finally replaced the pound of 240 pence with one divided into 100-decimal new pence. The new seven-sided 50 pence introduced in 1969 proved so popular that since then many countries have used this shape for their coinage.

During the second half of the 20th century, collector commemoratives were issued quite frequently. From the 1970s onward, new creative designs were used for these coins. Many were sold at a premium and were never placed in circulation.

Scotland

Scottish coins followed most of the same trends closely. Where royal copper coins were needed, however, Britannia was not depicted. Instead a thistle, scepters were used. After 1707, Scotland and England were joined as the United Kingdom and separate Scottish coinage

was ended. From 1937 to 1970, however, special Scottish shillings were struck, good throughout the United Kingdom. The current five pence and several brass pound coins also honor Scotland.

Ireland

Irish coins continued longer but were usually limited to base metal. From The Restoration (1660) until 1823, Ireland was usually provided with distinctive halfpennies, farthings and, ultimately, pennies with a crowned harp as their reverse. The first machine-made ones were struck in 1805. There were two important exceptions: After James II was forced to flee England in 1688, he managed to hold onto Ireland for several months. To help finance his war to keep the throne, he struck high-value coins in brass containing metal from melted cannon. These sixpences, shillings, half crowns and crowns were dated to the exact month and are called "gun money." Another exception came in 1804-13 when the Bank of Ireland struck silver five-, 10- and 30-pence and six-shilling tokens to ease the coinage shortage.

Ireland's first independent coinage was introduced in 1928, and this first year is the most commonly encountered. The country name given on the coins was changed from SAORSTAT EIREANN (Irish Freestate) to EIRE (Ireland) in 1939 because Ireland changed from a dominion to a republic. It phased in decimal coins beginning 1969.

In January 2002, Ireland replaced the pound with coins denominated in euros, the currency of the European Union. On the circulating denominations, one cent through two euros, there is one side that carries an Irish harp, the other a common European design.

The Empire & Commonwealth

Colonial coins struck during the 1700s and early 1800s, less common than the later ones, were similar in style to British issues. Ones struck for the 13 Colonies in America are discussed under the United States. One big exception is the coinage of the East India Company. Many of these are hardly distinguishable from local Indian states and Mughal Empire coins. Usually they are identified by certain symbols or their machine-made fabric, but they were originally intended to circulate alongside local coins, and their designs made this possible.

During the mid 1800s, colonial coins became increasingly more practical in

their designs, and many have no motif other than a large number indicating the value. Beginning in the 1920s in most territories, somewhat earlier in a few others, local color and creativity entered into colonial coin design. Native plants and animals were depicted. Some larger values bore the coat of arms of the individual colony. Many of the designs were so pleasing that they continued in use for decades, even after independence. As in the homeland, silver was phased out after World War II.

Many independent former colonies still recognize the British monarch as Queen. These British Commonwealth members often voluntarily depict the monarch on the obverse of their coins, as they did before independence. Most are listed here for convenience, except Canada, which is covered in depth in its own section.

Additional Specialized Books:

Dalton and Hamer, *The Provincial Token-Coinage of the 18th Century.*

Jinks, David, ed., *British Coins Market Values.* Current updated values but minimal numismatic information.

Pridmore, F., *The Coins of the British Commonwealth of Nations.* 4 vols.

Spink & Son, *Coins of England and the United Kingdom.* The basic reference.

Known Counterfeits: Vast numbers of contemporary counterfeits of 1700s copper were made, both by striking and casting. Those made in America and those in middle grade are worth more than the real ones. Many brass counterfeits of 1811-1820 silver were made at the time and have some small numismatic value. Other circulation counterfeits include shilling 1916; florin 1900, 1918, 1942; half crown 1818; three shillings 1815; and guinea 1798.

A great many sovereigns have been counterfeited, often originating in Lebanon. Some known examples include: 1887, 1910, 1911, 1913, 1918M, 1923SA (altered date) and 1927SA. Some were even found in lots bought in the Middle East to issue to British troops during the First Gulf War. Despite their commonness, *all* sovereigns should be examined carefully.

Recently, base-metal counterfeits of British trade dollars have been seen in abundance.

Collector counterfeits have been made of many coins with rare dates spanning the last 150 years, including the 1905 half crown and 1847 Gothic crown.

ENGLAND

F

Charles II, 1660-85.
1672 Farthing. Bust l. / Britannia std.
(C)... **60.00**

F
1673 Halfpenny. Similar.................. **65.00**
1670 Threepence. Bust r. / Three interlocking C's (S)........................ **25.00**

F
1677 Sixpence. Bust r. / Cross of shields, C's in angles (S)............................ **75.00**
1680 Crown. same......................... **300.00**
1676. Half Guinea. Bust r. / Cross of shields, scepters in angles (G)....... **600.00**
James II, 1685-88.
1686 Halfpenny. Bust r. / Britannia std. (Tin)... **400.00**

F
1685 Shilling. Bust l. / Cross of shields (S) **225.00**
1686 Half Crown. Bust l. / Cross of shields (S)................................... **300.00**
1688 Guinea. Bust l. / Cross of shields, scepters in angles (G) **800.00**
William and Mary, 1688-94.
1690 Farthing. Two busts r. / Britannia std. l. (Tin) **300.00**
1694, Similar but copper.............. **125.00**
1689 Twopence. Two busts r. / Crowned 2 (S) **50.00**

F
1693 Shilling. Two busts r. / Cross of shields, monograms in angles (S).. **200.00**
1689 Half Crown. Two busts r. / Crowned shield (S) **200.00**
1691 5 Guineas. Two busts r. / Crowned shield (G) **3,000.00**
William III, 1694-1702.

F
1699 Halfpenny. Bust r. / Britannia std. l.
.... **60.00**
1696 Sixpence. Bust r. / Cross of shields (S) **50.00**
1697 Shilling. Similar (S) **60.00**

F
1698 Half crown. Bust r. / Cross of shields (S)................................... **110.00**
1695 Crown. Bust r. / Cross of shields. (S)
.... **200.00**

GREAT BRITAIN

F

Anne, 1702-1714.
1714 Farthing. Bust l. / Britannia std. (C)... **500.00**

F
1708 Shilling. Bust l. / Cross of shields (S) **60.00**
1708 Half Crown. Similar (S) **120.00**
1712 Guinea. Bust l. / Cross of shields, scepters in angles (G) **500.00**

George I, 1714-27.   **F**
1719 Farthing. Bust r. / Britannia std.
  (C) **45.00**
1720 Halfpenny. Similar. (C) **50.00**
1718 Shilling. Bust r. / Cross of shields,
  roses and plumes in angles (S) **75.00**

1723 SSC Shilling Bust r. / Cross of   **F**
  shields, SS C SS C in angles (S) **50.00**
1716 Crown. Similar. (S) **500.00**
1718 Quarter Guinea. Bust r. / Cross of
  shields, scepters in angles (G) **220.00**
George II, 1727-60.
1754 Farthing. Bust l. / Britannia std.
  (C) **10.00**

1739 Halfpenny. Similar. (C) .... **23.00**   **F**
1757 Sixpence. Bust l. / Cross of shields
  (S) **25.00**

1750 Shilling. Similar (S) .... **65.00**   **F**
1758 Shilling. Similar (S) **35.00**
1759 Guinea. Bust l. / "Rose" shield (G)
  .... **500.00**
George III, 1760-1820.   **F**
1773 Farthing. Bust r. / Britannia std.
  (C) **20.00**
1763 Three pence. Bust r. / Crowned 3 (S)
  .... **20.00**
1787 Sixpence. Bust r. / Cross of shields,
  crowns in angles (S) **30.00**

1792 Guinea. Bust r. / "Spade" shield (G)   **F**
  .... **325.00**

Machine Made Coinage

1799 Farthing. Bust r. / Britannia std.   **VF**
  (C) **12.00**
1806 Farthing (reduced size). Similar.
  (C) **9.00**
1797 Twopence. Similar but broad border
  (C, 2 ounces!) **200.00**
  *The above usually comes with heavy
  rim bruises. Value is for undamaged
  examples..*

1817 Shilling. Bust r. / Arms within garter   **VF**
  (S) **30.00**
1817 Half Crown. Similar. **100.00**
George IV, 1820-30.
1826 Halfpenny. Bust l. / Britannia std.
  (C) **15.00**
1826 Sixpence. Bust l. / Lion on crown.
  (S) **45.00**

1821 Shilling. Bust l. / Arms (S) .... **80.00**   **VF**
1826 Sovereign. Bust l. / Crowned shield
  (G) **200.00**

1826 2 Pounds. Bust l. / Crowned arms.   **VF**
  (G) .... *Rare*

William IV, 1830-37.   **VF**
1831 Farthing. Bust r. / Britannia std. (C)
  .... **15.00**

                                                VF
1831 Halfpenny. Similar (C) **9.00**
1836 Four Pence. Similar (S) **30.00**
1832 Sovereign. Bust r. / Crowned shield
  (G) **600.00**
Victoria, 1837-1901.
1844 Half Farthing. Young head / Crown
  (C) **6.00**
1858 Farthing. Young head l. / Britannia
  std. (C) **6.00**
1884 Farthing. Bust / Similar (C) **2.50**
1886 Halfpenny. Bust / Similar (C) **5.00**

                                                VF
1881 Penny. Bust with Bun / Similar (C)
  .... **20.00**
1890 Penny. Bust / Similar (C) **9.50**
1900 Penny. Veiled bust / Similar (C)
  .... **4.50**
1881 3 Pence. Young head / Crowned 3
  (S) **9.00**
1838 4 Pence. Young head / Britannia std.
  (S) **20.00**

                                                VF
1887 6 Pence. Crowned bust / Arms (S)
  .... **9.00**
1893 Shilling. Veiled bust / Three crowned
  shields (S) **15.00**
1853 Florin. Crowned "Gothic" bust /
  Cross of shields, flowers in angles (S)
  .... **80.00**
1874 Half Crown. Young head / Crowned
  shield (S) **80.00**
1887 Double Florin. Crowned bust /
  Cross of shields, scepters in angles (S)
  .... **30.00**

VF

1893 Crown. Veiled bust / St. George slaying dragon (S) **45.00**
1880 Half Sovereign. Young head / Crowned shield (G) **150.00**

VF

1887 Sovereign. Veiled bust / St. George slaying dragon (G) **275.00**
1893 5 Pounds. Similar (G) **1,500.00**
Edward VII, 1901-10.
1903 Farthing. Head r. / Britannia std. (C) **2.00**
1910 3 Pence. Head r. / Crowned 3 (S) **2.50**

VF

1910 6 Pence. Head r. / Crowned value (S) **4.00**
1902 Florin. Head r. / Britannia stg. (S) **40.00**
1902 Crown. Head r. / St. George slaying dragon (S) **125.00**
1910 Sovereign. Similar. (G) **275.00**
George V, 1910-36.
1917 Farthing. Head l. / Britannia std. (C) .... **.50**
1928 Halfpenny. Similar (C) .... **.75**
1935 Penny. Similar (C) .... **.50**
1929 Sixpence. Head l. / Six acorns (S) **2.00**

VF

1911 Shilling. Head l. / Lion on crown (S) **5.00**
1928 Florin. Head l. / Cross of shields, scepters in angles (S) **4.50**
1935 Half Crown. Head l. / Shield (S) **6.00**
1927 Crown. Head l. / Crown in wreath. (S) **175.00**
1935 Crown. Head l. / St. George, armored, slaying dragon. (S) **20.00**
1911 Half Sovereign. Similar but saint nude (G) **140.00**

VF

1932 Maundy set. 1, 2, 3, 4 Pence. Head l. / Crown over value. (S) .... *Unc*. **185.00**

George VI, 1936-52. **XF**
1940 Farthing. Head l. / Wren (C) .... **.30**
1942 Halfpenny. Head l. / Ship (C) .... **.60**
1944 Penny. Head l. / Britannia std. (C) .... **.35**
1937 3 Pence. Head l. / Thrift plant (Brass) **1.00**
1946 6 Pence. Head l. / Crowned GRI (S) **1.50**

XF

1943 Shilling. Head l. / Scottish crest (lion std. on crown) (S) **2.50**
1948 Half Crown. Head l. / Shield (CN) **1.00**

BU

1951 Crown. Head l. / St. George slaying dragon (CN) **20.00**
Elizabeth II, 1952—.
1954 Farthing. Young bust / Wren **2.00**

BU

1967 Penny. Young bust / Britannia std. (C) .... **.25**
1966 3 Pence. Young Bust / Portcullis (castle gate) (Brass) .... **.25**
1963 Shilling. Young Bust / Crowned shield (CN) .... **.75**
1967 Florin. Young bust / Rose within border. (CN) **1.50**
1965 Crown. Young bust / Bust of Churchill (CN) **1.00**

BU

1958 Sovereign. Young Bust / St. George slaying dragon (G) **275.00**
Decimal Coinage **BU**
1971 1 New Penny. Bust in tiara / Portcullis (C) ....**.25**
1970 10 Pence. Bust in crown / Crowned lion (CN)..**.50**
1990 20 Pence. Bust in crown / Crowned rose (CN, heptagonal) ....**.75**
1981 25 Pence. Bust in tiara / Heads of Charles and Diana (CN) **2.00**
1973 50 Pence. Bust in tiara / Wreath of hands (CN, heptagonal) **2.25**

BU

2000 50 Pence. Older head in tiara / Britannia std. with lion (CN, heptagonal) **3.00**
1995 Pound. Bust in tiara / Welsh dragon (Brass) **3.50**
1988 50 Pounds. Bust in tiara / Britannia stg. (G, ½ ounce)........................ **550.00**
British Tokens **VF**
1667 Farthing. Shield with castle and lion / NORWICH FARTHING (C) **75.00**

BU

1792 Halfpenny. Elephant with castle on back / Lady Godiva on horse (C)
.... **20.00**
1788 Penny. Hooded head of Druid / Monogram (C) **17.00**
1813 Penny. Birmingham Work House / Shield (C) **15.00**
c.1980s R&W London / I (Brass)..........**.10**

SCOTLAND

F

Charles II, 1649-1685. 1677 Bawbee. Bust l. / Crowned thistle (C) **90.00**
1669 Merk. Bust r. / Cross of shields, C's in angles (S)................................. **150.00**
James II, 1685-89. 1687 10 Shillings. Bust r., 10 below / Shields in angle of X
.... **225.00**
1687 40 Shillings. Bust r., 40 below / Crowned shield (S) **400.00**

William and Mary, 1689-94. 1691
Bawbee. Two busts l. / Crowned thistle
(C)... **95.00**
1693 20 Shillings. Two busts l., 20 below /
Crowned shield (S) **650.00**

F
1691 60 Shillings. Two busts l., 40 below /
Crowned shield (S) **900.00**
William III, 1694-1702. 1695 Turner.
Crowned sword and scepter / Thistle (C)
65.00
1697 5 Shillings. Bust l. / Three thistles
(S) **120.00**
1695 40 Shillings. Bust l. / Crowned shield
(S) **300.00**

F
Anne, 1702-14. 1705 5 Shillings. Bust l., 5
below / Three thistles (S) **90.00**
1705 10 Shillings. Bust l., 10 below /
Crowned shield (S) **220.00**

IRELAND

F
Charles II, 1660-1685. 1682 Halfpenny.
Bust r. / Crowned Harp (C)............ **70.00**
James II, 1685-91. 1686 Halfpenny. Bust
l. / Crowned Harp (C) **80.00**

F
1690 Halfcrown. Bust l. / XII over crown
(C)... **60.00**
William and Mary, 1688-94. 1693
Halfpenny. Two busts r. / Crowned Harp
(C)... **70.00**
William III, 1694-1702. 1696 Halfpenny.
Bust r. / Crowned Harp (C).......... **120.00**
George I, 1714-27. 1723 Farthing. Bust r.
/ Hibernia std. with harp (C).......... **40.00**

F
George II, 1727-60. 1760 Halfpenny. Bust
l. / Crowned Harp (C) **25.00**
George III, 1760-1820. 1806 Farthing.
Bust r. / Crowned Harp (C)............. **9.50**

F
1766 Halfpenny. Similar (C)............ **15.00**
1805 5 Pence Bank Token. Bust r. /
Inscription (S) **20.00**

F
George IV, 1820-30. 1822 Halfpenny.
Bust l. / Crowned Harp (C)............ **10.00**
Irish Free State **VF**
1928 Farthing. Harp / Woodcock (C)
.... **1.50**

VF
1937 Penny. Harp / Hen and chicks (C)
.... **1.00**
1928 6 Pence. Harp / Wolfhound (N). **1.00**
1928 Shilling. Harp / Bull (S)............. **5.00**
1928 Florin. Harp / Salmon (S) **8.00**

Irish Republic

XF
1953 Halfpenny. Harp / Pig and piglets
(C)... **.25**

XF
1964 3 Pence. Harp / Hare (CN).......... **.25**
1939 Shilling. Harp / Bull (S)............. **4.50**
1962 Shilling. Similar (CN)................. **1.00**
1963 Half Crown. Harp / Horse (CN)
.... **2.00**

XF
1966 10 Shillings. Bust of Pearse / Statue
of Cuchulainn (S) .... *BU* **20.00**

Decimal Coinage

BU
1971 1 Penny. Harp / Celtic bird (C).....**20**
1986 20 Pence. Harp / Horse (Brass)
.... **1.50**
1988 50 Pence. Harp / Arms of Dublin
(CN)... **2.50**
1990 Pound. Harp / Stag (CN) **6.00**

Euro Coinage 2002 to date

2002 20 Cent. Harp / Map (B) **1.25**
2002 2 Euro. Harp / Map (NB clad N in
CN, bimetallic)............................... **4.00**

BU
2003 10 Euro. Harp / Games logo (S)
.... **40.00**

BRITISH COLONIES & COMMONWEALTH

AUSTRALIA

VF
1813 5 Shillings. NEW SOUTH WALES
counterstamped on Spanish colonial 8
Reales with large central hole (S) .... *Rare*
1927 Halfpenny. Bust of George V (C)
....**.75**
1949 Penny. Head of George VI /
Kangaroo (C)....................................**.25**
1910 3 Pence. Bust of Edward VII / Arms
(S) **5.00**

VF
1916 6 Pence. Bust of George V / Arms
(S) **70.00**
1936 6 Pence. Same. (S)..................... **4.50**
1943 6 Pence. Head of George VI / Arms
(S) **2.00**

VF

1942 Shilling. Similar / Ram's head (S) 4.50

1910 Florin. Bust of Edward VII / Arms (S) 150.00

1927 Florin. Bust of George V / Parliament (S) 9.50

XF

1937 Crown. Head of George VI / Crown (S) 22.00

1918 Sovereign. Head of George V / St. George slaying dragon (G) 275.00

Elizabeth II

XF

1961 Penny. Young bust / Kangaroo (C) 40

1964 3 Pence. Young head / Wheat (S) 1.00

1954 6 Pence. Young bust / Arms (S) 2.50

1961 Shilling. Young bust / Ram's head (S) 3.00

1960 Florin. Young bust / Arms (S)...5.00

Decimal Coinage **BU**

1981 1 Cent. Bust in tiara / Ring-tailed opossum................................50

1966 2 Cents. Bust in tiara / Frilled lizard (C)...50

1996 20 Cents. Bust in crown / Platypus (CN)...50

1966 50 Cents. Bust in tiara / Arms (S) 8.50

1988 2 Dollars. Bust in crown / Aboriginal man (B)........................4.00

BU

1993 2 Dollars. Similar / Koukaburra (S) 115.00

BU

1996 5 Dollars. Similar / Bust of Donald Bradman (ALB in Steel, *bimetallic*) 12.50

BU

1999 30 Dollars. Similar / Rabbit (S, 1 kilogram)..................................... 700.00

BAHAMAS

BU

1806 Penny. Bust of George III / Ship (C) .... *F* 40.00

1971 1 Cent. Starfish (C) 25

1966 10 Cents. Two fish (CN, scalloped) 25

1974 15 Cents. Hibiscus (CN)..............50

1972 25 Cents. Sloop. (N) 50

1966 1 Dollar. Conch shell (S) 9.50

1971 2 Dollars. Two flamingos (S) ... 20.00

BU

2000 2 Dollars. Queen mother with dog (Silver, gilt)....................*Proof only* 50.00

1967 20 Dollars. Lighthouse (G).... 280.00

BARBADOS

F

1788 Penny. Slave head wearing prince of Wales crown / Pineapple (C)........... 30.00

F

1792 Penny. Similar / King in chariot of hippocamps (C).............................. 60.00

BELIZE

BU

1989 1 Cent. Crowned bust (AL) 25

1979 50 Cents. Similar (CN) 1.75

1990 1 Dollar. Bust in tiara / Columbus' ships (Brass, decagonal) 2.25

1990 2 Dollars. Similar / EE monogram (CN).. 6.00

BERMUDA

F

c.1616 12 Pence. SOMMER ILANDS, Boar / Ship (C).........................20,000.00

1793 Penny. Bust of George III / Ship (C) 40.00

BU

1964 Crown Crowned bust / Arms (S) 12.00

1970 1 Cent. Bust in tiara / Boar (C) 20

BU

1996 2 Dollars. Crowned bust / Horsecarriage (S) ....**Proof only 35.00**

1996 60 Dollars. Bust in tiara / Map above ship (G, curved triangle) ....*Proof only* 1,100.00

BRITISH CARIBBEAN TERRITORIES

BU

1964 1 Cent. Crowned bust / Wreath (C) 35

BU

1962 2 Cents. Similar / Ship (C)......... 1.00

1964 10 Cents. Similar / Ship (CN).......65

1955 50 Cents. Similar / Queen stg. over arms of islands (CN)........................3.50

BRITISH GUIANA

VF

1813 Stiver. Bust of George III / Crowned
  wreath (C) **18.00**
1891 4 Pence. Bust of Victoria / Similar
  (S) **5.00**
1936 4 Pence. Bust of George V / Similar
  (S) **3.50**
1945 4 Pence. Head of George VI /
  Similar (S) **2.50**

BRITISH HONDURAS

VF

1888 1 Cent. Head of Victoria (C)
  .... **9.00**

VF

1972 1 Cent. Head of Elizabeth II (C,
  scallopped) .... **.40**
1907 5 Cents. Bust of Edward VII (CN)
  .... **55.00**
1936 10 Cents. Bust of George V (S)
  .... **13.00**
1952 25 Cents. Head of George VI
  .... **3.50**
1964 50 Cents. Bust of Elizabeth II (CN)
  .... **.50**
  The above are usually found worn.

BRITISH NORTH BORNEO

VF

1886 1 Cent. Arms with supporters /
  wreath (C) **10.00**

VF

1928 5 Cent. Similar / Value (CN)
  .... **5.00**

BRITISH VIRGIN ISLANDS

BU

1983 10 Cents. Bust in tiara / Kingfisher
  (CN) **1.00**
1973 25 Cents. Similar/ Cuckoo (CN)
  .... **1.50**
1985 20 Dollars. Similar / Spanish
  colonial cob coin (S) ..... *Proof only* **20.00**

BU

1975 100 Dollars. Similar / Tern (G)
  .... **250.00**

BRITISH WEST AFRICA

VF

1908 1/10 Penny. Titles of Edward VII /
  Six-pointed star (AL) **3.00**
1908 Similar (CN) .... **.50**
1920 ½ Penny. Titles of George V / Six-
  pointed star (CN) **2.00**
1936 Penny. Titles of Edward VIII /
  Similar (CN) .... **.75**
1956 Penny. Titles of Elizabeth II /
  Similar (C) .... **.60**
1940 3 Pence. Head of George VI /
  Wreath (Brass) .... **.75**
1913 6 Pence. Bust of George V / Wreath
  (S) **5.50**

VF

1936 Shilling. Bust of George V / Palm
  tree (Brass) **5.00**
1938 Shilling. Head of George VI / Palm
  tree (Brass) **1.00**
1938 2 Shillings. Similar (Brass) **2.00**

BRITISH WEST INDIES

VF

1822 1/16th Dollar. Rose-shaped arms /
  Crowned anchor (S) **15.00**
1822 1/8th Dollar. Similar (S) **18.00**

VF

1822 1/2 Dollar. Similar (S) **200.00**

CAYMAN ISLANDS

BU

1972 10 Cents. Elizabeth II / Green turtle
  (CN) .... **.50**
1992 1 Dollar Elizabeth II / Iguana (S)
  .... **Proof only 50.00**

BU

1975 100 Dollars. Elizabeth II / Five
  queens (G) **400.00**

CEYLON

VF

1803 1/12th Rixdollar. Large 12 /
  Elephant l. (C) **45.00**
1821 Rix Dollar. Bust of George IV /
  Elephant l. (S) **50.00**
1891 1 Cent. Head of Victoria / Palm tree
  (C) **4.00**
1910 5 Cents. Bust of Edward VII (CN,
  square) **2.00**

VF

1911 25 Cents. Bust of George V / Palm
  tree (S) **6.00**
1951 50 Cents. Head of George VI
  (Brass) .... **.35**
1957 2 Cents. Elizabeth II (Brass,
  scalloped) .... **.15**

CYPRUS

VF

1881 ¼ Piastre. Victoria (C) **22.00**
1908 ½ Piastre. Edward VII (C)..... **225.00**
1927 1 Piastre. George V (C)........... **30.00**
1934 1 Piastre. Similar. (CN, scalloped)
  .... **2.50**

VF

1901 3 Piastre. Bust of Victoria /
  Crowned 3 (S) **25.00**
1921 9 Piastres. Bust of George V /
  Crowned shield (S) **13.00**

VF

1928 45 Piastres. Bust of George V / Two
lions (S)................................ **40.00**
1947 Shilling. Head of George VI / Two
lions (CN) **3.00**

Unc.

1955 3 Mils. Bust of Elizabeth II / Fish
(C)..**.25**
1955 50 Mils. Similar / Ferns (CN) **1.00**

EAST AFRICA

VF

1898 1 Pice. Head of Victoria (C)
.... **10.00**
1908 ½ Cent. Titles of Edward VII /
Tusks (AL) **25.00**

VF

1930 1 Cent. Titles of George V / Tusks
(C)...**.75**
1956 1 Cent. Titles of Elizabeth II / Tusks
(C)...**.30**
1936 5 Cents. Titles of Edward VIII /
Tusks (C).......................................**.50**
1913 25 Cents. Bust of George V / Lion
(S) **9.50**
1963 50 Cents. Bust of Elizabeth II / Lion
(CN)...**.25**

VF

1937 Shilling. Head of George VI / Lion
(Billon).. **2.00**

EAST CARIBBEAN STATES

BU

1981 1 Cent. Bust in tiara / Wreath (AL)
....**.20**
1989 1 Dollar. Similar / Ship (CN, 10-
sided)... **2.00**

BU

1996 10 Dollars. Mature bust / Boat (S)
.... *Proof only* **50.00**

FIJI

VF

1934 Halfpenny. Titles of George V (CN,
holed).. **3.00**
1936 Penny. Titles of Edward VIII (CN,
holed).. **1.00**
1950 3 Pence. Head of George VI / Hut
(Brass).. **1.00**
1965 6 Pence. Bust of Elizabeth II / Sea
turtle (CN) ....**.30**
1934 Shilling. Bust of George V /
Outrigger (S) **5.00**
1943 Florin. Head of George VI / Shield
(S) **7.50**

BU

1976 1 Cent. Bust of Elizabeth II / Dish
(C)...**.35**
1987 50 Cents. Similar / Sailing canoe
(CN, 12-sided)................................. **1.75**
1995 1 Dollar. Similar / Rattle (Brass)
.... **3.50**

VF

1996 10 Dollars. Similar / Fijian Dancer
(S) ....*Proof only* **20.00**
1978 250 Dollars. Similar / Banded
iguana (G)............................. **1,100.00**

GIBRALTAR

VF

1813 1 Quarto. Lion holding key /
Crowned wreath (C)...................... **30.00**
1810 2 Quartos. Similar / Castle (C)
.... **20.00**

VF

1842 2 Quarts. Head of Victoria / Castle
(C)... **45.00**

BU

1967 Crown. Bust of Elizabeth II / Castle
(CN).. **1.50**
1988 5 Pence. Similar / Barbary Ape (CN)
....**.75**
1990 50 Pence. Similar / Five Dolphins
(CN, 7-sided)................................. **3.50**

BU

2001 Crown. Similar / Jumper (CN)
.... **8.00**
1989 5 Sovereigns. Similar / Una and lion
(G) ....*Proof only* **1,300.00**

GOLD COAST

XF

1818 ½ Ackey. George III / Arms (S)
.... **300.00**
1818 Ackey. Similar (S)................. **650.00**

GUERNSEY

VF

1830 Double. Shield (C)...................... **6.00**
1929 2 Doubles. Shield (C)................ **1.25**
1889 4 Doubles. Shield (C)................ **1.25**
1834 8 Doubles. Shield in wreath / Wreath
(C)... **10.00**

BU

1959 8 Doubles. Shield / Three lilies (C)
.... **1.25**
1966 10 Shillings. Elizabeth II / William
the Conqueror (CN, square)............. **2.50**
1971 2 New Pence. Shield / Windmill (C)
....**.35**

BU

1983 Pound. Shield / Sailing ship (Brass) **3.50**

1996 5 Pound. Elizabeth II / Queen Mother (S) ....*Proof only* **45.00**
1994 25 Pounds. Elizabeth II / Normandy invasion (G) **300.00**

HONG KONG

VF

1865 1 Mil. Crown / Chinese Inscription (C, holed) **15.00**

VF

1863 1 Cent. Victoria / Chinese Inscription (C)................................ **13.50**
1905 1 Cent. Edward VII / Chinese Inscription (C)................................. **4.50**
1932 5 Cents. George V / Similar (S) **1.50**

VF

1937 5 Cents. George VI / Similar (N) **1.25**
1885 10 Cents. Victoria / Similar (S) .. **3.00**
1948 10 Cents. George VI / Similar (Brass)......................................**.50**
1902 20 Cents. Edward VII / Similar (S) **40.00**
1866 ½ Dollar. Victoria / Ornament (S) **550.00**
1891 50 Cents. Victoria / Value (S) **50.00**
1866 Dollar. Victoria / Ornament (S) **330.00**
    Recent counterfeits of this coin are known.

BU

1967 5 Cents. Elizabeth II / Similar (Brass).. **1.00**
1975 20 Cents. Elizabeth II / Similar (Brass)..**.35**

BU

1960 1 Dollar. Elizabeth II / Lion (CN) **5.00**
1993 2 Dollars. Bauhinia flower (CN, scalloped) **1.25**
1994 10 Dollars. Similar (Brass in CN, *bimetallic*)..............................**5.00**
1977 1,000 Dollars. Elizabeth II / Snake (G) **600.00**

BU

1982 1,000 Dollars. Elizabeth II / Dog (G) **525.00**

INDIA - EAST INDIA CO.

F

1704-16 Pice. Crown / AUSPICIO REGIS ET SENATUS ANGLIA (C) **50.00**

F

1741 Pice. Similar, BOMB below crown (Tin) **45.00**
1179 AH (=1765) Rupee. Arabic inscriptions and ornament (S)........ **18.00**
1835 1/12th Anna. Arms / Wreath (C) ....**.75**

F

1857 ¼ Anna. Similar **1.00**
1835 ¼ Rupee. William IV / Wreath. (S) **5.00**

F

1840 Rupee. Victoria / Wreath (S).... **12.00**
1841 1 Mohur. Victoria / Lion and Palm tree (G).. **450.00**

INDIA - REGAL COINAGE

VF

1862 1/12th Anna. Victoria as queen / Wreath (C) **1.25**
1906 1/12th Anna. Edward VII / Wreath (C)...................................... **1.50**
1916 1/12th Anna. George V / Wreath (C) ....**.50**
1939 1/12th Anna. George VI / Wreath (C)...**.50**
1895 ½ Pice. Victoria as empress / Wreath (C)...................................... **1.75**

VF

1862 ¼ Anna. Victoria as queen / Wreath (C)...................................... **1.50**
1880 ¼ Anna. Victoria as empress / Wreath (C) **1.00**
1906 ¼ Anna. Edward VII / Wreath (C) **1.35**
1920 ¼ Anna. George V / Wreath (C) ....**.40**
1942 ¼ Anna. George VI / Wreath (C) ....**.35**
1943 1 Pice. Crown / Wreath (C)..........**.35**
1862 ½ Anna. Victoria as queen / Wreath (C)...................................... **20.00**

VF

1946 ½ Anna. George VI (CN).............**.30**
1945 1 Anna. George VI (Brass)..........**.25**
1901 2 Anna. Victoria as empress / Wreath (S)...................................... **2.50**
1918 2 Annas. George V (CN, square) **1.75**
1940 2 Annas. George VI (CN, square) ....**.30**
1919 4 Annas. George V (CN) **5.00**
1862 ¼ Rupee. Victoria as queen / Wreath (S) **5.00**
1892 ¼ Rupee. Victoria as empress / Wreath (S)...................................... **3.00**
1904 ¼ Rupee. Edward VII / Flowers (S) **3.00**
1936 ¼ Rupee. George V / Wreath (S) **2.50**

VF

1945 ¼ Rupee. George VI / Wreath (S) **2.00**

1946 ¼ Rupee. George VI / Tiger (N) ....**.75**

1919 8 Annas. George V (CN) **7.50**

1899 ½ Rupee. Victoria as empress / Wreath (S) **6.00**

1885 Rupee. Similar (S) **12.00**

1903 Rupee. Edward VII / Flowers (S) **13.00**

VF

1914 Rupee. George V / Wreath (S) **12.00**

1945 Rupee. George VI / Wreath (S) **6.00**

1947 Rupee. George VI / Tiger (N) **2.50**

1870 5 Rupees. Victoria as queen / Wreath (G) **600.00**

1870 10 Rupees. Similar (G) **750.00**

VF

1875 Mohur. Similar / Wreath (G) **500.00**

1918 15 Rupees. George V / Wreath (G) **400.00**

1918 Sovereign. George V / St. George slaying dragon, mintmark "I" on ground (G) **275.00**

INDIA - PRINCELY STATES

VF

Alwar. 1891 Rupee. Victoria / Arabic inscription (S) **15.00**

Bharatpur. 1910 VS (=1858) Rupee. Victoria / Arabic inscription (S) **85.00**

Bikanir. 1895 ¼ Anna. Victoria / Inscription (C) **12.00**

Bundi. 1989 VS (=1932) Rupee. EMPEROR GEORGE V, Dagger / Hindi inscription (S) **15.00**

Dewas, Junior Branch. 1888 1/12th Anna. Victoria / Wreath (C) **20.00**

Dewas, Senior Branch. 1888 1/12th Anna. Victoria / Wreath (C) **13.00**

Dhar. 1887 ½ Pice. Victoria / Inscription (C) **6.00**

VF

Kutch. 1936 5 Kori. Titles of Edward VIII (S) **12.00**

VF

1943 1/8 Kori. Titles of George VI (C, holed) ....**.50**

Sailana. 1912 ¼ Anna. George V / Inscription (C) **8.00**

For princely states coins not struck in name of British sovereign see India.

IONIAN ISLANDS

F

1814 50 Paras. Bust of George III and 50 counterstamped on Spanish 2 Reales (S) **450.00**

1834 Lepton. Lion / Britannia std. (C) **5.00**

F

1834 30 Lepta. Britannia std. / Wreath (C) **30.00**

ISLE OF MAN

F

1733 Penny. Eagle on cap / Three legs (C) **35.00**

1758 Penny. Crowned DA monogram / Three legs (C) **25.00**

1786 ½ Penny. George III / Three legs (C) **15.00**

F

1839 Farthing. Victoria / Three legs (C) **9.00**

BU

1971 1 New Penny. Elizabeth II / Celtic cross (C) ....**.35**

1980 10 Pence. Elizabeth II / Falcon (CN) ....**.85**

1990 1/5th Crown. Elizabeth II / Alley cat (G) **250.00**

1976 Crown. Elizabeth II / George Washington (CN) **2.50**

same (S) **20.00**

BU

1988 Crown. Elizabeth II / Manx cat (S) .... **Proof 20.00**

1985 1 Angel. Elizabeth II / Archangel Michael slaying demon (G, 1 ounce) **1,075.00**

JAMAICA

VF

1882 Farthing. Victoria / Shield (CN) **2.00**

1928 Farthing. George V / Shield (CN) **2.00**

1950 Farthing. George VI / Shield (Brass) ....**.25**

1869 Halfpenny. Victoria / Shield (CN) **2.50**

1907 Halfpenny. Edward VII / Shield (CN) **2.00**

VF

1937 Halfpenny. George VI / Shield (Brass) **1.00**

VF

1887 Penny. Victoria / Shield (CN) **15.00**

VF

1910 Penny. Edward VII / Shield (CN)
.... **2.50**
1920 Penny. George V / Shield (CN)
.... **2.50**
1937 Penny. George VI in high relief /
Shield (Brass) **1.75**
1950 Penny. George VI in low relief /
Shield (Brass) .... **.35**
1958 Penny. Elizabeth II / Arms (Brass)
.... **.25**

BU

1964 Halfpenny. Elizabeth II / Arms
(Brass)... **.15**
1966 5 Shillings. Crown in chain / Arms
(CN).. **5.00**

JERSEY

VF

1813 18 Pence. Shield / Wreath
(S) **90.00**
1841 1/52 Shilling. Victoria / Shield (C)
.... **45.00**
1909 1/24 Shilling. Edward VII / Shield
(C) **3.00**
1937 1/24 Shilling. George VI / Shield (C)
.... **1.00**
1877 1/12 Shilling. Victoria / Shield (C)
.... **2.00**
1931 1/12 Shilling. George V / Shield (C)
.... **1.00**

VF

1937 1/12 Shilling. George VI / Shield (C)
.... **1.00**

BU

1964 1/12 Shilling. Elizabeth II / Shield
(C).. **1.00**
1981 Penny. Elizabeth II / Shield (C)..... **.20**
1983 10 Pence. Elizabeth II / Prehistoric
stone structure (CN) **1.00**
1972 2 Pounds 50 Pence. Elizabeth II /
Lobster (S) **20.00**

MALAYA

VF

1943 1 Cent. George VI (C, square)...... **.20**

VF

1958 1 Cent. Elizabeth II (C, square)....**.20**

MAURITIUS

VF

(1822) 25 Sous. REÇU *au* TRESOR /
pour 25 Sous (S) **50.00**
1969 1 Cent. Elizabeth II (C) .... **.10**

VF

1949 2 Cents. George VI (C).............. **1.25**
1917 5 Cents. George V (C) **4.50**
1886 10 Cents. Victoria (S) **5.00**
1975 ¼ Rupee. Elizabeth II / Crown and
flowers (CN) .... **.30**
1950 ½ Rupee. George VI / Stag (CN)
.... **1.00**

VF

1934 1 Rupee. George V / Shield (S)
.... **12.00**
1975 25 Rupees. Elizabeth II / Butterfly
(S) .... *BU* **20.00**

NEW GUINEA

XF

1929 ½ Penny. Crown and scepters (CN,
holed).. **350.00**

XF

1936 Penny. Crown and *ERI* (C, holed)
.... **2.00**
1944 Penny. Crown and GRI (C, holed)
.... **5.00**
1944 3 Pence. Similar (CN, holed) **9.00**
1935 Shilling. Titles of George V, crown
and scepters (S, holed) **5.00**
1938 Shilling. Similar but George VI (S,
holed)... **5.00**

NEW ZEALAND

VF

1940 Halfpenny. George VI / Tiki idol (C)
.... **.50**

VF

1950 Penny. George VI / Tui bird (C)
.... **.50**

VF

1933 3 Pence. George V / Crossed clubs
(S) **3.00**
1952 3 Pence. George VI / Similar (CN)
.... **1.75**

VF

1943 6 Pence. George VI / Huia bird (S)
.... **6.00**
1952 Shilling. George VI / Maori warrior
(CN)... **8.00**

VF

1935 Florin. George V / Kiwi bird (S)
.... **30.00**
1940 Florin. George VI / Maori and two
vies of Auckland (S)...................... **30.00**
1943 Half Crown. George VI / Arms (S)
.... **15.00**

VF

1951 Half Crown. Similar (CN)......... **2.50**
1935 Crown. George V / Maori chief and
British naval officer shaking hands (S)
.... **3,000.00**

BU
1949 Crown. George VI / Fern leaf (S) **27.00**
1965 Halfpenny. Elizabeth II wearing wreath / Tiki idol (C) **1.00**
1965 Penny. Similar / Tui bird (C)...... **3.00**
1960 3 Pence. George VI / Crossed clubs (CN).. **2.00**
1956 6 Pence. Similar / Huia bird (S) **9.00**
1964 Shilling. Similar / Maori warrior (CN).. **2.50**
1965 Florin. Similar / Kiwi bird (S) **2.00**
1953 Crown. Similar / Crowned monogram (CN)........................... **12.00**
1987 1 Cent. Crowned bust of Elizabeth II / Fern leaf (C) **50**

BU
1967 2 Cents. Bust of Elizabeth II wearing tiara / Kowhai plant (C).........**25**
1967 5 Cents. Bust of Elizabeth II wearing tiara / Tuatata lizard (CN) **25**
1988 10 Cents. Similar / Maori mask (CN)...**25**
1993 50 Cents. Similar / H.M.S. Endeavor (CN).................................... **1.50**
1994 50 Cents. Similar (ALB in CN, *bimetallic*)...................................... **15.00**
1967 Dollar. Bust of Elizabeth II wearing tiara / Shield between branches (CN) **2.00**

BU
1990 Dollar. Similar / Kiwi bird (ALB) **2.00**
1996 5 Dollars. Similar / Kaka Parrot (CN).. **12.00**
Similar (S)......................*Proof only* **25.00**

BU
2003 5 Dollars. Similar / Fish (CN) **12.00**

NIGERIA

BU
1959 ½ Penny. Crown / Six-pointed star (C)..**75**
1962 Shilling. Elizabeth II / Palm branches (CN)................................ **3.50**
1959 2 Shillings. Elizabeth II / Peanut-plant (CN)....................................... **6.00**

RHODESIA

BU
1964 6 Pence - 5 Cents. Elizabeth II wearing tiara / Flame lily (CN) **1.50**
1964 2 Shillings - 20 Cents. Similar / Ancient bird sculpture (CN)............. **4.00**
1966 Pound. Similar / Lion holding tusk (G) ....*Proof only* **350.00**

RHODESIA & NYASALAND

BU
1964 ½ Penny. Giraffes (C, holed)...... **1.50**

BU
1957 1 Shilling. Elizabeth II / Antelope (CN)... **10.00**

SEYCHELLES

VF
1948 2 Cents. George VI (C)................**35**
1944 25 Cents. Similar (S).................. **3.50**
BU
1959 2 Cents. Elizabeth II (C)............ **2.50**
1972 5 Cents. Elizabeth II / Cabbage (AL) **25**

BU
1954 25 Cents. Elizabeth II (CN)....... **3.50**
1974 ½ Rupee. Elizabeth II (CN)....... **1.00**
1972 5 Rupees. Elizabeth II / Beach scene with tree and turtle (CN) **5.00**

BU
Similar (S)............................. **25.00**

SOLOMON ISLANDS

BU
1977 2 Cents. Elizabeth II / Eagle spirit (C)...**25**
1988 10 Cents. Elizabeth II / Sea spirit (CN)...**50**
1996 50 Cents. Elizabeth II / Arms (CN, 12-sided).. **3.00**
1992 10 Dollars. Elizabeth II / Crocodile (S) ....*Proof only* **35.00**

BU
1991 25 Dollars. Elizabeth II / Attack on PearlHarbor (G)......................... **300.00**

SOUTH AFRICA, UNION OF

VF
1931 1/4 Penny. George V / Two sparrows (C) **1.50**
1942 ¼ Penny. George VI / Two sparrows (C) **50**
1953 ½ Penny. Elizabeth II / Ship (C) **35**
1929 ½ Penny. George V / Ship (C).... **5.00**
1952 Penny. George VI / Ship (C) **50**
1953 Penny. Elizabeth II / Ship (C) **35**
1927 3 Pence. George V / Protea plant within three bundles of sticks (S) **2.50**

VF
1943 3 Pence. George VI / Similar (S) **1.50**
1924 6 Pence. George V / Wreath (S) **12.50**
1927 6 Pence. George V / Protea plant within six bundles of sticks (S)......... **4.50**
1957 6 Pence. Elizabeth II / Similar (S) **1.50**
1943 Shilling. George VI / Allegory of Cape of Good Hope (S)................... **3.50**
1953 Shilling. Elizabeth II / Similar (S) **3.00**
1932 2 Shillings. George V / Shield (S) **12.00**
1942 2 Shillings. George VI / Shield (S) **9.50**
1932 2½ Shillings. George V / Crowned shield (S) **12.00**

VF

1955 2½ Shillings. Elizabeth II / Similar
(S) **5.50**
1952 5 Shillings. George VI / Ship (S)
.... **12.50**

VF

1953 5 Shillings. Elizabeth II / Springbok
(S) **12.50**

SOUTHERN RHODESIA

VF

1936 Penny. Crowned rose (CN) **1.25**
1942 6 Pence. George VI / Two hatchets
(S) **2.25**
1947 Shilling. George VI / Stone bird
(CN)...**1.50**

VF

1932 2 Shillings. George V / Antelope (S)
.... **20.00**
1954 2 Shillings. Elizabeth II / Antelope
(CN).. **75.00**
1932 Half Crown. George V / Crowned
shield (S) **12.50**
1953 Crown. Elizabeth II / Cecil Rhodes
(S) .... *Unc.* **40.00**

STRAITS SETTLEMENTS

VF

1916 1/4 Cent. George V (C).............**5.00**
1926 1 Cent. George V (C, square) ......**.75**
1901 5 Cents. Victoria (S) **2.50**
1927 10 Cents. George V (S) **1.00**
1910 20 Cents. Edward VII (S)...........**7.00**
1920 50 Cents. George V (S) **5.00**

VF

1920 Dollar. George V / Ornamental
design containing Chinese and Malay
inscription (S)................................ **40.00**

CAUCASUS

The first modern, European-style coins struck in this region are the copper and silver issues of Georgia (1804-1833) while under Czarist Russian influence. It was not until the breakup of the Soviet Union that local coinage of the Caucasus region was again placed in circulation. The first coins were Azerbaijani and Armenian coins all struck in aluminum. Both were of fairly plain design. Well-made coins with attractive reverse designs were introduced by Georgia in 1993. A limited number of collector issues have been struck by Georgia and Armenia.

Nagorno-Karabakh is an ethnically Armenian area of Azerbaijan that broke away and declared its independence in 1991.

Known Counterfeits: None.

ARMENIA

BU

1994 10 Luma. Arms (AL) ....**.25**
1994 3 Drams. Arms (AL) ....**.85**
1996 100 Drachms. Stork with chess
board / Arms (CN).........................**6.00**

BU

1996 100 Drams. Bagramian / Arms (S)
.... **Proof 300.00**
1997 25,000 Drachms. Head of Anahit
(G) ....*Proof* **180.00**

AZERBAIJAN

BU

1992 10 Qapik. Eight-pointed star (AL)
....**.65**
1993 20 Qapik. Crescent and star (AL)
....**1.00**
1996 50 Manat. Romantic couple /
Mohammed Fuzuli (S)
....................................*Proof only* **60.00**

BU

1999 50 Manat. Horseman (S)
....*Proof only* **60.00**

GEORGIA

BU

1827 2 Abazi. Masonry crown /
Inscription (S) ....*F* **40.00**
1993 20 Thetri. Emblem / Stag (Steel)
....**1.50**

BU

1995 10 Lari. Eagle and Lion (Brass
around CN)................................... **16.00**
1995 500 Lari. Profiles of Stalin,
Roosevelt, Churchill and DeGaulle (G)
...................................*Proof only* **600.00**

NAGORNO KARABAKH

BU

2004 1 Dram. Emblem / St. Gregory
(AL). **1.00**

CZECHOSLOVAKIA

After 400 years of Austrian rule, Czechoslovakia became and independent state in 1918, following the breakup of the Hapsburg Empire. While most of the coins circulating here were regular money of the empire, special copper pieces were struck for Bohemia in the late 1700s. Also common were the coins struck by the local bishops of Olomouc in Moravia.

Additional Specialized Books:
Aicholz, Miller zu, *Oesterreichische Münzpragungen, 1519-1938*. Despite the title this is an excellent catalog for later Bohemian coins.

Known Counterfeits: Few.

BOHEMIA

F

1687 6 Kreuzer. Bust of Leopold I /
Double headed eagle, double tailed lion
on chest (S) **40.00**
1699 Ducat. Similar (G)................ **325.00**
1782 Groeschl. Crowned shield (C)
.... **12.00**

F

1731 Thaler. Bust / Two-headed eagle, double tailed lion in central shield on chest (S) **140.00**
1943 1 Koruna. Double-tailed lion / Ivy branches (Z) .... *VF* **.75**

OLOMOUC

F

1705 Kreuzer Bust / Arms (S).......... **20.00**

SCHLICK

F

1638 3 Kreuzer. Madonna and Child over arms / Double headed eagle (S)...... **35.00**

CZECHOSLOVAKIA

VF

1925 10 Haleru. Double-tailed lion / Bridge (C) **35**
1938 20 Haleru. Double-tailed lion / Wheat and scythe (CN).....................**35**

VF

1922 1 Koruna. Double-tailed lion / Woman with sheaf and scythe (C) ......**.50**
1934 20 Korun. Shield / Three figures stg. (S) **6.00**
BU
1949 50 Korun. Stalin / Shield (S)...... **8.50**
1965 10 Korun. Shield / Jan Hus (S) **15.00**
1966 5 Haleru. Shield / Wreath (AL) **25**
1980 2 Koruny. Shield / Symbol (CN)...**75**

BU

1981 100 Korun. Spaniel / Arms (S) **9.00**
1991 5 Haleru. CSFR over shield / 5h (AL) **25**

BU

1993 500 Korun. Shield / Tennis player (S) **35.00**

CZECH REPUBLIC

BU

1993 1 Koruna. Double-tailed lion / Crown (N clad Steel)..........................**60**
1993 50 Korun. Double-tailed lion / City view (Steel, Brass and Copper plated, *bimetallic*).. **7.50**

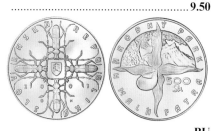

BU

2003 200 Korun. Vrehlicky / Quill (S) **17.00**

SLOVAKIA

VF

1939 10 Halierov. Shield / Castle (C) **2.00**
1941 1 Koruna. Shield / Wreath (CN) **1.00**
1944 10 Korun. Shield / King, bishop and knight (S) **6.50**
BU
1993 10 Haliers. Shield / Steeple (AL) **35**
1993 10 Koruna. Shield / Medieval cross (Brass).. **2.50**
1993 100 Korun. Shield / Three doves (S) **9.50**

BU

2001 500 Korun. Four beetles / Orchid (S) **40.00**

FRANCE

After centuries of deterioration, French royal coinage began to stabilize somewhat by the 1600s. This coincides with the introduction of milled coinage the same century. A silver-dollar-sized *ecu* and its fractions became common. Small values were struck in base silver and especially in copper. This included the old *denier tournois,* which had survived since

the 1200s. The gold *louis d'or* became so recognized for its stability that it saw wide circulation internationally. Most coins bore the king's portrait, with fleur-de-lis or a shield of arms on the reverse. Sometimes an elaborate cross or monogram would still be used, these being held over from the Renaissance. Despite the improved striking methods, imprecise means were used to manufacture blanks of exact weight, so many had to be adjusted with a file before striking to remove excess metal. The resulting "adjustment marks" are not damage, but if severe, do reduce the coin's value.

Among the most important uses of coinage for the study of French history is the effect that the French Revolution had on the iconography. An entirely new set of symbols replaced the traditional ones. Those reflecting new ideologies include one displaying a tablet inscribed, "Men are equal before the law." An allegorical head, initially representing liberty, was also quite popular. Even after Napoleon took the reigns as emperor, he maintained the revolutionary name of the country as the "French Republic" temporarily on the coinage. The revolution's most lasting change on the coinage was the decimal system. Used the world over today, it divides the monetary unit – the franc or the dollar, for example – into tenths or hundredths.

Most 19th-century French coins were quite conservative, depicting the monarch and a coat of arms or value. There was great artistic merit, however, in the beautiful coins of the 1898-to-1920 period.

In this dawn of the new European currency, the euro, it is all the more important to mention that French coinage was the basis of an earlier international currency, that of the Latin Monetary Union, from 1865 to 1920. During this period, the money of nations as diverse as Greece and Switzerland were struck on an international standard and held the same value.

The most common design to be used by the French republics is an allegorical female head or bust. This image, tracing its roots back to a 1790s allegory of liberty, is variously described toady as the personification of the Republic, of France, and as "Marie Anne" (the personification's nickname).

Inflation again hit France after World War I and the currency did not finally stabilize until 1960. During this time most of the coins were of baser metals, including bronze and

aluminum. Some denominations were distinguished with holes in their centers. Many mintmarks were used on French coins before 1960 and some of the dates and mintmarks can be valuable. Only common ones for the type are listed here. Coins before 1960, and some outmoded ones struck afterwards, have no legal-tender status.

In January 2002, France replaced the franc with coins denominated in euros, the currency of the European Union. Some coins were struck as early as 1999 and held until 2002. On the circulating denominations, one cent through two euros, there is one side that carries a French design, the other a common European design. On higher-denomination commemoratives, both sides are distinctively French.

In recent years a phenomenal amount of French collector issues have been struck, sometimes in odd sizes and at a rate of one every few weeks!

During and immediately after World War I, many municipal chambers of commerce throughout France struck small-denomination emergency tokens to facilitate commerce. Their designs run from utilitarian to breathtaking.

Coins from India are the earliest common French colonials. Many of these are hardly distinguishable from local Indian states coins. Usually they are identified by certain symbols, such as a fleur-de-lis or a cock. They were originally intended to circulate alongside crude local coins and their designs and crudeness made this possible.

Other colonial coins were struck occasionally from the 1890s through the 1930s, but were not abundant except in Indo-China. During and after World War II, they were struck in abundant quantities in base metals. Usually one side bore a female head representing an allegory of France. The reverse would allude to the individual colony. Since 1948, virtually all French colonial coins can be easily collected in mint state.

Additional Specialized Books:
Duplessy, Jean, *Les Monnaies Francaises Royales*, vol. II.

Known Counterfeits: Contemporary counterfeits of French coins have always been common. The gold 20- and 50-franc pieces should be examined with care. Counterfeits of smaller denominations are slightly less deceptive. A sampling of counterfeit French coins includes the one-franc 1867BB and 1915, and five-franc

1875A, 1960 and 1975, but hundreds of others exist.

KINGDOM

F
Louis XIV, 1643-1715. 1696 Double denier. Bust r. / Crown and three fleurs (C) **20.00**
1655 Liard. Crowned bust r. / LIARD DE FRANCE, fleurs (C) **20.00**

F
1676 2 Sols. Bust r. / 2 fleurs crowned (S) **40.00**
1707 10 Sols = 1/8 Ecu. Old bust r. / Crown over crossed scepters (S) **30.00**
1644 Quarter Ecu. Young bust r. / Crowned shield (S) **125.00**
1690 Ecu. Old bust r. / Cross of 8 L's (S) **100.00**

F
1646 Louis d'or. Young bust r. / Cross of 8 L's, crown ends, fleurs in angles. (G) **425.00**
1709 Louis d'or. Old bust r. / Eight crowned L's in form of cross, fleurs in angles (G) **425.00**
Louis XV, 1715-74 F
1720 1/2 Sol. Young bust r. / Crowned shield (C) **20.00**
1770 Sol. Bust r. / Crowned shield (C) **12.00**
1750 2 Sols. Crowned L / Crowned crossed floral L's (Billon) **12.00**

F
1779 6 Sols = 1/20 Ecu. Old bust l. / Crowned shield in wreath. Posthumous issue. (S) **20.00**

F
1729 24 Sols = 1/5 Ecu. Young bust l. / Similar (S) **30.00**
1741 Ecu. Bust l. / Similar (S) **95.00**

F
1758 2 Louis d'or. Head l. / Crowned shields of France and Navarre (G) **700.00**
Louis XVI, 1774-93 F
1786 Liard. Head l. / Crowned shield (C) **9.00**
1792 3 Deniers. Bust l. / Fasces (C).. **25.00**
1791 12 Deniers. Similar (C) **15.00**

F
1792 2 Sols. Similar (C) **20.00**
1783 6 Sols = 1/20 Ecu. Bust l. / Crowned shield in wreath (S) **35.00**

F
1791 30 Sols = ¼ Ecu. Bust l. / Angel writing on tablet (S) **50.00**
1783 ½ Ecu. Bust l. / Crowned shield in wreath (S) **50.00**
1792 Ecu. Similar (S) **120.00**
1786 Louis d'or. Bust l. / Crowned shields of France and Navarre (G) **400.00**
Republic, 1793-1804 F
1793 24 Livres. Angel writing on tablet / Wreath (G) **1,250.00**
1793 6 Livres. Similar (S) **125.00**

F
1793 2 Sols. Similar. **40.00**

F
1792 5 Sols. Soldiers swearing oath (C).
Common token of the time **14.00**
L'An 6 (1797-98) 1 Centime. Bust of
Liberty (C) **2.00**
L'An 7 (1798-1799) 5 Centimes. Similar /
Wreath (C) **8.00**
L'An 8 (1799-1800) 1 Decime. Similar /
Wreath (C) **10.00**
L'An 4 (1795-1796) 2 Decimes. Similar /
Wreath (C) **65.00**

F
L'An 6 (1797-98) 5 Francs. Liberty,
Hercules and Equality (S) **95.00**
Napoleon I, 1799-1815   F
1808 5 Centimes. N in wreath, raised
border (C) **100.00**
1810 10 Centimes Crowned N in wreath,
raised border (Billon) **9.00**
1814 1 Decime. Crowned N in wreath /
value in wreath (C) **18.00**
L'An 12 (1803-04) ¼ Franc. Bust as
Premier Consul / QUART in wreath (S)
.... **35.50**
L'An 12 (1803-04) ½ Franc. Bust as
Premier Consul / DEMI FRANC in
wreath (S) **19.00**
1809 ½ Franc. Bust as Emperor / same
(S) **15.00**

F
L'An 12 (1803-04) 1 Franc. Bust as
Premier Consul / Value in wreath (S)
.... **35.00**
1809 1 Franc. Similar (S) **20.00**
L'An 11 (1802-03) 5 Francs. Bust as
Premier Consul / Wreath (S) **90.00**
1811 5 Francs. Bust as Emperor / Similar
(S) **50.00**
1812 20 Francs. Similar (G) **250.00**
Louis XVIII, 1814-1825   F
1815 Decime. Crowned L in wreath /
Wreath (C) **12.00**
1817 ¼ Franc. Bust l. / Crowned shield
(S) **12.00**
1822 1 Franc. Bust l. / Crowned shield in
wreath (S)...................................... **17.50**

F
1824 2 Francs. Similar (S) **40.00**
1824 5 Francs. Similar (S) **25.00**
1816 20 Francs. Similar (G) **225.00**
Charles X, 1824-30
1827 ¼ Franc. Bust l. / Crowned shield
(S) **7.00**

F
1829 1/2 Franc. Bust l. / Crowned shield
(S) **11.00**
1825 1 Franc. Bust l. / Crowned shield in
wreath (S)...................................... **22.00**

F
1830 40 Francs. Bust r. / Similar (G)
.... **450.00**
Louis Philippe, 1830-48
1847 25 Centimes. Head r. / Wreath (S)
.... **6.00**
1840 ½ Franc. Similar (S) **5.00**
1846 1 Franc. Similar (S) **9.00**
1834 2 Francs. same (S) **25.00**

F
1848 5 Francs. Head r. / Wreath (S)
.... **20.00**
1831 20 Francs. Bust l. / Wreath (G)
.... **225.00**
Second Republic, 1848-52   VF
1849 1 Centime. Liberty head (C) **5.00**

F
1849 20 Centimes. Ceres head / Wreath
(S) **5.00**

F
1852 50 Centimes. Head of Louis
Napoleon / Wreath (S) **60.00**
1849 1 Franc. Similar (S) **45.00**

F
1849 5 Francs. Liberty, Hercules and
Equality (S).................................... **20.00**
1851 10 Francs. Cered head / Wreath (G)
.... **125.00**
Napoleon III, 1852-70
1862 1 Centime. Bare head. / Eagle (C)
.... **1.00**
1854 2 Centimes. Similar (C) **2.00**
1861 2 Centimes. Head with wreath /
Eagle (C) **1.50**

F
1855 5 Centimes. Bare head. / Eagle (C)
.... **4.00**

F
1862 10 Centimes. Head with wreath /
Eagle (C) **10.00**
F
1867 20 Centimes. Head l. / Crown (S)
.... **4.00**
1867 50 Centimes. Similar (S) **6.00**
1858 1 Franc. Bare head / Wreath (S)
.... **25.00**
1867 1 Franc. Head with wreath / Arms
(S) **12.00**
1856 2 Francs. Bare head / Wreath (S)
.... **275.00**
1866 2 Francs. Head with wreath / Arms
(S) **25.00**

F
1868 5 Francs. Similar (S) **20.00**
1862 10 Francs. Head r. / Wreath (G)
.... **115.00**
1868 20 Francs. Head r. / Wreath (G)
.... **225.00**
1869 100 Francs. Similar (G) **1,150.00**
Restored Republic, 1871-1958 **VF**
1895 1 Centime. Ceres head (C) **2.50**
1908 2 Centimes. Republic head (C)
.... **1.00**
1916 5 Centimes. Similar / Allegorical
group (C) **1.00**
1897 10 Centimes. Ceres head (C) **3.00**
1916 10 Centimes. Head r. / Allegorical
scene (C) .... **.75**

VF
1922 10 Centimes. Cap and RF (CN,
holed) .... **.75**
1945 20 Centimes. Similar (Z) **5.00**

VF
1904 25 Centimes. Republic head / Fasces
(N) .... **.75**
1916 50 Centimes. Sower (S) **2.00**
1939 50 Centimes. Head l. (ALB) .... **.50**

VF
1946 50 Centimes. Head l. (AL) .... **.25**
1872 1 Franc. Ceres head / Wreath (S)
.... **5.00**
1947 1 Franc. Head l. / Cornucopia (AL)
.... **.25**
1915 2 Francs. Sower (S) **6.00**
1921 2 Francs. Mercury std. (ALB)
.... **2.00**
1873 5 Francs. Liberty, Hercules and
Equality (S) **20.00**
1945 5 Francs. Head l. / Wreath (AL) ... **.35**
1901 10 Francs. Head l. / Cock l. (G)
.... **110.00**

VF
1952 10 Francs. Head l. / Cock and
branch (ALB) .... **.35**
1933 20 Francs. Head l. / Two ears of
grain (S) **6.00**
1953 50 Francs. Head l. / Cock and
branch (ALB) **1.75**

VF
1881 100 Francs. Winged genius (G)
.... **1,100.00**
1955 100 Francs. Bust with torch /
branches (CN) **1.00**
Vichy France **VF**
1941 20 Centimes. VINGT over oak
leaves (Z) **2.00**
1941 20 Centimes. 20 over oak leaves (Z)
.... **.75**

VF
1943 1 Franc. Ax between wheat ears
(AL) .... **.25**
1941 5 Francs. Philippe Petain / Ax (CN)
.... **100.00**

Fifth Republic, 1959-date **BU**
1968 1 Centime. Wheat ear (Steel) .... **.25**
1987 5 Centimes. Bust l. (ALB) .... **.10**
1967 20 Centimes. Bust l. (ALB) .... **.15**
1976 ½ Franc. Sower (N) .... **.30**

BU
1970 1 Franc. Sower (N) .... **.40**
1979 2 Francs. Modernistic sower (N)
.... **.65**
1974 10 Francs. Map / Girders (B) **2.00**
1989 10 Francs. Winged genius (Steel in
ALB, bimetallic) **6.50**
1989 10 Francs. Montesquieu (Steel in
ALB, bimetallic) **17.50**

BU
1986 100 Francs. Statue of Liberty (S)
.... **20.00**
1996 100 Francs. Clovis (S) **32.50**
1990 500 Francs = 70 Ecu. Charlemagne
(G) .... *Proof only* **550.00**

Euro Coinage 2002 to date   **BU**
1999 20 Euro Cent. Sower / Map (B,
  notched) **1.00**
2001 1 Euro. Stylized tree / Map. (CN
  clad N in NB, bimetallic) **3.00**

                                                BU
2004 1½ Euro. Book blended into
  building / Napoleon. (S) **45.00**

FRENCH COLONIAL

ALGERIA
                                                 VF
1956 20 Francs. Head r. / Two wheat ears
  (CN) **1.00**
1949 50 Francs. Similar (CN) **3.00**
1952 100 Francs. Similar (CN) **4.00**

CAMEROON
                                                 VF
1943 50 Centimes. Cock / Double cross
  (C) **3.50**
1926 1 Franc. Head l. / Palm branches
  (ALB) **2.00**
1948 1 Franc. Antelope head (AL) .... **.25**

                                                 VF
1925 2 Francs. Head l. Palm branches
  (ALB) **25.00**

COMOROS
                                                BU
1964 1 Franc. Head l. / Palm trees (AL)
  .... **1.25**

                                                BU
1964 5 Francs. Similar (AL) **2.25**
1964 10 Francs. Shells and Coelacanth
  fish (ALB) **3.25**

FRENCH AFARS & ISSAS
                                                BU
1975 2 Francs. Antelope head (AL) ... **5.00**
1975 5 Francs. Similar (AL) **4.00**
1975 20 Francs. Ocean liner and small
  sailing ship (ALB) **7.00**
1975 50 Francs. Head l. / Two camels
  (CN) **12.50**

FRENCH COCHIN CHINA
                                                 VF
1879 2 Sapeque. French inscription /
  Chinese inscription (C, holed) **6.00**

                                                 VF
1879 1 Cent. Seated figure (C) **18.00**
1879 10 Cents. Seated figure (S) **35.00**
1885 Piastre. Similar (S) .... *Rare*

FRENCH COLONIES
                                                  F
1721 9 Deniers. Crowned crossed L's /
  Inscription (C) **35.00**
(1779) Stampee. Crowned C / Blank (C)
  .... **15.00**
1841 5 Centimes. Bust of Louis Philippe
  (C) **6.00**

                                                  F
1828 10 Centimes. Bust of Charles X (C)
  .... **20.00**

FRENCH EQUATORIAL AFRICA
                                                 XF
1943 5 Centimes. Cap over RF (ALB,
  holed) **275.00**
1943 50 Centimes. Cock / Double cross
  (C) **7.00**
1942 1 Franc. Similar (Brass) **10.00**

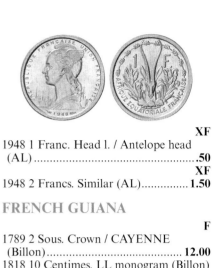

                                                 XF
1948 1 Franc. Head l. / Antelope head
  (AL) .... **.50**
                                                 XF
1948 2 Francs. Similar (AL) **1.50**

FRENCH GUIANA
                                                  F
1789 2 Sous. Crown / CAYENNE
  (Billon) **12.00**
1818 10 Centimes. LL monogram (Billon)
  .... **20.00**

FRENCH INDIA
                                                  F
(1723) ½ Fanon. Crown / Field of fleurs
  (C) **100.00**
1720-1835 Doudou. Fleur / Inscription
  (C) **12.00**
1753 Biche. Five fleurs / I753 (C) **25.00**
1776 1/5 Rupee. Arabic inscription, P on
  rev. (S) **20.00**

                                                  F
Arcot Rupee in name of Muhammed
  Shah, year 25 (S) **45.00**

FRENCH INDO-CHINA
                                                 VF
1887 2 Sapeque. French inscription /
  Chinese inscription (C, holed) **3.00**
1885 1 Cent. Std. figure / Chinese in
  rectangle (C) **4.00**
1899 1 Cent. Allegories of France and
  French Indo-China std. (C) **4.00**
1888 10 Cents. Figure std. (S) **30.00**
1921 10 Cents. Similar (S) **3.00**
1899 20 Cents. Similar (S) **30.00**
1894 50 Cents. Similar (S) **140.00**
1886 Piastre. Similar (S) **60.00**
1926 Piastre. Similar (S) **20.00**
                                                 XF
1942 ¼ Cent. (Z) **40.00**
1935 ½ Cent. Cap over RF (C) **2.00**
1943 1 Cent. Ears of grain (AL) **1.00**
1939 5 Cents. Head above two
  cornucopiae (CN, holed) **1.00**
1946 5 Cents. Bust with olive branch
  (AL) **1.00**
1941 10 Cents. Similar (CN) .... **.75**

XF

1941 20 Cents. Similar (CN) **1.00**
1936 50 Cents. Figure std. (S) **7.00**
1931 Piastre. Head l. (S).................. **20.00**
1947 Piastre. Bust with olive branch
(CN)... **2.00**

FRENCH OCEANIA

XF

1949 50 Centimes. Republic std. / Beach
scene (AL)...................................... **1.50**

XF

1949 2 Francs. Similar (AL)............... **1.50**

FRENCH POLYNESIA

BU

1965 50 Centimes. Republic std. / Beach
scene (AL)...................................... **1.50**
1987 1 Franc. Similar (AL).................. **.45**
1965 2 Francs. Similar (AL).............. **1.00**
1967 10 Francs. Carving (N).............. **1.75**
1991 50 Francs. Beach huts below
mountain (N) **2.50**

BU

1982 100 Francs. Similar (N-Brass).... **4.00**

FRENCH SOMALIA

BU

1959 1 Franc. Antelope head (AL) **5.00**
1959 2 Francs. Similar (AL).............. **5.00**
1975 10 Francs. Ocean liner and small
sailing ship (ALB)........................... **5.00**

FRENCH WEST AFRICA

XF

1944 1 Franc. Head l. / Two cornucopiae
(ALB)... **6.00**

XF

1948 2 Francs. Head l. / Antelope head
(AL) .... **.50**
1956 10 Francs. Similar (ALB) **1.50**
1957 25 Francs. Antelope head / Root
figure (ALB).................................... **2.00**

GUADELOUPE

F

1921 50 Centimes. Carib Indian (CN)
.... **12.00**

F

1903 1 Franc. Carib Indian (CN)..... **20.00**

MADAGASCAR

XF

1943 50 Centimes. Cock / Double cross
(C)... **12.00**
1958 1 Franc. Three bull heads (AL)
.... **.50**

XF

1948 2 Francs. Similar (AL)................ **.75**
1953 20 Francs. Map (ALB) **3.00**

MARTINIQUE

F

1897 50 Centimes. Bust of contemporary
woman (CN) **25.00**
1897 1 Franc. Similar (CN).............. **30.00**

NEW CALEDONIA

BU

1949 50 Centimes. Republic std. / Kagu
bird (AL).. **3.50**
1994 1 Franc. Similar (AL).................. **.50**
1949 2 Francs. Similar (AL).............. **4.50**

BU

1972 10 Francs. Small sailing ship (N)
.... **2.00**
1967 20 Francs. Busts of three bulls
.... **5.00**

BU

1972 50 Francs. Hut and trees (N) **5.00**
1976 100 Francs. Similar (N-C) **6.50**

NEW HEBRIDES

BU

1970 1 Franc. Bird (N-Brass)............... **.75**

BU

1973 10 Franc. Carved head (N)........ **1.25**
1966 100 Francs. Carving (S) **22.00**

REUNION

VF

1816 10 Centimes. LL monogram / ISLE
DE BOURBON (Billon)................ **85.00**
1896 50 Centimes. Bust of Mercury (CN)
.... **45.00**

BU

1948 1 Franc. Palm trees (AL)........... **2.50**
1955 10 Francs. Shield (ALB)............ **3.00**
1964 100 Francs. Shield (N)............... **4.00**

SAINT PIERRE & MIQUELON

BU

1948 1 Franc. Sailing ship (AL)......... **5.50**
1948 2 Francs. Similar (AL).............. **6.50**

TOGO

VF

1924 50 Centimes. Palm branches (ALB)
.... **6.00**
1948 1 Franc. Antelope head (AL)
.... **6.00**

VF

1924 2 Francs. Palm branches (ALB)
.... **27.00**
1956 5 Francs. Antelope head (ALB)
.... **3.00**

TONKIN

XF

1905 1/600th Piastre. French inscription /
Chinese inscription (Z)................. **18.00**

TUNISIA

VF

1938 5 Centimes. Arabic inscription /
French inscription (CN, holed) **2.00**
1945 50 Centimes. Wreath / Wreath
(ALB).. **35**
1946 5 Francs. Arabic inscription /
French inscription (ALB)................. **2.00**
1939 20 Francs. Two branches / Wreath
(S) **24.00**

GERMANY

The coinage of Germany is by far the most complex of the modern era. As more nobles and bishops were given the right to strike coins as a favor of the Holy Roman Emperor, the number of issuing authorities in greater Germany became almost bewildering. Certainly, at its greatest, it ran into several hundred. Most struck coins solely in their own names. Others, such as cities, stamped their own authority on one side, but paid homage to the Holy Roman Emperor on the other. The local side of a coin would usually depict the bust or arms of the local prince, or a city's patron saint. Some depicted symbolic animals or a "wild man" (a giant wearing nothing but a loin-encircling bush). The emperor was sometimes portrayed, but usually he was honored by inscribing his titles around a double-headed eagle. Usually the emperor was the head of the Austrian house of Hapsburg, but not always.

Following the Napoleonic wars, many of the ecclesiastical territories were absorbed by the secular ones. The greater states began to take over the smaller ones, and the Holy Roman Empire ceased to exist. For the first time, the number of coin-issuing German authorities began to decline. This process continued until the German states were finally replaced by a republic in 1918.

While there were a great many local coinage standards, some basic ideas remained consistent. A *thaler* was a large, silver-dollar-sized coin. A *ducat* was made of gold and uniformly contained 11/100 troy ounce of that metal. Good silver coins were often valued in terms of how many went to make a thaler. Thus the inscription *6 einen thaler* meant that the coin was worth one sixth of a thaler. *Guldens* were not always used, but usually resembled an American half dollar. The *albus* and

groschen were small silver coins. Other small coins, such as the *pfennig, heller* and *kreuzer*, could be either copper or billon, but when they were created in the Middle Ages, they were originally silver.

Almost 50 years before the German states passed into history, Germany became a unified nation. Each local prince retained his own territories and some aspect of local government, but after 1871 the national government fell to the hands of one German Emperor, who happened to be the hereditary King of Prussia, the most powerful of the German states. Throughout Germany, all copper and small silver coins (one pfennig to one mark) were uniform. Larger silver and gold coins (two through 20 marks) shared a common reverse design with the legend *Deutsches Reich*. The obverse bore the portrait of the local prince or the city arms.

During and immediately after World War I, hundreds of municipal governments and companies throughout Germany struck small-denomination emergency tokens or *notgeld* to facilitate commerce. They were usually struck in zinc, iron or aluminum, occasionally porcelain. Their designs run from traditional heraldry to humorous to utilitarian.

The "Weimar" Republic of 1918 to 1933 struck minor coins of fairly bland agricultural designs, and a good number of exciting commemorative silver pieces. Its coins were replaced in the 1930s by ones bearing the notorious Nazi swastika held by an eagle. During World War II, like so many other countries, zinc replaced most coinage metals needed for the war effort.

From 1949 until 1990 there were two Germanys, the Federal Republic (West), and the smaller, Soviet-dominated Democratic Republic (East). Each had its own coinage, the West with a traditional German eagle; the East, with typical Communist industrial symbolism. Both states struck numerous commemoratives, often quite similar in inspiration. With the fall of Communism, East Germany chose to join West Germany, which then attempted to bail the smaller state out of its economic morass.

In January 2002, Germany replaced the mark with coins denominated in euros, the currency of the European Union. On the circulating denominations, one cent through two euros, there is one side that carries a German design, the other a common European motif. On higher-denomination commemoratives, both sides are distinctively German.

The German Empire struck coins for two colonies and both are popularly collected. The issues for German East

Africa were struck in gold, silver and bronze. The large silver pieces bear an exciting bust of Kaiser Wilhelm II wearing an elaborate griffin-topped helmet. The large silver pieces of German New Guinea display a detailed bird of paradise, considered by some to be among the most beautiful images of the entire European colonial series. All German New Guinea coins are scarce and in high demand.

Prices: In many specialized markets and in Europe, many German coins can sell for prices in excess of those listed below. Also, the prices shown here are for common dates. Rare date and mint combinations can be quite valuable.

Spelling: There are many spelling variations connected with German coins. Thaler is the earlier form of *taler*. Kreuzer is the later form or kreutzer. Pfenning is a variant of pfenning. Also note that ü is a symbol for ue and both are quite common.

Additional Specialized Books: *Money Trend* magazine provides up-to-the-month pricing for this volatile market.

Known Counterfeits: A great many contemporary counterfeits exist of Prussian 1/24 and 1/12 thalers of the 1700s. Some also exist of 1/3 thalers, 1773A for example. Deceptive modern counterfeits exist of several 20-mark gold pieces. While rare patterns of Adolf Hitler portrait coins exist, virtually all those encountered are actually fantasy souvenirs made well after the war.

Some banks have re-struck classic 17th- and 18th-century coins with new dies. These are easily distinguished from originals because of their brilliant proof finishes. Many also have a small date of re-striking discretely placed on the coin.

Beware of damaged coins. Solder and other mount marks severely reduce the value of a coin. So does smoothing out an unpleasant surfaces by means of heavy polishing or scraping. This practice is particularly common on German coins. Early coins struck with roller dies will be slightly curved. This is not damage and is to be expected.

GERMAN STATES TO 1871

F

Aachen. 1759 12 heller. Eagle / Inscription (C).. **20.00**
Anhalt-Bernburg. 1806 2/3 Thaler. Bearon citywall (S) **30.00**
Augsburg. 1715 Heller. Pine cone / Cross with rose at center and leaves in angles (C).. **8.00**

F

Baden. 1870 Kreuzer. Shield between griffins / Wreath (C) **2.00**
Bavaria. 1750 12 kreuzer. Bust r. / Crowned round arms (S)................ **18.00**
1760 Thaler. Bust r. / Madonna and Child (S)... **40.00**
Many poor counterfeits of this thaler have recently come onto the market.
__. 1846 1 Pfennig. Arms (C)............. **2.00**

F

__. 1720 30 kreuzer. Bust / Lion with sword and shield (S) **30.00**
__. 1855. 2 Gulden. Bust r. / Madonna column (S)............................... VF **30.00**

F

Brandenburg-Ansbach. 1766 Thaler. Bust r. / Arms (S) **150.00**
Brandenburg-Prussia. 1676 18 Groscher (¼ Thaler). Bust r. with sword / Eagle (S) **35.00**
Bremen. 1781 Schwaren. Key / Inscription. (C)................................. **6.00**
Brunswick-Luneburg. 1660 Thaler. Shield / Wildman standing (S) **300.00**
Brunswick-Wolfenbuttel. 1823 1/24th Thaler. Horse leaping l. / Inscription (Billon)... **6.00**
Camenz. 1622 3 Pfennig. Wing / Inscription. (C)............................... **40.00**
Frankfurt. 1786 Pfennig. Eagle / Inscription (C)................................. **4.00**
Hamburg. 1727 4 Schilling. Double headed eagle / Castle (S)................ **20.00**
1861 Ducat. Knight stg. / Inscription (G) **200.00**

F

Hanau-Lichtenburg. 1759 4 Kreuzer. Lion, H D above / Value (S)........ **125.00**

F

Hannover. 1834 Thaler. Head of William IV of England / Crowned shield (S) **45.00**
__. 1855 6 Pfennig. Horse leaping (Billon) **4.00**
Hesse-Cassel. 1843 3 Heller. Shield / Inscription (C)................................. **2.00**

F

Hesse-Homburg. 1 Kreuzer. Arms / Wreath (S)....................................... **90.00**

F

Hohenzollern. 1 Kreuzer. Eagle / Wreath (C).. **15.00**
Isenburg. (1847) "Snipe heller." AJ in wreath / Snipe (C) **22.00**
Lindau. 1689 Pfennig. Linden tree / blank (C).. **30.00**
Lippe-Detmold. 1685 Thaler. Bust Simon Heinrich r. / Arms (S)................... **650.00**
1860 Thaler. Bust of Paul F.E. Leopold r. / Arms (S)..................................... **40.00**
Lübeck. 1732 8 Schilling. Double headed eagle / Shield (S)......................... **30.00**
Mainz. 1671 Ducat. Bust of Johann Philip r. / Shield (G) **350.00**
Munster. 1735 3 Pfennig. CA monogram / Inscription (C) **8.00**
Nassau. 1861 Kreuzer. Crowned shield / Wreath (Billon) **2.00**
Nurnberg. (1700) 1/16 Ducat. Shield / Lamb holding banner (G) square... **95.00**
Oldenburg. 1858 Groschen. Crowned shield / Inscription (Billon) **5.00**
Prussia. 1840 Pfennig. Crowned shield / Inscription (C)................................. **1.50**
1847 3 Pfenninge. Similar (C) **2.00**
1821 Silber Groschen. Head of Freidrich Wilhelm III r. / Value (Billon) **4.00**

1869 2½ Silber Groschen. Head of
 Wilhelm I / Value (Billon) **2.50**
1701 1/12 Thaler. Eagle surrounded by Fs
 and Rs / Crowned scepter (S) **35.00**

F

Rostock. 1729. 3 Pfennig. Griffin (C)
 .... **12.00**
Saxony. 1866 5 Pfennige. Crowned
 Baroque shield / Inscription **2.00**
1668 1/24th Thaler. Arms / Royal orb (S)
 .... **20.00**
1776 Thaler. Bust of Friedrich August r. /
 Shield (S) **45.00**
Schwarzburg-Sondershausen. 1846
 Pfennig. Crowned shield / Inscription
 (C) **2.00**

F

Silesia. 1809 1 Groschel. Monogram.
 (Billon) **22.00**
Stolberg-Werningerode. 1768 Ducat. Bust
 of Christian Ernst / Stag stg. l. (G)
 .... **600.00**
Trier. 1695 3 Petermenger. Crowned
 shield / Bust of St. Peter (S) **25.00**
Westphalia. 1812 2 Centimes. HN
 monogram / Inscription (C) **3.00**

F

1808 2 Franken. Bust of Jerome
 Napoleon / Wreath (S) **250.00**
Württemberg. 1798 ½ Kreuzer. Crowned
 FII / ½ (Billon) **9.00**
Wurzburg. 1791 20 kreuzer. Bust / Arms
 .... **35.00**
1848 3 Kreuzer. Crowned shield / Wreath
 .... **2.00**

GERMAN STATES 1873-1918

VF

(All reverses are the imperial eagle
unless noted.)
Anhalt-Dessau. 1914 3 Mark. Heads of
 Duke and Duchess (S) **60.00**

VF

Baden. 1908 3 Mark. Head of Friedrich
 II l. (S) **30.00**

VF

Bavaria. 1876 2 Mark. Head of Ludwig II
 r. (S) **70.00**
__. 1909 3 Mark. Head of Otto l. (S)
 .... **20.00**
Bremen. 1904 2 Mark. Shield (S) **65.00**
Brunswick-Wolfenbuttel. 1915 3 Mark.
 Heads of Duke and Duchess r. (S)
 .... **125.00**
Hamburg. 1896 2 Mark. Shield between
 lions (S) **25.00**
Hesse-Darmstadt. 1904 2 Mark. Busts of
 Philipp and Ludwig l. (S) **60.00**
Lippe-Detmold. 1906 2 Mark. Bust of
 Leopold IV l. (S) **260.00**
Lübeck. 1908 3 Mark. Double headed
 eagle (S) **70.00**

VF

Mecklenburg-Schwerin. 1904 2 Mark.
 Busts of Grand Duke and Grand
 Duchess l. (S) **40.00**
Mecklenburg-Strelitz. 1877 2 Mark. Bust
 of Friedrich Wilhelm l. (S) **300.00**
Oldenburg. 1901 2 Mark. Bust of
 Friedrich August l. (S) **225.00**
Prussia. 1913 2 Mark. Bust of Wilhelm II
 (S) **18.00**

VF

1913 3 Mark. King on horse, surrounded
 by followers / Eagle grasping snake (S)
 .... **20.00**
1908 5 Mark. Wilhelm II. (S) **22.00**

VF

1872 10 Mark. Wilhelm I (G) **145.00**
1888 20 Mark. Friedrich III (G)
 .... **275.00**
Reuss-Greiz. 1899 2 Mark. Bust of
 Heinrich XXII (S) **225.00**
Reuss-Schleiz. 1884 2 Mark. Head of
 Heinrich XIV (S) **300.00**
Saxe-Altenburg. 1903 5 Mark. Bust of
 Ernst r. (S) **200.00**
Saxe-Coburg-Gotha. 1905 2 Mark. Head
 of Carl Eduard r. (S) **300.00**
Saxe-Meiningen. 1915 2 Mark. Bust of
 Georg II l. (S) **75.00**
Saxe-Weimar-Eisenach. 1910 3 Mark.
 Heads of Grand Duke and Grand
 Duchess (S) **40.00**

VF

Saxony. 1913 3 Mark. Building (S)
 .... **20.00**
Schaumburg-Lippe. 1911 3 Mark. Bust of
 Georg l. (S) **65.00**
Schwarzburg-Rudolstadt. 1898 2 Mark.
 Bust of Günther l. (S) **260.00**
Schwarzburg-Sondershausen. 1905 2
 Mark. Head of Karl Günther r. (S)
 .... **55.00**
Waldeck-Pyrmont. 1903 20 Mark. Head
 of Friedrich l. (G) **4,000.00**

VF

Württemberg. 1914 3 Mark. Bust of
 Wilhelm II r. (S) **20.00**
__. 1904 10 Mark. Similar (G) **140.00**

GERMAN EMPIRE 1873-1918

VF

1915 1 Pfennig. Large eagle / Inscription
(C)..**.50**
1906 2 Pfennig. Similar (C).................**.25**
1874 5 Pfennig. Small Eagle (CN) **1.00**
1905 5 Pfennig. Large eagle (CN) ....**.50**
1919 5 Pfennig. Similar (Iron)..............**.25**

VF

1898 10 Pfennig. Similar (CN)..............**.25**
1875 20 Pfennig. Small eagle (S) **8.00**

VF

1890 20 Pfennig. Eagle in wreath /
Inscription (CN) **40.00**
1909 25 Pfennig. Large eagle / Wreath
(N) **9.00**

VF

1876 50 Pfennig. Small eagle / Inscription
(S) **12.00**
1918 ½ Mark. Eagle in wreath / Wreath
(S) **2.50**
1874 1 Mark. Small eagle / Wreath (S)
.... **6.50**

VF

1914 1 Mark. Large eagle / Wreath (S)
.... **4.00**

NOTGELD

VF

Aachen. 1920 10 Pfennig. Bear. (Iron)
.... **3.00**
Coblenz. 1918 25 Pfennig. Arms
(Iron) **2.50**
Darmstadt 1917 10 pfennig. Crowned
arms (Z) **2.50**

Hamburg. 1923 5/100
Verrechnungsmarke. Arms (AL) **4.00**
Leipzig. (1920) 20 Pfennig. Arms /
Strassenbahn... (Iron)...................... **4.00**
Similar but *wooden*........................... **6.00**
Saxony 1921 5 marks. Naked man
between ears of grain. (Porcelain, gilt)
.... **EF 12.50**

VF

Westphalia. 1923 ¼ Million Mark. Von
Stein / Horse rearing (AL) **8.00**

REPUBLIC 1919-1933

VF

1923 1 Rentenpfennig. Sheaf of wheat
(C)...**.50**
1925 2 Reichspfennig. Similar (C).........**.30**

VF

1932 4 Reichspfennig. Eagle (C) **9.00**

VF

1925 5 Reichspfennig. Stylized wheat
(ALB)...**.50**
1929 10 Reichspfennig. Similar (ALB)..**.50**
1924 50 Rentenpfennig. Similar.
(ALB) **12.00**
1931 50 Reichspfennig. Eagle (N) **4.00**
1924 1 Mark. Eagle (S) **12.00**
1922 3 Mark. Eagle within legend (AL)
.... **1.00**
1928 3 Mark. Eagle / Dinkelsbühl, Man
over city walls (S) **500.00**

VF

1930 5 Mark. Eagle / Graf Zeppelin (S)
.... **120.00**
1931 5 Mark. Eagle / Oak tree (S).. **100.00**

NAZI STATE 1933-1945

VF

1937 1 Reichspfennig. Eagle holding
swastika in wreath (C)......................**.50**
1940 5 Reichspfennig. Similar (Z)........**.25**
1938 50 Reichspfennig. Similar (N) . **30.00**

VF

1942 50 Reichspfennig. Similar (AL) . **1.50**
1934 2 Reichsmark. Schiller. (S)....... **70.00**

VF

1937 5 Reichsmark. Hindenburg / Eagle
holding swastika in wreath (S) **12.00**

FEDERAL REPUBLIC

Unc

1950 1 Pfennig. Oak sapling. (C plated
Steel) **1.00**
1993 2 Pfennig. Oak sapling. (C plated
Steel) ....**.10**
1949 5 Pfennig. Oak sapling. (Brass
plated Steel)................................... **30.00**

Unc

1980 10 Pfennig. Oak sapling. (Brass
plated Steel)......................................**.20**
1950 50 pfennig. Woman planting
sapling. (CN)................................... **9.00**
1977 1 Deutsche Mark. Eagle / Oak
leaves (CN)...................................... **1.40**
1951 2 Deutsche Mark. Eagle / Grapes
and wheat (CN).............................. **110.00**
1971 2 Deutsche Mark. Max Planck /
Eagle (CN)...................................... **3.00**

Unc
1952 5 Deutsche Mark. Museum, Stylized
eagle / Eagle (S)............................ **850.00**

Unc
1976 5 Deutsche Mark. Monster / Eagle
(S) **7.00**
1970 5 Deutsche Mark. Eagle /
Inscription (S) **9.00**
1983 5 Deutsche Mark. Karl Marx /
Eagle (CN clad N) **4.50**
1972 10 Deutsche Mark. Olympic flame /
Eagle (S).. **9.50**
1990 10 Deutsche Mark. Friedrich
Barbarossa / Eagle (S) **10.00**

Euro Coinage 2002 to date

BU
2002 5 Cent. Oak sapling / Map (C clad
steel)...**.50**
2002 1 Euro. Eagle / Map. (CN clad N in
NB, bimetallic)................................ **3.00**

BU
2002 10 Euro. Eagle / Map (S)......... **20.00**

DEMOCRATIC REPUBLIC (EAST GERMANY)

Unc
1952 1 Pfennig. Hammer, compass and
wheat (AL).. **6.00**
1948 5 Pfennig. Wheat on gear. (AL)
.... **50.00**
1989 10 Pfennig. Hammer and compass
within wheat. (AL)...........................**.60**
1950 50 Pfennig. Three smoke stacks.
(ALB).. **60.00**
1982 2 Mark. Hammer and compass
within wheat. (AL)........................... **3.00**
1971. 5 Mark. Brandenburg Gate. (CN)
.... **10.00**
1979 5 Mark. Albert Einstein (CN)
.... **80.00**
1972 10 Mark. Buchenwald Memorial
(CN)... **8.00**

Unc
1988 10 Mark. von Hutten. (S)........ **90.00**

GERMAN EAST AFRICA

VF
1890 Pesa. Eagle / Arabic inscription. (C)
.... **4.00**
1910 Heller. Crown / Wreath (C) **3.00**
1909 5 Heller. Similar (C) **55.00**
1916 5 Heller. Crown over DOA / Wreath
(C)... **13.00**

VF
1891 ¼ Rupie. Bust of Wilhelm II in
griffin helmet / Arms (S) **22.00**
1913 ¼ Rupie. Bust of Wilhelm II in
griffin helmet / Wreath (S).............. **15.00**
1893 2 Rupien. Similar bust / Arms (S)
.... **350.00**
1916 15 Rupien. Eagle / Elephant. (G)
.... **950.00**

GERMAN NEW GUINEA

XF
1894 1 Pfennig. Inscription (C)........ **90.00**

XF
1894 1 Mark. Bird of paradise (S)
.... **200.00**

XF
1894 5 Mark. Bird of paradise (S)
.... **1,250.00**
1895 20 Mark. Similar. (G)......... **8,750.00**

KIAO CHAU

VF
1909 10 Cent. Eagle on anchor / Chinese
Inscription (CN) **60.00**

HUNGARY

The reign of Leopold I the
Hogmouth (1657-1705) saw a far
greater change for Hungarian coins
than it did for the coinage of his
Austrian dominions. Of course, as in
Austria, modern coin production under
Leopold, then using roller dies, was
taken to a new height of uniformity.
Their excellent portraits are a perfect
example of the Baroque style. Collectors
should remember that coins struck
with roller dies usually appear slightly
curved and that this is not a flaw.
But in Hungary before the mid 1600s
only three denominations, the small
base silver denar, the big silver thaler,
and the gold ducat were common in
circulation. This period saw the increase
in production of a whole range of middle
denominations. For the most part, the
Madonna and Child still dominated the
reverse, with portraits on the obverse.
During the reign of Maria Theresa
(1740-80) copper replaced base silver
for the small denominations, and coats
of arms became more common. The
coppers in particular were ornamented
with impressive, high-relief portraits.
Unfortunately, the poor condition of
most surviving examples makes this
difficult to appreciate today.

From 1892 until the Communist
takeover, the Holy Crown of Saint
Stephen, a relic of Hungary's patron
saint, came to dominate the coinage,
with the Madonna or a portrait to give
diversity. The Communists replaced
the old religious symbols with national
heroes, architecture and images idealizing
industrial and agricultural labor.
Interestingly, the new post-Communist
republic combines both old and new
imagery harmoniously, with a pleasant
mixture of flora and fauna.

Additional Specialized Books:
Huszar, L., Münzkatalog Ungarn.
Known Counterfeits: Many gold
coins have been re-struck in quantity.
These include 1892 10 and 20 korona,
1907 and 1908 100 korona, and some
1895 pieces. Also note that all coins

marked UP are re-strikes, regardless of
type or metal.

Leopold I Hogmouth, 1657-1705   **F**
1662 Denar. Crowned shield / Madonna
and Child (Billon) **9.00**
1703 Duarius. Crowned shield / Small
Madonna and Child over denomination
(Billon).. **16.00**

    F
1671 6 Krajczar. Bust r. / Madonna and
Child (S)... **18.00**
1695 ¼ Thaler. Bust in diamond /
Madonna and Child stg. in diamond (S)
.... **30.00**
1661 Thaler. Bust of Leopold, Hungarian
shield and Madonna and Child in
margin / Double headed eagle (S)
.... **175.00**
1694 Ducat. Leopold stg. / Madonna and
Child (G).. **250.00**
1703 5 Ducat. Bust r. / Crowned imperial
eagle (G).. *Rare*

Other Rulers, 1705-1848

    F
1706 Poltura. Shield / Madonna and
Child (C) **15.00**
1711 Poltura. Joseph I / Small Madonna
and Child over denomination (S)
.... **15.00**
1705 10 Poltura. Crowned shield / PRO
LIBERTATE X (C)......................... **20.00**
1848 1 Krajczar. Crowned shield (C)
.... **2.00**
1849 6 Krajczar. Crowned shield (Billon)
.... **5.00**
1778 20 Krajczar. Maria Theresa in
wreath / Madonna and Child in wreath
(S) **15.00**
1839 20 Krajczar. Ferdinand I / Madonna
and Child (S).................................... **4.00**
1742 ½ Thaler. Maria Theresa / Similar
(S) **55.00**
1785 ½ Thaler. Angels over arms /
Similar (S).. **40.00**
1833 Thaler. Francis I / Similar (S)
.... **90.00**

    F
1765 2 Ducat. Maria Theresa stg. /
Madonna and Child (G) **400.00**
Francis Joseph, 1848-1916   **VF**
1868 1 Krajczar. Angels over shield /
Wreath (C) **1.25**
1870 10 Krajczar. Head r. / Crown of St.
Stephen (Billon) **7.50**
1879 1 Forint. Head r. / Crowned shield
(S) **12.00**
1909 2 Filler. Crown of St. Stephen (C)
.... **1.00**
1893 10 Filler. Crown of St. Stephen (N)
....**.50**
1915 Korona. Head r. / Crown of St.
Stephen (S)....................................... **4.00**
1908 5 Korona. Similar (S) **20.00**

    VF
1910 10 Korona Francis Joseph stg. /
Arms (G).. **120.00**
Regency, 1920-45   **VF**

    VF
1937 2 Filler. Crown of St. Stephen (C)
....**.25**
1927 1 Pengo. Crowned shield (S)...... **2.00**
1942 2 Pengo. Similar (AL).................**.35**
1938 5 Pengo. Bust of St. Stephen / Arms
(S) **15.00**
1943 5 Pengo. Bust of Nicholas Horthy /
Arms (AL) **1.00**

Republics, 1946-date   **BU**
1950 2 Filler. Wreath (AL, holed).........**.50**
1982 10 Filler. Dove (AL).................. **1.50**
1979 50 Filler. Bridge (AL)................ **1.50**
1949 1 Forint. Arms (AL)................ **12.00**
1971 5 Forint. Kossuth / Arms (CN) . **1.50**

    BU
2001 5 Forint. Egret (Brass).............. **1.00**
1956 25 Forint. Parliament / Arms and
gear (S)... **25.00**
1985 100 Forint. Turtle (S).............. **12.00**
1996 100 Forint. Crowned shield (Steel,
brass plated center, *bimetallic*).......... **5.00**

    BU
1979 200 Forint. IYC logo / child's
drawing of coin (S) **16.00**
2000 200 Forint. Rhodin's Thinker and
solar system / Arms (ALB) **5.00**
1961 500 Forint. Bela Bartok (G)
.... **1,400.00**
1992 500 Forint. Tellstar satellite (S)
.... **25.00**
2002 500 Forint. Rubik's Cube (CN)
.... **25.00**

    BU
2002 500 Forint. 1769 Chess automaton
(CN)... **18.00**

ITALY

    Much like Germany, Italy until 1861
was divided into a number of smaller
independent countries. During most of
the modern era, the south was unified as
the Kingdom of Naples and Sicily (more
properly called the Two Sicilies). While
artistically creative in the 1600s and
1700s, its more mundane later coinage is
commonly encountered. The island of
Sicily itself usually had separate coinage.

Central Italy was ruled by the Pope. Despite being one unified Papal State, many of the larger cities under papal rule did have special designs and sometimes even different coinage standards. This local variation ended by 1800. Unlike the other Italian states incorporated into the new unified Kingdom of Italy in 1860-61, the Pope was able to maintain his independence until 1870. After decades of dispute with Italy, the Papal State was restored to independence in 1929 as the much smaller State of the Vatican City. Since then, Papal coins have been routinely struck and can occasionally be found circulating not only at the Vatican, but in and around Rome. Most Vatican coins today are collected in mint sets.

Throughout this period most papal and Vatican coins have depicted the pope or his coat of arms, along with some religious iconography or a Latin saying reflecting some moral precept. There are three kinds of "special" coins. *Sede Vacante* coins are struck between Popes and have the arms of the Papal Secretary of State. *Holy Year* coins are struck to celebrate the Jubilee when pilgrims are encouraged to come to Rome. Lastly, *Lateran* coins were given to the crowds when the pope took possession of the Cathedral of St. John Lateran in Rome. This is his church as Bishop of Rome, not St. Peter's Basilica.

Papal medals are quite common and are struck for commemorative purposes only. They should not be confused with coins. They are usually large and have high relief. Most of those dated before 1775 are actually government re-strikes from the original dies from the late 1700s and after. Those after 1550 that appear cast are unofficial replicas, but not necessarily worthless.

Northern Italy – a mix of small states – was much more complex. Some, such as Venice, were international powers; others were controlled by petty princes. Ultimately, a good number of them fell into the hands of foreign powers such as Spain, France and Austria. The Duke of Savoy (who was also King of Sardinia) began to unify Italy by conquering these small states, and then moving south. One Italian state that has survived is San Marino. It has had coinage since 1864 but today most of its coins are sold to collectors. Like the Vatican's coins, they are struck to Italian standards and can be spent in Italy.

The first unified Italian coinage was struck to the international Latin Monetary Union standard (see France).

Italian coins of the 20th century are usually of high artistic merit. After World War I, the *lira* shrunk to one fifth of its value. Its value evaporated again after World War II and many coins of the 1940s to 1980s are aluminum or steel. (Lira is singular, lire is plural.)

In January 2002, Italy replaced the lira with coins denominated in euros, the currency of the European Union. On the circulating denominations, one cent through two euros, there is one side which carries an Italian design, the other a common European design. Because of their monetary unions with Italy, the Vatican and San Marino have euro coins struck out of Italy's allotment of coinage.

The colonial coins of Italy are popularly collected, and are in high demand. Most silver is found cleaned and most copper pitted, but despite this, collectors will often settle for these imperfect specimens.

Additional Specialized Books:
Berman, Allen G., *Papal Coins.*
Giganti, F., *Monete Italiane.*
Gill, Dennis, *Coinage of Ethiopia, Eritrea and Italian Somalia.*
Muntoni, *Le monete dei Papi e degli Stati Pontifici.*

Known Counterfeits: There are many contemporary counterfeits of Italian minor coins, including 1863M one lira, 1863N and 1911 two lire, 1927 and 1930 five lire, 1958-500 lire. Vatican and papal pieces include 1736 one grosso, 1796 two carlini, 1797 five Baiocchi and 1868 four soldi, and Naples including 1796 120 grana.

More deceptive counterfeits capable of fooling collectors are quite common. Mostly they are imitations of the old silver-dollar-size five- and 20-lire pieces. This is also true of similar Papal and San Marino five-lire pieces. The overwhelming majority of Eritrea five-lire and Talero pieces are counterfeit. Many Italian, Papal and Vatican gold coins have also been counterfeited, but less commonly than the large silver. A partial list of counterfeits includes: Two lire 1895 and 1898, and five lire 1914. Authentic common coins are sometimes found altered to rare dates.

The 20 lire depicting Mussolini is not a coin but a privately struck fantasy. Some trial euro coins exist, struck by cities. Vatican euro coins dated 2000 are unofficial.

ITALIAN STATES

Bologna. 1680 Quattrino. Lion with banner / BONONIA DOCET (C) **25.00**

F
1769 5 Bolognini. City arms / Cartouche (S) **30.00**
Genoa. 1814 10 Soldi. Arms / John the Baptist (S) **20.00**

F
Gorizia. 1733 Soldo. Crowned arms / Cartouche (C) **8.00**
Lombardy-Venetia. 1846 1 Centesimo. Two crowns (C) **4.00**
Lucca. 1664 Quattrino. L / Holy Countenance (C) **15.00**
Milan. 1665-1700 Quattrino. Charles II of Spain / Crowned MLNI DVX in wreath (C) **22.00**

F
Naples. 1693 Ducato. Charles II / Golden Fleece (S) **200.00**
1788 Grano. Ferdinand IV / Wreath (C) **15.00**
1791 Piastra. King and Queen / Band of zodiac over Sun and Earth (S) **175.00**
1845 6 Ducati. Ferdinand II / Winged genius (G) **325.00**
1857 2 Tornesi. Ferdinand II / Crown (C) **3.50**
Napoleonic Kingdom. 1813 5 Soldi. Head r. / Crown (S)..................................... **12.00**

F
Savoy (as Kingdom of **Sardinia**). 1794 5 Soldi. Bust r. / St. Mauritius stg. (C) **15.00**
1830 1 Lira. Bust r. / Arms (S)......... **25.00**
Sicily. 1737 Grano. Eagle / Cartouche (C) **25.00**
1793 Oncia. Bust r. / Phoenix in flames (S) **800.00**

F

Tuscany. 1680 Tallero. Cosimo III / Baptism of Christ (S) **220.00**
1710 3 Quattrini for Pisa. Crown over 6 balls / Cross (Billon) **15.00**
1859 2 Centesimi. Arms (C) **4.00**
Venice. 1684-88 Soldo. S M V M A IVSTIN, Doge and lion / Christ (C) **20.00**
1676-84 Zecchino (Ducat). ALOYSIVS CONT, Doge and St. Mark / Christ (G) **350.00**
1722-32 Scudo. ALOYSIVS MOCENICO...VQ, Cross / Bust of lion in shield (S) **125.00**
1741-52 Soldo. S M V PET GRIM D, Doge and lion / Christ (C) **15.00**

ITALY

VF

Vittorio Emanuele II, 1861-78 .
1861 1 Centesimo. Head l. / Wreath (C) **1.50**
1862 2 Centesimi. Similar (C) **1.50**
1861 5 Centesimi. Similar (C) **1.50**

VF

1867 10 Centesimi. Similar (C) **3.50**
1863 1 Lira. Head r. / Wreath (S) **5.00**
1874 5 Lire. Head r. / Arms (S) **23.00**
1863 20 Lire. Head l. / Arms (G) **215.00**

Umberto II, 1878-1900.
1897 2 Centesimi. Head l. / Wreath (C) **1.50**
1895 5 Centesimi. Similar (C) **35.00**
1893 10 Centesimi. Similar (C) **3.50**

VF
1889 50 Centesimi. Head r. / Arms (S) **300.00**
1886 1 Lira. Similar (S) **7.00**
1882 20 Lire. Head l. / Arms (G) **210.00**

Vittorio Emanuele III, 1900-46.
1915 2 Centesimi. Bust l. / Italia on ship (C) **1.30**
1921 10 Centesimi. Head l. / Bee (C) **1.25**

VF
1908 20 Centesimi. Bust l. / Flying woman (N) **2.50**
1940 20 Centesimi. Head l. / Allegorical head r. with fasces (Steel) .... **.40**

VF
1917 1 Lira. Bust r. / Italia in four horse chariot (S) **16.00**
1922 1 Lira. Italia std. (N) **1.00**
1924 2 Lire. Bust r. / Fasces (N) **2.00**
1914 5 Lire. Bust r. / Italia in four horse chariot (S) **4,000.00**
1927 5 Lire. Head l. / Eagle (S) **4.00**
1927 10 Lire. Head l. / Italia in two horse chariot (S) **20.00**
1927 20 Lire. Head r. / Naked youth before std. Italia (S) **200.00**
1943 20 Lire. Mussolini / Fasces and lion head (Silvered brass). *This is a common post-war fantasy.* .... *BU* **6.00**
1912 50 Lire. Bust l. / Italia and plow (G) **1,400.00**

Republic, 1946-date
BU
1954 1 Lira. Scales / Cornucopia (AL) **2.00**
1957 2 Lire. Bee (AL) **2.50**
1969 5 Lire. Rudder / Porpoise (AL) .... **.75**
1950 10 Lire. Pegasus (AL) **10.00**
1975 50 Lire. Vulcan at forge (Steel) ..... **.75**

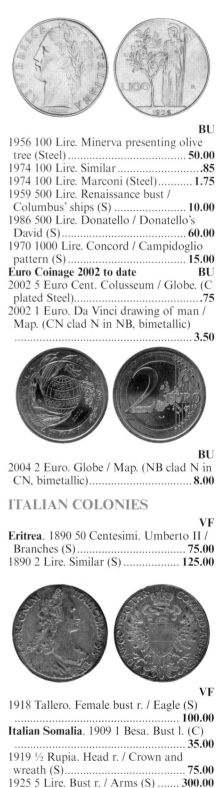

BU
1956 100 Lire. Minerva presenting olive tree (Steel) **50.00**
1974 100 Lire. Similar .... **.85**
1974 100 Lire. Marconi (Steel) **1.75**
1959 500 Lire. Renaissance bust / Columbus' ships (S) **10.00**
1986 500 Lire. Donatello / Donatello's David (S) **60.00**
1970 1000 Lire. Concord / Campidoglio pattern (S) **15.00**
Euro Coinage 2002 to date **BU**
2002 5 Euro Cent. Colusseum / Globe. (C plated Steel) .... **.75**
2002 1 Euro. Da Vinci drawing of man / Map. (CN clad N in NB, bimetallic) **3.50**

BU
2004 2 Euro. Globe / Map. (NB clad N in CN, bimetallic) **8.00**

ITALIAN COLONIES
VF
Eritrea. 1890 50 Centesimi. Umberto II / Branches (S) **75.00**
1890 2 Lire. Similar (S) **125.00**

VF
1918 Tallero. Female bust r. / Eagle (S) **100.00**
Italian Somalia. 1909 1 Besa. Bust l. (C) **35.00**
1919 ½ Rupia. Head r. / Crown and wreath (S) **75.00**
1925 5 Lire. Bust r. / Arms (S) **300.00**
    Note: The majority of the Tallero size coins of Eritrea and Italian Somalia found in the market are counterfeit.

SAN MARINO

	XF
1935 5 Centesimi. Arms (C)	**3.50**
1893 10 Centesimi. Arms (C)	**30.00**
1906 1 Lira. Arms / Wreath (S)	**60.00**

	XF
1937 10 Lire. Figure with sword and crown / Arms (S)	**30.00**
	BU
1972 1 Lira. Bust of St. Marino (AL)	**.25**
1974 20 Lire. Three towers / Lobster (ALB)	**.75**
1992 100 Lire. Similar / Columbus' ship (Steel)	**1.25**
1982 500 Lire. Similar / Garibaldi (S)	**13.50**
1996 10,000 Lire. Arms / Wolves (S)	**Proof only 40.00**
1979 5 Scudi. Three palm fronds / Three arms (G)	**500.00**

	XF
2002 1 Euro. Arms / Map. (CN clad N in NB, bimetallic)	**25.00**

PAPAL STATE

	F
Clement X, 1670-76. 1672 Piastra. Arms / Port of Civitavecchia (S)	**700.00**
__. 1675 1½ inch medal. Bust / Bricking up the Holy Door (C)	**125.00**
__. same, restrike	**40.00**
Innocent XI, 1676-89 ½ Grosso. Arms / NOCET MINVS (S)	**20.00**
Alexander VIII, 1689-91. 1690 Testone. Bust r. / Two oxen plowing (S)	**225.00**
Innocent XII, 1691-1700. Quattrino. Arms / St. Paul with sword (C)	**22.00**

	F
__. 1699 Testone. Arms / Inscription (S)	**120.00**
Clement XI, 1700-21. Grosso. Arms / DEDIT PAVPERIBVS (S)	**30.00**
Clement XII, 1730-40. 1738 Quattrino. Arms (C)	**18.50**
Benedict XIV 1740-58. 1750 Grosso. Arms / Holy door (S)	**32.00**
Clement XIII, 1758-69. 1766 Zecchino. Arms / Church std. on cloud (G)	**325.00**
Pius VI, 1775-99. 1797 2½ Baiocchi. Bust of St. Peter (C)	**22.00**
Pius VII, 1800-23. 1816 Quattrino. Arms (C)	**9.50**

	F
Sede Vacante, 1830. Scudo. Arms / Dove of Holy Spirit (S)	**150.00**
Gregory XVI, 1831-46. 1839 1/2 Baiocco. Arms / Wreath (C)	**4.00**
Pius IX, 1846-78. 1858 20 Baiocchi. Bust / Wreath (S)	**6.50**
1866 1 Soldo. Bust (C)	**2.00**

	F
1869 10 Soldi. Bust / Wreath (S)	**3.00**
1868 20 Lire. Similar (G)	**220.00**

VATICAN CITY

	BU
1930 5 Centesimi. Arms / Olive sprig (C)	**9.00**
1942 10 Centesimi. Pius XII / Dove (Brass)	**65.00**
1934 20 Centesimi. Arms / St. Paul (N)	**9.00**
1941 50 Centesimi. Arms / Archangel Michael (Steel)	**6.00**
1931 1 Lira. Arms / Madonna stg. (N)	**9.00**
1942 2 Lire. Arms / Justice std. (Steel)	**3.00**

	BU
1945 5 Lire. Pius XII / Caritas (S)	**135.00**
1962 5 Lire. John XXIII / Dove of Holy Spirit (AL)	**2.00**
1973 10 Lire. Arms / Fish (AL)	**1.00**
1985 20 Lire. John Paul II / Eagle (ALB)	**2.00**
1955 50 Lire. Pius XII / Hope (Steel)	**3.50**
1929 100 Lire. Pius XI / Christ stg. (G)	**600.00**
1978 200 Lire. Arms / Sermon on the mount (ALB)	**2.75**
1963 500 Lire. Sede Vacante, Arms / Dove of Holy Spirit (S)	**10.00**
1978 1000 Lire. John Paul I / Arms (S)	**25.00**
1990 1000 Lire. John Paul II treading over barbed wire / Arms (S)	**25.00**

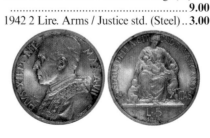

	BU
2000 2000 Lire. John Paul II praying/ Baby Jesus (S)	**40.00**
1998 100,000 Lire. John Paul II / Basilica of St. Mary Major (G)	**Proof only 600.00**
2002 50 Euro Cent. John Paul II / Map (B)	**50.00**
(1986-87) Official medal. John Paul II / St. Francis of Assisi (S, 44mm)	**150.00**
same but bronze	**75.00**
1986 Unofficial medal. John Paul II / Madonna and Child between saints (B, 50mm)	**25.00**

LOW COUNTRIES

These countries are Belgium, the Netherlands and Luxembourg. They are called this because most of their land is flat and hardly above sea level. They are sometimes also called "BeNeLux" after their customs and trade union. All three were controlled by the Spanish Hapsburgs until the late 1500s. At that time, the Netherlands became Protestant and declared its independence. The Spanish Hapsburgs continued to rule Belgium and Luxembourg until 1714, when they were transferred to the Austrian branch of the same dynasty. During the Napoleonic Wars, all three were part of the French Empire. After that, a newly independent Kingdom of the Netherlands was given all three territories, only to lose Belgium in an 1830 revolt due to cultural and religious

differences. In 1890, Luxembourg was lost when it was decided that the Queen of the Netherlands, as a woman, could not legally succeed to the Grand Duchy of Luxembourg.

In addition to royal portraits and heraldry, the coins of Belgium (called Spanish Netherlands and later Austrian Netherlands) and Luxembourg had a few distinctive motifs. This included an X-cross and some purely inscriptional types. A few small territories, such as Liege, had the arms of the local bishop or the bust of a patron saint. The new Kingdom of the Belgians used the international standard of the Latin Monetary Union (see France) until World War I. Interestingly, most Belgian coins are struck in two versions. Some have French and some have Flemish inscriptions, because both languages are commonly spoken.

The coins of the Netherlands have traditionally been struck by its constituent provinces. These almost always had a coat of arms on the copper. Some of the silver coins shared designs from province to province, such as arrows or a knight, but each individual province changed small details, such as the shield and its name in the legend. Thus they could circulate interchangeably throughout the Netherlands. The Lion *Dalders* are particularly common in this series. These are usually poorly struck on irregular blanks. Sea-salvaged examples are worth less, unless accompanied by documentation. After the new kingdom was founded in 1815, the national arms or the monarch's monogram or portrait were used on a more uniform national coinage. Since the 1500s, Dutch gold ducats with a standing knight have been particularly common in international commerce. The word BELGII on their reverse does not refer to Belgium, which did not exist when they were first struck, but to the ancient name for the region.

Belgian and Netherlands zinc coins struck during World War II were issued under the Nazi occupation. Fully brilliant specimens of these are virtually nonexistent.

In January 2002, Belgium, Luxembourg and the Netherlands replaced the currencies with coins denominated in Euros, the currency of the European Union. Some coins were struck years in advance, and held until 2002. On the circulating denominations, one cent through two euros, there one side carries a portraits of the monarch, the other has a common European design. On higher denomination

commemoratives both sides are distinctively local.

Both Belgium and the Netherlands struck colonial coinages. The issues of the Belgian Congo (earlier called Congo Free State) are particularly attractive. Some are enormous copper coins, others depict a powerful elephant. Dutch colonials for the Netherlands Antilles are of homeland types, although some have a distinctive inscription. Coins for the Netherlands Indies (today Indonesia) are far more distinctive. They either appear European or East Asian depending on which side one examines. Dutch colonials from World War II were struck by United States Government mints, and bear their mint marks.

Additional Specialized Books: De Mey, *Les Monnaies des Souverains Luxembourgeois.*

De Mey and Van Keymeulen, *Les Monnaies de Brabant 1598-1790.*

Mevius, J. *De Nederlandse Munten van 1795 tot Heden.*

Zonnenbloem, U., *Catalogus van de Zilvern Munten.*

Known Counterfeits: Low Countries coins have not been as extensively counterfeited as many other countries. A Holland 1791 2 stuiver exists and an occasional counterfeit gold ducat may be encountered.

BELGIUM under Austria

		F
1789 Liard. Joseph II / AD USUM BELGII AUSTR (C)		7.50
1790 Liard. Lion holding hat on pole (C) *Insurrection*		12.50
1766 Kronenthaler. Cross, crowns in angles / Double headed eagle (S)		60.00
1750 ½ Souverain d'or. Maria Theresa / Arms (G)		350.00

BELGIUM

		VF
1862 1 Centime. Crowned L / Lion with tablets (C)		5.00
1876 2 Centimes. Similar (C)		.75
1919 2 Centimes. Crowned A / Lion with tablets (C)		.35
1862 5 Centimes. Lion (CN)		.25
1832 10 Centimes. Crowned L / Lion with tablets (C)		100.00

		VF
1916 10 Centimes. Lion (Z)		.75
1944 25 Centimes. Monogram / Three shields (Z, holed)		.20
1844 1 Franc. Leopold I / Wreath (S)		140.00
1887 1 Franc. Leopold II / Arms (S)		15.00
1923 2 Francs. Belgium binding wound / Caduceus (N)		1.50
1869 5 Francs. Similar (S)		20.00
1877 20 Francs. Similar (G)		210.00
1932 20 France. Albert / Arms (N)		45.00
1934 20 Francs. Similar (S)		5.00
1935 50 Francs. Train station / Michael the Archangel (S)		80.00

Post-War Coinage

		BU
1971 25 Centimes. Crowned B (CN)		.15

		BU
1955 50 Centimes. Miner's head (C)		.50
1986 5 Francs. King Baudouin (AB)		.50
1994 5 Francs. Albert II (AB)		.50
1960 50 Francs. King and Queen / Crown over two shields (S)		10.00
1989 100 Ecu. Maria Theresa (G)		1,150.00

Euro Coinage

		BU
1999 1 Euro Cent. Albert II / Globe. (C plated Steel)		.50
2001 10 Euro Cent. Albert II / Map (B)		.75

		BU
2002 10 Euro. Albert II / Train. (S)		*Proof only* 40.00

BELGIAN COLONIES

		VF
Congo Free State. 1888 1 Centime. Star (C)		2.00
1887 2 Francs. Leopold II / Arms (S)		55.00

VF

Belgian Congo. 1910 5 Centimes. Star (CN)...**2.00**
1955 50 Centimes. Crowned shield / Palm tree (AL) ....**.25**
1926 1 Franc. Albert I / Palm tree (CN) **2.75**
1943 2 Francs. Elephant (Brass, hexagonal).......................................**8.00**
1944 50 Francs. Elephant (S) **55.00**
Rwanda-Burundi. 1961 1 Franc. Lion (Brass)...**50**

LUXEMBOURG

VF

1757 2 Liards. Maria Theresa / Wreath (C)..**85.00**
1789 ½ Liard. Crowned shield (C)... **20.00**
1854 2½ Centimes. Arms (C).............**3.50**
1908 5 Centimes. William (CN) **1.25**
1901 10 Centimes. Adolphe (CN) ....**.85**

VF

1924 10 Centimes. Ch monogram (CN) **50**
1924 2 Francs. Ch monogram / Iron worker (N)...................................**2.25**
1929 5 Francs. Charlotte / Arms at angle (S) **6.00**

Post-War Coinage

BU

1970 25 Centimes. Arms (AL) **10**
1957 1 Franc. Ch monogram / Iron worker (CN).....................................**40**
1946 100 Francs. Jean / Knight riding (S) **50.00**
1964 100 Francs. Jean / Arms (S).....**16.00**
Euro Coinage 2002 to date   **BU**
2002 2 Euro Cent. Henri / Globe. (C plated Steel).......................................**.50**

BU

2004 2 Euro. Henri / Map (NB clad N in CN, bimetallic).................................**7.00**

NETHERLANDS (PROVINCES)

F

Most coins below exist in several varieties with varying provincial shields and legends.
1794 Duit. Shield / D GEL RIE (C) ..**8.00**
1681 1 Stuiver. Shield between I S / GRON ET OML (S) **25.00**
1787 2 Stuivers. Shield between 2 S / TRA IEC TUM (S).......................**12.00**
1764 1 Gulden. Crowned shield / Woman stg. (S) **38.00**
1642 Lion Daalder. Bust of knight over shield / Lion (S)..........................**100.00**
1689 Ducat. Knight stg., shield at feet / Crowned shield (S) **120.00**

F

1729 Ducat. Knight stg. / MON ORD PROVIN... (G) **160.00**

NETHERLANDS (KINGDOM)

VF

1823 ½ Cent. Crowned W / Crowned shield (C).....................................**28.00**
1884 ½ Cent. Lion / Wreath (C) **3.50**
1876 1 Cent. Crowned W / Crowned shield (C).......................................**5.50**
1883 1 Cent. Lion / Wreath (C)..........**2.00**
1941 1 Cent. Similar (C) ....**.75**
1942 1 Cent. Cross (Z) ....**.50**
1877 2½ Cents. Similar (C)................**5.00**
1941 2½ Cents. Similar (C)................**1.75**
1827 5 Cents. Crowned W / Crowned shield (S)....................................**50.00**
1850 5 Cents. Willem III / Wreath (S) **5.00**
1907 5 Cents. Crown (CN)................**6.00**
1913 5 Cents. Orange plant (CN, square) **3.00**
1827 10 Cents. Crowned W / Crowned shield (S)....................................**27.00**
1849 10 Cents. Willem II / Wreath (S) **30.00**
1897 10 Cents. Wilhelmina as child / Wreath (S) **12.00**

VF

1918 10 Cents. Wilhelmina as adult / Wreath (S)....................................**2.50**

VF

1939 10 Cents. Wilhelmina mature / Wreath (S)....................................**1.50**
1826 25 Cents. Crowned W / Crowned shield (S)....................................**28.00**
1890 25 Cents. Willem III / Wreath (S) **150.00**
1943 25 Cents. Wilhelmina / Wreath (S) **1.25**
1942 25 Cents. Viking ship (Z)...........**1.50**
1818 ½ Gulden. Willem I / Crowned shield (S)..................................**280.00**
1858 ½ Gulden. Willem III / Crowned shield (S)....................................**25.00**
1922 ½ Gulden. Wilhelmina / Crowned shield (S)......................................**3.00**
1840 1 Gulden. Willem I / Crowned shield (S) **110.00**

VF

1848 1 Gulden. Willem II / Crowned shield (S) **26.00**
1892 1 Gulden. Wilhelmina as child / Crowned shield (S) **22.00**
1929 1 Gulden. Wilhelmina as adult / Crowned shield (S) **7.00**
1872 2½ Gulden. Willem III / Crowned shield (S) **22.00**
1930 2½ Gulden. Wilemina as adult / Crowned shield (S) **19.00**
1831 3 Gulden. Willem I / Crowned shield (S) **450.00**
1827 5 Gulden. Similar (G)...........**250.00**
1824 10 Gulden. Similar (G)..........**300.00**
1875 10 Gulden. Willem III / Crowned shield (S) **220.00**
1927 Ducat. Knight stg. / MO AUR REG BELGII... (G) .... *XF* **125.00**
Post-War Coinage   **Unc.**
1948 1 Cent. Wilhelmina old (C) **1.50**
1977 5 Cents. Juliana (C) ....**.25**
1948 10 Cents. Wilhelmina old (N)....**1.00**
1951 25 Cents. Juliana (N).................**1.00**
1982 1 Gulden. Beatrix (N)................**1.00**
1962 2½ Gulden. Juliana (S)............**12.00**

Unc.

1972 2½ Gulden. Juliana (N)............ **2.00**

1999 5 Gulden. Beatrix (B clad steel).... **3.50**

1997 10 Gulden. Beatrix / George
  Marshall (S) **22.00**

Unc.

1982 50 Gulden. Beatrix / Lion and eagle
  (S) **25.00**

Euro Coinage

BU

2000 5 Euro Cent. Beatrix / Globe. (C
  plated Steel).............................. **.75**

2000 50 Euro Cent. Beatrix / Map (B)
  .... **1.25**

2003 5 Euro. Beatrix / Van Gogh (S)
  .... **10.00**

BU

2004 5 Euro. Stylized half figure of
  Beatrix (S) **12.00**

NETHERLANDS COLONIES

Aruba

BU

1992 5 Cents. Arms (N clad Steel) .... **.30**

1995 5 Florin. Beatrix / Arms (N clad
  Steel, square)................................. **5.00**

1995 25 Florin. Beatrix / Sea turtles (S)
  .... **35.00**

Ceylon

F

1660-1720 2 Stuiver. IISt in wreath / same
  (C).. **22.00**

1791 1 Stuiver. T over Voc monogram / I
  over S T (C)................................... **38.00**

Curacao

VF

1821 1 Real. Caduceus and branch (S)
  .... **120.00**

1944 1 Cent. Lion / Wreath (C).......... **1.75**

1900 ¼ Gulden. Wilemina as adolescent /
  Crowned shield (S) **20.00**

1944 1 Gulden. Wilemina as adult /
  Crowned shield (S) **6.00**

Netherlands Antilles

BU

1965 1 Cent. Lion / Wreath (C).......... **1.50**

BU

1978 25 Cents. Shield (N) .... **.75**

1985 2½ Gulden. Beatrix / Arms (N)
  .... **4.00**

1977 25 Gulden. Juliana / Peter
  Stuyvesant (S) **200.00**

BU

1979 25 Gulden. Juliana / Children (S)
  .... **35.00**

1978 100 Gulden. Juliana / Willem I (G)
  .... **235.00**

Netherlands East Indies

VF

1789 Duit. Shield / VoC monogram (C)
  .... **6.00**

1807 Duit. 5 1/16 G, Shield / INDIA
  BATAV (C)..................................... **3.00**

1802 ¼ Gulden. Crowned shield / Ship
  (S) **70.00**

1859 ½ Cent. Crowned shield /
  Indonesian inscription (C) **4.00**

1945 1 Cent. Rice plant (C, holed)........ **.25**

1899 2½ Cents. Crowned shield /
  Indonesian inscription (C) **10.00**

VF

1945 Similar................................... **.50**

1913 5 Cents. Crown (CN, holed) **1.25**

1857 1/10 Gulden. Crowned shield /
  Indonesian inscription (S)................ **3.25**

1945 ¼ Gulden. Similar (S) **1.50**

1826 ½ Gulden. Willem I / Wreath (S)
  .... **40.00**

1840 1 Gulden. Similar (S)............... **42.00**

Surinam

BU

1764 Duit. Plant / SOCIETEI VAN
  SURINAME (C)...................... **F 60.00**

1972 1 Cent. Arms (C)....................... **1.00**

1962 1 Gulden. Juliana / Arms (S)..... **9.00**

POLAND

  Early modern Poland was mostly ruled by the royal House of Saxony, and its coins closely resemble the German States coins of the day. Mostly they were small coppers; small to medium-size coins of base silver; big silver thalers, and gold.

Most bore a bust, some had monograms on the obverse, and the royal arms dominated the reverse. Some of the most creative designs were memorial issues for the death of the king. Some of these depicted a butterfly.

  Poland may have been dissolved in 1795, but there were still Polish coins struck after that. The remnant state, the Grand Duchy of Warsaw, struck some heraldic types, though briefly. Krakow even more briefly did the same as an independent republic. Also, the part of Poland under Russian rule had its own distinctive coinage from 1816 to 1850. Some of these bore a portrait of the Czar, even when Russian coins did not. Others actually had the exchange rate on the reverse, giving values in both Polish and Russian currencies.

  Polish independence was restored in 1918 and the crowned white eagle became a national symbol always depicted on the coins of the between-the-wars republic. Portraits of an idealized Polonia, an allegory of the nation, and the forceful bust of Marshall Pilsudski also were very common.

  After World War II, the Communist government removed the crown and changed most of the minor coins to aluminum. Initially monotonous, later Communist issues depict diverse national heroes and local animals. Post-Communist are very similar in style to late-Communist issues, but with the crown replaced on the eagle's head.

  Poland has produced collectors' issues in quantity since the mid-1960s. The moderately priced circulating two-zlote commemoratives, issued every few months, have proven quite popular. There is also a strong market for coins depicting Pope John Paul II. Virtually unique among world coinage of the era, Poland has actually distributed quantities of rejected designs. These patterns, or *probas*, are usually far from rare like most other countries' patterns, and can usually be bought for $12 to $20 each!

  Additional Specialized Books:
  Gumowski, M., *Handbuch der Polnischen Numismatik*.

  Kopicki, E., *Katalog podstawowych typow monet i banknotow Polski*.

  Known Counterfeits: Polish coins have not been the victims of significant counterfeiting in the past, but may be slightly more so as a result of Eastern European counterfeiters. Counterfeits exist of the 1925 five zlotych and klippe (square) 1933 Sobieski 10 zlotych. An older-circulation counterfeit of the 1932 five zlotych is known.

KINGDOM

	F
1752 Solidus. August III / Arms (C)	15.00

	F
1767 Grosz. SR monogram / Square (Billon)	40.00
1780 Grosz. SR monogram / Arms (C)	15.00
1755 Tympf. August III / Arms, 18 below (Billon)	50.00
(1733) 16 Groschen. AR monogram, 16 gr below / Butterfly (S)	*XF* 1,500.00
1702 Thaler. Monograms around cross / Arms (S)	475.00

	F
1775 Thaler. Stanislaus Augustus / Arms (S)	125.00
1703 Ducat. August II / Crown over three shields (G)	550.00

GRAND DUCHY OF WARSAW

	F
1813 3 Grosze. Arms (C)	15.00
1814 1/3 Talara. Friedrich August / Arms (S)	55.00
1811 Ducat. Similar (G)	500.00

RUSSIAN RULE

1817 1 Grosz. Polish arms on Russian eagle (C)	9.00
1840 10 Groszy, Russian arms (Billon)	8.00
1838 2 Zlote = 30 Kopeks. Similar (S)	25.00
1817 5 Zlotych. Alexander I / Polish arms on Russian eagle (S)	65.00

KRAKOW

1835 5 Groszy. Eagle in Crowned city gate (Billon)	45.00

REPUBLIC

	VF
1923 10 Groszy. Eagle (N)	.45
same, Nazi restrike (Z)	.20

	VF
1925 2 Zlote. Eagle / Bust of girl (S)	12.00

	VF
1925 5 Zlotych. Eagle / Polonia and youth (S)	650.00
1934 5 Zlotych. Pilsudski / Eagle (S)	8.00
1925 20 Zlotych. King Boleslaus / Eagle (G)	*BU* 250.00

Postwar Coinage

	BU
1949 5 Groszy. Eagle (C)	1.00

	BU
1962 5 Groszy. Eagle (AL)	.20
1960 5 Zlotych. Eagle / Fisher (AL)	5.00
1967 10 Zlotych. Eagle / Marie Curie (CN)	2.50
1978 100 Zlotych. Moose / Eagle (S)	**Proof only** 22.00
1991 20,000 Zlotych. SAR monogram / Eagle (CN in Brass, *bimetallic*)	20.00
1992 5 Groszy. Crowned eagle (Brass)	.25
1997 2 Zlote. Beetle / Crowned eagle (Brass)	6.50
2002 2 Zlote. Turtles / Crowned eagle (Brass)	5.00
1997 10 Zlotych. Pope with Eucharist / Similar (S)	*Proof only* 30.00

(Reduced)

	BU
2002 20 Zlotych. Painter Jan Matejko (S, rectangular)	*Proof only* 30.00

PORTUGAL

Artistically, the coins of Portugal before the 20th century are distinctive in their consistent adherence to Baroque-style ornamentation. They are also distinctive in their relative lack of portraiture on silver and copper before the 1800s. The most common design is either a shield or a monogram. The reverse typically displays a cross or the denomination in Roman numerals.

Twentieth-century Portuguese coinage, both circulating and commemorative, places a heavy emphasis on the country's nautical heritage.

In January 2002, Portugal replaced the escudo with coins denominated in euros, the currency of the European Union. On the circulating denominations, one cent through two euros, there is one side that carries a Portuguese design, the other a common European design. On higher-denomination commemoratives, both sides are distinctively Portuguese.

During the 1600s, much Portuguese silver was revalued by the application of a countermark with a new value.

Portugal maintained its colonial empire longer than most European powers, and had an extensive colonial coinage. During the 1600s and 1700s, most of it was either of homeland types or bore a globe on the reverse. The coinage of Portuguese India up to the 1800s is interesting in its very European designs combined with primitive methods of local manufacture. Early in the 20th century, Portugal's colonial coinage was fairly uniform from colony to colony. By the 1930s, a distinctive formula was developed: One side bore an emblem of Portugal, the other a heraldic symbol of the colony itself. One of these was sometimes replaced by the value on smaller denominations.

Additional Specialized Books:
Gomes, *Moedas Portuguesas.*
Vaz, J., *Book of the Coins of Portugal.*
Known Counterfeits: Contemporary counterfeits of Brazilian copper are not rare and considered desirable; 1700s and 1800s gold should be inspected with care. The Azores crowned GP countermarked silver has been the victim of cast counterfeits. Some lack the flat spot that would naturally occur on the backside corresponding to the countermark.

KINGDOM

F

John IV, 1640-56. 80 Reis. Crowned IoIIII over LXXX / Cross (S)......... **75.00**
Afonso VI, 1656-83. 40 Reis. Crowned XXX / Cross (S)......................**55.00**
Peter II, 1683-1706. 1699 5 Reis. Crowned P∞II / V in wreath (C)....................**15.00**
John V, 1706-50. 1721 10 Reis. Crowned JV / X in wreath (C)......................**12.50**
Joseph I, 1750-77. 1760 4 Escudos. Bust of Joseph r. / Arms (G) **550.00**
Maria and Peter III, 1777-86. 200 Reis. Crowned shield / Cross (S) **30.00**

F

Maria alone, 1786-99. 1789 1000 Reis. Arms / Cross (G)...........................**300.00**
John, Regent 1799-1816. ½ Tostao. Crowned XXXX / Cross (S)...........**20.00**
John VI, 1816-1826. 1820 400 Reis. Portuguese shield on crowned globe / Cross (S)..............................**30.00**
Peter IV, 1826-28. 1828 40 Reis. Bust r. / Crowned shield (C) **25.00**
Michael, 1828-34. 120 Reis. Crowned shield / Cross (S) **25.00**
Maria II, 1834-53. 1850 10 Reis. Crowned arms / X in wreath (C) **3.00**

VF

Peter V, 1853-61. 1860 5000 Reis. Head r. / Arms (G).....................................**300.00**
Luiz I, 1861-89. 1884 20 Reis. Head l. / Wreath (C) **2.00**

VF

Carlos I, 1889-1908. 1891 20 Reis. Head / Wreath. (C) **2.00**

VF

1900 100 Reis. Crowned shield / Value (CN)...**1.50**
1892 500 Reis. Head r. / Crowned arms (S) **12.50**
Manuel II, 1908-10. 1909 200 Reis. Head l. / Crown in wreath (S) **6.00**

REPUBLIC

XF

1918 2 Centavos. Arms (C) **2.50**
same but (Iron) **300.00**
1919 4 Centavos. Bust of young girl (CN)...**1.50**

XF

1916 50 Centavos. Bust / Arms on armellary sphere (S) **10.00**
1910 Escudo. Bust with flag / Arms (S) **85.00**
1933 5 Escudos. Ship / Arms (S) **20.00**

VF

1942 same **5.00**
1934 10 Escudos. Similar (S)............**50.00**

BU

1968 20 Centavos. Cross of shields / XX (C)...**1.50**
1983 2½ Escudos. Corn ear / Arms (CN) **1.25**
1966 20 Escudos. Bridge / Arms (S)...**6.00**
1986 50 Escudos. Ship / Arms (CN) ..**2.25**
1991 100 Escudos. de Quental (CN) ..**3.00**
1997 200 Escudos. Francis Xavier / Ship (CN)..**5.00**
Euro Coinage 2002 to date **BU**
2002 1 Cent. Royal signature / Globe. (C plated Steel).....................................**.50**
2002 2 Euro. Royal cypher / Map (NB clad N in CN, bimetallic) **7.00**
2005 5 Euro. Pope John XXI (S)......**30.00**

PORTUGUESE COLONIES

Angola

VF

1698 20 Reis. Crowned Shield / XX (C) **35.00**
1762 2 Macutas. Crowned shield / Wreath (S) **45.00**

VF

1860 ½ Macuta. Arms (C)...............**25.00**
1921 1 Centavo. Arms (C)...............**12.50**

VF

1927 10 Centavos. Bust l. / Arms (CN) **4.00**
1953 1 Escudo (C).............................**1.50**
1952 10 Escudos. Portuguese arms / Angolan arms (S)............................**4.50**
1972 20 Escudos. Portuguese arms / Angolan arms (N)..........................**2.50**

Azores

VF

1750 5 Reis. Crowned II over V / Crown over five shields within wreath (C) **45.00**
830 5 Reis. MARIA II, etc., Arms (C) **15.00**

VF

(1887) 1,200 Reis countermark on Spanish 5 Pesetas (S). The example illustrated is counterfeit. Note that it lacks crispness. It was cast with the countermark "pre-stamped" in the mould. Authentic countermarks will also have a corresponding blank spot on the opposite side. This one does not.
1901 5 Reis. Arms / Wreath (C) **3.50**
1980 25 Escudos. Arms (CN).......*BU* **5.00**

Brazil

F

1695 320 Reis. Crowned shield / Globe over cross (S)..................................**40.00**
1768 5 Reis. Crowned V / Globe (C) **12.00**
1819 20 Reis. Crowned XX / Arms on globe (C) **9.00**

	F
1812 960 Reis. Crown arms / Armillary	
sphere (S)	**35.00**
1810 4000 Reis. Crowned shield / Cross	
(G)	**300.00**
1816 5 Onças 46 Oitavas. Arms and assay	
marks / Armillary sphere (G)	*Rare*

Cape Verde

	XF
1930 5 Centavos. Head l. (C)	**3.50**
1949 50 Arms (CN)	**2.50**
1967 2½ Escudos. Portuguese arms /	
Cape Verde arms (CN)	**2.50**
1953 10 Escudos. Similar (S)	**9.00**

Portuguese Guinea

	XF
1933 10 Centavos. Head l. (C)	**500.00**
1946 50 Centavos. Arms (C)	**15.00**
1952 2½ Escudos. Portuguese arms /	
Guinea arms (CN)	**3.00**
1973 5 Escudos. Similar (CN)	**10.00**
1952 20 Escudos. Similar (S)	**46.00**

Portuguese India

	Crude F
1706-50 5 Bazarucos. Shield between G A	
/ Wheel (Tin, 5.3g.)	**50.00**
1769 10 Bazarucos. Shield between G A /	
IO in Wreath (Tin)	**62.50**
1854 4½ Reis. Crowned shield / 4½ R (C)	
	12.50
1750-77 12 Reis. Crowned shield / *doze rei*	
in wreath (C)	**60.00**
1746 Pardao. John V / Arms (S)	**150.00**
1650 2 Tangas. Shield between G A / St.	
John between S I (S)	**70.00**
1796 Rupia. Maria I / Arms (S)	**30.00**
1857 Rupia. Peter V / Wreath (S)	**55.00**

	Crude F
1764 12 Xerafins. Arms / Cross (G)	
	850.00

Portuguese India, modern coinage

	VF
1871 3 Reis. Crowned shield / Wreath	
(C)	**11.00**

	VF
1881 1/8 Tanga. Luiz I / Crown (C)	**4.00**
1881 1/8 Rupia. Luiz I / Arms (S)	**6.00**
1901 ¼ Tanga. Carlos I ./ Arms (C)	
	16.00
1934 2 Tangas. Indian shield / Portuguese	
shield (CN)	**20.00**

	VF
1935 Rupia. Portuguese shield / Indian	
shield (S)	**16.00**
1961 10 Centavos. Arms (C)	**1.00**
1958 1 Escudo. Portuguese arms / Indian	
arms (CN)	**2.50**
1959 6 Escudos. Similar (CN)	**4.50**

Macao

	Unc.
1952 5 Avos. Arms (C)	**30.00**
1973 50 Avos. Portuguese arms / Macao	
arms (CN)	**3.00**
1952 1 Pataca. Similar (S)	**40.00**
1998 2 Patacas. (Brass, octagonal) Church	
and gateway	**5.00**

	Unc.
1992 5 Patacas. Junk passing cathedral	
(CN, 12-sided)	**6.50**
1989 100 Patacas. Arms / Snake (S)	
	50.00

Madeira

	BU
1981 25 Escudos. Head of Zarco / Arms	
(CN)	**6.00**

Mozambique

	VF
1853 1 Real. Arms / Wreath (C)	**22.00**
1820 80 Reis. Crown / Shield on globe	
(C)	**35.00**
1936 10 Centavos. Arms (C)	**10.00**
1945 50 Centavos. Arms (C)	**3.50**
1951 1 Escudo. Arms (CN)	**3.00**
1965 2½ Escudos. Portuguese arms /	
Mozambique arms (CN)	**.25**
1935 5 Escudos. Similar (S)	**24.00**
1960 5 Escudos. Similar (S)	**4.00**

	VF
1970 10 Escudos. Similar (CN)	**.70**
1955 20 Escudos. Similar (S)	**6.50**

St. Thomas and Prince

	VF
1971 10 Centavos. Arms (AL)	**.65**

	VF
1962 20 Centavos. Arms (C)	**1.25**
1951 50 Centavos. Arms (CN)	**3.50**
1948 1 Escudo. Arms (N-C)	**40.00**
1939 2½ Escudos. Portuguese arms /	
Colonial arms (S)	**32.00**
1951 5 Escudos. Similar (S)	**7.00**
1951 10 Escudos. Similar (S)	**8.00**
	BU
1971 20 Escudos. Similar (N)	**13.50**
1970 50 Escudos. Two shields / Cross of	
shields (S)	**12.50**

Timor

	XF
1951 10 Avos. Cross of shields (C)	
	8.50

	XF
1945 20 Avos. Bust r. / Arms (CN)	**75.00**
1951 50 Avos. Arms (S)	**9.00**
1970 20 Centavos. Arms (C)	**2.50**
1970 1 Escudo. Arms (C)	**9.00**

XF

1970 2½ Escudos. Portuguese arms / Timor arms (CN)............................**3.50**
1958 3 Escudos. Similar (S).............**12.00**
1970 5 Escudos. Similar (CN)............**8.00**
1958 6 Escudos (S) Similar (S)........**14.00**

RUSSIA

Russia has the dual distinction of being the last European country to abandon primitive medieval hammered coinage and the first country with a modern decimal-based coinage. When the silver-dollar-sized ruble was introduced in 1704, it was valued at 100 of the old kopeks. Modern Russian coinage is attributable to the personal will of Peter the Great, who was determined to make Russia into a modern country in a single lifetime. Before his reign, portrait coins were virtually unheard of in Russia, and large silver or gold coins were generally foreign imports. He was also the first ruler since the 1400s to successfully circulate copper coinage.

The standards of copper coins changed several times in the 1700s and 1800s, and new coins were often struck over old ones. Specialized collectors consider these particularly desirable, but not every one cares.

During the early and mid-1800s, portraiture was removed form silver coinage and replaced by a double-headed eagle. Throughout the century, the number of shields on its wings increased. Each shield represented an additional territory, such as Finland or Poland, which the Czar had incorporated into his empire.

One distinctive type of coin struck under Czarist Russia is the *novodel*. This is an official government "re-strike" with new dies. Some novodels are actually new issues of old coins that were never actually struck. They can sometimes be identified by their unusually uniform quality, not representative of the earlier coins they resemble. They were generally struck for wealthy 19th-century collectors and today are considered rare and desirable.

From 1921-23, coins were struck in the name of the Russian Soviet Federated Socialist Republic. These pieces carried the Communist slogan, "Workers of all countries unite!" and purely agricultural symbols. With the establishment of the Union of Soviet Socialist Republics and the addition of new territories, symbols of expansion began to appear. The new state symbol consisted of a hammer and sickle superimposed on a globe, with ribbons at its side. Each ribbon represented a republic added to the Soviet Union, much as the shields were added to the czarist eagle's wings. Among the most splendid depictions of Soviet iconography is the scene on the Soviet ruble of 1924. Nicknamed the "worker ruble," it shows an industrial worker pointing out the rising sun of Communism to a less-enthusiastic agricultural worker. This relates clearly to the difficulties implicit in Russia, an agrarian nation, being the first one to implement Communism, a system intended for an industrial society.

During the 1970s and 1980s, a wide range of commemoratives was released. Some base-metal pieces were widely distributed within the Soviet Union. Others, mostly platinum or silver, were not even made available to the average Soviet citizen. Much of the commemorative coin program continued after the fall of Communism, but other changes occurred. Most of the low-value circulating coins released over the last several years bear the double-headed eagle, former symbol of Czarist Russia, for the first time since 1918! Another post-Communist phenomenon is rapid inflation. This has caused a revaluation of the currency, followed by more inflation.

Following the fall of the Soviet Union, vast quantities of material flooded out of Russia, greatly suppressing prices.

However, the expansion of the Russian economy during the last few years has fueled a strong domestic coin market. The net flow of quality coins, struck between the introduction of modern-style coins by Peter the Great and the late1920s, is now back into Russia. For the last few years, prices of that material has been driven constantly upward.

After the fall of Communism, the republics within the U.S.S.R. became independent nations. Among the most important, besides Russia proper, is Ukraine. Ukrainian coins were released after years of being distributed unofficially in small quantities. Because of the initial difficulty in obtaining them, followed by abundant supplies, Ukrainian minor coinage was the subject of one of the most precipitous drops in value in the world numismatic market. The trident symbol depicted on them goes back to the early coinage of Kievian Rus', virtually all of which are considered museum pieces.

Belarus, between Russia and Poland has yet to actively circulate coinage, but has made available some collectors' issues.

Additional Specialized Books:
Spassky, I.G., *Russian Monetary System*.
Uzdenikov, V., *Russian Coins, 1700-1917*.

Known Counterfeits: Many new counterfeits of czarist coins have been appearing recently. More copper and gold has recently been counterfeited than silver. This includes Siberian coppers and many novodels. Know your dealer!
(Most of the massive quantities of 1700s copper coming onto the market recently are authentic, however.)

One distinctive aspect of Russian coinage has been the issue of *novodels*. These are re-strikes, often of coins that never existed. They are not counterfeits, however, but official government issues. Telling an original from a counterfeit from a novodel can often require an expert.

F

Peter I, 1689-1725. 1706 Denga. Two-headed eagle (C)............................**45.00**
1705 Kopek. Peter riding horse r. (C) **45.00**

F

1723 Ruble. Bust r. / Cross of four crowned Π's (S) **275.00**
Anna, 1730-40. 1734 Denga. Two-headed eagle / Cartouche (C) **20.00**
Ivan IV, 1740-41. 1741 Grivennik (10 Kopeks). Bust r. as child / Crown (S) **375.00**
Elizabeth, 1741-61. 1758 5 Kopeks. EE monogram in wreath / Two-headed eagle (C)..**40.00**

F

1752 10 Kopeks. Bust r. / Crown (S)..**40.00**
1752 Ruble. Bust r. / Two-headed eagle (S) **250.00**
1756 2 Rubles. Similar (G) **500.00**
Peter III, 1761-62. 1762 4 Kopeks. St. George spearing dragon / Drum, cannon and flags (C)................................**55.00**
Catherine II the Great, 1762-1796. 1792 5 Kopeks. EI monogram in wreath / Two-headed eagle (C)............................**15.00**

1783 15 Kopeks. Bust r. / *15* on Two-
 headed eagle (S) **40.00**
1769 Ruble. Bust r. / Two-headed eagle
 (S) **200.00**

F

Paul I, 1796-1801. 1799 2 Kopeks.
 Crowned *П* (C) **18.00**
1800 Poltina (= ½ Ruble). Cross of four
 crowned П's / Inscription in square (S)
 .... **150.00**
1798 Ruble. Similar (S) **135.00**
Alexander I, 1801-25. 1812 2 Kopeks.
 Two-headed eagle without border /
 Wreath (C) **5.00**
1803 5 Kopeks. Two-headed eagle in thick
 border with five dots / Inscription in
 similar border (C).......................... **90.00**
    The dots around the edge could be
used by the illiterate to tell the value.
Fivedots equalled five Kopeks.

F

1831 25 Kopeks. Two-headed eagle with
 wings down / Wreath (S) **20.00**
1820 Ruble. Two-headed eagle / Wreath
 (S) **50.00**
Nicholas I, 1825-55. 1835 Kopek. Two-
 headed eagle with wings down (C) ... **5.00**
1844 Kopek. Crowned H (C) **3.50**
1850 20 Kopeks. Two-headed eagle /
 Wreath (S)....................................... **7.00**

VF

Alexander II, 1855-81. 1875 ¼ Kopek.
 Crowned AII monogram in wreath (C)
 .... **3.00**
1855 Denga. Crowned AII monogram
 (C)... **4.00**

VF

1857 5 Kopeks. Two-headed eagle /
 Wreath (C) **5.00**
1869 20 Kopeks. Two-headed eagle /
 Wreath (S)....................................... **3.00**
1877 Ruble. Similar (S) **45.00**
Alexander III, 1881-94. 1889 ½ Kopek.
 Crowned AIII monogram (C) **2.50**

VF

1884 1 Kopek. Two-headed eagle in
 ornate border / Wreath (C).............. **6.00**
1894 50 Kopeks. Head r. / Two-headed
 eagle (S)... **55.00**
Nicholas II, 1894-1917. 1909 ½ Kopek.
 Crowned NII monogram (C) **1.00**

VF

1896 3 Kopeks. Two-headed eagle in
 ornate border / Wreath (C).............. **9.50**
1905 5 Kopeks. Two-headed eagle /
 Wreath (S) **2.50**
1896 50 Kopeks. Head l. / Two-headed
 eagle (S).. **12.00**
1899 Ruble. Similar (S) **45.00**
1902 5 Rubles. Similar (G) **150.00**
1902 37½ Rubles. Similar (CN) **25.00**
    This is a re-strike with original dies.
Look for the "P" added after 1902Г.
Beware: Some have been gold plated.

Communist Russia (РСФСР)

XF

1923 20 Kopeks. Hammer and Sickle /
 Wreath (S) **2.50**
1923 50 Kopeks. Similar / Star (S) **9.50**

Soviet Union (CCCP)

XF

1925 ½ Kopek. CCCP (C) **16.50**
1931 1 Kopek. Arms / Wreath (ALB)
 .... **1.50**
1936 2 Kopeks. Similar (ALB)........... **2.00**
1943 3 Kopeks. Similar (ALB).......... **1.00**
1952 5 Kopeks. Similar (ALB).......... **1.00**
1957 10 Kopeks. Arms / Octagon (CN)
 .... **2.00**

XF

1965 15 Kopeks. Arms (CNZ) .... **.40**
1967 20 Kopeks. Arms / Ship (CNZ) ....**.75**
1991 50 Kopeks. Dome and tower (CN)
 .... **.50**

XF

1924 Ruble. Industrial worker leading
 farmer towards sun / Arms (S) **25.00**

BU

1981 Ruble. Cosmonaut / Arms (CNZ)
 .... **2.00**
1991 5 Rubles. Cathedral / Arms (CN)
 .... **5.00**
1979 150 Ruble. Wrestlers / Arms
 (Platinum) **450.00**
Russian Federation   BU
1992 1 Ruble. Two-headed eagle (Brass
 clad Steel).. **.75**

BU

2000 2 Ruble. Battle (CN).................. **1.50**
1994 50 Rubles. Flamingos / Two-headed
 eagle (CN in ALB, *bimetallic*) **2.50**
1995 100 Rubles. Ballerina / Similar (G)
 .... *Proof only* **700.00**

SIBERIA

F

1768 Polushka (=¼ Kopek). Crowned E
 II monogram in wreath / Cartouche
 (C)... **100.00**

F

1772 5 Kopeks. Similar / Value on shield
 between sables (C)......................... **65.00**
    Illustration is of a novodel (see above).

UKRAINE

BU

1996 200,000 Karbovantsiv. Chernobyl
 memorial. Bell / Arms (CN)............. **5.00**
1993 2 Kopiyky. Arms / Value (AL)... **1.00**
2000 5 Hryven. Christ, crowds in
 background / Arms between two angels
 (CN)... **9.00**

BU

2001 10 Hryven. Stylized hockey player (S) **45.00**

SCANDINAVIA

Scandinavian coins first become common in the 1500s. By the 1600s, the small base-silver coins of Denmark are frequently found. During this period the coins of both Sweden and Denmark follow a typical European pattern of portraits, monograms, crowns and shields. Other features are distinctive. In both countries, standing figures of the monarch become more common than elsewhere in Europe. Monograms in Denmark are more likely to use modern than Roman numerals. In Sweden, the Divine name, the Tetragrammaton in Hebrew, is often depicted.

The single most distinguishing feature of Scandinavian coinage is the abundant use of copper. Large copper coins struck on crudely made blanks were common particularly in 1600s Sweden. Large slabs of copper, called "plate money," were also used instead of silver coins. Each piece, weighing up to several pounds, was usually stamped five times with circular dies: once in each corner to prevent clipping, with an additional stamp in the center. Most of the plate money on the market in recent years is from one shipwreck, the *Nicobar*, which sank off the coast of South Africa, and is corroded. These are worth less than non-sea-salvaged pieces. By the late 1700s, plate money had ceased to be struck, but large copper continued to be common throughout Scandinavia.

During the 1800s, Scandinavian coins were decimalized, and in 1872 a common monetary union was formed with all Scandinavian countries striking distinctive coins on a common standard. During this time, most countries used portraits only on silver and gold, with monograms on copper.

Norway has been part of either the Danish (1397-1814) or the Swedish (1814-1905) monarchy through most of the modern era. In 1905 it elected a king of its own, Haakon VII. Modern Norwegian coins usually resemble that of the kingdom with which it was united, sometimes with the distinctive Norwegian arms, a lion with a battle ax; other times differentiated only by a small crossed-hammers mintmark.

Iceland had no separate coinage until 1922, Greenland not until 1926. Before then, Danish coins circulated on both islands. In 1941, Iceland became independent and royal symbols, such as the crown, were removed from above the arms. Many recent coins show the guardian spirits of Iceland, sometimes supporting the country's shield. After 1964, regular Danish coins were reintroduced to Greenland and toady it is an integral part of Denmark.

All these countries have issued plentiful silver commemoratives in the modern era, with some base-metal ones more recently.

One convenient way to distinguish Swedish from other Scandinavian coins is that the word *ore* is spelled with "ö" in Swedish, "ø" in the others.

It is convenient to mention the names of the Scandinavian countries in their native languages:
Denmark..............................**DANMARK**
Greenland ....**GRØNLAND**
Iceland ....**ISLAND**
Norway ....**NORGE or** NOREG
Sweden.....................................**SVERIGE**

Denmark struck colonial coins for its possessions in the West Indies. They are generally artistic and not particularly rare. In 1913 Denmark sold these island to the United States and they became the U.S. Virgin Islands. Today these coins are popular with collectors not only of Danish coins, but with many U.S. collectors as well. The coins of Danish India are scarcer but less popular.

Swedish issues for the West Indies are quite rare. They consist only of countermarks on other countries' coins for local use.

Additional Specialized Books:
Hobson, Burton, *Catalogue of Scandinavian Coins.*
Sømod, J., *Danmarks Mønter*. Also covers Norway 1481-1813.
Tonkin, Archie, *Myntboken*. Annual editions with up-to-date Swedish pricing.

Known Counterfeits: Contemporary counterfeits exist of some 17th- and 18th-century Danish minor coins. Swedish plate money has been the victim of deceptive counterfeits. The rare Danish 1776 2 skilling is known altered from 1778.

DENMARK

F

1690s 2 Skilling. Crowned shield (S) **25.00**
1719 ½ Skilling. Crowned double *F4* monogram in wreath (C)............... **18.00**
1771 1 Skilling. Crowned double *C7* monogram (C)............................... **9.00**
1778 2 Skilling. Crowned C7 monogram / Crowned shield (Billon)...................**5.00**

F

1764 4 Skilling. Crowned double F4 monogram (Billon)....................... **12.00**

F

1702 8 Skilling. Frederick IV / Crown (S) **32.00**
1732 24 Skilling. Christian VI / Crowned shield (S) **110.00**
1711 Krone. Frederick IV on horse r. / Arms (S).. **135.00**
1786 Daler. Large wild man with club supporting Danish arms / Norwegian arms (S).. **600.00**
1738 Ducat. Crowned double *C6* monogram / Fortress (G) **650.00**

VF

1869 1 Skilling. Crowned CIX in wreath (C).. **4.50**
1856 16 Skilling. Frederick VII / Wreath (S) **8.00**
1855 1 Rigsdaler (S) Similar (S)....... **40.00**
1846 1 Species Daler. Christian VIII / Arms (S).. **110.00**

F

1876 1 Øre. Crowned CIX / Dolphin and wheat ear (C)............................... **700.00**
1899 Similar................................**2.50**
1907 2 Øre. Crowned F8 monogram (C) **2.00**
1919 5 Øre. Crowned Cx monogram (C) **5.00**
1897 10 Øre. Christian IX / Dolphin and wheat ear (Billon).......................... **6.00**
1924 25 Øre. Crowned CxR (CN, holed) **1.25**
1942 Similar (Z, holed) **1.50**
1925 ½ Krone. Crowned CxC monogram / Crown (ALB)............................... **8.50**
1875 1 Krone. Christian IX / Shield between Dolphin and wheat ear (S) **60.00**

F

1876 Similar..................... **125.00**
1923 2 Kroner. King and Queen / Arms
(S) **12.00**

BU

1908 10 Kroner. Frederick VIII / Arms
(G) **175.00**
1913 10 Kroner. Frederick VII / Arms
(G) **175.00**
1873 20 Kroner. Christian IX / Dania std.
l. (G) **300.00**

Post-war Coinage   **BU**

1962 1 Øre. Crowned *FRIX* monogram
(Z) **1.25**
1973 10 Øre. Crowned *M2R* monogram
(CN)................................**.25**
1957 1 Krone. Frederick XI / Shield
(ALB)............................. **4.00**
1968 10 Kroner. Frederick XI / Princess
Benedikte (S)..................... **15.00**
1992 200 Kroner. Queen and Prince /
Stylized house (S)......................... **37.50**

GREENLAND

XF

1926 25 Øre. Crowned shield / Bear (CN)
.... **15.00**
same but holed................................ **75.00**
1960 1 Krone. Crown over two shields /
Wreath (CN) **13.00**

XF

1944 5 Kroner. Crowned shield / Bear (B)
.... **82.50**

ICELAND

1931 1 Eyrir. Crowned Cx (C) **6.00**
1942 2 Aurar. Similar (C)................... **1.00**
1963 5 Aurar. Shield in wreath (C)........**.75**
1981 10 Aurar. Ox / Cuttle-fish (C).......**.20**
1922 25 Aurar. Crowned shield (CN). **4.00**
1940 1 Krona. Similar (ALB) **2.00**

BU

1984 1 Krona. Giant / Cod (CN)..........**.50**
1970 10 Kronur. Arms (CN)................**.75**
1974 500 Kronur. Four spirits / Woman
leading cow (S)................................**8.00**
1987 50 Kronur. Four spirits / Crab
(CNZ) **3.00**

BU

1995 100 Kronur. Four spirits / Lumpfish
(B)................................. **6.00**
2000 1,000 Kronur. Leif Ericson (S)
.... *Proof* **65.00**
    This was sold in a two piece set
with the United States Leif Ericson
commemorative.

NORWAY

F

1643 Skilling. Lion with battle ax / I
SKILL ING DA (Billon) **47.00**
1714 2 Skilling. Crowned double *F4*
monogram / Lion with battle ax (Billon)
.... **18.00**
1778 4 Skilling Danske. Crowned *C7*
monogram / Crowned arms, crossed
hammers below (Billon) **24.00**
1655 8 Skilling. Crowned F3 monogram /
Lion with battle ax (S) **100.00**
1740 24 Skilling. Crowned *C6* monogram
/ Similar (S) **45.00**
1763 24 Skilling. Crowned *F5* monogram
/ Similar (S) **30.00**
1684 Mark. Crowned *C5* / Lion with
battle ax, in wreath (S) **275.00**
1689 4 Mark. Crowned double *C6*
monogram / Lion with battle ax, in
wreath (S)........................... **125.00**

F

1723 4 Mark. King on horse / Crowned
arms (S)........................... **900.00**
1673 ½ Specie Daler. Christian V /
Crowned shield (S) **2,300.00**
1749 1 Riksdaler. Frederick V / Lion with
battle ax, mountains behind (S) ... **300.00**

VF

1870 1 Skilling. Arms (C) **7.50**
1825 8 Skilling. Carl XIV / Arms (S).. **42.00**
1847 24 Skilling. Oscar I / Arms (S) ... **25.00**
1891 2 Øre. Arms, O^{cr} II at sides (C)
.... **5.50**

VF

1876 5 Øre. Arms, O^{cr} II at sides (C)
.... **9.50**

VF

1917 10 Øre. Crowned H7 monogram
(Billon)............................**2.50**
1939 50 Øre. Cross of monograms /
Crown (CN, holed)............................**.75**

VF

1905 2 Kroner. Arms / Tree within border
of hands (S) **55.00**

Post-war Coinage   **Unc.**

1957 1 Øre. Crowned H7 monogram (C)
.... **2.50**
1964 10 Øre. Crowned Ov monogram /
Bee (CN) **1.00**
1992 1 Krone. Harald V / Crown (CN)
....**.75**

VF

1964 10 Kroner. Arms / Building (S)
.... **15.00**

VF

2002 20 Kroner. Harald V/ N.H.Abel (S)
.... **20.00**
1993 100 Kroner. Harald V / Figure
skater (S)...................................... **60.00**

SWEDEN

F

1666 1/6 Öre. C R S, Three crowns /
Crowned lion (C) **15.00**
1720 ½ Öre. F R S, Three crowns /
Crowned arrow shield (C) **9.00**

F

1650 1 Öre. Arms / Crossed arrows (C) **50.00**
1690 1 Öre. Crowned CXI / Three crowns (Billon) **18.00**
1748 2 Öre. FI SG V R, Crowned shield / Crown over crossed arrows (C) **7.00**
1759 2 Öre. AF SG V R, Crowned shield / Crown over crossed arrows (C) **7.00**
1669 4 Öre. Crowned C / Three crowns (S) **30.00**
1719 1 Mark. Ulrica Eleonora r. / Crowned shield (S) **200.00**
1676 2 Mark. Charles XI l. / Three crowns (S) **80.00**
1753 4 Mark. Adolf Frederick r. / Arms (S) .... **200.00.**
1697 8 Mark. Charles XII r. / Crowned shield (S) **600.00**
1778 1/24th Riksdaler. Crowned G^{III} / Crowned shield (Billon) **20.00**

F

1779 1/12th Riksdaler. Similar (S) **28.00**
1718 Daler. Jupiter and eagle (C) **18.00**
1719 Daler. Hope (C) **18.00**
1725 Riksdaler. Frederick I r. / Arms (S) **225.00**
1781 Riksdaler. Gustav III r. / Arms (S) **85.00**

VF

1721 2 Daler "Plate money." Crowned FRS in each corner, 2 DALER SILF. MYNT in center (C) **500.00**

VF

1728 ½ Daler "Plate money." Crowned FRS in each corner, ½ DALER SILF. MYNT in center (C) **350.00**
1721 Riksdaler, Anniv. of Liberation War, busts of Gustav Vasa and Gustav II Adolf **4500.00**

VF

1709 Ducat. Carl XII r. / Crowned CC monogram (G) **1,400.00**
1776 Ducat. Gustav III r. / Arms (G) **775.00**
1821 ½ Skilling. Crowned CXIV / Crossed arrows (C) **65.00**
1848 1/16th Riksdaler. Oscar I / Arms (S) **9.00**
1806 Riksdaler. Gustav IV / Arms (S) **320.00**
1866 1 Öre. Carl XV / Wreath (C) **4.00**
1920 1 Öre. Crowned GvG monogram / Three crowns (C) .... **.50**
1935 same (C) .... **.30**
1890 2 Öre. Crowned OII monogram (C) **2.50**
1917 2 Öre. Crowned GvG monogram / Three crowns (Iron) **4.00**

VF

1901 5 Öre. Crowned OII monogram (C) **4.00**
1941 5 Öre. Crowned GvG monogram / Three crowns (C) .... **.35**
1898 10 Öre. Crowned OII monogram (Billon) **5.00**
1934 10 Öre. Crowned shield (Billon) **1.00**
1943 25 Öre. Crown (Billon) **1.00**
1856 25 Öre. Oscar I / Wreath (S) **14.00**
1907 50 Öre. Crowned OII monogram / Wreath (S) **7.00**
1938 50 Öre. Crowned shield (S) **1.75**
1940 50 Öre. Crowned Gv monogram / Wreath (CN) **1.00**
1898 1 Krona. Oscar II / Arms (S) ... **30.00**
1936 1 Krona. Gustav V / Arms (S) **5.00**

VF

1897 2 Kronor. Oscar II crowned / Arms (S) **12.00**
1944 2 Kronor. Gustav V old / Arms (Billon) **4.50**
1874 10 Kronor. Oscar II / Arms (G) **150.00**

Unc.

1895 20 Kronor. Similar (G) **325.00**
1953 1 Öre. Crown / Crown (C) **2.00**

Unc.

1967 2 Öre. Similar (C) .... **.45**

Unc.

1979 5 Öre. Crowned CXVIG monogram (C) .... **.25**
1988 10 Öre. Similar (CN) .... **.15**

Unc.

1956 25 Öre. Crown (Billon) **3.50**
1968 50 Öre. Crowned GVIA monogram (CN) **1.00**
1979 1 Krona. Carl XVI / Crowned shield (CN) .... **.75**
1964 2 Kronor. Gustav VI / Crowned shield (Billon) **5.00**
1952 5 Kronor. Gustav VI / Crowned GVIA monogram (Billon) **30.00**

Unc.

1972 10 Kronor. Gustav VI / Signature (S) **14.00**
1976 50 Kronor. King and Queen / Arms (S) **20.00**
1990 200 Kronor. Carl XVI / Ship Vasa (S) **40.00**
1993 1000 Kronor. Queen / Arms (G) **200.00**

SPAIN

During the 1500s through early 1800s, Spanish coins were among the most important international trade coins in the world, particularly those struck at Spain's colonial mints in the Americas. They were so respected that they were the

standard of value on which the original United States dollar was based.

Spanish coinage until the mid-1800s was based on the *real* introduced by Ferdinand and Isabella. It was originally a silver coin larger than the modern quarter, although it had shrunk to the size of a nickel and was thinner by the 1600s. From then until the Napoleonic Wars, it remained quite stable. During most of this period it carried the coat of arms of Spain on the reverse, a portrait or variation on the arms on the obverse.

Gold coins were plentiful, as well. They were denominated in *escudos*, worth 16 *reales*. They more often bore portraits than the silver did.

Copper coins were denominated in *maravedi*, 34 of which were worth one *real.* At this time, the copper coinage was poor. There was often a shortage of new copper, causing old, worn-out coins to continue in use long after they should have been replaced. Often these coins would be counter-stamped to revalidate them. A number indicating a new value, and sometimes a date, would be impressed. When this was done repeatedly, the coins took on a mutilated appearance and sometimes ceased to remain flat. This practice of making *resellados* ended in the 1700s, but the practice of forcing worn-out copper into continued use persisted.

Spanish coins from the mid-1800s until recently have carried two dates. The large date is the year of authorization but not when the coin was actually manufactured. The real date was usually indicated in tiny incuse numbers on the six-pointed star, which is a Madrid mintmark.

SECRET and ACTUAL DATE ON SPANISH COIN

After a few monetary experiments in the mid-1800s, Spain joined many other European countries in 1869 in striking its coins according to the international standard of the Latin Monetary Union, and continued to do so until 1926. Most of the issues during this period uniformly bore the royal portrait and the coat of arms.

The final years of the monarchy and the period of the civil war not only saw a deterioration of the value of the coinage,

but also an opening up of the designs to new ideas under all three governments. Despite the extremely modernistic eagle supporting the shield, Gen. Francisco Franco's later coinage, mostly of base metal, was fairly conservative in pattern.

The restoration of the monarchy not only promised a progressive government for Spain, but also changes in the coinage. Since the 1980s, new shapes have been used to distinguish denominations, and a plethora of designs have been used to promote the recognition of various cultural sights and events throughout Spain. There have also been a vast number of collector issues sold at a premium. These, too, have had unusual and progressive designs.

In January 2002, Spain replaced the *peseta* with coins denominated in Euros, the currency of the European Union. Some coins were struck years in advance and held until 2002. On the circulating denominations, one cent through two euros, there is one side which carries a Spanish design, the other a common European design. On higher-denomination commemoratives, both sides are distinctively Spanish.

COLONIAL COINAGE

The *real* issued in the New World was struck to the same standards as in Spain, but the designs often varied. The first issues of the early 1500s displayed the Pillars of Hercules and a coat of arms. In terms of style, they seemed no different than European coins. The first copper coins struck in the New World, minted in Santo Domingo (now capital of the Dominican Republic), featured monograms. They were far more carelessly made.

When the quantities of silver and gold being mined and shipped back to Spain became so great that they could not be struck into nicely finished coins, a rough, improvised coin was devised. Called "cobs" by modern collectors, these coins were struck to the same exacting weight standards but the designs were only hastily impressed, with no complete image being found on any one coin. The blanks on which they were struck were neither round nor flat. Originally it was intended that these be shipped back to Europe and melted, but the pressing need for money in the Spanish American colonies caused them to be pressed into service as regular coinage.

While dates were engraved on the dies of these cobs, they are usually not

clear on the coins. Specialized references, however, sometimes permit the dating of these pieces by the correlation of mint marks and assayers' initials, which are more often legible.

Many of the cobs on the market are recovered from shipwrecks or found on beaches near shipwrecks. Generally, sea-salvaged coins are either pitted or covered with black compounds called "horn silver." This is bonded to the metal and cannot be removed without removing part of the coin. Such corroded coins are worth far less than other cobs and Spanish colonial coins. The exception is for those coins with pedigrees from known shipwrecks. If satisfactorily documented, the novelty value of their history can far exceed their value as low-grade Spanish Colonial coins. Be careful of false documentation and made-to-order pedigrees. When possible, documentation from the original salvagers is desirable.

From 1732 onwards, more careful methods of manufacture were implemented. Initially the improved silver carried the crowned shield of Spain on one side, two globes between the Pillars of Hercules on the other. Later the designs were changed (1760) to bear the king's portrait and a Spanish shield. The face value of each silver coin was indicated in numbers of reales indicated as 8R through 1R, with the half real simply as "R" without a numeral. The improved gold had carried a similar design since the 1730s. Copper in the Spanish colonies was not common, and at most mints not struck at all.

Despite the vast expanse covered by the Spanish colonies in the Americas, most of the coins struck were of similar design from mint to mint. Some mints, however, are far scarcer than others, so it is important to recognize their marks. Usually the mintmark is incorporated into the reverse legend. The colonial listings below follow a large representation of the mintmarks which appear on the coins listed. Later Spanish colonial coins of the Philippines and Puerto Rico resemble Spanish coins made at the end of the 19th century. On these, the name of the colony is clearly indicated.

Additional Specialized Books:
Cayon, *Las Monedas Españolas del Tremis al Euro.*
Sedwick, Daniel, *The Practical Book of Cobs.*
Known Counterfeits: Gold coins of Isabella II have been counterfeited. So

have many 19th-century silver-dollar-sized coins. These include, among others: 20 reales 1852, 5 peseta 1870 (69), 1871 (73), 1897, 1899 (the "star" dates are the ones in parentheses). Many are not silver but a nickel alloy. Other gold coins of Alfonso XII and XIII have been re-struck by the Spanish mint but they bear the accurate "secret" dates of (19)61 and (19)62.

Counterfeits of Spanish colonial cobs are plentiful in both gold and silver. Examine any example for casting seams, raised pimples or a cloudy appearance. This is different from the graininess found on authentic sea-salvaged coins. Also note that no two cobs are precisely identical, so if you have a pair of identical coins, there is a good chance both are counterfeit. Many of the two-globes and portrait pieces have also been counterfeited, both at the time of issue and recently. Most of the recent counterfeits are poor-quality metal and will not ring correctly.

Be careful not to purchase Puerto Rican coins with solder marks on the edges.

EUROPEAN COINAGE

Carlos II, 1665-1700.

F

1682 2 Reales. Arms in octolobe / Crowned CAROLVSII monogram (C) **45.00**
1685 4 Reales. Crowned shield / Arms in octolobe (S).................................. **375.00**
1687 4 Reales. Similar / Cross over MA monogram (S) **600.00**

Carlos III Pretender, 1701-13

1711 2 Reales. Similar / Crowned CAROLVSIII monogram (S) **50.00**

Philip V, 1700-46

1719 4 Maravedi. Crowned shield / Lion holding globes (C)........................ **15.00**
1707 1 Real Crowned shield / Floral monogram (S) **35.00**
1726 1 Real. Crowned shield / Arms in octolobe (S).................................. **25.00**
1734 4 Reales. Similar (S).............. **225.00**

F

1729 8 Escudo. Bust r. / Crowned shield (G) **2,200.00**

Louis, 1724

F

1724 2 Reales. Crowned shield / Arms in octolobe (S)................................... **75.00**

Ferdinand VI, 1746-59

1757 2 Reales. Crowned shield / Arms in octolobe (S)................................... **40.00**
1747 ½ Escudo. Bust r. / Crowned shield (G) **100.00**

Carlos III, 1759-88

1780 8 Maravedis. Bust r. / Castles and lions in angles of cross (C) **17.00**
1788 2 Reales. Bust r. / Crowned shield (S) **30.00**
1786 4 Escudo. Bust r. / Crowned shield in collar (G) **300.00**

Carlos, IV, 1788-1808

1800 4 Maravedis. Bust r. / Castles and lions in angles of cross (C) **13.50**
1793 1 Real. Bust r. / Crowned shield (S) **18.00**

Joseph Napoleon, 1808-13

1810 4 Reales. Bust l. / Crowned shield (S) **30.00**

F

Ferdinand VII, 1808-33 2

1833 2 Maravedis. Bust r. / Castles and lions in angles of cross (C) **3.00**
1809 4 Reales. Bust r. / Crowned shield (S) **135.00**

Isabel II, 1833-68

1846 2 Maravedis. Bust r. / Castles and lions in angles of cross (C) **8.50**
1837 4 Reales. Bust r. / Crowned shield in collar (S) **28.00**
1868 2½ Centimos. Bust r. / Crowned shield (C).. **5.00**
1868 Escudo. Bust r. / Crowned shield between pillars (S) **15.00**

Latin Monetary Union Standard

VF

1870 2 Centimos. Hispania std. / Lion holding shield (C)............................ **2.25**
1879 5 Centimos. Alfonso XII / Arms (C) **4.50**

VF

1900 50 Centimos. Alfonso XIII as child / Arms (S)... **3.50**
1891 1 Peseta. Alfonso XIII as baby / Arms (S)... **25.00**
1871 5 Pesetas. Amadeo I / Arms (S) **22.00**

VF

1883 5 Pesetas. Alfonso XII / Arms (S) **20.00**
1878 25 Pesetas. Alfonso XII / Arms (G) **335.00**

Republic & Civil War

VF

1938 10 Centimos. Arms (Iron)...... **650.00**
1937 25 Centimos. Yoke and arrows / Crowned shield (CN, holed)............... **.50**
1937 1 Peseta. Head l. / Grapes (Brass) **1.25**

Franco Regency

BU

1953 10 Centimos. Horseman / Arms (AL)... **3.00**

BU

1959 10 Centimos. Franco (AL)............ **.10**
1964 1 Peseta. Franco / Arms (ALB) .... **.75**
1949 5 Pesetas. Similar (N) **3.00**
1975 25 Pesetas. Franco / Eagle holding arms (CN)..................................... **1.00**
1966 100 Pesetas. Franco / Arms in octolobe (S).................................. **12.00**

Kingdom Restored

BU

1983 1 Peseta. Juan Carlos / Arms (AL) .... **.20**
1990 50 Pesetas. Juan Carlos / Globe (CN, notched) **1.50**
1994 100 Pesetas. Juan Carlos / Prado Museum (ALB).............................. **3.00**

BU

1999 2000 Pesetas. Alfonso XII / Train (S) .... *Proof* **33.00**
1989 5000 Pesetas. Arms / Ship Santa Maria (S)..................................... **45.00**

Euro Coinage

BU

1999 20 Euro Cent. Cervantes / Map (B, notched).. **.85**

BU

2000 1 Euro. Juan Carlos / Map. (CN clad N in NB, bimetallic) 4.00

BU

2002 10 Euro. King and Queen / Men on horses (S) .... *Proof* 50.00

COLONIAL COINAGE

F

Santo Domingo, Hispaniola

1506-1516 and later. 4 Maravedis. Crowned Y / Crowned pillars (C) 450.00

C

Cartagena, Colombia

1634 8 Reales cob. Crowned shield / Pillars over waves (S)................ 2,500.00

C or C[A]

Chihuahua, Mexico

1812 8 Reales. Ferdinand VII / Arms (cast S) 60.00

D

Durango, Mexico

1814 1/8th Real. Crowned FoV monogram (C)................................ 30.00

1814 1 Real. Ferdinad VII / Arms (S) 450.00

1821 8 Reales. same (S).................... 60.00

G[A]

F

Guadalajara, Mexico

1821 8 Reales. Ferdinand VII / Arms (S) 55.00

1821 8 Escudos. Similar (G)........ 2,600.00

G[O]

Guanajuato, Mexico

1822 8 Reales. Ferdinand VII / Arms (S) 55.00

ME

Lima, Peru

F

1689 1 Real cob. Pillars over waves / Castles and lions in angles of cross (S) 60.00

1740 2 Reales cob. Similar (S).......... 65.00

1697 4 Reales cob. Similar (S)........ 300.00

F

1714 8 Reales cob. Similar (S)........ 200.00

1696 8 Escudos cob. Similar (G). 2,500.00

1754 ½ Real. Crowned shield / Two globes between pillars (S)............... 20.00

1761 4 Reales. Similar (S)............... 125.00

F

1772 8 Reales. Similar (S).............. 250.00

1796 ¼ Real. Castle / Lion (S) 18.00

1812 ½ Real. Ferdinand VII / Arms (S) 12.00

1793 2 Reales. Charles IV / Arms (S) 35.00

1805 4 Reales. Similar (S)................ 50.00

1782 8 Reales. Charles III / Arms (S) 40.00

1821 2 Escudos. Ferdinand VII / Arms (G) 400.00

1775 8 Escudos. Carlos III / Arms (G) 1,500.00

Mo

Mexico City, Mexico

F

1653 ½ Real cob. CAROLVS monogram / Arms in octolobe (S).................... 150.00

1714 1 Real cob. Crowned shield / Arms in octolobe (S)............................... 65.00

1613 2 Reales cob. Similar (S)........ 165.00

1733 4 Reales cob. Similar (S)........ 200.00

1664 8 Reales cob. Similar (S)........ 250.00

1714 8 Escudos cob. Crowned Shild / Cross, fleurs in angles (G) 5,000.00

1755 ½ Real. Crowned shield / Two globes between pillars (S)............... 22.00

1736 2 Reales. Similar (S)................. 40.00

1768 4 Reales. Similar (S)............... 150.00

F

1769 8 Reales. Similar (S).............. 250.00

1780 ½ Real. Carlos III / Arms (S).. 15.00

1817 1 Real. Ferdinand VII / Arms (S) 15.00

1788 2 Reales. Carlos III / Arms (S).. 30.00

F

1805 4 Reales. Carlos IV / Arms (S) 75.00

F

1780 8 Reales. Carlos III / Arms (S).. 40.00

1808 1 Escudo. Carlos IV / Arms (G) 265.00

1736 4 Escudos. Philip V / Arms (G) 2,000.00

F

1805 8 Escudos. Carlos IV / Arms (G) 1,400.00

NG or G

Nueva Guatemala, Guatemala

F

1743 ½ Real cob. Crowned shield / Two globes between pillars (S).............. 60.00

1752 8 Reales cob. Similar (S)........ 150.00

1758 2 Reales. Similar (S)................. 80.00

1772 2 Reales. Carlos III / Arms (S).. 50.00

1812 2 Reales. Ferdinand VII / Arms (S) 40.00

F
1805 8 Reales. Charles IV / Arms (S)
.... **100.00**

NR or SF

Nuevo Reino / Santa Fe de Bogotá Colombia

F
1652 2 Reales cob. Crowned shield /
  Pillars over waves (S)..................... **750.00**
1663 2 Escudos cob. Crowned shield /
  Cross, fleurs in angles (G) **1,400.00**
1795 1 Real. Carlos IV / Arms (S) ... **50.00**
1777 1 Escudo. Carlos III / Arms (G)
.... **200.00**

P

Popayan, Colombia

F
1810 1/2 Real. Ferdinand VII / Arms (S)
.... **40.00**
1772 1 Real. Carlos III / Arms (S)
.... **150.00**
1814 8 Reales. Ferdinand VII / Arms (S)
.... **900.00**
1776 8 Escudos. Similar (G)........ **1,250.00**
1814 8 Escudos. Ferdinand VII / Arms
  (G) **1,200.00**

PTS or P

Potosi, Bolivia
1662 ½ Real cob. PHILIPVS monogram /
  Castles and lions in angles of cross (S)
.... **100.00**

F
ND (1556-98) 2 Reales cob. Crowned
  arms / Arms in octafoil (S)........... **120.00**
1749 2 Reales cob. Pillars over waves /
  Cross, castles and lions in angles (S)
.... **75.00**
1648 8 Reales cob. Crowned shield / Arms
  in octolobe (S)............................ **265.00**

F
1695 8 Reales cob. Pillars over waves /
  Cross, castles and lions in angles (S)
.... **250.00**
1770 1 Real. Two globes between pillars /
  Arms (S)...................................... **27.50**
1770 8 Reales. Similar (S)............... **250.00**
1799 ¼ Real. Lion / Castle (S) **20.00**
1808 1 Real. Carlos IV / Arms (S) ... **18.00**
1776 2 Reales. Charles III / Arms (S)
.... **22.50**
1823 4 Reales. Ferdinand VII / Arms (S)
.... **40.00**
1795 8 Reales. Charles IV / Arms (S)
.... **40.00**
1822 1 Escudo. Ferdinand VII / Arms (G)
.... **350.00**
1784 2 Escudos. Charles III / Arms (G)
.... **450.00**
1822 8 Escudos. Ferdinand VII / Arms
  (G) **1,200.00**

$

Santiago, Chile
F
1792 ¼ Real. Carlos IV / Castles and
  lions in angles of floral cross (S) **25.00**

F
1817 ¼ Real. Lion / Castle (S) **20.00**
1810 2 Reales. Imaginary bust of
  Ferdinand VII / Arms (S)............... **75.00**
1797 8 Reales. Carlos III / Arms (S)
.... **175.00**
1749 2 Escudos. Ferdinand VI / Arms (G)
.... **1,500.00**
1810 2 Escudos. Bust of Carlos III with
  titles of Ferdinand VII / Arms (G)
.... **650.00**

Z or Z$

Zacatecas, Mexico
F
1820 1 Real. Ferdinand VII / Arms (S)
.... **20.00**

F
1820 8 Reales. **40.00**

Philippines
1805 Octavo. Crowned shield / Lion with
  two globes (C)............................ **65.00**

VF
1868 10 Centavos. Isabel II / Arms (S)
.... **15.00**
1864 20 Centavos. Similar (S)........... **75.00**
1868 50 Centavos. Similar (S)........... **20.00**
1868 2 Pesos. Similar (G) **130.00**
1880 10 Centavos. Alfonso XII / Arms (S)
.... **325.00**
1885 20 Centavos. Similar (S)............. **9.00**
1885 50 Centavos. Similar (S)........... **15.00**
1882 4 Pesos. Similar (G) **1,200.00**
1897 Peso. Alfonso XIII / Arms (S)
.... **40.00**

Puerto Rico
VF
(1884) 1/2 Dollar. Fleur-de-lis
  countermark on United States Liberty
  Seated half dollar (S) .... *F* **275.00**
1896 5 Centavos. Arms (S)............... **50.00**
1896 10 Centavos. Alfonso XIII / Arms
  (S) **70.00**
1895 20 Centavos. Similar (S)........... **80.00**
1896 40 Centavos. Similar (S)........ **350.00**

VF
1895 Peso. Similar (S) **450.00**
Hacienda Vega Redonda. 1890s 2 Almud
  token (Brass) *This is the most common of
  the many different Puerto Rican hacienda
  tokens. Most others are far scarcer.*
.... *EF* **20.00**

SWITZERLAND

While the Swiss cantons (provinces) gradually formed a union during the 13th through 15th centuries, each one maintained its own coinage. During the early modern period most had a range of small silver denominations, with some striking silver-dollar sized talers and gold. Copper was not generally favored so very small denominations were usually struck in billon, a base silver-copper alloy.

During the Napoleonic era, a Swiss Republic was established (1798-1803) and even after its demise the various cantons maintained similar standards. After a new Swiss Confederation was founded, a uniform national coinage was created, replacing the issues of the cantons in 1850. It was based on the French franc, which became an international standard under the Latin Monetary Union.

Shooting competitions have been major events in Switzerland for centuries. Many of these festivities were commemorated, especially in the 19th century, by special silver talers, and later, five-franc pieces of high artistic merit. These are much prized by collectors and should be examined carefully for signs of cleaning, which reduces their value.

The regular coinage of Switzerland is perhaps the most conservative in the world, reflecting its extreme stability and resistance to inflation. Bearing a female representation of Helvetia, the allegory of the nation, or the Swiss cross, the designs of many denominations have not changed in more than 130 years. Like most countries however, Switzerland moved from silver to base metal in the 1968. Interestingly, Swiss coins rarely bear any language spoken in Switzerland. Because of the awkwardness of inscribing the coins in the four different languages spoken there, most coins are inscribed only in Latin. Switzerland in Latin is *Helvetia*; Swiss is *Helvetica*.

Additional Specialized Books:
Richter, J., and Kunzmann, R., *Neuer HMZ-Katalog.*

Known Counterfeits: Pre-1850 coins of Switzerland are not often counterfeited. Gold 20 francs of the late 19th and early 20th centuries should be examined with reasonable care. A partial list of years counterfeited include 1897, 1900, 1902-04, 1911, 1912, 1915, 1919, 1922, 1927, 1930, 1931, 1933, 1935, all with the B mintmark. The 1935 with the LB mintmark is an official re-strike form 1945-47.

CANTONAL ISSUES

F

Aargau. 1811 5 Batzen. Shield / Wreath (S) **17.50**
Appenzell. 1808 1 Batzen. Shield / Wreath (Billon) **22.00**
Basel. 1749 ¼ Thaler. City view / Basilisk (S) **100.00**

F

Bern. 1764 20 Kreuzer. Crowned arms / 8 B's cruciform (Billon) **18.00**
1809 1 Batzen. Shield / Wreath (Billon) **10.00**
Freiburg. 1830 5 Rappen. Shield / Cross, C at center (Billon) **10.00**
Geneva. 1791 3 Sols. Shield / Cross in quatrilobe (Billon) **10.00**
1840 1 Centime. Arms (C) **4.00**
Glarus. 1808 1 Schilling. Shield / Wreath (Billon) **38.00**
Graubunden. 1842 1/6 Batzen. Three oval shields / Wreath (Billon) **9.00**

F

Luzern. 1796 40 Kreuzer. Arms / 40 in Cross (Billon) **160.00**
1846 1 Rappen. Shield / Wreath (C) **6.00**
Neuchatel. 1817 1 Kreuzer. Crowned arms / Cross (Billon) **9.00**
St. Gall. 1790 6 Kreuzer. Bear l. / Wreath (Billon) **20.00**
Schaffhausen. 1809 ½ Batzen. Arms / Wreath (Billon) **22.00**
Schwyz. 1655 Schilling. Two-headed eagle / Saint (Billon) **18.00**
Solothurn. 1830 2½ Rappen. Shield / Cross, C at center (Billon) **9.00**
Thurgau. 1808 1 Kreuzer. Shield / Wreath (Billon) **22.00**
Ticino. 1835 3 Soldi. Shield / Wreath (Billon) **9.00**
Unterwalden. 1812 ½ Rappen. Shield / Wreath (Billon) **32.00**
Uri. 1811 ½ Rappen. Shield / Wreath (Billon) **48.00**

F

Vaud. 1823 10 Batzen. Shield / Soldier (Silver) **70.00**
Zug. 1783 1 Schilling. Arms / Saint Wolfgang (Billon) **22.00**
Zurich. 1842 2 Rappen. Arms / Wreath (Billon) **6.00**
1810 Ducat. Lion with shield (G) **600.00**

REPUBLIC

1802 1 Rappen. Fasces / Wreath (Billon) **10.00**
1801 10 Batzen. Figure with flag and sword / Wreath (S) **75.00**

CONFEDERATION

VF

1851 1 Rappen. Arms / Wreath (C) **20.00**
1895 1 Rappen. Similar **8.00**
1899 2 Rappen. Similar (C) **8.00**
1942 5 Rappen. Head of Helvetia (CN) **1.00**
1850 10 Rappen. Arms / Wreath (Billon) **18.00**
1920 20 Rappen. Head of Helvetia (CN) .... **.50**
1906 ½ Franc. Helvetia stg. / Wreath (S) **3.00**
1894 1 Franc. Similar (S) **12.00**
1907 1 Franc. Similar (S) **6.00**
1939 2 Francs. Similar (S) **6.00**
1865 5 Francs. Woman and child / Shield in Cross (S) **150.00**
1934 5 Francs. 18th century soldier / Arms (S) .... *Unc.* **60.00**
1950 5 Francs. William Tell / Shield (S) **10.00**
1883 20 Francs. Head of Helvetia / Wreath (G) **210.00**

Unc.

1963 2 Rappen. Cross / Wheat ear (C) .... **.45**
1993 5 Rappen. Head of Helvetia / Wreath (CN) .... **.20**
1956 1 Franc. Helvetia stg. / Wreath (S) **4.50**
1967 Same **3.50**
1963 5 Francs. Red Cross commemorative. Nurse and patients in form of cross (S) **12.00**
1984 5 Francs. High altitude balloon and deep water submarine (CN) **7.50**

WORLD PAPER MONEY

Paper money was created to make several things possible. The original reason for the invention of paper money in China in the 1200s was to permit the government to spend an increased amount of money, without having to incur the expense of actually making coins of that value. Such deficit financing has, over the last few centuries, been the cause for hundreds of countries printing billions of pieces of paper money. Most governments have had the ability to force their citizens to accept their paper money through coercion, but they have not always had to. Historically, most government notes have been backed up by full or partial reserves of precious metal, and such notes have been redeemed for that bullion under specified conditions. This has been less and less the case over the last 30 or so years. There are also advantages to the general public in the use of paper money. It permits the convenient transportation of a fixed amount of value. Because it is physically small, it is also easier to hide, making such transportation and storage not only more convenient, but also more secure. Unfortunately, when a government that has issued paper money is overthrown, its paper, unlike its precious-metal coins, often becomes worthless. Many countries even declare their own paper money obsolete every 10 or 20 years as a matter of course.

There are no surviving examples of the first paper issued in China 700 years ago, but specimens are known of notes printed on Mulberry bark paper in the 1300s during the Ming dynasty. The first European notes were printed in France in the 1600s when the French king wished to raise funds without having to part with gold or silver bullion. It was at that time a failure, and it was not until more than a century later that paper money became accepted in any serious way by the European population. This was during the French Revolution, when the government printed *assignats* backed up by confiscated church property.

Because of the potential for counterfeiting, most paper money is made with a number of deterrents incorporated, all of which are intended to make reproduction difficult. Many of these devices have recently been incorporated into United States paper money and are explained in that section. Several countries have even considered replacing paper (actually combinations of paper and cloth) with plastic notes. Australia has circulated these plastic notes for years with great success. Multicolored inks and intricately engraved designs may have been intended to thwart counterfeiters, but they have had the secondary result of encouraging collecting.

Over the last decade the market in collectible paper money has been quite strong. Many prices have increased, and at shows, over-the-counter sales are far more brisk than they were a decade ago. Like coins, the value of a piece of paper money varies based on its state of preservation. The proper handling and grading of world paper is similar to that for U.S. paper, and the reader should refer to the discussion in that section. The nature of paper money design incorporates extremely minute differences in details between varieties. The dates of the notes listed here are the series or law dates appearing on the notes themselves. However, dates appearing on paper money are not necessarily the actual dates of printing, which often can be told only by an analysis of the signatures printed on the notes. Dates in parentheses here are actual issue dates, which do not appear in the notes.

Note that many collectors consider grades below strictly Uncirculated unacceptable for common notes. Grades below this may be worth a fraction of the prices indicated for Unc. It is important to realize that most examples of world paper money in low grades – such as G to VG – may have virtually no wholesale value.

A book such as this can do no more than introduce the collector to this hobby. Thus, it is particularly important for anyone interested in collecting world paper money to acquire one or more of the excellent specialized books listed here.

Illustrations shown here are not to actual size. A typical piece of world paper money will usually range from 3" to 7" on its side. Those notes either much longer or shorter than this length will be noted in the text as either *large* or *small*.

Specialized Books:
Bruce, Colin R. II, ed., *Standard Catalog of World Paper Money, Specialized Issues.*

Bruce, Colin R. II, and Shafer, Neil, eds., *Standard Catalog of World Paper Money, Modern Issues.*

Monetary Research Institute, *MRI Bankers' Guide to Foreign Currency.*

Pick, Albert, *Standard Catalog of World Paper Money, General Issues.*

Known Counterfeits: Good counterfeits of British notes were made during World War II by the Germans, and Allied counterfeits of Ottoman notes were made during World War I. Many counterfeits are not made by the same process as the real notes they imitate. Often the counterfeits will lack the precise detail of the originals. Notes of significant value should be authenticated by an expert.

AFGHANISTAN

	VF
1299SH (1920) 1 Rupee, Coins / blank	**8.00**

	Unc.
1340 SH (1961) 10 Afghanis, King / Mosque	**5.00**
1352 SH (1973) 10 Afghanis, President / Arch	**2.25**
1357 SH (1978) 50 Afghanis, National seal (Inscription in wreath) / Building	**20.00**
1370 SH (1991) 500 Afghanis, Horsemen racing / Fortress	**1.50**

	Unc.
1372 SH (1993) 5,000 Afghanis, Mosque with minaret / Hexagonal mosque	**2.00**

Note: The 1996-2001 Taliban regime issued no paper money.

1381 SH (2002) 1 (New) Afghani, Bank seal / Mosque with two domes	**.50**

ALBANIA

	F
(1926) 5 Franka Ari, Boy in fez	**60.00**
(1939) 20 Franga, Roma std.	**12.00**
	Unc.
1957 10 Leke, Arms	**2.00**
1964 1 Lek, Peasant couple / Mountain fortress	**1.50**
1976 5 Leke, Bridge / Freighter ship	**1.25**
1992 1000 Leke, Skanderbeg / Arms and tower	**22.50**

	Unc.
2001 1000 Leke, Bogdani / Church	**15.00**

ANGOLA

	VF
1861 1000 Reis, Portuguese Arms	*Rare*
1921 1 Escudo, Francisco de Oliveira Chamico and steamship / Woman looking out at ships	**75.00**
1956 20 Escudos, Porto r. / Gazelle running	**4.00**
	Unc
1962 20 Escudos, Dock / Gazelles running	**32.00**
1976 100 Kwanzas, Antonio Neto / Agricultural workers	**6.00**
1995 1000 Kwanzas Reajustados, Jose Dos Santos and Antonia Neto / Antelope	**3.50**

ARGENTINA

	F
1884 5 Centavos, Avellanda, *small*	**13.00**
(1900) 1 Peso, Argentina std. (grey-blue-pink)	**175.00**
	Unc.
(1935) 1 Peso, Similar (blue on pink paper)	**5.50**
(1960) 5 Pesos, Young Jose de San Martin / People in plaza	**5.50**
(1983-84) 1 Peso Argentino, Old Jose de San Martin / Mountain lake	**.75**

Unc.
(1991) 100,000 Australes, M. Quintana / Progress std. with torch.. **45.00**
(1991) 500,000 Australes, M. Quintana / Progress std. with torch.. **75.00**

AUSTRALIA

VF
(1923) 1 Pound, George V **600.00**

VF
(1938-52) 1 Pound, George VI / Shepards and sheep...... **10.00**
Unc.
(1961-65) 10 Shillings, M. Flinders / Parliament building **250.00**
(1974-83) 1 Dollar, Elizabeth II / Aboriginal art **4.00**

Unc.
(1988) 10 Dollars, Ship / Aboriginal youth .... **Unc. 25.00**
1994-01 20 Dollars, Biplane and Rev. J. Flynn / Sailing ship and M. Reiby **47.50**

AUSTRIA

F
1759 10 Gulden, Inscriptions.. *Rare*
1847 10 Gulden, Austria, Atlas and Minerva **150.00**
1858 100 Gulden, Austria l., Danube r........................ **450.00**
1880 100 Gulden, Boys with sheaf and book................ **800.00**

VF
1919 2 Kronen, Mirrored female heads .... **.25**
(1919) 1000 Kronen, Imperial eagle, female bust r........... **2.00**
1927 10 Schilling, Mercury / Harvest............................. **30.00**
1936 100 Schilling, Woman with Edelweiss................... **600.00**
1945 10 Schilling, Woman / Mountain............................. **2.00**
Unc.
1956 20 Schilling, A. von Welsbach / Mountain village **15.00**
1967 20 Schilling, C. Ritter von Ghega / Railway bridge over Semmering Pass **4.50**
1986 20 Schilling, M. Daffinger / Albertina Museum, Vienna **3.25**
1986 50 Schilling, Sigmund Freud / Josephinum Medical School **7.00**
1988 5000 Schilling, Wolfgang A. Mozart / Opera House, Vienna.. **575.00**

BAHAMAS

	VF
1870s Bank of Nassau 5 Shillings, Victoria I	**Scarce**
1919 1 Pound, George V and ship	**600.00**
1936 4 Shillings, George VI and ship	**40.00**
(1953) 4 Shillings, Elizabeth II and ship	**7.50**
	Unc.
1965 ½ Dollar, Elizabeth II / Underwater scene of fish	**17.50**
1974 ½ Dollar, Elizabeth II / Smiling woman at market	**4.50**

	Unc.
2001 ½ Dollar, Elizabeth II / Smiling woman at market	**3.00**
1996 100 Dollars, Elizabeth II / Swordfish	**245.00**

BAHRAIN

	Unc.
1964 100 Fils, Boats / Palm trees	**9.00**

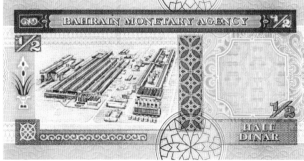

	Unc.
1973 (1986-98) 1/2 Dinar, Weaver / "Aluminum Bahrain" facility	**4.00**
(2001) 20 Dinars, Emir / Ahmed al-Fateh Islamic Center	**100.00**

BELARUS

	Unc.
1992 50 Kapeek, Knight / Squirrel	**.30**
1995 50,000 Rublei, Medieval gateway / Modern star-shaped gateway	**8.00**

BELGIUM

	VF
1851-52 100 Francs, Two cherubs	*Rare*
1910-20 20 Francs, Minerva and lion	**20.00**

	VF
1919 1000 Francs, Allegorical figures	**400.00**
1927-32 100 Francs, Albert and Elizabeth	**9.50**

VF

1935-47 50 Francs, Woman on two horses / Woman holding
ship and cornucopia **3.00**
1952-59 100 Francs, Leopold I **5.00**

Unc.

1964 20 Francs, King Baudouin / Molecule **2.00**
(1978-81) 100 Francs, H. Beyaert / Geometric design **25.00**
(1995-2001) 100 Francs, J. Ensor and theatrical masks / Beach
scene **7.50**

Unc.

(1980-96) 1000 Francs, Andre Gretry / Tuning forks **90.00**
(1992-97) 10,000 Francs, King Baudouin and Queen Fabiola /
Greenhouses at Laeken **600.00**
(1997) 10,000 Francs, King Albert II and Queen Paola / same
as above **450.00**

BERMUDA

F

1914 1 Pound, Arms **1,950.00**
1920-35 5 Shillings, George V / Ship **800.00**

VF

1937 5 Shillings, George VI and Hamilton harbor **40.00**
1952-57 5 Shillings, Elizabeth II and Hamilton harbor
.... **7.50**

VF

1952-66 5 Pounds, Elizabeth II / Arms .... **Unc. 950.00**

Unc.

1970 1 Dollar, Elizabeth II / Two sailboats **27.50**
1988 2 Dollars, Elizabeth II / Two towered building and
map **9.50**
1996 100 Dollars, Elizabeth II / House of Assembly **175.00**
*Many Bermuda notes after 1978 marked SPECIMEN
trade below their nominal values.*

BOLIVIA

VF

1902 1 Boliviano, Arms and Vegitation **5.00**
1928 1 Boliviano, Bolivar and mountain **1.00**
1942 500 Bolivianos, Miner **85.00**
1945 500 Bolivianos, Busch / Miners **1.50**

Unc.

1962 5 Pesos Bolivianos, G. Villarroel / Oil refinery **12.00**
1981 500 Pesos Bolivianos, Avaroa / Puerto de Antofagasta in
1879 .... **2.00**

Unc.

1986 50 Bolivianos, M. Perez de Holguin / Early church
.... **17.50**

BOSNIA-HERZEGOVINA

Unc.

1992 50 Dinara, Bridge **1.50**

REPUBLIKA BOSNA I HERCEGOVINA РЕПУБЛИКА БОСНА И ХЕРЦЕГОВИНА

100 STO DINARA СТО ДИНАРА

NARODNA BANKA BOSNE I HERCEGOVINE НАРОДНА БАНКА БОСНЕ И ХЕРЦЕГОВИНЕ

100 000

STO DINARA СТО ДИНАРА

	Unc.
1992 100 Dinara, Shield containing arm with sword	1.75
1994 500 Dinara, Shield containing six fleurs-de-lis	6.00

BRAZIL

	F
1833 1 Mil Reis, Arms l., Commerce std. center / blank	9.00
(1860-68) 5 Mil Reis, Arms between Justice and Commerce	140.00

	F
(1870) 1 Mil Reis, Pedro II and arms	250.00
(1885) 2 Mil Reis, Pedro II and Church / Rio de Janeiro Post Office	150.00
Estampa 3A (1893) 500 Reis, Woman with sheep	40.00
Estampa 11A (1907) 5 Mil Reis, Woman std. with flowers and fruit	250.00
Estampa 17A (1925) 10 Mil Reis, Pres. Manuel Ferraz de Campos Salles	12.00
	VF
(1943) 10 Cruzeiros, Getullio Vargas / Allegory of Industry	7.00
Estampa 1A (1955-59) 50 Cruzeiros, Princess Isabel / Allegory of Law	4.00
Estampa 2A (1954-61) Similar	1.50
	Unc.
(1961-62) 5 Cruzeiros, Bust of male Indian / Flower floating	1.25

	Unc.
(1972-80) 1 Cruzeiro, Liberty head in circle / Bank building in circle	.50

	Unc.
(1981) 200 Cruzeiros, Princess Isabel / Women cooking outdoors	.50
(1988) 5000 Cruzados, Bust of C. Portinari / C. Portinari painting	4.00

	Unc.
(1991-93) 10,000 Cruzeiros, Vital Brazil and snake being milked for venom / One snake swallowing another	1.00

BULGARIA

	F
1885 20 Leva, Arms	575.00
(1904) 5 Leva, Value / Arms	20.00
1922 5 Leva, Arms / Bee hives	4.50

	F
1942 500 Leva, Tsar Boris III / Allegorical woman	**7.00**
1943 200 Leva, Tsar Simeon II and Arms / View of Tirnovo	**7.50**

	Unc.
1947 20 Leva, Bank building	**10.00**
1951 100 Leva, G. Dimitrov and arms / Woman with grapes...	**.25**
1962 1 Lev, Arms / War monument	**1.75**
1974 2 Leva, Arms / Woman picking grapes....................	**1.75**
1991 20 Leva, Portrait of medieval duchess / Boyana church	**.25**

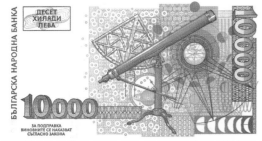

	Unc.
1997 10,000 Leva, Dr. P. Beron / Telescope.....................	**17.50**

CAMBODIA

	VF
(1955) 10 Riels, Temple of Banteay Srei / Phnom-Penh central market	**10.00**

	Unc.
(1963-72) 100 Riels, Preah Vihear Temple / Areal view of Preah Vihear Temple.......................................	**1.00**
(1973) 1000 Riels, Children at desks / Ancient stone face .	**1.00**
1998 5000 Riels, King Sihanouk / Phnom-Penh central market	**6.50**

CANADA

A much fuller treatment of Canadian paper money is provided here than for any other country, except the United States. This is due to the wide popularity of collecting in North America.

As in the U.S., many of Canada's earlier notes were actually issued by banks and not by the government. Earlier examples of these notes have little or no printing on the back. They were gradually eliminated by the 1940s. Fractional notes, with face values under one dollar, were common well into the 20th century. They are frequently found in quite worn condition.

Note that the prices here are for the most common dates appearing on the notes, and the most common variety for each design described. There are sometimes many varieties, and a specialized reference should be consulted.

Additional Specialized Reference:

Charlton, J.E., *Standard Catalogue of Canadian Charter Bank Notes.*

Charlton, J.E., *Standard Catalogue of Canadian Government Paper Money.*

Known Counterfeits: The series of 1954 is known to have been counterfeited in the 20-, 50-, 100-, and 1,000-dollar denominations. Counterfeits are also known of some of the earlier private bank notes.

Many Canadian notes have small colored discs called plachets imbedded in the paper. This is a counterfeit deterrent. Those that are simply printed on are counterfeit.

Notes issued by Banks

	F
1859 Bank of Canada 4 Dollars, Queen Victoria..........	**100.00**

	F
1859 Bank of Western Canada 4 Dollars, Lion, Prince Albert, Queen Victoria	**75.00**

Twenty Five Cents

	VF
1870 Bust of Britannia, *small*	**65.00**
1900 Britannia std, *small*.	**15.00**

	VF
1923 Bust of Britannia, *small*	15.00

One Dollar

	F
1866 Champlain and Cartier	1,400.00
1870 Cartier, and Woman with child and globe	950.00

	F
1878 Countess of Dufferin	250.00
	VF
1897-98 Countess and Earl of Aberdeen, Lumberjacks between / Parliament building	600.00
1911 Earl and Countess of Grey / Parliament building	200.00
1917 Princess of Connaught	95.00
1923 George V	45.00
1935 George V	50.00
1937 George VI	8.00
	Unc.
1954 Elizabeth II with "Devil's face" in hair / Prarie scene	37.50
1954 similar, no "Devil's face"	7.50

	Unc.
1967 Elizabeth II / Parliament	3.50

	Unc.
1973 Elizabeth II / Floating logs in river near Parliament	3.50

Two Dollars

	F
1866 Indian woman, Britannia scene, sailor	2,500.00
1870 Gen. Montcalm, Indian chief, Gen. Wolfe	3,000.00
1878 Earl of Dufferin	2,750.00
1887 Marchioness and Marquis of Lansdowne	1,500.00
	VF
1897 Prince of Wales and fishermen in boat / Wheat threshing scene	600.00
1914 Duke and Duchess of Connaught / Arms	300.00
1923 Prince of Wales	140.00
1935 Queen Mary	90.00
1937 George VI	15.00
	Unc.
1954 Elizabeth II with "Devil's face" in hair / Quebec scene	75.00
1954 similar, no "Devil's face"	15.00

Unc.

1974 Elizabeth II / Inuit scene 9.50

Unc.

1986 Elizabeth II / Two robins 3.50

Four Dollars

F

1882 Duke of Argyll 1,700.00

VF

1900 Countess and Earl of Minto, ship in lock between /
  Parliament building 2,000.00
1902 similar but ship on Canadian side of lock 1,700.00

Five Dollars

F

1866 Victoria, arms, sailing ship 6,000

VF

1912 Locomotive 500.00

VF

1924 Queen Mary 2,500.00
1935 Prince of Wales 150.00
1937 George VI 15.00

Unc.

1954 Elizabeth II with "Devil's face" in hair / Otter
  Falls 90.00
1954 similar, no "Devil's face" 30.00
1972-79 Sir Wilfred Laurier / Fishing boat 30.00

Unc.

1986 Sir Wilfred Laurier / Kingfisher 8.50
2002 Sir Wilfred Laurier / Children skating, tobogganing,
  and playing hockey 7.50

Ten Dollars

	F
1866 Sailors, lion and beaver	11,000.00

	VF
1935 Princess Mary	150.00
1937 George VI	17.00
	Unc.
1954 Elizabeth II with "Devil's face" in hair / Mt. Burgess	85.00
1954 similar, no "Devil's face"	45.00
1971 Sir John MacDonald / Oil refinery	40.00
1989 Sir John MacDonald / Osprey	15.00
2001 same / Peacekeeper and Memorial	13.00
2005 same with holographic strip	12.50

Twenty Dollars

	F
1866 Princess of Wales, Beaver, Prince Albert	Rare
	VF
1935 Princess Elizabeth	750.00
1937 George VI	30.00

	VF
1954 Elizabeth II with "Devil's face" in hair / Laurentian Hills	140.00
1954 similar, no "Devil's face"	65.00
1969-79 Elizabeth II / Lake Moraine and Rocky Mountains	55.00

	VF
1991 Elizabeth II / Loon	30.00
2004 Elizabeth II / Sculpture	25.00

Twenty Five Dollars

	VF
1935 George V and Queen Mary	1,600.00

Fifty Dollars

1935 Duke of York	1,150.00
1937 George VI	65.00
	Unc.
1954 Elizabeth II with "Devil's face" in hair / Nova Scotia coastline	250.00
1954 similar, no "Devil's face"	150.00

	Unc.
1975 W.L. MacKenzie King / Mounted Police in formation	
....	**185.00**
1988 W.L. MacKenzie King / Snowy owl......................	**75.00**
2004 W.L. MacKenzie King / Famous Five & Thérèse	
Casgrain	**65.00**

One Hundred Dollars

	VF
1935 Duke of Gloucester..	**800.00**
1937 Sir John MacDonald	**140.00**
	Unc.
1954 Elizabeth II with "Devil's face" in hair / Okanagan	
Lake	**250.00**
1954 similar, no "Devil's face"	**220.00**
1975 Sir Robert Borden / Nova Scotia harbor scene.....	**220.00**
1988 Sir Robert Borden / Canada Goose.....................	**135.00**
2004 Sir Robert Borden / Maps	**125.00**

Five Hundred Dollars

1896 Genius, Marquis of Lorne and Parliament building	
....*Cancelled*	**5,500.00**
1911 Queen Mary	**8,500.00**
1925 George V	**4,250.00**
1935 Sir John MacDonald	*Rare*

One Thousand Dollars

1896 Queen Victoria ....*Cancelled*	**6,500.00**
1901 Lord Roberts...................................*Cancelled*	**3,500.00**
1911 George V .... *VG*	**3,500.00**
1924 Lord Roberts...................................*Cancelled*	**5,000.00**
1925 Queen Mary	*Rare*

	VF
1935 Sir Wilfred Laurier	**1,300.00**
1937 similar	**1,250.00**
	Unc.
1954 Elizabeth II with "Devil's face" in hair / Landscape	
....	**3,750.00**
1954 similar, no "Devil's face"	**1,300.00**

	Unc.
1988 Elizabeth II / Two pine grosbeaks......................	**1,350.00**

Five Thousand Dollars

	VF
1896 J.A. MacDonald ....*Cancelled*	**6,500.00**
1901 Queen Victoria ....*Cancelled*	**3,500.00**
1918-24 similar.......................................*Cancelled*	**4,000.00**

Fifty Thousand Dollars

1918-24 George V and Queen Mary ....*Cancelled*	**6,000.00**

CHILE

	F
1881 5 Pesos, Village and Gen. Freire	**450.00**
1918-22 5 Pesos, Chile std. with shield.........................	**20.00**
1929 1000 Pesos, Condor...	**200.00**

	VF
1939-47 20 Pesos, Capt. Valdivia / Park scene...................	**3.50**
1958-59 5 Pesos, O'Higgins...	**.25**
	Unc.
(1962-70) ½ Escudo, Bernardo O'Higgins / Early	
explorer	**3.00**

	Unc.
1970-76 10 Escudos, J.M.Balmaceda / Battle scene	2.00
1975-81 50 Pesos, Capt. A. Prat / Sailing ship	2.00
1989-95 10,000 Pesos, Capt. A. Prat / Hacienda	45.00

CHINA, EMPIRE

	F
1368-99 300 Cash, Three strings of coins, *large*	*Rare*
1856-59 5000 Cash, Inscription with dragons	60.00

	VF
1904 5 Dollars, "Imperial Bank of China," Confucius stg. / same in Chinese, Confucius stg.	125.00
(1910) 10 Dollars, Prince Chun l., Dragon above Great Wall	900.00

CHINA, REPUBLIC

	VF
1914 5 Yuan, Locomotive / Bank building	25.00
1931 5 Yuan, Temple of Heaven	5.00
1937 5 Yuan, Sun Yat-sen / Skyscraper	.25
(1940) 10 Cents, Temple of Heaven	.75
1947 1000 Customs Gold Units, Sun Yat-sen / Building	2.50

Republic, on Taiwan

	Unc.
1946 1 Yuan, Bank building and Sun Yat-sen / Naval battle	15.00
1954 1 Yuan, Sun Yat-sen / Bank building	25.00
1961 1 Yuan, Sun Yat-sen / Presidential Office Building	3.00
1972 50 Yuan, Sun Yat-sen / Chungshan building	6.00
1987 100 Yuan, similar	7.00

	Unc.
1999 50 Yuan, Bank building / Paper money. Made of polymer plastic	4.00

CHINA, PEOPLE'S REPUBLIC

	Unc.
1948 5 Yuan, Sheep	30.00
1953 2 Fen, Airplane	.25
1953 5 Fen, Freighter	.30
1962 1 Jiao, Farm workers	.50
1972 5 Jiao, Textile workers	.75
1980 1 Jiao, Two Taiwanese	.50

	Unc.
1990 2 Yuan, Two portraits / Rocks at sea	.75
1990 50 Yuan, Three portraits / Waterfalls	12.50

	Unc.
1999 10 Yuan, Mao Tse-tung / Gorges	2.50
1979 10 Fen Foreign Exchange Certificate, Waterfall	.50

COLOMBIA

	F
(1819) 2 Reales / 25 Centavos Donkey with pack	100.00
1860s 1 Peso = 10 Reales, Steamship	200.00
1888 1 Peso, Arms and Bolivar	20.00
	VF
1929-54 1 Peso, Santander and Bolivar / Liberty	1.00
1953-61 10 Pesos, Gen. Nariño / Bank	35.00
	Unc.
1959-77 1 Peso Oro, Bolivar and Santander / Condor	3.00
1974-75 200 Pesos Oro, Bolivar / Coffee picker	20.00

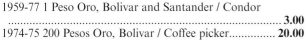

	Unc.
1997-2003 5,000 Pesos, J. Asuncion Silva / Woman amid trees	6.00

COSTA RICA

	F
1871 2 Pesos, Arms l., woman r.	1,200.00
1910-14 1 Colon, Columbus and Arms	70.00
1914-32 10 Colones, Coffee pickers	75.00
	VF
1942-48 10 Colones, Carazo / Sailing ship	35.00
1951-62 10 Colones, Echeverria / Oxcart	25.00
	Unc.
1963-67 5 Colones, B. Carrillo / Coffee worker	45.00

	Unc.
1968-92 5 Colones, R.Y.Castro / Port scene	2.00
1977-88 100 Colones, R. Jimenez / Supreme Court building	15.00
1996 5000 Colones, Ancient sculpture / Ancient stone sphere and animals	45.00

CROATIA

	Unc.
1941 10 Kuna	10.00
1991 1 Dinar, R. Boskovic and geometry / Zagreb Cathedral	.10
1995 10 Kuna, J. Dobrila / Pula Arena	4.00

CUBA

	F
1857-59 100 Pesos, Allegorical scene	*Rare*
1872-83 5 Centavos, Arms / Allegory	7.50
(1905) 10 Pesos, T. Palma	*Rare*
1934-48 10 Pesos, Cespedes	80.00

	VF
1949-60 1 Peso, Jose Marti	4.00
1949-60 10 Pesos, Cespedes	4.00

	Unc.
1961-65 1 Peso, Jose Marti / Castro entering Havana	7.50
1971-90 20 Pesos, C. Cienfuegos / Soldiers on beach	10.00
1995 3 Pesos, Ernesto Che Guevara / Guevara cutting sugar cane	1.50
(1985) 1 Peso Foreign Exchange Certificate, San Salvador de la Punta castle	3.50

CZECHOSLOVAKIA

	VF
1919 1 Koruna, Arms	1.50
1920 100 Korun, Bohemian lion and Pagan priestess / Female portraits at each side	95.00
1932 1000 Korun, Figure scanning globe	50.00
(1945) 1000 Korun, King George Podebrad / Castle	3.00
1953 25 Korun, Equestrian statue / View of Tabor	7.50

	Unc.
1961 3 Korun, Arms	2.00
1973 500 Korun, Soldiers in rain gear / Medieval fortress	30.00
1986 10 Korun, P. Orszagh Hviezdoslav / Orava mountains	2.00

DENMARK

	F
1713 5 Rigsdaler, Crowned F4 monogram	Rare
1819 1 Rigsbankdaler, Inscriptionsand ornaments	100.00
1819 100 Rigsbankdaler, Inscriptions	4,000.00
1875-90 10 Kroner, Arms	800.00

	VF
1916-21 1 Krone, Value / Arms	3.00
1910-42 50 Kroner, Fishermen pulling net into boat / Arms within vine	37.00

	Unc.
1950-60 5 Kroner, B. Thorvaldsen and three graces / Kalundborg city view	23.00
1972-78 10 Kroner, S. Kirchhoff / Eider bird (duck)	5.00

	Unc.
(19)97-(20)00 200 Kroner, J.L.Heiberg / Lion	50.00
(19)97-(20)03 500 Kroner, N. Bohr / Medieval relief of knight fighting dragon	125.00

DOMINICAN REPUBLIC

	F
(1810) 4 Escalins, Arms	Rare
1848 2 Pesos = 80 Centa with 40 Pesos overprint, Boy l., Arms center	225.00
1867 10 Pesos, Arms	225.00
1947-59 100 Pesos, Woman with coffee pot	VF 90.00

	Unc.
(1961) 10 Centavos Oro, Reserve Bank building	15.00
1978-88 5 Pesos Oro, Sanchez / Hydroelectric dam	5.50
1992-94 1000 Pesos Oro, National Palace / Columbus's fortress	125.00

ECUADOR

	VF
1928-38 5 Sucres, woman std. with fruit and sickle	45.00
1939-49 100 Sucres, Woman scanning globe	60.00

	Unc.
1957-88 10 Sucres, Conquistador	4.00
1957-80 100 Sucres, Bolivar / Arms, American Banknote Co.	12.50

	Unc.
1961-65 100 Sucres, same but T.DeLaRue	50.00
1976-82 1000 Sucres, Ruminahui / Arms	25.00
1995-99 50,000 Sucres, E. Alfaro / Arms	10.00

The Sucre has been demonitized and replaced by the US Dollar.

EGYPT

	VF
1899 50 Piastres, Sphinx	3,750.00
1917-51 25 Pistres, Nile scene	8.50
(1940) 5 Piastres, King Farouk	3.00
(1952-58) 5 Piastres, Queen Nefertiti	1.75

	Unc.
1961-66 25 Piastres, Arms	6.00
1967-78 50 Piastres, Al Azhar Mosque / Ramses II	3.50
1976-78 25 Piastres, Statue and Sphynx / Arms	3.50
1995-, 50 Piastres, Al Azhar Mosque / Ramses II	.75
1978-99 1 Pound, Sultan Quayet Bey Mosque / Four statues from Abu Simbel	1.50
1989-2002 5 Pounds, Ibn Toulon Mosque / Ancient Egyptian relief	5.00

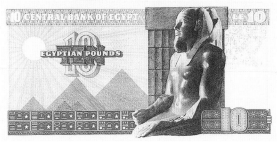

	Unc.
1969-78 10 Pounds, Sultan Hassan Mosque / Ancient Egyptian statue	25.00

	Unc.
1994-97 100 Pounds, Mosque / Sphinx	60.00
1940 (1998-99) 5 Piastres, Queen Nefertiti, signed M. Elghareeb	1.25

EL SALVADOR

	VF
1934 5 Colones, Woman reclining with branch / Columbus	50.00
1955-58 2 Colones, Coffee bush / Columbus	10.00

	Unc.
1963-66 1 Colon, Columbus / Central Bank building	30.00
1974-76 25 Colones, Columbus / Port	45.00

	Unc.
1983-88 100 Colones, Columbus / Monument	30.00
1997 200 Colones, Columbus / Monument	9.00

ERITREA

	Unc.
(1997) 10 Nakfa. Portraits of three girls / Bridge.	**1.00**

Note foil at left with color-shifting camels to deter counterfeiting.

ETHIOPIA

	F
1915-29 10 Thalers, "Bank of Abyssinia," Leopard	*Rare*
1932-33 5 Thalers, Head of gazelle	75.00
1932-33 100 Thalers, Elephant	175.00
	VF
1945 1 Dollar, Haile Selassie and Farmer plowing	13.00
1945 100 Dollars, Haile Selassie and Palace	175.00
(1961) 1 Dollar, Haile Selassie and coffee bushes	15.00

	Unc.
(1966) 1 Dollar, Haile Selassie and Harbor	20.00
(1966) 100 Dollars, Haile Selassie and Church cut from rock	125.00
1969EE (1976) 50 Birr, Science students / Castle at Gondar	50.00
1969EE (1991) 100 Birr, Menelik II / Man with microscope	45.00
1989EE (1997) 1 Birr, Portrait of boy / Tisisat Waterfalls on Blue Nile	.75

EUROPEAN UNION

Unc.

In 2002, this currency replaced the issues of those European Union countries that chose to become part of the "Euro Zone." The designs are uniform across borders, but the prefix of the serial number indicates the country where a particular note was issued as follows:

L	Finland
M	Portugal
N	Austria
P	Netherlands
R	Luxembourg
S	Italy
T	Ireland
U	France
V	Spain
X	Germany
Y	Greece
Z	Belgium

All notes have arches on the obverse, and a bridge on the reverse. These motifs are interpreted with a different style of architecture on each denomination. They are archetypal images, and no specific building or bridge is intended.

These values are for crisp notes. Circulated ones are worth only their face value. Values in all grades may fluctuate with the currency markets.

	Unc.
2002 5 Euro, Classical	10.00
2002 10 Euro, Romanesque	20.00
2002 20 Euro, Gothic	40.00
2002 50 Euro, Renaissance	95.00
2002 100 Euro, Baroque	180.00
2002 200 Euro, Late Nineteenth Century	400.00
2002 500 Euro, Twentieth Century	900.00

FIJI

	VF
1873 50 Cents, C R	150.00

	VF
1942 1 Penny, Coin / Coin, *small*	**2.00**
	Unc.
(1980-93) 1 Dollar, Elizabeth II / Crowds at fruit market	**2.50**

FINLAND

	F
1790 8 Skilling Specie, Arms	**1,500.00**
1862 20 Mark, Arms with supporters	**500.00**
1897 5 Markkaa, Allegorical bust / Arms	**75.00**
	VF
1918 25 Penniä, Group of four flowers	**1.50**

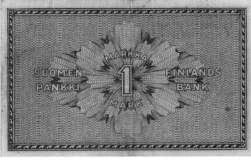

	VF
1918 1 Mark, Flowers	**1.50**
1939 50 Markkaa, Allegorical group of six people, ship in background	**15.00**
1945 1000 Markkaa, Allegorical group of 13 people with heavy rope	**75.00**
	Unc.
1963 1 Markka, Wheat / Lion rampant with sword	**1.50**
1975 500 Markkaa, President Kekkonen / Arms	**150.00**
1986 100 Markkaa, Jean Sibelius / Swans	**40.00**
1986 (1991) same but optical varialble divice added	**27.50**
1993 (1993-97) 20 Markkaa, V. Linna / Tampere Street	**7.50**

FRANCE

	F
1701-07, 200 Livres, Crowned monogram	**3,500.00**
1789-90, 1000 Livres, Louis XVI	**2,200.00**
	VF
1792 10 Sous, Value in triangle between allegorical figures	**4.00**

	VF
1792 50 Livres, Republic std.	**16.00**
1864-66 50 Francs, Two cherubs	*Rare*
1889-1927 50 Francs, Two cherubs, two portraits and ornate oval border	**70.00**
1939 20 Francs, Science and Labor / Scientist	**15.00**
1941-49 10 Francs, Miner / Farm woman	**.75**
1944 5 Francs, Flag	**.40**
1946-51 50 Francs, Leverrier / Neptune	**3.50**
	Unc.
1966-70 5 Francs, Louis Pasteur / Louis Pasteur	**200.00**
1963-73 10 Francs, Voltair / Voltair	**20.00**
1980-97 20 Francs, Claude Debussy / Claude Debussy	**10.00**
1981-94 200 Francs, Baron de Montesquieu / Baron de Montesquieu	**70.00**

The backs of the above four notes are mirror images of their fronts.

1995-99 200 Francs, G. Eiffel / Base of Eifel tower	**40.00**

GERMANY

	VF
1874 20 Mark, Herald wearing tabbard	*Rare*
1908 100 Mark, Eagle / Medallic woman's head supported by two women kneeling	**.75**
1910 1000 Mark, Inscription / Arms with supporters, *large*	**1.00**

	VF
1923 100,000 Mark, Inscription / blank	.50
1939 20 Reichsmark, Woman with edelweiss	5.00
1944 1 Mark, Large M	.75
1948 5 Deutsche Mark, Europa on Bull	20.00

	Unc.
1960 5 Deutsche Mark, Young Venetian Woman by Albecht Dürer / Oak leaves	14.00
1970-80 10 Deutsche Mark, Young Man by Albecht Dürer / Sailing Ship	12.00

	Unc.
1991-93 1000 Deutsche Mark, Brothers Grimm / Open book	775.00

GERMAN NOTGELD

	Unc.
Frankfurt: G.M.Holz, 1921 25 pfennig, Golem, *small*	5.00
Schneidemuhl, c.1919 75 pfennig, Biplane, *small*	1.00

These very common emergency notes were issued mostly by cities. Austria, Hungary and other countries saw the same phenomenon during or after World War I.

GHANA

	Unc.
(1965) 1 Cedi, Kwame Nkrumah / Bank building	7.50
1979-82 5 Cedis, Old man with hat / Men cutting tree	3.00
1994-96 5000 Cedis, Arms / Freighter in harbor	25.00

GREAT BRITAIN

	F
1694 5 Pounds, Inscription (handwritten)	*Rare*
1751 10 Pounds, Inscription (handwritten details)	*Rare*
1797 1 Pound, Inscription and Small arms	*Rare*

	F
1815 1 Pound, Building. Issued not by the Bank of England but by Sunderland & Wearmouth Bank	150.00
1855 5 Pounds, similar but "payable to the bearer"	*Rare*
1902-18 10 Pounds, similar	775.00
1917 1 Pound, St. George and George V / Parliament	110.00

	VF
1928-48 1 Pound, Britannia seated / coins with St. George and dragon	27.50
1944-47 5 Pounds, Inscription and small arms	125.00
(1957-67) 5 Pounds, Head of Britannia and St. George / Lion	55.00

	Unc.
1960-70 10 Shillings, Elizabeth II / Britannia std.	10.00
(1978-84) 1 Pound, Elizabeth II / Sir Isaac Newton	9.00
1990 (1990-02) 5 Pounds, Elizabeth II / G. Stephenson	22.00

GREECE

	F
1822 100 Grossi, Inscription and seals	500.00
1822 1,000 Grossi, similar	975.00
1852 10 Drachmai, Arms	*Rare*
1897 5 Drachmai, Arms and Stavros / Athena	175.00
1922 100 Drachmai, Stavros, reclining women, arms / Acropolis see between columns	95.00

	VF
(1946) 10,000 Drachmai, Aristotle	150.00
1955 50 Drachmai, Pericles / Pericles speaking	15.00

	Unc.
1964 50 Drachmai, Arethusa / Shipyard	2.50
1978 50 Drachmai, Poseidon / Sailing ship	2.00
1983 500 Drachmes, Capodistrias / Fortress at Corfu	4.50
1996 200 Drachmes, R. Velestinlis Ferios / Secret school of Greek priests	3.75

	Unc.
1997 5,000 Drachmes, Kolokotronis / Church at Calamata	35.00

GUATEMALA

	F
(1882) 5 Pesos, Locomotive	175.00
1934-45 5 Quetzales, Freighter between two quetzales	50.00

	VF
1948-54 ½ Quetzal, Building l., Quetzal flying at center / Two figures	9.50

	Unc.
1966-70 100 Quetzales, Indio de Nahuala / Mountain	400.00
1971-83 10 Quetzales, Gen. Granados / National Assembly of 1872	22.50

	Unc.
1989-92 50 Centavos, Tecun Uman statue	5.00
1994-95 100 Quetzales, F. Marroquin / Univ. of San Carlos de Borromeo	35.00

HAITI

	F
1790s 4 Escalins, Arms	*Rare*
1851 2 Gourdes, Arms	100.00
1875 1 Piastre, Pres. Domingue l., Agriculture r.	35.00
1914 2 Gourdes, J.J. Dessalines and arms / Mining scene	60.00

	Unc
1919 1 Gourde, (1964-67) Castle / Arms	7.50
1973 1 Gourde, Francois Duvalier / Arms	2.00

	Unc.
1973 5 Gourdes, Francois Duvalier / Arms	**7.50**
1979 5 Gourdes, Jean-Claude Duvalier / Arms	**4.00**
1989 1 Gourde, Toussaint L'Ouverture	**.60**
1992 5 Gourdes, Statue of several figures / Arms	**1.50**

HAWAII

	VF
(1880) 10 Dollars, Sailing ship, cowboy, locomotive	**10,000.00**
1895 5 Dollars, Woman, building, bull's head	**15,000.00**

HONG KONG

1931-56 10 Dollars, Chartered Bank of India, Australia and China	**F 95.00**
(1935) 1 Dollar, George V	**350.00**
(1949-52) 1 Dollar, George VI	**22.00**
1952-59 1 Dollar, Elizabeth II	**2.00**
	Unc.
1961-95 1 Cent, Elizabeth II, *small*	**.25**

	Unc.
1961-70 10 Dollars, The Chartered Bank	**60.00**
1973-76 500 Dollars, Hongkong and Shanghai Banking Corp	**375.00**
1985-91 10 Dollars, Standard Chartered Bank	**6.00**
1994-00 20 Dollars, Bank of China	**6.00**
1993-2001 100 Dollars, Hongkong and Shanghai Banking Corp.	**250.00**

HUNGARY

	VF
1920 20 Korona, Matyas Church	**.50**
1929 10 Pengo, Deak / Parliament	**10.00**
1939 5 Pengo, Girl / Man playing balalaika	**3.00**
	Unc.
1965-89 50 Forint, Rakoczi / Battle scene	**9.00**
1990 500 Forint, Endre Ady / Aerial view of Budapest	**9.50**

	Unc.
1992-95 100 Forint, Kossuth / Horsecart	**3.00**
1997-03 10,000 Forint, St. Stephen / View of Esztergom	**120.00**

ICELAND

	VF
1792-1801 1 Rigsdaler, Inscription, triangle above	*Rare*
1928 10 Kronur, Sigurdsson	**25.00**
1957 5 Kronur, Viking / Farm	**1.50**
	Unc.
1961 10 Kronur, J. Eiriksson / Ships at port	**6.00**
1961 (1984-91) 1000 Kronur, Bishop Sveinsson / Church	**27.50**

Unc.

1986 2000 Kronur, J.S. Kajarval / Leda and the Swan **40.00**

INDIA

	VF
1861-65 10 Rupees, Queen Victoria	*Rare*
1910-20 10 Rupees, Inscription	*F* **40.00**
1917 1 Rupee, George V	**90.00**
(1937-43) 5 Rupees, George VI	**20.00**
	Unc.
1957 1 Rupee, Coin, *small*	**5.00**
1966 1 Rupee, Coin, *small*	**3.00**
(1962-67) 5 Rupees, Asoka pillar	**10.00**

Unc.

(1997-2002) 5 Rupees, Mahatma Gandhi / Tractor **1.00**
(1996) 10 Rupees, Mahatma Gandhi / Tiger **1.00**

INDONESIA

Unc.

1945 1 Rupiah, President Sukarno / Smoking volcano
.... **6.00**
1964 2½ Rupiah, President Sukarno **7.50**
1964 50 Sen, Soldier, *small* .... **.25**
1980 5000 Rupiah, Diamond Cutter / Three Torajan houses
.... **20.00**

Unc.

1993-94 50,000 Rupiah, President Soeharto / Airplane over
airport **35.00**

IRAN, Empire

F

1890-1923 1 Toman, Lion and Nasr-ed-Din Shah **200.00**
1924-32 50 Tomans, Nasr-ed-Din / Lion.................... **1,750.00**

VF

1315AH (1936) 10 Rials, Reza Shah / Mountains......... **150.00**
(1948) 50 Rials, Shah Mohammad Reza / Five ancient
figures **50.00**

	Unc.
1340SH (1961) 10 Rials, Shah Mohammad Reza / Amir Kabir Dam	10.00
(1965-69) 20 Rials, Same / Painting of hunters	10.00

	Unc.
(1974-79) 50 Rials, Same / Tomb of Cyrus the Great	8.00
(1971-72) 5000 Rials, Same / Trees before Golestan Palace	600.00

IRAN, Islamic Republic

	Unc.
(1979) 50 Rials, Same / Tomb of Cyrus the Great. The Shah's portrait overprinted with arabesque by the Islamic Republic	12.00
(1981) 200 Rials, Imam Reza Shrine / Tomb of Ibn-E-Sina	6.00
(1982-2002) 1000 Rials, Ayatollah Khomeini / Dome of the Rock in Jerusalem	4.00
(1986-c.2004) 2000 Rials, Revolutionaries before mosque / Kaaba in Mecca	3.00
(1993-) 5000 Rials, similar / Flowers and birds	6.00

IRAQ

	VF
1931 1 Dinar, King Faisal I	250.00
1931 (1935) 1/4 Dinar, King Ghazi	110.00

	VF
1931 (1941) 1/4 Dinar, King Faisal II as child	120.00
1947 1 Dinar, King Faisal II as adult / Horseman	50.00
(1959) 1/4 Dinar, State seal / Palm trees	5.00
(1959) 5 Dinars, Same/Hamurabi receiving laws	12.50

	Unc.
(1971) 1/4 Dinar, Ship at port / Palm trees	9.00
(1971) 1 Dinar, Oil refinery / Doorway	17.50
1978-80 25 Dinars, Horses / Courtyard	22.50
1986 25 Dinars, Saddam Hussein / Monument	2.50

	Unc.
1994 100 Dinars, Saddam Hussein / Building with tower	1.00

Unc.
(2003) 50 Dinars, Grain silo / Date palms.........................**.50**
(2003) 1,000 Dinars, Medieval coin / University **2.50**

IRELAND

F
1808 1 Pound, Hibernia std. .... *Rare*
1890-1917 10 Pounds, Hibernia stg. l. and r................. **275.00**
1929-39 5 pounds, Man plowing with horses **110.00**
Unc.
1962-68 10 Shillings, Lady Hazel Lavery / Face of river god
.... **45.00**

Unc.
1977-89 1 Pound, Queen Medb / Medieval writing......... **12.00**
1993-99 10 Pounds, James Joyce / River allegory **30.00**
1995-01 50 Pounds, D. Hyde / Statue of Parnell **150.00**

ISRAEL

VF
(1948-51) 500 Mils, Anglo-Palestine Bank **100.00**
(1952) 1 Pound, Bank Leumi Le-Israel **15.00**

Unc.
1958 ½ Lira, Woman with oranges **5.00**
1968 5 Lirot, Albert Einstein / Atomic Reactor **9.00**

Unc.
1973 10 Lirot, Moses Montefiore / Jaffa Gate **1.50**
1975 500 Lirot, David Ben Gurion / Golden Gate **45.00**
1978 1 Sheqel, Moses Montefiore / Jaffa Gate................. **2.00**
1983 1,000 Sheqelim, Maimonides / View of Tiberias **20.00**
1986 1 New Sheqel, Same **2.00**
1985-92 10 New Sheqelim, Golda Meir / Jews in Moscow
.... **12.00**
1985-92 50 New Sheqelim, S.Y.Agnog / Buildings **50.00**
1999-2002 200 New Sheqelim, Zalman Shazar in
photographic style.. **90.00**

ITALY

VF
1874 2 Lire, Bust of Italia .... *F* **8.00**
1888-1925 10 Lire, Umberto I....................................... **12.00**
1926-36 50 Lire, Woman with three children / Woman
standing **55.00**
1935-44 10 Lire, Victor Emmanuel III / Italia.................. **2.00**
Unc.
1966-75 500 Lire Eagle and Arethusa **25.00**
1982 1,000 Lire, Marco Polo / Doge's Palace **3.00**
1990 1,000 Lire, Montessori / Teacher and student........... **3.00**

Unc.
1985 5,000 Lire, V.Bellini / Opera scene 7.50
1971-77 5,000 Lire, Columbus and Hippocamp.............. 95.00
1962-73 10,000 Lire, Michaelangelo / Piazza del Campidoglio
.... 60.00
1975 20,000 Lire, Titian / Painting................................ 340.00
1984-90 50,000 Lire, Bernini / Equestrian statue............. 60.00
1997 500,000 Lire, Raphael / Painting "School of Athens"
.... 400.00

JAMAICA

F
1904-18 2 Shillings 6 Pence, George V / Woman with hat
....1,250.00
1939-48 10 Shillings, George VI / Value.......................... 40.00
Unc.
1960 5 Shillings, Elizabeth II / River rapids 100.00
1978-81 10 Dollars, G.W. Gordon / Bauxite mining 7.50
1991-93 100 Dollars, D. Sangster / Dunn's River Falls ... 10.00

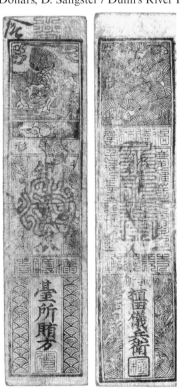

JAPAN

VF
ca.1800-60s, "Hansatu" various denominations.............. 25.00
(1872) 1 Yen, Two phoenixes and two dragons 125.00
(1930) 100 Yen, Pavilion and Shotoku-taishi / Temple
complex.. 50.00
1938 50 Sen, Mt. Fuji .... .75
(1947) 10 Sen, Dove / Diet building .... .25
(1950) 1000 Yen, Shotoku-Yaishi / Yumedono Pavilion
.... 30.00
Unc.
(1969) 500 Yen, Iwakura Tomomi / Mt. Fuji 10.00
(1963) 1000 Yen, Hirobumi Ito / Bank of Japan............. 16.00

Unc.
(1984-93) 1000 Yen, Soseki Natsume / Two cranes 15.00
(1993-) 5000 Yen, Inazo Nitobe / Mt. Fuji..................... 65.00
1958 10,000 Yen, Yumedono / Pavilion watermark 100.00

JORDAN

Unc.
1959 ½ Dinar, Young King Hussein / Collonade............. 95.00
(1975-92) ½ Dinar, King Hussein / Jerash 3.25

	Unc.
(1975-92) 5 Dinars, King Hussein / Petra	22.50
1977-92 20 Dinars, King Hussein / Electric power plant	85.00
1992 20 Dinars, King Hussein / Dome of the Rock in Jerusalem	95.00
2002 5 Dinar, King Abdullah I / Palace	12.50
2002-04 50 Dinars, King Abdullah II / Palace	110.00

KENYA

	Unc.
1966-68 5 Shillings, Jomo Kenyatta / Woman picking coffee	85.00

	Unc.
1978 10 Shillings, Jomo Kenyatta / Cows	5.00
1980-88 50 Shillings, Daniel Arap Moi / Airplane over airport	12.50
1995 20 Shillings, Daniel Arap Moi / Runner and stadium	2.50

KOREA, SOUTH

1962 100 Hwan, Mother and child	325.00
1962 10 Jeon, Value, *small*	.40
(1975) 1000 Won, Yi Hwang / Do-San Academy	5.00

KUWAIT

	Unc.
1960 (1961) 1/4 Dinar, Amir Shaikh Abdullah / Port	45.00
1968 1 Dinar, Amir Shaikh Sabah / Oil refinery	40.00

	Unc.
1968 (1980-91) 1 Dinar, Arms / Old fortress, red-violet and purple	7.00
1968 (1992) 1 Dinar, Arms / Old fortress, green and deep blue	9.00

Because many notes were stolen by invading Iraqi forces, the Kuwaiti government declared the paper money worthless and reissued it with similar designs but different colors after liberation. The above pair of notes is an example.

1968 (1994) 1/2 Dinar, Boys playing game	7.00

LAOS

	Unc.
(1957) 100 Kip, King and dragons / Woman with bowl of roses	10.00
1997-2003 5000 Kip, Kaysone Phomvihane / Cement factory	3.00

LATVIA

	VF
(1919) 5 Rubli, Head l. / Flame	20.00
1937-40 10 Latu, Fishermen / Man sowing	9.00
	Unc.
1992 1 Rublis	.30
1992-2001 5 Lati, Tree	10.00
1992 50 Latu, Sailing ship / Crossed keys	120.00

LEBANON

	VF
1925 25 Piastres, Water mill	350.00
1939 5 Livres, Cedar tree r. / City view	110.00
1942 25 Piastres, Umayyad mosque	25.00
1948 5 Piastres, Value	3.50

	VF
1952-64 1 Livre, Crusader castle / Columns at Baalbek	8.00
1952-63 100 Livres, Beirut harbor / Cedar	35.00
	Unc.
1964-86 10 Livres, Ancient arch / Rocks in water	1.00
	Unc.
1964-88 50 Livres, Temple of Bacchus / Building	2.50
1988-93 500 Livres, Beirut city view / Ancient ruins	3.00
1994 5,000 Livres, Geometric pattern	12.00

LITHUANIA

	Unc.
1991 0.10 Talonas, Arms, *Small*	.25

	Unc.
1992 500 Talonu, Bear *Small*	4.50
1993 500 Talonu, Wolves *Small*	2.50
1993 2 Litai, Bishop / Castle	6.00
2001 10 Litu, Two pilots / Early monoplane	9.00

LUXEMBOURG

	VF.
1856 10 Thaler, Seated woman and three cherubs	*Rare*
1944 5 France, Grand Duchess Charlotte	3.00
	Unc.
1961 50 Francs, Grand Duchess Charlotte / Landscape	10.00
1967 10 Francs, Grand Duke Jean / Bridge	5.00
1972 50 Francs, Same / Steel workers	7.00
1980 100 Francs, Same / City view	7.50
(1986) 100 Francs, Same	4.50

MACEDONIA

	Unc.
1992 10 Denari, Women harvesting	.75
1993 20 Denari, Tower / Turkish bath	2.50

Unc.

1996 50 Denari, Archangel Gabriel / Byzantine coin
.... Unc. **3.00**

MEXICO

A much fuller treatment of Mexican paper money is provided here than for any other country, except the United States and Canada.

As in the U.S., many of Mexico's earlier notes were actually issued by banks and not by the government. They were eliminated by the issues of the Bank of Mexico in about 1920. This introductory reference only deals with federally issued notes.

Note that the prices here are for the most common dates appearing on the notes, and the most common variety for each design described. There are sometimes a wide number of varieties, and a specialized reference should be consulted.

Additional Specialized Reference:

Bruce, Colin R. II, *Standard Catalog of Mexican Coins, Paper Money Stocks, Bonds and Medals.*

Empire of Augustin Iturbide

	F
1823 1 Peso, Arms	30.00
1823 2 Pesos, Arms	40.00
1823 10 Pesos, Arms	75.00

Empire of Maximilian

1866 10 Pesos, Allegorical figures	*Rare*
1866 20 Pesos, Allegorical figures	*Rare*
1866 100 Pesos, Allegorical figures	*Rare*
1866 200 Pesos, Allegorical figures	*Rare*

Issues of the Republic and Estados Unidos

Fifty Centavos

	F
1920 Minerva	15.00

One Peso

	F
1823 Arms, cut cancelled	50.00

	F
1920 Plenty with Cherubs	22.00
(1936)-43 Aztec calendar / Statue of Victory	3.00
	Unc.
1943-48	6.00
1948-50 similar	4.00
1954 similar	4.00
1957-70	1.00

Two Peso

	F
1823 Arms, cut cancelled	75.00

Five Pesos

	F
1925-34 G. Faure / Victory statue	20.00
1936	50.00
	Unc.
1937-50 similar	5.00

	Unc.
1953-54 similar	4.00
1957-70 similar	2.50
1969-72 Josefa / Aquaduct	1.50

Ten Pesos

	F
1823 Arms, cut cancelled	150.00

The above one-sided note was printed on old Church documents to conserve paper.

	F
1925-34 Two winged Victories / Statue of Victory	20.00
1936 similar	50.00
	Unc.
1937-42 Woman with large headdress / Road to Guanajuato	15.00
1943-45 similar	10.00
1946-50 similar	9.00
1951-53 similar	5.00
1954-67 similar	3.00

	Unc.
1969-77 Hidalgo / Dolores Cathedral	.75

Twenty Pesos

	F
1925-34 Freighter at dock by locomotive	40.00
1937 Josefa / Federal Palace courtyard	VF 35.00
	Unc.
1940-45, similar	15.00
1948 similar	15.00
1950-70 similar	5.00
1972-77 Morelos / Pyramid	1.50

Fifty Pesos

	F
1925-34 Navagation std. / Statue of Victory	120.00
1937-40, Zaragoza / City view	250.00
	Unc.
1941-45 de Allende / Statue of Victory	25.00
1948-72 similar	3.00
1973-81, Juarez / Aztec deity	1.00

One Hundred Pesos

	F
1925-34 Maritime Commerce and Youth / Statue of Victory	175.00
1936 Madero / Bank building	40.00

	VF
1940-42	60.00
1945 Hidalgo / Coin	15.00
	Unc.
1950-61 similar	25.00
1974-82, Carranza / Stone altar	1.00

Five Hundred Pesos

	F
1925-34 Electricity std. / Statue of Victory	950.00
1936 Morelos / Miners' Palace	375.00
1940-43 Morelos	VF 100.00
	Unc.
1948-78 similar	8.50
1979-84, Madero / Aztec calendar	2.50

One Thousand Pesos

	F
1925-34 Wisdom with globe / Statue of Victory	2,250.00
	VF
1936 Cuauhtemoc / Pyramid	600.00
1941-45 Cuauhtemoc / Pyramid	100.00
	Unc.
1948-77 similar	8.00

	Unc.
1978-85, de Asbaje / Santo Domingo plaza	2.50

Two Thousand Pesos

1983-89, J. Sierra / 1800s courtyard	2.25

Five Thousand Pesos

1980-89 Cadets / Chapultepec castle	3.00

Ten Thousand Pesos

1943-53 Romero / Government Palace	VF 60.00
1978 Romero / National palace	75.00
1981-91 Cardenas / Coyolxauhqui	6.00

Twenty Thousand Pesos

1985-89 A. Quintana Roo / Pre-Columbian art	12.50

Fifty Thousand Pesos

1986-90 Cuauhtemoc / Spaniard and Aztec fighting....... **45.00**

One Hundred Thousand Pesos

1988-91 Calles / Stag.. **85.00**

Reform, 1000 Pesos = 1 New Peso

Ten Nuevos Pesos

1992 Cardenas / Coyolxauhqui **7.50**
1992 Zapata / Statue of Zapata **4.00**
1994-96, same without Nuevos **3.00**

Twenty Nuevos Pesos

1992 A. Quintana Roo / Pre-Columbian art **12.50**
1992 Juarez / Statue **6.50**
1994-96, same without Nuevos **5.50**
2000, same with commemorative bank inscription **9.50**

Unc.
2001, as 1994-96 but plastic polymer **4.50**

Fifty Nuevos Pesos

Unc.
1992 Cuauhtemoc / Spaniand and Aztec fighting........... **27.50**
1992 Morelos / Fisherman **15.00**
1994-98, same without Nuevos **10.00**
2000, same with commemorative bank inscription **17.50**
2000, as 1994-98 but vertical security strip added **10.00**

One Hundred Nuevos Pesos

1992 Calles / Stag.. **40.00**
1992 Nezahualcoyotl / Xochipilli statue...................... **25.00**
1994-96, same without Nuevos **22.50**
2000, same with commemorative bank inscription **35.00**
2000, as 1994-96 but vertical security strip added **18.00**

Two Hundred Nuevos Pesos

1992, de Asbaje / Temple of San Jeronimo **45.00**
1995-98, same without Nuevos **37.50**
2000, same with commemorative bank inscription **70.00**
2000, as 1994-98 but vertical security strip added **32.50**

Five Hundred Nuevos Pesos

1992, Zaragoza / Puebla Cathedral **110.00**
1995-96, same without Nuevos **95.00**
2000, same with commemorative bank inscription
.... **150.00**
2000, as 1995-96 but vertical security strip added **80.00**

One Thousand Nuevos Pesos

2002, Hidalgo / Fountain and church **150.00**

MOROCCO

VF
1944 1 Franc, Star / City of Fez. *Small*........................... **3.50**
1943-44 10 Francs, Star.. **5.00**
1951-58 1,000 Francs, Mosque and city view **45.00**
Unc.
1965-69 5 Dirhams, King Muhammad V / Man with sheaf
.... **35.00**
1970-85 10 Dirhams, King Hassan II / Woman sorting
oranges... **5.50**
1987(-1991) 10 Dirhams, similar / Mandolin and pillar
.... **3.50**
1987 (c.1991) 200 Dirhams, similar / Sailboat................ **35.00**

Unc.
1996 20 Dirhams, Hassan II and Mosque / Fountain **4.50**
2002 20 Dirhams, Mohammed VI / Coastal town **4.50**

NETHERLANDS

F
1846 10 Gulden, Inscriptions .... *Rare*
1904-21 25 Gulden, Arms and ornate border **450.00**
1939-41 20 Gulden, Queen Emma and sailing ship / Church
.... **10.00**

	VF
1943 1 Gulden, Queen Wilhelmina / Arms	4.00

	Unc.
1966 5 Gulden, Vondell / Mondernistic depiction of building	10.00
1972 1,000 Gulden, Baruch d'Espinoza	750.00
1982 50 Gulden, Sunflower and bee	35.00
1985 250 Gulden, Lighthouse	150.00
1992 100 Gulden, Abstract pattern	75.00

	Unc.
1994 1000 Gulden, Abstract pattern	600.00
1997 10 Gulden, Abstract pattern	7.50

NEW ZEALAND

	VF
1934 1 Pound, Kiwi, Arms and Maori chief	135.00

	Unc.
(1967-81) 1 Dollar, Elizabeth II / Bird	17.00
(1981-92) 1 Dollar, similar but older portrait	5.00
(1992-99) 5 Dollars, Sir Edmond Hillary / Penguin	8.50

	Unc.
1996 20 Dollars, Elizabeth II 70th birthday inscription	200.00

NICARAGUA

	F
1894 10 Centavos, Arms, *small*	75.00
1938 50 Centavos, Liberty / Arms	30.00

	Unc.
1962 1 Cordoba, Building / Cordoba	7.50
1972 20 Cordobas, Woman lighting cannon / Treaty signing ceremony	10.00

	Unc.
1979 1000 Cordobas, Sandino	45.00
1985 1000 Cordobas, Similar	2.00
(1991) 50 Cordobas, Chamorro / Polling place	12.50

NIGERIA

Unc.

(1967) 1 Pound, Bank building / Man beating plant **8.00**
(1973-78) 1 Naira, Bank building / Workers stacking bags of
grain **12.50**

Unc.

(1984-05) 10 Naira, A. Ikoku / Women carrying bowls on
heads **3.00**

NORWAY

F

1695 25 Rixdaler Croner, Inscription with wax seals
.... **2,000.00**
1877-99 5 Kroner, Oscar II **800.00**
1940-50 1 Krone **8.50**

Unc.

1972-84 10 Kroner, F. Nansen / Fisherman **6.50**
1984-95 50 Kroner, A.O. Vinje / Medieval stone carving
.... **15.00**
1996-2000 50 Kroner, P.C. Asbjornsen / Water lilies **10.00**

Unc.

1999-2002 500 Kroner, S. Undste / Wreath **90.00**

OMAN

(1970) 100 Baisa, Dagger and swords **5.00**

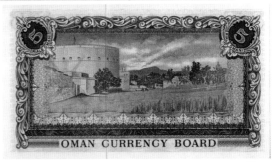

Unc.

(1973) 5 Rials, same / Nizwa Fort **70.00**
(1977) 1/2 Rial, Same / Castle **8.00**
1985-92 50 Rials, Sultan / Castle **300.00**
1995 200 Baisa, Sultan / Port **3.00**
2000 5 Rials, Sultan / Nizwa city view **27.00**

PAKISTAN

(1953) 5 Rupees, Small boat / Mountain scene **12.50**

	Unc.
(1964) 50 Rupees, Mohammad Ali Jinnah / Two boats...	**10.00**
(1973) 1 Rupee, Archway	**3.00**
(1982-) 1 Rupee, Tomb of Allama Iqbal, *small*	**1.00**
(1986) 50 Rupees, Mohammad Ali Jinnah / Gate of Lahore fort	**6.00**

PALESTINE

	F
1927-45 500 Mils, Rachel's Tomb l. / Tower of David	**125.00**
1927-44 1 Pound, Dome of the Rock l. / Tower of David	**125.00**

	F
1927-44 1 Pound, Crusader tower / Tower of David	*Rare*

PANAMA

	VF
1941 1 Balboa, Balboa	**950.00**
1941 5 Balboas, Uracca	**3,000.00**

PARAGUAY

	F
1856 ½ Real, Flowers and seal	**80.00**
1903 1 Peso, Woman in straw hat	**7.50**
	Unc.
1943 5 Guaranies, Gen. Diaz	**15.00**
1952 1 Guarani, Soldier / Building	**4.00**

	Unc.
1952 (1963-95) 500 Guaranies, Gen. B. Caballero / Freighter	**1.25**
1995 5000 Guaranies, D.C.A. Lopez / Lopez Palace	**5.00**

PERU

	F
1879 5 Soles, Women with children	**12.50**
1922 1 Libra, Woman seated	**45.00**

Unc.
1958 5 Soles, Liberty (or Peru)........................... **7.00**
1962-68 5 Soles de Oro, Liberty (or Peru) std. / Arms **4.00**
1977 50 Soles de Oro, Tupac Amaru / Town of Tinta....... **1.25**
1994-95 10 Nuevos Soles, J. Abelardo Quiñones / Biplane
flying upside-down... **7.00**

Unc.
1994-95 20 Nuevos Soles, R. Porres Barrenechea / Torre Tagle
Palace... **14.00**

PHILIPPINES

F
1852-65 25 Pesos, Isabel II .... *Rare*
1908 50 Pesos, Woman with flower, "Banco Español Filipino"
.... **650.00**
1928 50 Pesos, similar, "Bank of the Philippine Islands" .. **80.00**
Unc.
(1942) 10 Centavos, "Japanese Government," *small*............ **.50**
(1943) 5 Pesos, Monument, "Japanese Government"........ **2.00**
(1949) 2 Pesos, Rizal **2.00**
(1969) 1 Piso, Rizal / 1898 Independence declaration **1.00**
(1970s) 10 Piso, Mabini / Barasoain church **2.00**

Unc.
(1985-94) 10 Piso, Mabini / Barasoain church **1.50**
(1987-94) 500 Piso, B. Aquino / Scenes of Aquino's life
.... **30.00**

POLAND

F
1794 5 Groszy, Eagle and mounted knight **15.00**
similar, *F. Malinowski* on back..*Copy*
1917 20 Marek, White eagle... **20.00**
VF
1931 20 Zlotych, E. Plater / Woman with children............ **2.00**
1948 50 Zlotych, Bust of fisherman................................ **1.50**
Unc.
1962-65 1000 Zlotych, Copernicus / Diagram of Copernican
view of solar system.. **20.00**
1977-82 2000 Zlotych, Mieszko I / Chrobry..................... **1.00**
1994 20 Zlotych, Boleslaw I / Medieval coin.................. **10.00**

PORTUGAL

F
1798-99 2400 Reis, Walled cities and cherubs .... *Rare*
1891 500 Reis, Arms / Arms **95.00**
1918-20 50 Centavos, Woman holding ship / Justice **5.00**
1920-25 5 Escudos, J. das Regras / Church and convent
.... **95.00**
1944-52 500 Escudos, Joao IV / King with crowd ..... *VF* **40.00**
Unc.
1960 50 Escudos, Pereira / "The Thinker" statue **95.00**
1971 20 Escudos, G. de Orta / Market in Goa **5.00**
1967 1000 Escudos, Queen Maria II / Maria II and building
.... **65.00**
1987-93 5,000 Escudos, Antero de Quental / Six hands with
rope... **120.00**

Unc.
1989-91 10,000 Escudos, Moniz / Nobel Prize and snakes
.... **220.00**
1996-2000 1,000 Escudos, Cabral / 1500s Sailing ship..... **20.00**
1997-2000 500 Escudos, Joao de Barros............................ **9.00**

PUERTO RICO

	F
1813 8 Reales, Paschal lamb .... G	**1,600.00**
1889 10 Pesos, Paschal lamb and Coast watchers / Arms	
.... *Rare*	

	F
1895 1 Peso, Bearded Bust l. / Crowned arms of Spain ..	**65.00**
1909 10 Dollars, Ponce de Leon / Liberty	**2,500.00**

QATAR

	Unc.
(1973) 1 Riyal, Arms / Port of Doha	**15.00**
1980s-1996 10 Riyals, Arms / National Museum	**8.00**

	Unc.
1980s-1996 500 Riyals, Arms / Oil platform	**225.00**
(2003) 1 Riyal, Arms / Three different birds	**1.25**

ROMANIA

	F
1877 5 Lei, Two women std................................	**380.00**
1877 50 Lei, Ancient Romans	**850.00**
	VF
1914-28 5 Lei, Woman with distaff / Woman picking apples,	
child at side	**8.50**

	VF
1947 100 Lei, Three men with torch and grain	**5.00**
	Unc.
1966 1 Leu, Arms, *small*	**2.50**
1991 500 Lei, Bust of Brancusi / Brancusi std.	**6.00**

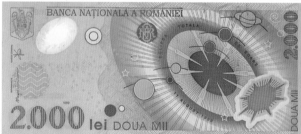

	Unc.
1999 2000 Lei, Solar system / Path of solar eclipse. Made of	
plastic with a transparent window.	**2.00**
2000 50,000 Lei, Enescu / Neoclassical building	**4.50**
2005 5 Lei, similar	**2.00**

RUSSIA

	F
1787-1818 5 Rubles, Inscriptions	750.00
1866-80 5 Rubles, Monogram / D. Ivanovich Donskoi	450.00

	F
1872 100 Rubles, Catherine the Great	*Rare*
	Unc.
1909 5 Rubles, Arms	2.50
1918 100 Rubles, Two-headed eagle	3.75
The above is from the Russian civil war.	
1938 5 Rubles, Pilot	6.00
1961 3 Rubles, Kremlin tower	1.00
1991 50 Rubles, Lenin / Dome at Kremlin	6.00

	Unc.
1997 50 Rubles, Statue of River Neva / Naval Museum	4.00
1997 100 Rubles, Chariot monument / Bolshoi Theater	7.50

RWANDA

1964-76 50 Francs, Map / Miners	2.50
1978 100 Francs, Zebras / Woman and child	7.00

	Unc.
1978 5000 Francs, Woman with basket / Mountain lake	150.00
1988-89 1000 Francs. Two Watusi warriors / Two gorillas	20.00

SAUDI ARABIA

	Unc.
1373AH (1954) 10 Riyals, Two dhows in Jedda Harbor	250.00
1379AH (1961) 1 Riyal, Hill of Light / Arms	45.00
1379AH (1968) 5 Riyals, Airport / Ships at oil dock	60.00
1379AH (1976) 50 Riyals, King Faisal / Arches in mosque	75.00
1379AH (1977) 10 Riyals, King Faisal / Oil platform	25.00

	Unc.
1379AH (1984) 1 Riyal, King Fahd / Landscape	Unc. 1.25
1419AH (2000) 200 Riyals, King Abd al Aziz with glasses / Gate of Al Mussmack Palace	85.00
1379AH (1983-2003) 500 Riyals, King Abd al-Aziz and Kaaba in Mecca / Courtyard of Great Mosque	200.00

SOUTH AFRICA

	VF
1867-68 1 Pond, Arms, "Zuid-Afrikaansche Republiek"	*Rare*
1920 1 Pound, Arms	**150.00**
1928-47 10 Shillings	**40.00**
1928-47 1 Pound, Sailing ship	**17.00**
	Unc.
(1961-65) 1 Rand, Jan van Riebeeck / Lion crest	**28.00**

	Unc.
(1966-72) 1 Rand, Jan van Riebeeck / Sheep and plow	**8.00**
(1978-93) 10 Rand, Jan van Riebeeck / Bull and ram	**12.00**
1984-93 20 Rand, Elephant / Mining scene	**16.00**
1994-99 100 Rand, Water buffalo / Zebra herd	**30.00**

SPAIN

	VF
1874 50 Pesetas, D. Martinez	*F* **2,000.00**
1925 (1925-36) 100 Pesetas, Philip II / Philip II in scene	**9.50**
1935 500 Pesetas, H. Cortez / Cortez burning his ships	**125.00**
1949 1000 Pesetas, de Santillan / Goya painting	**165.00**
1951 5 Pesetas, Balmes / Building	**43.50**
	Unc.
1965 100 Pesetas, Gustavo Becquer / Woman with parasol	**15.00**
1965 1,000 Pesetas, St. Isidoro / Medieval sculpture	**110.00**
1970 100 Pesetas, Manuel de Falla / Residence of kings of Grenada	**7.50**

	Unc.
1971 500 Pesetas, J.Verdaquer / Mt. Canigo	**50.00**
1976 5,000 Pesetas, Charles III / Prado Museum	**200.00**
1985 10,000 Pesetas, Juan Carlos I / Prince of Asturias	**175.00**
1992 1,000 Pesetas, Cortes / Pizarro	**25.00**
1992 5,000 Pesetas, Columbus / Armillary sphere	**90.00**

SUDAN

	VF
1961-68 1 Pound, Dam	**20.00**
1964-68 10 Pounds, Bank building / Camel rider	**75.00**
	Unc.
1970-80 25 Piastres, Bank building / Textile machine	**7.50**

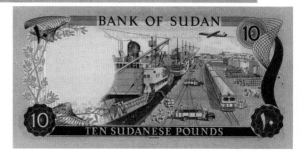

	Unc.
(1970-80) 10 Pounds, Bank building / Port scene	35.00
1981 10 Pounds, Pres. Nimeiri / Sugar factory	85.00
1987 50 Piastres, Instruments, Map and Peanut plant / Bank building	.75
1993 10 Dinars, People's Palace / Dome and tower	3.50

SWAZILAND

	Unc.
(1974) 1 Lilangeni, King Sobhuza / Row of princesses	Unc. 6.00

SWEDEN

	F
1666 10 Daler Silvermynt, Inscription	7,000.00
1802-34 8 Schillingar Specie, Inscription	100.00
1906-17 5 Kronor, Svea std. / Gustav Vasa	25.00
1918-52 5 Kronor, similar	2.00

	Unc.
1954-61 5 Kronor, Gustav VI Adolf / Svea stg.	4.00
1965-81 5 Kronor, Gustav Vasa / Stylized rooster	2.00
1985-2003 500 Kronor, Carl XI / C. Polhem	80.00
1991-2005 20 Kronor, Selma Lagerlöf / Boy flying on goose	3.50

	Unc.
1996-2003 50 Kronor, Jenny Lind / Violin	8.50

SWITZERLAND

	F
1907 50 Franken, Helvetia and child	1,400.00
1924-49 100 Franken, Female portrait / Man chopping tree	*VF* 55.00

	Unc.
1979-2002 10 Francs, L. Euler / Water turbine	12.50
1961-74 50 Francs, Little girl r. / Apple harvesting	75.00
1994-95 50 Francs, S. Taeuber-Arp / Her abstract art	50.00
1975-93 100 Francs, Francesco Borromini	105.00
1954-74 1000 Francs, Female head / Dance Macabre	1,150.00

SYRIA

	VF
1919 5 Piastres, Baalbek / Lion head	60.00
1935 5 Livres, Azam Palace	150.00
1944 5 Piastres, Citadel of Aleppo	5.00
1958 1 Pound, Industrial worker / Water wheel	3.00
1963-73 5 Pounds, same / Citadel of Aleppo	4.00

	Unc.
1977-91 10 Pounds, Palace and woman / Water treatment plant	1.50
1997 200 Pounds, Saladdin / Cotton weaving and energy plant	8.00
1997 1,000 Pounds, Pres. Assad / Oil , harvesting and fishing industries	40.00

TANZANIA

	Unc.
(1966) 5 Shillings, Young Julius Nyerere / Mountain	12.50
(1978) 20 Shilingi, Julius Nyerere / Cotton knitting machine	4.50
(1985) 20 Shilingi, Old Julius Nyerere / Tire factory workers	2.50
(1992) 200 Shilingi, Pres. Mwinyi / Two fishermen	6.00

THAILAND

	Unc.
1955 1 Baht, Rama IX and temple / Building	2.50
1968 100 Baht, Rama IX / Royal barge	15.00

(1969-78) 100 Baht, Rama IX / Statue of Narasuan on
Elephant **10.00**
1987 60 Baht, Rama IX enthroned / Royal family with
subjects.. **4.00**

Unc.
1997 50 Baht, Rama IX / Rama VI seated, *plastic polymer*
.... **3.00**

TIBET

F
1942-59, 100 Srang, Two lions / Seated figure.................. **5.00**

TURKEY

XF
1259AH (1843) 250 Kurush, Inscription......................... *Rare*
1334AH (1918) 10 Livres, Inscription in ornamental border,
large **300.00**
same, WWI British military counterfeit......................... **5.00**
Note: The counterfeits far outnumber authentic notes.
1930 50 Kurush, Ismet Inonu / Building.......................... **8.00**

Unc.
1930 (1961) 5 Lira, Ataturk / Three women with baskets
.... **60.00**
1970 (1971-82) 10 Lira, Ataturk / Lighthouse view........... **4.00**
1970 (1984-97) 10 Lira, Ataturk / Children giving flowers to
Ataturk .... **.50**

Unc.
1970 (1997) 100,000 Lira, Ataturk / similar **4.00**
1970 (1995) 1,000,000 Lira, Ataturk / Dam **20.00**
1970 (2000) 20,000,000 Lira, Ataturk / Ancient city **45.00**
2005 20 New Lira, Same... **40.00**

UKRAINE

Unc.
1918 500 Hryven, Head between tridents...................... **25.00**
1991 1 Karbovanets, Libyd / Cathedral .... **.25**
1992 100 Karbovantsiv, Libyd and her brother Vikings on
ship / Cathedral.. **1.75**
1994-95 1 Hryvnia, St. Volodymyr / City of Khersonnes
.... **1.00**
(1996) 50 Hryven, Hrushevsky / Parliament **20.00**

UNITED ARAB EMIRATES

Unc.
1973 5 Dirhams, Arms / Fujairah Fortress **50.00**
1982-2001 5 Dirhams, Sharjah market / Tower **2.50**

Unc.

1993-2004 10 Dirhams, Dagger / Farm **8.00**
1993-2003 100 Dirhams, Fortress / Dubai Trade Center
.... **60.00**

VENEZUELA

F

1811 1 Peso, Seal..**1,000.00**
1861 8 Reales, Inscription .... *Rare*

Unc.

1945-60 10 Bolivares, Bolivar and Sucre / Arms **45.00**
1961 10 Bolivares, Bolivar and Sucre / Carabobo Monument
.... **35.00**
1974-79 20 Bolivares, J. Antonio Paez / similar................. **8.00**
1985-98 50 Bolivares, A. Bello / Bank building................. **1.50**

Unc.

1991-92 1000 Bolivres, Bolivar / Signing of Declaration of
   Independence **4.00**
1994-98 1000 Bolivres, similar... **2.50**

VIETNAM

F

(1946) 100 Dong, Farmers with buffalo......................... **70.00**

Unc

1976 5 Hao, Arms / River scene..................................... **3.00**
1980 100 Dong, Ho Chi Minh / Junks sailing amid rocks
.... **8.00**
1994 50,000 Dong, Ho Chi Minh / View of docks............ **8.00**

WEST AFRICAN STATES

(1959-65) 1000 Francs, Two busts / Bust of man with graying
   beard **35.00**

YUGOSLAVIA

VF

1920 10 Dinara, Progress moving wheel / Mountain scene
.... **50.00**
1931 50 Dinara, King Alexander / Equestrian statue........ **3.00**
1939 10 Dinara, King Peter II / Woman in local costume
.... **8.00**

Unc.

1944 1 Dinara, Soldier, *small* **1.00**
1963 100 Dinara, Woman in folk dress / View of Dubrovnik
.... **2.00**
1974 20 Dinara, Freighter ship **1.50**
1985 5000 Dinara, Tito / View of Jajce............................ **3.50**

Unc.

1991 1000 Dinara, Nikola Tesla / High frequency transformer
.... **7.00**
1993 10,000,000,000 Dinara, Same **10.00**
2000 20 Dinara, Petar II of Mentenegro / Statue.............. **2.00**

ZAMBIA

Unc.

1963 1 Pound, Elizabeth II & Fisher with net / Bird .... *Rare*
(1968-69) 2 Kwacha, Pres. Kenneth Kaunda / Mining facility
.... **120.00**

(1973) 5 Kwacha, Pres. Kenneth Kaunda / Children..... **450.00**
(1980-88) 10 Kwacha, Older Pres. Kenneth Kaunda / Bank
   building **5.00**
1992-2003 500 Kwacha, Bird / Elephant head and cotton
   pickers... **3.00**

INDEX

More Solid Investments

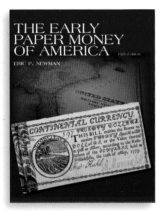

by Eric P. Newman
Make savvy decisions regarding Colonial American paper money with more than 1,100 detailed illustrations, descriptions and researched collector values presented in this unique guide.

Hardcover • 8-3/4 x 11-1/4 • 496 pages
1,000 b&w photos • 100 color photos
Item# Z0101 • $95.00

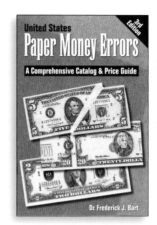

by Dr. Frederick J. Bart
More photos, updated listings and prices reflective of the increase in values are featured in this unique and essential paper money reference. In addition, you'll discover countless listings for new discovers and revised market report sections.

Softcover • 6 x 9 • 288 pages
500 b&w photos
Item# Z2544 • $26.99

Edited by George S. Cuhaj
Accurately identify and assess notes printed between 1368 and 1960, from all corners of the globe, with this comprehensive and easy-to-use guide. In addition to 6,000 detailed photos of notes, this edition also contains a BONUS DVD. The DVD allows you to search using key words and enlarge pages, by up to 400%, to gain a closer look at notes.

Softcover • 8-1/4 x 10-7/8 • 1,200 pages
6,000 b&w photos
Item# Z2756 • $80.00

Edited by George S. Cuhaj; William Brandimore, Market Analyst
Concise, compact and in full-color, this new edition of the only paper money reference of its kind bears the same reliability and ease of use as previous editions, with current pricing for monetary issues including large and small-size notes.

Softcover • 6 x 9 • 432 pages
50 b&w photos • 1,300 color photos
Item# Z2408• $26.99

by Allen G. Berman
Perfect if you're a new collector fixated on state quarters, or a veteran collector looking for a more portable price guide, this book features extensive listings and 500 color photos for quick identification.

Softcover • 5 x 8 • 272 pages
500 color photos
Item# Z0302 • $17.99

Numismatic news you can use at www.numismaticnews.net AND www.numismaster.com